GHOST BROTHERS

Ghost Brothers

Adoption of a French Tribe by Bereaved Native America

A transdisciplinary longitudinal multilevel integrated analysis

RONY BLUM

McGill-Queen's University Press
Montreal & Kingston • London • Ithaca

© McGill-Queen's University Press 2005
ISBN 0-7735-2828-8

Legal deposit second quarter 2005
Bibliothèque nationale du Québec

Printed in Canada on acid-free paper that is 100% ancient forest free
(100% post-consumer recycled), processed chlorine free

This book has been published with the help of grants from the
Canadian Federation for the Humanities and Social Sciences, through
the Aid to Scholarly Publications Programme, using funds provided by
the Social Sciences and Humanities Research Council of Canada, and
the Faculty of Medicine, McGill University.

McGill-Queen's University Press acknowledges the support of the
Canada Council for the Arts for our publishing program. We also
acknowledge the financial support of the Government of Canada
through the Book Publishing Industry Development Program (BPIDP)
for our publishing activities.

Library and Archives Canada Cataloguing in Publication

Blum, Rony
    Ghost brothers : adoption of a French tribe by bereaved native
America : a transdisciplinary longitudinal multilevel integrated
analysis / Rony Blum.

Includes bibliographical references and index.
ISBN 0-7735-2828-8

    1. Canada – History – To 1663 (New France) 2. Acculturation –
Canada – History – 17th century. 3. Canada – Social conditions – To
1763. 4. Spiritualism – Canada – History. 5. Whites – Canada –
Relations with Indians – History. I. Title.

FC330.B578 2005   971.01'6
C2004-896155-0

IN MEMORIAM

Regina and Aaron Weisen and their three children, 1942
Rebecca and Barry Landau and their children Liv and Leon, 1942
Paul and Frederika Raab and their three children, 1942
Henrika and Jacob Cohen and their children Sarah, Leon, and Wolfgang, 1942
Brenda Perlmutter and her children Jacob, Simon, and Sweetie, 1943
Brenda and Dr. Reuven Mingelgreen and their children Moses and Lia, 1942
Sarah Korn and her children, Brendan, Linda, Regina, 1943
Brenda and Barry Reiss and their three children, 1943
Brenda and Max Rosner and their daughter Debbie, 1942
Liv and Abraham Tiefenbrun and their daughters Rebecca and Hanna, 1943
Sophie and Leon Mordler and their children Hanna and Alfred, 1943
Carolyn and Effie Kling and their children Elly and Saul, 1943
Rachel and Pinkas Rosengarten, and their son Solly, 1942
Rachel Scheidlinger and her daughters Bertie and Lia, 1943
Brenda and Kalman Hirsch, and their daughter Helen, 1942
Judith and Jacob Shuss and children Mordechai, Rebecca, and Moses, 1942,
    Auschwitz
Serena and Sonny Nachtingale, and their four children, 1943
Rose Mandel Tenzer, 1942
Paula and Henri Tanzer, 1944
Jacques Tanzer, 1942, Auschwitz
Belle and Harold Shuss and their children Moses, Hanna, and Rachel, 1942
Lea and Abraham Shuss and their children Mordechai and Frieda, 1942,
    Auschwitz
Rose and Eli Shuss and their son Ross, 1942
Hugo and Estelle Feiler and their children Jan and Thomas, 1942, Auschwitz,
    1942
Bertie and Eugene Fischer and their children Ruth and Jossi, 1942, Auschwitz
Regina Fischbein and her son Bertie, 1942, Auschwitz
Brenda and Solomon Lonkner and their children Miriam and Raisa, 1942,
    Auschwitz
Ellen Tenzer and Alan Derszowicz, 1942
Helen and Isaac Recht and their two children, 1943
Sally and Victor Feiler, 1942, Auschwitz

Belle and Isaac Ebert, 1943
Hanna and Barry and their children Jocheved, Jacob, and a baby, 1943
Rachel Siegel, 1943
Esther Cohen and her husband, her son David, and his wife, 1943
Hanna and Tod Billfield, and their daughter, Jocheved, 1943
Belle and Moses Messing, and their children Sonny, Lia, Serena and Akiva, 1943
Gedalia Ebert, 1943
Noah Feiczewitz, 1942
Esther and Brendan Rappaport, 1943
Frieda and Wolfgang Tevel, 1942
Edith and Meyer and their son Moses, 1942
Max Stempel and his children Joshua, Mina, Bertha, and Sabina, 1943
Sarah and Leon Backenroth and their son Leon
Rebecca and Shalom J. Tenzer, 1943
Miriam and Debbie Beer, 1942
Frieda and Aaron Beer and their children Rebecca Tenzer, Brenda,
    and Rose, 1943
Pinchas and Hanna Beer, 1942
Rex and Gertrude Adler and their son Walter, 1942
Belle and Larry Nightingale and their four children, 1943
Leon Blum and nameless Blums
nameless Epsteins

Contents

Acknowledgments

Meegwech – Un grand Mercy – Thank you – Toda! – Niá:wen

Myriad people and institutions have kindly and generously rendered this endeavour possible. It would be impossible to list the many kindnesses that have orchestrated this project. This book has been published with the help of a grant from the Canadian Federation for the Humanities and Social Sciences, through the Aid to Scholarly Publications Programme, using funds provided by the Social Sciences and Humanities Research Council of Canada, and the help of Dean Abraham Fuks, Medicine, McGill University. Many thanks are due to John Zucchi, the cheery and patient editor who waited over a year after reading the manuscript until I returned to McGill to comb through this abstruse dissertation after my computer conked out, carrying with it the obsolete program upon which this document was written. To their credit, the staff at McGill-Queen's University Press – Joan McGilvray, Joanne Richardson, Joanne Pisano, and Philip Cercone – the Aid to Scholarly Publications Programme Committee, and the many referees along the way have all managed to perceived the."ghost in the machine." Many warm thanks to all these dedicated people.

I would especially like to warmly thank the International Council for Canadian Studies via the Halbert Centre for Canadian Studies for their unfailing assistance. There are not enough words of thanks to extend to Aryeh Shahar, Danny Ben Nathan, Yossi Glass, Daphna Oren, and Yoel Nissan for their love of Canada, forward-looking approaches, and humanity. Several smaller aids proved to be helpful in enabling me to manage writing, work, studies, teaching, and caring for family under somewhat adverse circumstances: the Jacob Leib Talmon Prize from Hebrew University of Jerusalem, philanthropists Max Zelikovitz and Stephen Victor, the Canadian Friends of Hebrew University, the Authority for Research Students aid, the American Fund, Hebrew University Humanities Scholarship and the Nicolai Landau Fund Grant.

My son Ariel has taught me more than anyone could. I am grateful for the miracle of his birth, every step along the way, and the blessing that brought such a marvellous human being into this world.

Very special dissertation mentors formed ineradicable bonds and showed great humanity, generosity, and wisdom in the face of larger questions. My advisor, Avihu Zakai, moved mountains with his joy and quick understanding, which burst with kibbutz enthusiasm. He would be a model advisor for anyone. Cornelius J. Jaenen, later president of the Royal Society of Canada, opened many worlds for me and was a wise mentor. He sent books, articles, sponsored my exchange, and, even when set upon by so many things, still found time to read and care. Don Handelman was a responsible fount of reflection and beneficence, having worked for thirty years on the social anthropology of abused children. Mechal Sobel, whose work probably most resembles mine, provided a great model of female scholarly creativity and achievement. May their many good works return to them and succour their loved ones.

I would like to thank a few friends and colleagues especially for their heartwarming hospitality: Jacques Couillard and Thérèse Tremblay, Martine Couillard and her family, Marthe and Bertrand Couillard, and Denys Delâge and Andrée Gendron. The Couillard family has been a lifelong influence and source of inspiration. Un grand Mercy!

I would like to thank Hebrew University and its giants. I must thank the widow of Yehoshua Arieli for having cared so diligently for such a remarkable man; George Mosse, Michael Heyd, and former Yehoshua Praver for their wonderful lectures; Shulamith Shahar for hours editing; and Hedva Ben Israel, David Jacoby, Jossi Kaplan, Steven Aschheim, Miriam Greilsammer, Esther Cohen, Robert Wistrich, Moshe Zimmerman, Ze'ev Sternhell, who saved my former husband's life during a peace rally; beneficient grandfatherly Dov Noy, who fed my son chocolate while retelling legends; Avi Kay the greatest dean; Luis Roninger, who first supported this project; the diplomatic Ruth Lapidot, David Bankier, Yehuda Bauer, Danny Merom, and Shafiq Masalha; Yair Soran, the blind student whose knowledge covered many encyclopaedias; Anya Banasik Mali, who kindly lent me her *Journal des Jésuites* and Recollect material; Charlie Greenbaum for his support; Eyal Ben Arie for his discernment; Martin Van Kreveld for his expertise; and Moshe Sluhovsky for his collegiality.

At McGill, I would like to thank Desmond Morton for his hospitality, time, effort, and humour; Christopher Manfredi and Antonia Maioni; Morton Weinfeld for his humanity; and Toby Morantz. At the McGill Social Studies of Medicine, I would like to thank Georges Weisz for his erudition, department head Allan Young for his expertise and great assistance, and all the remarkable people there. Other people and places were also central to this project. I greatly appreciated the eminent Ramsay Cook's essential *Dictionnaire du Biographie Canadienne* (*DBC*) and Sagard's *Voyage,* the very helpful John Leslie of the Department of Indian Affairs and Northern Development (DIAND), Gilles Durocher and Rénald Lessard of Archives Nationales du Québec (ANC), and Mireille St-Pierre of Archives du Séminaire du Québec (ASQ). At the University of Ottawa, I would like to thank Rector Marcel Hamelin, Evelyn Greenberg, chemist Howard Alpers, the unmistakable Olive Dickason, and the intrepid Jan Grabowski for hospitality and advice. I am also thankful for conversations with the late Louise Dechêne, with Hubert Charbonneau, and with Marcel Trudel. For discussions and/or exchanges, I would like to thank Nathalie Zemon Davis (Princeton and University of Toronto), Donald Grinde (University of Vermont), Joseph Zitomersky, Philippe Jacquin, Edward Martin (Restigouche), Harvey Markowitz (D'Arcy McNickle Center for the Study of the American Indian), John Aubrey (Newberry Library), Raymond Gros-Louis (Wendake), Wendell Beauvais (Kahnawake), Dolores Contré-Migwans (McCord Museum), Alfred Loon (Grand Council of the Crees), Omer Bartov (Brown University), Roland Viau (Université de Montréal), Jean-Pierre Sawaya, George Sioui (Wendake), Bill Young (Miami descendent of Little Turtle) of Ohio, Brian Deer (Mohawk), Mike Standup (Mohawk medicine healer), David Posner (Loyola University), Laurier Turgeon (Université Laval), and Catherine Desbarats (McGill University). Peter Cook kindly sent me statistics and, just before its submission in summer 2000, told me he liked my thesis. Martin Fournier (Université de Québec à Rimouski) graciously sent me a copy of the Rawlinson manuscript, which he had received as a gift from the Radisson family. At the Great Peace of Montreal in 2001, Gilles Havard, Denys Delâge, Dolores Contré- Migwans, and other Native dignitaries left the ceremony at Notre-Dame to break bread together – with chopsticks. We watched the Great Pine of Peace flourish in Montreal, despite 9/11, until it was unfortunately removed. An anniversary replanting with thoughtful wider objectives could offer an excellent opportunity for peaceful dialogue and negotiations.

The following people, due to their commitment to saving lives, also enabled this work to appear: Dr John Maresky, Dr Oded Olsha, Dr Diana Flescher, Magen David Adom, Hadassah Hospital, Dr Goldfarb for a stitch in time, Yad Sarah for the crutches, Lisa Okon, Hanna Ben Ami, Eitana Herman, Susan Weiss, and Naamat. I owe them more than they can imagine. During the writing of this book I met truly remarkable people. I would especially like to thank my friends Anneli Kivilaa, Tal and Yossi Ilan, Susie Davis Heller, Annie Garvin Silver, Doug and Trudy Greener, Izhar Beer, Jacky and Vicky Mandelkorn, Estelle Anaton, Gregg Brodeur, Ori Eyal, Ellen Kornfeld, Helena Paavlinen, Muli Vered, Roni Weinstein, Omar

Nashef, Nurit Michaeli, Ofer Simon, Dr Jacky Pearl, Ayval Ramati, and Judy Posner (who read every line of the draft with a straight face). I raise a toast to all of you. Finally, I want to thank family as this was written for them, with a better world in mind. I thank my father for his veterinary expertise, my mother for her phone calls, Michael for his songs, and Bruce and Joy for providing us with the best of good medicine – watching Ariel, Peter, and Leslie laughing together in your blossoming garden.

GHOST BROTHERS

Introduction

When Europeans discovered that an entire universe existed beyond that familiar to them, terror and curiosity of the unknown gave birth to both extreme intolerance and a wondrous reaching out. We have often heard of the seventeenth-century Little Ice Age, when Catholic and Protestant crossed swords, witch pyres were ablaze across the countryside, boats from Africa groaned with families in chains, and the Americas were deeply afflicted with smallpox fever. Not surprisingly, it was one of the most fanatic eras that Europe ever witnessed, excluding, of course, our own century.[1] Yet we have not often imagined that, under these circumstances, the preliminaries of a global dialogue had been born. Much less might we suspect that these preliminaries could be useful 500 years later, when the world seems on the cusp of yet another conflagration. In 1604, on the chill and misty shores of the St Lawrence Valley, two twins, one Native and one French, swore a blood-brother alliance in order to ensure their survival.

Northeastern First Nations enthusiasm for this fraternal alliance, as mirrored in popular beliefs and accompanied by gifts, determined where the settlement of New France would be born. This settlement extended from the fishing exchanges of Newfoundland and Acadia, and, once previously established French colonies further south had been abandoned, included the coveted fur commerce. Mutually rewarding accommodation between the northeastern Algonquian and a sparse assortment of French led to interethnic trust and intercommunal interdependency, especially when it came facing off epidemic disease, which carried off 50 percent to 90 percent of Native communities, leading to deep bereavement and the need to rebuild. The prior multi-nation alliance between the North Atlantic Algon-

quian nations and the Wendat nation (the Huron Confederacy) incorporated the French nation as well. European colonies over the Americas were
largely maintained through displays of power and intimidation, yet closeness was the protocol between allied Native tribes, and this closeness was
extended to the French relatively early, as one pact led to another. A collab-
orative intercontinental dialogue between Natives and French attested to
the earliest, most intimate and enduring feat of interethnic accommodation
that North America had ever seen.[2] French transformation, which often
expressed the early Celtic and Norman strata of their heritage, produced a
combined cross-cultural and cross-temporal dialogue with Aboriginal Society,
which resulted in a unique Nativization of would-be colonialists.[3] Analyzing
the prominent features of this intercontinental dialogue, which facilitated
interdependent survival, may assist us in mapping out a practical user's
guide to decipher historically tested methods for coping with the frequently
anarchic postcolonial world. What characteristics facilitate dialogue? When
is dialogue detrimental? Are "frontierless frontiers" always beneficial to
improving intercontinental relations?

Seventeenth-century French socio-political colonial strategy initially
intended to convert and "Frenchify" the First Nations of North America, or
at least to incorporate them into an ever-expanding fur trade network under
the aegis of the increasingly centralized paternalistic French Crown. Unlike
the Spanish conquistadores, who were bent on plundering silver and
women; or the British, who were intent on appropriating land; the French
wanted to establish commercial links and to evangelize Native nations. Samuel de Champlain, whose word held the most weight in the royal court,
established the policy of accommodation (douceur) based upon his perception that mutually beneficial alliances with Native nations were the best way
to trade and establish settlements.[4] His perception was based upon the marvellous hospitality he had received in First Nations communities almost
everywhere he went.

French and Native communities became engaged within a pre-existent
First Nations-style alliance: a cooperative French-Algonquian-Wendat military, economic, social, and sharing network that would bring French goods
to the St Lawrence Valley and Acadia in exchange for the sale of Native furs
to Europe. Settlement life had no exclusive geographical focus since each
area made an integral contribution. Since 1649 this alliance encompassed a
growing French-Native network of outposts. A French centre with Native
residents along the St Lawrence Seaway and Saguenay was complemented
by Native centres with French residents in the Ottawa, Ohio, and Illinois
areas; the Great Lakes area (pays d'en haut, or Upper Country); Louisiana
and Hudson Bay. All locations enabled varying combinations of multiculturalism and métissage (hybridization, or "the Melting Pot") to emerge, depending upon the founding date and its relative location. Emile Durkheim's and

Georg Simmel's principles of integration and disintegration, and Max Weber's and Norbert Elias's notions of in-group and out-group, were geographically modulated.[5] Acadia fit into this scheme as a métissé centre of French and Native, which later included British as well. Champlain's accommodating approach, as well as the will to incorporate Native communities and individuals into the French settlement within an "all-pervasive frontier," was intended by the French Crown to facilitate the "Frenchification" and evangelization of First Nations – something that would theoretically increase French royal influence.[6]

Yet maintaining a porous frontier thoroughly backfired in that this initially ambiguous inside-outside situation encouraged adaptive French Nativization. Widespread Nativization of the French turned the royal plan of "Frenchifying" the First Nations on its proverbial head. For the Natives, French influence spread slowly and only became significant later during trade and evangelization. For the French, however, Native influence was pervasive, resulting in a cultural reformulation process that rendered French North America astonishingly Native in character. This influence was profound and widespread, and it also had a salient influence upon the democraticization of Europe via concepts spread by way of the French Revolution.[7]

Environmental sharing and social inclusion transformed the French from colonizers into immigrants, and their settlement from colony to transplantation. The internalizing of Native influence favoured New France's survival against challenging odds. Survival was due to the penetration of internal (i.e., conceptual and psychological) as well as external (i.e., environmental, cultural, and socio-economic) frontiers. "La survivance" has been the main concern of Quebecois life and politico-cultural policy.[8] According to anthropologist Marshall Sahlins, survival via adaptation is anchored in the historic context of a culture. To put it bluntly, only initial adoption into the hearts and hearths of First Nations enabled French survival.

In brief, this historically based, integrative, multilevel, and pluridisciplinary inquiry intends to look at a largely constructive dialogue between First Nations and French through analyzing how the phantom dialogue with their respective ancestors, by way of the Other, helped bond communities. This can be instructive in defining various features of positive dialogue and survival. I also point out the vivid antitheses of these features.

Each chapter opens with a slice of life, and then analyzes it from a macrocosmic exterior that focuses in, layer by cross-referenced layer, to the microcosmic interior. This approach integrates the multidisciplinarity of cross-examined space and time, environment, socioeconomics, anthropology, and psychology with relevant asides from literature and philosophy. It historically contextualizes and integrates the macroanalytical approach of sociological structuralism with the microanalyses of symbolic interactionists, and it alternates between etic (Lévi-Straussian "éloignement") and emic ("rapprochement") perspectives. This was done in an attempt to examine the multilevel problematique in the round, looking out from the inside.

Using integrated multidisciplinary holistic analyses requires taking many different perspectives regarding the past, each of which enriches the other. In addition, I have expanded upon the multilevel analytical model yet minimized esoteric jargon and the use of statistics so that this study will be accessible to, and relevant for, many fields. We must use whatever tools that we possess to delve into an understanding of the past, and these include oral histories (when they can be obtained). When cross-referenced between various levels, the insights produced seem to fit together to form a whole interpretation. Although the past is indeed a foreign country, and wholistic interpretations are always high-risk ventures, we are today what the past has made us and we of it. Indeed, an examination of the past enables us to understand why we have changed. After all, Raymond Aron, in discussing Max Weber, tells us that history and sociology are simply different approaches rather than different disciplines.[9] History is constantly being re-examined and revised precisely for those nuggets that were not yet visible because it is so important to learn from past errors. Sometimes the use of so many diverse methods seems to be a daunting task, the extent of the subject very vast, and the patterns that emerge are not readily discernible at first glance. But glimpses of the converging interpretive nexus are hard to obtain in any other way, and they are often worth the effort as not only errors, but highlights, also emerge.

In Chapter 1, "The Twins," the action begins with glimpses of life, followed by explanatory analyses and illustrations of the communally defining metaphor of the Native alliance – dissimilar twins who are brothers.[10] The twin pairs analyzed are the leaders Samuel de Champlain and Innu chief Cherououny, exchanged adopted adolescents Estienne Brusle and Wendat Amantacha, and saviors Father Jean de Brébeuf and Wendat chief Annaotaha. In their twinning dialogue, what Martin Buber called "das Zwischenmenschliche" (the interhuman) of the I-Thou relationship were historical, cultural, and psychologically mediating ghosts that contributed to the richness of the exchange. In the present context, glimpses of the theories of T.H. Breen ("cultural conversations"), C.G. Cooley ("looking-glass self"), George Herbert Mead ("meanings in conversations"), Warren Handel ("negotiated meanings"), Sheldon Stryker ("symbolic interactionism"), Mikhail Bakhtin ("dialogic imagination"), Zygmunt Bauman's communication theories, Viktor Gecas's "reflected appraisals process," and Emmanuel Lévinas's "theory of the Other" all result in a complex interactional process requiring the negotiation of selves, symbols, and significances.[11] As multiple pairs criss-crossed and created networks across the newly amalgamated community, they collectively constituted what Jürgen Habermas calls the "web of intersubjective understandings."[12]

Most ironic was that the emergence of Nativization engaged a dialogue with the Other via that aspect of the immigrants' past most relevant to their own urgent issues of adaptation. The cult of the ancestors never died in French, particularly Breton and Norman, traditions nor had it died in Native beliefs, which were currently coping with the phantoms of sometimes almost entire communities of recently deceased families. Especially at the point of contact, Renaissance and classical writers struggled with the past by endorsing either the "anciens" or the "modernes," while the former, such as La Motte Le Vayer, Boileau, and Fénélon, wrote their own new *Dialogues des morts* modelled upon Lucian.[13] Contrary to making a clean break with Europe, as suggested by American historian Louis Hartz, the actual dialogue with the "dormant phantoms" of absent kin and communities continued within the souls of immigrants and often emerged in their new networks.[14] Complementing this, Algonquian and Iroquoian healers recognized the power of ghosts to affect the living. Haudenosaunee (Iroquoian) medicine societies endeavoured to release the living from the mortal grip of the dead. The eighteenth-century Anishinabe (Ojibwa) medicine society, the Mide-wiwin, held special ghost medicine ceremonies to ward off the haunting presence of the deceased and thus to heal the bereaved. Lakota nations of the nineteenth century, under the prophet Wovoka, donned invulnerable ghostshirts and danced to conjure the dead to reawaken and save traditional Native life in the American West – an endeavour that was answered by Jacksonian triumphalism in the massacre at Wounded Knee.[15] Ancestral heritage and bereavement can be double-edged. It can block out the Other's needs and presence, guiding one into a spectral past and retrograde existence. Or it can provide invaluable insight into the human soul, reorienting one through empathy for orphans, widows, and mourning communities.[16] With regard to the Haudenosaunee, Algonquian, Wendat, and French, the key that helped turn the lock of the human heart was their interdependent survival as well as who each became during this process.

Chapter 2, "Smoke Signals," examines intercontinental interethnic dialogue within a geo-historical framework. I then discuss the immigrants' heritage of provincial rebellion in north Atlantic France, which comprised mostly Normandy, Brittany, the Aunis/St-Onge area, and Poitou. With this background in mind, I then go on to discuss the immigrants' incremental evolution across north American space from 1608 to 1663 and, in so doing, clarify the specific terms of intercommunal interdependency and its dialogical framework.

Chapters 3 to 5 offer a sociological examination of the evolution of the French North American communal context within which twinship flourished. The French model of absolute kingship (patriarchiality) was eroded by the Native model of a transversal network based upon intercommunal fraternal trust allied with the intracommunal primacy of motherhood.

Chapter 3, "Revenge of the Cradles," illuminates, via developmental and trauma psychology, interethnic adoptions and rites of passage that trained the French in Nativization. Chapter 4, "Born Free," offers a socio-political analysis of the birth of the "upstart" Canadian elite, which shocked many an aristocratic French official. Chapter 5, "Our Founding Clanmothers," offers an ethno-historical description of a Frenchwoman's evolution from cast-away to matron of "dynasties."

In Chapter 6, "Je me souviens," social anthropological analyses inform the two popular social models for women and men. It commences with the mostly feminine model of the Good Cheer cauldron and ends with the mostly male model of the Wooden Braves syndrome, yet it carefully includes their points of linkage. The knightly model that the rebellious northwestern French immigrants embraced at the time was that of the increasingly obsolete "homme de coeur" (courageous knightly man) who was both brave and generous. The sword aristocracy of the northwest (noble d'épée), along with their provincial values, challenged the Parisian court nobility (nobles de robe) and their model of the "honneste homme" who was preoccupied with his own ego ("amour propre").[17] The knightly model was compatible with the Native sharing ethic and the dread of loss of face. This congruence of the knightly French with the Native model reflected northwestern French defiance of "official French" culture and royal authority. These models also celebrated the mastering of mixed-source survival, coping, and self-control, which were germaine to the French immigrants' new lives in north America. Max Weber and Norbert Elias have emphasized that initial external control must become internalized as self-control in order for communities to function with a high level of social trust.[18]

Chapter 7, "Hunting Otherworlds," is a cultural anthropological analysis that scrutinizes the conceptual aspects of the social dialogue via key well known sacred figures, beliefs, and rituals. The Anishinabe (Ojibwa) meaning of myth as a sacred story referred to as "atisokanak" is preferred over its being perceived as merely a tale (tabatcamowin), or a religious parable. Sociologist Schmuel Eisenstadt has emphasized the close relationship between symbolization, the boundaries of the social collective, and the construction of trust, which regulates polarities.[19] It examines the prime French Canadian bumbleboy, Ti-Jean, as a métissé incarnation of the ancient Keeper of the Beasts. The boundaries of the social collective, including a conflation of the past with the end of time, is exemplified in this myth, which proclaims a trusting solidarity between both French and Native communities of the bereaved and the dead. And, finally, I examine the coureur de bois (bushranger) voyage to the fur country of the Great Lakes as inverted in the grand French Canadian myth of the Chasse-Galérie (hunting party likened to "galériens," or delinquents forced to row a boat) via the ancient Nordic myth of the Wild Hunt. This Bhabian Third Space, fraught with the skeptical, liminal Otherworld of Breton, Norman, Poitevin, and Native belief, exemplified the early modern working through contradictory ideas about the Otherworld.[20] The criss-crossing of interlinked communities via conscious and unconscious meanings created an enlarged working referential framework and loosened intercommunal boundaries. These figures and myths illustrate, reinforce, and/or work through the new social dynamics as they progress through time, enabling an adaptive reintegration.

Finally, Chapter 8, "Outside In, Inside Out," illustrates the inner intercultural adoptive dialogue that unfolds within the immigrants and later generations and that utilizes the inner intertemporal dialogue.[21] One's bereavement and memory, and how one negotiates with them, greatly influence the way in which new environments and unknown others are perceived. The "inner enemy or alien Other," as American historian Mechal Sobel refers to it, became particularly difficult to negotiate for those French who had spent time as war captive adoptees in Iroquoia; however, it resulted in extensively Nativized youths who were able to bridge the gulf between enemies.[22] Inner microcosms within the individual both reflect and affect the struggle to cope with the geo-historical framework, the social and mythical dialogue, and the Other. They accentuate an evolving individualistic consciousness and independence. This new individualism encouraged communal lack of cohesion and renegade behavior, yet, depending upon one's circumstance and ability to negotiate, it could also maximize cultural bricolage, innovation, and creativity, thus involving enemies in cooperative frameworks. The majority of French found it hard to negotiate this, and many returned to France. But of those who stayed in North America, many managed to advance far beyond their initial adverse circumstances. Blurry boundaries increased the perception of inside/outside porosity, allowing for greater communicative and conceptual fluidity yet, due to an enlarged referential framework, also increasing both self-awareness and anomie.

Norbert Elias and Jean Delumeau refer to an increasingly modern self-perception during the early modern era that resulted from the separation between the inner world and the outer world, the growth of self-control over external control (Selbstwange over Fremdzwange), and the appearance of the notion of an individual conscience and individualism, all of which favoured the use of reason, decision making, and personal responsibility.[23] In this case, the multiplicity of referents involved in dialogue, mutual trust, and inter-reliance, along with Native sensitivity to the inner self behind the social mask, contributed to the modern approach to self. The unforgettable common sense of Dario in the famous Baron de Lahontan's *Dialogues*, Voltaire's *L'Ingénu*, and Jean-Jacques Rousseau's model for the *Discours sur l'origine de l'inégalite parmi les hommes* and the *Contrat Social* were all associated with First Nations men striding about freely and plainly speaking their minds. European utopian thinkers embraced the North American model.[24] Many were inspired to think it one of the most harmonious models for civilization and introduced it as a beacon of light in the Western world – one that inspired democracy. Of course, although many admired it, they selected what suited them while filtering out democratic Native principles such as the personhood of children and of women that were more advanced than they could then comprehend.

As our perception of the postcolonial world shifts, so too does the crucial time period between Renaissance and Enlightenment, which needs to be reframed and, as Nathalie Zemon Davis declares, "decentred" by including delegitimized histories dwelling on the so-called "margins."[25] The need for fresh interpretive evaluations of colonial situations from both etic and emic perspectives is clear. In ethnohistorical analyses we can benefit from postcolonial hindsight while retaining the continuity of human experience.

We too often pride ourselves upon having discarded the pre-literate, irrational cult of the ancestors for the "reason" of the present. Today, postcolonial concerns should lay in examining the past for fresh ways of healing, cooperating, and maximizing well-being rather than in unearthing additional fuel for old hostilities. It is especially important to reexamine old colonial twinships as the speed of global communications immediately connects us with twinships and métissages that were impossible only a decade earlier. Old colonial and minority wounds have festered globally, spawning many spins on the past. We can begin to redress this by examining twinship, by sailing away from the Nu-pieds rebellion in Normandy and trying on another nation's moccasins for size.

CHAPTER ONE

Intertwined Twintalk

"*C'est fait, on est frères ... Haudenosaunee, Hurons [Wendat],* Algonquins, et François, on n'est qu'un seul peuple."

Wendat Chief Atironta to Champlain[1]

Symbolic brotherhood and sisterhood was instituted through commercial, military, social, and familial Native alliances and was cemented by intercommunal bonding rituals. Fraternal twinships provided the basis for these alliances in both French and Native communities. "Twinning" in this context refers to a profoundly intertwined dialogue between two allies whose functions corresponded to each other yet whose comraderie or enmity goes beyond the purely utilitarian "I-it" exchanges into the *Zwischenmenschliche* (interhuman) dialogue defined by Martin Buber, which Emmanuel Lévinas has sometimes adjusted in his own "face à face," to place the Other before himself. The "I-Thou" relationship, as Buber sees it, tries to understand the whole human being beyond the mere utilitarianism of the "I-it" function, beyond Viktor Gecas's "reflected appraisals" approach, and into the dialogue approach of Sheldon Stryker's "symbolic inter-actionism."[2] Father LeClercq's Native chief "twin" declared the two to be brothers, that their hearts were one, he accompanied him everywhere, and he wore Leclercq's clothes, gloves, and rosary at all public functions to reinforce bonding.[3] Haudenosaunee captives even had blood drawn from them to mix with the blood of their captors not only so that they could know their enemy well but also in order to induce a cessation of hostilities as they would then be blood brothers.[4] In an I-Thou relationship, ancestral, socio-cultural, conceptual, and psychological mediating "ghosts" influence the dialogue between two people. In other words, inchoate socio-cultural models, ancestral and gender masks, rituals, and beliefs, as well as variables like bereavement, infuse any given dialogue with depth and meaning, or as Viktor Frankl and Emmanuel Lévinas consider it, "higher meaning." These "ghosts" dredge up collective historical memory intergenerational transmission a collage of utopian dreams, dreaded shadowy alters, and unresolved psychological states as Feinberg, Tisseron, Pirlot and Le François in *Evolution Psychiatrique*, have claimed. For initial inter-Atlantic contact, the rules governing an appropriate interchange were as yet uncharted, especially since the colonial accounts from other areas did not seem to reflect the current reality and since most immigrants were functionally non-literate. In this multivalent dialogue, the richness of communication was not limited to any discernable unidimensional self or Other; however, despite the intermittent polarization of positive or negative perception, people explored each other's, and their own, human inner worlds.

GHOSTLY DIALOGUE

The tightly knotted real or symbolic kin relationship that bound alliances involved a combination of twinships between members of the same sex from each community and interethnic partnering, or métissage, between French male/Native female. Brotherhood (fraternité) struck a resonant chord with the Frenchmen, who trusted their ties to their "buddies" over their ties to women. The intense and long-lasting alliance between Algonquians and Wendat, which now included the French, involved strands of twinships whose intercommunal ghosts "dialogued" with one another directly or by reference, depending on the paths their lives took, whether parallel, polarized, inverted, or collaged. Non-verbal dialogue complemented the verbal interchange in committed fraternal twinships, where meaning reverberated in the slightest acts and culturally mediated metaphor echoed, especially for Aboriginals, whose gifts were "words," pregnant with significance. Thus, ghosts wound themselves about the nexus of twinships between Champlain and Cherououny, Bruslé and Amantacha, and Brébeuf and Annaotaha, who usually metaphorically represented aspects of the past but who also reflected glimmers of emerging alternative inner worlds and identities that remained latent until prompted to appear, especially by life-death encounters. These alternates, or "ghosts," represented the appropriated or rejected characteristics of the absent complementary twin. The simultaneous expansion of a heightening Other-conciousness with a deepening self-conciousness revolutionized a widened cultural and mental frame of communal reference.

Native-French twinships could be intense, as they were factored into a conceptual and emotive network that was already replete with "phantoms." Northeastern First Nations are currently derived from a mix of Native and some European ancestry. This study may perhaps assist in the recognition of some hazy ghosts of the past that can help them clarify the trajectory of their ancestral past and its effect upon their current lives within the context of an important oral tradition. Even among egalitarian Natives, the French thought in terms of hierarchies. Recollect brother Gabriel Sagard thought the Wendat aristocratic owing to the harmony of that society, which was regulated by bonding, taboos, and rigourous self-control.[5] He considered the Algonquian and Innu to be more akin to the Third Estate, with the former being "bourgeois" and the latter being peasants. In the Algonquian-Wendat alliance, the Wendat were the elder brother. Of the Wendat Charlevoix wrote: "of all Canada, they have the most intelligence but ... [also excessive] dissimulation ... [they are] feared and respected by the other wildmen [*sic*] for their industriousness, their fertile genius for efficiency and resourcefulness, their eloquence and courage ... yet they have more faults and virtues [than the others]."[6] French and Wendat twinships were coloured by overly utopian expectations, which were sometimes accompanied by extreme disappointments, which led to mutual accusations of perfidy. According to Sagard, "our Hurons [Wendat] have some admirable qualities above our own ... they possess moral virtues ... conduct themselves in a humbly dignified and modest manner ... they rarely take offence and pardon each other easily .... because they love [one another]."[7] The French therefore preferred Frenchifying and missionising wealthy settled agricultural Wendat over doing the same to most other hunting/gathering Algonquians. They invested more in distant Wendake, despite Innu proximity and their fascination with those Mi'kmaqs who used the cross as their emblem.[8] However, they took their cue from the alliance configuration itself. The Algonquians admired the Wendat, for although there were only around 30,000 of them in the confederation, 300,000 mostly Algonquians spoke Wendat due to their centrality in the commercial nexus.[9] For some French the Wendat served as an inverse mirror to criticize French social, political, and legal mores as well as providing a challenging religious alternative. The unflattering image of themselves stimulated French political reflection. Although many other aboriginals were admired or reviled by an entire literature, dialogue with the Wendat caused the French to doubt themselves.

Overstretched French expectations of Wendat utopian behaviour was not based only upon ideas of the Noble Savage, as was the case in the metropolis. In Canada there was the realistic perception that Christianity had been successfully challenged by an alternative worldview. Typically, Charlevoix reports of the Wendat Ahatsistari: "[He has] good sense, natural eloquence, and an elevated nobility of sentiments."[10] Sagard began to fear that the French might lose God's favour: "God would be pleased with them better than our miserable Frenchmen who chase him from our houses, by our tumults, our quarrels, and our never-ending debates ... This is why I am frightened that in the end, a punishment like that of the Jews does not happen to us."[11] This contrition gave way to confusion as recurrent theories expounding upon the possible Israelite origin of the Amerindians were debated.[12] If the Natives were pre-Adamites or the ten lost Hebrew tribes, then how could they have better socio-political sense than the pious Counter-Reformation French? Other French writers reflect the utopian dialogue between Wendat and French missionaries, and their rivalry with regard to the latter's attempts to match higher Native norms of sharing.[13] In addition, the utopian vision of the lost tribes enflamed Jewish belief in the coming of the Messiah as well as Puritan millennial beliefs in the Second Coming and the New Jerusalem.[14]

By contrast, the French-Algonquian relationship was less bombarded by distance, conceptual expectations, and melded multiple images than was the French-Wendat relationship. There was an older, more intimate and frequent contact, material borrowing, and fusion than occurred with the French-Wendat configuration. Therefore, "ghosts" were often those of not only the traditional past but also of their own shared past. There were myriad Algonquian nations, so variations and alternatives were endless; however, to the French, it had a "family look."

I will illuminate the twinning of two adult heroes, two youths, and two adult leaders in exceptional life-death encounters. The incidents to be recounted were fraught with risk, emotion, and conflicted interests, where the true Buberian exchange emerges from beneath the mask of social forms. The greatest risk in such emergence would be to be misinterpreted as then communication would be reduced to a series of bungled misreadings. Youths as well as the adults were either involved in trading and/or evangelization. The first set of twins is Samuel de Champlain and Innu chief Cherououny. The second set is Estienne Bruslé and Wendat Attigneenongnahac Amantacha (baptised Loüys de Ste-Foy). The third set is Father Brébeuf and Wendat chief Annaotaha. The first set is French-Algonquian and involves two rather ordinary men who became chiefs through their gift for intercultural understanding. However, while one began with hostility and ended with amicability, the other began with amicability and ended with hostility. Both participated in crystallizing the French legal approach to murder within the interethnic alliance, a very telling indication of how unfortunate incidents were regulated. The second set is French-Wendat and involves a friendship between two notably promising youths. The French youth specialized in trading, the Wendat youth in religion. However, after either was murdered outside their respective birth communities, the collective commemorations of their memory were held in opposite regard: while the first failed to be an effective intercultural liaison, the second succeeded. The third set is French-Wendat and involves especially heroic men, with the Wendat being a trader and the Frenchman a missionary. These heroes were martyred for the sake of one another's birth communities and received exceptional honour. All six of our twins knew each other, and all save one, Champlain, died by human hands.

Samuel Champlain had many Algonquian chiefs as partners, but there was none who could aptly be called his unlike twin outside of Cherououny. Cherououny was an Innu chief who chose to accommodate himself to French cultural and diplomatic protocol. But in the end, even though they behaved in similar ways, the naive Champlain and the wily Cherououny had opposite approaches to the unknown.

To begin with, the Innu were originally the key fur-trading allies of the French until the latter were introduced to the Wendat. Both Innu and Algonquians were avid to insert themselves in disputes between French and Wendat in order to improve their trade rights. Bruslé, for example, experienced an Innu ruse to claim payment for passage from both French and Wendat at Cap de Victoire.[15] As fur trade rivalry mounted between 1608 and 1633, cultural misunderstandings added to an intimate but tense dialogue. The Wendat-Innu dialogue awoke dormant French snobbery when the Wendat called the Innu "babelling geese." This was a reference to Innu spontaneity as compared to Wendat reserve.[16] The Innu, due to their precarious northern hunting and fishing existence, possessed excellent survival skills and sharing values, yet their lack of a well-elaborated agricultural village system tended to jeopardise their status vis-à-vis both Wendat and French. Although the Innu were perhaps the most intimately intertwined communally and geographically with the French, they frequently felt obliged to underline the seniority of these ties.

Second, there was a cultural gap between what the French and what the Innu considered to be required generosity. The Innu shared everything among themselves, including their medicines when in the French hospital (Hôtel-Dieu).[17] Even if the French greatly admired this, it made them uncomfortable to know that, if they were to avoid reproach, they too would have to reciprocate everything and keep nothing private.[18] Several misunderstandings occurred to illustrate this, as when the Innu were upset over the pettiness of French gifts and decided that whatever the French were holding back they would simply appropriate.[19]

Nevertheless, when the French returned to Canada in 1633, the French-Innu relationship was characterized by great interdependency as the French initiated winter feeding of Innu destitute and put the elderly, ill, and some children in the hospital. Innu adults reciprocated by bringing them fresh winter game.[20] Additionally, French male commoners were quite close to the Innu with whom they hunted and fraternized, and whom they admired for their resourcefulness and stoic manliness in extreme winter conditions. The Innu girls, on the other hand, were eager to learn dainty French beadwork, crochet, lace, and crafts.

Within this interdependent yet tense framework, Innu reaffirmations of brotherhood sometimes created conflict and even divided chiefs with regard to how best to handle interethnic dialogue. The biggest conflict occurred in 1628–29, when the Kirke brothers conquered Quebec. Some chiefs led the British/Huguenot Kirke brothers to lay siege to Quebec in order to punish the French for relying upon Wendat traders rather than upon themselves. Erouachy, Mahican Atic Ouache (Miristou) and the Tadoussac chiefs reached out to the British, while Chomina, Negabamat, and Napagabiscou defended the French.[21]

The main misunderstanding, and one that had repeated social consequences, involved the French perceiving themselves as authoritarian but generous fathers while perceiving the First Nations as naughty children. Natives perceived the French as the still-feminine younger brother in the alliance, yet with a coat of many colours like the biblical Joseph. The royal pardon for capital crimes was as important in the French pantheon of social reintegration strategies as was the royal "healing touch," which cured scrofula on feast days which Marc Bloch made famous.[22] Thousands crowded around the king to have their lymph nodes touched and head crowned by his magical sign of the cross.[23] These extraordinary symbols served to offset the ordinary business of paternalistic tyranny, symbolized by the arbitrary royal order (lettre de cachet) that threw the recipient into the Bastille, which became the bête noire of the French Revolution.[24] How the French and Natives negotiated these discrepancies over time transformed their perceptions and reconfigured their relationships.

THE BUMBLER AND THE DISSIMULATOR

Samuel de Champlain was in an utter quandary. Famous around Native council fires for his accommodation, he was laughed down by his own men for his unassuming affability, credulity, and lack of refinement. Brimming with frustration, he reviewed his former bosses. The consequences of unassertive leadership, among other things, brought down Biencourt de Poutrincourt, Gravé du Pont (Pont-Gravé), and Pierre du Gua, sieur de Monts in Acadia, not to mention the part it played in Cardinal Richelieu's taming of the royals.[25] Champlain's ability to be accomodating was his most beloved feature, yet now that he was in a position of authority it became his nemesis. How could he become a respected governor when he was famous as the world's friendliest explorer? Everyone joked about his famous Ordre du Bon Temps! He had married a wealthy heiress whose father was the secretary of the king's chamber. Yet her parents twice dispossessed her due to their snobbish attitude towards Champlain's life work.[26] Even adding the noble "de" to his otherwise common name couldn't elevate his standing. Marc Lescarbot, the erudite Parisian lawyer, also thumbed his nose at Champlain for believing in the frightful Algonquian Gougou monster – which surely was dangerous. And then there was Duval, the cad, who brewed mutiny even before the Quebec habitation was built. And that rascal interpreter De Vignau, who, after exhausting everyone canoeing and portaging for days to reach Allumette Island, led them to a non-existent "mer de nord" (north sea).[27] And that pair of turncoat interpreters, Jean Nicolet and Etienne Bruslé! Bruslé! His face flushed crimson as Etienne's Haudeno-saunee captivity stories had formerly evoked his indulgence, when he had really been double-dealing in furs.[28] And now was the fatal blow, as he navigated the Scottish Kirke brothers' vessel to besiege Quebec. Now everyone was starving.[29]

After years of braving the saltwater, Champlain was now finally lieutenant-general of Quebec. Yet why did he continually wind up in the pickling barrel? He would make himself heard by evasive chiefs, disdainful Parisian officials, and rough-hewn mariners. Even his friends among the Innu chiefs had sometimes chortled at him, but now they ruled for his downfall. They hadn't listened to him during the attack on Iroquoia, leaving him wounded and fuming.[30] Maybe Kichespirini chief Tessouat had lied to him about De Vignau, wanting to prevent direct French trade with the "north sea." After all, they didn't call him the Borgne de l'Isle for nothing.[31] No matter. He founded this colony and refused to be anyone's fool.[32]

These might have been the indignant and hungry Champlain's thoughts as he answered the Kirkes from behind his doomed defensive wall: "I will answer you by the mouths of my canons." It was 1628. The Innu were edgy about ceding primacy in the fur trade to the Wendat, and Champlain already knew he had bungled relations with them. It seemed hard to maintain a comfortable equilibrium with chiefs who never presumed to rule, for, as Gilles Deleuze writes, the very nature of a horizontally run alliance among equals, as opposed to a vertically run hierarchy among non-equals, was complex and in continual disequilibrium.[33] Champlain's actions were an attempt to bolster the security of his newly founded French haven in what he perceived to be a Native ocean. Native alliances were feted with mountains of steaming moose and beaver meat, yet one had to keep abreast of subtle innuendo. Champlain was an inexperienced administrator and relative newcomer, yet he was now responsible to the French Crown for every blunder within the subtle web of Native alliance and intrigue. Surely he felt himself inadequate to the task. His dream was to become a fatherly mediator among the Aboriginal nations, with cultural and diplomatic liaisons (interpreter and traders) whose fidelity he could depend upon.

Ironically, this forced him to swear the filial fidelity of a younger brother. The deaths of two Frenchmen, discovered prior to the siege, put the French-Innu dialogue in difficulty due to the power of "phantoms" during bereavement. Innu chiefs like Erouachy were disturbed over Champlain's bid to assert his authority following the deaths of two Frenchmen, Henry and Dumoulin, who were killed by an Innu. Recollect Brother Gabriel Sagard thought the culprit was Miristou (Mahican Atic Ouache), but Champlain thought it was another man, whom he imprisoned at Quebec. He swore indignantly that French lives were not meaningless.[34] He wrote that when he conferred with Innu chief La Fourière over these two murders, he had saved over 100 of their families from starvation. Champlain's outrage was increased when he overheard the unlikely Haudenosaunee version, which blamed the Algonquians for the crime. Champlain fumed and was no longer going to countenance the "gall of impassive assassinations" by Innu, into whose hands the French had literally entrusted their existence.[35]

After all, premeditated murder was not liable to royal pardon in France or Britain, with, as Nathalie Davis tells us, only "ordinary hot-heads" (chaude colle) who "accidently" overdid it receiving any sympathy.[36] Even so, there was still a legal precedent for a French pardon. In Rouen, the Privilege of St-Romain was a tradition that involved the cathedral canons pardoning the most deserving criminal in prison.[37] Besides, his men had previously pardoned another murder by the Innu. In 1616 Cherououny murdered two Frenchmen, who were presumed to have drowned in their canoes. The lifeless bodies of locksmith (Antoine Natel or Recerche) and Charles Pillet were found in a forest stream two years later, weighted down by stones. Horrified, the Innu withdrew from the Quebec habitation. Taking counsel, the French decided to wait for the ships from France before tackling the situation. Brother Sagard even claimed that 800 frightened Algonquians of diverse nations planned to kill all the French, thinking to avoid counter-revenge, but then called it off when they realized the French did not suspect them. Chief La Fourière was sent to reconcile matters with the French. While Champlain thought they were ready to negotiate because they had been deprived of dialogue and good hospitality (conversation et bon accueil accoutumé), Sagard wrote that Innu diplomacy was the result of forty canoes full of hungry women and children.[38]

While Native custom offered gifts to "wipe away the community's tears," the French deferred to Recollect judgment, despite their preference for consulting Champlain and the sea captains. They opted to interrogate the suspected murderers. The Innu considered the horrifying possibility of a perpetual war with the French and, thus, decided to send them forth. In Champlain's absence, tempers rose. Champlain's version noted that the Innu considered the French to be rather effeminate. One of the assassins, Cherououny, dared to brave French justice by entering the habitation with his father. Although the French only held the assassins responsible, they were quite startled when they realized that their great friends the Innu had been collectively hiding the crime. The Innu claimed that it was "too late" once they knew about it, so they kept quiet while "reprimanding the culprits that brought misfortune upon them, their families and their friends" so as not to ruin relations with the French.[39] The Recollects countered by saying that, after ten to twelve years of inexpressibly close friendship, after showing

compassion for Innu needs, and after Champlain having fought Innu enemies, the French were shaken by these murders. Ostensibly, Father Joseph
Le Caron told the murderer's father that his son deserved to die together
with Father Paul Huet. The missionaries' view was opposed to that of merchant Beauchesne, who led the French who were willing to settle. The
French were also shocked to learn that, prior to the murders, the victim had
rounded up his friends to beat Cherououny. The Innu, however, pointed
out that they had freely brought the murderer to the French. Cherououny's
father wept for grace for his "worthless, young and crazy son." Cherououny
publically confessed his crime and commended his life into French hands,
calling upon the merchant Beauchaine to kill him right then and there.

Ultimately, the French pardoned Cherououny in a formal hybrid ceremony that mixed Native condolence gift-giving, a royal pardon, and priestly
absolution. This reconciliatory action contrasts greatly with the Puritan
decision to exterminate the Pequots after John Stone's murder a decade
and a half later in 1637. As Stone had hunted escapee Natives, in that case
the Native motivation for murder was surely greater than in the case involving Cherououny's personal revenge. The French accepted the traditional
Innu presents, which were given to reintegrate the white/First Nations
interethnic community. The first gift was twelve moose skins; the second was
the cleansing of the bloody murder site; the third was two beaver robes to
strengthen the arms of those who buried the dead; the fourth was to cleanse
the murderers and to give them back their lost sense; the fifth was to efface
all French resentment; the sixth was to strengthen the inviolable peace with
the French by casting away hatchets; the seventh was 2,000 blue and black
wampum beads that were to enable the French to open their ears to the
sweetness of peace and to pardon the murderers; and the eighth gift was a
chain of wampum, along with ten robes of beaver and moose, to induce the
union of the French and Innu.[40] Then, after some deliberation, Father
Joseph LeCaron pardoned Cherououny but stipulated that two children,
Nigamon and Tebachi, be adopted by the French as formal hostages.[41]
Emery de Caen threw a sword into the St Lawrence to wash away ill will, but
evidently the rumour went about that the Innu now believed that the price
of a Frenchman could be covered by several pelts.[42] Even so, Cherououny
was henceforth dubbed the Reconciled (le Réconcilié).

What were the reasons for the French accepting the condolence gifts and
instituting the pardon? Given that they were furious, it was not out of a
desire to accommodate (douceur). First, the French were very few and were
interpenetrated by Innu. If they took vengeance, this would render them
continually on the defensive in their intercultural dialogue with the Innu
and perhaps with other bands. Vengeance would also harm the trust
required for the fur trade. Second, the Innu themselves had responded to
the French request for the murderer responsibly, which, presumably, would

hold oblige them "to be friends and serve [sic] the French."[43] In other words, building French and Innu interdependence forbade punishing the murderers of the French. In their deliberations, Champlain and Recollect Superior Le Caron lauded the trust and dialogue that the Innu and French had enjoyed for over thirty years, while Sagard emphasised the survival value of peace. Even though the former pointed to the Buberian I-Thou relationship, while the latter clung to the I-it relationship, for the French, both trust and survival were intimately linked.

Nevertheless, Innu secrecy about this grave crime exemplified the opposed views of French and Innu regarding what this intercommunal trust consisted of. The French suddenly discovered that, despite Innu affability, they would not always reveal personal secrets. This deep reserve disconcerted the French for they could never be sure whether the Innu were really upset. The Innu, by contrast, distrusted volatile French "feminine" emotionality. Neither could perceive the other as truly sincere. While the French engaged in camaraderie, in constant banter, argument, or weeping, they guarded their own possessions jealously. Innu closeness, on the other hand, never limited the independence of the individual with verbal intimacy, yet sharing and extensive mutual aid to family and community were unquestionably primary obligations.[44]

The difference between French and Native conceptions lay within the uniqueness of the individual. One historian has postulated that, whereas the French mourned a lost "self" and punished a guilty "self," Native peoples offered equivalent gifts because they valued the "personhood" of the lost individual and the "person" of the murderer. How can a society that so profoundly respected the sacredness of human individuality and uniqueness suddenly foist a "personhood" upon someone when he/she is deceased? Probably because Native justice focused upon assisting the victim, not on punishing the perpetrator. Killing the assassin of an allied band would only create more bad blood and would not bring back the dead. Gift exchange was favoured as a method of reintegrating the social life of necessarily allied peoples through the triumph of reason over passion. Obviously, the gifts were not offered as mere "blood money" according to rank ("wergild" in medieval Germanic usage). The sacred quality of human life translated into social reconciliation between allies but into blood revenge between enemies.

Native society had a more subtle grasp of the gap between interiorization and exteriorization than did French society. Thus, as cited by White, while living in Iroquoia a Wendat could declare himself fully Haudenosaunee, yet with a Wendat heart.[45] Philosopher Paul Ricoeur thinks of identity as a paradox because the unchanging self over time (identité-idem) and the polysemy of one's otherness (identité-ipse) appear to be contradictory concepts.[46] Full conscious recognition of the dissociative gap between the two was confusing for the average early modern Frenchman, if he was not busy constructing outer social masks for the court, even if women became famous for the rigours of their bare-faced confessions to their spiritual directors.[47] The Native courtesy of deferring to one another's social faces was not a notable feature in France, nor was the inner search for truth. On both social and psychological levels, Native cultures applied their knowledge of these sensitivities in highly effective adoption strategies, diplomatic subtlety, dream therapy, and conversionary techniques, all of which were continual sources of astonishment to the French. The missionaries learned greatly from what they observed and put some lessons into practice. It is possible that the French-Native dialogue contributed to the increasing recognition of the distinction between the "innerness" of the self and the exteriority of the world, especially that of the "Other," as the mark of modernization.[48]

After all was said and done, Champlain still called Cherououny a murderer, especially after the latter became chief. Champlain forced him to depart from a feast that he himself hosted in 1622, which, by Native standards, was a truly offensive act. He pretended to desire to kill him and refused to take his hand as Cherououny was dancing during peace talks with the Haudenosaunee. Champlain's approach contrasts greatly with John Smith of Virginia's attack upon the Powhatans for lesser offences, although this nation initially fed and kept them alive in their new country. Champlain wrote that it was divine justice when Cherououny later died as a captive in Iroquoia for, in his eyes, the murders were spiritually unabsolved.[49] The absent grieving French families of these lone immigrant youth were but "ghosts" at the proceedings. In French eyes, Dumoulin and Henri's rowdiness and insults were considered to be merely mischieveous, while in Native culture an arbitrary loss of face was usually followed by courteous silence, even though it could bring blood revenge or suicide. Not having accepted or fully digested this, Champlain was not satisfied. Therefore, he ostracized Cherououny so as not to jeopardize intercommunal relations.

At least, he did so until the second murder incident was revealed in 1628. This time Champlain tried to see that the new assassin was treated in the manner in which he thought Cherououny should have been treated. He wanted, at all costs, to bury his own former "ghost" identity of being a buffoon. This time the suspected murderer was hauled into jail, and even his son was held as hostage, together with a French accomplice. But Chief Erouachy, and Chief Cherououny himself, forced Champlain to kiss the dust by pardoning the assassin. Interdependency triumphed.

What was the link that repeatedly set Champlain and his erstwhile double, Cherououny, at odds? When Cherououny faced his Recollect judges, he knew that because they desired converts, they always preferred attrition, contrition, confession, and absolution over death.[50] He bargained his life upon the wise policy of a show of classic Native dread of loss of face mixed with a healthy dose of unflinching honesty, which the French found utterly disarming. The cultural dexterity with which Cherououny handled this dangerous situation contrasts greatly with Champlain's cultural flatfootedness.

The subtle French diplomat resplendent in Versailles who possessed "génie colonial" was preceded by the adventurous but blundering buffoon. Awkward newcomer twinned with agile Native was a social reality that repeated itself over and over again. The newcomer became the invariable life of the party as he tipped over his birch bark canoe, fell headlong into an icy precipice when snowshoeing, and speared his hand when torch-fishing Innu-style. If the early Algonquian model from folklore and Euro-Canadian history was characterized by imperturbable wiliness, then the early French model was characterized by jovial bumbling.

After 1648, the French accepted reparations for crimes committed by First Nations perpetrators. Jan Grabowski, Richard White, and John Dickinson remind us that Natives who killed and were pardoned by French allies constituted a veritable motif that was repeated many times over. Dickinson reminds us of French acceptance of Wendat reparations for the murder of Jacques Douart in Wendake.[51] White cites Vaudreuil, who virtually reiterated Champlain's remark that the blood of Frenchmen was not to be paid in beaverskins. He also expected the Odawa to put "great trust in [his] kindness ... [to experience] a real repentance ... and a complete resignation to [his] will,"[52] which corresponds closely to Champlain's approach. In other words, the French focus was upon murder as an indication of disrespect for French authority, which required Catholic contrition before a suitably paternal pardon could be contemplated. The Natives, on the other hand, focused upon the grief of the deceased's mother and relatives by offering gifts to soothe the bereavement of the family. This pattern was identified by White as the French demanding the surrender of the killer while requiring remorse (ostensibly to satisfy the post-Trentine Church), deference (ostensibly to satisfy the French king), and then, as local symbolic representatives of both Church and Crown, they accorded a pardon with these minimal requirements, plus reparation gifts to "cover" the dead and mend the communal wound.[53] After all, "younger brothers" have to listen attentively to those "older" and wiser.

THE LONER AND THE LAMB

The wind swept through their hair, they had downed a few pints of firewater and had just dumped that insufferable old fogey Champlain, who was determined to starve Quebec to death. And those bearded Scotch seamen had the most hilarious accent, one had to rib them at any price! So Etienne Bruslé pretended to his Scottish captors that young Wendat friend Amantacha, baptised by the Jesuits as Loüys de Sainte-Foy, actually was a

Wendat prince who held many beauteous furs and gold. Snickering, the two marvelled at the outlandish outfit that the Kirke brothers offered Amantacha, as Bruslé firmly guided their vessel nearer and nearer to hungry Quebec. The two, as prisoners of war, were sailed back home by the Kirke brothers, one as a pauper, the other as a prince. And they laughed until they cried when they stood face to face with the enraged Champlain and Amantacha's horrified, and impoverished, father.

The youths had been sent by their own communities to become inter-preter-liaisons (truchements). Their identities were still fluid, as socio-cultural mores of each other's communities challenged their still flexible childhood and youthful cognitive schemae, or Weltanschauungen, in order to find the appropriate collaged identity (identité bricolée) within the novel intercommunal situation.[54] Anthropologist Claude Lévi-Strauss's idea of a mythmaker as a craftsperson (bricoleur)[55] must also be applied to the con-struction of identity, as events and myths contribute to locating a sense of self. Estienne Bruslé was one of the first French youths to be sent, at around age eighteen, to live among the Amerindian allies, and he became an inter-preter according to Native alliance procedure.[56] He was among a group of fifteen to twenty young men from 1615 to 1628 to be sent to Wendake, among them: Du Vernay, Grenolle, Guillaume Chaudron, La Criette, La Montagne, La Vallee, La Marche, and Auhaitsique, who was familiarly refer-red to only by his Wendat name.[57] Bruslé's Zwischenmenschliche twin was his great admirer Amantacha (Loüys de Ste-Foy), who was sent to France in 1626 in order to be an Attignawantan, or Bear Clan, intermediary for the French upon his return. Due to the complexity of an adolescent bricolage of identity, he incorporated wide-ranging cultural transpositions, which were low on communal commitment. Amantacha also initially floundered, espe-cially when accompanied by Bruslé, yet he eventually committed himself to the good of both communities. He expressed his fidelity to both, so his own métissage culturel would promote Wendat and French intercourse; at the same time, he aspired to one of the primary guiding principles of psycho-social evolution: he chose to commit himself to a measure of communal responsibility.[58]

Bruslé clung to his Wendat lifestyle as if it were his lucky charm, the magic spell that opened all doors within the circumference of his two cultural worlds. Having been born in Champigny-sur-Marne (ca. 1592 to ca. June 1632), he lived with the Wendat from the age of eighteen, between 1608 and 1632, excluding two years that he spent in France (1622–23 and 1626–28).[59] He was famous for espousing Wendat rather than French orien-tations, including the Wendat view of Wendat-Innu rivalry,[60] and he offered sacred Native tobacco to a "metamorphised man" rock to ensure an excel-lent voyage.[61] Prior to a canoe accident, the only Christian prayer he recalled was grace before meals.[62] Yet it appears that Bruslé successfully utilized the Wendat cultural mode without being satisfactorily integrated into either the French or the Wendat socio-cultural web. This upset both communities, causing them to suspect him of perfidy and, in the end, to condone his death. Initially, his adaptability pleased Champlain and the Wendat chiefs, who sent him on important errands and allowed him unprecedented travel freedom. However, the Wendat appeared uneasy when he remained with Susquehannock allies all winter in 1615. His companions claimed that he had been captured by Haudenosaunee enemies (Seneca) and that he returned to the Susquehannock alone.[63] Had he simply been abandoned? Even the Seneca appeared puzzled about his identity – a lone, bearded (i.e., European) youth who was Wendat-speaking yet had a French accent, who refused to be called an "Adoresetoüy" (Man of Iron, i.e., Frenchman)?

Nonetheless, even if he was becoming confused and isolated culturally, he initiated and reciprocated kindnesses, even to his quasi-enemies. He taught the Jesuits the Wendat language after they saved his life, even though they were instrumental in removing him from Wendake for three years and reducing his wages.[64] Even though Bruslé sided with the British Kirke expedition during the siege of Quebec in 1628–29, he lent 100 écus without interest to none other than Louis Hébert, the model of fidelity to Governor Champlain. Bruslé therefore seems to have adopted a Wendat cultural mode without its socio-cultural anchoring. His personality took on a chameleon-like quality to some friends, and this disconcerted them because he did not fit into any recognizable mould. Psychologist Erik Erikson writes that a sense of ego identity becomes more necessary whenever a wide range of possible identities can be envisaged, for it involves a psychological process that reflects social processes and/or a social process that reflects psychological processes. Yet youth is the prime time of identity confusion due to a confusing array of choices and an ostensible moratorium on adult responsibilities.[65] Bruslé's identité bricolée was constantly shifting: risky explorations, the unwillingness to identify himself as a Frenchman, switching allegiance from Catholic to Huguenot, Champlain to Kirke, from tribe to tribe and from woman to woman (married to Parisian Alizon Coiffier plus many Wendat partners).[66] Sagard attributed this long-standing non-commital mindset to his idea of "Nativization."[67] Yet French reservations regarding his métissage may have only added to those of the Wendat.[68] Erikson writes that fidelity bolsters adolescent ego strength, which can arise only in the interplay of the individual life stages within a true community.[69] This was precisely what was ambiguous between French and Wendat prior to permanent settlement in 1632, when overall interethnic policy was only in its formulation stages.

Bruslé left once again for Wendake and never returned. Archaeologist Bruce Trigger theorizes that he attempted to divert trade to the Seneca or to join them, thus again conjuring charges of perfidy.[70] Did Amantacha try to save him? Therein lies the ambiguity of where commitment ends and the choice between perfidy or self-destruction begins. To what extent were unlike twins tied together at the expense of their own self-destruction? Bruslé's death was so controversial that talk of including him at the great Feast of the Dead aroused contention between Chief Anenkhiondic and murder suspect Chief Aenons.[71] Jesuit refusal to include Bruslé's bones in the great reburial caused angst over not having fraternal relations with the French, even symbolically. The feast was celebrated every twelve years in order to join the bones of the dead in a common grave so that all the parts of the soul that reside in the bones (astiken) could be together until they could be reincarnated, relinking the chain of Wendat dead and living in one community.[72] These beliefs were much like those associated with the European plague-linked dance macabre, both having been instituted during community-shattering epidemics. Perhaps the telling forensic condition of the corpse caused Chief Aenons to be suspicious. Brébeuf publically condemned Bruslé in Wendake, yet he privately anguished over Bruslé's fate, and perhaps his own. If anyone understood Bruslé, it would have been Brébeuf as they were together for seven years in Wendake (1623–29).[73] So eventually both communities felt Bruslé to be a perfidious insider rather than a friendly outsider. If he was regularly misunderstood, no wonder he ended up a lone wolf. But after his death, if the Wendat wanted to be forgiven by his spirit, then so did the French. His bones ultimately received a Christian burial.

High expectations, bordering on the utopian, that tied French and Wendat together haunted both whenever one failed the other. Phantom lore was extremely prominent in northwestern France, as can be seen in several Livres d'heures, La Légende dorée, the miribilia literature (Miracles du Protomartyr Etienne, Perlevaus, Amadas et Idoine, and the "aître périlleux," or haunted cemetery).[74] In Wendake, where great value was placed upon the community, the spirits of the dead never hovered too far. They were seen in dreams and by shamanic orendiouane and oki.[75] When a community is abruptly faced with devastating epidemics that cut the ties with its elders, painfully severing the living from the dead, the cult of the dead can become especially significant. If at the same time this dismembered community forges significant links with a foreign community whose ways are difficult to decode, then the interweaving and juxtaposition of the living community with the accompanying communities of the deceased is even more essential as an anchor of identity. The searching dialogue that took place involved a constant intercommunal comparison as well as a continual working through of the past. The Feast of the Dead cemented stability in an epidemically ravaged and militarily menaced community whose commercial livelihood depended upon favourable intertribal relations.

The belief in the visitation of phantoms thus has deep roots and there are profound reasons for its continued existence in French Canadian folklore. Ghost tales fill this folklore: "le revenant," "la dame blanche" (Montmorency Falls), "le fantôme de Blanche de Beaumont" (Rocher Percé)," "le noyeux," "les fantômes du manoir," "le fantôme du Cap Rosier," "l'Hôte à Valiquette," "le fantôme de la Roche" "le fantôme de l'avare," "le fantôme de la tempête" (Repentigny), "la voleuse de la barette" (la Pocatière), "trois gouttes de sang," "la chambre du revenant," "le revenant au presbytère de Gentilly," "le revenant de Pascal Dion," and "la grande oie blanche" of L'Islet, according to which the young son of a captain waded to a rock beyond the shore, was swallowed by the tide, and returned as a snow goose.[76] In these tales, generally the ghost returns to right a wrong or pay off a debt, such as in "Michel Morin" (La Pocatière).[77] Several later historical figures across the continent were immortalized in French North American lore (sometimes via Métis or Amerindian tales) by their tragedies, such as Admiral Walker, who is still looking for his lost ships ("le fantôme de l'Île-aux-Oeufs"), "bones of the prophet" (île au pêche or Peach Island), "the phantom Priest" (Recollect Brother Constantin Del Halle of St. Anne's Church, b.1670), and "ghost of Mongaugon" (Governor Hull's surrender at Detroit in 1805).[78]

North Atlantic French lore, especially in the Breton and Norman areas from whence the immigrants came, were fraught with phantom tales that had evolved since their origin as pre-Christian Celtic and Norse traditions. As French historian Le Roy Ladurie has noted, French "folklore horizontale" kept the dead close to the living.[79] The meaning of one's heritage can become strengthened when one is faced with an uncertain environment, particularly when this enviromnemt reinforces supportive communal ties between the dead and the living in an "incomplete society." Historian Jean Delumeau mentions that many early modern European jurists and physicians believed that corpses could bleed in the presence of the assassin (like in Shakespeare's *Richard III*) and ensure justice (like in *Hamlet*), and haunted houses were accorded payment exemptions.[80] The link between the living and the deceased was especially strong in north Atlantic France. Breton spirits ("spontails") return during the Celtic Feast of the Souls (Goël ann Anaon, formerly Samhain [Halloween]), Christmastime, or after the fires of the summer solstice Feast of St John the Baptist.[81] Spontails dominated the night, as the living did the day, and the latest deceased in a village (Ankou) were feared for their death-barrow, into which the unwary living were thrown. When the deceased were placed upon a stone before burial, the buggy was hurried home to prevent the dead from returning.[82] If they disturbed the living, they were unearthed, chopped into pieces, or weighted with a stone, and the heart was frequently burned. Breton spontails return in the form of ghosts or animals, usually in the form of birds, bees, butterflies, crows, or ravens, who were called "badb," meaning the fury of the early Celtic war goddess Morrigan, who was reincarnated as King Arthur's sister.[83]

Norman revenants embodied the Germanic idea of the soul as an envelope ("hamr"), or twin-brother. This twin had Roman roots as a "larvatus," or "mascus" (witch), and its Celtic counterpart was a "taidhbhse."[84] Those born with a caul were supposedly gifted with shamanic powers as they were born with a natural shroud that enabled them to pass through to the realm of the dead.[85] The Greek-Roman roots hailed from the "empousai," who were angry souls associated with Hecate and Miasma, inanimate agents of pollution that embodied the rage of the slain.[86] Hence the preoccupation with "dames blanches," or ghosts, in north Atlantic France, such as "La dame blanche de Tal-ar-Groas" and "Le fantôme du Maner bihan."[87] Elves ("gobelins" in Norman) were ancestors who returned after death because of some sin, and they often became horses like the cheval Bayard. We must remember that death was one's constant companion in seventeenth-century Normandy. About 50 percent of the population died before age twenty. Furthermore, between 1600 and 1670 11 to 15 percent of the French population perished of the plague, whereas between 1628 and 1632, plague victims constituted 25 to 30 percent of all deaths in France.[88] Aside from the plague, tax revolts, the Wars of Religion, the Fronde, poverty, and illness account for additional mortality. Therefore, the connection between the deceased and the living was particularly intense in north Atlantic France due to local traditions that were exacerbated by increased mortality. The concrete presence of the dead was also evident for ossuaries (garnals) were kept in Brittany. To this day, charnel houses still exist in both Brittany and Normandy.

The dead returning to haunt the living was a concept shared with the Wendat. After Bruslé's death, the Wendat collectively felt guilty. The avenging spirit of Bruslé's sister was assumed to have been responsible for the drought of 1636 and other disasters that almost prevented the missionaries from returning to Wendake.[89] The chiefs of Ossossané and Téanaostaia strove to right this wrong by including Bruslé's bones among those buried during the Feast of the Dead in order to mingle his remains with those of the community, thus uniting them, in death, as one family. Chief Aenons staked his reputation on serving and protecting Father Brébeuf, while insisting that he was not Bruslé's killer. And curiously, when Chief Aenons' son lost a large wampum collar in gaming, he committed suicide because: "I have someone inside me telling me continually, hang yourself, hang yourself" ("i'ay quelqu'vn dedans moy qui me dit continuellement, pends toy, pends toy"), and Bruslé was again invoked.[90] The Attignawantan (Bear Clan) conscience was decidedly haunted by guilt and closely resembled ghostly Breton remorse. The phantom dialogue of the missing community link appeared inevitably whenever accounts re-opened old wounds.

The Algonquians, avid to benefit from the distrust generated by the murder, tried to insert Bruslé's death as a bone of contention between the French and the Wendat. They told Brébeuf of the Algonquian death threats to the Attignawantan due to Bruslé. Algonquian Kichesipirini chief Tessouat whispered that Champlain wanted four heads for Bruslé and tried to coax Brébeuf into leaving the Wendat due to their "perfidy." He promised to make him a "great chief" who would dominate the Algonquian councils.[91] (It seems that Tessouat imagined that Brébeuf's gullibility and agenda were similar to those of Champlain.) The Nipissing also told the Jesuits that the Wendat epidemic was due to 2,400 wampum shells having been stolen from Bruslé.[92] However, the Algonquians never dreamed that the French would ever repudiate one of their own because such an act was so unthinkable in their own cohesive community. The Wendat community accepted a measure of responsibility for Bruslé, an unusual character whom they had partially raised. How did he become an object of anger, jealousy, and suspicion? Bruslé was evidently better loved in his death than he had been during his short life.

Amantacha was twenty years younger than Bruslé and admired him as a model. Soranhes of Téanaostaia, of the Attigneenongnahac (Cord) tribe, brought sixteen-year-old Amantacha to Récollet Father Joseph Le Caron, who was obliged to entrust him to the Jesuits and Henri Lévis de Ventadour. He travelled with thirty-four-year-old Estienne Bruslé.. Presented to the British as the son of the king of Canada, he was baptised in the Rouen cathedral in 1627 with godparents Henri II d'Orléans, the duc de Longueville, and the duchesse de Villars. On his return two years later, Admiral Roquemont de Brison hijacked him with Bruslé and took them both to London, after which they returned to Quebec with the Kirkes. Bruslé tricked the British into bowing to the princely incumbent Amantacha, yet, when his half-starving father appeared, they stripped their splendid English threads off the boy's back.[93] Amantacha fell captive twice to the same Seneca that Bruslé had visited while waging war. The first time, they tortured him and cut his finger off, while his father escaped to the woods. The latter wandered for thirty days, starving, until he had a vision of a cauldron from which his son, Amantacha, told him to eat. His hunger was assuaged until he was found by the Neutrals.[94] Yet in 1636 Amantacha was assumed dead in Iroquoia. Champlain continued to think of Amantacha as perfidious, as one of many entries in his rather long list of disappointments. But the Jesuits, with whom Amantacha lived after 1636, accorded him their high regard.[95]

Bruslé and Amantacha were close friends despite their twenty-year age difference, owing to the prolongation of Bruslé's youthful oscillation between intercultural and interhuman "ghosts." They had symmetrical functions in Wendake and Paris, respectively, and were friends. Their symmetrically twinned cultural immersions, and a bicultural friendship, helped them appreciate many aspects of one another. Bruslé's ruse that Amantacha was a prince linked them in a playful entente through cultural inversion. French, not Native, culture was hierarchical, and Louis XIII himself was actually about Amantacha's age. At any rate, why should Bruslé deny himself the preposterous bluffing permitted the Jesuits, who pretended the same when Amantacha was in France? In the end, was not this coddled Amantacha really a prince of the forest? Bruslé and Amantacha returned to Wendake together after Champlain was defeated in 1629. They also died within a short period: Bruslé was killed in Wendake around 1632, and Amantacha was supposedly killed by the Haudenosaunee in 1636. While Bruslé retained the reputation of ostracized traitor in both communities, Amantacha was seen as a hero in his. They suffered similar but inverted fates: one being killed as an enemy within his adopted community, the other being killed in enemy territory. Yet, ironically, their fame after death reversed itself. Amantacha was just another hero, while Bruslé haunted the consciences of both Wendat and French long after his lonely heart was buried.

THE MARTYR AND THE WARRIOR

The smoke in the distance signalled trouble, even before the shrieks were heard. They caught us at the most vulnerable moment, the women and children are alone, and the lake is frozen. Nadouek (Enemy)![96] Again! How on earth did they get here in the dead of winter? How many of them are there? With trepidation, Chief Annaotaha girded for a struggle and led the Wendat warriors in the direction of the cries, fearful for the families and wise Echon (Father Brébeuf). Simultaneously, with the cries, Brébeuf grabbed his cross, and all his senses alive, looked out upon Chief Annaotaha departing upon the snow. Despite his heavy cassock, he rushed to administer the last rites to his quickly gathered little flock. Terror struck and women were screaming their children's names as they grabbed them one by one as they ran. Winter winds swept their dishevelled hair, and they scanned the treacherous ice covering the horizon. Hobbling a distance, the white-haired elders covered their eyes, then raised their hands in despair. Mohawk war whoops grew nearer and nearer as the flock scampered hopelessly about. They were trapped. Annaotaha had already sung his farewell song and led his men to the front. Brébeuf crossed his Christian children and prayed silently to His Father. He had prepared a million times in his dreams for this glorious martyrdom. His great heart was pounding. The hour had come.

Such was surely the gist of reflections that flit across Annaotaha's and Father Brébeuf's minds, Brébeuf huddled beside his flock of new Wendat Catholics surrounded by Mohawk quivers, shot, and flamebrands. Both he and Chief Annaotaha were later killed in separate incidents by the Haudenosaunee. Jesuit missionary Father Jean de Brébeuf missionized

Wendake and converted the prominent Chief Annaotaha. Brébeuf was born in Condé-sur-Vire, Lower Normandy, in 1593, of the English counts of Arundel. He spent several months among the Innu before going to Toanché in Attignawantan (Bear Clan) country as a missionary from 1626 to 1629. He was taken prisoner by the Kirkes and, on board ship from France, he was accused by the Huguenot Jacques Michel of wanting to convert "beavers" instead of souls (i.e., to engage in the the fur trade rather than missionization).[97] By 1634 Brébeuf had returned to Wendake, which was in the throes of an epidemic that devastated Ihonatiria in Attignawantan country, and decided to base missions in Ossossané (La Rochelle, or L'Immaculée Conception) and Téanaustaié (St-Joseph II). Due to the 1635 epidemic and a lean harvest in 1636,[98] the Jesuits were accused of sorcery by a Wendat shaman (or arendiouane) named Tehorenhaegnon in 1637. In consequence, Brébeuf wrote a letter of adieu to Rome and held a farewell feast before his death in Wendat fashion (Ouenda Athataion.) This courageous act won him respect and warded off the murder itself. He visited the Neutrals, as Bruslé had, accompanied by Wendat who, frustrated in their rivalry, urged the former to murder him due to his alleged witchcraft. The traditionalist Wendat preferred that the death of a Frenchman not be perpetrated by their community, as it had been with Bruslé.[99] He returned to St-Louis in 1643, and in 1649 he was caught by the Haudenosaunee while trying to distract them from fleeing Wendat families. According to Father Ragueneau, he was tortured with a searing necklace of axes and boiling water was poured over him in imitation of baptism by antagonistic Wendat who become thoroughly Haudenosaunee. After more torture, his heart was eaten. Annaotaha barely escaped after trying to protect him. Father Brébeuf gave his life to enable the Wendat to become Christian, but Wendat adopted by the Haudenosaunee tortured and ate him to acquire his courage.

Both Chief Annaotaha and Father Brébeuf became unprecedented social models in their own communities by acting as "warriors of God" (guerriers de Dieu). Brébeuf was sent as a "soldier of God" by the militant Society of Jesus exhibiting a Norman aristocratic sense of courage (honneur) and a readiness to sacrifice himself as a lamb in imitation of Christ. Yet he innovated when defying apostate Wendat, who challenged his God, and expressed rage over the slaughter of the cream of his flock. He demonstrated the Wendat warrior code to his spectator Wendat neophytes in a way that could not fail to reconvert them. French honneur and Native dread of loss of face surprisingly converged. In this sense, both French and Natives insisted upon never losing face, yet each interpreted the loss differently.

On the other hand, twinning occurred in cultural as well as social spheres. Between Brébeuf's death in 1648 and the Battle of the Long-Sault of 1660, the French became plagued by Wendat returning spirits (revenants), or, in Breton usage, spontails. Many settlers were horrified that the French governor did not intervene in 1653 when the Haudenosaunee massacred the Wendat remnants that had sought French protection and settled on Ile d'Orléans after the Fall of Wendake.[100] However, French missionaries were in Iroquoia, and the governor feared for their lives if he intervened.[101] The populace was horrified by this inaction and offered plots of land to the survivors, among them Chief Ignace Tsaouenhohoui. Even after this massacre, in 1657, as Father Raguenau was travelling with the remaining male Arendaronons who were to live with the Haudenosaunee Onondaga, the latter suddenly began to massacre the former before his very eyes. This remains a tragic part of Wendat history.

Yet, upon sober reflection, is it reasonable to expect one Jesuit father to save many warriors who are unable to defend themselves? In 1684 Father Raguenau had hidden for several days in Ste-Marie fortifications while two fellow fathers were being tortured to death. One of them was Brébeuf, whose eulogy he wrote after gathering up what was left of his friend's remains. Ragueneau, no matter how adventurous, was no Brébeuf. The Wendat had perhaps already realised this in 1648 when they presented ten large collars of wampum to Father Ragueneau as the testimonial of the voices of their massacred women and children in order to encourage Brébeuf to be reincarnated in him.[102] They surely hoped that the outrage might stiffen his resolve, but it probably had the opposite effect. The Wendat, for their part, were judged by trader Nicolas Perrot to never have forgiven this lack of French protection, as Bruce Trigger observed.[103] Yet the French were still haunted by Wendat avenging spirits. By 1662 flying snakes with flaming wings and a thundering globe of flames were sighted. In 1663 a great earthquake sent everyone running to confession during carnival week.[104] Some believed it was divine retribution for abandoning the Wendat while they were under French protection. Others saw it as punishment for neglect of religious duties, particularly by those who were engaged in the fur trade and military service. Survivor's guilt, followed by temporary amnesia and dissociation, is almost axiomatic as a psychological response to disaster. Traumatic memories can be "forgotten" due to their indigestible impact.[105] By the same token, Marcel Proust's *Time Lost* demonstrates, among myriad other things, how unanalyzed traumatic or fabulous memories can be retriggered by the slightest sights, tastes, or scents. These fragments catalyze the urge for comprehension, and post-event comprehension of these memories can cause one to significantly reinterpret one's entire life.[106] Even after the Wendat were no longer the key intermediaries, French sentiment regarding their noble Natives still ran high among the elite due to their inspirational Christian utopian missions.

Whereas Annaotaha had always been a famed war chief, in 1660 he became, through contact with Brébeuf, a warrior at the Long-Sault, where he was willing to defend Christianity and its priests, and to accept certain martyrdom. This was out of fidelity to Brébeuf, and perhaps out of gratitude for his sacrifice for Wendake, which flew in the face of the defection of forty other Wendat warriors to the Haudenosaunee at the Long-Sault.[107] The 1660 Battle of the Long-Sault has perennially spurred controversy over the interpretion of the French-Wendat relationship and its evolution over time. Was Dollier de Casson so incensed with the defection of the Wendat that he underplayed Annaotaha's role while aggrandizing that of Dollard?[108] Marie de L'Incarnation recorded that the respected Eustache Tsaouonhohoui reported that Dollard fired the first shot due to his distrust of Wendat diplomatic negotiations conducted in Huron, which excluded the French.[109]

Dollard des Ormeaux has been glorified, when the real savior of New France was Chief Annaotaha. His self-sacrifice for New France mirrored that of Father Brébeuf for Wendake. And it was none other than Annaotaha who tried to save Brébeuf himself a decade earlier. And he did this despite the fact that forty Wendat warriors opted to switch sides, leaving him virtually alone fighting for the French and Algonquians. This twinship in martyrdom is, in a sense, his monument to Brébeuf and New France as well as a token of his devotion to the Wendat souls that he could not save during the Fall of Wendake. In addition, he probably had become slightly frenchified in that he considered soldiers obliged to fight losing, as well as winning, battles (as typified in the French chanson de Roland).

Three pairs of twins modelled the criss-crossing lives and personalities of the social scene in the French-Native skeine that wove across the continent. The first paired a wily Native with naive newcomer; the second paired a roguish Frenchman with a Native innocent; and the third paired a Frenchman intent on becoming Native with a Native twin who became somewhat frenchified. In the first instance, the newcomer is initiated but manipulated. In the second, the Old World tried to corrupt New World innocence. And in the third, immigrant and Aboriginal join together. In New France typical twinship types such as these crocheted a net of trust. Hilarity was prime as they laughed at each other's, and their own, foibles. These common understandings facilitated Nativization. As the boundaries of both communities were opening to include each other – Algonquian, Wendat, and French – the symbolic representation of social twinships reinforced the complexities of these processes.

CHAPTER TWO

Smoke Signals

Infinitely layered echoes of past, present, and future phantoms, which reflect the interaction and transformations of internalized life and communal events within the self and society, take place within the crux of a multilevel framework that extends through time and space. Twins held the keys to one another's lives, but their relationship also symbolically represents the communal reality. I look at communal twinship on a macro level, examining it via time and space. First, I look at political and socio-economic twinships and their demographic character. Then I map out the geographical context and spatial negotiations within which the interethnic dialogue took place. And finally, I reflect upon the key historical turning points that interactively framed the meaning of the dialogue. A unique confluence of multilevel facilitating contexts helped twinning to develop and French Nativization to ensue.

IMMIGRANT HERITAGE

The uniquely northwest Atlantic character of early immigration resisted royal Parisian centralization and "offical French" culture. Northwest provincial geographical, historical, political, socio-economic, and cultural environments usually opposed the centralizing, standardizing, and revenue-collecting impetus of the Parisian royal family. The four major features of French immigration were: a small number of immigrants, a high percentage of northwesterners, a majority of male youth, and heavily urban rather than rural emigrants.[1] Early British settlement was more akin to Louis Hartz's idea of a transplanted "fragment" of Europe due to its greater and more demographically balanced immigration, close-knit communities, and accessible seaboard settlement. The Hartzian analyses of Bernard Bailyn, David Hackett Fisher, and even Alden Vaughan have presented British American immigrant culture as homogeneous "fragments" of European heterogeneity.[2] In New France, however, the "fragment effect" was lessened by proportional lack of sizable family or communally complete settlements, the isolation of settlement, and the commercial nature of much settlement activity, which required dependence upon Native communities. The slight, youthful, masculine, and seasonal nature of French immigration prevented the formation of a tightly knit, self-sufficient ethnically European community located not far from others. "Nativization" was not a complete adaptation of Native ways and values but the engagement of a real dialogue, on the French side, of those northwestern French elements most tenacious of the older culture and ancestral identity. This heritage hailed the past and was perceived by immigrants to be their refuge in the flux of their adaptation to, or rejection of, the New World.

Dialogue is optimal between relatively commensurate forces whose everyday functioning depends upon a foundation of basic trust between parties. Approximately two-thirds of immigrants to New France hailed from the northwestern provinces of France from 1604 to 1763, especially during the period until 1666.[3] They brought to the French-Native dialogue their heritage, which contained a prior antagonistic struggle between the northwestern provinces and the official French Parisian court culture. Paris established its hegemony through abrogating the authority of local elite administrative, financial, and legal institutions. The abrogation of provincial authority, through the establishment of alternative functions that had been under the jurisdiction of the provincial elites while attenuating their powers, jeopardized trust and dialogue between those provinces and Paris, despite their need to cooperate economically.

A micro-shifting interplay of memories and perceptions complemented this general framework in an immigrant's memory. His family at home, his parish friends, his birthplace, his contact with French-based northwestern traders, Parisian French officials, and new French immigrants in dialogue with the Canadian-born and Native nations surely shifted as his life evolved in the New World. All of these differential factors assisted him to orient himself in his new home or, with each fresh period of reevaluation, incited him to leave. His family and friends' absence were usually the most powerful incentives for him to return, after founding a family himself, through the missing interlinkage of generations. Yet, if his province was stigmatized or mistreated by official "France," he may have felt quite Breton, Norman, Saintongois, or Poitevin rather than "French," particularly if he lost a brother, father, or friend in the hostilities. Therefore, the northwest versus "France" struggle was the mental framework within which the French-Native dialogue began.

The underlying political, economic, social, cultural, and sometimes religious background of the northwestern French immigrants who, until 1663, comprised about 81.9 percent of French immigrants to Canada, traditionally resisted official Parisian elite culture.[4] This resistance was exacerbated by social and political crises that swept France during this period. In northwestern France, with its unique provincial history, legal tradition, and folkways, the basis was laid for insubordination to the Crown and the rejection of Parisian court culture. Normandy and Brittany both had their own legal customs and provincial sovereign courts (parlements). Normandy was especially upset at being demoted from a "pays d'états" to a "pays d'élection," thus becoming subject to all French taxes. The Breton marshes, Poitou, the southern chastellenies of Saintonge and Angoumois, and the marshlands of Riez of the Northwest also had traditions of insurrection.[5]

Moreover, economic and political crises during this period reinforced the rebellious tradition of northwestern France. A "little Ice Age" that resulted in a recurrent cycle of failed crops, inadequate nutrition, and epidemics was accompanied by intermittent Wars of Religion, followed by widespread hunts of heretics and "witches."[6] Increasing taxation as well as legal and administrative centralization followed these difficulties, which set off endemic insurrections against Crown agents for imposing these unnecessary burdens during troubled times.[7] Common cause against the Crown proved stronger than interprovincial rivalries in northwestern France, and Canadian immigrants hailed in large proportions from seaboard urban milieux that espoused and celebrated regional traditions.[8] Resistance remained high because northwest France traditionally sought British aid against the French Crown, as had been the case during the Hundred Years War. The traditions of resistance to imposed Parisian centralization and culture were reinforced during this time of crisis.

A large proportion of the immigrants came from regions on the vanguard of resistance to the Crown politically, culturally, religiously, and economically.[9] According to Marcel Trudel, in 1663, out of an approximate total of the known immigrant population of 3,106 from all provinces, Normandy sent the greatest number to Canada: 442 (21.7 percent.)[10] The areas of highest immigration were the north Atlantic area: Normandy, Brittany, Perche, and Picardy: 765 (37.6 percent); central Atlantic area: Aunis, la Saintonge, Poitou, Limousin, Angoumois: 616 (30.3 percent); the inland Northwest: Maine, Anjou, Auvergne, Nivernais, Berry, Orléanais, Touraine: 285 (14 percent). Only 229 (11.3 percent) were from Paris and Ile-de-France, leaving us with a total of 81.2 percent northwesterners, according to Marcel Trudel.[11] Northwest France not only contained the Huguenot area designated by the Edict of Nantes (1598) but it was also the epicentre of the initial insurrections that later spread farther south in what was called the Croquant Revolt. These two factors complicated northwestern France's relations with the Crown and reinforced separate regional identities within the provinces, which nevertheless often united in the attempt to oust emergent Crown administrative, legal, and financial dictates and French court culture and identity.

The northwestern revolts attempted to reestablish ancient provincial aristocratic privileges over growing Parisian royal centralization.[12] Instability, of course, had already been introduced by the Wars of Religion, the anti-tax league (1578–79), the Gautiers Revolt (1587),[13] and the Salic Law, which in delegitimatizing queenly authority introduced even more instability. On the coattails of these hostilities, the northwest experienced epidemics during the 1620s and a famine (1630–31) that entailed difficulties of subsistence where taxes, including the direct taxes introduced between 1625 and 1634, seemed exorbitant at a time when investment and production were reduced and rent incomes were hard to pay. New impositions were fiercely resisted.[14] Naturally, the local nobility often encouraged the revolts to protect their people from the encroaching monarchy, while reinforcing their own status.[15] Whereas earlier generations of landowners had existed upon their rents, by the seventeenth century rents became worth less. Noble exemptions, powers of justice, and administration were being curtailed,[16] and many poor, sometimes illiterate, country nobles (hobereaux) were forced out of the ranks of the aristocracy generally by bourgeois-cum-noble royal officials. Royal officials were sent to discredit the country nobles, who were mocked by the wealthy court nobility who lapped up more prestigious titles, offices, and benefits.[17] Louis XIV contributed greatly to the redundancy of the local nobility.[18] The proud insubordinate hobereaux, as well as the grand seigneurs who resisted the Crown, such as the dukes of Montmorency, La Trémoille, Mercoeur, and the princes of Rohan and Condé, were admired by the petit peuple and were more popular in northwestern France and Canada than Cardinal Richelieu, whose name graced the river that led to the then dreaded Haudenosaunee League. The much admired Condé was student to Father Paul Ragueneau, a prominent Jesuit missionary in New France, and Montmorency had a magnificent waterfall in Canada named after him, after being beheaded in the most grotesque manner by the king for his insubordinate duelling.[19]

Brittany was the most autonomous region to have ancient ties to Canada through fishers, fur traders, and venturers. These included Jacques Cartier and in Leslie Choquette's demographic sample constituted 16.9 percent of immigrants, due to the inclusion of seasonal residents and steady immigration.[20] Brittany was a relatively barren, sparsely populated region, where agriculture was necessarily varied and self-sufficient.[21] According to Marc Bloch, Breton agricultural land was characterized by enclosures and lack of communal grazing, which indicated and/or reinforced an independent frame of mind.[22] Yet the seasonal traders hailed overwhelmingly from

French-speaking Upper Brittany (95 percent from 1608 to 1760), while poor isolated Finistère and Brest were the ports of departure for Breton-speaking Canadian immigrants.[23] This autonomous tradition, particularly of the coastal seafarers, sprang from the combination of a Celtic heritage and an exceptional history of political autonomy, and was reinforced by continuous socio-economic maritime commerce. Nominae, the Celtic hero, had led the Breton knights under his banner in 848 AD and defeated French king Charles the Bald at Ballon, a much honoured tradition. The fifteenth-century Declaration of Plessix elaborated that only the Breton language would be used locally and that only Breton courts would adjudicate quarrels. No service was required in the royal armies outside the Armorican peninsula, and church benefices were limited to Brittany.. No alterations of customs, institutions, or juridical procedures would take place without local consent. In short, the juridical sovereignty of the Parliament of Brittany would prevail. A pact of union between Brittany and France was negotiated only in 1532 by Francis I. Flashes of Breton independence continued to manifest themselves during the succeeding centuries, sometimes more, sometimes less. During the French Revolution, in order to regain those ancient Breton rights, the Marquis de la Rouerie and the Association Bretonne roused 3,000 peasants (Les Chouans) to arms. During the 1870–71 Franco-Prussian War, the Breton contingent was distrusted and was sent to the disastrous battle of Le Mans. And again, during the Second World War, there was an effort to revive special privileges for Brittany. The Breton Celtic dialect interfered with French literacy, especially inland, until the nineteenth century when Fouquet's 1874 study revealed a French literacy rate of 73 percent.[24] The traditional Breton prophecy foretells that "Pa vo beuzet Paris, Ec'h adsavo ker Is" (When Paris is submerged, the island of Ville d'Is will resurge).[25]

During the seventeenth century, the Breton nobles d'épée were powerful enough that they, rather than the magistrates of the nobles de robe, received parlement (consultative, not legislative) offices and royal support.[26] Due to their relative autonomy, they rarely sided with the Crown.[27] The king knew not to meddle with the great nobility (grands) such as the Rohans or La Trémoille, who could muster 3,000 armed cavalry in twenty-four hours and commanded annual incomes of over 30,000 livres.[28] While Brittany was usually counted upon by the rest of northwestern France to defend interests in opposition to the Crown, the Breton nobility was widely admired by many northwestern insurrectionists who sought their support.[29] The late François Furet and Jacques Ozouf remarked that the Bretons' first spontaneous revolt was to emigrate, which served to "bolster its conscious desire for liberation."[30]

In the 1598 Edict de Nantes the La Rochelle area was declared, a Huguenot area of refuge, a veritable state within a state. Marguerite de Navarre and

Theodore de Bèze (author of "Du Droit des Magistrats," which proclaimed the right to resist an unworthy ruler) formulated the "Confession de foi de La Rochelle" in 1559, which was signed by Jeanne d'Albret, young Henri IV, Coligny, Louis de Nassau, and several great seigneurs. By 1628, however, Cardinal Richelieu and Louis III besieged La Rochelle.[31] At the same time an exclusively Catholic immigration was formally organized to sail to Canada (1627–32) in order to "remedy the ills that have begun under his predecessors, and to leave others to his successors."[32] Centres of resistance at La Rochelle and surrounding Poitou, Aunis, and Saintonge were crushed, levelled, and stripped of privileges in 1628-29 by Cardinal Richelieu. Ordered for destruction were the citadel of Xaintes, the castles of Saint-Mexant, Loudun, Chinon, Mirebeau, the new fortifications of Tours, and, particularly, the citadel of St-Martin de Ré. The colonization of Canada and the crushing of La Rochelle were two connected Counter-Reformation aims of Louis XIII and Cardinal Richelieu. John Bosher points out that the charter of the Canadian colonizing and fur trading company, the Hundred Associates (Cents-Associés), was formulated in camp while setting siege to La Rochelle. He equates the enforced catholicization at both La Rochelle and New France as two arms of the same Counter-Reformation movement planned by the Montmorencys, the Lavals, the Lévis, and members of the secret Compagnie du Saint-Sacrement.[33]

The Rochelois sought northwestern and British aid even after their defeat at Ile-de-Ré, and they mustered seventy vessels, which were intimidated by the French royal fleet. One hundred and twenty British vessels failed to save the city. Richelieu wrote: "in Montagu's papers, it appeared that there was a conspiracy between England, Lorraine, Soissons, Rohan, and La Rochelle against the state – they intended to revolt and make war ... with the consent of the reigning queen ... As the year began, the Rochelois hurried to the King of England, pleading with him to take them under his protection and to assist their deliverance from the oppression that they said they suffered ... the English have drawn up a treaty with them ... to rescue them by land and sea at his own expense ... the Rochelois and their brothers of the Loire provinces, to incite them to take up arms."[34] The fifteen-month siege generated bitterness against the Crown because the inhabitants were reduced to boiling leather and aniseed, and baking straw bread to survive.[35] The humiliation of La Rochelle included the destruction of their famous urban privileges and fortifications, both of which were the finest in France.[36] John Bosher points out that of the original 25,000 inhabitants, only 5,000 had not died or escaped. Jean-Marie Bercé writes of under 6,000 survivors, while de Foletier mentions that out of 28,000 inhabitants, only 5,000 remained.[37] In 1629 Richelieu even defeated Henri de Rohan, capturing the last Huguenot stronghold. After 1629 La Rochelle was "re-Catholicized" but was subject to economic woes. The tax rate was high in general for areas rich in salt, and there was a high proportion of anti-governmental salt-smuggling. Rumours that the salt tax (la gabelle) was about to be exacted infected western France from Poitou to the south. Aunis and the Saintonge, like Poitou, Maine, and Anjou, experienced endemic insurrections, and the year 1653 witnessed a great influx of Canadian immigrants from these areas.[38] The northwestern nobility was extraordinarily interested in vindicating the revolts and in reinstating their image as regional protectors.[39] The most commonly represented immigrant occupations from this region were farmers and woodsmen (199, or 16.4 percent of 1,206 men) as well as unskilled manual workers (148, or 12.3 percent), the professions heavily involved in Western French grain riots and rural tumult.[40] Robert Mandrou has demonstrated, using Gabriel Debien's examination of Rochelois workers enlisted between 1634 and 1714, that Canadian immigration from Aunis corresponded with local famine and riot.[41] Ironically, this misery was not due to the Huguenots but, rather, to the new Catholic proprietors (among them Cardinal Richelieu himself, who obtained the lucrative right to tax salt), privileges connected to the governorships of Aunis, Ile de Ré, and La Rochelle, and the acquisition of numerous properties in Aunis and the Saintonge.[42]

Normandy was particularly coveted by the Crown but was exceptionally rebellious. Rouen possessed commercial, industrial, and agricultural wealth; social prominence; proximity to Paris; and a reputation for insubordination; which infuriated the Crown.[43] Normandy's notable privileges dated from eleventh-century concessions to powerful dukes: the Norman Charter (1458) and the custom of Normandy were still in force in 1583.[44] During the Wars of Religion, a Huguenot Rouen was besieged, resulting in 1,000 dead (1562), and, in 1591–92 mortality rates rose to 40 percent in certain areas.[45] This reinforced its Catholic population but did not enhance Rouen's relations with the Crown. The sack of Rouen appeared to one contemporary as merely another example of the way "these inept Parisians, almost idiotic by nature" ("ce peuple inepte de Paris, presque sot de nature") had always preyed on the hard-working Normans, bleeding them dry of food and precious metals.[46] Therefore, when the Norman Nu-Pieds revolted, following rumours of the introduction of the salt tax into the Cotentin peninsula in 1639–40, the militia and the Rouen councillors, who themselves were often of the grand nobility (like the duc de Longueville and Harcourt), revolted.[47] They were called Nu-Pieds because they worked barefoot at the salt mines.[48] These 20,000 armed men suffered a cruel suppression that caused deep resentment throughout the region.[49] Unsettled conditions in the British Isles at the time further contributed to increased anxiety in a region that was part of a north Atlantic trading network.[50]

Northwestern France often opposed the Crown, a situation that gave Canadian immigrants a sense of separate identity from that of France proper. The Norman Nu-Pieds rebels called on Brittany and Poitou for help,[51] and Chancellor Séguier, who suppressed the revolt, quotes the manifesto of the supposed Jean Nu-Pieds: "Caesar in the Senate, was attacked by Brutus, / For having sworn against the Romans. / Catalina was killed after a pile of abuse, / That he did at Humanity's expense; / And I suffered a languishing people / Under tyranny and a pile of horizons / Oppress everyday with their parties! / I swear to prevent it, even Barefoot as I am. / I am not afraid at all of the menacing axes; / My people are good soldiers and in supporting me, / will furnish me with enough lines of companies / To stay tough, the peasants will help, / Against these Salt taxers, true tyrants from Hiranie, / Who want to oppress peoples and nations / Through solicitors and so many tyrannical actions, / against which are opposed Normans, Poitevins, and Bretons." ("César, dans le sénat, fut occis par Brutus, / Pour avoir conjuré contre tous les Romains. / Catilina fut tu, après un tas d'abus, / Qu'il avoit entrepris aux despens des humains; / Et moy je souffriray un peuple languissant / Dessoubz la tyrannie, et qu'un tas de horizains / L'oppressent tous les jours avecques leur partys! / Je jure l'empescher, tout Nuds-piedz que je suis. / Je ne redoubte point leurs menaces hachées; / Mes gens sont bons soldatz, et qui, en m'appuyant, / Me fourniront assez de compagnies rangées / Pour soustenir hardis, assistez de paisans, / Contre ces gabeleurs, vrays tyrans d'Hiranie, / Qui veulent oppresser peuples et nations/ Par des solliciteurs de tant de tyrannies, / Où s'opposent Normandz, Poittevins, et Bretons.")[52] Marshall Gassion used 10,000 royal mercenaries to prevent perfidy and after their leaders were tortured thirty-eight were hanged or banished without due legal process, in a province proud of its legal tradition. Norman outrage mounted when the parlement was suppressed for several months on grounds of collusion, the municipality of Rouen was stripped of its functions and its finances were confiscated, the Corps de Ville of Rouen was replaced by the Six Bourgeois (Six Burghers), the Cour des Aides was closed, and the bourgeoisie was forced to pay a fine of 1,085,000 livres in tax-farming loss, while Caen owed 60,000 livres. The rights, communal liberties, and walls of Avranches, Vire, Caen, and Rouen were destroyed.

The Nu-Pieds word "liberty" meant provincial freedoms, and the infringement of these rights were again protested during the Fronde (1648–53), especially by the local nobility, village and town magistrates, and parish clergy.[53] In fact, not only did Richelieu profit from provincial exploitation, but the detested Concini, advisor of Queen Regent Marie de Medici, and now governor of Caen, invested in land in Lower Normandy in 1616.[54] These bourgeois upstarts were a focus of contempt on the part of the local nobility and the populace.

Deeply affected as they were by economic crises and revolts in their region, most Canadian immigrants were from social and professional milieux that suffered especially from central royal power. According to Trudel's occupational breakdown, until 1663, of the 1,206 men whose profession is known,[55] the masons recruited to build settlements was 15.2 percent of the total (183 men). They were undoubtedly recruited from the numerous journeymen who could not obtain a mastership due to closing of ranks within the guilds.[56] Seafarers, whose ranks swelled during hard times, comprised 122 men of the whole, or 11 percent.[57] Toolmakers comprised seventy-two men or 6 percent. Among them most probably were metalworkers, tanners, and peltworkers from Normandy, professions notable for their presence in the ranks of the Nu-Pieds[58] and that tied them to Canadian commerce. In contrast to these moderately skilled crafts, highly sophisticated urban professions such as those found in the famous Norman textile and stocking industries were hardly needed in Canada. These professions, such as bonnetmakers, lacemakers, linenworkers, and so on, were generally made up of women and rarely came to Canada. Women came to Canada either as missionaries, mothers, or prospective brides.[59] Normandy in particular was overrepresented, and Normandy and Aunis steadily exported both brides and married women.[60] Missionaries generally came from Normandy, Brittany, or Paris.[61]

It can be reasonably assumed that some of the Nu-Pieds participants' families escaped to Canada for there was a list of 197 persons who had fled Rouen when Chanceller Séguier arrived there. Of the 3,106 immigrants identified, there were numerous young single men, who, if they stayed in Canada, might attract other family members to join them. Among those Nu-Pieds who were documented and caught are names such as Pierre Blondel, a literate engagé, who in Normandy is listed as a councillor. Some Norman Morels or "dit Morel," the supposed name of Jean Nu-Pieds himself, also appeared in Canada.[62] René Voyer D'Argenson, the governor of New France, suffered personally from the Nu-Pieds suppression because his brother René II, who sympathized with the rebels, was later badly received as a new councillor in the Rouen parlement.[63] Other immigrants were probably family or admirers of the renowned rebels Lafontaine and Lalande.[64] Although many of the urban Nu-Pieds leaders were caught, rural participants simply fled the province and were not always registered as absentees during Séguier's purge in 1640.[65] This permitted some to escape overseas.[66] La Rochelle was known to serve as a gathering place for the surrounding area.

It is no surprise, therefore, that families involved in crushing the revolt were generally shunned by the Canadian elite. Well known families in this category included Jean Fortin de Beaupré, who was held responsible for the 1639 salt-tax in Avranches,[67] and the Baron Du Mesnil-Garnier, the seigneur and magistrate at Coutances, whose property was attacked in 1639.[68] Intendant Charles La Roy de La Poterie of Caen, probably the financial successor of Leneuf de la Poterie who joined forces with the royal Marshall

Gassion and twelve regiments, was the intendant of Justice who tortured and condemned to death the rebels at Avranches and Caen.[69] Antoine l'Heritte "dit Bassompierre" and Louis Delamare "dit Gassion" were surely insultingly nicknamed after the marshals who cruelly suppressed the revolt. And, surprisingly, the Québécois term "broc" (pitchfork)[70] was a typical appellation of a Croquant.

In short, the immigrant pool in Canada included northwestern rebellious, ambitious, and "anti-French" male youth, despite the careful political and religious plans of Richelieu and the Jesuits to exclude such colonists. Plans for a model immigrant population that would cooperate with Crown dictates excluded non-Catholics, criminals, and prostitutes. However, these plans did not anticipate that northwestern immigrants, partisans of the northwestern provincial nobility and antagonistic to the Crown, would come to Canada.[71] The local nobility, admired for their military courage, generosity, and believed to have defended the rights of the common people, were honoured as knightly "hommes de coeur" or self-sacrificing men protecting the defenceless. They provided a model for male youth aspiring to gain wealth and social standing in an unstable French socio-economic world where mobility for male youth was rapidly rising.

NEGOTIATING SPACE

Two centuries of Anglo-American North American history has chiefly been a criss-crossing of ad hoc struggles beginning with a European east/Native west divide that was later split between the abolitionist north versus the slave-holding south. By contrast, early French North American history has largely occurred along east-west waterways, from settlements in the northern valley to riverine trade nodes in the continental heartland. William Ecces's thesis of a "frontierless frontier" during the French regime seems perfectly true, and Harold Innis capitalized upon the watery lifeline foundations of Canada as opposed to the American frontier that buffered tightly knit colonies from dispossessed First Nations.[72] Yet, a qualification remains. Where winter threw a thick white mantle, the frontier was everywhere. If the ethnic "frontier was in every habitant's backyard" in other seasons, chill tempests physically grounded every habitant in snow barriers in a winter twice as long.

The icy harbors prohibited transatlantic traffic with the metropolitan, beyond one large summer shipment. The frozen St Lawrence Seaway, Ottawa River, and other tributaries forced isolation upon each settlement until the spring waters trickled forth. Yet it was precisely due to a frosty and thickly forested environment, favouring trade at the warmer Great Lakes, that Native-French cooperation was required for survival. If the British divide, originally placed at the Appalachian mountains, ran between rela-

tively homogeneous, densely settled, insulated agricultural ethnic populations, the French winter frontier trapped French and Native together, as
well as liberating both to trade over the vast river network in the spring. If
the English frontier was ethnic and geographical, then the ambivalent
French "frontier" was religious and seasonal.

Quebec, Three Rivers, and Montreal (originally Ville-Marie) were not
founded upon "conquered Stadacona and Hochelaga." These towns disappeared during the century that intervened between Jacques Cartier and
Samuel de Champlain's time, ostensibly due to intervening catastrophic epidemics brought from Europe. The three large French settlements were
founded due to repeated Native requests and French promises.[73] Settlers
avoided large sedentary Native settlements, which enabled them, bit by bit,
to become familiar with smaller non-sedentary bands who desired trade,
instead of fearing for their fields.[74] The Mi'kmaq and Innu especially demonstrated their goodwill to the French, and this was a decisive factor in the
placement of early French settlement.[75]

The Little Ice Age of the seventeenth century, besides encouraging immigration due to ruined fields in Europe, was an additional factor that kept the
mercury especially low. The result of this hibernating isolation encouraged
the growth of what Jan Grabowski has dubbed the local "petit commerce,"
which complemented the "grand commerce" of the fur trade that extended
over long distances. "Petit commerce" involved the exchange of furs for
local goods and took place between settled Natives and French residents of
the Laurentian Valley.[76] The French were required to learn local Canadian
self-sufficiency through acquiring specific nations' skills appropriate to each
location as well as to learn Native canoeing, hunting, snowshoeing, and
reconnaissance for Haudenosaunee parties. Practice was needed to make
perfect, for twenty-nine French youth drowned from 1646 to 1662, mostly
while canoeing, while there were seventy drownings between 1632 and
1662.[77] Establishing agricultural self-sufficiency took time due to the short
warm season available for forest clearing. And by the 1650s, the funnelling
of male muscle to the Great Lakes area meant that the French-First Nations
"petit commerce" was essential for survival. French trade brandy (eau de
vie), beer, homemade spirits (bouillon), wine, British rum, and French articles and food were traded for Native pelts, handicrafts (especially moccasins
and leggings), and food (especially fresh game and cornmeal).[78] Native
transport, reconnaissance, hunting, and delivering of news and letters even
on the frozen St Lawrence rendered the French communications network
dependent upon the tribes and left immigrants anxious to acquire their survival methods.

New France was not a simple "conquering colony" but a complex arrangement of nodes of economic activity, government, society, and culture that
expressed interdependent configurations of metissage and multicultural-

ism. For the British colonies, geographer D.W. Meinig's theory of the "distance decay of European culture" defines degrees of New World acculturation according to physical distance from the cultural hearth of origin. It is akin to Edward Shils's centre-periphery theory but emphasizes the degrees between the two poles rather than the dichotomy, which would correspond with Davis's Metropolitan-Hinterland thesis.[79] The St Lawrence East-West axis could be seen as possessing degrees of fading Frenchness in relation to increased distance from the metropolis. And, conversely, instead of being seen as the "distance decay of Europeanness," it can also serve as the "distance decay of Native culture" from west to east. The periphery was not a periphery at all but, rather, the main source of New France's wealth and thus a centre. For these extended settlements, immigration was not pushed by land speculators to farmsteaders, as it later was in the British colonies. The Great Lakes region and beyond were areas of French exploration and commercial objectives. Therefore, in the Laurentian settlements proper, multiculturalism was generalized, with Three Rivers and Montreal requiring it to a greater degree than Quebec, and with enclaves of reserves near all three settlements. Along the fur routes and in the fur country of the Ottawa, Great Lakes, and Illinois country, and to a lesser extent in the Saguenay, métissage was the norm. The enclaves of mission reserves along the way were a curious mixture of tribes and bands that had chosen the Catholic and agricultural life. They fought valiantly for New France and were allowed great commercial mobility and freedom to contraband and foster the "petit commerce," which attracted the French to the reservations as well.[80]

Three Rivers was a major centre of the fur trade and cultural métissage during the seventeenth century.[81] The majority of the French immigrant population lived in the Quebec region (2,857 people of 4,219 known in the population by 1666), while Three Rivers had 602, and Montreal 760.[82] According to Grabowski, the de facto legal double standard favoured the Natives, who were given preferential treatment, at least in Montreal.[83] Medievalist John Bartlett cites that on the margins of medieval Europe, the Sepulvedo, Sachenspiegel, and Iura Prutenorum legal codes usually recommended that the accused be judged according to his own law.[84] This multicultural legal orientation definitely seemed to be in vogue on the St Lawrence, especially among the young male population heavily involved in the fur trade. Even using only official congé records, Louise Dechêne recorded that 54 percent of Three Rivers men were involved in fur trade travel even in 1708–17, with 30 percent for neighboring seigneuries (Champlain, Batiscan, Cap de la Madeleine). Montreal men were involved at a rate of 25 percent, although nearby Montreal seigneuries (Boucherville, Varenne, Cap St-Michel, Trinité) had a rate of 38.9 percent official involvement.[85] Three Rivers was founded in order to be near the rendezvous of the Mauricie-area Natives, who repeatedly requested the establishment of a French habitation on the site that was founded in 1634. The habitants of Three Rivers were so immersed in Native affairs that they requested special trading conditions in 1647, which included individual rights to trade. If the company clerk (commis) kept the company store well stocked and sold canoes and moccasins at a reasonable price, it was allowed that the habitants could have a schooner and that they could sell corn to the Natives with the proceeds converted into money.[86]

Many of the earliest and most famous interpreters, traders, and coureurs lived in Three Rivers: Jean Nicollet (interpreter cum diplomat and explorer, father of a Nipissing Métis girl), Jacques Hertel (interpreter that stayed with Natives during the Kirke occupation, one of the founders of Three Rivers), Thomas Godefroy de Normanville (interpreter, stayed with Natives during Kirke occupation, twice captured by Haudenosaunee they finally caught him in the end), and Jean Godefroy de Lintot (interpreter, member of Communauté, first family man of Three Rivers). Pierre-Esprit Radisson (too famous to detail), Chouart des Groseilliers (ibid.), Pierre Boucher (interpreter cum governor of Three Rivers), Guillaume Cousture (interpreter, adopted war captive of Haudenosaunee, became important diplomat), as well as interpreters François Marguerie and Guillaume Pépin.[87] This Three Rivers sample undoubtedly became tightly interlinked through marriage in such a little town, thus pooling much of their diverse knowledge of different tribes. Both the St-Maurice forges and the canoe-building industry were erected here, and both were essential to the fur trade.

Montreal was originally intended: "to assemble a people made up of French and Amerindians who will be converted so as to render them sedentary to train them to practice the mechanical arts or farming, to unite them under a common discipline in the exercise of the Christian life ... and to have celebrated praises of God in the desert."[88] Louise Dechêne noted that, for 1708–17, out of 586 voyageurs in Montreal, 206 came from one family, while voyageurs came from 380 nuclear families total. We can surmise that not only does voyageur knowledge begin to shift to certain regions of Montreal and its surroundings, but it also became specialized in certain families. In addition, certain professions tended to enter the fur trade: artisans, especially carpenters, surgeons, blacksmiths, arquebuse (an early lighted-fuse-driven firearm) makers, traders and their sons, officer's sons, and, in lesser proportion, farmer's sons.[89] A fur trade heritage and trade canon grew first in Three Rivers, then in Montreal.

Frederick Jackson Turner's Frontier thesis, presented in Chicago in the 1890s, has come full circle with the publication of Richard White's *The Middle Ground* (1990). White's thesis emphasizes the frontier's uniqueness in establishing mixed-ground rules in the French-Native encounter in the Great Lakes region. A curious point about White's thesis is that he focused

on Chief Pontiac and worked backward, as is articulated in the introduction,
yet history works in reverse. Lack of a St Lawrence background and base has
cut this "Middle Ground" off from its raison d'être, thus "dropping in" on a
temporary situation. The Middle Ground was only an interlude in US history, but in Canada, it was its veritable foundation. The Great Lakes area
must be recognized as part of the Native sphere of New France, which, in
tandem with the French sphere, composed what was called New France.
Perhaps, the term "Middle Ground" should refer to the cultural compro-
mises that were found with far-flung French and Native populations that
had extremely incomplete demographic equations and who often wound
up completing one another and eventually gave birth to the Métis. A middle
ground is also intended time-wise, for it is between initial contact and later
Caucasian domination – a negotiating interlude that was later destroyed. Yet
this middle ground was not born with Pontiac: it had an entire set of ground
rules from New France that must be examined in proper context. It was only
transformed, but not destroyed, with the 1761 Cession of New France. Thus,
although the middle ground was subsequently somewhat ruined in the
Great Lakes area as land surveyors encroached, most of the Natives fled
northward. For Canada, continuity of the tradition was the norm in the
Hudson's Bay Company and North West Company, where the fur trade was
continued from its eastern base a bit over a century ago. Thus, the Middle
Ground, in effect, moved northward to what subsequently became western
Canada, whose very establishment was affected, as mentioned, by those
Métis and Nor'Westers left stranded when the buffalo thinned and the
North West Company was subsumed by the Hudson's Bay Company.

The mission reserves (réductions) allowed distinctive enclaves to grow
within New France, whose inhabitants were Christian Natives called "domiciliés." There were also traditionalist bands that lived close to and in the habitations themselves. Due to their honoured place in French society, these
mission reserves could not be properly called either centres of métissage or
centres of multiculturalism, although both of these phenomena were present. Here a type of the Bhabhian missionary "third spaces" was created,
which, due to its encapsulation, provided an innovative communal experiment that was endemic within both French and Native spheres, a syncretic
Counter-Reformation utopia.[90] Multivalent reserve life allowed enormous
cultural leeway. It housed destitute or persecuted Natives, hosted other visiting Native groups, and accommodated French families, where they were
freer to manage a lucrative contraband trade with Albany.[91] Grabowski notes
that, during the seventeenth century, numerous Natives were not far from
the three habitations, especially from Three Rivers and Montreal.[92] Many
reserves are still integrally part of "culture Québécoise de vieille souche," in
striking contrast to the marginal national role of US reserves, which were not

missions but areas of containment whose purpose was to permit land purchase in the States. This is not to say that either is currently thriving, as they often constitute communities of the lowest life expectancy and highest suicide rates in North America today (and are struggling to heal themselves).[93]

The borderlands-to-borders thesis of Stephen Aron and Jeremy Adelman postulates that First Nations could play Europeans off against one another in borderlands between empires, thus manoeuvring on their own terms.[94] They recast the revised frontier thesis of New Western historians that has recently been reformulated. Aron and Adelman distinguished between frontiers as a meeting area with unclear borders (Turner), while borderlands were presented as contested boundaries between colonial domains (Bolton).[95] The three borderlands that they presented were the Great Lakes, the Missouri Valley, and the Rio Grande. These were the main ones: they operated simultaneously and their fates were linked. Olive Patricia Dickason made this point herself in her dissertation on the Mi'kmaq of Louisbourg and Acadia, these two areas functioning as the borderlands between French and British.[96] Nonetheless, New France's Native centres were not merely borderlands to extend their spheres or to offer land, as in Spanish and British colonies, but were the essential source of New France's survival. This is precisely the reason why, when the British took over the French sphere and Montreal trade, they could not dictate terms. Indeed, if the French Crown had not attempted to interfere so often, perhaps a regularized cross-trade with anglophone colonials could have been established with many Radissons declaring themselves instead of hiding their contraband to Albany. The British also attempted to arrive at agreements with New France regarding captivity policies[97] but hampered these efforts by deporting the Acadians, which lent urgency to French raids on New England. Politics between the settlement and metropolis were also strained, and part of the metropolis's aim was precisely to send out imperial policies and troops to both squelch entente and force Canadians to bide by French authority. New France often resisted imperial policies, exploring-trading expeditions were approved rather than sent, and so much effort was invested in organizing and mediating intertribal and renegade Canadian affairs that the imperial concept simply was not the foremost item in early New France.

In conclusion, New France was one sprawling but coherent entity that was based upon the premise that métissage and multiculturalism were integrally complementary, not opposing, policies. This modularity encouraged worlds like the Great Lakes "Middle Ground" and the Montreal and Three Rivers "Common Ground" to exist in tandem as coherent modular aspects of the whole, and this afforded a diversity of communal arrangements. In sum, French-Native North America had an alternate vision of what North America could become.

NEGOTIATING TIME

French-Native dialogue was also negotiated within a temporal framework. During the course of approximately fifty years, from the earliest period of Laurentian immigration accompanying the founding of Quebec in 1608, the colony consisted of commercial and missionary operations that preceded colonial royalization in 1663. Over a period covering two generations, the ground rules for this dialogue were laid, when the French were the most dependent upon Native aid. During this period, there were three crucial dialogic turning points that encouraged an intensely interdependent dialogue. French immigrants embraced the policy of accommodation (douceur), which, via intercultural dialogue, induced French Nativization.

Nativization was the key to French survival in North America. Yet, although colonial implantation in Canada was a French choice, the interacting negotiation of a Native-immigrant dual ethnic entity was not a smooth endeavour, as our twins have shown. Negotiation skill and frequent demonstration of good will were required in order to allay suspicions and reciprocally destructive hostilities. By contrast, in the British colonies hostilities began early. Since the 1620s Virginians set out against the Pamunkey, and by 1637 New England, began military measures with the intention of warding off possible trouble from neighboring Algonquian tribes, which began with the Pequot tribe massacre. Dialogic turning points in New France were also brought on by historical crises that left few options for the immigrants. These dialogic turning points were benchmarks that demonstrated how fragile French settlement was when neglected by the metropolis, how deeply entwined French-Native interdependence had become, and how essential this was to the survival of early New France.

The three crucial turning points that will be dealt with are the Kirke conquest of Quebec 1629,[98] the twin disasters of 1648, and the Eight Day Miracle of 1661. The 1629 conquest of Quebec was due to a faulty French-Native dialogue, yet the result was the formation of a highly Nativized pioneer nucleus, which subsequently ameliorated the interethnic dialogue. The twin economic disasters of 1648 were the simultaneous occurrence of the fall of Wendake and the hostilities of the Parisian Fronde, which forced the French to penetrate deep into Native fur country to replace Wendat traders. This also required a more intense Nativization. And, finally, the battle of the Long-Sault in 1661 definitively showed that having Native ties was insufficient for a strong settlement: Nativization itself was required.

The harsh lesson of the Kirke conquest of Quebec taught the French that holding their own in the French-Native dialogue was not going to occur according to French rules but, rather, to Native rules. Disturbances in effective French dialogue with their first and most veteran allies, the Innu, had rude consequences and degenerated into a "dialogue of the deaf." Two intertwined results became evident. The breakdown endangered the question of French settlement altogether and forced the French to cognitively adapt, if they wished to stay. These defining negotiations were essential to feeling out the framework, and limits, of the dialogue.

Innu chiefs like Erouachy were disturbed over Champlain's bid to assert his authority after the deaths of two Frenchmen, Henry and Dumoulin, who had been killed by an Innu in 1626. Sagard thought the culprit was Miristou (Mahican Atic Ouache), but Champlain thought it was another man, whom he imprisoned at Quebec, insisting that French lives were not meaningless.[99] Champlain was not condemning him out of senseless ethnocentricity but upon solid experience evaluated according to his evolving understandings. In 1616 a similar incident had occurred, and the Recollects decided to pardon the crime, albeit with great consternation.

In addition to tension over how to treat the murderer, it has been suggested that Champlain upset the Innu over his retention of two girls entrusted to his care, and the rumoured release of a Mohawk woman captured in the 1610 Richelieu battle.[100] Champlain had already confronted Chief Iroquet for having cut off the latter's finger while she was helpless. This analysis matches well with French accounts of the Algonquian politeness etiquette, which prized public magnanimity while sometimes gunnysacking private turmoil. Yet the suggestion that Champlain might have been afflicted with pedophilia is a case worth reexamining. Three Innu girls were originally entrusted to Champlain's care, one of whom was the daughter of Mecabou (Martin). Their names were La Charité, Lespérance, and La Foy, to be taught in the Catholic faith. La Foy decided to return to her parents, while the two others remained for two years under famine conditions with Champlain. He taught them French knitting, which was widely admired by Innu girls, and Catholicism, which was more daunting. The two girls publicly resisted the clumsy attempts of interpreter-liaisons Estienne Bruslé and Nicolas Marsolet to seduce them, and perhaps wanted to sail to France when the French left Quebec in 1629. Sagard wrote that they were so upset at being prevented from voyaging to France that "ces pauures filles ne faisoient que pleurer & ne vouloient ny boire, ny manger, de regret."[101] Champlain wrote long passages about their refusal to eat or drink, their threats to Marsolet that, if they could not canoe to France, then they would live at Guillemette and Guillaume Couillard's home. He also tried to offer 1,000 livres worth of goods as a gift to reconcile the Innu chiefs, via Marsolet, which they refused. Guillaume Couillard and Gros Iean de Dieppe (an Algonquin interpreter who opted for the Kirkes) both knew of the Innu council and, according to Champlain, declared to him that the chiefs had never discussed the girls. Champlain's account of Lesperance's speech at a dinner at which he, the Kirkes, Sagard, the captains, and Marsolet were present tells that she accused Marsolet of betraying the French and attempting to sexually harass her. Trigger writes that this had an "artificial and highly theatrical ring to it and that all or part of it may be Champlain's invention."[102] Marsolet, according to Sagard, was speechless and tried to pass Lesperance off as crazy. Champlain wrote that, before he left, he fit each of them out, probably through the good services of Marie Rollet Hébert, with little dresses fashioned of his coat. Sagard also writes that : "il n'a iamais esté soupconné d'aucune deshonnesteté pendant tant d'années qu'il a demeuré parmy ces peuples...c'est pourquoy ces filles l'honoroient comme leur père."[103]

Marsolet, for his part, wrote to the Kirkes to the effect that the Innu chiefs held council at Three Rivers and requested the return of the girls under threat of death. Marsolet had offered gifts to Lespérance on the way to Tadoussac, ostensibly for favours. Unfortunately, we do not have his account, but after having navigated the Kirkes to conquer Quebec, after most of the French left the settlement from 1629 to 1632, he resided with Innu and Algonquian friends. Marsolet was worried that if any Innu hurt the English, they might again rehash the issue of the girls and that he personally would bear the brunt of everyone's anger. Only after the French returned in 1632, and he married a Frenchwoman, did he try to rehabilitate his family's reputation in the settlement by preparing an over-elaborate fête-Dieu bread, which the Jesuits vetoed. He wound up fomenting a civil mutiny over fur taxes, which was quickly negotiated out of existence.

Was the founder of Quebec, or his ill-viewed interpreter Marsolet, a child abuser? Most historians have studiously erased this puzzling incident from the official register, although a spat over prepubescent girls is highly atypical of most male French writing of this time and place. Non-aristocratic women and children were almost never named; usually they were not even mentioned. It is axiomatic, therefore, that the only thing of which we can be absolutely certain is that these were exceptional girls. It is also axiomatic that we tend to trust those who have risen to positions of public trust and to discredit those who have either been antisocial or misunderstood. Interpreters were young Frenchmen often notoriously avid to grab Native beauties. Why were they having a tug-of-war over the girls? Marsolet may have been coarse to Lesperence, but he was surely never lacking for bed partners. He definitely could not have been forceful because he spent the next few years with the Innu, and female harassment and child abuse were anathema in northeast Native culture at that time. So why was he so avid to return the girls to the Innu? Obviously, Champlain and Sagard's accounts against him are in accord. But why would they both accuse him, yet offer long apologies to exculpate Champlain, if he was never the one in question? Why did the girls really refuse to eat or sleep, and why did they cry? Why was Marsolet, and apparently the Innu chiefs, so avid to have them back? And why did Champlain do everything possible to retain them?

The drama of the Innu girls influenced both returning and remaining French, and further defined the limits of the dialogue. The girls, theoretically, could readily have left Champlain, as had La Foy. For sure, Champlain could not have easily abused the girls' filial trust under the watchful eyes of Marie Rollet Hébert, the Recollects, or the Innu without serious consequences. We do not have Marie Rollet's or Guillemette Hébert's accounts, the women who, being fluent in Innu and having taken in the girls after Champlain's departure, undoubtedly would have known or guessed the girls' true story. The Hébert-Couillard families were certainly close to Champlain and perhaps might have overlooked his "peccadillos." But Innu girls had minds of their own, to the sometime despair of French educators and suitors alike. Marie was famously responsive to children of all kinds. Her home became a veritable multiethnic school, but these girls were never again mentioned, which indicates that they probably left.

The Kirke record does not record any counter-accusation of Marsolet against Champlain. Champlain was always rather monosyllabic about femininty, even when women ceremonially danced nude in front of him. Lesperence's accusation of Marsolet is dramatic, but Champlain was not gifted in melodrama. And although the settlement had starved, the girls refused food and sleep, which is quite unusual. In addition, Champlain's marriage to twelve-year-old Hélène Boullé was cited by Trigger, but this complicates rather than reinforces the pedophile thesis. Would he have put his marriage, the pedigree girl for whom he had waited for two years, and his entire Canadian enterprise at risk for two children? Doughty masculine souls have sometimes flinched before this insanity. Why not Champlain? The later distant relationship with his wife, Hélène Boullé, followed the classic French marriage pattern, which involved social standing and dowry rather than romance.

One obstacle. "His little Innu girls" had to be displayed knitting, reciting their rosaries, and speaking French so that the devout and monied aristocratic ladies could fawn over them in court and provide him with financial backing for his Canadian enterprise. Pedophilic abuse is perpetrated in secret, not as the pièce de resistance in the effort to advance one's lifelong work. Even if Marie Rollet had missed something, the eyes of these scrutinizing, confessing court ladies emphatically would not. And a final obstacle to the pedophile idea: Champlain risked his relationship with the prominent Chief Iroquet to succor a helpless Haudenosaunee woman captive, declaring that women's only defence is their tears and that a man who violates that is a coward. We may safely conclude that it is highly unlikely that Champlain belied the trust that the girls and their parents placed in him.

Were the girls crying out of sheer homesickness and a desire to see their mothers? Were Marsolet and the chiefs anxiously jockeying for their return due to immense pressure brought to bear upon them by the mothers? After all, it had already been observed that many Natives who journeyed to France had simply died overseas. Perhaps we should view the girls as Champlain's last grandfatherly dedication, at the ripe age of sixty or seventy, to his vast Canadian project. They were his last great hope to cherish after witnessing the fall of Port Royal to Samuel Argall and the fall of Quebec to the Kirkes. And to preserve their Christian discovery of the value of cherubic chastity from men like Marsolet or even Innu suitors, he may have placed their future squarely in the hands of the Couillarts.

This was the background preceding the Kirke siege of Quebec in 1628, which lasted until 1629. When a pair of French Huguenot brothers born in Dieppe, of an English father, decided to lay siege Quebec in 1628, some Innu chiefs helped them.[104] The Kirkes' design benefited from recent French-Innu misunderstandings as well as from Catholic-Huguenot rivalry. The Huguenots, for example, had informed the Innu that the Catholic French were making them ill, which touches a raw nerve.[105] Catholic defectors like Huguenot Jacques Michel, who steered the Kirke ship, and irreligious interpreters Estienne Bruslé and Nicolas Marsolet navigated the way to defeat Champlain.[106] Religious factionalization was high due to rivalry over monopolies. Not only were the Innu in the thick of illness and dialogic short-circuit with the French, but, since 1610, Innu traders were increasingly being replaced by the Wendat. It is no wonder that some Innu chiefs, like Erouachy, aided the Kirkes.[107]

It is also notable that other chiefs, like Negabamat and Chomina, not only battled the Kirkes but also led the Recollects to escape and brought the French provisions from the Innu, Wendat, and Abenaki.[108] During the siege, between eighty to one hundred starving inhabitants of Quebec were distributed among the Innu, Wendat, Mi'kmaq, and other tribes, each of whom offered to host twenty to twenty-five French and sent sacks of cornmeal, moose meat, gunpowder, and eels as well as some of their own children to them to be cared for.[109] The sons of Mahigan Aticq Ouche, Mecabou and Chappé Abenau, spent the winter in Quebec, while their parents hunted.[110] Even the Abenaki, who barely knew the French, offered to host them while the latter promised to reciprocate with a barrel of sea biscuits and two beaver robes for each host when the ships arrived.[111] Seeing that the immigrants were reduced to spoiled sea biscuits, peas, and beans, the Innu taught them how to boil roots and herbs to mix with their dwindling supplies in order to survive.[112] By 1629 the majority of the French were forced to return to France during the Kirke occupation. The siege, the defeat, and the three-year occupation of Quebec from 1628 to 1632 clearly indicated how utterly dependent the early settlement was upon successful interethnic dialogue.

Chomina has been considered to have been a drunkard due to his nickname, "le Raisin" (the Grape), and his "subservience" to Champlain.[113] His loyalty to Champlain is certain, for he denounced the assassin of the two

Frenchmen to Champlain, warned them of Chief Erouachy, and brought them nourishment in necessity. Yet, the label of a simple drunkard would belie Chomina's capabilities and independence. Chomina also had other nicknames, such as "Le Cadet" (the Younger), as had many other Natives, especially after their baptism. Champlain's bid to nominate him for Innu chieftainship is due not to his being unforgivably "ethnocentric"[114] but to his attempt, as a bumbling newcomer, to reciprocate due loyalty. Champlain has also been charged with "cultural prejudice." The problem is, it is difficult to prejudge the (Native) culture within which one is immersed. "Cultural preference" might be an appropriate term, but how could one be faulted for preferring one cultural pattern over another, as everyone does this? Lack of racial prejudice seems to be a sufficient gauge for Champlain and still leaves him several notches above many other colonial founders in his openness and effort at interethnic dialogue, which only faltered with age.

This very trying British occupation intensified French-Native dialogue and catalyzed a profound Nativization among those immigrants determined to hold onto Quebec until the French could regain it. The handful of people who remained in Quebec were Champlain's friends, who had already invested everything in the Canadian venture.[115] Widow Marie Rollet Hébert formed the nucleus around which the settlement gathered, which included: her daughter Guillemette Hébert and husband Guillaume Couillard, their four children, Olivier le Jeune, La Charité and Lesperence, Guillaume Hébert, Guillaume Huboust (second husband of Marie Rollet), Adrien Duchesne the surgeon, Jacques Junier, and the young interpreters. These were Estienne Bruslé (Wendat), Jean Godefroy de Lintot (Algonquian), Thomas Godefroy de Normanville (Algonquin, Wendat, and Haudenosaunee), Jacques Hertel de la Fresnière (Algonquian), François Marguerie dit Delahaye (Algonquin), and Nicolas Marsolet de St-Aignan (Innu) Jean Nicollet (Nipissing, Algonquin). The few who stayed at Quebec, or who enjoyed the hospitality offered them among the tribes, never certain from summer to summer if and when the French ships would return, were thrown upon their own resources and those of their Native friends.[116] The Couillart-Hébert family and the interpreter-liaisons who initially hosted or were hosted by the Amerindians later became key figures who hosted groups of post-1632 immigrants and engagés, instructed them in Native survival techniques, and were ennobled and enfiefed for their contributions. Louis Hébert received the first fief, Sault-au-Matelot, from the duc de Montmorency (4/2/1626), The Hébert-Couillart family were the only serious planters of Quebec, having cleared and seeded six to seven arpents.[117] They distributed their bounty during the siege by giving to the Jesuits two barrels of peas, and by giving barley, peas, and corn to the Recollects and others. These foods were rationed out in a small soup bowl (eight and a half ounces, or "escuellée") per week.[118]

The first residential seminary of Native and French children (and one African, Olivier le Jeune) was hosted by Marie Rollet Hébert in her own home. This seminary included the two little Innu girls who perhaps desired to follow Champlain to France. Sagard wrote: "Champlain entrusted them to Guillaume Couillard, son-in-law of Dame Hébert, so that he could care for them and govern them as if they were his own girls, which he promised to do and did, be cause he was a very honest and God-fearing man."[119] The Native education essential for survival received via dialogue, and the means for its educational transference from veterans to newcomers, occurred en route.

TWIN DISASTERS OF 1648

A critical juncture occurred in 1648 when the French were obliged to handle two major crises in their intercommunal dialogues. The French Crown and Wendat traders, the settlement's two economic pillars in the east and west, unexpectedly collapsed just when a Canadian elite was beginning to assert its existence. When the economic mainstays of the settlement on both French and Wendat ends crashed, the entire colonial enterprise was placed in jeopardy. At stake were the budding Canadian institutions into which Queen Regent Anne d'Autriche introduced a popular element. She was only too glad to delegate responsibility for one more headache in order to obtain parliamentary cooperation for she, Cardinal Mazarin, and Particelli d'Emery were none too popular.[120] The mostly bourgeois-run Community of Habitants (Communauté des Habitants) of 1645 replaced the Parisian-based aristocratic Hundred-Associates company, and by 1647 a partly elective Council of Quebec (Conseil de Quebec) was founded to handle legislation. Both institutions contained a large proportion of socially mobile veteran pioneers anxious to participate in shaping the settlement.

The first disaster was the Parisian Fronde, which involved a series of upheavals against the French Crown authored by various factions, including, among others, the parlement, the nobility, and the clergy. The second disaster was the Fall of Wendake, which entailed the partial annihilation of the Wendat and the diaspora of the remnants of the Wendat confederation. The combined results of these disasters was that the French in Canada were faced with reduced metropolitan investment, financial support, and markets for pelts, while the Fall of Wendake induced French male youth to replace Wendat traders in the fur trade from the Great Lakes.

In sum, the French were forced to take charge of both ends of the commercial process. While they failed abysmally at finding solid French support and markets on their own, they had a specially good flair for linking themselves up with initially unknown Native fur sources deeper in the continent. Why was their western Native rapport remarkably better than their French connection, although, according to their heritage, the opposite should have been the case? At the dialogue crossroads of two radically different worlds, one can never espouse Meinig's "distance decay" theory unless it is applied in reverse as well. It is important to note that the immediate concern of French Canadians was to find the pelts, not to market them. Rather than basing themselves in the former life and selves that they had known in the Old World, French Canadians embraced Nativization during crises such as these.

The Fronde jeopardized the entire Canadian enterprise through lack of investment and financial support. France was warring with itself, and colonial ventures were the last thing that concerned a troubled Queen Regent Anne d'Autriche as she was fleeing with her son, Louis XIV, from Parisian mobs.

The Fronde entailed a reverent sight for our northwestern rebels, who saw the mounted nobility sallying forth with the regional saltbags past the salt tax checkpoints along the Loire and elsewhere in the west. The aristocratic radical individualism that Paul Benichou has emphasized during the "Great Century"[121] remained a live wire fanned by popular adoration. Indeed, the populace usually preferred the known requirements of the local noble over the abstract, unpredictable demands of the Crown. The governor duc de Longueville rekindled an aristocratic uprising in Normandy that proved to be tenacious,[122] the Rohan duchesse de Chevreuse roused agitators, while the Bordeaux Ormée rallied around the prince de Condé and incited a British-inspired republicanism and egalitarianism.[123] Pierre Corneille and the Companie du Saint-Sacrement were pro-Condéen, which reinforced the anti-Crown and anti-Mazarinism of the French Canadians.[124] Although the French elite, especially the Jesuits, were distraught by the crumbling of their own influence, Richelieu's patronage network, and the Crown, initially the petit peuple were ecstatic.[125] If the earlier revolts had a common groundswell, then the Fronde was led by the grands seigneurs, the parlementaires, and even the high clergy, who all promised great benefits to the populace. Their promises, incidentally, appeared to be fulfilled when the intendants, the taille militiamen, and the tax-farm agents disappeared. Rouen became an important centre for the reimpressions of Mazarinades. If dashing tales of the Fronde, the intrigues between the Condéen, Orléannais, and Rohan (Retz) clans, and the Mazarinades satisfied the Canadian immigrants' propensity for anti-Crown activity, they themselves were never obliged to endure the post-Fronde hardships.[126]

Despite the nobility's vision of autonomous regional authority and a weak centralized Crown, precisely the opposite occurred due to the absence of a strong king with which to do away (as was the case in England at this very moment).[127] Yet in France the revolt never entirely revolutionized the country. The horror of regicide was associated with the recent memory of Henri IV's assassination – a man who was widely regarded as a great king and whose body became the focus of a cult (for although buried in St-Denis, his heart was preserved at the famous Jesuit collège of La Flèche).[128] It was there that many Jesuit missionaries and the later philosophes (like Voltaire) studied, and the Jesuits had much to lose through the disintegration of royal power. Although the Fronde was not a revolution, it was a factionalized civil war among the elite, and it caused a moderate amount of agricultural destruction and political havoc as well as much bewilderment.

Simultaneously, the main Native middlemen in the French-Native Great Lakes fur trade, the Wendat, witnessed the fall of their confederacy and the diaspora of the remnants from the Wendake homeland. The Haudenosaunee-Wendat struggle predated French settlement, and Daniel Richter has written that the Haudenosaunee endeavoured to either incorporate or annihilate the Wendat.[129] Due to the Haudenosaunee threat, by the early seventeenth century the Algonquians and the Wendat suggested to Champlain that he initiate the French "tribe" into their pre-existing trade and military alliance as brothers to bolster their defences.[130] By 1648, however, the conflict between the Haudenosaunee and the Wendat escalated, and afterward the conflict sharpened. The Haudenosaunee fought the Great Lakes Algonquians and the French due to a constellation of factors that have recently been debated with renewed verve, which is another book altogether.[131]

In the last two decades, revisionist historiography has charged the Jesuits with helping bring down the Wendake through disease, division, and refusing them adequate defense and arms.[132] The time has come to reevaluate this question. We must first reconsider the terms of early immigrant French survival. These twin crises in 1648 elaborated upon the lesson of the Kirke Conquest of 1629. How could anyone imagine that France might bail out the Wendat, when the Crown had not bailed out its own settlement and was itself in dire disequilibrium? The crops failed, fish were scarce, an epidemic claimed several lives, and the Jesuits lost court influence in the person of the duchesse d'Aiguillon due to the death of Cardinal de Richelieu and the ravages of the Fronde.[133] The French Crown, occupied with the Fronde, reluctantly sent 100 soldiers only in 1653, and they did not arrive until October, after an entire summer of Haudenosaunee ambushes upon the settlement.[134] In addition, disease and the Haudenosaunee were chasing, exterminating, and incorporating a great number of tribes in the area. The Neutrals, the Tionnontati (Petun or Tobacco Nation), the Kichespirini (Allumette Islanders), the Weskarini (Petite Nation), the Nipissing (nation des sorciers), the proto-Anishinabe (Ojibwa), the Maskouten (la nation du Chat), the Miami, the Illinois, the Potawatomi, the Winnebago (les Puants), the Attikameg (Poisson blancs), the Odawa (Ottawa), the Innu, and others all suffered death and dislocations due to Haudenosaunee policy of this time.[135] Sixty armed French with extra munitions were hardly adequate, but

350 to 450 potential fighting men was a considerable number to send to Wendake to fight off the Haudenosaunee.[136]

The fall of Wendake was facilitated, of course, by the Haudenosaunee perception of demographic weakness due to the epidemic scourge among the Wendat in the 1630s, as Denys Delâge has insisted.[137] Before this, the French plague crisis of 1628–31 carried off 1.5 million out of seventeen to twenty million French, and this was followed by a famine in 1630, which was severe in the Norman Cotentin and ports of Brittany.[138] The profound effect of a high death rate upon Wendake could be compared with the effects of the bubonic plague of the fourteenth century upon European communities, whose rate of depopulation was not as catastrophic was that of the Wendake.[139] Why should the missionaries, a European factor of only middling importance, be implicated in the Wendat tragedy when more primary questions have heretofore been neglected. Then, with the Haudenosaunee threat on the confederacy's tails, factionalization certainly followed.

The Wendat Confederation was a recent union, which was founded to defend Wendake against the Haudenosaunee, and was still shaky.[140] Haudenosaunee factionalization was pulling apart Wendat unity by offering different deals to different tribes. Some tribes had captives in Iroquoia that they were anxious to bargain for, while others had none and were well insulated geographically. When threatened with annihilation, Wendat communal factionalization was expressed by the formation of Haudenosaunee collaborationist camps versus resistance camps. As early as 1647 the Attignawantan (Bear) tribe was wary of the Haudenosaunee yet the Arendaronnon (Rock) tribe sent converted chief Jean-Baptiste Atironta to make peace, in order to free Arendaronnon captives held by the Onondaga.[141] This vital strategic split definitely characterized geopolitical rather than religious differences. The Jesuits only exacerbated preexisting divisions that were already ruptured due to the Haudenosaunee campaign's threat to people's literal survival.

The divisions within the Haudenosaunee League itself made for further cleavages. The Onondaga and Oneida were ready for peace with the Wendat, while the Seneca were not. Iroquoia itself had also suffered from smallpox epidemics between 1646 and 1647.[142] Yet none could rival the Mohawk fear of the Susquehannock (Andastes) and their consequent aggressivity towards the Wendat.[143] Pre-Jesuit Wendake was not a static idyll: but had tensions of its own, particularly as it had a vast trading network among many different tribes. Therefore, the aggravation of the split between converted Wendat and traditionalist Wendat under the Haudenosaunee menace was mostly a result of, not a reason for, prior Wendat factionalization.[144]

The threat of imminent annihilation through Haudenosaunee hostilities[145] was hardly conducive to unity. Father Charlevoix estimates that Haudenosaunee strategy was to divide and conquer by concluding a tactical peace. They would then attack the farthest villages simultaneously and pass this off as border incidents irrelevant to the central peace accord, which would lull the Wendat into a false sense of security.[146] The threat of extinction in and of itself is a powerful factionalizer, but when the threat is due to human aggression, factionalization becomes even more extreme, as reconcilers and opponents sweat it out together.[147] During the Second World War European Jewish communities were threatened with extinction, and those who were informed of the gas chambers in the death camps or warned of the coming of the Einsatzgruppen quickly split into antagonistic camps.[148] Each had different plans for collective salvation, and the odds of escaping death were almost nil.[149] Victims typically focus their anguished anger at other victims, even those more traumatized than themselves, instead of fingering the actual aggressor. This, of course, was a consequence of displaced rage, bereavement, and deep fear.[150]

Neither "genocide" nor "ethnic cleansing" are appropriate terms for these kind of phenomena. Use of the term "genocide" gives unwarranted prominence to the unscientific belief that social categories have fixed genetic or racial bases. We are all one race and are extremely similar genetically, which Raphael Lemkin did not know when he coined the term. It also furthers the mistaken idea that ancestry, or group identification, determines behaviour. Last, it erroneously implies that the killing of an entire socially or historically constructed people, independently of their own self-identification, can ever have any ostensible "reason" outside of some collective pathology at work within the perpetrators.

"Ethnic cleansing," like "genocide," is also an unfortunate term. No murder can "clean" anything, and no group is any cleaner than any other group. This term sees the phenomenon from the perpetrator's point of view rather than from the victim's point of view. The same obtuseness to human suffering is also reflected in the term "target," which also emanates from a killer's perspective. Political objectives are the supposed "targets" of war, not human beings. Contemporary war strategists, technology, and the media have further obfuscated the distinction between civilians and the military by using "sensationalist misnomers" instead of truly considering the human dimension. For this reason, I attempt to clarify the meaning of Wendat suffering in its own context, applying hindsight but not permitting current misnomers to obfuscate any further. It seems appropriate to employ the term "holocaust" to the Wendat historical experience. Holocaust refers to the obliteration of people of one's identified group, together with its culture. When a holocaust threatens one's entire tribe, the trauma is experienced, remembered, and reconstructed both collectively and individually.

The Haudenosaunee appear to have intended this catastrophe to have been simply a large "mourning war" (see below). And this particular mid-century mourning war specifically coveted the talented and famous Wendat, who were to be removed, converted, reoriented, and incorporated into the Haudenosaunee League. It seems that the League intended to employ Wendat talent and skills to its own benefit, certainly a more intelligent and humane plan than that of the Nazis, who wished to obliterate the accomplishments of European Jewry (to the loss of humanity). Yet it appears that the Wendat resisted this co-optive plan, and the resulting clash of wills brought about a tragedy.

The only thing that could perhaps have averted the fall of Wendake would have been aid from their Susquehannock allies. The Wendat delegation, headed by Charles Ondaaiondiont, petitioned the Susquehannocks in June 1648. Ondaaiondiont saw himself as the voice of a dying Wendake and spoke of his coming from the land of the dead.[151] Could it be that the Susquehannocks, having sent a delegation to the Haudenosaunee, were apprised of the latter's strategy but failed to inform the Wendat of their intelligence? And is this in any way connected with the Wendat delegation to New Sweden in 1648? The missing Susquehannock link here could explain why stronger Wendat allies, and they had many, failed to avert the fall of Wendake.

On the other hand, Wendat men decided to leave for winter trade even though they were well aware of the Haudenosaunee danger. They obviously focused not upon French support but upon French trade. During the winter of 1648 the Seneca took twenty-four captives and killed seven Wendat at St-Ignace, including Ignace and Saonaretsi. When the survivors returned to near St-Ignace, before they had a chance to organize themselves, they were attacked by around a hundred Mohawks and about forty were taken as captives. By 15 March 1648, when most of the men were gone, they captured the town of about 400 people at dawn.[152] A Haudenosaunee-adopted Wendat-led ambush killed four to five Wendat and rounded up seven Wendat captives on one of the distant islands, but they escaped. The fourteen-year-old daughter of Antoine Otiatonnety escaped from certain death at the hands of the Seneca and found refuge with the Neutrals. According to the Jesuit Relation of 1648–49, the St-Joseph Mission was taken by summer 1648.

When the great attack took place, it should have surprised no one. Even so, the exact timing of an endemic security problem, and the flat denial of imminent life-threatening danger, is quite common. By 15 March 1649 St Louis was left with only eighty fighters, together with the Jesuit mission Ste-Marie, where Father Jean de Brébeuf and Father Gabriel Lallemant were overcome by 1,000 Haudenosaunee. The mission was burning by 9:00 AM the same morning, as was the town of St Ignace. According to Wendat accounts, Father Brébeuf withstood exceptional torture. Gabriel Lallemant was tortured and killed the next day. Wendat chief Annaotaha had refused to allow the warriors to abandon the Jesuit Fathers Brébeuf and Lallemant, but to little avail. When a massacre ensued, the Wendat turned to Wendat warriors rather than to the paltry French mission for aid. Father Ragueneau wrote that, of the forty-six Frenchmen scattered at missions in Wendake, those of Ste-Marie (estimated from thirty at maximum to less than twenty, with priests being unable to bear arms) waited all night for the Haudenosaunee to enter. The defence went well while 300 Attignawantan of Ossossan and Ste-Magdeleine fought off 200 Haudenosaunee, taking thirty captives.[153] Wendat escapees sought aid from Wendat warriors, not from the Jesuits, for of the 500 escapees of St-Louis only two male converts arrived at Ste-Marie, although it was only a distance of two miles (one lieue) and was relatively well fortified. One elderly woman who escaped from the flames ran all the way to Scannonaenrat, at a distance of around fifteen kilometres (around nine miles), instead of seeking refuge at Ste-Marie. She probably knew that there were many warriors there, 700 of whom set off after the retreating Haudenosaunee, who were loaded with captives and spoils. After pursuing them for two days without reaching them, lacking provisions, apprehensive of confronting an enemy encouraged by success, and lacking an equal number of firearms, they turned back.[154] So the backbone of Wendat resistance would evidently have been Wendat and Susquehannock warriors, not Frenchmen.[155]

The fall of Wendake was tactically effected through a novel Haudenosaunee strategy applied to a badly defended area, as Cornelius Jaenen has already suggested.[156] The Haudenosaunee force during the dawn attack of 16 March 1649 was massive (around 1,000 warriors)[157] and unprecedented (unscouted by Wendat reconnaissance).[158] The attacks were lightning strikes lasting only three days while the Haudenosaunee defended their rearguard reinforcements in St-Ignace.[159] Haudenosaunee forces concentrated on precisely those areas that lacked Wendat reconnaissance and forces, and were designed to cut Wendake in two. This spelled disaster for local families, who lost over 780 people to the Haudenosaunee (through death or captivity), of whom only 380 were warriors. Four hundred of the dead were children, women, and the aged.[160] When trapped the Wendat were extraordinarily courageous. About eighty armed converts of St-Louis, led by the Wendat hero Chief Annaotaha, defended their turf and the Jesuits, and fell captive to the enemy while doing so.[161] In conclusion, neither missionary-instigated factionalization, nor the refusal of French aid, nor any special perfidy on the part of the French caused the fall of Wendake.

Despite this, the holocaust deeply affected the French-Wendat dialogue. The fall of Wendake completely reversed the former dependency of French upon Wendat, caused Wendat standing to reverse, and initiated a diaspora to escape Haudenosaunee recruitment and/or persecution. The pre-existing Algonquian-Wendat alliance and trade web, which funnelled goods from the northeast to the northwest, had, since the French joined it, become the route for French goods to the inland tribes. With the fall of Wendake, the majority of Wendat fled west, while some joined the Haudenosaunee in order to rejoin family. Christian Wendat followed the French to the St Lawrence. Father Ragueneau estimated that, from the spring of 1647 to the spring of 1649, over 9,000 Wendat sought board at Ste-Marie. For the French at that time, extensive sharing was more easily offered than military aid.[162] (There were about 1,000 converts by 1647, 1,800 by 1648, and over 3,500 by 1649, including the Tionnontati.)[163] Those who moved to the Island of St-Joseph with the Jesuits were approached by twelve Wendat chiefs, who asked them to "have pity on their misery, without us they see themselves as prey to the enemy, only with us they consider themselves strong enough to defend themselves courageously: We should have compassion for their widows and poor Christian children, that all those who stay infidel have all resolved to embrace our faith, and we would make of this island, an island of Christians."[164] Some chose New France as their new abode, where they were first succored by the French population; they erected their own neighbourhood on Ile-d'Orléans, leased to the Jesuits for this purpose by Eleonor de Grandmaison.[165] The socio-cultural effect of the Wendat diaspora enhanced the importance of their historical-cultural inheritance as creation and historical myths function to piece together (bricoleur) something coherent out of the nightmarish past. Whereas with a less sophisticated tribe the diaspora might have tended to weaken traditions, with the capable and sophisticated Wendat it forced them to cling to their collective identity and to reweave versions of the traumatic past to make retroactive sense of them.[166] The tragic fall of Wendake in 1648–49 also cost New France several key things: the Wendat trade network between the St Lawrence and the Great Lakes that kept the settlement afloat, the flower of their missions, and prominent Jesuit fathers Jean de Brébeuf and Gabriel Lallemant.[167] Wendat network traders had been either killed, adopted by the Haudenosaunee, or dispersed.[168]

The French-Wendat geographical negotiation was further catalyzed when French youth began the fur-laden canoe transports, as coureurs de bois, to the Great Lakes. The replacement of Wendat traders by the French among the Algonquian peoples of the Great Lakes also situated the Algonquian-French dialogue as the constellations of economic power and necessity evolved. The Jesuit Relation of 1652–53 states: "all our youth is planning to go fur trading, to find dispersed nations here and there, and they hope to return laden with several years-worth of beaverpelts." ("toute notre jeunesse Françoise est en dessein d'aller en traite, trouver les Nations dispersées, ça et là, & ils esperent d'en revenir chargez des Castors de plusieurs années.")[169] The later geographical dispersion required of the men and youths, who branched out to the west and south, touched the Gulf of Mexico. This was the beginning of the implantation of limited French-Native mixed-marriage settlements along trading posts that later became French forts. This diaspora of Frenchmen via trade or soldiery gave birth to largely Métis children in the west and an increasing gap between the French population on the St Lawrence (and those further west and south) due to the breakdown of the centralizing institutions in New France. The dearth of furs motivated the French Canadians to push exploration into trade regions even further from Haudenosaunee tomahawks. Ventures up the Gaspésie, the rivers north of Lac St-Jean, up the Mauricie to Labrador, Lake Superior, and Lake Nekouba continued the search for fur trading partners after 1663, beyond the well established trading post of Tadoussac.[170] The new trading map of 1653 was not a testament to metropolitan French power and influence; rather, it documents the startling extent of French initiative and adaptation to the Native world. In this sense, the fall of Wendake resulted in both a Wendat diaspora due to the need for elementary survival, while encouraging a French male diaspora due to dire economic need, with continuing reciprocal cooperation between the two.

After the fall of Wendake, the Wendat role of mediator, with the Huron language as the lingua franca of the fur trade, was slowly replaced by French. This involvement in the First Nations commercial heartland was in stark contrast to the separateness preferred by the population of New England. The French tried to insinuate themselves as mediators among the Great Lakes nations, as Champlain earlier had endeavoured to do among the earliest allies, with only partial success. The fatherly protection of the French king (Grand Onontio), who gave his "children" Catholicism and the metal cauldron, would eventually predominate. By the eighteenth century, Bacqueville de La Potherie wrote that, initially: "it sufficed that a nation had some French to believe itself immune to its neighbors' insults, they became the Mediators of all the quarrels" ("il suffissoit à une Nation de posséder des François pour se croire à l'abri des insultes de ses voisins, ils devenoient les Mediateurs de tous les differens"). This policy reflected the French desire to become what the Potawatomi had originally envisioned them to be upon their first encounter: "you are one of the first spirits ... because you make iron, it is you who should dominate and protect all men, blessed is the sun which illuminated you and rendered you unto our land" ("tu es un des premiers Esprits...puisque tu fais le fer, c'est toi qui doit dominer & proteger tous les hommes, loué soit le soleil qui t'a éclairé et t'a rendu sur notre terre").[171] Yet this replacement of Wendat by French not only reversed the French-Wendat symbiosis and shifted the French-Algonquian constellation of relations, it also had two other consequences.

First, especially in the Native heartland, the French were forced to reevaluate the exact degree to which they were willing to Nativize or return to France.

This eventually divided the population into Nativizing versus returning French. Second, Haudenosaunee hostility intensified against the French. What was the proportion of Nativizing to returning French? The Trudel hypothesis states that 36.4 percent of all immigrants returned to France. Peter Moogk hypothesized that 69.9 percent returned to France.[172] Whichever calculation we choose, the proportion is in great contrast to the rootedness of British settlement in North America. These calculations assume that the resident population is deduced from passenger ship lists obtained from those actually staying in the settlement proper, which nevertheless does not account for those who opted for Native marriage or adoption elsewhere on the continent (which was not always documented). At any rate, with all options, this spells out a very large return rate of immigrants, meaning that Canadian survival skills became available only to vereran Canadians.

The second consequence, the escalation of hostility in the French-Haudenosaunee equation, became the basis of the next disaster that we shall examine. Although the French Canadians at a vulnerable early point in the colonial venture were faced with devastating odds by having their fur sources, middlemen, investors, and markets jeopardized, they already seemed to be more adept at seeking the Native end of the commerce than that of the mother country. Simultaneously, the relationship of dependency upon their most prominent allies, the Wendat, reversed itself when the French replaced the latter in the middleman function, which reversed power perceptions within the French-Wendat dialogue and set the Haudenosaunee upon the French. In addition, this precarious state of affairs narrowed down those French capable of increased Nativization from those returning to France.

EIGHT DAY MIRACLE OF 1660

As the French Canadians replaced Wendat middlemen, the Haudenosaunee escalated ambushes en route and targetted New France itself. Haudenosaunee, especially the Mohawk, attempted to circumscribe the military and commercial options of New France in order to keep their own arena large. From the fall of Wendake in 1648 until 1661, they escalated their attacks upon the French. Previously, the Haudenosaunee had intermittently tried to secure a French alliance but failed.[173] By 1645, Father LeJeune reported that Governor Montmagny was finally pressured into a peace with the Mohawks, whose secret clause only made peace with converted allies.[174] As can be expected, this diplomatic trick did not curry favour with anyone when it became generally known. In 1655–57, when hostilities were halted, missionaries were sent to Iroquoia, but this alliance was also short-lived.

Due to hostilities with the Haudenosaunee during the early years, the French suffered a casualty total of 296 (Dickinson) or 267–71 (Brandão) deaths, wounding, torture, becoming lost, and/or captivities. Of this total, fatalities were estimated at 96 (Brandao) or 221 (Dickinson) or 159 (Trudel) from 1608–66.[175] Until 1642 there were only four or five deaths due to the Haudenosaunee, yet hostilities escalated so that during 1660–61, according to Dickinson, there were a total of between 58 and 62 deaths in the three main settlements – Quebec (22 deaths, 11 captives), Three Rivers (5 deaths, 23 captives), and Montreal (31 deaths, 25 captives). Brandão lists 211 persons affected – killed (96), lost (9), and captured (106) – as a result of 88 raids.[176] Over time, only 26 were killed/captured/lost (a 2.8 average annually), until 1650, when raids markedly escalated to 153 (13.9 yearly), which by 1662 began to decline to yearly averages of 7.6 fatalities.[177]

Psychological terror was caused by the anticipated Haudenosaunee fire torture, which was rumoured to terminate in cannibalism. In continental Europe, only alleged witches were burned, and cannibalism was anathema to the Church, so these were viewed as unusually frightening. Despite this, the ecclesiastical and administrative pleas for military aid from Paris went virtually unheeded, with the exception of a minuscule party of soldiers (camp volant). Other people's tortures always seem more shocking than one's own – especially for newcomers who never know what to expect. The psychological element of fear exerted upon the family and friends of tortured and dead French Canadians, indeed upon the entire small community during this long war of attrition, should not be underestimated. The context of uncertainty was significant. Perceptions count acutely in war, particularly interethnic war, where enemies can demonize one another.[178]

Deep fear was multiplied when the gap between initial conception and later events became too evident. Montreal was erected with the intention of being a New Jerusalem, designed to encourage the mixing of French and Native in a utopian religious atmosphere. Marie Morin writes: "The men set up tents ... like the real Israelites ... they called each other brothers and sisters, tried to defer to one another in everything, to serve the all the others ... to console them, to serve the sick ... and as our Israelites did not have any oil to light their lamp day and night in front of the hostel, they put several fireflies in a fine glass vial ... one never saw public sins or hate or rancor, all were as one heart for charity, always ready to serve and speak to others with respect and affection." (les hommes travaillerent a dresser des tantes ... comme des vrays Israelites ... ils ne s'apellois que freres et soeurs, s'étudies a ce deferer en tout, a servir tous les autres ... les consoler, a servir les malades ... et comme nos Israelites n'avois point d'huille pour faire brusler une lampe jour et nuit devant l'hostel, ils s'aviserent de metre dans une phiole de verre fin plusieurs mouches qu'on apelles a feu ... On ne voyet point de pechés publics ni des heines ou rancunes, tous n'estois qu'un couer en charité, toujours prets a ce servir et a parler des autres avec estime et affection. [sic].)[179] Instead of a peaceful interethnic métissage, warlike defence was required to protect the flat vulnerable post from the Haudenosaunee. The mental gap between the utopian Ville-Marie in the French religious psyche, and the terrifying French-Haudenosaunee mis-dialogue actually there, forced a coming to terms between conceptions and imminent reality.

The Eight Day Miracle of 1660 occurred precisely after an innovative trade council (Conseil de la Traite), which was established in 1657. It again put Canadian institutions in jeopardy. Governor Du Bois d'Avaugour called this council a "Conseil Général," and it consisted of the governor; the fur trade director; four councillors elected by the Communauté des Habitants; and, at Prince de Condé's insistence, a Jesuit and Bishop Laval. Ironically however, like the earlier innovations in Canada, the Conseil de la Traite was established at a precarious juncture when the Haudenosaunee returned to the warpath in earnest and almost severed the jugular of New France.

Recurrent rumours of Haudenosaunee intent on devastating the young settlement spread panic and reinforced fortifications. A Haudenosaunee captive under torture reported that 900 to 1200 warriors were planning to attack Quebec, to make off with the governor-general's head, to capture the "white girls" ("filles blanches," i.e., Hospitallers), to make a fort of their hospital, and to scorch the entire settlement. Bishop Laval ordered the Ursulines to go live with the Jesuits inside the walls for protection, which seemed to Mother Marie de L'Incarnation unnecessary (but then her desire for self-sacrifice must be considered). Torture is the worst method one can use to learn the truth from a captive, nevertheless it seems that some plan was afoot.[180]

The crisis in French-Haudenosaunee dialogue peaked at the Battle of the Long-Sault (1660), which culminated in the deaths of sixteen Montrealers, four Algonquians (among them Chief Metiouemig), and Wendat chief Annaotaha. The young French Dollard des Ormeaux had joined Chief Annaotaha with four Algonquians and forty Wendat to hold off around 800 Haudenosaunee warriors who were intent on attacking Montreal. This lasted for about a week.[181] The sixty-one men fought a preliminary Haudenosaunee force from a dilapidated and abandoned French "fort" at the Long-Sault just west of Montreal (although it was possibly at the Chaudières Falls), as fleeing Haudenosaunee rushed reinforcements to the spot.[182] The battle ceased as negotiations opened between dwindling Wendat and Haudenosaunee-adopted Wendat. According to the Wendat escapee account, the French became nervous during these negotiations and opened fire upon the Haudenosaunee. The escapees claimed that Chief Annaotaha cried that the French had brought about their own deaths.[183] Haudenosaunee losses, reported by Dollier de Casson, were supposedly half their numbers, yet the Dutch reported them to be at 14 dead and 19 wounded, leaving a total of 18 dead and 25 prisoners.[184] The final outcome of this disproportionate battle was that New France was no longer menaced that year, sparing the huge fur convoy that Pierre-Esprit Radisson brought on sixty canoes worth 200,000 livres tournois from the Great Lakes. According to Dollier de Casson and Mother Marie de l'Incarnation, New France was spared owing to this defence of the Long-Sault.

Each community represented in this battle had its own motives for participating in the defence of New France. The French motive of self-defence is obvious. Despite this, Dollard's specific motives are somewhat unclear, leaving much debate to divide historians (mostly clerical Francophone) who claim that Dollard was the hero who saved New France.[185] Other historians have argued that Dollard, the commander of the Montreal garrison, was not even apprised of the Haudenosaunee presence there.[186] One has suggested that Dollard expected to raid the Haudenosaunee who were supposed to be descending with northern furs.[187] Nonetheless, a mere booty raid does not seem to be worth the effort to amass sixty-one men to write up their wills and go west of Montreal. Why, in this case, did not traders like Lambert Closse also participate, for surely in the tiny Ville-Marie of the time, he would have known all about this expedition? Dollier de Casson writes that he was "a self-sacrificing hero and generous as a lion ... the sworn enemy of cowards" (un homme de tout coeur et généreux comme un lion ... l'ennemi juré des poltroons).[188] He was killed the following year in another raid. André Vachon argues that Dollard had tried to protect the fur-laden canoes that he knew Radisson and des Groseilliers were about to bring in.[189] Two of his contingent, Tavernier and Valets, wrote their wills before leaving Montreal, with the latter specifying their intent to ambush small bands of Haudenosaunee and our enemies (les petites bandes Haudenosauneees et nos Ennemis). He certainly suspected a Haudenosaunee force in the vicinity but seemed unaware of its actual size.[190]

The menaced Wendat presumably participated in this pre-emptive manoeuvre to deter repeated Haudenosaunee attempts to capture the remaining families of old Wendake that had settled in New France, as Wendat Eustache Tshaouonhohoui mentions.[191] Chief Annaotaha, who had tried to save Father Brébeuf in Wendake, was a celebrated and experienced hero, and the Long-Sault defenders certainly recognized his authority, as Dickinson deduced, for French Dollard was young, only resident for two years in the country, and yet was responsible for commanding a sensitive entry zone like Montreal.[192] This incident was fraught with intense French-Wendat mutual commitment, which apparently had difficulty standing up to the Haudenosaunee menace.

We should be extremely cautious regarding the specific veracity of the accounts. The account of each contains the seeds of underlying assumptions, attitudes, and interpretation of those events, where self-justification may be a primary motive. The Haudenosaunee would have been interested in minimizing their losses, and the Wendat would have been wary of accusing themselves when relating the events back to the French, even to highly sympathetic Mother Marie de L'Incarnation. The French participants, most of whom were barely seven years in Canada, were not fathers of families, did not all understand Huron, and did not unconditionally trust the Wendat. French aggression was due to their newcomer alarm and unfamiliarity compounded by the lack of Canadian dependents, while the Wendat had much to gain by negotiating. Theoretically, even if they had been captured and transported alive to Iroquoia, they thought the Wendat would have been saved by their own relatives, leaving the French to boil in the cauldron.

Haudenosaunee motives for massing such a force have been debated, but John Dickinson has informed us that the main prey the Haudenosaunee were after were the remaining Wendat, presumably for adoption and the reunion of the Wendat community within Iroquoia.[193] This would explain why all the French were killed and some Wendat were spared. A different suggestion that 800 Haudenosaunee warriors had circled a wide arc to Montreal in the dead of winter only to capture a few French and allies and, thus, force the French to keep their neutrality, does not seem plausible In accord with Richter and Viau's "mourning war thesis," which Claude Gélinas also seconds, Dickinson's idea has explanatory power.[194]

The perturbed Wendat-Haudenosaunee love-hate relationship overshadows other conflicts in this incident. After so much strife, the Wendat had no illusions about Haudenosaunee motives. Perhaps initially they had wanted to pre-empt the Haudenosaunee, yet switched their strategy when they saw the Haudenosaunee-adopted Wendat. If the choice was between winning kin or losing French confidence, the die was already cast. Even in such a clear-cut situation, Dollier de Casson rails against supposed Wendat perfidy, yet hails Chief Annaotaha as a hero. He imagines that Wendat twinship with the French should have been more important to them than survival itself, hardly a reasonable expectation. The Wendat eye was fixed upon their enemies, who had obliterated old Wendake, massacred families, and dispersed the remnants. Henceforth all Wendat dialogue moved within the shadow of this predicament.

This brings us to the complex question of Chief Annaotaha's motives. Dollier claims that he stood by the French until the end, but the Wendat claimed that he accused Dollard of rashness. In this case, it would seem that Dollier must have been correct because he would have every reason to blame the chief alongside his own warriors (which he did not do), but the Wendat had an obvious interest in justifying Wendat volte-face against the French. Why did Annaotaha stand with the French against his own men?

Here we have the real hero of New France who followed neither furs nor his own kin. He died mirroring Father Brébeuf, as a Wendat statesman who was willing to sacrifice his life for the French-Wendat twinship because it was for the future benefit of both peoples.

Yet Dollard des Ormeaux became the savior that every French Canadian historian must pronounce upon.[195] Why? Dollier de Casson's astonishment that Annaotaha, with a handful of inexperienced Frenchmen and four Algonquians, could prevent a crushing force of Haudenosaunee from demolishing the settlement, became eclipsed by ecstatic cheers for the "feminine" French tribe finally defying the terrifying Haudenosaunee, despite many Wendat turnabouts. They were proud of finally being recognized as a "tribe" that could hold its own against the most powerful nations amongst them. The fame of the martyred Dollard and his Montreal men spread among the French and Native nations. Mostly clerical nineteenth- to early twentieth-century French Canadian historians, from Ferland to Groulx, have pointed to the Long-Sault as the triumph of civilization over savagery. But they inverted the original message. French acquisition of enough "savage" courage to cause enemy retreat was, at the time, excellent reason to celebrate.

To conclude, the survival of the nativity of French settlement in North America depended wholly upon positive relations with Native peoples. This contrasts starkly with Virginia and New England, who struck harshly at the very nations closest to them, with less vital risk. The weaving of these relations created an engaging and committed dialogic interaction, which resulted in a much stronger degree of Nativization of the French than the Frenchification of Aboriginal nations. This phenomenon, on the French side, went hand in hand with the later success of encouraging at least a syncretic Christianity among First Nations. Prior to arrival in North America, the political, economic, spiritual, and cultural resistance of Canadian immigrants' provincial traditions and current political situation provided further impetus to cast off perceived Parisian centralization of tyranny, and a French identity through emigration to improve their own lot.

Yet after the immigrant arrived, a novel situation had been created that demanded delicate negotiation. In order to achieve the original colonial aims of trade and evangelization through Frenchification, the interethnic dialogue took place in differing geographical contingencies with a variety of peoples. The climate enhanced local winter autonomy while the summer thaw of a continuous skein of waterways encouraged seasonal powwows with the coming of the French ships. Thus, the environmental negotiation necessitated banding together for survival due to freezing isolation, while the distance between locales allowed for relative local autonomy and, thus, greater plurality of cultures on the St Lawrence, with a predominant métissage at its blurry edges. The negotiation of interethnic dialogue over time taught the French (who had decided to stay by 1663) the essential nature of dependable Native ties and the adaptive advantage of Nativized responses to historical challenges. The anti-French propensities of the majority of immigrants, combined with the environmental and historical necessity of Nativization, were what ensured the tenacity of early settlement and Nativization.

CHAPTER THREE

Revenge of the Cradles

Gluscap boasted aloud after having conquered the giants Kookwes or Kewawkqui, the medicineman Boo'in or Medecolin, and the evil spirit of the night Pamola. There was nothing left to defeat, he marvelled to himself. No one was more powerful than he. The baby chortled. The Woman laughed, and declared that Wasis the baby was unconquerable. Gluscap told Wasis to come to him. The infant utterly ignored him. Infuriated, Gluscap employed his most terrible powers. The earth shook, the waters whipped into a tumult, and the night never ended. The baby only opened his jaws wide and emitted an incessant wail. Gluscap left in defeat.

Algonquian parable

The most salient key to why an intercommunal dialogue took place between French and Native was the necessary interdependence of French and Native communities for survival.[1] Life together brought forth common partying, commercial negotiation, inveterate friendships, canoeing, diplomatic power tactics, romantic ties, common enemies, and competing educational systems. French members were referred to as uncle, aunt, and brother. This unusually intimate French-Native intercommunal interdependence owed its urgency to extremely sparse French immigration. Due to this anemic immigration, an incomplete society full of surplus young males matched nicely with Native societies suffering from a lack of males. The men suffered especially due to waves of epidemics along the trade routes and fur-trade wars. The communities shared informal local bartering, significant fraternal twinning, physical métissage, some Native conversions, and the inroads of French Nativization. Each one of the ethnic communities' predicaments was eased through joining together in mutual aid. In contrast, large-scale British colonization farther south often resulted in mutual hindrance.

Anemic French immigration was a major liability to the new settlement. According to William Eccles, Gary Nash, and Richard White, French policy was born of this weakness.[2] French habitations, isolated for a major part of the year due to ice, relied upon economic, communications, transport, military, and allied reinforcement in order to function. By way of comparison, while Virginia in 1627 had 2,000 colonists, and New England 310, New France had only 107. By 1663 the disparity was much greater, for in round numbers, New England had 40,000, Virginia had 30,000, (total British population: 70,000), New Holland 10,000, and New France (including Acadia) had a mere 3,500. And by 1674, while New France had only 8,000 souls, Virginia had 35,000 and New England 52,000.[3]

The onslaught of European diseases to which allied Native communities had little immunity was due to centuries of virtual isolation, and it struck their communities with particular force. Europeans had acquired a shield of immunities through surviving the devastating bubonic plague and other diseases ostensibly contracted from sustained contact with domesticated animals and through commercial ties with the Far East and Africa.[4] Even so, longevity was not pronounced. We must remember that in seventeenth-century Normandy, about 50 percent of the population died before age twenty, and between 1600 AND 1670, between 3,360,000 and 2,205,000, or 11 to 15 percent, perished of the plague. This figure amounted to 18 to 27 percent of the total urban mortality rate. Between 1628 and 1632, it constituted 25 to 30 percent of mortality rates in all France.[5] Father Brébeuf remarked that, whereas prior to the 1630s epidemics there were twenty villages and 30,000 Wendat, there was severe depopulation thereafter.[6] William Eccles writes of over 15,000 Wendat dead in the 1630s, while Bruce Trigger approximates a 50 percent depopulation for Wendake alone.[7] The First Nations underwent even more severe depopulation, at a rate of 55 to 90 percent. European diseases had been clawing at the fabric of Native communities since the sixteenth century. Smallpox, scarlet fever, bubonic plague, and other European diseases claimed myriad victims.[8]

Disease especially claimed the lives of many Amerindian elders and children, the main links in the sociological and cultural chain. The sociological impact of contact can only be understood within the light of widespread communal mourning, drastically reduced or destroyed families, and sometimes conflicting communal interpretations of the tragedy that invariably followed. The epidemic devastation was complemented by a host of other contact ills in Native communities. French-British fur trade rivalries exacerbated pre-existing Haudenosaunee competition with the Algonquian-Wendat alliance as the level and scope of aggression increased. In addition, although alcohol was an ordinary French accompaniment to mealtimes, shipboard life, and deal-making, it quickly became a self-destructive substance for First Nations, and this also accelerated population decline.[9]

French-Native interdependence was also legitimated by the official military reciprocity common in Amerindian intertribal alliances, which entailed rules of extensive sharing, commercial ties, reciprocal hospitality, exchange of children and youths, interethnic romancing (métissage), and seasonal months-long settlement isolation when the St Lawrence froze over.

French-Native socio-economic and military policies were formulated during the establishment of Acadia and Quebec, which expressed the objectives of both communities. Algonquian communities, especially the Mi'kmaq, Maliseet, Haudenosaunee, and Wendat, welcomed the French into their network of alliances with the objective of gaining exclusive trading rights for European articles as well as additional defence from the dreaded Haudenosaunee nations. Official French objectives in investing in settlement in North America were to extensively explore trade routes, gain exclusive trading rights over Native furs and fish, and to Frenchify and convert the Natives. After a few years, the goal of conversion took precedence over Frenchification as the latter was harder to obtain, and a utopian plan of creating a strong French Creole through métissage of Frenchmen with Native women appeared. The constant give and take of image and reality involved a process of "ghostly" negotiation involving the selection of collective memories that constituted a coherent "ghostly" past relevant to the contact. The conception of good and evil in each community also influenced glimmers of the desired "ghost" of a utopian future, that of a feared Hell, and actual social reality.

Social dialogue and mutual influence between the French and Native communities was enhanced by many interethnic exchanges beginning in the tender years, which increased interdependence. Exchanges of children and youths were normative aspects of Native alliances between nations, and were also the rule between the French and their allies. This method of social and cultural immersion acted like a "baptism" into another world. Exchanges and adoptions were extremely powerful in facilitating intercultural understanding, creating a cadre of multiculturally adroit young people and also Nativizing French educational, ritual, and social norms for young French North Americans.

The children of New France were cherished as the new "françois-canadois," who were free of the corrupting atmosphere of Europe. Their status and treatment within the settlement was far above that of French children, who were subject to severe discipline and castigation. These new françois-canadois were the first fruits of settler effort and were prized for their independent behaviour, despite the horror of royal administrators at seeing French seeds gone wild.

Native chiefs considered children from other communities a top priority – trainees and valuable cultural liaisons and translators. The adoption and exchange of children and youth were required by Native alliance protocol.[10] And simultaneously, the Recollects and Jesuits initially missionized children, whom they considered more malleable than their parents.[11] Yet while very few Native children became Frenchified, all the immigrant children acquired various degrees of Nativization. A growing body of multiculturally raised, multilingual youth grew up within the context of mutual respect between French, Métis, and Native centres.

Subsequently, the incorporation of the Native approach to French Canadian wilderness training and religious education benefitted the majority of the newcomers. The tradition was also continued as veterans taught incoming newcomers. Several institutions gave them a formal as well as an informal education relevant to their adjustment in Canada. Hallowell remarked that a well developed learning theory is relevant to promoting further knowledge of the whole process of cultural transmission as well as processes involved in acculturation and cultural change.[12] French youth assumed a nom de guerre, were baptized on the traversée several times, and worked in a three-year "engagement" for a veteran habitant, much as a compagnon in France would on his tour de France.[13] While in the settlement a newcomer learned the Native allies' mainly Algonquian survival lessons through hunting, fishing, canoeing, and warring together with their allies. And when thoroughly habituated and deemed capable of it, the more seasoned newcomer, but usually Canadian-born, spent seasons, if not years, in the Great Lakes area as a rite of passage. These series of "baptisms" were accompanied by nicknames, renaming, adoptions (some by Haudenosaunee torture fire), and the assumption of the identity of defunct family members to mend the social fabric torn by death. All these rites of French initiation and education in New France were benchmarks upon the waterway of a complex internalization of Native cultural lessons that excluded winterers and merchants, admitting only those capable of jumping these rigorous hurdles.

Adoption broke down the elementary barriers of contained, culturally unified families or the family enclave of Catholic religious communities. Ethnohistorian James Axtell emphasized that the adoption of Amerindian children by immigrants was initially a system of "didactic persuasion."[14] Persuasion, however, was greatly tempered with genuine doting tenderness of "attachment transference or expansion." Socio-cultural and biopsychosocial immersion were intimately achieved during early childhood or adolescence via emotional attachment, communication, and implicit social modelling. The critical early childhood stage of a "symphonic interaction" between nature and nurture, and the neural pruning at the adolescent stage, reinforced brain patterns formed within the Other's community.[15] This transformed the early mother-child bond into an emotional means of identification, empathy, and communication with others. It also led to skills at socio-cultural adaptation that could be applied to a variety of milieux as well as to the expansion of the boundaries of the developing complex self.[16] Each adoptive family could influence their charges with their admiration, approval, consternation, or mockery. Implicit guidance acts as a powerful catalyst upon a developing mind anxious to obtain familial, peer, and communal approval and love.[17] Unspoken directives were doubly powerful with orphans, whose only familial framework was the adoptive unit and whose identity was necessarily complex due to lack of a protective parental buffer in the early years.

The *Jesuit Relations* of 1636 and 1638 provide us with an example of this cultural moulding. A twelve-year-old girl whose parents gave her to the Jesuits was truly a marvel. In their eyes, she was not "Native" except for her complexion and hair colour, otherwise "with her docility, her modesty, her obedience she could pass for an aristocratically raised little French girl" ("sa docilité, sa modestie, son obeyssance la feroient passer pour une petite Françoise bien née"). To confirm their point, she refused to return to her tribe after her two years of studies.[18] By implication, Native girls were comparatively lively and independent, perhaps not docile enough for the Jesuit fathers.[19] In Native America, protection of the young was supreme, and their independence of thought and will was inviolable. Mother Marie de l'incarnation also noted that Native girls were accustomed to liberty but that this was accompanied by a delicacy and refinement of which few well raised young ladies in France were possessed.[20]

There may be another reason that the attachment of French young was so critical to their acculturation. A reevaluation of French early modern motherhood has speculated that French parents valued their children far more than French historian Philippe Ariès estimated in his controversial book (*Centuries of Childhood*, 1962). Yet, in the French documents that might be oblivious to their own cultural specificity, French writers were astonished that French mothers were seen as "porcupines" by Native mothers. Why did French mothers hand over their newborns to wet nurses?[21] In other words, Native mothers probably provided a modicum of intimacy, devotion, and communication that was basically lacking in the French youth, which means that not only was adoption perhaps not an attachment transference but something that touched an emotional cord in the youth that had previously never been accessed. The medieval attitude towards infanticide still exerted an impact upon societal mores, and early modern laws seemed more concerned with regulating women's behaviour than protecting children. A February 1556 royal edict forbade infanticide upon pain of death by drowning.[22] French children died at a 50 percent rate from birth to fifteen years old, and this could sometimes induce mothers to become depressed or commit suicide.[23] Fertility in New France was officially encouraged by an edict of 1666, which offered tax exemptions to all non-noble Catholic parents who had ten to twelve live children, and yearly pensions of 1000–2000 livres tournois, which was promised to noble families.[24]

In early modern France reason was thought to be crystallized in the young brain only by age seven or eight.[25] La Rochefoucauld referred to childhood as a time of folly. La Fontaine, the great defender of beasts, however, characterized children as stupid, severe, and cruel. La Bruyère reflected that children quickly became adults.[26] The most common family was the "splintered family," where, due to the death rate, one marriage in four was a remarriage with children of two or three unions brought together, and every second child had a stepmother or stepfather.[27] The paradigm of unlike stepbrothers and stepsisters was about as common as it is today, and thus brotherhood between perfect strangers was not uncommon.

Under these conditions, if stepparents were not exquisitely sensitive to the needs of children in their care, additional alienation could have arisen. The authoritarianism wielded by French fathers of this period would not be so readily acceptable to his stepchildren. Since 1566 French legislation sought to augment paternal power over wife and children, and it increased penalties, including death, for those who dared to contract a clandestine marriage.

Male youth rebellion was at an unprecedented height as their professional and educational possibilities for advancement expanded far beyond that of their more parochial fathers and even their own sisters. First on the front line of this unprecedented advance of male youth were the schools, which in France became battlegrounds in the struggle between Protestantism and Catholicism, and between Catholic Jesuits and equally Catholic Jansenists.[28] Severe discipline and beatings did not endear their wards to their head- masters. The schools were also used as one of the principal tools of colonial missionaries to Christianize the Native peoples of North America.

Guiding, rather than forcing, children was the Native educational way. Aiding them to develop individually for their own future, not obedience, was the goal. Group norms were of course highly important, but limitations were imposed by taboo rather than through penalty, for adults as for children. Group harmony, responsibility, and caring were paramount in order to encourage the expression of individualism in Native culture. Algonquian educational philosophy emphasized that every child has his or her manitou (guardian spirit), which, if offended, would abandon the child and cause sickness or suicide: "les peres & les meres n'ayant point de chastiment pour leurs enfans ... & i'en ay veu qui se font empoisonnez, d'autres se sont pendus, ou pour auoir receu, ou de peur de recevoir, vne correction ... et cela pour quelques petites fautes."[29] LeClercq wrote that "La Nature leur inspire assez de tendresse & de charité envers leurs Enfans ... elles aiment leurs enfans."[30] Consequently, punishment was rarely used,[31] but children were guided through persuasion, logic, scary stories, taboos, and teasing.[32] Savignon, the Wendat youth who sailed to France, was horrified by parents who restrained and beat their own children.[33]

A famous incident illustrates this philosophy. When a French child, while playing a drum, hit an adult Nipissing with his stick, Native adults present requested a gift from the French for this behaviour. According to their philosophy, the child was not responsible for the act, but his caretakers, meaning all French adults within that town, were. Yet this occurred at an early date in contact, 1634, and some French newcomers assured them that the child would be whipped. The Nipissing men were so horrified that they supplicated that the child be pardoned on the grounds that he did not yet know what he was doing. When they realized that the French were determined to carry out their intention, one of them stripped himself and threw his beaver-skin robe over the child, crying to the Frenchmen, you can hit me if you like, but you will never strike this child![34] This incident illustrates clearly to what lengths Native people were willing to go to protect children as such, even if they were neither theirs nor acting like angels. French children surely quickly sensed that they could count on them in a stitch if faced with patriarchal severity. This attitude in a distant and relatively unfamiliar tribe like the Nipissing indicates to what extent Native people were willing to risk their diplomatic relations with the French in order to protect the latter's own children and reeducate their abusive parents.

Yet what was most instructive for the French was how Native children protected their own play group harmony by imitating adult-modelled communal values – by protecting one another. The barón de Lahontan, then a military officer, relates that, when two children began to argue, their friends formed a neutral loving circle around them without taking sides until both calmed down. If the dispute degenerated to blows, the other children took them both home to cool off.[35] This behaviour opened fresh vistas of emotional intelligence for the frequently temperamental French. This was doubly true for the Normans, who were so enamoured of legal chicanery that they even sued members of their own families.

Jesuit Father Charlevoix remarked that Native children were raised in absolute independence.[36] Wilcomb Washburn has noted that the permissive educational atmosphere began at birth, when the baby was nursed on demand for several years. The infant was not forced to walk or talk, was never spoken to in babytalk, was neither weaned nor toilet- trained (even into the third year), and was "treated from birth as an individual who belongs to the group and has a place and role in it."[37] Childcare was the Native mother's first responsibility, with her brother as the male child's role model and from whom he inherited standing, backed up by her tribe, which acted as the child's collective godparents. This profusion of parental supports reinforced parenting in the event of the death of the father in war, his absence after a divorce, or the death of the mother in childbirth. The child always remained with his/her mother, uncle, and the mother's tribe. The security that collective maternal godparenting provided to lone mothers waiting for their husbands to return from war or hunting, or for a new husband if widowed or separated, enhanced the security and love surrounding their children. Surely, the communal style of child-rearing provided more support for young people than did a French village full of godparents since the community felt itself responsible for all children.[38] All pitched in to help the little one fashion child-size bows and arrows, dolls, and so on. The very first animal caught, even if it was a sparrow, caused a celebration.[39]

The Native idea of what constituted fatherhood was clearly born out when First Nations were urged by French explorers to form a confederation with the French king as their common father. As egalitarianism was strong and motherhood the primary notion of parenthood, many nations continued to refer to the French as brothers, with the Great Onontio, or French king, as their father, whom they assumed would only offer the carrot and never weld the big stick.[40]

Native alliance procedure included the exchange of children and youth as a guarantee of fidelity and desired kinship.[41] Religious training was offered by Jesuit educational strategy to induce conversions: therefore intimate ethnic interpenetration was encouraged through these practices.[42] Montesquieu wrote that there are two salient ways to encourage cultural change, either by law (which establishes precedents) or by education (which helps shape the next generation's world). Nevertheless, none of these are as effective as an alternative living model. The Algonquian generally gave young children of both sexes to families, the hospital, and other religious institutions, especially while they were winter hunting. On the other hand, Wendat and Haudenosaunee gave children in a more representative status as they were usually were in a better economic situation and were farther from the St Lawrence. Even as late as 1675, Louis XIV wrote to Governor Frontenac that he was pleased that Native children sought guidance from the missionaries, and he advised that well-off settlers also send their young off to the wigwams.[43]

The great majority of these children were pubescent girls (perhaps 200 or more), mostly Haudenosaunee, who were drawn to pretty French handiwork, crafts, and lacework. It can be conjectured that many of these girls simply assimilated into immigrant life for several had also visited France, and it was noted that many, apparently, desired to "become French." The precarious winter hunting life and childbirth in subarctic weather may have appeared especially daunting to girls on the brink of adolescence. The few boys sent (twelve documented – at most) were either Wendat or Haudenosaunee, and the Jesuits hoped they might later attain chiefdom. Yet many of them returned from France in a state of anomie and identity crises that did not quickly pass, as was the case with Savignon and Amantacha.

Cornelius Jaenen has succinctly pointed out that the failure of Frenchification lay in the rigidity of the French learning experience and unfamiliar European concepts (such as the measurement of time, punishment, the unaccustomed loneliness of the boarding school, and the apparent irrelevance of French curricula to the North American reality).[44] By Jesuit and Ursuline standards, Native children were very delicate and often actually died when cooped up for too long or reprimanded too severely. In response, even the most rigorous Jesuits modified their approach and spared the rod, which lightened on the limbs of French children as well.[45] French immigrant and Canadian-born children enjoyed running to play with Native children, who were never scolded and ran free from formal lessons and farm chores. This was fun! Immigrant papas knuckled under the squeals of laughter, despite themselves.. Even Lahontan expresses the new French Canadian attitude when he writes that "gentleness is frequently more effective than punishment, especially harsh ones."[46]

As a result of the creeping Nativization of French children, by the late seventeenth century French officials were anxious to reverse the hard-won integration. Now they strove to separate their pet converts from those pesky French "petits sauvages." Native children learned awful habits from French children, and the French learned about "indiscipline" from their Native friends.[47] Of course, by the time the king caught on, it was too late. The reining in of Canadian youth to fulfill French expectations did not help re-Frenchify them any more than the Frenchification plan worked with the Amerindian children. In fact, it only pushed them further away from French metropolitan expectations. Parallel to this, French evangelization of Native communities was enjoying a slow but steady success and became stronger over the next century.

Educational liberality crescendoed for Canadian-born French: their allies saw to that. As many Frenchwomen were from orphanages themselves, and lacked a normative model of mothering, they were certainly open to alternatives, particularly given that institutions had their share of abuses. Denise Lemieux and Peter Moogk both elaborate on this freedom and the comparatively liberal Canadian education.[48] Some French Canadian children were even raised on Native reserves, like Iean (Jean) Amiot, who was brought up in Sainte-Marie-aux-Hurons.[49] Antoine-Denis Raudot wrote in 1709 that "fathers keep their children busy only when they are able to do so ... they love their children too much to compel them to do something against their will."[50] Roger Magnussen states that the oral tradition held sway over the written tradition, which was mirrored by the absence of culturally reinforcing institutions, such as printing presses, booksellers, and lending libraries. He adds that "the Canadianization [sic: meaning Nativization] of the colony gave rise to different values and behaviors ... reared in a frontier environment [sic], they preferred the forest and the field to the school as their place of learning." And Montcalm's aide de camp, Bougainville, seeing this, was quite surprised. The Canadian ability to sign actually fell from 1680–99 to 1750–65, and the number of schools was reduced.[51]

Here we can catch a glimpse of the educational significance of the French Canadian trickster Ti-Jean, who needed courage and strength instead of learning in his harrowing adventures. By the eighteenth century, French Canadian children's lack of regard for European-style authority and deference towards their parents shocked French administrators as much as did their Native-style half-nakedness during summertime and their strength and solid build. Their behaviour was often described as self-confident and reckless, just like the behaviour of Native youth.[52] Lemieux suggests that not only did the Native models afforded by the Jesuit Relations serve to transform European ideas concerning childhood but also that in New France these living models influenced the Canadian concept of childhood, motherhood, and education.[53]

It appears that the increasing independence and indulgence of children was a North American-wide phenomenon for Richard Rapson has reported similar descriptions of British American children by British travellers even as late as 1935. The British interpreted the North American self-reliant young as being the result of increased democratic values, but we could perhaps conjecture that the Native model had some impact there as well.[54] The moderation of educational severity and the youthful push for freedom could certainly be attributed to the adaptive advantage of Native educational philosophy. Thus, despite French intent to both Frenchify and evangelize Native peoples, beginning with malleable children, only the latter goal had any lasting effect a century later. For French children, the immediate advantage of Nativization both to their juvenile status and their adaptivity was great. The cultural dialogue was thus cross-fertilized with children whose identities and orientations were taken from both worlds.

RITES OF PASSAGE

In this environment, the possibilities of adolescence swept away old paradigms. The French immigrant community resembled a male youth camp, where the great majority of immigrants (60.5 percent) were between the ages of fifteen and twenty-nine. By July 1663 75.8 percent of approximately 3,106 immigrants were male. A total of 37.4 percent of these men were single or widowers.[55] Male-female proportions were extremely imbalanced, as was the case in early Virginia: approximately 80.2 percent of settlers were men while 19.8 percent were women; that is, there were about four times as many males as females.[56] Only after 1663, when Louis XIV shipped over the filles du roy (orphan girls raised on royal subsidies), did gender proportions begin to approach an equilibrium.

Pubescent boys are the most exposed to their outside environment, least encumbered by obligations, and likeliest to overstep tradition, due to their low personal vulnerability. They are precisely the weakest link in the transmission of tradition. Psychiatrist Erik Erikson has highlighted modern adolescents' challenge to paternal authority as well as that of medieval students, early modern journeymen, soldiers, and compagnons.[57] Sociologist Schmuel Eisenstadt's generation theory has similarly emphasized that rapid social change was particularly characteristic of the youthful elements in societies. And sociologist Karl Mannheim has underlined frequent misunderstandings between youth and adults.[58] The abundance of young males significantly raised the propensity towards openness to dialogue. First, biologically, adolescence is a prime moment of transformation. French historian Philippe Ariès has reminded us that the attitude towards childhood and adolescence can be more historically constructed than we realize. Yet Dutch sociologist Norbert Elias argues the opposite point: that sober adulthood had to construct itself in early modern times in juxtaposition to the un-selfconcious puerility of adults during the Middle Ages.[59] In principle, we should expect a heavily male youth immigration to seek a transformation of their heritage, compounded with the will to seek Native romance. In practice, historian Nathalie Davis's concept that urban French male youth sought to maximize their social standing by using youthful licence to redelineate social sanctions has been seconded by historians Robert Muchembled, Susan Desan, and Norbert Schindler.[60] From all angles, pubescent androgen crescendos are recognizable anywhere. French immigrant youth, at a crucially malleable stage of identity-formation, lacked a "complete" community of family and village (or urban sector) within the piecemeal Canadian habitations around which to crystallize their identity, communal function, and masculinity without recourse to the hearths of allied Native tribes.

Most Canadian immigrant youth hailed from urban Atlantic port areas, which were particularly well exposed to printed matter and new cultures, including various Amerindians and even Inuit, especially in Rouen.[61] Youth were also heavily represented in the Nu-Pieds insurrections and indubitably joined immigrant ranks, as mentioned.[62] Immigrations and insurrections both required young male energy. Even in north Atlantic France these youth had been exposed since childhood to Aboriginal peoples (i.e., in the French ports) and to resisting official "French" cultural dictates. Therefore, these youth had many incentives to be open to cultural options that rejected socio-political absolutist tendencies, repressive patriarchy, and peasant identity that, in the same breath, promised adventure, social status, and even romance.

In Native culture, in order for a child to become an adult, he or she had to conduct a quest for a guardian spirit (manitou or pawaganak [Anishinabe or Ojibwa]). The Algonquian focus on the youth rite of passage prepared an adolescent to seek his guardian spirit, who would help him kill or trap game. The girls' powagan protected them. The teen smeared ashes on her face and fasted all alone in a hut at a distance from the community in order to dream. His or her manitou appeared, usually in the guise of an animal. This inward search for self-reliance, trust in their place in Nature, and ultimate meaning was sought.[63] According to late anthropologist Wilcomb Washburn, the spiritual function of this quest was to reinforce freedom and independence.[64] If a male youth had not found his powagan, he was denied admission to the company of male hunters.

Native skills, which were essential for survival, were acquired directly through becoming liaison-interpreters (truchements), diplomats, or traders, or participating in joint trading, hunting, fishing, exploratory, and contraband enterprises. Indirectly, youth also acquired Native skills through indentureship (engagements) with French veterans. Canadian male youth underwent a rite of passage to Native folk cultural communities by passing through a series of metaphorical "baptisms" into Great Lakes Native life. These were staged along the metaphorical historical canoe route from "French" Montreal to "Native" Green Bay, which is now in Wisconsin. The voyage bound pubescent crews with Nativized French veteran guides along the rapids with interculturally mixed charms to ward away disaster as they approached the Great Lakes woods. This was done in solitude. Native adolescent rites of initiation similarly sought guardian manitou protection, alone in the depths of the woods. Both rites of passage helped train a fairly large bicultural cadre that mediated between peoples, blurring insider-outsider status.. Ultimately, identification largely hinged upon a religious lifestyle (Christian versus traditional Native) rather than upon ethnicity (Native versus European). Young French Canadians often teamed up with Native friends against the directives of post–1663 Crown officials, which legitimated and gave direction to their new path.

"Courir la dérouine" was the name of the great youthful pilgrimage to the fur-rich Great Lakes. Prior to the "coureur de bois" were the interpreter-liaisons and the later mission workers (donnés). These youth were in socio-economic and cultural training in Native upcountry, in contrast to the newly arrived youth fresh off the boat, who were called interns (engagés) and received training in a veteran host family, where they learned settlement life and skills. Five to twenty men were sent annually as interpreters to various allies and often spent years among one or several nations. From 1639 Jesuit concern for the youths' tendency to Don Juanery and dubious "Frenchness" led to taking them on their missions as "donnés." The donné system supposedly afforded greater social control over these youths, but the Jesuits could not exert absolute control over their entire staff, particularly when their missionary work depended upon the interpreters for very basic survival skills.

Survival skills and traditions were initially absorbed by new French settlers and/or engagés by living in French pioneer homes, which bridged the gap between French and Amerindian lore. Engagement contracts were considerably better than those of indentured servants in Virginia and Maryland. There were more British indentureships until these were replaced by those made up of imported and enslaved Africans. By contrast, early French engagés were few, consisting of only 129 men (1632–63), whose utility could not have been replaced by forced slave labour. Not being agricultural, engagés required training.[65] In the British colonies there were many indentured servants who worked not for three years, as in New France, but for five, and who were treated like convicts (who worked for seven). By the late 1700s a British officer reported to his father in Britain that "they sell the servants here as they do horses, and advertise them as they do their beef and oatmeal."[66]

The linking of the double stigmas of poverty and criminality were trademark in self-righteously Protestant Britain, until even Dickens's writing of *Oliver Twist*, but the Catholic Church opened its arms to paupers and orphans. Their employers' investment and hospitality aided the newcomers acceptance into an inclusive community and encouraged great initiative. Engagement in a host family involved a training period during which the engagé was to become an urgently needed settler ("habitant"); it was not an introduction into a life of service.[67] The pioneers Guillemette and Guillaume Couillart's home hosted sixteen adult engagés before 1663, while Guillemette's mother, Marie Rollet Hébert, opened the first mixed ethnic boarding school for children.[68] It seems that hosting and teaching became a family tradition, as grandson Louis Couillard de Lespinay's also hired two engagés. Notwithstanding the hope invested in engagés, exploitation sometimes occurred. Norman nobleman Legardeur de Repentigny's imperiousness earned him rebellion by his servants, who sang the upside-down world ("monde-à-l'envers") refrain "Poor Bonhomme, you are not the master in your home when we are there!" ("Pauvre bonhomme, t'es pas le maître dans ta maison quand nous y sommes!")[69]

Finally, there were incentives in French communities to Nativize that did not exist in Native communities to Frenchify. French youth often gained a second family, especially a Native mother and sisters, to feed and fuss over them, as well as greater liberty to court forest beauties, than was the case on the St Lawrence. Even if Haudenosaunee girls became agents of Frenchification for their nation, the French did not treat them as diplomats of public standing due to their as yet limited understanding of female capacities. Thus, while Native boys frequently suffered from anomie after residence with the French, French male youth resident among the tribes later became prominent members of society, diplomats, seigneurs, and traders. The ability to relate and Nativize made or broke French North American futures.

Consider the case of Etienne Brûlé, whose behaviour was disapproved of by the missionaries due to his Don Juanery but were powerless to stop him due to his perceived standing among the Wendat.[70] Only later, when his assassination by one of the Wendat became known, did the French dare to repudiate him and his ways.[71] Interpreter-liaison Nicolas de Vignau became anathema due to Tessouat's (Le Borgne de L'Isle) anger over his revealing their voyage to the "northern sea" (mer du nord), which the Kichespirini chief tried to hide from Champlain due to trade rivalries. Champlain disregarded the word of his own young interpreter boy, who had no apparent motive for telling this kind of lie, and accepted that of the enraged chief, who desired to attract all French commerce to his tribe. Champlain thus abandoned the terrified youth in the forest, probably to his death, and he was never mentioned again.[72] Therefore, while the exchanged youth and children were precious diplomatically, it was the alliance that was all-important until Native values set in. A cadre of multicultural personnel as initial intercommunal liaisons was thus built through these exchanges.

For French Canadian male youths' seasonal fur trading in the Great Lakes area functioned in conjunction with the Algonquian dream quest as the male rite of initiation into full Canadian manhood. One could not be relied upon, either in trade, or in arms, or even in marriage, if one had not spent at least a season there. It became the male passport to full communal appreciation. By 1652, even when some Wendat, together with the Odawa, took over the bulk of trade, the tradition of French canoeing up to trade directly with the Great Lakes Algonquians, instead of waiting for them to come to the Montreal fur fair, had been irreversibly established.

Rites of passage usually aim at effecting motivational change appropriate to adult social roles.[73] Distance and frozen waterways induced the Great Lakes trapping and trading area to function as a moratorium area – a time in one's life free from the ordinary pressures of society and agricultural necessity. This rite functioned as a youthful training interlude, like university studies or army service.[74] Erik Erikson recognized the desire of youth for travel (Wanderschaft) and the fact that a long moratorium can result in identity confusion.[75] Identity confusion could be especially pronounced if youth were expected to acquire a degree of Nativization as part of their full communal initiation, such as was the case in New France. For French youth, the freedom afforded them in the Great Lakes area, far from king, governor-general, bishop, and French social constraints, was unprecedented. In any culture-jump, former measures of conduct and interpretation are necessarily suspended. The cultural framework at the waning of medieval European society hampered young men in their natural tendencies to expand their horizons, test their capacities, and seek sexual intimacy in their own locales. While uprooting forests was pure drudgery, settlement life afforded fewer daredevil challenges, and frowned upon pubescent romantic exploration outside the yoke of holy matrimony. In contrast, Native life required extensive travel, hazardous challenges, and abundant opportunities to appreciate Native courting rites.

The settlement was thirsty for furs, yet the independent, sometimes undisciplined, mentality that was attendant upon the fur trade was denounced by incoming French officials who enforced the royal policy after 1663.[76] Later intendants and governor-generals complained about the slowness of land clearing and planting, which they attributed to a Canadian nonchalance that either mimicked the French nobility, the Native men, or both. The

Jesuit fathers complained that French youth endeavoured to live like Wendat chiefs, who could sometimes marry their wife's sister, if she insisted upon it. To French ears, female-willed sororial polygamy smacked of male-initiated enslaved polygamy as practised in harems of the Middle East. And this intrigued them. These critiques were indicative of how Nativization was linked in the French mind with the aristocratic pursuits of idleness, the hunt, and war, without the attendant fear of losing a French title of nobility due to being gainfully employed (dérogéance).

In the name of agricultural implantation, population increase, and sexual continence, the post–1663 royal administration joined hands with missionaries in trying to prevent the mass exodus of youth seeking a free-for-all. A battery of ordinances and rules (règlements) were brandished to forbid youth to engage in the fur trade or even to leave their farms for twenty-four hours without permission.[77] Officials had little way of controlling this without an extensive police force or border controls, none of which then existed. Several strategies were tried, none of which was ultimately effective.[78] The coureurs de bois were required to attest to their good morals, to bring a certificate from the missionaries about their lifestyle, and to get married. They were threatened with corporeal punishment if they "debauched" Native women or girls and with lettres de cachet if they left without permission.[79] Intendant Talon tried to force men to marry and settle down before they could either engage in the fur trade, hunt, or fish. In 1676–79 additional coureurs de bois were prohibited from travelling west. Soon permits (congés) were instituted that permitted only eight men with their crews to leave for each congé. These were officially limited to twenty-five, thus totalling around 200 men. But often several more canoes left, and a great traffic gathered, which could be resold for prices rising from 800–1,200 "francs" a few years later.[80]

By 1690 the fur market was flooded, but this fact did not discourage the youthful exodus from the St Lawrence. Intendant Denonville wanted to install fortified posts at strategic points in the West to supervise the coureurs, DeMeulles thought of multiplying posts on the rivers, and others wanted to force the coureurs to sleep in the forts and observe a curfew. During the eighteenth century, Intendant François Bigot sent all the post commanders a voyageur blacklist to send the guilty back to Montreal. Governor Frontenac sent a hit team to hunt up the coureurs and drag them home, after which the governor officially "pardoned" them. Intendant Duchesneau envisioned sending the entire militia to track them down to the limits of Lake Superior, and a canoe patrol was set up to guard the St Lawrence all the way to Lake Ontario.[81] Intendant DuChesneau sent officers Daniel Greysolon DuLuth, Henri de Tonti, La Nouë, and Le Chevalier de Troyes to catch them; La Salle himself ordered his men to pillage them;[82] and Natives allies were enlisted in the chase.[83] Some youth avoided this harassment by not returning at all or by simply migrating to other locations. Late historian Louise Dechêne cites 668 coureurs of Montreal and notes that perhaps 150 to 200 remained on location or died there.[84]

Dutch and British markets were the first beneficiaries of this manhunt. Intendant Champigny was afraid that 200 to 300 men would desert to the British in the Great Lakes area to get better returns on their furs.[85] Intendant De Meulles wrote that Fort Frontenac was used by the coureurs as a refuge and entrepot before descending to the Dutch and British with their furs.[86] Not surprisingly, this traffic was mostly spearheaded by Christian Natives of the mission reserves, with French accomplices: "The domiciled Natives take most of their beaver to [Fort] Orange ... they take afterwards to Montreal where they trade them with Great Lakes Native nations who usually descend annually, even the merchants. They also go to wait for the Great Lakes Native nations at the passages to trade pelts. This commerce injures the royal interest, but it is not possible to stop it by force, it would even be dangerous to do so."[87] After all, they were the mission's prizes in more ways than one. Twenty-four-hour absences were the maximum time possible before the law cracked down on illicit trading of both French Canadian and reserve Natives, especially in Montreal.[88] However, these trading interdictions led to locally based and domiciled Natives to capture frustrated traders whose mobility was reduced.[89] This result was a far cry from the original goal of conversion as an enabler of Frenchification, a facilitator of trade interests and land claims, and loyalty to the French Crown.

After 1649, when coureurs de bois went seasonally en masse directly to the far tribes to trade (or, as it was called, woodroving, or, literally, "running the woods" [courir la dérouine]), the settlement gradually suffered a young male deficit. Quite a reversal of early settlement ratios. After the 1680s the lack of women almost levels off, and in a decade able-bodied men were lacking in the St Lawrence in those areas where coureurs were recruited. Perhaps this is due to the fact that, whereas the Québec area had the largest average land holdings (208.1 arpents), these were diminished around Three Rivers (60.9 arpents), while Montreal had the most diminutive holdings (27.7 arpents). Trifluvians (of Three Rivers) and Montrealers were forced to search for additional income or moved there especially to work in the trade.[90] Intendant Duchesneau even thought that woodroving was the reason settlement demography became reduced.[91]

Chronologically, by 1672 there were 400 coureurs, and Aubert de la Chesnaye thought that there were around 500 in 1676. In 1679–80 there were about 800 yearly, which Stanley Diamond estimates to have been 33 percent of able-bodied males. Patoulet, former secretary of Minister Colbert, noted after the 1681 census that 1,475 married men and 65 widows were missing. Six hundred men left in 1685, and Nicolas Perrot notes that he left Montreal with 143 Canadians and 600 coureurs in 1694, and 300 in

1695. Patoulet wrote that "these volunteers are vagabonds who never marry nor work the land ... and who commit an infinity of disorders by their licentious libertine lifestyle. These men always live in the Native manner and go five or six hundred lieux north of Quebec to trade pelts that the barbarians [sic] bring themselves into our habitations."[92] Louise Dechêne calculated 150 departures for the west between 1708 and 1717.[93] And there were many departures that were left unregistered, for between 1670 and 1745 upwards of 3,000 men left for the Great Lakes. Filteau estimates that 300 men went to trade annually, yet Eccles thought 500 to 600 men left out of a total population of 10,000.[94]

French Canadian youth were censored in scalding terms by later French officials, governors, and intendants. Denonville, Courcelles, Duchesneau and even military officers (all the way to the marquis de Montcalm), who themselves came from the French élite, considered the behaviour of French Canadian youth and militia captains (capitaines de milice) an outrageous challenge to their own status and authority.[95] Independent-minded habitants and freewheeling coureurs de bois were seen by French administrators as "ensauvagé" (having become wild).[96] Canadian titles of nobility were chortled at and seigneuries were rescinded.

Youth received the bulk of this scorn. Denonville's famous "complainte" of Canadian youth in 1685 runs thus:

These disorders ... are greater in the gentlemen's families, or those who would like to be [gentlemen] through laziness or vanity, because they have no resources to subsist on except in the woods, because they are unaccustomed to hold the plough, the pickax, and the ax, their entire resource being nothing but a firearm, they must pass their lives in the woods ... We thought for a long time that the proximity of the Natives to our habitations was a great opportunity to accustom these people to live like us and to instruct them in our religion, but I have perceived ... that exactly the opposite has occurred because instead of them becoming familiar with our laws, I assure you that they have lent us their shortcomings, while they have acquired the worst and most vicious of our bad qualities ... other Natives are vagabonds and wandering about particular seigneuries without being organized in villages like the others, you would not believe the problems created by this [for] ... the discipline of the colony, because not only the seigneurs' children get used to living a libertine lifestyle like they do, but they debauch the Native girls and women, that they keep with them and bring with them to the hunt in the woods, where frequently they suffer hunger to the point of ... devouring their own dogs.[97]

He complains elsewhere:

It seems to me that this is the place, Monseigneur, that we have to take into account the disorders which occur not only in the woods but also in our settlements. These disorders are due to the youth of this country only through the laziness of the children, and the great liberty which the light control of fathers and mothers and Governors have exercised over youth in allowing them to go into the woods on pretext of hunting or trading. This has reached such an extremity, Monseigneur, that as soon as the children can shoulder a rifle the fathers can no longer restrain them and do not dare to make them angry. You may judge what evils may ensue from such a manner of living ... They have to pass their lives in the woods, where there are neither priests nor Governors to constrain them. There are, Monseigneur, among those men some who distinguish themselves above others in these disorders and against whom I have promised to employ the authority which the King has entrusted to me to punish them severely. Governor de la Barre suppressed a certain gang called the Knights, but he did not take away its manners or disorderly conduct ... I could not express sufficiently to you, Monseigneur, the attraction that this savage life of doing nothing, of being constrained by nothing, of following every whim, and being beyond correction, has for the young men.[98]

Intendant Duchesneau also speaks in similar terms: "several of these gentlemen and officers ... and the land-owning seigneurs, as they are accustomed to what one calls in France the life of a country gentleman that they themselves practiced or witnessed make hunting and fishing their biggest occupation and because for their vituals and their clothes and those of their wives and children ... [they can] forego so much like the simple habitants, that they do not apply themselves entirely to their farms and fields, they get mixed up in commerce, become endebted on every side, and incite their young habitants to run the woods."[99] In other words, the Nativized past, although discredited by French officials, clearly reflected the advent of the French Canadian "revenge of the cradles."

CHAPTER FOUR

Born Free

These Indians are perfectly convinced that man is born free and no power on earth has a right to infringe his liberty.

Father Francois-Xavier Charlevoix

Man is born free, yet is everywhere in chains.

Jean-Jacques Rousseau

French settlement society on the St Lawrence underwent a "metamorphosis." Nativization eased and legitimated the levelling among men. The hierarchically vertical ordering of society in a tightly knit, geographically restricted area of France gave way to a transversal political and socioeconomic organization spread out geographically. Social utility and wealth, rather than Old World pedigree, became powerful. Aboriginal life on Turtle Island enabled the eco-conservation of untouched resources stretched out as far as the eye could see, while coercive measures were introduced very slowly and were hard to enforce. Transversalization increased the gap between Quebec society and those further afield at Three Rivers, Montreal, Gaspésie, and Tadoussac. The Quebec bastion contained French administrators, stronger French regulations, and a more agricultural lifestyle but was more immune to the fur traffic and Haudenosaunee incursions. The French periphery that interfaced that of the Natives, including Three Rivers, Montreal, and Tadoussac, frequently ignored the authority of Quebec, and especially that of the Crown, when convenient. Deep in the Aboriginal centres – the Illinois country, Ottawa valley, and Great Lakes – the French cast a wide network and introduced intertribal and interracial mixed marriages and forts. The fur trade in these areas induced French society to imitate that of the Wendat socio-economically and geographically by segregating the hunting-trading work of men and agricultural labour of women over vast distances that increased with the diaspora. Yet, like the Algonquians, the opposition between severe winter isolation and annual festive coming of French ships and coureurs to Three Rivers and Montreal functioned like an Algonquian-style powwow. The sun king of France lolling in his "bed of justice" sharply contrasted with the fraternal sons of liberty who convened at woodsy campfires over North America.

The old French elite fragmented into factions that haggled over prestige and power. As a result, many of their functions were superseded by the new rising Canadian elite. Due to old elite fragmentation, the need for settlers, and the Native context, commoners scaled social heights. The rising Canadian elite was not far from its own commoner roots and its responsibilities to the early community. Commoners also established new ground rules by calling themselves "habitants," which distanced them from the despised French peasant. Seigneurs were required to care for their relations with their censitaires instead of despising their vassal. Male levelling was matched by reciprocal agricultural and entrepreneurial functions for women, which precluded their automatic subordination. Thus, French Canadian society of the early seventeenth century appeared less vertically hierarchical and became more horizontally levelled, which extended geographically across the continent.

In general, the metamorphosis of society was faciliated by the youthfulness of the settlement, which looked to ancestral "ghosts" for rerooting and reorientation in the novel situation. This was a rebellious, but ultimately non-confrontational, way to conduct a dialogue (over time and distance) with the suffocating patriarchy of France.

French society was elaborately hierarchical, and this became more entrenched during Louis XIV's consolidation of power after the Fronde. His motto, "I am the state," and his symbol, the sun king, all vividly point to the new ideal of self-adoration ("amour-propre"). The nobility was not amused, but they were only 1.5 percent of the population, while the Third Estate garnered a full 90 percent to 85 percent, the remainder being filled by clergy. During the 1500s, promotion to the nobility was eased by the growth of venal offices. By mid-century, this also gave way to a closing of ranks. Officials combed the countryside for false titles of nobility.[1] Nevertheless, the popularity of the urban bourgeois, who possessed talent and refinement without a pedigree, rose as the country nobility simultaneously lost seigneurial, judicial, and administrative rights. Prices rose as land rents crashed. Untutored country nobles (hobereaux) of ancient standing were forced to derogate their titles to wealthy court nobility, who often sprung from bourgeois merchants. Country aristocrats were appalled, and together with noble parlementarians led or fanned the fires of rebellion in north Atlantic France.[2]

The one point upon which male nobility, both sword and robe appeared to agree upon was paternal power within the family. This turning of the screws was cinched in the cult of St Joseph, the king as the state's father, and the father/husband as king within his castle-home. Penetrating paternalism gathered strength in early modern Europe, whose first source lay in the

Reformation, which repudiated Mary as a genetrix. In France the Counter-Reformation saw a swell of support for the cult of Mary, but both the king and St. Joseph still provided a patriarchal counterweight to this in both government and the church.

The second source of paternalism sprang from the exclusive authority that Roman law invested in fathers (patria potestas) and statesmen, ostensibly for keeping order.[3] The political instability of seventeenth-century France was attributed by the French elite to a string of queenly run "regencies," where queens were merely official vessels for the flowering of the prince incumbent, the Dauphin. The Salic example that nullified queenly authority also disturbed stability, an example that was not imitated by other countries like Sweden (Queen Christina) and Britain (two Marys and one Elizabeth). The Crown and royal noble de robe magistrates, therefore, were singularly intent on reinforcing the king as father of the state, and the father as king within his home, in the fond hope that order would then prevail, yet specifically so that they then could legitimate their own power base. Even the great noble d'épée Frondeurs resisted royal authority, especially in the person of Mazarin, without upsetting the conceptual order. Yet rebellion was not revolution. They labelled the assassination of Charles I of England the "blackest of all parricides" in their Mazarinades, and John Milton's *Paradise Lost* was suppressed.[4] Parricide was punished a century earlier in France by having one's right hand cut off, having one's chest branded, being hung from the feet, and being strangled by a heavy stone.[5] The Counter-Reformation Gallican church reinforced this tradition by foisting the banner of St Joseph as the last answer to French political, religious, social, and familial instability.

Waves of culture shock were generated by the meeting of hierarchical French and Native egalitarian freedom – and individualistic reason. It has been suggested that Haudenosaunee political conceptions contributed to the basis of the US Constitution via Benjamin Franklin at the Albany Plan of Union in 1754.[6] Native political and legal conceptions swept beyond North American shores and were used to justify the toppling of the socio-political foundations of France via Rousseau's *Social Contract* (1763).[7] Native individualism and egalitarianism astonished but intrigued the French, who participated in many negotiations and witnessed the levelling of artificial distinctions, titles, and privileges. One of the most salient lessons taught in Amerindian society was that all members of society are human beings with equal human rights, and a chief has only the authority of which he or she can convince his listeners, who are presumed to possess reason or common sense. French philosophes were enthusiastic about the former, while the British colonists rallied to the latter.[8] Sagard declared: "They act only according to their reason ... to which they easily cede, and not according to their passions, because violence has no credit in their thinking."[9]

Haudenosaunee oral canon still insists that a "good mind" was essential for peace, consensus, and the common weal.[10] Brébeuf noted that "there are none who are incapable of having an intelligent conversation and do not reason very acutely and in excellent terms."[11] Lafitau wrote: "They have a sound intelligence, a vivid imagination, easy conception and abstraction, and an admirable memory."[12] Lacking common sense or reason were the temporary attributes of young children, the bereaved, and the furious, who were all gently counselled to be aware that they temporarily did not "have sense" ("n'avoir pas de bon sens"). Father LeClercq also wrote: "they think themselves equal in life as in death, without distinction even of the chiefs."[13] Champlain noted: "They have no special chiefs who rule absolutely ... they give honnour to the oldest and most valliant, whom they call Captains."[14] As Perrot wrote: "Natives do not know what obedience is. The father would never dare to use his authority on his son, nor the commanding chief on his soldier."[15] And La Potherie: "[Natives have] never desired to suffer subordination ... this is a general phenomenon with all the Natives, each is master of his actions without anyone daring to contradict him."[16]

For important decisions affecting the community, consensus was required. Among the Haudenosaunee, men and women held their own separate councils with representatives, but women could also voice their objections at male councils.[17] Gilles Deleuze emphasized that alliances weave a transversal network in opposition to vertical hierarchical structure, and Foucault's conception that power interests are structured into the building of institutions seems a particularly apt observation.[18] When the power elite is spread out over the nodes of transversality, this structure in itself defuses many potential social conflicts because smaller nodes ostensibly have tinier hierarchies.

American historian David Hackett Fisher, in *Albion's Seed* (1993), has argued that the arriving elite of British North America had a key role in shaping the colonies. In contrast, vying French factions struggled for dominance in New France. The Jesuits, in particular, seemed to serve as a negative model of internecine rivalry for the habitants. Rivalry between clerics, seigneurs, traders, and governors dated back to early Acadia, and the interdiction of Huguenot immigration in 1627 with the Hundred-Associates, although set up by Cardinal Richelieu to avoid Huguenot trader-Catholic missionary competition, only served to set off intra-Catholic competition.

The Jesuits, due to their royal connections in France, seemed to have a particularly hard time getting along peaceably with the other orders, as they squeezed out the Recollects, hassled the Sulpicians, made life difficult for the Montreal Hospitallers, and chased away Grand-vicaire Thubières de Queylus by importing Bishop Laval.[19] Laval also strove to endear himself to the population by reducing the authority of the respected Mother Marie de l'Incarnation[20] and chasing away the popular governor of Montreal,

Chomedey de Maisonneuve. The Jesuits and Laval invariably interjected themselves into the going dispute in order to improve their standing by driving wedges between others. Sometimes the Jesuits did not even get along with each other, as Governor d'Argenson teamed up with Father Lalemant, while Bishop Laval and Father Ragueneau stood diametrically opposed.[21] For all their talents, the Jesuits and bishop played too heavy a political hand, and being constantly recalled to the metropolis only underlined where their ultramontanist fidelity really lay. Bishop Laval was squarely against the establishment of the Montreal Hospitallers (filles de St-Joseph) but relented as he witnessed their talent for healing.[22]

Pride and prejudice powered the famous disputes between the governor general and prominent clerics, which often resulted in the governor's recall to France. By 1665, after the French king amused himself with Canadian affairs, the religious establishment was denounced by prominent traders like Legardeur de Tilly, Mathieu Damours, and Juchereau de la Ferté.[23] The disenfranchised Recollect missionaries were more popular among the habitants than the shrewd but political Jesuits, and the populace unanimously requested postmortem masses of the former. The recalled founder of early Montreal (Ville-Marie), the remarkably generous Governor Maisonneuve, and recalled Governor d'Argenson were loved more universally than was the remarkably severe Bishop Laval. The later Governor Frontenac particularly was dead set against the Bishop-Jesuit political axis and was famously recalled to France due to disputes with them in 1680. The wily Frontenac, however, glossed over this kerfuffle and made a comeback with flying colours.[24]

The official political power of French North America consisted of French officials, missionaries, officers, the bishop, and prominent Native allied chiefs like Algonquian Iroquet, Innu Erouachy, Wendat Atironta (Champlain's friend), Wendat Annaotaha (Brébeuf's friend), the famous Tionontati-Wendat Kondiaronk of Michilimackinac, Wendat Eustache Ahasistari (who suffered seven weeks of Haudenosaunee torture with René Goupil and Father Isaac Jogues), influential Onondaga Garakontié, and the bishop.[25]

Sociologist Schmuel Eisenstadt delineates three basic types of elites: the power elite, articulators of cultural models, and articulators of group solidarity. In the French-Native axis, there were some cross-overs between these newly founded elites. The articulators of cultural models included missionaries, especially Fathers Brébeuf and Ragueneau; medicine healers like Innu Pigarouich; articulate traders like Aubert de la Chesnaye; and prominent French and Native women like Marie Rollet Hébert, Katéri Tekakwitha, , Erie Cathérine Gandeacteua, Anne Gasnier Bourdon, Madeleine de la Pelletrie, and Marie-Barbe de Boullongne, wife of Governor General d'Ailleboust. And the solidarity elite was largely composed of adopted French, Canadian, and Native children, trading and adopted French Canadian youth, Native women pairing off with Frenchmen, cabaret owners, and the pre-1663 power elite, who endeavoured to reinforce the French tribe within the alliance network.

Nativized pioneers became the emerging Canadian elite, which had characteristics of all three elites. Figures such as Louis Couillard de L'Espinay, Jean Bourdon, Pierre Boucher, Charles Aubert de la Chesnaye, Guillaume Cousture,[26] the Godefroy brothers, and Jean Nicollet were leaders in the tiny community. Nativized pioneers replaced many functions of the splintered French elite. This replacement was catalyzed by Native models, lack of a printing press (which prevented centralized organization over the vast geographical extension), and severe winters, which isolated the settlements from one another. The functions of cultural articulation and intercommunal solidarity were often somewhat joined because, in order to rise socially to articulate cultural formulae, one was required to Nativize or be Native, which enhanced intercommunal trust. Thus, the plurality of elites, and the inclusion of non-traditional members, opened possibilities for usually excluded groups, which distributed tasks more widely.

Initially, being of Norman origin was a factor in social mobility. They adapted better than the other represented provinces, with only a 13.4 percent dropout rate as opposed to a median average of 29.9 percent for other provinces.[27] In 1653, when a recruitment of workers was requested from France, Normans were sought on the pretext that they did not drink and that they were well adapted to the cold. It is true that, in the central western regions like Poitou, Angoumois, Saintonge, and Aunis, the vine was an important element in the diet, and there were many holidays celebrated with a period of uncontrolled drinking, such as May Day and the feast of St John the Baptist (June 26).[28] Normandy was the oldest and most populous of the French provinces represented in Canada at this time, had the highest number of notables, and could be considered as the "charter group" in New France, against which the incoming groups were often compared.[29]

An explanation for the preference shown the Normans could be made on two levels. Sociologically, the veteran group that settles in a specific place tends to arrogate a preferred status and stigmatize "outsiders," as Norbert Elias has theorized.[30] Historically, after Cardinal Richelieu interdicted the wintering of Huguenots from 1627, the favouring of intensely Roman Catholic Rouen and Dieppe over rival Huguenot La Rochelle should come as no surprise. The rich merchants of Rouen particularly were involved in the Canadian fur trade, especially from 1650 to 1670, with Jean Rozée, Jacques Duhamel, Pierre Le Breton, Robert, and Toussaint Guénet,[31] most of whom were among the founders of the earlier Hundred-Associates. Normans proved themselves via economic initiative, as most of the interpreters and early coureurs, first fishers or sea dogs (Louis Couillard de Lespinay, Simon Guyon de Courville, Charles Legardeur de Tilly, and Jean-Paul Godefroy), and earliest tanners (François Bissot de la Rivière on the Pointe de Lévy in 1668) hailed from Normandy.[32] Of the twelve first managers of the Communauté des Habitants, six came from Normandy (Jean Bourdon, Jean Godefroy de Lintot, Pierre Legardeur de Repentigny, and the two Leneuf brothers Michel Leneuf de La Poterie, and Michel Leneuf du Hérisson, and perhaps Guillaume Couillart (but he may have been from Brittany).[33] Last, a certain common sense was expected of Normans, who, according to their custom, were allowed the "clameur de Haro," which was akin to a citizen's arrest (directed mainly at seducers and thieves (Haro being the hero of carnival).[34] And common sense and reason were highly appreciated in Native communities. It would seem that the Normans had the easiest adaptation at this point, due to a long familiarity with conditions, a relative majority of immigrants, the high prestige of Canada in the province, the Norman feeling that they were a charter population, and their relatively easy adaptability to Native life. Apparently, they did not come to Canada in distress, for Normandy, despite the Nu-Pieds rebellion, was relatively well-off. Father LeJeune writes of the popularity of Canada among Norman religious women's communities,[35] and perhaps others were inspired as well. But it is also possible that, due to so many Natives being brought to Rouen and Dieppe,[36] and the tales told about Canada in their communities, they had a better idea of what they were getting themselves into than did immigrants of other provinces.

Norman pioneers often received titles of nobility and functions in the founding institutions of French North America. The phenomenon of everyone wanting to acquire nobility sprang not from the intensification of a pre-existing hierarchical mentality but from the desire to make those privileges more widely available. Criteria for obtaining nobility in Canada usually rested upon heroism or social utility. Being a survivor of Haudenosaunee captivity, showing great courage in battle, being the reliably generous and wise neighbour, or gaining prestige in the fur trade were the best grounds for public recognition.

The Communauté des Habitants, founded in 1645, was established to transfer responsibility for the fur trade from the French company of the Hundred Associates, which was then in financial straits.[37] A series of institutional innovations in New France, based upon French institutions yet carrying different weight and emphasis, were initiated by the settlers. This included beaver-skin currency, which was later followed by paper cards, which sought to redress the Canadian-French trade imbalance.[38] In France, a Communauté des Habitants was the institution that managed the town communes by exercising a limited amount of political, judicial, military, policing, and fiscal powers for the upkeep of the municipalities, but whose power became increasingly limited, especially when the powerful office of intendancy was introduced under Louis xiv.[39] The French immigrants obtained administrative and ecclesiastical support, and petitioned the Queen to syndicate a Communauté des Habitants to replace the Hundred Associates and, especially, to manage the fur trade. This proposal seemed innocuous due to its institutional precedent, but in the North American context, the Communauté was initially the only body to run New France from 1645 to 1651, together with the governor.

The setting up of this Communauté had many aspects, not the least of which entailed raising the status of the settler to "habitant," or permanent resident. They were clearly different from both migrant winterers (hivernants) from 1645 and from temporary engagés, soldiers, administrators, missionaries, and transatlantic French merchants (who were called "françois" as opposed to the habitant "canadois"). Instead of submitting to one's low social status, one was respected for one's contributions to New France. But at this stage the growing cognizance of the gap between "françois" and "canadois" was often blurred by French writers, administrators, and officers, who labelled all francophones as French.[40] Yet, by the Seven Year War, French officials and officers complained bitterly over the difference.

The twelve managers of the Communauté in 1645 were, according to original social status, composed of four nobles from France (a Legardeur, the Leneuf brothers, and the governor's lieutenant, Chavigny de Berchereau), all the rest being of bourgeois to commoner standing. The salient point about most of these directors was the early date of their arrival, their prominent involvement in the settlement, their personal capacities, and their knowledge of Native communities (note Guillaume Couillart, Jean Bourdon, Robert Giffard, the Godefroy brothers, Jean Guion, Noël Juchereau des Chastelets, and Mathurin Gagnon, most of whom were then or later rewarded for their contributions by ennoblement, a seigneury, or an official function.) Rosario Bilodeau wrote that those who were at the head of the Communauté were later at the head of French Canadian society: "Ceux qui sont ... sa tête [de la Communauté] seront aussi ... la tête de la société canadienne."[41] The Communauté management was composed primarily of six families: the Couillarts, the Giffards, the Godefroys, the Juchereaux, the Legardeurs, and the Leneufs, only two of whom were noble in France. Although the Jesuits supported their efforts to obtain local fur trade control, Father Jérome Lallemant seems apprehensive about the import of the takeover for the Jesuits.[42] The replacement was sometimes disorganized due to the irregular supply of furs, the high fixed rates owed the Hundred Associates and alternate investors, mismanagement, and the loss of fur shiploads through piracy on the high seas.[43] Nevertheless, the habitants looked to fur trade veterans and Native peoples for guidance, whether noble or not. Due to their pressure, habitants were eventually free to trade and to go into the woods for pelts.[44]

There was a shift in basic values underlying the shift in social status. In order to count the number of needed representatives for the Communauté's assembly of Quebec, the immigrants were ostensibly divided into "principaux" (principals), "médiocres" (middling), and "commun" (commoners). These innovative criteria for determining the condition of each member were "condition, faculté" and "mérite," meaning birth, capacity, and communal worth, categories dramatically different from ordinary French social status of noble, bourgeois, and commoner, which hailed from relatively rigid historical estates.[45] Although during the late 1500s in France there had been an increasing amount of bourgeois magistrate ennoblement, this social mobility had been arrested by complaints of encroachment on the part of the great nobility, who tried to close ranks. The "paulette" rendered ennoblement inheritable, yet was bitterly resented by the waning aristocracy, who attempted to restrict the galloping growth of the robe nobility. The Crown and the aristocracy both had vested interests in limiting their privileges to an exclusive club. In Canada, however, a new set of standards emphasized usefulness and public esteem, both of which required a priori Nativization. Naturally, the acquisition of money and skills was the straightest path from commoner status to nobility status. Therefore, the keys to social mobility had shifted from money and magistracy in France to Native knowledge, heroism, and money in North America, in that order.

Social levelling through institutional change was effected through setting up a Conseil de Québec.[46] By 1648 it was allowed, together with the Communauté, relative autonomy and was a popular element in the settlement. The Conseil de Québec permitted a legislative and administrative council of the governor general, the former governor general, the governors of Three Rivers and Montreal, the Jesuit Superior (who eventually relinquished this honour due to collegial complaints of Father Ragueneau's politicking), and popularly elected syndics of Quebec, Three Rivers, and Montreal (in an advisory capacity), as well as two councillors (or three, if the former governor was not present) elected for three-year terms by regular council members and the syndics.[47] Its task was to install officers for the Communauté des Habitants, examine financial matters, manage the fur trade, and install a secretary to manage the registers. Although Marcel Trudel sees the Conseil de Québec as run mostly by the nobility (thirty-seven out of sixty-nine persons) and the bourgeoisie (twenty-four out of sixty-nine persons), leaving commoners only eight functions, and only in auxiliary posts (statistics include the later Conseils as well), one must not historically "upstream" these statistics (i.e., interpret them according to today's standards). This degree of self-rule was unheard of in seventeenth-century northwestern France. Gilles Durocher, French regime archivist at the National Archives of Canada, calls the 1647 decree "Canada's first constitutional document" (i.e., Canada's first form of representative government).[48]

The Communauté des Habitants had brought a measure of prosperity to some of the more enterprising habitants, but due to variable fur catches after 1649 and the fall of Wendake, its exigent investors were not reimbursed. So in 1657 a Conseil de la Traite replaced the earlier Conseil in overseeing and regulating all fur trade affairs. The directors that we know include d'Ailleboust de Coulonge, former governor; Denis-Joseph Ruette d'Auteuil, Nicolas Juchereau de Saint-Denys, Jacques Maheust, and Jean Bourdon. Of these only two were nobles from France (d'Ailleboust and d'Auteuil), while the three others were notable due to their capacities and merit.

Naturally, Governor General Montmagny, a high-status Knight of Malta, was not thrilled with the new situation and promulgated several ordinances to limit what he perceived as a habitant-backed free-for-all.[49] We must deduce that habitant freedom of assembly and initiatives were so great as to push through an innovation that was not entirely to the taste of the Governor General himself. This royal administrative clampdown angered the habitants, causing a mutiny that was handily headed by formerly renegade Nicolas Marsolet and his wife Marie Lebarbier, in a desperate drive to regain lost social status. Mme Marsolet's recent ostentatious decorations on the blessed bread "pain bénit" had been removed by the Jesuits due to fear of neighbourly envy. Another mutineer, René Maheust, accused the directors of corruption,[50] which was surprising since blatant corruption was quite normal for titled functionaries in France. It appears that social jousting was the driving force of this failed mutiny. As Raymond Cahall rightly states: "This democratic introduction was one of the most salient things that Louis xiv wanted to abolish. He reinforced the clerical and absolutist character of the [Conseil's successor, the] Sovereign Council of 1663 by providing only three seats, the Governor General, the intendant, and the Bishop. The Bishop and the Governor General together appointed five councillors, an Attorney General and a clerk."[51] The habitants of Three Rivers, who were famous for their level of Nativization and initiative, refused to be manual drudges of the Jesuits and also mutinied.[52] Craftsmen in North America, unlike in France, had a decent chance of obtaining master craftsmanship status.

The growing hunger for egalitarian self-amelioration crystallized in the later horse craze.[53] This satisfied both the problem of mobility and thirst for the accoutrements of an homme de coeur, as they had seen Nu-pieds insurgents and Frondeurs galloping off upon their swift steeds. Governor General LaBarre suppressed a youth group dubbed the Chevaliers (Knights) for becoming too arrogant, and the habitants rode around so rambunctiously that a rash of ordinances was needed in an attempt to prevent accidents.[54] When the Marquis de Montcalm ordered horsemeat for the troops, Canadians who hosted them were horrified.[55] Perhaps it is not insignificant that the

Canadian dialect, Joual, was based upon the great habitant passion for the horse (cheval) which was in itself the symbol of according privileges for all.

The result of this dialogue entailed more than the creation of a Canadian elite out of formerly Third Estate veteran settlers. Settlers were needed, which increased the aspirations of immigrants and accelerated levelling. The New World seigneurial system pared down lordly rights, increased noble responsibilities, and allowed the "censitaire" unheard of rights denied the French peasant.[56] Almost as likely to be from a village, town, or city as from a rural area, he refused any appellation less than "habitant."[57] Alexis de Tocqueville insisted that, in the New World, the old feudal distinctions of the aristocracy were due to land-based privileges, and that being abolished, there was little left to establish a permanent aristocracy, except money. This settlement strategy resulted from Crown inducements and liberalities to swell colonial demography, the perennial royal fear of investing the nobility with autonomous powers, and the staunch resistance of the habitants to onerous impositions due to their witnessing the egalitarianism of Native culture. Fernand Ouellet, who argued that Canadian levelling did not occur, only winds up highlighting this early reality by rightly pointing out that, as the settlement aged, there were fewer and fewer seigneuries available to commoners.[58] This however, does not attest to the ephemeral quality of Nativization but to the metropolitan attempt to force the settlement to fit the royal plan (while struggling with and attempting to stigmatize early Nativization). Many commoners were already ennobled by that time. By mid-eighteenth century, fertile seigneuries were used, together with the charms of French Canadian girls, as bait to induce French officers to settle down to reinvigorate the tiny Canadian settlement. As in most young societies, social mobility was more fluid in the pioneer years than it was when it became more institutionalized. A core of prestigious families who, due to their experience or due to their high status before immigration, married amongst themselves and barred mobility for newcomers. This typically colonial stopgap was mostly a reflection of limited economic growth and isolation from metropolitan centres, but it did not preclude overall social levelling.

Several controversial issues that erupted in New France exposed the often conflicted premises and aims of French Canadian immigrant regional variations, societal sectors, successive immigrant waves, and the growing gap between French and Canadian. These variations were compounded by the dialogue with a multinational Native population across a vast geographical expanse. Even against a background of noisy legal disputes, the topics that touched the raw nerve of these differences caused a great ruckus and arrayed forces on either side of the conflict. The disruptive disputes often exposed the shifting power equations between those who jockeyed for social esteem. Pioneer settlers, Canadian-born, and local (sometimes Christian)

Natives received the social recognition of being "insiders," while French administrators and officers invested by the Crown with disproportionate power were tagged as "outsiders." Even so, the clergy and many Christian Natives (domiciliés) were simultaneously "inside" and "outside" while possessing an independent stance on religious issues. Renegotiation of social esteem was especially fierce by the later seventeenth century between the old French elite, the recently born Canadian elite, and the prominent bishop and/or Jesuits.

Zwischenmenschliche twinning and couple métissage were enhanced through joint Native-French hunting expeditions, fishing ventures, religious celebrations or ceremonies, social festivities accompanying the "petit commerce," and mixed parties (usually involving alcoholic beverages and smoking), all of which served to further tear down social barriers and psychological inhibitions. While alcohol undermined the traditional life of Aboriginal nations, the French Canadian clergy saw French smoking as a sign of Nativization and called it "barbarization," as it was thought to dry up the brain and intoxicate like wine.[59] Intimate contact ensured many intensely personal relationships, where drunkenness, quarrelling, and cross-infection were the possible risks. Passing around drinks to all at informal interethnic pairing-off parties proved to be an aid to métissage. The Jesuits complained that: "Drunkenness would be as common in these countries, as it is in the depths of Switzerland, if there had been drinks." ("l'yurognerie qui seroit aussi commune en ces contrées, qu'elle est dans le fond de la Suisse, s'il y auoit des boissons.")[60] Jan Grabowski cites the overabundance of cabarets, and Cornelius Jaenen notes that such activity even pulled the population away from attendance at mass.[61] Yet, the great dispute as to whether or not to sell liquour to the Natives divided the settlement throughout its existence.[62] Champlain had forbidden selling alcohol to the Natives on the pain of 50 livres and corporal punishment.[63] In 1642 the Mi'kmaq requested that it not be sold to them.[64] In 1657 the King's Council of State forbade liquour traffic, with a fine for the first offence, whipping and banishment for the second.[65] Because this ban was hard to enforce, a cabaret was established in Three Rivers that same year, and it sold wine: one glass for a summer beaver pelt, two glasses for the thicker winter pelt. Among those opposed to its sale was the clerical bloc headed by Bishop Laval, the Jesuits, the Sulpicians, and certain traders and officials like Governor Denonville, Governor Champigny, Intendant Duchesneau, Governor Vaudreuil, Governor Pierre Boucher (Three Rivers), merchant Jacques LeBer, Governor Meneval (Acadia), and explorer Jolliet, who remarked that anyone selling brandy to the Natives deserved to die.[66] Denonville remarked that there were seigneuries with only twenty inhabitants, yet they partied at ten cabarets, and that in Three Rivers, of twenty-five homes, eighteen to twenty sold alcohol. The pro-sale camp was composed of Colbert,

Frontenac, Talon, de Lagny, LaSalle, and some coureurs who argued that economic exchanges were vital to the economy and that if the French did not supply the Natives then they would turn to the British.[67]

The relationship of the French to Native peoples was still a debatable issue that many tried to define. Was it a paternalistic relationship with the French (as the French maintained) or was it an equal brotherhood-style partnership on every issue outside of religion (as the Natives maintained)? Should the French disclaim their right to ban anything to their allies and allow Native dignitaries to hold the last word over their own communities? Or were the French and Native allied communities to be considered as one integrated entity in New France? After many severe rulings with lax applications, anything stronger than beer was legally anathema. Extralegal activity was frowned upon but ignored. This indicates that New France regarded its role in the Native alliance as exceeding the authority of Native chiefs. But when band or tribe dignitaries wanted the alcohol ban respected, thinking of liquour as poison and wine as blood, this was not legally negligible.[68] This major test case demonstrated the legal double standard that favoured Native peoples escaping French punishment through "cultural clause" loopholes, as Jan Grabowski has demonstrated.[69]

We should not ignore the fact that the French themselves were often found to be indulging along with Native peoples. Bishop Laval threatened excommunication for the sale of liquour because it caused the destitution of families, the sale of children, and murders.[70] Daniel Vuil was shot for selling alcohol to the Natives the same year.[71] When the governor general issued a permit to sell liquour to the Natives in 1662, the violence was renewed. In 1663 the Sovereign Council implemented a fine of 300 livres for the first offence and lashing and banishment for more. This proved ineffective,[72] and the ordinances became increasingly severe.[73] In 1667 a fine of fifty to 200 livres was required for the first offence, and serious offenders spent a month in prison and fifteen days on a wooden horse.[74] Many sellers, as well as drunken French and Natives, were arrested for alcohol and attendant crimes. And apparently two sellers were then executed.[75]

A remarkable turning point occurred in 1667 in Three Rivers, at that time the centre of the fur trade on the St Lawrence. The "Affaire Gamelin" involved Michel Gamelin (Ottocociniche [Alg.]: doctor) being caught in violation of alcohol restrictions. His case revealed that all the major authorities of the town were heavily implicated, including the mother-in-law of the Three Rivers governor and the sister-in-law of the royal judge, along with the intermediary governor of New France. Almost a third of the population was involved, or 622 persons from Three Rivers, Champlain, Batiscan and Cap-de-la-Madeleine.[76] At this juncture it appears that, despite popular support for the opposition, practicality won out over ethics. In 1668 Talon founded a beer brewery and lifted all restrictions.[77] As long as restrictions were lifted, there were murders and rapes, sicknesses and starvation, despite protestations from the sachems, with only intermittent interdictions.[78] In 1678 the king ordered an assembly of twenty of the principal habitants engaged in the fur trade to decide once and for all about the alcohol question.[79] Oppositionsts LaChesnaye and LeMoyne were not invited by Governor Frontenac, although they were the most prominent men of Montreal. Even so, five of the traders were absolutely opposed to selling under any pretext whatsoever.[80] The final decision forbade the sale of alcohol to Native peoples in their homes and elsewhere, but the French Canadians could still serve liquour to Natives in their own homes.[81] After 1680 interdictions targeted French Canadian habitants who tried to sell directly to reserve Natives at Lorette, Sillery, and Prairie de la Madeleine; to those camped close to the towns; during trips; to those in the surrounding forests; and to those in the south and north French-Native spheres.[82] And of course Bishop St-Vallier condemned the heavy drinking of the settlers.[83] Echoes of the dispute reverberated even in France.[84]

In the end, the majority agreed that selling liquour to the First Nations was bad policy, but it proved to be extremely difficult to stop due to French drinking and socialization habits, and the fact that there was profit in it. In this dispute, allegiances could vary, but all admitted that their Native colleagues were especially vulnerable to alcohol poisoning, and all felt paternalistic to some degree. The struggle often involved crossed aims: veteran commoners who had ameliorated their status, French nobles who sought to establish greater control over the settlement, and clerics bent on establishing worldwide Catholicism and extensive theocratic political power. Ironically, the final result was to unite the immigrants.

In this three-pronged struggle, the French elite was the most challenged axis, in seeking to maximize their own influence by delegitimatizing Canadian autonomy and stigmatizing its proponents. In this conflict, the greatest source of contention was the libertarian political and sexual aspects of French Canadian Nativization. Other aspects of Nativization were outwardly disdained by French officials and clerics, yet unadmittedly admired and employed by them, as the need arose.

By 1663 the Nativized Canadian oligarchy had become an autonomous political force that the Crown tried to contend with, first with the stick, and then reluctantly with the carrot.[85] Louis XIV had been forced as a fourteen-year-old to flee Paris with his mother during the Fronde. His Canadian colonial policy, no less than his domestic policies, kept its clamp on potentially rebellious elites. Thus, Louis XIV's policy of "Colonial Reorganization" entailed an effort to re-Frenchify New France. Minister of the Marine Jean Colbert advised the governor general to incrementally suppress the office of syndic, prevent general assemblies, and forbid general petitions.[86] Yet French royal administrators, especially those with express plans to curb

Canadian autonomy, found that once they were in Canada, they depended upon the cooperation of the oligarchy to realize at least some of their plans and to avoid clashes that cost them dearly. Governor Mézy expressly sent the immensely popular Jean Bourdon to France in shame, but it cost him his own job, despite his own famously pious Norman connections.[87] Péronne Dumesnil was sent to investigate the financial irregularities of the Canadian elite and, due to his snooping around to discover corruption, was hassled by most of the Canadian elite and chased from the country. His son also lost his life in dubious circumstances.[88] Ruette d'Auteuil, a noble from France, also wound up becoming anathema when he decided to complain about the upstart Canadian elite.[89]

The disputes taught the Canadians that the Crown was aiming at their autonomy, while the latter realized that douceur was not only an essential policy towards Native allies but also towards his own insubordinate Canadians. The dialogue negotiated between the king and the Canadian elite was nuanced by the dialogue between France, the Canadian elite, and Native chiefs. The French policy of suppressing the Canadian elite was untenable as long as Native policy was guided by accommodation (douceur). Tyrannical royal officials undermined the goal of convincing the Natives that the Great Onontio was benevolent. Thus, Louis xiv, via the astute Minister of the Marine Colbert, was forced to recognize his limitations and coat his stick thick with maple taffy. He imported mostly orphan girls as brides (filles du roi), used the efficient Jean Talon as intendant, and brought in the celebrated General Prouville de Tracy to finally chase the Haudenosaunee. Despite these well-chosen moves, the power struggle and cultural misunderstandings between the Canadians and the French widened over the course of the late seventeenth century.

As misapprehensions increased, the king reevaluated the situation. Around the 1680s, when the coureurs de bois had evolved a distinctive lifestyle, French officials did nothing but complain about their incorrigible liberty, licence, and insubordination. In France, aristocratic culture had begun to emphasize pedigree rather than military might, "amour propre" rather than "homme de coeur." French officials generally held an outsider status vis-à-vis the emerging Canadian elite, and closely associated the older noble d'épée lifestyle with that of the First Nations. They probably did not dare to snub them too openly in Canadian society, but in dispatches to the king or minister, the Canadian nobility, officers, and seigneurs were viewed as incorrible "coqs du village" and "parvenus." Louis xiv spent enormous effort trying to rein in these "incorrigibly insubordinate" Canadians, who had already established a more egalitarian precedent and resisted Crown intervention.[90] Royal officials and the clergy often perceived the Canadians as being almost half-wild (demi-sauvage), and ennobled Canadians were little better than those "false" country nobles (hobereaux) who were being stripped of their titles.[91] Intendant Champigny wrote: "the principal faults of people established in Canada lies principally with the nobles and those who coopt this title to themselves without being it ... it is evident that one must not give aristocratic titles to none of them, unless one wishes to augment the number of beggars .... The Intendant will know how to discover the these so-called nobles for misrepresenting their titles"[92] In 1684 a royal edict levied a 500-livres fine on any Canadian who had a "false" title of nobility as there were more nobles in Canada than in all the other French colonies combined.[93] The king effectively cancelled previously autonomic institutions like the Conseil de Québec through weeding out the commoner elements while adding extra weight to royal officials and the bishop. He simply replaced the Communauté des Habitants. And, by counterbalance, the king satisfied the protests against his earlier disciplinary tactics by skilfully instituting a yearly Assemblée Générale, where habitants could vent their spleen annually – even if it found no sympathetic echo within Louis' agenda.

The Canadian elite effectively resisted restrictions on the sale of liquour to the Natives, regulations limiting the opening of cabarets, and surreptitious fur trading and petit commerce between Natives and Canadians. As for the coureurs de bois, during the beaver-pelt sale crisis of 1701–21, when the king tried to forbid access to the Great Lakes, many coureurs, cut off from family, risked their lives by marrying into the socially reconfigured intertribal villages neighbouring the French forts. Fur contraband was also a popular amusement. The habitants continued strip farming along the seaway shore rather than submit to French blueprints for circular village settlements. As Canadian society at every level was permeated with defending its own turf, several governors and administrators colluded to their own benefit or even, as the Governor comte de Frontenac did, set their own rebellious example by attempting to pour the lion's share of fur profits into their own pockets and protecting dubious explorers (like La Salle) to explore new markets for themselves alone. The king's efforts at re-Frenchification especially targeted the prominent and influential coureur de bois.

An expanding geographical disparity began to become more important than simple vertical hierarchical position. The perennial Haudenosaunee conflict, which accelerated after 1649, peaked during the 1661 Long-Sault Battle and was calmed for awhile after the Great Peace of Montreal in 1701, constituted a central dynamic of French Canadian society. It was the major force weeding out those who judged New France a losing battle, could no longer identify with what this battle represented, or felt that the sacrifices were not worthwhile. At any rate, this menace did not leave anyone indifferent, but some areas were more rudely exposed than others. Quebec, the Gaspésie, Lac St-Jean, and Acadia were generally safe from this threat, while Three Rivers and Montreal, not to mention the trade route settlements into Native centres, were constantly under fire. Historically based clashes between the respective governments of Montreal and Quebec did not provide an atmosphere of cooperation and understanding. In addition, even when the jurisdiction of Montreal became part of the Quebec-administered territory of the entire St Lawrence, the bulk of royal officials stayed in Quebec, while the majority of Three Rivers- and Montreal-area habitants were directly or indirectly involved in fur trade matters. Royal plans tried condensing an already far-extended settlement, organizing French round-style villages instead of the rectangular strip plots preferred by the habitants, developing local industries useful to the mother country, and limiting the fur trade while stigmatizing the coureurs. The famous tension between habitants and the coureurs de bois must be seen against this backdrop, where the former were favoured by royal officials in Quebec whereas the latter had their Native-centred bases of approval. In other words, geographical location also resulted in conflicting perspectives due to winter isolation, proximity to economic lifelines, sources of external threats, and differential metropolitan ties.

Ironically, the king led his Canadian flock back into the French fold through the medals-and-ribbons tactic originally deployed upon Native chiefs to endear them to the Great Onontio! Crown perception of the Canadians being more Native than French enticed them with prestigious rewards for courage. These included the Croix de St-Louis, gifts of land and titles, and military offices.[94] During the eighteenth century, the goal of re-Frenchification came closer but still stigmatized and marginalized too many Native cultural habits that were too deeply rooted. After the Cession/conquest of New France in 1759, this socio-cultural split expressed itself by the French elite escaping to France while leaving behind bereft veteran Canadians who were firmly attached to North America.[95] It also appears that the fleeing French, while pressing to redeem their worthless French royal banknotes for their own fortune, never applied their ardour in testimonial influence at court to succor the helpless French Canadians, who were at the mercy of an ostensible British conquest. As luck would have it, Conquest/ Cession relations were quite amicable, considering the circumstances. But then, French Canadian ancestors had looked to the British, not the French, Crown for respite – from the tyranny of growing French absolutism.

St Joseph, the great paternal figure that the Recollects and Jesuits were anxious to install and whose cult was on the rise in France, apparently irked young men anxious to resist their fathers, the governor, and royal authority.[96] Yet the French authorities, both clerical and administrative, insisted upon playing the father to their Native allies rather than seeing their allies as brothers, as the chiefs insisted.[97] There was no flood of conversions due to St Joseph. In Native culture, socio-economic and customary gender reciprocity, not paternalism, was the rule. The Recollects and Jesuits expended the abortive effort to install St Joseph as the colony's patron saint.[98] The Natives were not impressed by the incredible fire and snake-spewing Jesuit-designed contraption built to convert them on St Joseph's feast day, and they balked at attaching St Joseph as the patriarch of the Wendat, for only the Innu could conceptually identify with a male father figure, Atahocan, who even then was eclipsed by the general creator, Messou.[99]

The power struggle between the clerical and Canadian fur traders' vision of New France was most starkly demonstrated by the burning question of alcohol. This debate over Native policy literally sundered the community into two bitterly opposed camps. Pro-alcohol traders, coureurs, and habitants opposed the church and other habitants who militated against it.[100] This issue redebated the wisdom of both paternalistic and fraternalistic Native policies.

Nobility itself was transformed. The Canadian aristocrat had precious few privileges, myriad responsibilities, and became bourgeois-gentilhomme who abhorred indigence,[101] preferring the court of the Native maiden to that of the sun king. This commercially minded nobleman was not unlike the Wendat traders. Yet there were many more new types in the New World, which indicated a new kind of masculinity. Both habitant (as opposed to the French peasant) and coureurs de bois were new male models and shared a new-found pride. The missionary "soldier of God" (soldat de Dieu), Father Brébeuf, defied his torturers more like a chief than like a lamb. The cancelled role of French Canadian syndic was replaced, in 1669, by a capitaine de milice, who was often a commoner yet commanded seigneurs if he was able. Even more remarkable is that, by 1690, Father LeClercq called them "capitaines français" (French chiefs), meaning, by implication, that the other kind of capitaines were "capitaines sauvages" (Native chiefs).[102] All these types demonstrate a brusque departure from "official" French metropolitan social ideals as enunciated by Jean de La Bruyère (Les caractères, 1688), Jean-Baptiste Poquelin dit Molière (1622–73), and Marie-Madeleine de la Fayette (La princesse de Clèves, 1678). The new social roles expressed the independent spirit of immigrant deviation from French norms, a new meaning to nobility, and a fresh significance to the concept of masculinity. Individualistic freedom, the use of reason, and independent decision making enhanced a deepening consciousness of the inner "self" as an individual rather than as an insignificant notch on a predetermined hierarchy (as had often formerly been the case in France). Yet this independence was cultivated not only due to a self-awakening but also to the fact that the new initiative was essential for communal survival.

In conclusion, the hierarchical society of France was transformed into a series of more egalitarian transversal male nodes that interlinked with allied feminine, as well as Native, communities in a network over North America. This was due to lack of a coherent and reliable French authority, an alternative Native example, isolation, and the rising French Canadian elite. In order to be socially mobile in Canada, the most salient criterion was Native knowledge, by which wealth and standing could accrue through the adaptation of useful skills. Therefore, not only were interethnic boundaries ambiguous, but social boundaries were metamorphosed by general levelling, social mobility, and the rise of a complementary elite. Tough, reliable Canadian manhood was a far cry from the dandies trotting about the corridors, and whining at the boudoirs, of Louis XIV's court.

CHAPTER FIVE

Our Founding Clanmothers

The contrast between the standing of Frenchwomen and Native women before their respective communities were joined was striking. Frenchwomen were one of the prime banes of the early modern era in France, with endless debates and treatises slighting their capacities (*la Querelle des femmes*, debate over the Salic Law; *Le Caquet des Accouchées, Les Evangiles des Quenouilles*) to their being chased and burned as witches.[1] Native women, by contrast, were in charge of the majority of family and baseline economic functions. In New France, Native women's salutary influence upon the French settlement included providing a reverse model in which women were honoured for their centrality to the functioning of the family and society, and as individuals possessed of extensive obligations and rights. Frenchwomen provided Native women with lacemaking, knitting, and handiwork that pleased the Innu women, and the religious models of St Anne and St Mary included the option of marrying a dead ancestor (Jesus), who was alleged to be perfection itself. In New France the female pioneer population was mostly restricted to a few settler wives and selected clergy, who were greatly outnumbered by the men. Only by 1663, when orphan filles du roy arrived, did demographic proportions approach parity. Thus, the men relied upon Native womens' survival skills, some of which were passed on to pioneer Frenchwomen.

Unlike Native women, Frenchwomen had no secure standing in their government, economy, society, or homes. The fifteenth- to seventeenth-century debate over female rulers led to a reinforcement of social and political control over the "gentle" sex. Jean Bodin hailed the patriarchal state, while Richelieu decided that female government was detrimental.[2] In France, measures were constantly initiated by royal officials, legal experts, scholars, craftsmen, and provincial parlements during this era to ensure that male dominance was enhanced within the economy, community, and home as the prime building block of the state. Historian Sarah Hanley has called this the "Family/State Compact," which dramatically reduced women's rights since the waning of the Middle Ages.[3] Therefore, whereas Frenchmen, especially elderly men of standing, were vituperatively dominant in French society, both children and women were regularly disadvantaged (particularly elderly women, who became wards of their own offspring). Yet women were the key transmitters of culture to the next generation.

Frenchwomen were officially barred from higher education and were increasingly excluded from professions and guilds, whereas earlier there had been exceptions, especially for widows, which condemned them to begging and social stigmatization.[4] The permitted female guilds were few in number. Their legal capacity was undermined by the sexus imbecillus clause, included in the legal custom de Paris, which was drawn from Roman law, as was their political capacity (which was drawn from Frankish Salic law). Historian Robert Muchembled writes of the devalourization of the status of early modern Frenchwomen.[5] Although the brain was considered to be the same in the two genders, it was the body that threw thinkers into a tizzy. Rabelais' *Pantagruel* and Molière (les Femmes savantes, and L'école des femmes) ridiculed women entering the exclusively male world of learning. Few countered them.[6]

Young Frenchwomen were particularly irked by patriarchal authority when forced into the marriage bed of the wrong man. The so-called "précieuses" literature of the duc D'Urfé (L'astrée) and Madeleine de Scudéry (Clélie) often portrayed this choice as black comedy, with the antihero usually being a monstrously decrepit, yet jealous, groom. Boys' possibilities were expanding through improved education and urban employment during this era, but their sisters could rely neither upon a solid education, nor gainful employment, nor inheritance, nor a husband who might cherish them for themselves.

There appeared to be a French taboo on ensuring the financial security of women. They were regularly disinherited of land and goods in order to enrich their brothers, and they wound up dependent upon their own sons. Disease and the dangers of childbirth resulted in the "splintered family" type during the early modern era, which put daughters in jeopardy in order to advance their brothers. Elementary rights regularly accorded even the poorest man simply did not apply to women as Frenchwomen suffered from legal strictures that Native women could not even conceive of. French provincial legal codes resisted faint-hearted Parisian reforms and attempts at extended jurisdiction, which sometimes improved undue provincial strictures but officially repressed female status due to their Roman legal base.

The Breton law code evenly divided inheritances among girls as well as boys, and accorded widows full inheritance, yet it lost out to the encroaching Latin-based law code. Legally, widowhood suddenly condemned one to starvation. The legal custom of Paris allowed widows merely half of their own husband's inheritance, and in Normandy, even this pittance was hewed down to a mere one-third. Early modern European legislation, unlike medieval laws, proved particularly severe to women accused of infanticide, prostitution, or witchcraft.[7] Infanticide was a frequent accusation, and it covered abortion by ergot or sevin as well as stillborns.[8] Witchcraft was punished by burning, infanticide by hanging, while prostitutes endured public whipping, branding, or (by 1684) permanent disfiguration through nose and ear slitting. The latter were sometimes deported to a colony, although not to Canada.. In France, if wives managed to escape a murderously jealous spouse, the latter continued to abuse her legally by stripping her of her own children and, indeed, everything but the clothes upon her back.[9] Other women were often too intimidated to help her, yet if she found assistance from some male defender, she could be accused of adultery. This entailed having her head shaved and being thrown into a convent against her will. In Normandy, accused women were lashed while running naked in the streets, while in Poitou they were dragged through the streets by a mule's tail and bound to the stake in the public square. As Nathalie Davis reminds us, Rabelais declared that Frenchmen served the goddess Jealousy.[10] The disproportionate villainy that was attached to the rare wife who dared to defend herself in the thick of threats and blows contrasted starkly with the celebrity of murderous "shrewtamers."[11] A late sixteenth-century Breton writer, Noël du Fail, had his hero say: "I would really like ... Martin Punishing-Rod to be in charge" ("Ie voudrais bien ... que Martin Baston trotteroit").[12] Legally, women were overburdened with obligations yet possessed rights akin to those of inanimate property. As for male adultery, the so-called popular tale of Griselda forbade wives to be anything less than magnanimous. No wonder popular belief characterized Carnival as an overstuffed youth astride a bloated sausage loaded with beefy meats, lard, and cakes, while Lent was invariably characterized as a haggard matron starving on wilted vegetables and a skimpy fishtail.[13]

The French absolutist hierarchy, which cut the lower rungs off most privileges, accorded well with French mental strictures that failed to associate femaleness with humanity. Together, both insidiously obstructed familial and communal trust. Frenchwomen, nevertheless, insisted on doing charitable works, learning science and humanism, establishing female professional bastions like linen and silkworks, and spicing up court and literary life.[14] While British Quaker women asserted their spiritual equality with men, French religious women far outran Frenchmen in charitable works.[15] Historian Elisabeth Rapley describes seventeenth-century Protestant societies as assimilationist and Catholic societies as pluralist, yet both systems disadvantaged and controlled women. The first accomplished this through subordination, the second through segregation – and both by varying degrees of disinheritance, intimidation, and violence if women did not acquiesce.[16] Although woman was the closest and most intimate "Other," French society disgraced her instead of relying upon her.

Native communities, by contrast, benefited from freely exercised female capacities. The Haudenosaunee Hiawatha told his people to choose a wisewoman to be the Peacemaker, or Genetaska. She welcomed disputes into her kiepuk (sanctuary) to allow the parties time off to rest, eat, and recover their sense. Then she heard both sides and arbitrated. Lafitau wrote that women have the chief authority in Iroquoia.[17] Even as late as the eighteenth century, the British wrote of Haudenosaunee women: "women are treated in a much more respectful manner than in England & that they possess very superior power" and "the women are admitted to the council fire & have the liberty of speaking."[18] Charlevoix, even in the eighteenth century, noted that the Iroquoian and Wendat matrons were clan heads, name councillors, and had chief authority through their own councils, called Hotouissaches, which ratified or rejected decisions. Further to this, the Iroquoian near-matriarchal organization is well-known.[19] Economic complementarity between female agriculturalists and male hunters and traders was the Native norm. Women were also occupied with birthing, childcare and education, home-building, carrying loads, collecting firewood, clothesmaking, toolmaking, cooking, and gathering edible nuts, roots, vegetables, fruits, and plants. Wives were the central decision-makers if projects, moving, and travel were required.[20] Many writers were surprised that Native women endured childbirth without crying out and that their tasks had made them "so strong that few men in Europe can match them."[21]

Marriage, instead of being between a man and his dowry, as Sarah Gibson reminds us was the situation in France, in northeast Native nations it was a matter of cooperation between a very familiar couple. "Every possession of the man Except his horse & his rifle belong to the Woman after Marriage. She takes care of their money & gives it to her husband as she thinks his necessities require it."[22] Fathers Brébeuf and LeClercq marvelled that Wendat and Mi'kmaq men were never observed by the French to quarrel with or boss around their wives.[23] The Mi'kmaq husband was required to live under the roof of his intended on trial for a year providing for her family and proving his hunting ability, which, together with warring, was the prime Native index of manhood. In Innu culture doing something that one's wife did not wish was indisputably unacceptable and was the patent excuse whenever a man endeavored to be let off some social hook.[24] Marriages were arranged by clanmothers, who were responsible for guiding the couple into a harmonious relationship.[25] Marriage was rarely difficult between such familiar partners, but, if it was, then they generally parted amicably, another fact that astonished French writers.[26] Haudenosaunee mothers kept everything except the bridal gift, which ensured that her children would not suffer.[27] Husbandly possessiveness, enshrined in France through the wife having the legal status of a chattel, was utterly bewildering to Native men, who thought it a form of French insanity.[28] After all, it was the jealousy of Aataentsic's husband that caused the uprooting of the Tree of Light (paradise) and caused her descent to Turtle Island (America). Indeed, the Seneca practised polyandry, while some Wendat and Algonquian chiefs were permitted sororial polygamy if their wives desired it in order to have help with their work.[29] If a husband hurt his wife, she could retaliate, and in some cases he was killed by her brothers.[30] If women were murdered in any conflict, the presents due to her relatives were forty instead of the thirty offered for a man because women engender life and "cannot so easily defend themselves" against male warriors. When a daughter was born, the rejoicing was great.[31] William Fenton writes that the Haudenosaunee, then and now, value a woman's life as twice that of a man due to her generativity.[32] After his trip to France, Wendat youth Savignon concluded that Frenchwomen could be bought from their fathers for three beaver pelts due to their low status.[33]

These cultural contrasts came into inevitable friction during dialogue due to unavoidable interdependency between the French and their allies. The crux of that interaction was also the most typical: that of female Native with male immigrant. Both received the highest creditation of their respective communities and therefore expected similar treatment in the alternative community. On the other hand, this potential clash of cultures took place precisely at a conjuncture of young male and female, which served to considerably soften the shock and induce each to attempt to seduce the other into their own norm or to try out the alternative norm. Yet due to the ultimate dependency of the French upon the surrounding Natives who outnumbered them, and the greater need of uprooted foreign young males for already well adjusted local young females, the cards were heavily stacked against the French norm winning out.

Thus French North American society, in contrast to that of France, also benefitted from an ameliorated reliance upon women's capabilities.[34] Candidates for immigration were pre-selected, particularly the women, in contrast to many colonies.[35] This screening reflects the royal plan to "socially engineer" a semblance of a utopian society, even though women were considered to be naturally disorderly.[36] In addition, men greatly outnumbered women until 1663, which certainly improved the choice of suitors. In France, women usually outnumbered men.[37] From 1632–1663, about 420 female immigrants arrived. After 1663, 800 filles du roy arrived with only 265 additional other women from 1673–1730, leaving the majority during the seventeenth century to be filles du roy.[38]

The legal environment reflected a shift in practice, if not in theory. The civil authorities gave severe sentences to rapists and prostitutes, yet light sentences to drunks, debauchés, and adulterers.[39] This policy created a safe social environment for families by ensuring public safety yet leaving personal matters to be sorted out with one's own conscience. That contrasted greatly with Puritan policies, in which private conscience was a public affair.

Immigrant women reformed the impoverishment of women to the best of their ability. The education of girls was constantly placed on the colonial agenda through the outreach efforts of Marguerite Bourgeoys and the prominent example of the Ursulines. Canadian girls were better formally educated both than Canadian boys or feminine counterparts in France, a situation deplored by some 'educated' Frenchmen like Franquet.[40]

Furthermore, single women were not pushed to the margins of society.[41] Women were rapidly swept back into circulation through rapid remarriages, averaging 8.8 months.[42] It is similarly significant that their longevity improved dramatically, especially in Montreal. Those few but prominent pioneer women were widely admired and/or coveted by settlers, missionaries, and sometimes Native men, who had difficulty conceiving of women lacking full rights of personhood.[43] Hélène Boullé, Champlain's young wife and the founding Mother of the Québec Hospital, Mother Ste-Marie, were admired by settlement and Native men. Jeanne Mance was "a woman of almost heroic chastity and semi-masculine resolution," whose plan to found the Montreal Hotel-Dieu attracted the attention of the Queen, the princess, Chancellor Séguier's wife, and other wealthy devotees. Marguerite Bourgeoys was a "mighty woman of the gospels." Marie-Barbe de Boullongne, wife of Governor d'Ailleboust, was named "Chaouerindamaguetch" (she who pities our poverty) by the Algonquians. Naturally, there is always a gap between the attitudes towards elite and less privileged women, but elite examples here were significant as models in Quebec. Mother Marie de L'Incarnation's shrewd advice as founder of the Quebec Ursulines was so widely sought that Bishop Laval attempted to circumscribe her power. Nevertheless, her Native disciples and those of Mother Marie de St-Joseph looked to them for motherly spiritual guidance: "Jean Baptiste ... let a few words fly ... he ran to the Ursulines asking of the Mother who knows their tongue ... he told her the four words. Marie you will tell ... my Confessor ... Jean Baptiste ... sinned ... he is greatly sorry, he will be very careful to avoid refalling." ("Iean Baptiste ... laissant aller quelques paroles ... il s'en court aux Vrsulines demande la Mere qui entend leur langue ... il luy dit ces quatre paroles. Marie tu diras ... mon Confesseur ... Iean Baptiste ... . peché ... il en est grandement marry, il se tiendra sur ses gardes pour ne plus retomber.")[44]

Women seemed to have a markedly tenacious staying power in North America when compared to men. This was true in both religious and secular communities. Only 8.2 percent of the women, as opposed to 35.2 percent of the men (at least) returned to France by 1663.[45] Their prodigious progeny, encouraged by official policy, were additional reasons to prevent using the dangerous seventeenth-century inter-Atlantic voyages frequently.[46] Also, over 50 percent of immigrant women were filles du roy who were orphans, widows, or institutionalized neo-Catholic girls, many from the Parisian La Salpetrière, and had no viable home to which to return.[47] Although the male clerics regularly returned to France at a rate of 45 percent between 1632 and 1659 (thirty-six of a total of eighty), religious women were committed to Canada, with only four out of thirty women returning to France, or 13.3 percent. For religious women, the motivation that accompanied the voyage to Canada was extremely strong, which caused Father LeJeune to chuckle patronisingly: "this ardour is commendable, but ... the Ursulines ... if one opened the door to their desires, we would have a city of religious women, and would have ten schoolmistresses for one schoolgirl." ("Cette ardeur est loüable, mais ... Vrsulines ... si on ouuroit la porte à leurs desirs, on composeroit vne ville de Religieuses, & il se trouueroit dix maistresses pourvne escholiere.")[48] A city of religious women seemed absurd to LeJeune, but Ville-Marie (Montreal) was founded as just that, with benefactress Madeleine de la Peltrie, who could not stop joyously embracing the little Native girls. Their lifelong commitment surpassed his own as he returned to France in 1649, while their sepulchres have become veritable Canadian shrines.[49] Nuns and other pious women were in useful and close personal contact with the population and Native allies rather than being wastefully sequestered as in France.

French Canadian society wound up mirroring Wendat socio-economic reciprocity more than French metropolitan-style hierarchy. This was due to economic necessity and the interethnic dialogue that was enacted over wide geographical distances. In the new settlement, women were responsible for the bulk of agricultural work as the fur trade required male mobility, especially outside of Quebec, after the Fall of Wendake. The eminently hierarchical society of France was also forced to adopt the Wendat-style gender-based complementarity of labour. Instead of the hierarchy dividing up the population vertically, the horizontal situational occupations of men and women, especially in the Trois-Rivières and Montreal areas, diverged radically and had much in common with Wendat gender-divided occupations. The male traders-female agriculturalists division of labour placed mothering, education, and agriculture in female hands, while the coureurs de bois mimicked the Wendat trader lifestyle. By 1663 one could speak of an adequate agricultural land base for settlement, with 54.5 percent of seigneurial land in female hands thanks to eleven widows who retained their seigneuries.[50] This accident, however, is less haphazard than one might guess. Iroquoian women owned and worked the land, like Norwegian women, whose men worked at sea far from home.[51] During the seventeenth to eighteenth centuries, agriculture, caring for the war wounded, commercial affairs (including contraband, laundering, later manufacture of canoes and trade articles, businesses [such as running taverns]), and the preservation of family assets were ordinary female occupations, especially for widows. Jan Noël has emphasized that, by the eighteenth century, the textile and lumber industries, and several fur trade posts, were founded and run by women (often widows), who thoughtfully provided inheritances for their daughters.[52] Instead of a man confiscating his wife's assets through early modern Latinized patriarchal-style marriage, wives, and thus mothers and children, legally retained their asset rights under all circumstances. The Canadienne and her children enjoyed better protection than contemporary divorce laws accord Canadian women, who typically suffer an overall financial loss of 75 percent while their spouses gain over 45 percent (1992).[53] And, very recently, the provincial law of Ontario has discarded the traditional preference for mother custody, which places mothers in a position nearer that of women under Moslem Sharia law – who can be thrown out of their own homes without children or money when husbands will it or want to add another wife – than that of women under Native law (under which motherhood is sacrosanct).

Despite a gendered division of labour, the establishment of necessary patterns of mutual aid within one's own gender were weaker among French Canadian women than among Native women. In Haudenosaunee communities, for example, these divisions were reinforced by matrilocal marriage, matrilineal inheritance, and joint female ownership of the land and longhouse.[54] While Frenchmen developed a certain culturally mixed code that paralleled same-gender isolation, with the male bonding involved in the swearing of fidelity, confrérie bonding, and guild solidarity, Frenchwomen were initially fundamentally divided between poor urban filles du roi, French orphans, veteran immigrant Frenchwomen, and native-born Canadians. The men also had much greater opportunities for male bonding through woodroving and/or being twinned with male Natives. For Frenchwomen, their sororial cooperation experience related to tasks in the orphanage or to living in a religious community. The overwhelming majority of women were urban and, thus, the village farm cooperation would have been unfamiliar to them. Canadian strip farms afforded them privacy without isolation, surrounded, as they were, by their numerous children. Thus, most of the friendly twinning that occurred between women was within the context of religion or family.

The French obsession with feminine sexuality contrasted greatly with the Native concern with their human worth. Only with the introduction of royal officials after 1663 was a woman accused of adultery, and condemned to be shaved and lashed, while her accomplices sat in jail in hand and foot irons, reduced to a penance ration of bread and water.[55] Throughout the seventeenth century, owing to the Native welcome offered children born out of Catholic wedlock, only two women were executed for alleged infanticide.[56] Governor Frontenac accused the Jesuits and the Confrérerie de la Sainte-famille of trying to install an Inquisition in New France that was a thousand times worse than that in Italy or Spain through getting women to spy upon one another and rustle up intrigue. The inculcation of mutual mistrust among isolated, largely single mothers with many toddlers – people obviously in need of significant family and communal support – received little practical application since it was not suited to the building of a young community. Inquisitional procedure itself, projecting the illusion of purification, destroys the fabric of personal and social trust, without which a viable communal life cannot exist. A suspicious husband once threatened to kill his wife, who had been unjustly accused of infidelity. Frontenac intervened, induced the witness to retract the story before a notary, and personally mediated a reconciliation between husband and wife. Frontenac recounted that the entire community was edified by this peaceful regulation of unnecessary misunderstandings conjured by clerical meddling.[57] Several husbands apologized and pleaded to exonerate their wives of adulterous accusations before the Sovereign Council. Historian Jan Noël rightly contrasted New France both with the treatment of feminine adultery in New England (branding) and Portuguese Brazil (death), to say nothing of France.[68] So much for Canadian liaisons dangereuses.

If restricting the freedom of settlement women was not easy, lording it over new Native converts evidently had its rewards. Father LeJeune told his disciple that, in France, women do not control their husbands, and an Innu convert threatened an assembly by saying that if wives did not obey their husbands, they would not be allowed to eat.[59] The Fathers "bettered" them by instigating men to imprison or beat their wives if disobedient.[60] Nonetheless, female preachers were encouraged to offset hostility to patriarchy, like Erie nation Catherine Gandeacteua, founder of the Prairie de la Madeleine mission.[61]

MÉTISSAGE

Métissage penetrated the most intimate social unit, the family.[62] The volatile complementary gender surpluses of the two joining communities resulted in many French males finding First Nations partners.[63] There was a contradictory juxtaposition of solidarity and rivalry, as each group's roles were negotiated in time and space. Inevitably, it was not in the centres, but along the margins, where cultural and social creativity were greatest. Widespread interethnic romancing, several extra-ecclesiastical marriages, and some Catholic mixed marriages were common, especially on the margins of the

French centre (Gaspésie, Lac St-Jean area), in the Native centres (Ottawa Valley, Great Lakes region, Illinois country, and later in Louisiana),[64] in the Métis area of Acadia, and also in the reductions (reserves or neo-Christian agricultural villages).

Official policy favoured the blending of the French with the First Nations to create one people (métissage).[65] Royal policy based itself upon Champlain's assessment that this was both possible and beneficial. The Hundred Associates Charter naturalized as French, with full legal capacity and the right to move to France, any Native or his descendant who converted to Roman Catholicism: "Ordonne sa Majesté, que les descendans des François qui s'habitueront au dit pays, ensemble les sauvages qui seront amenés ... la connoissance de la foi et en feront profession, seront censés et réputés naturels françois, et comme tels pourront venir habiter en France quand bon leur semblera, et y acquérir, tester, succéder et accepter donations et légats."[66] These legal rights are much more extensive than in New England, Virginia, or New Spain. Métis children had the same rights as their parents in North America and in France. When Three Rivers was established Champlain declared that the French and Natives would intermarry, and form one people.[67] In 1637, when the Jesuits asked the Attignawantan (Bear tribe) Wendat chiefs if Frenchmen could marry Wendat women, the chiefs were surprised and responded that they had always done so, without any special permission from them.[68] The goal of the Société de Notre Dame de Montreal, which founded the city, was to integrate French and Natives to form a single people in a Christian atmosphere.[69] By the 1660s, Colbert and Louis XIV encouraged intermarriage so as not to "depopulate" France as well as to encourage a hardy mixed-blood people to form in Canada.[70] Official doweries rewarding mixed marriages dated from 1680, with 3,000 livres being granted for dowries of 50 livres each for Roman Catholic French-Native marriages (later on, 1,000 livres were budgeted to teach French domestic techniques to Native girls). Even so, few claimed the dowry, which was in the budget until 1702.[71]

Early French policy favouring métissage contrasted sharply with the spirit of official British policy, which frowned upon mixed unions.[72] The British prohibited intermarriage between Europeans, Natives, and Africans in 1662 in Maryland, 1691 in Virginia, 1692 and 1705 in Massachusetts, 1715 in North Carolina, 1717 in South Carolina, 1721 in Delaware, 1725 in Pennsylvania, and 1754 in Georgia. An isolated instance of British tolerance of intermarriage cropped up in Acadia only because they found the Mi'kmaq and Maliseet so attached to the French Acadians.[73] Governor Latour's, Governor D'Aulnay's, and the St-Castin Métis lines are well-known, and Olive Dickason points to indirect references to the prevalence of métissage, particularly in Acadia. Colonel Vetch, English commander at Port Royal (1710–13), noticed that the Natives had a strong influence over the Acadians due to their family ties, and Abbé Maillard wrote in 1753 that he did not expect more than fifty years to elapse before the French would be so mixed with Mi'kmaq and Maliseet that they would be indistinguishable. A letter published in 1758 in London by a M. de Varennes stated: "We employ a much more effectual method of uniting them to us ... intermarriage ... . They [Acadians] were a mixed breed ... of the savage women with the first settlers." As Bailey has noted, citing Abbé Maurault, "there was more or less intermarriage between these settlers and this tribe [Mi'kmaq] which more firmly cemented the bonds ... métissage was an important feature of ... the founding of Port Royal. The Bretons and Basques, more than any other European people seem to have exerted the widest influence upon the Malecite [Maliseet] and the Mi'kmaq. Malouidit ... [is the] name given to the metis among the Malecite ... while the [physio-logical] measurements of living Malecites and Mi'kmaqs ... are now unques-tionably mixed with French Canadian blood." And Abbé Maurault believed that "marriages with Indians were so frequent [1607–75] ... when European women were [so] scarce that there were few Acadian families with no Indian blood in their veins."[74]

Within the French area, interethnic romantic occasions were enhanced by the French opening of cabarets, where both French and Natives merrily toasted each other's health. Alcohol was an indispensable aid to northwest-ern French mariners, helping them to dispel the monotony of ship life; and French mid-Atlantic Poitou, Saintonge, and Aunis were famous grape-grow-ing regions. Even Champlain of Brouage complained that alcohol was the only blessing absent in Canada. Alcohol was a traditional fixture in north-western French immigrant social life prior to inter-Atlantic contact. Most Canadian cabarets were female-owned. Usually they were the woman's sole means of support. Often women bereft of their husbands and sons (who boasted of their erotic conquests) sought economic security through com-panionship. The importance of these cabarets cannot be overstated, for they seemed to have constituted the nexus of what Jan Grabowski called a "Common Ground" in mid-seventeenth-century Three Rivers as well as in eighteenth-century Montreal.

Cabaret parties particularly appear to demonstrate the initial gap between Native and French understandings regarding the same events, par-ticularly alcoholic parties in which couples paired off. The exchange over a few drinks was generally amicable, even though initial Native interpreta-tions were antithetical to those of the French. On one hand, it is possible that Natives sought truly religious experiences through a shamanistic voy-age via alcohol to the "country of souls" (realm of the dead) in order to visit family members recently smitten by the epidemics.[75] On the other hand, Frenchmen felt they had submitted to satanic temptation by participating in what they saw as a drunken mess. Some cynical Frenchmen even plied

Native men with drinks in order to get cheaper fur prices; and they plied Native women with drinks to procure more feminine favours.[76] Yet the French benefited from Native legitimation of the human need for intimate bonding – a need that was so repressed in French traditions.

Romancing Native-style was colloquially referred to as "courir l'allumette." A Native youth took a lighted twig from the campfire and sought his sweetheart after dark at her bedside. If she accepted him, then she blew out his light. If not, she would cover her face with her fur blanket. Veteran Canadians advised newcomers never to question her decision, for she might then think him a brute.[77] Unlike Frenchwomen, in whom, theoretically, chastity and subordination had been instilled, First Nations women were expected to accept or refuse their sweethearts according to their own hearts. Lahontan writes that, while the French blinded themselves in sexual passion, the Natives were more sensitive to caring tenderness "which was not subject … to all the excesses … caring always … to protect the freedom of their own heart … they are not … as savage [or wild] as we are." ("qui n'est pas sujette … [a] tous les excès … veillant toujours … se conserver la liberté du coeur … ils ne sont pas … si sauvages que nous.")[78]

Native communities had a much more severe taboo on rape than did European communities.[79] Officially, Christian Natives were subject to French Canadian laws forbidding murder, rape, theft, drunkenness, "et autres fautes," but traditionalist Natives were not.[80] In the seventeenth century, there was a rare case of a drunken Native man, Robert Hache, who was indicted for raping a Frenchwoman, Marthe Hubert, thus violating the norms of both communities. The French treated him as any other Frenchman, threw him in jail, and sentenced him to be hung and strangled. He escaped from prison but was returned. When the Algonquian chiefs learned his fate, they attended the Sovereign Council and Tek8erimat argued that they were simply ignorant that rape was punished in this fashion (which was highly unlikely, by that time). They still could appeal that he be pardoned for this first offence in order to reconcile the "ancient [French and Algonquian] friendship." A second offender would suffer the full French penalty.[81] The double legal standard that, by the eighteenth century, provided Natives with a loophole due to their greater "innocence," indicates French willingness to protect legitimate Native perceptions and defend them against the exploitation of ill-intentioned Frenchmen.[82] The Native-French accord over French rules pertaining to rape also converged with Native taboo; thus, even in a multicultural setting, common threads could emerge. Official recognition of Native understandings provided a bridge that facilitated raised consciousness and officially recognized a legitimate biculturality. This stated, one should not ignore that, with increasingly mixed perceptions, the "Native mentality defence" legally extricated Natives from New France criminal proceedings when proximity and biculturality were widespread enough to belie protested ignorance of French taboos. The alternate legal standard afforded Natives in New France actually provided them with twice the number of loopholes afforded Frenchmen, and it contributed to the diffusion of Native standards in New France.

The utopian "first stage" (1608–80) of interethnic mixing in the Laurentian French heartland conceived of physical métissage as the solution to fulfilling Counter-Reform aspirations, toughening up feeble Frenchmen, and serving as an antidote to remedy sparse immigration. By the late 1600s, the practical "second stage" of mixing recognized the pluses, minuses, and failure of Frenchification. Yet, it now provided a double framework for Native peoples of all stages of familiarity with the immigrants to find an appropriate cultural niche, while requiring even highly Nativized French to uphold only the French standard on the St Lawrence heartland. This de facto multiculturality resulted from fresh arrivals and troops from France as well as the desire of various Native groups to convert and settle on mission reserves. Nevertheless, in the Native centres inland, the "first stage" was less utopian due to French experience in the Laurentian first stage. All the pluses and minuses of mixing were known beforehand. Yet, due to the attraction of diverse kinds of tribeswomen, the necessity of wide political networking, and the anticipated burden of unskilled Frenchwomen, métissage was the practical solution in Native centres.

Marrying a Native girl meant something different in the French centre than in the Native centres or even in any of the peripheries. And each Native centre had its own set of norms. In the St Lawrence Valley, when M. de la Barre had an extramarital love affair with a Native woman that resulted in her pregnancy, he was sent back to France.[83] Métissage in the Great Lakes was a double-edged phenomenon. Rancorous enmities and social fragmentation characterized the Great Lakes, which was in flux at this juncture. White records the murder of thirty-nine unprotected French in 1684 in the Great Lakes area due to liquor-induced quarrels and robberies between them and unallied tribes. From the late 1690s to the early 1710s, while the Great Lakes were officially closed to coureurs due to the fur glut on the world market, French mixed marriages were effected to free traders from the strictures of French control. In the Great Lakes region, and later in the prairie-Rockies-Northwest, Native/French marriages, from the late 1600s, were the norm. Métis communities developed near the French posts, and their descendants became the freemen and essential workers of the fur trade, without whom little could be accomplished. Jacqueline Peterson (*The People In-Between*, 1980), Marthe Faribault-Beauregard (*La population des forts français d'Amérique*, 1982), and others have documented the main pays d'en haut families, who created mixed-blood settlements that were visible by 1700 and grew thereafter, adjacent to French forts and Native tribes, but notably "in-between" both.[84] As Richard White has pointed out, Métis born into Catholic wedlock tended to identify more closely with the French, while Métis born according to Native custom were more likely to stay closer to their various tribes. The Jesuits explained as much to the French court in defence of their matrimonial blessings.[85]

Opposition to, or support of, métissage seemed to depend upon the nature of the tribes involved, the kind of coureur on location, and the style of interethnic contact. While in the Great Lakes area, métissage occurred mostly with egalitarian and atomistic Anishinabe and Odawa women, who were accustomed to independence and winter hunting band isolation. Métissage in the Illinois country was composed of the marriages of renegade coureurs with subordinated Illinois, Kaskaskia, and Miami women, whose views on chastity and Christianity concurred with those of the French. Illinois women, unlike the northeastern Natives, valued chastity before marriage, and their jealous spouses sliced off the tip of their noses if they were adulterous, precisely as prescribed by the draconian medieval European Lombardian laws and those of the Alamans.[86] But this furious "castration" of unownable female beauty found a resonant chord in the hearts of jealous Frenchmen. Father Gabriel Marest, missionary in Illinois country, noted: "The Illinois are much less barbarous [sic] than the other Indians. Christianity and their intercourse with the French have by degrees somewhat civilized them."[87]

French girls and women became resourceful when too many men ran to "courir la dérouine." The 1681 census figures for 25- to 29-year-olds show 100 women for 105.6 men in Quebec and 100 women for 83.8 men in Three Rivers. In Montreal there were 100 women for 66.3 men (in the city proper this rose to 100 women for 97.1 men, while in the surrounding area it dropped to 100 women for 46.3 men). Notably, for the south shore of Montreal, for ages 20 to 29, there are 27 males for 60 females.[88] Governor Frontenac wrote: "a thousand disorders ... the bachelors are responsible to no end for licentiousness ... and this particularly so in the distant settlements ... the women are very glad to have several husbands while many of the men cannot find wives ... wives became involved in scandals, so that the husbands arrived home to find additions to their families that they could not account for [trans. mine]." This is the courtier Governor Frontenac writing, not the missionaries, and even his jaded perspective found the situation out of control – when it involved the women, at least.[89] Several intendants and governors also mention this as a perennial problem. Intendant Duchesneau wrote that, when her spouse was absent in the Great Lakes, the French-women fell into the arms of other men – or is it the reverse? Other officials charged that, with so many husbands away, the morals of the Canadian women had deteriorated almost as much as had those of the coureurs de bois, who changed girls every week.[90]

Young French immigrant couples, having been forced together in a pressure-cooker to marry, were now having difficulty sticking together when continually separated. Yet fertility was not marred, indeed, it flourished.[91] Denys Delâge has wondered whether our interpretation of the folkloric expression "les sauvages emènent les bébés" contains a historical kernel of truth, and Peter Moogk reminds us that Québecois children even today are affectionately called "les petits sauvages."[92] The clergy visited homesteads if they could tramp though the snow, but many births did not see a priest for a year or longer, due to the great distances, and in the interior, this often took several years. One of the central goals of the Confrèrie de la Sainte Famille initiated by Barbe de Boullogne (Mme d'Ailleboust, wife of the governor general) and Father Chaumonot in 1663 was at least to keep the wives in line by creating a mainly female tattle club willing to confess not only their own sins but also those of all their neighbors, relations, and friends. This, at least, kept the clergy informed of rumours.[93]

In the rural areas, homes were arranged single file along the St Lawrence, instead of close village-style, which facilitates gossip. Winter tempests obscured visibility and limited mobility. In the fields and their homes, women worked in short Native-length skirts, shoulders and breasts bared, while men worked trouserless, and the children ran naked in the heat.[94] Bishop St-Vallier was particularly scandalized that Native-style partial nudity had become so common that he had to remind women to cover their arms and bosoms before receiving communion.[95] Urban Frenchwomen abandoned by their husbands kept their joie de vivre and rarely missed an evening party (la veillée) with dancing.[96] There were soldiers, French newcomers, and Natives who chose to live in the French settlements, the mission reserves, or in wigwams close to the towns.[97] Innu hunters returned to the Three Rivers and Quebec vicinity if little winter game could be secured, and in summer they returned to fish for eels; in Montreal there were later seasonal fur fairs and the meeting of different tribes. The mission reserves were close by, and some French married Natives and began to live there.

The Native influence upon Frenchwomen was further facilitated when, after the 1690s, Native war captives (largely from Louisiana, Pawnees from Missouri, and Wisconsin Fox) were brought into the settlement. By 1709 slavery was deemed legal, but captives received the common family name, being called a servant or domestic. Some female slaves bore children out of Catholic wedlock. Native male slaves perhaps also discretely fathered some children when the men were gone. Also, during the early 1700s, the raids on English Deerfield and other border hamlets permitted the incorporation of more captives, both Native and English, who were adopted and instructed in Roman Catholicism.

Growing partisanship regarding métissage polarized society by the eighteenth century. Opposition to métissage was sometimes born from preconceived prejudice, especially among the new administrators who still utilized

French constructs for understanding the "sauvages amériquains."[98] Such opposition could also spring from some of the rising Canadian élite, who identified their potential with metropolitan support and whose familiarity with Métis and the tribes only made them fearful of being swallowed in a great Native sea. The continual influx of immigrants in an immigrant society guaranteed that a continual comparison of metropolis/settlement penetrated the French/Native dialogue. Canadian veterans with elite status generally define the rules, boundaries, and definitions of settlement identity while often publicly rejecting, yet privately desiring, a metropolitan refinement. Incoming immigrants form strong sentiments of either acceptance or rejection of North America, which can oscillate confusingly over a long time as they struggle to decide where they finally stand. Veteran commoners and bourgeois could still hope for social advancement within Nativized settlement norms, as a wealthy merchant or post commander could within the Native world.

The classic "colonial elite bottleneck" emerged by the eighteenth century, when many veteran elite had nowhere to rise to (in European terms) in an economically and demographically limited settlement, except the mother country. Therefore, the Canadian elite was forced to choose between re-Frenchification or Nativization. Ironically, while disaffected new administrators joined forces with elite Canadians aspiring to metropolitan standards in condemning expressions of Nativization, enthusiastic French gentilhommes joined their voices with habitants-turned-coureurs eager to better their fortunes in the fur trade.[99] On top of this social polarization, individuals varied and could reverse their evaluations of the situation and their role within it. Thus it should not surprise us that Vaudreuil, the elite scion of an illustrious Canadian family, not only was opposed to métissage but quit the colony after the Cession, while Lamothe Cadillac, a new French nobleman in Detroit, was proud of himself and favoured métissage, which he interpreted as a successful adaptation to a challenging new situation.[100]

One's view of métissage often depended upon where one stood. A substantive royal policy shift became evident when an Arrêt declared that Amerindians were excluded from the successions of the French and an interdiction was laid against contracting marriage with "Sauvagesses." In the Illinois country, Native women were taking back to their villages all their deceased husbands' assets, in accordance with Illinois custom.[101] This volte-face was all the more remarkable for the earlier interethnic fluidity: Pierre Boucher and his Wendat wife, Marie-Chrestienne, held a community of goods, and if she survived him, half of the inheritance was hers according to the Parisian "coustume," which was that adopted in New France.[102]

By the eighteenth century, French administrators on the St Lawrence became opposed to métissage due to their ultimate lack of control regarding its effects. Missionaries consecrated mixed marriages in the west to pre-

vent debauchery, while western post commanders, including Henri de
Tonti, Sieur de la Forest, and Cadillac, supported them to the hilt.[103] As
Métis proliferated in Tadoussac, the Great Lakes region, Illinois country,
and Louisiana, French critics of the "one race" policy emerged.[104] In
Tadoussac, for example, Nicolas Pelletier was criticized for not consulting
relatives, the bishop, and the governor before marrying an Innu girl in June
1677.[105] Vaudreuil and Bégon wrote to the minister as follows: "One should
never mix a bad blood with a good one, the experience that we have in this
country is that all the Frenchmen who have married Native wives have
become lazy libertines, and became intolerably independent" ("Quil ne
fault jamais mesler un mauvais sang avec un bon, l'expérience que lon en a
en ce pays que tous les françois qui ont épous, de sauvagesses sont devenus
libertins feneans, et d'une independence insupportable").[106] Isabelle
Perrault has attributed this to the increasing royal marginalization of the
coureurs de bois.[107] Native blood, however, was considered more noble than
that of the French by other sectors of the population, which included Jesuit
historian Pierre-François-Xavier Charlevoix, Jean-Jacques Rousseau's in-
structor.[108] Women thought the coureurs de bois to be dashing. When the
canoes entered Montreal, habitant boys drank their gloom away, while village belles danced with the coureurs. The most significant variables influ-
encing one's views on métissage were (1) whether there were any vested
interests and (2) one's geographical proximity to either centre. Meinig's
metropolitan decay model could be conditionally operative here as intimate
knowledge of the conditions relative to the occurrence of métissage still
tended to increase understanding of the practical problems it solved, such
as companionship, diplomatic solidarity with tribes fractured by dislocation
and the need to regroup, and an appreciation of its economic utility.

Initially, the French formally adopted interethnic romance and métissage
in order to encourage Frenchification. Two of the three French settlements,
Three Rivers and Montreal, were officially founded to cradle métissage, and
Louis XIV declared every converted Amerindian a naturalized Frenchmen
or Frenchwoman who could enjoy legal rights of their own and, alterna-
tively, reside in France. Freely chosen métissage in Native communities was
standard Native alliance behavior. Since the earliest days of settlement, a
Native wife or partner was the choice of several prominent members of the
pioneer community, which legitimated and modelled métissage. The
orphan girls must have relied heavily upon elderly Frenchwomen and
Native women for assistance, especially concerning childbirth, breastfeed-
ing, and childrearing. Native women were also sought by Frenchmen as
partners in informal settings in geographically marginal settlements and
were used by the authorities as exotic bait to attract French youth to trade in
the Native centres.

Only by the eighteenth century did negative evaluations of métissage appear, usually emanating from French royal representatives. "Metropolitan reorganization" occurred only when Frenchwomen initiated cabarets and got involved with Native men right under the very noses of officials, which further induced the latter to repeatedly ban cabarets and surreptitious Native drinking.

The French approach initially reflected a practical openness at the highest ranks. Embracing Catholicism accorded First Nations every civic dignity. But when social and cultural ambiguity scuttled royal aims of Frenchification and the harnessing of Native good will under the aegis of the French Crown, then official attitudes shifted. Even so, re-Frenchification could not hold unchallenged authority over the varied intercultural social configurations that coalesced in New France. The French North American permanent settler population was perceived to have become half-savage, but the Crown was as yet incapable of foreseeing the cultural and social complexity of the outcome.

NOTRE DAME

If St Joseph was gaining in popularity during the Counter-Reformation, the real pull of Roman Catholicism lay with Mother Mary. Mother Mary was almost as popular in Canada as in Rouen. Louis XIII, whose relationship with his own mother, Marie, seemed complex: he both rebelled against her and placed the entire French kingdom under her protection before commencing a war in 1635.[109] Anne d'Autriche dedicated a statue of silver angel and golden child to our Lady of Loretto after giving birth to Louis XIV in 1638.[110] Marian worship was especially strong in devoutly Roman Catholic Counter-Reformation Normandy, particularly in Rouen. A contemporary wrote: "There is no gate of the city, no street, no corner, virtually no noteworthy house which is not adorned with the figure of that divine intercessor."[111] Nineteen confraternities were dedicated to her, and the prestigious confraternity annual poetry contest, which included a big banquet and a play, was also dedicated to her.[112] After 1596 this tradition was reestablished by the president of the Rouen parlement, Grulart, and fully one-half of its members were parlementarians.[113] Many of the Canadian missionaries, including Father Jean de Brébeuf, Mother Marie de l'Incarnation, Marguerite Bourgeoys, Father Chaumonot, and Madeleine de la Peltrie, among others, had visions of Mother Mary in France.[114] Apparently, the cult of Mary was strongest among celibate male misogynists like Bernard de Clairvaux, who strove to maximize the gap between real women and Mary, the ideal.[115] Yet in Canada devotion to Mary appears to have been generalized and mirrored by the Wendat and Abenaki, who sent a wampum to Chartres that remains there still.[116]

The Jesuits often named their missions and chapels Ste-Marie or Notre-Dame, in true Counter-Reformation style, and installed Mary as patron of this or that Native nation. Charlevoix said that "Mother Mary" was responsible for miracles, including saving French lives from the Haudenosaunee. When Dutch pirates raided the Gaspésie, the habitants were horrified when the crowns of the Virgin Mary were placed on the head of a sheep before sacrificing it.[117] The registers of the Confrérie de la Sainte-Famille of the parish of Notre-Dame de Québec record many Wendat. The Wendat received from Bouvart "Virgini Raritvrae votvm Hvronvm," and Chartrain gave to the Abenakis "Matri Virgini Abnaqvaei."[118] A later book of Wendat religious songs might indicate preferences: Marie Oki is mentioned many more times than any other, and St Joseph was almost never mentioned.[119] Wendat Notre-Dame-de-Lorette chapel became a place of pilgrimage for the French, and Native converts were derisively called "Marians" by Native traditionalists. Marian worship and pilgrimage, even now, is still the most popular in Quebec, with from eighteen apparitions to twenty-five vocables, while St Anne had fifteen and St Joseph only six.[120] Marie was the most popular girl's name in Rouen, as it was in New France, with Anne a close second (1565–1602).[121]

If, in Canada, Mary became an important mediator between Father and Son, then grandmotherly St Anne became a veritable genetrix. This burst of grandmotherly popularity was in direct contrast to the French Counter-Reformation practice, where writers criticized the veneration of St Anne and the female Trinity of Emerentia, Anne, and Mary, which was replaced in pamphlet pictures by Mary and her parents or Mary as an adolescent cared for by a fatherly Joseph. Even Bishop Laval was well advised to obtain reliquiae of St-Anne for Canada.[122] St Anne's initial popularity was as patron of the mariners, including Cartier and his sailors, who prayed to her during storms and after safe voyages. The shrine of Ste-Anne-de-Beaupré was named after the 1630s worship of Ste-Anne-d'Auray in Britanny, built without hands and unburnable. The Parisian Ste-Anne-la-Royale was dedicated to Anne d'Autriche and was also popular.[123] The cathedral of Ste-Anne de Beaupré was founded by a ship's crew floundering in a storm. The chapel causes the blind to feel they can see, the deaf to hear, the lame to walk; and a heap of crutchs and a white dove (symbol of the Holy Ghost) on the altar bring hope and healing to the afflicted.[124] A French Canadian custom arose whereby all passing boats saluted the site with cannonballs in thanks for a safe journey. She was also greatly loved by the common people as patron saint of childbirth as the birthrate in Quebec surpassed that in France.[125] At Montreal's "la bonne Ste-Anne-du-Nord" at Bellevue, engagés put themselves under its protection.[126] In 1648 workers requested the establishment of a confrérie du Saint Rosaire. And in 1657 the furniture makers of Quebec asked to establish a confrérie de Ste-Anne.[127]

Ste-Anne-de-Beaupré became a prime site of pilgrimage and miracles for First Nations as well. The Wendat of Lorette adopted her as their patron saint.[128] The Wendat likened St Anne to the Wendat grandmother genetrix Aataentsic and brought wampum and other treasures to her shrine. She was also extremely popular with the Mi'kmaq. The Atlantic Algonquian demiurge Gluscap lives with his grandmother, Kesegoocsk, and the Cookumijenawanak (Grandmother's Place) in present Nova Scotia (Shubenacadia River on the rock) is considered by the Mi'kmaq to be the spot par excellence to fish – spot that sometimes supplies them with smoked eels all winter.[129] According to the Mi'kmaq, the chapel of St Anne was built without hands and is unburnable. St Anne, the Mi'kmaq patron saint, is even now called Nukumijinen (Our Grandmother) or Se'tan. And according to legend, she was born 300 years ago, was married to Suasin (Joachim), and her daughter Ma'li (Mary) was the mother of Niskam (Jesus).[130] The site is today a famous site of Mi'kmaq marriages, ship celebrations, healing rites, the reliquiae of St Cyrance, the annual Mi'kmaq festival of ancient Wigubaltimk and Neskouwadijik, dances, and St Anne's legendary miracles.[131] Even among the Great Lakes Algonquians, St Anne's power was enshrined in the famous French Canadian legend. An Anishinabe woman and her child were trapped in their canoe by the Haudenosaunee at Lac-des-Deux-Montagnes on their way to the Montreal fur fair. They were saved by praying to St Anne, the Grande Dame Blanche. Her husband, coureur de bois Cadieux, could not escape. Cadieux has been traced to Jean Cadieux (1671–1709), and his "Complainte" has been retold by Métis and Great Lakes Natives in thirty-seven different versions. J.G. Kohl found it around Lake Superior in 1860.[132] The pope originally designated St Anne as the patron saint of French Canada, until the Canadians decided to adopt St John the Baptist in 1909.[133]

The French elite ideal for women, which can be extracted from the oft-repeated Jesuit training of Native girls, consisted of chastity and submissiveness. Of the inverse defamations that plagued the legal records, the worst denunciation that was employed for Frenchwomen was "putain" (prostitute), yet no racial slurs for Native women appear.[134] Nonetheless, the pioneering "amazone de Dieu" belies Jesuit ideals yet was adapted to Canadian reality. The extreme fortitude and resourcefulness of the Quebec Hospitallers, the take-charge attitude of Jeanne Mance ("vertu assez héroique et de résolution assez mâle"),[135] the perceptive intelligence of Marie de l'Incarnation of the Ursulines ("illustre" ... "Thérèse de la Nouvelle France"),[136] and the managerial ability and application of Marguerite Bourgeoys ("de bon sens et de bon esprit")[137] and her Filles de Notre-Dame are all lavishly praised by men who otherwise, at least theoretically, prefer female deference. Dollier de Casson and Marie de L'Incarnation admire several other staunch women who fended off the Haudenosaunee. The wife of Dollard des Ormeaux ran to recharge the male defenders of Montreal with the Haudenosaunee on her heels. "Parmanda" Primot's story: "three of these barbarians [*sic*] threw themselves on her to kill her [with] ... ax blows, when this woman saw, she began to defend herself like a lion ... they tried to scalp her ... but our Amazon, feeling herself being grabbed, suddenly recovered her senses ... stood up and more furious than ever seized this cruel man with so much ferocity in a place that modesty forbids us to mention, that he could barely escape, he axed at her head, but she clutched him so strongly until she fainted upon the ground ... this Iroquois tried to escape as quickly as possible" ("trois de ces barbares [Haudenosaunee] se jetèrent sur elle afin de la tuer ... coups de haches, ce que cette femme voyant, elle se mit à se defendre comme une lionne ... ils la jetèrent bas comme morte et alors un de ces Haudenosaunee se jeta sur elle afin de lui lever le chevelure ... mais notre amazone se sentant ainsi saisie, tout d'un coup reprit ses sens, se leva et plus furieuse que jamais elle saisit ce cruel avec tant de violence par un endroit que la pudeur nous défend de nommer, qu'a paine se peut-il échapper, il lui donnait des coups de hache par la tête, toujours elle tenait bon jusqu'... ce que dérechef elle tomba evanoüie par terre ... cet Haudenosaunee [essayait de] ... s'enfuir au plus vite").[138] Father Charlevoix chronicled the arrival of women to Canada, who were celebrated as if they were heroines: "raised in abundance and delicacy ... they left their gentle and calm life to come to teach their children and care for their ill ... which was for the entire city a holiday ... The governer general received these hero-ines at the riverside ... [and] the head of the troups ... sounded the canon ... he brought them to the centre of public acclamation to the church for thanksgiving" ("élevée dans l'abondance & la délicatesse ... quittaient une vie douce & tranquille pour venir instruire leurs Enfans & prendre soin de leurs Malades ... fut pour toute la ville un jour de Fête ... le Gouverneur reçut ces Heroînes sur le Rivage ... la tête des Troupes ... & au bruit du canon ... il les mena au milieu des acclamations du Peuple à l'Eglise en actions de graces").[139]

The women of Quebec were more traditional, while the women of Mon-treal acquired more Native norms and were called "demie-sauvagesses." This gap began with the wealthy benefactresses who founded Montreal and were prominent in hospital charity and female education. Seasonal male absences encouraged women to hold the home ground and defend the vulnerably flat outpost of Montreal from Haudenosaunee raids. Sulpician autonomy also spared the city two decades of governorial, Jesuit, and bishopric domination, which otherwise could have entrenched French patriarchal norms. William Eccles and Denys Delâge remark that, in the eighteenth century, the Montrealers dubbed the Quebecois "sheep," while they themselves were referred to as "wolves."[140] Quebec meant civilization as opposed to the "wilder-ness" of Montreal. The historical crises of 1648 and 1661 were salient watermarks catalyzing this perceived cultural oppositioning. We must remember that, after 1665, downriver Montreal was not populated primarily by country girls but by Parisiennes. The post–1665 request for sturdy country women who could endure the rigours of Canadian life, rather than the delicate urban girls who made up the previous contingents of the filles du roi ships, indicate not only that the conditions in northern north America were more rigorous than the harshest conditions in France, but that urban elite ideals for women were doubly inappropriate to Canadian circumstance. Decidedly, French and Canadian men commended French Canadian women who demonstrated notable fortitude, initiative, and resourcefulness, indicating the growth of an alternative, more energetic, Nativized female norm. In 1664 Marie de L'Incarnation tried to use her monastery as a refuge for French girls because otherwise she saw them Nativizing and becoming even more "wild" than the Natives themselves ("elles seraient aussi sauvages, et peut-être plus que les sauvages mêmes").[141]

RAGING GRANNY VERSUS THE GREAT SERPENT

Together with the social tie of twin fraternity was the twinning of myths and rituals as evolving themes reflecting previous historical realities. Mythical symbols themselves are fragments of histories or rituals, reoriented within a unique bricolage that represents important community problems. One of the key methods of decoding meaning involves the reconstruction of those primordial events and their successive layers of significance. French north Atlantic provincial dualistic beliefs were in a dialogue with Native folk wisdom, and this was an essential key to the integration of two unlike societies. The sacred unlike twins mirrored concrete social twinships. This conceptual duality provided a psycho-socio-cultural space for working through social duality. Sociologist Schmuel Eisenstadt's recent formulation specifies that socially relevant myths of duality often concern themselves with the human being and the choice between good and evil – like that of the present "raging Granny," or genetrix, versus the Great Serpent.[142]

Great Serpent Oyalerowek, in the famous Wendat Tree of Dreams (l'arbre des songes) so popular in Quebec, came from the Wendat mission reserve of Lorette. This myth, seemingly didactically constructed by the Jesuits, presents the moral dilemma of choosing between two poles, Good and Evil, of which the assumedly prelapsarian Wendat had been innocent. This scenario was presumedly set in order to develop their sense of Counter-Reformation free will and, it was hoped, their choice of Good. This concept countered the Protestant concept of predestination and illustrated the social paradigm of the nasty Bruslé, with the good Amantacha, as well as both Father Brébeuf and Chief Annaotaha alone against the Haudenosaunee, whom they conceived of as "evil."

In addition, Eisenstadt writes that there is a close relation between symbolization, the boundaries of the social collective, and the construction of trust, all of which regulate exchange between the polarities.[143] The genetrix versus Great Serpent symbolism reflects clearly the construction of meaning by articulators of cultural models (i.e., the missionaries). French missionaries were troubled by the Native manitous, or okis, which the Counter-Reformation Church perceived as akin to pagan Celtic or Germanic gods and spirits whom they determinedly banned and demonized, yet whom the Nativized French habitants were careful to appease. If the local French fairy was no longer there to protect the fountain, at least St Anne was, as well as the local Aboriginal manitou.

A mythical genesis occurred in French Canada. Elements of parallellism and polar duality of beliefs were the result of the French-Iroquoian, including the Wendat, dialogue. In contrast, fusion, métissage, and collage of beliefs was the ordinary outcome of the French-Algonquian dialogue. Why were these two dialogues so different?

There was also a French-Algonquian dialogue that often resulted in the métissage of opposite elements due to French familiarity with North Atlantic Algonquian and innovation with Great Lakes Algonquians. The Atlantic Algonquians must be distinguished from lakeland Algonquians. Each had a different relationship with the French under different circumstances. Atlantic Algonquians lived interdependently with the French in close geographical proximity or within the habitations, but lakeland Algonquians were frequently fleeing from the Haudenosaunee and had constructed mixed-band settlements together with the French. The result was a mix of peoples. In the Atlantic area, the fusion of French and Atlantic Algonquian tales was so extensive that separate elements may be indistinguishable, yet Bailey signals that it is essential to ascertain the time and circumstances of that fusion.[144] By contrast, the lakeland Algonquians were often unfamiliar, their myths were collaged, and intact nuggets of each culture were still clearly visible. The lakeland diffusion of collaged French-Algonquian cycles extended over the North American continent. Therefore, in both the Atlantic and inland Algonquian cases, cultural hybridity was the norm, yet while it was more fused along the Atlantic, in the Great Lakes area it was patchier and noticeably bricolé.

Dialogue between the French in New France and the Wendat was typically utopian. The French embraced a good/evil duality. Bipolar contrasts were intended to be didactic and conversionary, with the Wendat at the good pole, while the "misguided" Haudenosaunee and erring French were at the opposite pole. This illustrates no small effort on the part of the Jesuits to provide instruction for the French. This duality also reflected the pre-1649 struggle between Attignawantan (Bear tribe) Christians and Attignonnahak (Deer tribe) traditionalists. The Bear tribe refugees who came to Ile d'Orléans were Christians, open to the polarity between Mother Mary or St Anne versus Satan, which mirrored the previous juxtapositions. Interpretation of the traumatic partial annihilation campaign and diaspora they underwent was most often defined as a struggle between good and evil. If this were not the case it would have been difficult to extract any narrative and personal meaning in what they had suffered (which is an important element in the meaning-making required in order to overcome trauma). Oppositions and contrasts frequently helped interpret the extremely traumatic events of attempted tribicide, complemented by partial incorporation through cultural reprogramming, and the extinction of a prosperous and safe cultural homeland – Wendake. An evolving conceptual reorientation, along with the reweaving of versions from various perspectives, occurred as the dispersed Wendat attempted to keep their connections and map out a new future. These important contrasts were also used by the Jesuits to construct meaning for the Christian Wendat. For the converted, the Jesuits were key articulators who helped guide them through the intricacies of combined cultural models.

Christian saints and Native manitous struggled in the bid for ultimate control. While Native traditionalists were more sceptical of than hostile towards Christianity, missionaries often set up a conceptual rivalry in their bid to attain converts. Yet between the two extremes of syncretism and polarity, most French and Native realignment of loyalties generally tolerated a degree of co-existence. The following myth creates a world where both Mary or Anne and the Great Serpent co-exist for both French and Wendat. The historical configuration begs to be decoded behind the myth, bringing us closer to its significance. Thus, the "ghosts" of Mary and the Great Serpent co-exist and exert a phantom influence upon mutual interethnic dialogue.

As the unlike twin was a myth that became history, so history was also mythologized. A mirror version of the Amantacha-Bruslé twinship, the paradigm of the unworthy Christian Frenchman with his worthy neophyte Wendat twin was embodied in the famous "Tree of Dreams" (l'arbre des songes.) This tale was formulated in the Wendat mission reserve of Lorette for Christian neophytes, but it became widely popular in French Canadian folklore because the Wendat of Lorette have been renowned for being part and parcel of Quebecois "vieille-souche" culture. The myth runs thus: a pious elderly Amerindian, Haouroukai, slept under a tree at the mouth of the St Charles River (Oria8enrak: trout river), dreaming that the Wendat Christian agricultural village patron, Our Lady of Lorette (Notre-Dame de Lorette), opened the doors of heaven for him when he died. When an arrogant French Canadian youth (in some versions, a Wendat), Otsitot, imitated him to obtain the same grace, the manitou serpent called Oyalerowek rose from the water, called him Carcajou, offered him money, clothes, endless food, a bottomless liquor bottle, and the chief's daughter (all of which signified the five Catholic cardinal sins) if the youth would worship him. The youth accepted, and before his death by drunkenness, the serpent prevented the absolution of his sins by the "black robe" (Jesuit).[145]

In decoding this sacred story, we must first consider the implied twinning of Aataentsic with the French maternal genetrix in the guises of Mother Mary or her mother Anne. Grandmotherly Aataentsic was the creator of all humankind, the foundation of clan matrilineality, and her name means "fertile earth," which in the Mohawk Iroquoian dialect was "Awenhai." Before giving birth, she literally fell from the heavens to earth, landing on the back of a turtle, who proceeded to create a suitable earth island for her birthing bed at the nativity of her unlike twins. Turtle Island became North America. After giving birth, Aataentsic mirrored the moon, which clearly demonstrates her correlated opposite function from Mary in the guise of a Diana-like figure. In Wendat lore Aataentsic still retained the more ancient attributes of power over life and death, and the power to do both good and evil.

The bad French twin with the good Wendat twin, their saviours being a Jesuit version of a corrupt pagan Leviathan Manitou and the saintly Mary, respectively, reversed the equation entirely. The symbol of the serpent as Manitou is a bricolage of both European and Native heritages.[146] Early pagan and Christian significances nuanced the rich Breton, Norman, and Poitevin meaning of the serpent for the French in Canada.

Initially, neolithic European and Levantine goddesses were often part serpent, as were Greek and Roman sibyls.[147] A serpent guarded a pure water fountain where Cadmus, Europa's brother, killed the sacred snake, with the result that, in revenge, Jupiter struck down his entire family and metamorphosed him and his wife into serpents. During the plague of Athens, Thucidides related that, due to drought, the serpents poisoned all the wells and springs. Discord and the Medusa had serpents as hair. Lucretius wrote of the "simulacrum" as an immortal double that appeared like shed skins of serpents on Feralia, the Day of the Dead.[148] The biblical pythoness of Ein Dor conjured the spirit of Samuel for King Saul, who foretold his downfall at Mt Tabor.[149] In the final analysis, the serpent was thought capable of divining the future, but it was also the Hebrew and Christian symbol of Satan.[150]

Celtic and Nordic lore literally bristle with sea serpent tales, like Beowulf.[151] The Nordic sea monster (Midgard Serpent) encircled the world from jaw to tail, and at the Final Conflagration (Ragnarok) he flooded the world and drowned the combatants.[152] In Norman folklore, the serpent of Villedieu des Bailleul was a church dedicated to St John the Baptist, given by Henri I to the chevaliers of Jerusalem.[153] Leviathan was the form of Satan invoked most frequently by the possessed nuns of Normandy and Poitou during the witchhunt years, and it characterized the all-encompassing jaws of Hell.

In Brittany, Celtic goddesses and druidesses, divined with snakes wound around their arms, and a serpent's egg (Anguinum) was the Druidic symbol.[154] The wisdom of serpents (seraphim) come from this, and the Christian Ophites. This corresponds with the St Patrick legend, which holds that, through his prayers, he banished all the snakes in Ireland. Carnac in Brittany was built in serpentine fashion, which can be seen from the Mont-St-Michel.[155] The Maypole and Easter eggs symbolized the ancient serpent with its eggs at springtime. Gerhild Williams demonstrates how, by the later Middle Ages, the fairy-serpent was perceived as a satanic succubus, particularly as she was supposedly raised at her aunt Morgana's in Avalon.[156] In Poitou, this heritage was transformed during the course of the Middle Ages through the perennial legend of the serpentine fairy Mélusine, who evidently prevented the church of Parthenay-le-Vieux in Poitou from being completely built, saved the tower of Bruges from destruction by King Louis x, predicted the death of Henri iv, and prevented the chateau of Lusignan in Poitou from being destroyed.[157]

The serpent was not loved in Native culture either. It was the Algonquian symbol for their enemies, the Haudenosaunee. In an Atlantic Algonquian myth, Gluscap, the culture hero, struggled with the sea monster, squeezing him into a bullfrog, and freed floods of fresh water for the thirsty people.[158] Nanabozo, the Anishinabe demiurge, also struggled with the evil Great Serpent Meshekenabek of Manitou Lake, which sent all the little snakes running. Nanabozo warned the Anishinabe that snakes want revenge, so they took refuge in the Lake Superior area. When it began to flood, he sent small animals to dive for a bit of earth, from which he made land.[159] A similar Cree tale was told of Misikinipik, the horned serpent under the world and waters, who fought the thunder beings.[160] The Kickapoo River has Algonquian Great Serpent mounds, and these are also found in Brush Creek, Granville, and Tarlton, Ohio; Prairie du Chien, Wisconsin, and Prairie de la Porte, Iowa.[161] The Algonquians told of the manitou of Belle Isle and Detroit, who was shattered by the missionaries, after which each stone became a rattlesnake to guard the site from marauders.[162] The Odawa of Odanak also contributed a sea serpent tale to later French Canadian lore.[163] In Haudenosaunee lore, Ototarho, the fierce chief, was only convinced to lay down the tomahawk by Hiawatha by having his snake-hair combed, thus straightening out the tangles. There are also many Wendat sea-serpent myths, in which the serpent is called grandfather and receives gifts of tobacco.[164] It is no wonder that, before the general confessions following the 1663 earthquake, French guilt for Wendat massacres expressed itself in visions of flaming serpents. The Wendat who fled west from the Haudenosaunee found refuge with the Odawa and around the Great Lakes, and later continued to migrate to Ohio, while some eventually reached Oklahoma. These Wyandots, or Wyandottes, have continued to recite serpent monster myths, saying that they originate with the cosmogonical bad brother Tah-weh-skah-reh (Wyandot version of Ta8iscaron, the bad twin of good Ioskeha). An alternate version is that they come from the Hooh-keh giants, who followed the Wyandot migration by wriggling after them, and were transformed into huge serpents who plagued and tormented the Wyandots for centuries. Their bodies incised the rivers, to the Great Lakes, where they now live in the depths of the waters.[165] The origin of the later Wyandot Snake Clan was linked to a grandmother's ambitious delaying of her granddaughter's choice of manitou in her fasting rite of passage, wherein the sea serpent carried off the lone girl. In some versions, she successfully escaped from her snake husband.[166] This tale appears as the inverse mirror-image of the European Mélusine tale, itself based upon Celtic fairy beliefs and in the power of druidesses to shapeshift.

The streets of Lorette today are still ostensibly marked by the contortions of the Great Serpent, Oyalerowek, who formerly infested Lorette and was exorcised by a Jesuit missionary with a cross and Holy Water – signifying the opposition of Christianity to a Native manitou who appears to the missionary as Satanic.[167] This opposition could also be interpreted as the triumph of Christian sexual mores over the lascivious Oyalerowek as the phallic Wendat snake. It could also be seen as the mythologizing of an inverted tale of Father Brébeuf, the Jesuit, finally winning the battle over the Haudenosaunee serpent, chasing him into water instead of himself being consumed by the opposite element – fire. From another angle, we can see the switch from the male-serpent struggling in a concrete battle to a less direct rivalry between the masculine sexual imagery of the snake and the motherly influence of Mary or Anne. In the Jesuit version, the polarities of water and fire refer to John the Baptist. John the Baptist's prophecy refers to baptism first by water, then by fire, and, finally, by the Holy Ghost.

From the sociological angle, the symbol of the snake was a "ghostly" collage of both European and Native sources with a historically and socially relevant thrust. The legend reflects the contrast between "wolverine and satanic" Bruslé and the "neophyte and saintly" Amantacha. These twins' functions were symmetrical and their relationship reciprocal, but their behavior was reversed. This primary twin pair has been overlaid in the myth by others: the drama between Brébeuf and the Haudenosaunee, the Christian God and the Native manitou, Mary/Anne and the Great Serpent, and Christian and Native mores. "L'arbre des songes" thus appears as mythicized history, which helped reinforce the Frenchification of Lorette Wendat socio-cultural heritage.

As mentioned, for both French and Algonquians, a serpent was the worst epithet they could use. The French called the coercive tax farmers serpents, while the Algonquians called the Haudenosaunee serpents.[168] Thus, the social switch from victimizing the stranger to victimizing the war captive was also effected on a conceptual level. The expletive of "serpent" was not used upon members of the community, according to both André Lachance's and Peter Moogk's study of insults.[169] Nevertheless, it is notable that, as a popular French Canadian myth, even from Lorette, it was the French youth and not the pious Native youth who succumbed to temptation.

This tale was conjured through a dream, and the French youth died of alcoholic overindulgence. The dream was an important guiding institution in Native culture, while alcohol was a social tool in French culture. As Mechal Sobel has adroitly observed, the dreamscape provided a protected space for negotiations with the Other and a reacceptance of part of the "abjured self."[170] Yet there are also resemblances between the two consciousness alterations that permit a kind of consciousness "voyage." This the Wendat interpreted as felicitous, while the French missionaries usually perceived both dream and liquour "voyages" in exceedingly dubious terms (unless they were their own). Dreams were the Wendat indication either that the patient had unfulfilled wishes (ondinnonc) of the soul (onraon) or that the dead were interfering with one's health. Brébeuf aptly described the dream as being "the oracle that these poor peoples [sic] consult and listen to, the prophet that predicts the future, the Cassandra who warns them of menacing troubles, it is their regular physician ... their Mercury when they travel ... the principal God of the Hurons" ("l'oracle que tous ces pauures Peuples consultent & escoutent, le Prophète qui leur predit ls choses futures, la Cassandre qui les advertit des malheurs qui menacent, le Medecin ordinaire ... leur Mercure dans leurs voyages ... le principal Dieu des Hurons").[171] European dream tales like John Milton's *Paradise Lost*, but especially John Bunyan's *Pilgrim's Progress* (1678) (which was so popular in New England), served to expand consciousness in the dreamspace for social and cultural negotiation. In the latter, the hero is continually tempted by Satan, yet instead of going to Hell like the French youth, he simply wakes up. Alcohol was used by Europeans to celebrate, especially among seafaring Atlantic coast residents, but it was condemned. Native peoples, by contrast, used drunkenness to simulate the journey to the "country of souls." The Wendat saw both dreams and alcohol as opportunities to bond with ancestors, reevaluate one's situation, and resolve communal predicaments, particularly since consciousness was significantly raised through the 1649 genocide and diaspora. And "firewater" can refer to baptism by both fire and water.

If there is a historical basis for this myth, it can be conjectured that it was cobbled together by the Jesuits to guide history back into myth.[172] The missionaries sought didactically to caution against syncretism on the part of settlers who were liable to transfer their submerged Celtic fairy and dolmen beliefs from north Atlantic France to the local pagan manitou in Canada. The tale also reflects late seventeenth-century official stigmatization of the

"Nativized" coureurs de bois, the purpose of which was to encourage a compact Laurentian agricultural colony, as the mid-seventeenth century fur trade had encouraged a Wendat-type division of labour in French society, with men trading far from home while the women farmed. Additionally, the tale appears to underline the missionary conviction that the ultimate value of a human being rests upon his or her worthy behaviour and choices rather than upon any religious background. This attitude reinforced communal trust and Jesuit admiration for utopian aspects of Wendat behaviour, and it underlined the ultimate European challenge.

CHAPTER SIX

Je me souviens

Models, symbols, and myths that developed in settler society were the fruit of Native influence and dialogue. The Native sharing ethic and "dread of losing face" shaped early French North American cultural ideals through their convergence with provincial French aristocratic ideals of libéralité (generosity) and honneur (bravery), both of which evinced settler reverence. Intertwined, these combined qualities comprised the older French ideal of an "homme de coeur" – a generous man willing to risk himself to protect the defenceless.[1] This ideal reflects the lengthy vulnerability of small European tribes to invasions from the East and later (after the decline of the Roman Empire) to internal dissention. The rise of knightly warlords who shared power with educated missionaries offered the populace protection while the latter offered the former their fidelity and labour within the evolving feudal system. By the early modern era, early colonization enabled further economic growth and urbanization, which saw the rise of a wealthier aristocracy and its subsequent struggle to establish its primacy, stability, and standardization. For the Mi'kmaq, this medieval homme de coeur ideal exactly corresponded with the meki'k mkamlamun (Great Heart), a name of honour.[2] Frenchwomen focused upon charitable works, while Frenchmen focused on bravery. Yet this older aristocratic model was delegitimized in Paris for it was the provincial ideal of the sword nobility. Instead, the Crown rewarded the value of courtly polish and egotism (amour-propre) of the robe nobility (noble de robe) while forbidding the duels identified with the older sword nobility (noble d'épée). Insubordinate aristocrats and their knightly values were especially admired by north Atlantic insurgents who, to resist the incursions of royal administration, taxes, and Parisian culture, returned to the familiar provincial aristocratic culture of the past.[3] Early French Canadian youth joined the ideal of the homme de coeur with Native models to create upwardly mobile identities in their new environment.

CARITAS

The Native sharing ethic was initially seen by French missionaries as charity, yet it was generally viewed by the poorer immigrants as both charity and aristocratic liberalité. Charity was sorely tried with an unprecedented flood of the destitute in the metropolis during the seventeenth century. Good works increasingly became the exclusive domain of devoted women often inspired by Olivier Maillard in Brittany, St Vincent de Paul, or St. François de Sales. During the Middle Ages sharing food with a stranger was a standard indication of heroic or saintly generosity, which, it was hoped, would fall upon a wandering fairy, angel, or Christ himself. Medieval charity lessened in the seventeenth century as growing contingents of roaming beggars (mostly women and children) and bandits flooded the roads due to inadequate alms. Townspeople were frightened, and the uprooted poor were forced to wear insignia.[4] The Parisian parlement imprisoned, sent to galleys, branded, and banished beggars and vagabonds. Even the Rouen parlement deliberated during the Nu-pieds revolt over punishment for the poor.[5] While men usually organized the social control of the working poor, women generally organized aid to the sick and helpless in hospitals, orphanages, and infirmaries. These were increasingly dealt with by founding hospitals and general alms offices. French wills still often gave donations to the poor: 60 percent in Paris, 25 percent in Lyon; and in Normandy, Easter was the perfect Sunday for alms.[6] Yet funerals were sometimes mobbed by the poor to the point where people were crushed to death.

Despite this, the ideal of charity was alive and well among those who financed Canadian enterprises, especially among idealistic wealthy widows. French devotees, Ursulines, the Filles de la Charité, and the Hospitallers were extremely generous in their medical, religious, and gastronomical services to Native neighbours, by which they hoped to demonstrate Catholic good works. Generosity seemed to herd Natives, like the French poor, gently into the Christian fold.

The ancient provincial French noble d'épée "libéralité," although requesting political rewards from their aristocratic "betters," still benefitted those on the lower rungs.[7] On the other hand, French noble privileges were based upon the wealth that was already present or accrued, yet simultaneously gained through hosting banquets and gift-giving. Naturally the king was the most "generous" peer of all, for while his taxmen bled the population all year long, he pardoned their theft of royal funds every Easter.[8]

Thus, in seventeenth-century France, giving and sharing was essentially the realm of either mostly charitable religious women who selflessly cared for helpless unfortunates or "largesse" on the part of the great nobility.[9] Sharing norms were much paler among the people, although in areas with large common pastures and fields such as Lorraine, both sharing and witchcraft accusations were high. In northwestern France, the sheer amount of bocages, hedged fields, and impenetrable marshland largely prevented intense neighbourliness and the high degree of friction that could be generated during stressful times. The main exceptions to this general tenor were the unusually fertile areas of Normandy, where neighbourly and familial legal chicanery was pronounced. As Breton Noël du Faïl wrote, "There was never a feast day when someone in the village didn't invite all the rest to dinner to eat his hen, gosling, and ham. But nowadays ... the hens and goslings are scarcely fat enough when they are carried off to be sold for money to pay Monsieur the Lawyer ... to mistreat his neighbor."[10] Nevertheless, while sharing was on the wane in general, this societal function of caring for the needy was taken on largely by pious women. As common sharing became eclipsed by parsimony or calculation, collective admiration of the liberal seigneur led the common folk to doubly aspire to become rich and to gain hard-won prestige.

NATIVE SHARING ETHIC

Sharing is the diametric opposite of charity because common distribution obviates the need for charity: weak and strong both contribute to, and are served from, the same pot. Sharing was the first secret of Native survival and was the Native characteristic most valued by the French regime. The giving of mutual hospitality intensified bonds between French and Native.[11] Champlain remarked that Innu chief "Anadabijou ... received us very well, according to the custom of the country" ("Anadabijou ... nous receu fort bien selon la coustume du pays"); of an Innu that had been received by Louis XIII: "his speech on the good reception that he had by the [French] King ... and that they were assured that His Majesty had good intentions, and desired to people their homeland ... [Anadabijou said] that they had to be very happy to have His Majesty as a great friend." ("sa harangue de la bonne reception que leur auoit fait le Roy ... & qu'ils s'asseurassent que saditte Maiesté leur voulloit du bien, & desiroit peupler leur terre ... [Anadabijou said] ils deuoient estre fort contents d'auoir saditte Maiest, pour grand amy.") Sagard noted that hospitality was reciprocal: "The wildmen [Natives] have a noble character in that they give liberally ... . a type of contract ... I give you so you can give to me." ("Les Sauvages ont de cela de noble qu'ils donnent liberalement ... vne facon de contract ... Ie te donne a fin que tu me donnes.")[12] Extended hospitality was similarly offered to French guests among the tribes, where they had the opportunity to witness ordinary sharing, Native-style. Brébeuf commended the Wendat: "This nation is very hospitable ... and you can stay as long as you want, and will always be well treated ... it is the custom of the country, and when you leave, it is for a ho, ho, ho, ouecti, or a great thank you" ("ceste Nation ... est fort hospitaliere ... & vous y demeurez tant qu'il vous plaist, tousiours bien traité ... la facon du pays & au partir de la vous en voyla quitte pour vn ho, ho, ho, outoécti, ou vn grand mercy"). And "they give much to one another ... they give feasts to the whole village, and their hospitality toward all kinds of strangers is remarkable. During these feasts, they present the best of what they have prepared ... they never refuse their door to a stranger ... they share with him the choicest of what they have." ("Ils s'entredonnent beaucoup ... ils ont font festin à tout le village; l'hospitalité envers toute sorte d'estrangers y est remarquable. Ils leurs presentent en ces festins ce qu'ils ont preparé de meilleur ... Ils ne refusent iamais la porte ... vn Estranger ... ils luy font part de ce qu'ils ont de meilleur.")[13]

Joseph LeCaron noted that he was excellently recieved by the Wendat but not by the Tobacco nation, who probably had less to give.[14] LeClercq admired the fact that the Mi'kmaq gave "charitably to those that have nothing ... widows and orphans receive presents ... . the children and seniors ... it would be an eternal reproach, if they knew that a Wildman [Native] had food in abundance, and did not share it with those who did not have enough" ("charitablement à ceux qui n'ont point ... les veuves & les orphelins recoivent des presens ... enfans les anciens ... un reproche eternel, si on scavoit qu'un sauvage aiant des vivres en abondance, n'en eut pas fait largesse à ceux qu'il scauroit dans la disette").[15] Pierre Boucher marvelled at the Algonquians, among whom he had found a wife: "they are very charitable, and easily lodge strangers and voyagers, without a thought to any reward, and there are several who leave their own beds ... to give them ... to eat the best of what they have, and frequently ... a man they have never seen, and perhaps will never see again" ("Ils sont fort aumosniers, & logent facilement les Estrangers & Voyageurs, sans esperance d' aucun salaire, & il y en a plusieurs qui Quittent leurs lits ... leur donnant à manger ce qu'ils ont de meilleur, & cela assez souuent à vn homme qu'ils n'ont iamais veu, & qu'ils ne verront peut-estre iamais"). And regarding Wendat and Haudenosaunee (Iroquois) care of the poor: "When there is some family who has fallen in want, there are some chiefs who go about the towns gathering wheat [i.e., cornmeal] for the subsistence of these poor people, each gives according to his own capacity" ("Quand il y a quelque famille qui est tombé en necessité de vivres, il y a des Capitaines qui vont par le Bourg ramasser du bled pour la subsistance de ces pauures gens, chaqu'un donne ... selon son pouvoir").[16] Sagard marvelled that "they have no poor beggars among them ... they send of their goods to the homes of the needy ill, widows, and orphans" ("ils n'ont aucun pauvres mendiants parmy eux ... enuent de leurs biens iusques dans les maisons necessiteux malades, veuues & orphelins").[17]

The worst insult one could give to someone was to call them "Medousaouek" (Huron: avaricious).[18] For the Natives a true Aienda8asti (Huron: civilized man) was, first and foremost, generous.[19] The baron de Lahontan commented: "The Savages are utter strangers to distinctions of property, for what belongs to one is equally another's" and elsewhere criticized the French: "those [Natives] that were in France often tormented me about all the ills that they saw and all the disorders that are committed in our cities over money" ("Ceux qui ont été en France m'ont souvent tourment, sur tous les maux qu'ils y ont vu faire & sur tous les désordres qui se commettent dans nos Villes pour de l'argent"). According to trader Nicolas Perrot: "The hospitality that they practice surpasses every European norm" ("L'hospitalité qu'ils exercent surpasse toutes celles du commun chez les Europeans").[20] The Natives roundly scolded the French for their shocking avarice and attributed it to lack of common sense : "they pillage and steal from one another ... anytime that they find the occasion to do it with impunity ... they lie without scruples as soon as it concerns their own interest" ("ils se pillent & se volent ... toutes les fois qu'ils trouvent l'occasion de le faire impunément ... mentent sans scrupule dès qu'il s'agît de leur interet").[21] Lafitau perceived that the Native peoples "exercise toward strangers and the miserable a charitable hospitality, that would utterly confound all the nations of Europe" ("exercent envers les etrangers et les malheureux une charitable hospitalité, qui a de quoi faire confondre toutes les nations d'Europe").[22]

Native right to rule was not founded upon the prestige of wealth but the prestige of magnanimity. Pierre Boucher wrote : "Generosity is esteemed among them, this is why the chiefs are ordinarily poorer than the others ... they give everything, to attract the affection of their people" ("La libéralité parmy eux est estimée; c'est d'ou vient que les Capitaines sont ordinairement plus pauures que les autres ... ils donnent tout, pour attirer l'affection de leurs gens").[23] Antoine Denis Raudot wrote that "war chiefs ... [are the] most poorly dressed of the nation, giving everything to make themselves liked."[24] And Bacqueville de la Potherie commented: "It is a beautiful quality among the wildmen [Natives], to be considered generous ... it is the role of the chiefs to prodigiously give everything that they possess to others" ("C'est une belle qualité parmi les Sauvages, de passer pour libéral ... c'est le propre des Chefs de prodiguer tout ce qu'ils ont").[25] LeClercq remarked that chiefs particularly were judged according to their poverty after giving to the poor, sick, and strangers: "show that you have a veritably dignified chief's heart" ("fais paraitre que ton coeur est un véritable coeur de Capitaine & digne").[26] Natives were always willing to host the French for exchanges or when the latter were in need, especially dating from the 1628 Kirke conquest of Quebec, where almost eighty French were hosted by different allies. This attitude is well summed up by Bruce Trigger: "All forms of generosity were publicly noted and acclaimed and were a major source of power and influence. The desire to win prestige therefore provided a major stimulus for economic activities ... Failure to redistribute was penalized by hostile gossip, denunciations, and in extreme cases accusations of sorcery."[27] Champlain tells us that, in Wendake, if someone did not receive a gift, a stone was placed next to the offender, and the injured party left so as not to lose face and returned singing to feign nonchalance.[28] Innu chief Erouachy was so upset at the puny gift of figs offered by the French traders when their ships arrived from France prior to 1632 that he advised his men to plunder the ship and offer few pelts in return.[29] Wealthy converts were even threatened with death for refusing to ritually share.[30] Even today, the "sharing ethic" is still prominent in Native culture. The Native belief in the need for sharing was intertwined with the primary importance of familial and communal trust and goodwill.

Hunters, of course, were consistently in a better position to give than were others. According to John Price, because sharing is a largely unconscious function in society, "the language and analysis of sharing is poorly developed. However, sharing is expressed in ethical rituals ... the ritual sharing of large game animals is usually made in sharing terms, not in reciprocity terms ... while food sharing is uncommon among herbivores and fruit-eaters generally ... [due to] an unequal exchange, because some people are consistently in a better position to give. Sharing is characterized by the attitude that each person will do what is appropriate, not by an expectation of an equivalent return."[31] Price's point concerning the importance of sharing behaviour among carnivores generally is interesting when we consider how ubiquitous it was among the Innu. A ruckus was caused at the Quebec Hospital in 1640 when Innu routinely shared their medicines, regardless of their illnesses.[32] Yet this value has two expressions. One was that of simple sharing, or equitable distribution, which usually applied to the family, adoptee, band or tribe, and even intertribal sharing and hospitality among allies.[33] The second was reciprocal gift-giving, which involved a formal ceremony generally related to diplomacy, trade, barter, and military endeavours.

But the most sensitive act of gift-giving was that offering reconciliation after a murder within the tribe or between allies. In Wendake, two categories of gifts were required. The first were Andaonhaan, to neutralize vengeance; the second were Andaerraehaan, to give to the cadaver. The first category consisted of nine subcategories: (1) condayee (gift worth a thousand wampum beads) to remove the ax from the wound and place it in the avenger's hand, (2) to wipe the head wound blood, (3) to aid the village to heal, (4) to put a stone on the earth's cleavage caused by murder, (5) to clear the roads and remove the bushes, (6) to give sacred tobacco, (7) to give back sense to the aggrieved, (8) to provide drink for the aggrieved mother, and (9) to provide a mat for her to sleep upon during her mourning. The Andaerraehaan were to relieve the cadaver from pain.[34]

AROUND THE KETTLE

In seventeenth-century north America, however, the sharing ethic was driven through sheer necessity and was widely admired by French and Natives alike.[35] The bid for French aristocratic libéralité, and the fainter echo of clerical hospitality and handouts to encourage Native conversions, also encouraged the development of this ethic.[36] LeClercq remarks that the Native sharing ethic was a "beautiful lesson ... for the rich who lacked pity and those hearts of stone, who have only guts of iron for their close ones and comrades ... that they are only depositaries of Providence and would not have put these riches into their hands, if they would not put it to saintly use of alms and charity" ("belle instruction ... pour les riches impitoïables & ces coeurs de roche, qui n'ont que les entrailles de fer pour leurs semblables ... dont la Providence ne les a fait que dépositaires, & ne les a mis entre leurs mains, que pour en faire un saint usage d'aumônes & de charité").[37] The first French Canadian model of Native-style sharing was the home of Guillaume Couillart and Guillemette Hébert Couillart, who fed the entire settlement by sharing their pioneer crops during the 1628–29 Kirke occupation of Quebec. Champlain entrusted them with his adopted Innu daughters, and they were among the first to be ennobled and enfiefed in Canada for their public service to the entire community.[38]

Sharing among and between habitants and Native allies became customary due to the tone set by the Natives. The French initiated seasonal winter feeding of starving Innu during bad hunting seasons,[39] cared for adopted First Nations children even during the worst starvation of 1628–29, provided free Catholic education for Native children, and held an open-door winter hospital policy, which cared for the invalid, elderly, and children of the Innu and other Algonquians who winter hunted. The latter reciprocated by bringing back fresh game. The French also fed, clothed, and helped house several hundred Wendat after the fall of Wendake. Wendat chief Atironta, his wife Catharine, two year-old Mathieu, and Jacques Acharro, all Wendat, lived at the Quebec Hospital. The Jesuits gave the Wendat wheat and eels in 1645, and gave the Algonquins (probably Noel or Iean Baptiste) several food items in November 1645, including cloth and two barrels of peas, as well as spending about a thousand écus on the Sillery reserve mission.[40] French Canadians preferred taking refuge in hospitable Native communities, while French traders and administrators opted for returning to France[41] In 1680, forty to fifty starving Gaspesians sought succor from Mme Denis of River Ste-Croix, who gave them bread, flour, peas, meat, and fish.[42]

Generosity modelled by Natives and French elite, also finally benefited those on the lower rungs. The governor, the Ursulines, and the Jesuits all gave the French Canadian poor alms of over 200 écus before Christmas.[43] Besides the Quebec and Montreal hospitals, the Quebec General Hospital was founded after Louis XIV took the settlement; and in 1688, three Bureaux des pauvres were erected in the main towns.[44] Self-amelioration was a central aim of all immigrants, yet self-aggrandizement at the cost of the community was frowned upon. A negative model of inflated privilege was the immensely unpopular Governor Jean de Lauson, who obtained huge quantities of land for his own family while in office. Needless to say, the settlement burst into rejoicing when he returned to France. De Lauson held 66 percent of 9,600,000 arpents, which was 96.4 percent of seigneurial land then held in Canada. This was over six times more land than was held by the next titled noble seigneur in New France.[45] His hoarding was regarded as a sign of privilege and power in France, while in Native communities and the French north American settlement proper, it was viewed as grossly inappropriate behaviour that was both an abuse of privilege and an insult to the community.

Examples of social models that received political standing for their famed generosity were Marie Rollet Hébert, Marie Barbe de Boullongne (the governor-general's wife), Anne Gasnier Bourdon, Governor Maisonneuve,[46] Jeanne Mance,[47] Madeleine de la Peltrie,[48] Marguerite Bourgeoys, and Catherine Ganeacteua, Erie, founder of Prairie de la Madeleine.[49] Even Bishop Laval, generally avoided for his meddling and severity, set an example of generosity so illuminating that the popular Pierre Boucher exclaimed: "he is everything to everyone, he becomes poor to enrich the needy, and resembles the bishops of the Primitive Church" ("il est tout ... à tous, il se fait pauvre pour enrichir les pauvres, & ressemble aux Evesques de la primitive Eglise").[50] In Canada, this norm was generalized, especially when the "mérite" criterion became the official classification for the Communauté des habitants. Canadian wills during the French regime usually donated to the poor. The donated total for good works (203,566 livres [average 410]) was twice the amount of that for prayers for themselves. The French North American donated an average of 205 livres, which was literally four times more than what was donated in Provence in France.[51]

Outsiders to the community were treated well, unlike in France, where they were feared. The stranger was feted with hospitality and presents, while the Haudenosaunee enemy was the focus of fear. These opposite approaches to outsiders were used in tandem, as the stick and carrot, in all Native diplomatic negotiations.

The second mode of Native-style sharing was by reciprocal gift-giving. Innu gift-giving protocol required was as follows: "When a wildman [Native] has given you something for a great thank you .... you have to return something else for another great thank you. Otherwise, they will think you ungrateful." ("Quoy qu'un sauvage vous donne pour un grand mercy ... il leur faut rendre quelqu'autre chose pour un autre grand mercy. Autrement, vous serez tenu pour un ingrat.") Father LeJeune learned the hard way: "I will give you ... of everything that I have and you will give me all that you have" ("Je te donneray ... de tout ce que j'ay et tu me donneras de tout ce que tu as"). Uninitiated French were reproached for their stinginess. Natives said that these French loved their things better than their friends, unlike themselves, who desired brotherhood and to share everything.[52] Cornelius Jaenen cites several direct French settler borrowings of Native generosity. They developed a full Native repertoire of names for certain standard gift-packages, such as an Aouapon package for a warrior (blanket, shirt, mittens, shoes, and breeches) and an apichimon package for his winter apparel (bearskin, snowshoes, tumpline, and warm mittens). Chiefs received fancy uniforms. Native wampum was given, and gifts were employed as metaphorical "words" (paroles), Native-style, to appease revenge, to comfort relatives of the dead, to use in child-naming ceremonies, in marriages, in peace negotiations, as friendship tokens, in healing the ill, and so on.[53]

Although Native gift-giving significance and protocol was closely observed during the seventeenth century, as Cornelius Jaenen has pointed out, by 1707 the French Crown finally realized that this arrangement was going to cost increasing sums. Metropolitan amusement suddenly sobered, but it was too late to withdraw from proper protocol. By 1709 the gifts were offered unilaterally, as a royal patriarchal gesture to inspire reverence. A mere five years later, the king attempted to wholly abolish them.[54] British imitation of this French policy was employed to mollify former French allies disillusioned with the British (whom they called "Red Dogs") during the king's annual gifts.[55]

Greed can, paradoxically, increase with one's wealth. An attitudinal shift regarding gifts also appeared in the Native viewpoint. Laurier Turgeon wrote that the Europeans (Basques, Bretons, Normans) of the sixteenth century were drawn into northeast American Native protocol and that, at that point, gift objects seemed to fill a symbolic rather than a purely utilitarian function.[56] This validates Marcel Mauss's idea, which qualifies the context of gift-giving as being less an exchange of objects per se than of services, yet it tends towards a substantivist interpretation of the significance of these early exchanges.[57] Eventually, gift-giving was institutionalized in New France, and the objects were used profitably, thus implying a more formalist interpretation as their intrinsic value was increasingly recognized. Certainly, the aim of the Jesuits was obtained when, at Sillery in 1648, a Christian Native chief proclaimed: "In the past, when we were well treated, we said to our hosts, this feast will carry your name over the earth, all the nations will consider you as generous people who know how to conserve human life, but I have quit these customs. Now ... it is to God that I address [myself], when one does something good for me." ("Autrefois quand on nous auoit bien traitez, nous disions ... nos hostes, ce festin va porter vostre nom par toute la terre, toutes les nations vous regarderont d'oresnauant comme des gens libéraux qui sçauez conseruer la vie aux hommes: mais i'ay quitté ces coustumes, c'est maintenant ... Dieu ... qui ie m'adresse quand on me fait du bien.")[58] Perhaps the governor general would not be quite as pleased, but the open-table policy of the Jesuits was hardly a negligible factor in gaining converts. Perrot wrote bitterly in the early eighteenth century that there was no ignominy or insult that could not be ignored for a fine present, material possessions being their "principal idols."[59] Perhaps social cohesion was the central factor in enhancing the symbolic character of gifts, for the fragmented tribal entities located in the Great Lakes area with whom Perrot was so familiar valued their possessions more than those of the east due to the social breakdown of their communal frameworks and, thus, their greater need of French goods. Incremental Frenchification regarding the importance of acquisition may also have become a factor in this.

In short, in both sharing and gift-giving, the French became increasingly generous in North America through their extreme dependency upon the Native sharing ethic, its high value among the Natives, the prestige of French aristocratic generosity (libéralité) among the immigrants, and the Roman Catholic ideal of caritas. The cultural convergence of Native values with those specific to the Canadian immigrants and missionaries perpetuated a Native, rather than a French, sharing ethic.

Symbols and folklore reinforced this amalgamated norm as breaking bread together coalesced with steaming cauldrons of Native corn soup (sagamité). The fête-Dieu bread was blessed by the priest (pain bénit), distributed among all the ceremony participants, symbolizing that the entire community must break bread together. Disputes forbidding ostentation in presenting the bread reflect its symbolic egalitarian and charitable importance in the eyes of the habitants.[60] According to Therese Beaudoin, the pain bénit supposedly had medicinal qualities that protected against epilepsy (le mal de St-Jean), and abbé La Trudelle cites that a really infirm or poor person was referred to as getting along on pain bénits.[61] It is also significant to note that possessions were often countered and exorcised by the feeding of the victim with pains bénits or eucharists, which allegedly aided in the chasing of demons by fortifying one's spiritual strength to fend them off (as well as ordinary illnesses). Every Sunday, pain bénit was fed to newly converted congregants. "La guinolée" of Quebec, on New Year's Eve or the twelve nights (Chanteleur), is a door-to-door request for alms for the poor. This approach differed notably from that of the Parisian "aguilanneuf" collection, but especially from the Norman "aguigettes," or the Poitevin "guillaneu," where destitute children were forced to beg openly in the night chill.[62] Marie-Barbe de Boullongne (Mme d'Ailleboust, spouse of the governor general) and Jeanne Mance, founder of the Montreal Hôtel-Dieu, asked to be called "sister," in conformance with the early church and also Native norms, where strangers were called brother and uncle. The ubiquitous figure of the wanderer, "quêteux," in French Canadian folklore, who was bedded upon the fur pelt of the family sled or carriole (light cart), facing the warm fire,[63] and apparitions of revenants (who evened up moral debts), abound. In the tale of the phantom of the tempest (fantôme de la tempête,) a man did not open his door to the weary stranger, trudging through the snowstorm. At dawn, his icy corpse still clung to the threshold. His punishment was to pass every New Year's Eve as a spirit returning from the dead.[64] Wronged souls visited terrible vengeance and woe be to the unwary French egotist who was so anxious to assert his self-love ("amour-propre").

WOODEN BRAVES

Generosity (libéralité) was a female ideal, but to be a man, honneur (bravery) was needed. For both French and Native males, death was preferred to losing face.[65] The initial discrepancy lay in what constituted this loss of face. French aristocratic honour and Native masculine social face were astonishingly convergent on many points, but some aspects challenged each other. The result was a honing of French north American ideas of courage, manhood, community focus, and the enemy. The settlement "military ethos" admired heroic models, who were honoured due to noble d'épée precedent, adaptive Native example, and the perennial Haudenosaunee threat.[66]

During the "great century," the notion of masculine military honneur was growing increasingly obsolete among the aristocracy of the Parisian court as pedigree replaced military prowess as what provided one with a claim to noble entitlement and social status. Honour (honneur) was the noble's claim to the privilege of legitimated violence.[67] The rebellious provinces, on the other hand, were attached to the dated concept of honneur because their local nobility were defending provincial rights against Parisian royal centralization initiatives, particularly those implemented by the bourgeois-born intendants and taxmen. They thus had living models through whom to admire the old French concept of honneur. Quintessentially male and aristocratic, medieval knighthood gave place to the grand heroic gesture (geste) and furious duelling defiance (défi.)[68] Duelling between male social peers was highly esteemed. The right to exercise violence had been reserved for the aristocracy, and by the seventeenth century, even this estate was not necessarily engaged in it. Desiderius Erasmus himself challenged aristocratic claims to public utility in serving European societies through warfare.[69]

The homme de coeur ideal fell hard. The nobility traditionally literally preserved their hearts, and Charlemagne cut out the brave hearts of Roland, Olivier, and Turpin and wrapped their bodies in deerskin.[70] William the Conquerer's heart was laid to rest in Reims, King Henri IV's heart was preserved at La Flèche, and Anne de Bretagne's at Nantes.[71] Human hearts were even being sold in Auxerre during the Wars of Religion, as mentioned by Cornelius Jaenen.[72] And it is possible that the popular early modern tradition of the sacred heart of Christ (sacré coeur) was reinforced by the Aztec sacrifices of New Spain, which filtered back into Spanish Catholicism.[73] Augustinian thought described the heart as being the "inner man."

Provincial traditions of the Third Estate, especially those of the north Atlantic west, challenged the falling away from military duties. The pre-Fronde era "fierce independence" of the great north Atlantic nobility and their Nu-Pieds admirers-imitators challenged the new Parisian attachment to personal "gloire" and "amour-propre.".[74] A Nu-Pieds poem entitled "A la Normandie" calls upon the sword nobility to recall their original raison d'être: "If you do not conserve your Charter [of the Normands], you have no heart [homme de coeur] ... / And you, country nobles / Will you suffer this faceslap, / ... It is an attack on your rank, / Jean Nudz-piedz is your reinforcement / he will avenge your quarrel." ("Si vous ne conservez voz Chartes [la charte aux Normands] / Normanz, vous n'avez point de coeur [homme de coeur] ... / Et vous, noblesse du pays [provincial, not court nobility] / ... Endurer vous ce soufflet, / .... C'est attaquer vostre rang, / Jean Nudz-piedz est vostre support / Il vengera vostre querelle.")[75] The Norman tradition of fierceness in battle was recounted by medieval Orderic Vital.[76] Despite royal endeavours to curb the fierce insubordination of the old aristocracy, and the decline of the military function of the nobility, noble-backed insubordination enjoyed universal admiration, particularly when their own rights were at stake. Balthasar Castiglione wrote that the French love military endeavours far more than erudition, and even by the reign of Louis XIV, of the 318 medals struck, 218 were of Mars.[77] Literature also praised the popular *Amadis de Gaule* (1508) and *Roland furieux* (1516), which praised the knightly homme de coeur.

Montaigne associated ignoble cruelty with cowardice and low birth: "Cowardice, mother of cruelty" ("Couardise, mère de la Cruauté").[78] Nevertheless, unoccupied court noblemen, by the seventeenth century, rose to defend their own social faces in fits of "amour-propre." In France the Edict of 1626 renewed the interdiction on duelling, but its penalty soon took the life of the comte de Bouteville of the Montmorency family, who was much mourned in Canada. At the time Isaac de Razilly remarked: "What power has your king? ... [H]e was unable to vanquish a gentleman of his own subjects [the Prince of Rohan] without the assistance of Britain ... . Hollande ... Malta." ("Quelle puissance a votre Roi ... il n'a pu vaincre un gentilhomme de ses sujets [prince de Rohan] sans l'assistance de l'Angleterre ... Hollande ... Malte.") And French Persac declared to the British Buckingham that "in our nation, we are not accustomed to serve up persons condemned to death to do good actions [i.e., military feats], because we fight over this job" ("dans notre nation, on n'a pas accoutumé de se servir de personnes condamnés à mort pour faire de bonnes actions [meaning military feats], car on se bat pour avoir de l'emploi").[79] However alive the degraded military tradition was, French royal centralization was intent on suppressing it. This naturally backfired and gave young and rebellious immigrants to Canada extra incentive to keep it aflame.

Medieval tournaments that helped establish the acquisition of honneur were jousts that consolidated fidelity towards king and one's lady while affording a controlled environment to test one's mettle and prove male aristocratic social parity. By definition, aggression excluded the Third Estate, women, and children, who were war prizes. Thus, honneur was limited to only a fraction (about 1 percent) of the population, with few female beneficiaries. Seventeenth-century French women thus lacked a tradition of protection from men and had much to be apprehensive about. They often found their fields awash in blood and their children and themselves the inauspicious prizes of rapacious soldiers during the Wars of Religion, the revolts, and the Fronde. Women had to defend their virtue, while noblemen had to defend their honneur. While most women's mettle was tested through protecting their children, home, and reputation, devout women endured self-inflicted flagellations, fastings, and fleshly mortification, while defending their maidenhead.[80]

The male Native public persona in French eyes consisted of pride, which, on one hand, encouraged male heroism but, on the other, forbade the display of upset. Charlevoix tells of the first converted Haudenosaunee war captive, who, at his "feast of adieu" prior to his death, unflinchingly declared: "I am a man and am persuaded that I fear neither death, nor anything that you could make me suffer with" ("je suis un Homme & soyez persuadé que je ne crains ni la mort, ni tout ce que vous pouvez me faire souffrir de maux").[81] Lafitau said that the Natives had a "courageous mettle ... a constancy in torments which is heroic" ("un courage à l'épreuve ... une constance dans les tourments qui est héroïque").[82] LeClercq remarked that Native heroism was selfless and pointed to a few Mi'kmaq who immediately dove into the water to save some drowning Recollects: "a generosity that we can never acknowledge nor admire enough" ("Une générosité que nous ne pouvons assez reconnoître ni admirer").[83] The French marvelled at their capacity for endurance in the wilds, for rough games like lacrosse (much rougher than today's game), and hot coal wrestling.[84] Even torture was endured with comparative magnanimity compared to French standards. The Jesuits noted that, "during these torments, the patient kept singing, as it is reputed that it is a disgrace if they scream and complain" ("pendant tous ces tourmens, le patient chante tousjours, resputans ... déshonneur s'ils crient et s'ils se plaignent").[85] LeClercq wrote: They suffer patiently the most rigourous chastisements" ("Ils souffrent patiemment les châtiments les plus rigoureux").[86] This was readily identifiable for the French as belonging to the old local aristocracy. The brave and generous conscience of the Augustinian "inner man," who mirrored the "homme de coeur," had some affinity to the Mi'kmaq *meki'k mkamlamun* (Great Heart) and the later Innu Mistabeo, or Great Man (the soul-spirit that leads to the game).

On the other hand, it was noted that Native masculine pride prevented the display of anger, whether it be at friends, family, or when flinching under torture. Especially, it was forbidden to argue, attack, or defend themselves from upset women and children; they were to accept the responsibility that accompanied the privilege of generally superior physical strength.[87] Women usually endured childbirth stoically, but emotional expression was still the realm of the feminine. Sagard was amazed: "they have an absolute power over their passions" ("ils ont un pouuoir absolu sur leur passions").[88] Lafitau explained: "they act out of cold reason ... due to honour and greatness of the soul, they are never angry, seem always to be masters of themselves ... always have the heart high and proud" ("ils agissent de sens froid ... par raison d'honneur et par grandeur d'âme ils ne se fâchent jamais, paraissent toujours maîtres d'eux-mêmes..ont le coeur haut et fier.").[89] And he continued: "they are never angry with one another" ("Jamais ils ne se fâchent entre'eux").[90] In the play that Jean Bourdon wrote to welcome GovernorGeneral d'Argenson (with all the allies present), the player representing the Algonquian welcomed him in their tongue: "I know what it is to cry, I have too much courage and intelligence ... I leave the frightened souls and leave weeping to the women ... [I will spill] for your service not my tears but my blood until the last drop" ("je ne scais ce que c' est de pleurer; j'ai trop de courage et de force d'esprit ... Je laisse aux âmes lâches et aux femmes les larmes ... [je verserai] pour votre service non des larmes mais mon sang jusqu'à la dernière goutte").[91] Chiefdom especially required self-management. A Haudenosaunee chief was expected to uphold the ideal: "the thickness of their skins shall be ... seven spans of the hand" (*wasogondadensta djowenhgada*).[92] Three Rivers governor Pierre Boucher, who had a Wendat wife, remarked that Native men thought that "a man who cannot command himself is incapable of commanding others" ("vn homme qui ne peut pas se commander soy-mesme est incapable de commander autruy").[93] Even in the Great Lakes area, Perrot wrote that Natives would never openly affront someone who was publicly insulting them. Displaying emotion was only permitted while defending the reputation of the dead.[94]

Due to Native conceptions of pride, the French feared vengeance if they mistreated them without a clear cause. The French noted that, if Natives thought they were in the wrong in a misunderstanding, they would disavow any slighting of the other's social face and personal feelings, saying "I was wrong to offend you" ("j'ai tort de t'avoir offensé").[95] This was a penitent social gesture unthinkable to Parisian court nobility entranced with their own "amour-propre." The "pardon" was graciously bestowed to the "erring petit people" by the grands as a grand "geste."[96] Native sensitivity to unmerited affronts was never immediately discerned. If the deliberation was too long, it sometimes poisoned their spirits so that they attempted suicide.[97] Vengeance was undertaken by family members, but clemency was generally shown towards women and children.[98] Even the Wendat gave the head of the slain captive Haudenosaunee to the most loutish ("malotru") to devour.[99] Another motive for vengeance was due to disputes over women.[100] And of course disease, the thinning of game, and economic rivalries created by the fur trade propelled new conflicts. Tactics included the taking of captives for bargaining purposes, the demographic replenishing of numerous deaths, the plunder of fur convoys, and disputes over game-filled hunting territories.

As Robert Young has argued, not only was gender racialized in colonial situations but socially constructed "race" was frequently genderized.[101] Being a man was "the greatest [male] praise that Indians can give one another. It means they are very brave and know how to die with fortitude."[102] All the French allies admired their own enemy, the Lakota, as being more "virile" than either they or the Haudenosaunee. The Haudenosaunee sometimes mocked the Wendat for being "ashamed like women."[103] And the Wendat laughed at the Innu for being "babbling geese," which was another way of saying that they did not possess masculine reserve. But they all collectively ridiculed furious French manhood. It was ironic that, although French immigrants had a male surplus and Native communities had the contrary, the French still became conceptually feminized in Native eyes.

French manhood itself was being challenged in military alliances or encounters between French and Native. Seventeenth-century Frenchmen took all available wealth and authority from women and children, yet were not obliged to defend them. The primary role of First Nations men was to ensure the sustenance and protection of women and children, and it was upon this that they based their concept of worthiness as men. In France, the social usefulness of men weakened as the nobility replaced military obligations with that of pedigree, the homme de coeur with amour-propre, and the knight with the courtier.

Thus, during early settlement, the French were definitely the most "feminine" tribe. The Jesuits especially, due to their lack of firearms and sexual activity, were forced to prove to the Natives the worthiness of their masculinity. The missionaries tried, as Jean Bodin had, to link the Christian God with

French paternalism, an idea absent in Native culture. In the later Wendat songbook "Recueil de chants hurons" (Paul Tsaouenhohi Picard) God is called Skaïsten (Father) and his name is decorated with bow and arrows.[104] Father Druillettes told the Kiskakon and Iskouakite that Jesus was the French god of war.[105] To convert the Haudenosaunee, the Jesuits compared the Haudenosaunee war deity Agreskoué to the great king of France, the "chief of the chiefs" ("Capitaines des plus grand capitaines"), whose military power allegedly dwarfed that of the Haudenosaunee.[106] But they omitted mention of the king sending soldiers to battles from which he himself was absent. In Native eyes, he would hardly be considered a worthy warrior, let alone a respected chief.

French North Americans learned how to mask their emotions more effectively because of their admiration of Haudenosaunee steeliness. Even the allies jeered at volatile Frenchmen, to their great discomfiture. They were such sissies that they even argued with their own wives! Savignon similarly chuckled at the "feminine lack of courage" of quarrelling Frenchman.[107] This mocking positively jolted Frenchmen, for the higher one's social rank in France, the greater allowance that was made for one's emotional expressions. A peasant, for example, would not dare to publicly exhibit the same arrogant tantrums regularly thrown by the touchier nobility.[108] However, on the French scale, Normans prided themselves upon their sobriety, which stood in contrast to the more explosive southerners. Becoming a wooden warrior was just like toughening up.[109]

Haudenosaunee utilized French excitability to their own strategic benefit.[110] The Jesuits complained: "they think us incapable of doing any harm ... our generosity will not protect us from their treason and cruelties ("tant ils nous croiront incapables de leur faire aucun mal ... nostre bonté ne nous mettra pas à couuert de leurs trahisons, & de leurs cruautez.").[111] This strategic manoeuvring widened the number of behavioural models that toned down "Gallic vivacity." The necessity of survival provided adequate incentive, so that by 1666, Mother Marie de L'Incarnation referred to the French Canadian irregulars who accompanied Prouville de Tracy on the military trek to Iroquoia as follows: "all our young French Canadians who are very valliant, and who run the woods like the wildmen [Natives]" ("tous nos jeunes François-Canadois qui sont tres-vaillans, & qui courent dans les bois comme les sauvages").[112] The French Canadians, precisely on this mission, reversed the tables so completely on the Haudenosaunee that the "Flemish Bastard" (Haudenosaunee-Dutch Métis) and other captives wept openly when caught by them.[113]

In New France, the switch from infighting to outfighting signalled the evolving context of insider and outsider in an ambiguous community. Native culture funnelled aggression outside rather than inside the collectivity.[114] Initially excluding the Haudenosaunee as the outsider, facilitated the construction of a frame of reference for New France. And the outsider was viewed with a combination of heroic admiration and horror, a mix of awe and revulsion. Infighting, especially duelling, was understood differently by both French and Native peoples. The code of blood revenge within the community familiar to Frenchmen was often expressed in aristocratic duels. On the St Lawrence settlement the only French play repeatedly reenacted was Corneille's "Le Cid".[115] In "Le Cid," the only element that could override the place of honneur (in this case: blood revenge in a duel) was love. Three duels take place in the play but cede to the greater grandeur of having honourably fought the Moors, who were outside enemies. Cardinal Richelieu was the main opponent of the warring nobles dividing France, and he also abhorred "Le Cid." Saint-Beuve wrote: "We thought we were hearing the proposal of a Montmorency, a Lesdiguières, of a Rohan, as this was the way the last great seigneurs spoke. We heard it not without a certain shiver the echo of this great old and feudal arrogance that Richelieu had just overthrown and levelled" ("On croyait entendre le propos d'un Montmorency, d'un Lesdiguières, d'un Rohan: c'est ainsi que les derniers grands seigneurs encore avaient parlé. On écoutait sans un certain frémissement l'écho de cette altière et féodale arrogance que Richelieu achevait à peine d'abbattre et de niveler.") These proud seigneurs represented the indomitable northwestern nobility who were so avidly admired by French Canadian immigrants. David Posner has remarked that Corneille's Le Cid was the theatre of aristocratic revolt, which expressed Jacob Burckhardt's thesis of "Entwicklung des Individuums," the genesis of modern concepts of selfhood, which led to Renaissance self-fashioning.[116] Self-fashioning in New France certainly required the juxtaposition of the mirrors of Other and self in order to advance.

Two duels occurred in 1646. The first one was a quarrel between two Ursuline workers. The second one involved a duel between two soldiers in Three Rivers and was watched avidly by Native men. As a result this duel, LaGroye was wounded and Lafontaine was imprisoned. As for later incidents, in 1669 François Blanche dit Langevin, soldier, was condemned to death for killing Daniel Lamaire dit Desrochers, and in 1671 two officers of the Carignan-Salières regiment duelled.[117] From this brief list, we can see that duelling was rare. Those who duelled were incoming French soldiers and manual workers attempting to boost their social status by playing ostentatious games of one-upmanship. Native ridicule for intragroup sparring was a more effective damper on French North American behaviour than its formal interdiction in France (since 1626). By 1679 the Superior Council of New France outlawed duelling for good.

If the "antagonistic acculturation" of the French by hostiles relations with the Haudenosaunee encouraged more rigorous standards of honneur, the Wendat holocaust of 1648–49 haunted French consciousness as they them-

selves scrambled to acquire the "wooden warrior" look. Charlevoix writes
that nothing mortified the Wendat so much as the "memory of their incredible blindness" to Haudenosaunee stratagems to divide and conquer.[118]
When the Wendat were singled out by the Haudenosaunee for annihilation
as a confederacy, waves of fright rippled along the St Lawrence as the
French became the former's commercial successors. In addition, they had
lost many of their prize converts. Angst for the Wendat defeat, and sympathy
for the surviving Wendat who sought refuge on l'Île d'Orléans, ran high.[119]
Survivor's guilt is an almost axiomatic psychological response to disaster. To
make things worse, the disempowered victim is often the one blamed. In
adults great trauma often causes losses of the awareness, amnesia, and
numbness, as, bit by bit, the meaning of what has happened sinks in.[120]
When these remnants were massacred and survivors were carried off by the
Onondagas right next to Quebec itself in 1656, Governor Montmagny had
avoided interfering due to the founding of the recent Jesuit mission in
Iroquoia. The French settler population, however, was outraged.[121] We must
keep in mind that the Haudenosaunee of today are composed of many
adopted nations and are not inheritors of this tragedy.

Some writers have suggested that the French were unwilling to protect the
Wendat and that Montmagny's non-interference was an act of perfidy.[122] Yet
Montmagny did not express the will of the settlers or the religious communities. Until Prouville de Tracy arrived in 1666 with the Carignan-Salières regiment, the Canadians almost never switched from defensive to pre-emptive
offensive strategy with the Haudenosaunee, due precisely to the very thin-
ness of their forces – and a large dose of fright. We could postulate that, if
the massacre and carrying off of prisoners had taken place near Three
Rivers or Montreal, then intervention would have occurred due to the readiness of these settlements for Haudenosaunee attacks and the distance of
both settlements from Governor Montmagny. Quebec residents were less
inclined to pitch into battle, as evidenced by the terror that gripped the settlement when it was rumoured that the Haudenosaunee were targeting
Quebec itself, from 1656–61. Most habitants and missionaries, however,
were scandalized and identified with the Wendat, for they sensed they would
receive similar treatment in the future.[123] Dollier de Casson wrote: "this
entire country is in a powerful revolt ... menacing all the French to run the
same disgrace and to follow the same treatment" ("tout ce pays ... était fort
épouvanté ... menaçant ensuite généralement tous les Français d'encourir
la même disgrâce et de suivre le même traitement").[124] The Quebec Hospitallers wrote that the Haudenosaunee "cruelly butchered the Hurons
[Wendat] ... without our being able to oppose it, because it was the planting
season, and there were no men in Quebec, all being busy in the countryside.
It was a very painful thing to be obliged to abandon them to the fury of these
barbarians [sic] these poor Christians whose throats were cut despite the

measures we took, and the expense that we took to guarantee their safety from this misfortune, as we built them a fort, even with a canon. But it was useless, because the Haudenosaunee surprised them, and they received no help from the French .... we received this sad news with a feeling of general desolation." ("Firent une crüelle boucherie des Hurons ... sans qu'on put s'y opposer, parce que lon étoit dans la saison des semences, & qu'il y a avoit point d'hommes dans le québec, tous étant occupez a la campagne. Ce fut chose bien affligeante que d'être obligez d'abandonner a la fureur de ces barbares ces pauvres chrétiens qui furent égorgez malgré les mésures que l'on avoit prises, et la dépence que l'on avoit faites pour les garantir de ce malheur, en leur faisant bâtir un fort, ou l'on avoit même mis du canon. Mais tout cela fut inutile, parce que les Haudenosaunee les surprirent, et qu'ils ne reçurent aucun secours des François ... On apprit cette triste nouvelle avec une désolation generale.")[125] Unreasonable expectations, sprung from a closely meshed identification, could bring deep disillusionment, for at least in Quebec the women and children were no match for the warriors: – but this scenario would not have happened in Montreal. In 1657 the assassination of all but one of the male Arendaronons by the Onondaga took place under the eyes of Father Ragueneau, who had hid for several days behind the walls of Ste-Marie while Father Brébeuf was being tortured at a stone's throw. Obviously, he was too terrified to intervene. He had previously barely escaped death in 1640 when an ax lodged in his hair instead of his skull, which could surely bring on the jitters.[126] Understandably terrified, Father Ragueneau was not the indomitable Father Brébeuf, just as perfidious Governor Montmagny was not loyal Governor D'Ailleboust. Even if the French admired the Native ideal of never losing face, not everyone could live up to this – especially Jesuits who preferred returning to France instead of winding up like Brébeuf.

William Eccles has emphasized that the "whole fabric of Canadian society was imbued with the military ethos." By 1760, 3,300 men, or a full 32.20 percent, of the permanent settlers (who totalled around 10,250 souls) were professional soldiers.[127] Several seigneurs were even obliged to leave some of their lands due to the incursions, among them, Jean Bourdon, Jean Godefroy de Lintot, Pierre Legardeur de Repentigny, Jacques Hertel, François Chavigny de Berchereau, and Jacques Leneuf de la Poterie.[128] In Three Rivers, Governor Pierre Boucher armed a militia as early as 1651, while Governor Maisonneuve ordered one for Montreal in 1663. By 1669 all males between the ages of sixteen and sixty were organized into militia units, and during the eighteenth century the influx of soldiers increased even more.[129] While Canadians were arming through general conscription, the French were disarming insurrectionists who closely resembled them.

French Canada had a long list of legendary models of defensive bravery. Heroism was a social model that improved male standing and served as the "capacité" criterion for political functions in the Communité des habitants. As early as 1641 Three Rivers defended beleaguered Algonquians.[130] Marie Morin writes that the men of Montreal had the reputation in Canada, and even in France, of being excellent soldiers. The Haudenosaunee did not consider the French to be owners of the area they considered within their reach, yet even they remarked that three men of Montreal frightened them more than six men from elsewhere.[131] Father Daniel, seeing women, children, and the elderly massacred in Wendake in 1648, tried to distract the Haudenosaunee by posing as a target so the others could escape.[132] Father Jean de Brébeuf sang the traditional Native death song when accused by the Wendat of sorcery when they were attacked by a virulent epidemic in the 1630s, and then he defied his Haudenosaunee tormentors at the stake during the fall of Wendake.[133] Commoner Pierre Boucher's courage at Three Rivers saved lives time and again, and he was rewarded by receiving a governorship.[134] The founder of Montreal, Governor Maisonneuve, was renowned as a courageous defender of the city, declaring that: "my honour is to defend Montreal ... [even] when all the trees of this island will be changed into as many Haudenosaunee warriors" ("il est de mon honneur [to defend Montreal] ... quand tous les arbres de cet Isle se devraient changer en autant d'Haudenosaunee").[135] Guillaume Cousture survived Haudenosaunee captivity and became an indispensable diplomat. Adam Dollard des Ormeaux, although not the savior of New France, was still a key hero of the Long-Sault of 1660. François Hertel of Three Rivers, in Haudenosaunee captivity in 1661, returned to become a hero.[136] And in the eighteenth century, the Lemoyne brothers were legendary for their military prowess.[137] Also fourteen-year-old Madeleine de Verchères defended the Verchères Fort almost single-handedly from a Haudenosaunee siege, imitating her mother who did the same several years earlier.[138] Even the French commander Prouville de Tracy was greatly admired for chasing after the Haudenosaunee, and he was almost adored by otherwise prudent Mother Marie de L'Incarnation.[139] All have become legendary heroes of French North America.

Military tactics adopted Native bushfighting, often mentioned in battle accounts, which included ambush tactics, disguises, feasting and ceremonies.[140] There were a handful of later governors, intendants, and military officers who appreciated Canadian daring and knew how to apply its strengths to best effect. Frontenac, for example, understood the fur trade strategy and utilized the coureurs to revive his dilapidated fortune. He also made tactical use of the Canadian militia instead of requiring them to perform as drilled French regulars. The Chevalier de Lévis, Malartic, and artillery lieutenant Joseph Fournerie de Vezon unanimously praised the bravery, marksmanship, endurance, and speed of the Canadian militia, and these officers intelligently utilized their bush-fighting strengths instead of submitting them to French discipline. The Chevalier de Lévis incorporated

2,264 Canadian militia into his eight battalions of land troops and two battalions of marine troops.[141]

If the French were rattled at being considered women by the Natives, it was nevertheless the case that the dread associated with loss of face was still closely linked with aristocratic ideas of bravery and the social self.[142] For Frenchman even of de Tocqueville's time, Native and old aristocratic honour seemed linked: "War and hunting are the only pursuits that appear to him [Native] worthy of a man. The Indian ... cherishes the same ideas, the same opinions, as the noble of the Middle Ages in his castle ... Thus, however strange it may seem, it is in the forests of the New World, and not among the Europeans ... that the ancient prejudices of Europe still exist."[143]

The Beau Sauvage tale from the Mauricie area illustrates the value of honneur in the pursuit of love. Ti-Jean, the bumpkin of French Canadian lore, appears as a handsome Native youth and is forced by kings and queens to perform incredible feats before winning the hand of the beautiful French princess.[144] Histories are curiously tongue-tied about romances involving French women with Native men, yet this tale is not. The Canadian princess prefers the Native warrior, who is willing to risk his life to love and protect her, over the power and wealth of the rival French-style king.

We should perhaps consider the contemporary French Canadian affection for dangerous sports as a faint glimpse of this ideal: their penchant for bareback racing, canoeing through rapids, kayaking over waterfalls, lacrosse, broomball, daredevil skating, ski games, sheer cliff tobogganing, extreme skidoo, and, of course, hockey, are often unequalled elsewhere. The height of the Winter Carnival in Quebec today is the daring but dangerous ice-canoeing attempted across the ice-floe-thick St Lawrence Seaway.

The mixed French Canadian ideals of generosity and courage developed from the dialogue between ancient northwestern French noble and Native values. Generosity was the prime characteristic of the old French nobility and missionaries, while hospitality, gift preparation, and giving was the special preserve of allied Native women, Frenchwomen, missionary women, and diplomats. Unlike in France, Native and settlement femininity was largely defined in terms of motherhood, which required selflessness and fortitude without the comfort of a familiar infrastructure. Thus, the values of generosity and bravery were those most required of pioneer women, and they were bolstered by the examples of veteran founding women and Native women.

Courage was also valued by north Atlantic French noblemen and Native warriors, to the awe of the Canadian immigrants, who were originally considered to be too feminine. This had three main effects. Seeing themselves as the Other's feminine Other forced them to see the world through female eyes, which can be an instructive exercise. Possibly, this could have deepened their appreciation for women as subjects instead of objects. The second effect required them to keep their volatility under better control in order to provide a dignified stance that properly represented the Great Onontio with so many Native "children" to care for. The "benevolent paternity model" eventually offered by veteran French officers and Canadians (especially after 1663) certainly benefited dialogue, diplomacy, and mediation. It also led to an increased standing for the French among the tribes of the west. The third effect of being seen as the feminine tribe was that it eventually toughened them up as they engaged in Native-style feats of exceptional heroism in order to prove themselves in an ocean of potential and formidable foes.

Both generosity and courage helped define and shape dual Canadian notions of femininity and masculinity as each one bore a complementary communal responsibility. The transversal shift from French patriarchy to an alliance between the sexes, where obligations were born horizontally, enhanced trust within the community and heightened the likelihood for communal survival.

CRYING OUT IN THE WILDERNESS

Sin was a major headache to most Frenchmen. This was especially true in ambiguous liminal environments, where sometimes sin metamorphosed miraculously into virtue. The internalization of repentance, which struggled with egotism as opposed to generosity, and the pride of bravery as opposed to humility was typified by the natural simplicity of John the Baptist.

The repentant John the Baptist fused so closely with his twin, the Atlantic Algonquian Gluscap, that he became not only French but also Algonquian. Therefore the unlike twinning between John the Baptist and Gluscap initially involved contrasts and reversals that ultimately resulted in parallelisms and fusion. The prime feature of these tales is the humility of penance and the redemption of generosity. Repentance and penance were both re-examined as widespread "contrition of the heart," and the "imitation of Christ" flourished during the Reformation and Counter-Reformation. The consciousness that the "I" can also be an "Other" reawoke, especially in the light of renewed interethnic contact.[145] Many tales told during the nineteenth century resembled parables. This particular twinship exemplifies human soul-searching within oneself and demonstrates how the symbolic boundaries of the collectivity have been bound up with symbols of personal identity. This model reflected not only the newly converted repentant yet generous shaman, but the aged coureur de bois anxious for the absolution of his numerous youthful sins. Even today, both John the Baptist and Gluscap are symbols of their respective communities. But they are both unaware of the degree of fusion between them.

During the early French-Algonquian contacts, Gluscap had been the proud creator who assisted Atlantic Algonquian peoples and, indeed, punished them severely if they erred. Of all the great explorers, was the first to discover the New World of Europe. He sailed his grandmother Kesegoocsk to Planchean (France) to have her baptized, and told the Mi'kmaq about England. He was fired at, but never injured. He begged European warships for scissors, clothes, thread, and utensils for his grandmother.[146] When the Perry expedition discovered the North Pole, he saw Gluscap sitting at its top and spoke to him. He was the original creator of the world.[147] The deity of the Mi'kmaq, Ktcinisxam, made Gluscap out of earth and breathed life into him. Gluscap taught humankind agriculture, hunting, and language.[148] He formed the sun and the moon, animals, the fish, the fairies and dwarves (from tree bark), and humans (by shooting arrows into the heart of a tree).[149] Gluscap himself is a sun deity of the far northeast, wears a magic belt, and possesses a canoe that could become as capacious or compact as need be.[150] He lives with his grandmother Kesegoocsk and Abistanaooch (Marten) his helper. He lives in the west in the Realm of the Dead ,where Coolpujot (boneless creature who creates the seasons), and Kuhkw (Earthquake) also live. He created geographical formations in his beaver hunts and feasts (e.g., Annapolis Gut and Cape Split, Aylesford Bog, the huge beaver bones at Bras d'Or Lake in Cape Breton, Cape Chignecto's Isle of Holt, and the rocks there called Ooteel, Isle of Hant, Owokun [Boar's Back], and Ooteomul [Spencer Island], which is his overturned kettle). And he dispersed the cedar trees covering Nova Scotia and New Brunswick.[151] The cry of the loon calls out to Gluscap.[152]

It is possible that the Viking contact during the course of the Middle Ages resulted in a degree of cross-fertilization between northern Native peoples and Scandinavians. It is likely that if this did occur, as postulated by Charles Leland, the degree of convergence and rapid identification was facilitated because the Normans treasured their Nordic heritage. This influence as yet lacked the later orientation of Christianity, which ultimately twinned the north Atlantic Algonquian with the north Atlantic French. Leland saw Gluscap as a product of diffusion of Norse myth among Native nations, thinking his attendant wolves and birds were like those of Odin, god of the dead.[153] Gluscap created human beings out of the ash tree, as in the creation of man and woman (aske und emble) in Norse mythology. Both Odin and Gluscap have whale-hunting and freezing competitions. Both also participated in the cosmic Final Battle (Ragnarok, or Armageddon), wherein Gluscap made arrows, killed humankind, and burned the world, and both Odin and Gluscap fought the formidable Wolf-Destroyer.

The fusion of biblical and Norse myth is quite similar for the Normans, who were deeply enamoured of their Viking tradition as well as the saints. Bailey writes that Gluscap was, for the Mi'kmaq, Maliseet, Passamaquoddy, Penobscot, and Abenakis, "a forerunner of Christ, a sort of Hebrew prophet," and that the two had a rivalrous relationship.[154] He paralleled John the Baptist in humility, healing with gifts, and disappeared from the people who needed acceptance and understanding from the world, God, Nature, and the self. Whenever Gluscap's pride overpowered his magnanimity, Nature provided the antidote. According to Frank Speck, Gluscap prophesied the coming of the Europeans who would baptize the Mi'kmaq. And despite the coming of Christ to Turtle Island (North America), which induced Gluscap to exit, the Mi'kmaq's guardian would return if they needed him.[155] In one tale, he fought a great serpentine sea monster in order to rescue fresh water for humankind; this is similar to Mary and/or Anne, who opposed the Wendat Oyalerowek (Great Serpent).[156] The Gluscap twist was that, unlike Mary (who provided a silent example of holiness for humankind in order to indirectly combat the symbol of "Satan"), Gluscap literally struggled with the beast. This tale also parallels that of the Nordic Thor, god of the sky, who fought with his thunderbolt hammer the world leviathan whose length spanned the earth from mouth to tail. Again, the Gluscap twist was that Thor did this to demonstrate his power, while Gluscap did his deeds out of care for the survival of his people. Gluscap also caused a world flood, yet instead of drowning humankind, he metamorphosed them into rattlesnakes, demonstrating that his forgiveness was greater than that of YHWH of the Old Testament.[157] Thus, the dialogue "ghosts" of the four saint/deity versus sea monster tales at the judgmental Endzeit were within each other's frame of reference, modifying or fusing meanings and weaving a common north Atlantic French-Atlantic Algonquian-Wendat web of understandings. One must nevertheless note that, while the French-Wendat lore frequently provided legitimated versus discredited contrasts, the French-Algonquian lore often fused French and Native values in métissé figures. Thus, whereas French-Wendat lore was polarized into good and evil multicultural categories, French-Atlantic Algonquian lore was deeply métissé.

Gluscap's role matched that of John the Baptist, whose twin fusion resulted in the image of a humble wiseman. For them, the world, God, the manitou, and Nature were accepted as unchanging realities that the human can best deal with through comprehension rather than power or magic. One Mi'kmaq tradition has it that the world was created by Christ, Gluscap, and Hadam (HaAdam in Hebrew means human). Gluscap and Hadam walked upon the water, but only Gluscap didn't sink, leading him to tell humankind that their descendants would live in sin. Gluscap's rules were intended for human beings, who would perish without them.[158] Gluscap and Christ conducted a freezing contest, similar to that of Odin and the giant. Similarly, Christ took Gluscap to the ocean and told him to close his eyes, at which time Christ moved an island in the middle of the lake closer to the shore. Gluscap told Christ to close his eyes and moved the island back to its original spot, thus demonstrating that, while Christ concentrated on performing miracles, Gluscap concentrated on returning Nature to its proper ecostasis.[159]

Gluscap's function was to protect humankind from wild beasts, giants, windigos (chenoos), and sorcerers. He sent a Megumawessu (a great sorcerer) to the "Country of souls" (Boo'in), where his representative was obliged to kill a dragon (Che-pitch-calm [Mi'kmaq] or Wee-wil-l-mecqu [Passamaquoddy]).[160] The evil sorcerer Porcupine forced Gluscap to sit in a cave full of fire, from which he escaped. Finally, when Gluscap is finished filling his wigwam with arrows; he will come in his canoe; meet the Great Wolf; make the last war with giants, goblins, elves, and sorcerers; and burn the world with the final fire.[161]

The parable that most characterizes Gluscap's wisdom and common sense is that of "Gluscap and his visitors."[162] It has many versions but definitely points out that the attainment of moderate desires accomplished through working with oneself far outstrips unrealistic grandiose wishes, which are self-destructive. In addition, it is axiomatic that, in Atlantic Algonquian lore, the unprotected and weak manage to defeat strong bullies, reinforcing the ideal of seeing right triumph over might and the gentle person over the bully. It also reinforces the ideal of producing riches from scarcity, mirroring the John the Baptist's slant on Jesus' Sermon on the Mount.[163] One version describes three visitors, a Maliseet and two Penobscots, who journey seven years to reach Gluscap. This journey is classically arduous, especially for the wicked, but the return home is easy. One of the visitors desires skill in the hunt, which Gluscap grants through the gift of a magic flute. The second man wanted the love of many women. The third man wanted to be the source of merriment due to his skill in belching and breaking wind, which was then popular among the Abenaki. Gluscap warned all the men not to touch the presents until they had arrived home. The second and third men imprudently opened their gifts before they reached their destination. Only the first man arrived home and became happy. The second man died through being suffocated by the crush of women who desired him after he opened his gift in the woods. The third man was also impatient and ate the magic root. Villagers and game avoided him due to his uncontrollable digestive system, and he therefore committed suicide.[164] According to the Mi'kmaq version of this myth collected by a missionary, after Gluscap left the Natives, four men sought him for a long time and found a wigwam peopled by a grandmother (like Anne), a middle-aged man, and a strong young hunter. After the hunter had prepared a meal and washed the face of his grandmother, restoring it to youthful beauty, they knew they had found Gluscap. The first man told Gluscap that he was bad-tempered and that he desired to become good-tempered, the second desired to become an excellent hunter, and the third wanted to be loved and respected. To all Gluscap granted small gifts of ointment that were not to be opened until they arrived home. The fourth man requested a long life. Gluscap took the men to a barren hilltop and planted the last man as a cedar tree. Gluscap explained that the man would live long because no one would disturb him up there. His seeds dispersed and covered Nova Scotia and New Brunswick with cedar trees, the sacred tree of the western nations that was used in totem poles. But Gluscap helped the other three to achieve their dreams because they were moderate and required working upon the self.[165]

These parables exemplified humble penance and giving as the spiritual antidotes to those striving to fit the desired homme de coeur ideal. This spirituality became important in Atlantic Algonquian culture and was intimately fused with the asceticism, self-searching, and divination of the Judeo-Christian European heritage of the Hebrew prophets, early Christians, and, especially, John the Baptist. The inner strength of humble gentleness was embodied in the fusion of Catholic, Nordic, Celtic, and Atlantic Algonquian beliefs. The Catholic espousal of the Sermon on the Mount's preaching that the "weak shall inherit the earth," the Nordic saying "beware of the mistletoe" (which embodied the unsuspected power of the soft berries that killed Baldur), the Celtic belief in the healing power of mistletoe, and Gluscap's declaration that only soft cattail down (in some versions, rushes) could kill him, are cases in point. James Scott's "weapons of the weak" address the embodiment of alternative viewpoints in popular cultural forms such as folklore.[166] Thus, Gluscap has been transformed by this dialogue from a proud and combative demiurge essential to medicine healers into a lone wilderness prophet-in-exile due to his supposed ceding to the coming of Jesus.

John the Baptist appeared as the twin of the repentant Gluscap, who converted to Christianity. He became a "voice crying out in the wilderness," transforming savage beasts into gentle lambs. The lamb-like gentleness and humility was essential to the angelic ability to fly above passion and ire, like the Holy Ghost, to reach out to other worlds, and to mediate between Heaven and Hell.

In Isaiah (40:3), this voice cries out in the wilderness to clear the way straight for YHWH, which, in its own historical context, was a veiled allusion to Bible study as the wilderness of impenetrability. This idea reflects the Essenian ethos, which was expressed in the Dead Sea scrolls, where myriad acts of hygienic, communal, and spiritual purification were performed. John the Baptist, who lived at this time and had many attributes of the Essenes, called out: "Do penance, for the kingdom of YHWH is upon you," while threatening that every tree that failed to produce good fruit would be cut and thrown on the fire. Josephus considered Essenian prophecies to "rarely ... prove wrong."[167] Repentance and the Hebrew mitzvah (good work) of brotherly sharing were good fruits, and "taxmen," "bullies," and "blackmailers" were forewarned. The Essenes shared everything with their unity-brethren (Yahad). Josephus wrote: "everyone gives what he has to anyone in need and receives from him in return something he himself can use

and even without giving anything in return they are free to share possessions."[168] In other words, the Essenes lived communally in the kind of generalized trust and sharing ethic common to Native communities, which
enhanced the value of libéralité.

Water and fire were the media through which the divine presence made
itself felt. St John the Baptist healed physical and spiritual illness by boiling
the therapeutic St John's wort (artemisia vulgaris, or armoise commune)
after gathering seven of them before dawn, and bathing children in the
rivers or basins filled with the herb and dew collected before 24 June.[169]
Youth gangs caroused through villages setting up bouquets and maypoles,
choosing a mock prince among them, drinking, and charivariing with
torches.[170] The classic bonfire was lit, and, as in an ancient fertility rite, girls
tried to jump over the flames to see who would get married.[171] This holiday
not only assures that the grain will grow but also that health will be restored
if a smouldering branch is brought home and kept all year. John the Baptist
only claimed to baptize with water, but the "lamb of God" would baptize with
eternal fire and the Holy Spirit.[172] One had to be tested by the classic ordeals
of water and fire before the Holy Spirit could enter.

St John's Eve not only rejuvenated nature but relinked the living with the
dead in one community. The holiday falls directly on the summer solstice,
the longest day of the year. In ancient times, the Roman feast was held at this
time, and Demeter searched for Proserpine with a torch. This was also the
Celtic feast of Beltane (Aiche Baa-tinne), dedicated to Baal (or Bel, or
Belenus), the sun, as a male principle, while autumnal Samhain (Aiche
Shamain) was to the female principle, the moon.[173] This fire was preserved
in the ancient Scot tradition of passing through the fire and circling flocks
and fields with torches to ensure fertility.[174] In Celtic Cornouille, the souls of
the dead came out after the fires were extinguished, and money from sold
cinders was spent to pay for mass for the dead. It was thought that whoever
bought these cinders would not die during the year. In Brittany the souls of
the deceased returned to warm themselves by the fire, and it was forbidden
to sweep after dark. The dead returned thrice yearly: at Christmas, on All
Saint's Eve, and on St John's Eve. The last dead of the year became the grim
reaper (Ankou) and wandered around with a barrow.[175] In Normandy the
legend of Hellequin, discussed in greater detail in the next chapter, was perhaps connected with Proserpine. This guess is based on Hellequin's alias, "la
mère Harpine," which linked him to the return of the dead. Rites connected
to the celebration were taken as precautions to ensure long life.[176]

Therefore, the rowdy St John the Baptist feast day was celebrated with
rebellious intent. This was due to post-Trentine suppression of its magical
content, owing to its pagan Celtic and Roman origins.[177] In Poitou and Normandy the feast-fires were especially suppressed by the Jesuits due to the
drinking, violence, and sexual licence that accompanied them. In 1665

Bishop Meaux tried to Christianize the celebration by having one official fire in order to regulate disorders. This was part of a post-Trentine effort to replace pagan-originated fires by auto-da-fés, which burned heretical books and pagan ritual objects.[178]

St John the Baptist has had potent political significance. Some Essene Hebrews retreated to the Judean desert as ascetic communitarians, secluded from the political Pharisees and Sadducees, near the wilderness fortress of Machaerus. The Early Church sprang from some Essenes, while others retained Judaism, but all shared basic values and a large number of similar beliefs. Herod Antipas finally beheaded John the Baptist because of the latter's wide influence, and he feared an uprising when the populace learned his death for he was very popular among the Jews.[179] The Norman Nu-Pieds insurrection (1639–40) appropriated St John the Baptist as the Nu-Pied protector: "ces mutinez qui portaient pour estendart l'image de St. Jean Baptiste et pour devise: FUIT HOMO MISSUS A DEO CUI NOMEN ERAT JOANNES." And the legendary Jean Nu-Pieds himself portrayed St John the Baptist's emblem upon his orders, with two bare feet upon a crescent.[180] And not only the king, but the Jesuits, strenuously opposed the Nus-Pieds, the Croquants, and the Bonnets-Rouges.[181] Interestingly, John the Baptist allegedly stated that he was not fit to remove Jesus' shoes. Barefootedness was a symbol of repentance that the Recollects and Discalced Carmelites showed God, both of whom missionized in Canada. So which is it, penitence or rebellion? Or both?

The dialogue between north Atlantic French conceptions, especially Norman, and those of northeastern First Nations took on a unique Nativized French Canadian relevance. John the Baptist in Canada was an utterly transformed symbol from that of John the Baptist in France. His symbols and celebrations also became intimately associated with relevant Native meanings through the linking of French past with Native present. A tipi of cedar covered with spruce, the former being the sacred wood of totem poles, was constructed for celebrations in St-Jean-Port-Joli and St-Jean of Ile d'Orléans.[182] Ashes and twigs from the saint's bonfires were saved, just like the famous match (allumette) used in Native lovemaking, which enhanced fertility associations.[183] A related legend from Ohio tells of Didier Duchesne's daughter, Fanchette, hearing of an enchanted spinning wheel after her grandmother died. On St John's Eve she kept vigil all night with cedar (sacred Native) and fir branches so that her soul would not leave her body to wander to the site of her future death. At sunrise, the sun danced thrice, she had a vision of her future husband, whom she could not marry until Christmas due to the mobility of the souls.[184] Flowers of the eldertree (sureau), cut the day of the St John celebration, were thought to be good for the eyes and skin diseases. St John's wort was picked in the morning, and the dew gathered during the St John festivities reputedly healed wounds.[185] In addition, John the Baptist was beheaded in a similar way to how Haudenosaunee victims were beheaded before being cannibalized. When the Montreal hero, Lemaître, was beheaded during a Haudenosaunee ambush, Montrealers at the time associated his type of death with that of John the Baptist.[186] Thus, the martyr-dom of the repentant only heightened his holy prominence.

Ironically, the Jesuit frowning upon the disorderly, religious, political, and Native associative contents of the feast of St John the Baptist only served to enshrine it, with the result that today it is the most significant celebration of French Canada. John the Baptist was the patron saint of the Norman pays de Caux parish in France.[187] But in Canada, the *Journal des Jésuites* records Jérôme Lalemant's reluctance to light the fires of St John the Baptist, and his departure from festivities was generally at 9:00 PM, leaving the popula-tion to celebrate with the Natives in their own way. By 1650 the Jesuits refused to attend. At this salient celebration, the French Canadians again turned the tables upon their own metropolitan French elite and inverted the hierarchy at this most rebellious feast, which became, in the words of Cornelius Jaenen, a kind of "colonial national holiday."[188]

The saint had a twin in Gluscap, and the lambskin corresponded to his twin's wild pelt.[189] In ancient times, sheep fleece was an object of power, much as hair was to Samson; hence Jason sought out the golden fleece. Zeus had a sacred fleece that supposedly purified a murderer (Dios koidion).[190] In Canada beaver pelt packs were worth gold (louis d'or). In medieval France wool was a magic substance and was used as an offering to local spir-its.[191] After childbirth, noblewomen's stomachs were sometimes encased in the skin of a freshly killed sheep to reduce the organs, thus associating sheep and lambs with health and the life/death cycle.[192] One must particularly note that Hellequin, like John the Baptist, was traditionally dressed in a sheepskin.[193] We presume this sheep pelt later to have become the late medi-eval penitent's self-mortificatory "hairshirt" (hure or haire). Molière refers to Tartuffe, doyen of false piety, as ostentatiously donning his hairshirt.[194] As for pelts and hairshirts, the all-important Wendat were called "Hurons" by the French, referring to both their pelt clothing, the boar's head coiffure, and their ascetic (in French eyes perhaps repenting) demeanor.

Repentance was the great issue of the European post-Plague waning of the Middle Ages, and it was the great divide between Roman Catholic and Protestant. In brief, Hieromymous's translation was "do penance," which, embraced by the post-Trentine Church, put the emphasis upon free will, including good works and intercessory prayers (suffrages) to remit another's sin while in purgatory. Erasmus's translation of "repent" was embraced by Luther, and the subsequent Protestants placed the emphasis upon the concepts of predestination and election, with faith and contrition of the heart being capable of providing sufficient grace. Yet it was the great unavoidable subject for epidemic-infested Native communities and soul-searching missionaries and settlers newly aware of their own communal and conceptual frailties through self-examination forced by circumstance. Relevant correspondences were not unremarked by the simplest of writers. For, as Sagard, remarked, "these poor peoples live just as our ancestors after the first sin."[195] This was expressed not only by missionaries and converts wearing "hures" to repent but also by them celebrating an elaborate Feast of the Dead, which literally wrapped the bones of their ancestors in a beaver pelt-lined great pit to accomplish their resurrection to a happy afterlife in the "country of souls."

The social face so dear to the youth enthralled with the homme de coeur ideal soon enough became lost in humility and repentance as he aged. Rigorous-souled ascetic and repenting figures such as Gluscap and St John the Baptist, and Native convert piety, aided the generalized and widespread French North American search for rites of repentance and absolution prior to death. Cornelius Jaenen remarked on the difference between French and Canadian burial rites. In France a corpse was exposed upon a bed; in New France the body was exposed at a Celtic-style wake. Burial was usually in the parish cemetery, but several priests and seigneurs asked to be buried in the pauper's section of the church face down in perpetual repentance (until a public outcry against the odour abruptly ended the practice). Jaenen remarks tellingly: "Very few, after lives of transgressing the commandments of God and the church in the fur trade, the army, the social life of the towns, or the isolation of the backwoods seigneuries, failed to seek reconciliation and the comfort of the last rites."[196] Fur trader Aubert de la Chesnaye and Peuvret de Mesnu donated their considerable fortunes to the poor of the hospital. Marie-Anne Cliche categorized two groups of wills: those who donated more to good works (clergy, administration, officers of justice, seigneurs, and traders) and those who donated more to masses for themselves (military officers, craftsmen, censitaires, and clerks).[197] The choice between being charitable or guaranteeing an open gate to Heaven must not have been an easy one.

After the fall from Grace, Adam and Eve were required to clothe their nudity, became aware of their transgressions, and repented their sin of disobedience to God. They literally "shed their pelts," left their innocent sinfulness behind, and acquired a conscience, which permitted their access to Heaven. Pagans like Hellequin, pre-Christians like St John the Baptist and Gluscap, were required to carry their pelts with them so that they would never forget from whence they emerged. Jesus himself seemed to be the earthly incarnation, or "pelt of God." Baptized and unctioned souls flew straight to Heaven because they were cleansed of beastly impurity. Thus, the enormous attention devoted to bereavement, the dead, ancestors, and "ghosts" was also therapeutic, enabling reevaluation of the self by way of one's past conscience, as well as the Other's and his ancestral conscience, to regenerate and resurrect life itself.

The later transition from focusing on Saint Anne to focusing on John the Baptist is historically and socially significant. During colonial times, the comforting grandmotherly Anne salved fears of the ocean and the rivers of the fur trade. Only later, when the fur trade was the only redeeming feature of a farm life wracked with wheat blight in 1837, did the repentant medicineman, John the Baptist, rise in prominence in a clerically directed mea culpa for the passing of the Golden Age of the French regime, while stigmatizing the "unrepentant libertarian" coureurs de bois. The symbol of St John the Baptist became, by 1834, a nationalist Quebecois emblem. He was adopted as French Canada's patron saint in 1908.[198] The traditional pure lambswool of the saint's garment juxtaposed against Amerindian wild animal pelts clearly echoes the eighteenth-century Nativized Montreal wolf versus the French Quebec lamb conjugation cited earlier.[199] The banner of the patriotic St-Jean-Baptiste-Society expresses the French-Native dialogue and contains a medallion of Frontenac, a golden beaver upon a maple tree branch, the other side of which sports the tricolour with the fleur-de-lys. Native and French elements combine here but are as of two sides of the same Janus-like emblem: the beaver and sugar maple are Amerindian borrowings of the early immigrants and are considered to be the heart of "old French Canada," while the tricolour and fleur de lys are almost totemic qualifiers indicating a specific tribe.

The famous modern Québecois expression "100 percent wool" (la laine pure 100 percent) alludes to the myth of an exclusively French ancestry and distinguishes the "Québecois vieille souche" from the newcomer. This expression has a layered meaning due to a cross dialogue with Normandy, Brittany, the Counter-Reformation, the First Nations, and the British in an evolving context. The first layer refers to the colonial context: lambswool as the French tribe's vulnerable and repentant animal totem twinned to fiercer Native animal pelts in the wilderness as well as to the symbol of pelt-induced resurrection and rebirth. The second layer refers to the rebellious political import of John the Baptist insurrectionist symbolism. The third layer refers to the lamb emblem of the Norman city of Rouen.[200] The fourth layer refers to the pagan magical and properly medicinal and supposed fertility-enhancing properties of lambs and sheep.[201] The fifth layer could refer to the metaphorical and religious importance of sheep to the shepherds of Normandy, who were willing to use eucharists and to face death annually rather than to let the wolves get to this famous Norman specialty.[202] The sixth layer, reinterpreted by the clergy after the 1763 Cession of New France, refers to the innocent blood of the dead lamb (i.e., Jesus Christ), signifying the "Saintly Canadian Martyrs" sacrificed for the great mission in North America. This includes those converted and Frenchified like old Haudenosaunee war horse La Barique, who, wounded in battle, was nursed by the French and later become pro-French, or "doux comme un agneau."[203] Mission neophytes were famous for their severe self-imposed penitence.[204] The source of this symbol was the ancient Passover, the paschal lamb sacrifice applied upon the entryways of the Hebrews before God allowed their exodus from Egypt (echoing how Abraham allegorically saved his son Isaac from God's might by historically replacing child sacrifice with beast sacrifice). This is what most distinguishes Judeo-Christian heritage from that of the more ancient fertility beliefs. This was meant to preserve them from the angel of death sent to smite Egyptian firstborn sons.[205] The seventh layer, by the nineteenth century, provides the French Canadian denial of anglophone disparagement expressed by snorting at the "French-speakin' injun."

In conclusion, the French and Native social masks required men (as hommes de coeur) to show self-sacrificing courage while women were required to sacrifice themselves for their children. Thus, generosity aided survival in Native North America and social mobility in French Canadian society. However, at the interior core of the "continually running" French Canadian was a far more timid creature, confessing his sins anxiously before God for ultimate legitimation of his half-wild existence, especially, as Cornelius Jaenen has noted, before his feet were forever stilled. The final humility of repentance and vulnerability allowed the immigrant and Native convert to reveal an inner "lamb-like" nature in an atmosphere ostensibly surrounded by "wolves" so that, although they had been Nativized and could be as "wary as serpents (the Haudenosaunee)" on the outside, they could still retain the teachability of children (like Gluscap's nemesis, Wasis) "innocent as doves (Holy Spirit)" on the inside. Thus they were able to enter the "kingdom of heaven" ("I send you out like a lamb among wolves, be wary as serpents, innocent as doves" [NT, Matt. 10:16]). Returning to the wild asceticism of John the Baptist or modest Gluscap metaphorically cleansed one (like baptism) in preparation for the finality for death. Sociologically, the French were deeply moved while witnessing Native humility, as it appeared that the latter confessed and submitted to European authority. This literally allowed wily allies like Cherououny to get away with murder if they requested pardon like children before the chief of the "feminine tribe" and the "black robe's Great Father," an act repeated over and over into the eighteenth century. But it also entailed mature self-examination on the part of the French, who saw themselves as parents.

Thus, inside the rugged exterior of the pioneer lay the spiritual uncertainty of absolution. Despite general French-Native consensus regarding good, there was confusion concerning the true nature of evil. Were they, the French North Americans, to live or be judged according to New World standards or French standards of evil? Or had they really pioneered something in-between? If they ventured too far away from their Old World kin would they ever find them in the afterlife? Could souls travel the Atlantic ocean?

Mythological and religious syncretism had allowed both a certain duality and the fusion of a common pantheon of twins and rites during life. But now, before the day of judgment, before joining and answering to their ancestors, what was the final word? A resuscitated Wendat woman reported to her community that in Heaven the French tortured their converts as captives while Wendat traditionalists danced in the Native "country of souls."[206] A French Canadian legend expressed a similar worry: L'arrivée was stuck in Purgatory because he was refused entry to both Heaven and Hell, by both St Peter and Satan, because of debt.[207] Anxiety over rejoining kin in familiar communities in the afterlife troubled both French and Native as the novelty of their interlaced multiethnic community might find locked gates, with the result that they would be scattered to heaven, hell, and the "country of souls." A soul lacking kin and community was truly a lost soul, ripe for joining the ranks of haunting revenants. If the social models metaphorically exhorted action (like the war chiefs), then the twinned Gluscap and John the Baptist counselled wisdom (like the elders). Gluscap's increasing humility and John the Baptist's repentance were "voices crying out in the wilderness" of moral uncertainty, awaiting the final baptism by water, fire, and the Holy Ghost.

CHAPTER SEVEN

Hunting Otherworlds

Belief and rituals stress an aspect of a communal shared past (Urzeit), which embodies its view of the end of time (Endzeit), in order to orient the community in the present and to enable it to make sense of how to face the future. The relinking of common meanings reinforces the boundaries of communal trust. In a multiethnic "frontierless" Fourth World society, who is inside and who is outside the community? Where does communal trust begin and end? And what does this all mean after life ends? Christian belief emphasized inherent good and evil, while most Aboriginal beliefs demonstrated the ambiguity of power and how it could wield both good and evil. When belief met belief, the view of good was often shared, but the nature of evil was more debatable. "One man's wine" sometimes seemed literally to be "another man's poison," as demonstrated by Innu Betsiamites who, due to its effect on them, believed wine literally to be French poison. On the other side, so many customs tabooed in Europe were freely practised and, to French astonishment, appeared to have a beneficial effect upon health and society. Even the missionaries wondered if innocence could bring better results than the necessity of choosing between good and evil and that it failed so often due to human weakness – which induced them to try to protect their "innocent" Aboriginals on missions away from the "corrupted" French. And the free will so vehemently embraced by the Counter-Reformation, especially by the Jesuits, was contingent upon the knowledge of what good and evil were – a knowledge that enabled one to really choose between them (and that appeared to be increasingly multivalent). For those who vied to be entrusted with communal survival for the future, how did a communally significant fragment of their shared past, filtered through some semblance of a shared interpretation about the end of time, reorient immigrant-adoptees in their confusingly new environment?

Each communities' interpretation of the end of time, through twinned corresponding ancestor and foundation myths, is the point of entry into a central "world of interfaced meanings." We shall examine each community's main pre-contact sacred mythical foundation and ancestors through to the central unifying sacred myth, which is still being dealt with today in French North America. Here we are tracing not the specificities of the chronological cross-section of events but the longitudinal "longue durée" of conceptualization.

As the two communities met, French ancestral myth had its roots in pre-Christian lore, which entered into para-Christian legend in the guise of Hellequin of the Wild Horde. Hellequin mediated between this world and the otherworld by leading his hunters (who in later Christian lore were sinners instead), who galloped across the sky to the otherworld. Concurrently, Gluscap's brother, Carcajou (of the north Atlantic Algonquian culture area), was cast as the evil one yet had the power of resuscitation and thus mediated between the living and the dead. The qualities and stories of Hellequin and Carcajou matched, were compared and contrasted as twins, and, over time, were melded through the forge of common life and dangers. A uniquely New World mythical being, Ti-Jean, evolved through mediation of the ancestral heritages of both French and Algonquian. The famous Ti-Jean emerged not only from a combined sacred mythical heritage but also from a pressing social necessity. The comically well-meaning, bungling, but ultimately triumphant Ti-Jean resembled Champlain and was prototypical of so many maladroit newcomers. These stories were also excellent social icebreakers, together with alcohol, tobacco, and the aroma of roasting meat over a crackling campfire. They eased cultural discrepancy by providing a common laugh.

Following this, we shall trace the foundation and still central sacred myth of French North America, that of the Chasse-Galérie. The mediators who flew between this world and the Other became associated, due to the constant stream of coureurs de bois who travelled along the riverine fur trade route, with the ubiquitous Chasse-Galérie. The concrete east-to-west route taken by the coureurs and later by the voyageurs became mirrored in reverse in the mythical west-to-east route through the sky taken by the phantom Chasse-Galérie canoe. The role of inversion enables us to sort through conflicting meanings of the liminal, ambiguous, hybrid Third Space and helps make sense of Purgatory and the Native otherworld (Wendat Atisken andahatey or the Innu Tchipai meskenau). The Chasse-Galérie myth deals with the social conundrum of the human within a "frontierless frontier," as well as with our relationship with nature itself, where the interwoven past (Urzeit) and the end of time (Endzeit) become conflated and sacrally mythicized. Positive solutions were drawn from the past to help people face the conundrums of the present and future, enhancing the intercommunal trust that bound the French-Native network.

HELLEQUIN AND THE GREAT RABBIT

The Wild Man of the Woods, ancestor of Hellequin, was keeper of the animals and leader of the spirits of the dead, and he was at the crux of related traditions in north Atlantic France. Ethnohistorian Olive Patricia Dickason has clearly linked him to the image of the "homme sauvage" in New France.[1] Ancient Celtic as well as Nordic lore were still alive in the Breton and Norman areas, some being so ancient that the distinction between Celtic and Nordic beliefs is not entirely clear-cut. Celtic and Nordic versions of the Hellequin myth indicate its antiquity and wide distribution. A central source of Hellequin was the ancient mysterious antlered Celtic divinity Cernunnos, who was the keeper of the forest game and was usually portrayed seated cross-legged with a stag or ram-headed serpent whose boar led hunters to the otherworld.[2] Early Christian missionaries identified Cernunnos with Satan, yet belief in him survived among the common people. For centuries his persona continued roaming through European folklore, usually in the form of King Arthur or his several wilder or mysterious alters: the giant herdsman of the Lady of the Fountain was one.[3] The second was his mysterious alter-ego, the enchanter Merlin as Merlin-Ambrosius according to the Babylonian Talmudic tradition of Ashmodai (rebel of YHWH or Asmodeus), or Merlin-Silvestris of Celtic tradition (Myrddin or Taliesin of Welsh, Suibhne of Irish, and Lailoken of Scottish folklore).[4] Homines sylvestris, or the druids of Pliny and Caesar's descriptions, antedate this tradition and were later reflected in the Welsh poem "Ymddiddon Myrddin" ("Merlin's Conversation"), which has Taliesin or Myrddin (the Welsh variant of Merlin) call the insane dying warriors "gwyllon." This is because 140 slain nobles passed "occult information from the realm of the dead" to Merlin, thus enhancing his magical powers.[5] Merlin's underworld link was associated with the Dis Pater god, Don, of the Underworld, supposed by Caesar to be ancestor of the Gauls.[6] Another Celtic offshoot of the Cernunnos tradition had the Irish St Patrick transforming himself into a stag, and the Scottish St Kentigern legend was connected to St-Corneille, or Cornély, patron of the beasts.[7]

Traditions in the Breton highlands attribute similar traditions to rex Artus (King Arthur), king of the ancient Britons, according to Gervais de Tilbury.[8] In Brittany the Welsh tradition of Gwyn ap Nudd, lord of the dead, led the Cwn Annwyn (Gabriel hounds, or hounds of Hades) over wastelands at night bearing away the souls of the dying.[9] The ancient Briton legend of King Herla, who made a pact with the king of the dwarves (who were ancestral spirits), was also associated with King Arthur. The dwarf king entered Herla's wedding as he was getting married to the daughter of the king of the Franks, gave many gifts. He even gave Herla fancy gifts for the his (the dwarf king's) own wedding. The dwarf king afterward gave King Herla a bloodhound but forbade him, on pain of death, to dismount before the dog descended from the skies, thus condemning him to wander forever in the heavens. This was King Herla's punishment for making a pact with the king of the dead.[10] The king of the hunt was also associated with the Devil himself as king of the dead.[11] In the Vendée this story was referred to as the "carosse du roi Hugon." This being hunted after on the Toussaint (Halloween) and ran from Rome to Nantes. He was often sighted above the forest of Chantemerle, Clazay, and at Deux-Sèvres. Sieur Galléry hunted the game of the gods.[12]

In Normandy the Mesnie Hellequin (Wild Chase, or familia Herlichini, or Wilde Jagd) flew across the skies, with Hellequin leading a horde of revenants as an apparition that appeared to priest Walchelin (or Gauchelin), as recounted by Orderic Vital in a history of the Normans from 1123 to 1137.[13] Even today the Norman Cauchois have a cult of the dead, which begins on November first, and they go to the cemetery with crysanthemums.[14] The dead were anticipated from November third to eleventh, or from the day after Halloween (la Toussaint) to the feast of St Martin, when "bears and savages leave their caves." This was the same as the ancient Roman Feralia (day of the dead), which was held for the "manes" (good spirits of the dead).[15] Orderic Vital's army of revenants was composed of three groups: the Third Estate (commoners), the First Estate (clerics), and the Second Estate (nobility). The commoners walked or rode horses heavy with stolen goods, accompanied by a cavalry of noblewomen, who rode past the priest with breasts pierced by incandescent nails (note that noblewomen were automatically demoted from their estate and unclothed) The second troupe was armed with crosses and begged Walchelin to pray for them. Finally, the army of knights (chevaliers, or exercitus militum, or Totenheer) rode clothed in black and spewing flames, each bearing his torment, such as burning irons or blood "heavier than the tower of Rouen or Mont St-Michel" (landmarks in Normandy and Brittany, respectively). The priest Walchelin received a signum (sign) from his brother to repair the latter's sins. He had to remain silent for three days to ensure his brother's redemption from Purgatory – a sure sign of official apparitions in Norman lore. Walchelin was also warned of his own impending death. The apparition, as recounted by Vital, also has very ancient roots and appears to be related to Tacitus's Germanic Harii spectres who engaged in combat by night. This belief continued in the Mannerbünde of the ancient Germans; In Normandy it continued as the Chasse sauvage (Wild Hunt). In Scandinavian versions, the tradition of Nordic "berserkers" was expressed in warrior societies whose members dedicated their lives to Odin, were remarkably immune to pain, and wore wolf or bear skins.[16] A famous tale in the Norse "Speculum Regolae" involved men frightened in battle who went insane and ran off to the woods. They were called "gelt" and acquired feathers and agility, as discussed in the Irish miribilia. The tradition of the Mesnie Hellequin was very strong in Normandy, and he was called Carlequin, mère Harpine, Chéserpine, Karlequinus (Charles Quint) and Proserpine.[17] In the Orbec region of Normandy he was called Cain, while in Rémilly-sur-Lozon (Manche) the hunt was called Chasse à Charlemagne.[18] He was a major myth, especially in sixteenth-century Rouen, and a figurine of the Wild Man was placed above house doors or by the fireplace to guard against the invasion of the Underworld as well as on the portal of Rouen cathedral to represent the condemned wanderers doing penance.[19] Father Brébeuf himself, who hailed from Condé-sur-Vire in Normandy, was not only graced by visions of giant palaces, angels, and Mary and Joseph erecting a huge cross over Iroquoia but was also haunted by troops of ghostly demons in the guise of men, bears, wolves, lynx, and skeleton-like spectres.

The Mesnie Hellequin supposedly appeared in borderland and crossroads areas, such as the border of Wales, Mount Etna ("mouth of Hell"), the island of Avalon (Arthur's abode), or Mont-Chat in the Franche-Comté.. His mesnie flew from St Catherine's Monastery in the Sinai desert to Normandy.[20] In the Roman Britannia of the sixth century it was believed that the wilderness between the Roman walls was the home of wild beasts and departed souls, which was exactly where Merlin fled: the Caledonian woods. Wilderness forests, islands, borderlands, mounds, and crossroads were sacred spaces where the Mesnie passed, and to which the demoted druids returned.[21] The Mesnie Hellequin, according to Guillaume d'Auvergne, medieval bishop of Paris, was located in the sacred space of Purgatory, where souls repented for their sins in order to gain entry into Heaven.[22] This sacred space was an in-between space for in-between souls, neither quite alive nor completely dead, as they sought reconciliation with their creator. In this place the frontiers between worlds were thinner and more permeable than elsewhere. The terror inspired by the Mesnie guarded aristocratic, and later royal, rights over the forests and was thus useful in keeping the population from crossing the line of habitation. Jean-Claude Schmitt signalled that any lapse of royal power, such as that which occurred in early seventeenth-century France, was often occasioned by the identification of the troop in the reverse mode of an infernal royalty.[23] Even today Hellequin survives in modern European carnival celebrations, which, by always including Arlequin, link church and state through their intimate connection with Lenten repentance and the monde à l'envers.[24]

In north Atlantic France, the belief that the spirits of the dead were linked to the living via beasts was still very strong in the seventeenth century. It was believed that revenants were capable of metamorphosing into animal form in the sacred in-between space of Purgatory. The hunting of animals was associated with accompanying the Mesnie Hellequin as the cohort of dead souls returned.[25] Breton "spontails" returned in the form of animals, especially birds (ravens and crows), bees, or butterflies; and the ancient Celts, Nordics, and Romans used bird omens to guide their actions. One Breton tradition relating to King Arthur's death holds that he and Queen Guinevere were both buried in the canton of Barentin between Mortain and Domfront, and that their souls flew off as white crows.[26] In Nordic tradition Odin travelled shamanically as a bird to the otherworld.[27] Northern tales of swan maidens were like Mi'kmaq tales of Pulowech.[28] Elves ("gobelins" in Norman), were also ancestors and returned after death because of some sin, at which time they often became horses instead of birds.[29] Popular in Western France was the Vendéen tale of the Route du Sel, in which a French Hansel and Gretel were abandoned in the forest by their hungry parents. They are subsequently taken in by a wolfman's wife; the boy is eaten and the girl gathers his bones together and metamorphosed into a bird. The childrens' parents are damned and finally the children are saved.[30] This may reflect on a cultural level what Géza Roheim wrote on a psycho-physiological level. Women, like beasts, were thought not to possess souls and, therefore, were likely repositories for such between-world action.[31] Both British queens, for example, were thought by their countrypeople to be capable of transforming men into beasts. Mary Tudor, Queen of Scots, was contentiously labelled by Anglicans a Circe who killed men and then metamorphosed them into animals (wolves, swine, and lions). Spencer epitomized Queen Elisabeth in the figure of the Fairie Queen (fairies, like elves, being ancestors), who magically influenced the moon with a wand and was called Titanesse, the name Ovid gave to one of his heroines in *Metamorphoses.*

Carcajou, the fallen brother of Gluscap, has always been presented as a troublemaker. These twins were akin to those of the Iroquoians, who had a good brother (Ioscaha, or Sapling) and an evil one (Ta8iscaron, or Flint). The present examination focuses upon Carcajou, his role in the afterlife, and the ghosts of the deceased, symbolically including them in the community through cultural métissages. Both brothers, as well as the Anishinabe Nanabozo, were descended from the turtle, but their grandmother was a bear, thus adding to the reverence of bear rites. The Atlantic Algonquian demiurge Gluscap was the creator of the animals, and he had a trickster twin brother named Carcajou. He was also called Kakajo, Glouton, Wolverine, Wolf, Indian Devil, Lox, Lucifer, raccoon, lynx, and Malsumsis. He was the chief, or father, of the wolves (the Mi'kmaq and Menomini both associate him with the wolves) and was called the Destroyer as he mediated between this world and the otherworld.[32] Among the later Innu (Innu-Naskapi), Mistabeo, or Mistanabi, the male inner "Great Man," was identified, with

Carcajou, as one's soul-spirit, which led one to the game, revealed itself in dreams, and must be nurtured through smoking or drinking bear grease.

The two brothers discussed how they were going to be born, and Gluscap preferred the normal route. But Carcajou decided to leave by his mother's side or armpit, which killed her. Both formed the beings and things of this world, but Carcajou formed the mountains, valleys, serpents, and inconveniences. Each held the key to the other's life and death. Carcajou asked Gluscap what would kill him, and he said the bulrush or cattail. Yet when Carcajou applied it to Gluscap, it killed him only temporarily. When Gluscap recovered, he killed Carcajou with bird down. Notice that the brothers could only wound one another with softness.

Carcajou corresponded with the French Hellequin, a central figure of French north Atlantic folklore, who was leader of the Wild Hunt. Hellequin blew his horn while racing over the night sky with his menagerie of dead souls. Wolverines were not a species that existed in Europe, and therefore Carcajou was an addition to rather than a transformation of the French Canadian pantheon. The wolverine's characteristics were famous among the Algonquians: it stole freshly killed carcasses hunted by other animals, indicating unusual cowardice joined with exceptional deception and cruelty. Both Carcajou and Hellequin were negative models – foolish tricksters and comic antiheroes feeding upon the exploits of more positive personae.

Carcajou was a pivotal figure and, because his feet were of both genders, could even change his gender at will.[33] His overweening pride and desire to promulgate mischief were the core of his tales. He was also so rude to the ferryman, the crane, that he was temporarily drowned.[34] Carcajou raced with the stone giant.[35] Fiery and prickly objects constantly plagued Carcajou (thorns, briars, flint, hornets' nests, and itchberries caused him to almost scratch himself to death). He was constantly dying and being returned to life. After several deaths he was revived by his brother and then remarked that he must have been asleep.[36] This refers to his shamanic ability to symbolically "die" while asleep and then subsequently be revived, like the historic Celtic druids, King Arthur, Nordic völva, and Nordic Odin.

In the Atlantic area French north Atlantic Hellequin lore paired up with the lore of the Atlantic Algonquians (mostly Mi'kmaq, Maliseet, Innu, and Abenaki). Because the inter-Atlantic contact in this area had been continuous since the sixteenth century via Norman, Rochelois, and Breton fishers, the fusion appears to be earlier and the most extensive than anywhere else in French North America. When there was dualism in the myths, such as competitions between European and Native powers, often the outcome demonstrated the triumph of a mix of Native and European values as evidenced in both Native and European personae.

Among the lakeland Algonquians, who lived where the woodlands were replaced by lakes and grasslands, Hellequin twinned up with Nanabozo rather than with Carcajou. The hunt was believed to be regulated by the Great Rabbit, Michapou (Anishinabe),[37] or Messou or Mecabau (Innu), who was associated and often fused with Nanabozo (Anishinabe), Wiske'djak (Cree), or Mahtigwess (Mi'kmaq). Hennepin mentions the otkon (oki) in the wood who regulated the hunt and who was called "Lady of Hunting."[38] The Great Rabbit was the most prominent among a host of Great Brother animals of the Great Lakes. These beings could graciously allow game to be caught or they could withhold it.[39] The Great Rabbit originated death but could also restore life.[40] Nanabozo's wolf brother, from his adopted family, guided dead souls on a four-day journey.[41] Nanabozo could metamorphose himself into any animal, and he revoked the gift of animal speech due to their plotting against humans.[42] If the learned French generally scoffed at Algonquian hunting and culinary rites, the non-literate habitants took no chances of offending the Great Rabbit or any of the Great Brother animals. Sagard wrote that the Innu venerated the Great Brother animals who regulated the taking of game. In the eighteenth century, Bacqueville de La Potherie declared that the habitants held the Great Keeper of Bears, Dogs, and Beavers in special veneration, which implies their ordinary respect of all such keepers.[43] One had to dream of the animal before it would allow the hunter to catch it.[44] Ground animal bones were important ingredients for medicines and magic, and hunting charms (such as rabbit's feet) were saved as good luck charms, much to the disdain of many of the erudite Jesuits, who tried to suppress and laugh off such "superstitions."[45]

Later tales of Nanabozo typically portray him as a comic trickster who falls victim to snares that he had laid for others.[46] The later Nanabozo plays the anti-hero, a Jungian trickster or shadow. This is closer to the Wendat ondinnonk (soul-wish revealed in a dream) or, as Géza Roheim has suggested more prosaically, the Freudian id.[47] Great Rabbit, or, in his most familiar guise, Nanabozo, seems to be the model for the American Bugs Bunny. He was constantly dissimulating his Rabelaisian desires and rabbit identity to escape being punished or devoured. In French lore the rabbit was the symbol of fertility and was frequently portrayed in etchings and paintings. The invulnerable rabbit or rabbit-fairy was also a staple of Norman beliefs, which coincided with the Algonquian view of Great Rabbit as full of protective magic.[48] Has the founding Algonquian Great Rabbit become our foolish Bugs Bunny?

Hunting and gathering Algonquians conceived of human beings as part of Nature as their lives staple depended upon their respecting the capacity to renew game.[49] Beast pelts and bones were fastidiously utilized, and those that were not used were carefully treated with elaborate taboos and rites so as not to hinder the catching of other animals.[50] The animal origin and end of humans, and the Algonquian powagan, or guardian spirit (Mi'kmaq:

téomul, or pou-he-gan), corresponds with Celtic and Nordic customs. The latter believed that the animal double needed a pelt or mask in order to travel to the otherworld. Upon the abortion of embryos, the Mi'kmaq wrapped death bows and arrows in a thin skin scrawled over with representations of babies, birds, moose, bears, and beavers.[51]

Calvin Martin quoted eighteenth-century fur traders Alexander Henry and David Thompson, who indicated that some Algonquian trappers apparently suspected the bears of having sent famine and disease due to the over-kill of game. Martin rightly discussed endemic diseases of both animals and humans (such as tularemia and typhus).[52] Human/beast relations in both Native and French cultures of this era were far more important than one can perhaps imagine today.

The belief in animals possessed of souls akin to those of human beings, and the belief that human beings were capable of metamorphosing into beasts, was common in both communities. Beasts were included in the pantheon of intermediaries between the living and dead communities, particularly when life was so dependent upon the wildlife that was diminishing as the fur trade was expanding and as disease was increasing in Native communities.[53] Beasts featured ritually both as the disease-containing and disease-healing elements in the medicine rites of Algonquian, Wendat, and Haudenosaunee. Bits of their bones, sinews, and dried fluids composed the main panoply of sacred objects in medicine bags.

If beasts enabled the prolongation of life or threatened its end, they also provided shamanic mobility between the world of the living and the world of the dead. In order to world-jump, the trickster took on just another one of his myriad disguises, which healers symbolically simulated by the use of an animal pelt or a mask. The pagan pelt of European heritage, in contrast to the European Christian hairshirt, did not involve shedding one's pelt, or sinfulness, to become reborn. Pre-Christian pelts returned to the past to heal the wounds of the living. Human metamorphosis into animals has a long history in France, where it is linked to the Roman idea of "larvatus," or "mascus" (witch). This was based upon the fact that those born with a caul were supposedly gifted with shamanic powers, being born with a natural shroud that enabled them to enter the realm of the dead and to return. Norse hamingja, or fylgja (double or "following" one), was an animal or woman who accompanied a person throughout life and was seen after death in the dreams of family members.[54] Norman revenants were related to the Germanic idea of the soul ("hamr," or envelope) due to their being covered by former animal skins (in Norman dialect: "haire," or "hure").[55] This pelt or mask permitted not only a world-jump but also the return trip. In Western Europe animal bones were wrapped in skins to ensure the resurrection of the animal. The Nordic deity Thor's restored goats after eating them by saving their bones and skins and raising his hammer over them.[56] The Norman custom of fashioning death masks of wax before burial was akin to the earlier custom of wrapping bodies in pelts. The church condemned pagan resurrection. The medieval penitentials condemned widespread masquerading in calfskins on the first (Kalends) of January. The Burgundian Penitential forbade disguising oneself as a calf or sitting on a stag as though such actions were demoniacal. Penance for such actions lasted for three years, as did the Roman and Reginas Ecclesiastical Discipline. The Corrector of Burchard of Worms liberalized this penance, changing it to thirty days on bread and water.[57]

Finally, it appears that Native peoples may not have been half wrong about the beast/human ecostasis and the animal link to disease and healing. European immunity to European diseases was usually acquired through lengthy contact with domesticated and barn animals' diseases, which mimicked human diseases yet protected against them (e.g., cowpox conferring immunity against smallpox). With regard to Native Americans, however, it was physical distance from wild beasts (excepting the dog and bear) that ensured their safety.[58] Now the HIV virus and perhaps others transfer diseases from animals to humans, while the use of animal organs and tissues is a potential human life saver. The ecostasis that depended upon the interdependence of human and beast used to be embodied in the beliefs that underlay shamanic practices. And, frankly, these make more ecological sense than does the sociobiological "Darwinian" (Spencerian) misconception, which holds that the species, gender, and race that is the strongest must necessarily subjugate all the others rather than using its strength or intelligence to maintain a life-giving biodiversity.

Rites and myth in French North America often revolve around the deceased, ancestors, and beasts. In French Canada the Day of the Dead – November second (Jour des morts) – was traditionally devoted to the souls in Purgatory. There were masses for the dead financed by money from farm produce (la criée des morts). The dead were called as witnesses, albums and prayers were brought out, sacrifices were made to the dead, and tithes were paid to the treasury of souls ("trésor des âmes"), especially for the most abandoned soul in the parish.[59] After the Mass for the Dead, the food is brought to be sold for the criée, the bell is rung all night, ploughing is banned between Halloween and November second so as not to bleed the earth, and month-long prayers are said for the well-being of the dead.[60] After Halloween, the Wendat of the late 1670s flocked to church to console Mother Mary for the loss of her only son.[61] As is attested to by the wills of New France collected between 1633 and 1760, 75 percent of the population requested the Recollects, not the Jesuits, to say mass for their souls in Purgatory.[62]

Mythologically, the classic fallen twin was epitomized in the emergence of the famous French Canadian trickster, Ti-Jean, whose characteristics draw from Hellequin, Carcajou, and Nanabozo, and whose tales have spread through all of Turtle Island.[63] The French Canadian legend of Ti-Jean was highly fused as a result of métissage in the Atlantic area, while in the Great Lakes area a patchier bricolage melded traditions. Ti-Jean was a clumsy and foolish simpleton, like Til Eulenspiegel of the Netherlands, or Dum Hans of the Germanic areas. The tales generally involve a simpleton winning the hand of a princess or chief's daughter after fighting wild beasts, monsters, or cannibals with the aid of magic obtained, through his warm-hearted and/or bumbling qualities, from cunning forest people.[64] Whereas metropolitan French tales usually wind up with the commoner becoming elevated to a prince, the French Canadian versions finish with the simpleton bringing his princess back to nature.

One version that provides metaphorical keys to meaning comes from the Ile d'Orléans. Ti-Jean was a prince who saved himself from being devoured by wild beasts upon Île d'Orléans and thereafter won the hand of the princess. This tale clearly links him to all his mythical predecessors. The location of Île d'Orléans specifies both Wendat ghosts returned as animals and Ti-Jean as Hellequin, Carcajou, Nanabozo, who commands the forest beasts as in the Lorette legend "Rêve du chasseur."[65] Of course, his reward is a high status matrimonial match, which is classic in French tales.[66] The echo of Old Testament Daniel taming the wild beasts also provides the Endzeit aspect, which was nuanced by the Mi'kmaq and Norman final conflagration (Ragnarok), when every deity struggles with his beast-nemesis before the renewal of the world.[67] And is Ti-Jean the early shadow of the later Algonquin Kawichet, spirit of the hunt?[68]

French Canadian lore was so thoroughly mixed with that of the Atlantic Algonquian that many Native nations have their own locally flavoured Ti-Jean tales. For example, the Mi'kmaq tell of a Ti-Jean who exchanged his cow for magic food, belt, and a flute, which helped him tame the wild beasts and win the hand of the princess. Another tale tells of a servant who made off with the wife and wigwam of his master by way of a magic box and coat. His master found the coat, regained everything, and subsequently flayed the servant.[69] The Maliseet told of a simpleton called Strong John who succeeded in killing a monster for the hand of a princess.[70] Bernard Assiniwi tells of the Algonquin "Chagnan," a goofball type remarkably similar to Ti-Jean.[71] The Native allies so thoroughly enjoyed the inanities of Ti-Jean that they spread his fame all over the continent. Stith Thompson and Claude Lévi-Strauss have marvelled at the infusion of European folklore into Algonquian tales and attribute it mainly to French Canadian coureurs and voyageurs. But again, it must be emphasized that the process of collage and métissage began long before the French approached the Great Lakes. Bailey comments, referring to the Maritimes and New England, "Ti-Jean ... contributed to the Paul Bunyon cycle of the Maine lumberjacks to an as yet unestimated extent."[72] And farther west Jean Morisset remarked: "In his last work, Claude Lévi-Strauss was surprised to state ... to what extent French Canadian folklore has penetrated West Coast Native legends ... so they have Ti-Jean ... Ti-Jean-le Fripon, Grand-Jean-L'Intrépide, etc." ("Dans son dernier ouvrage, Claude Lévi-Strauss s'étonne de constater ... quel point des légendes indiennes de la Côte-Ouest ont puisé dans le folklore franco-canadien ... Ainsi Ti-Jean (Ti-Jean-le-Fripon, Grand-Jean-L'Intrépide, etc.)."[73]

Why did Ti-Jean appeal to Algonquian nations and beyond? Ti-Jean provided a social model of the greenhorn newcomer who stumbles over his own feet yet, due to his good intentions, winds up on top. This model, like Carcajou, is the inverse of the early wise and/or cunning Gluscap and the early Nanabozo. The greenhorn could always earn big laughs among the immigrant as well as among the veteran Native population. His antics were repeated over and over in the social sphere as Native paired up with French on hunting, fishing, and canoeing expeditions. Yet the archetypal social model was Champlain, whose image closely resembled that of Ti-Jean, while cunning Algonquian chiefs like Cherououny were the spitting image of the pre-contact Gluscap. This equation of foolish greenhorn leader paired with sophisticated chiefs was repeated with other chiefs as well (e.g., when Champlain met Kichesipirini chief Tessouat, Innu chief Erouachy, Algonquin chief Iroquet, and Wendat chief Aenons). Even though later governors general were unlike Champlain in that they were seasoned nobility, they were still greenhorns with regard to Native protocol and could often be wound about a Native chief's finger, as Governor General Montmagny was wound around the finger of Mohawk chief Kiotsaeton. Clearly, due to common social interactions, the Ti-Jean myth was relevant and thus perpetuated.

As he moved westward and southward, Ti-Jean was drawn not only from later comic Hellequin, Carcajou, and Nanabozo traditions but also from other trickster types. Further west, among the Siouan peoples, the antics of the foolish Coyote trickster, and farther south, among the Navaho, of Loki also closely resemble those of Ti-Jean. All these areas have complementary Ti-Jean tales. He was a well known character in Native tales and was called Ticon or Jijean (Anishinabe), Kicon (Cree), Laptiss (Nez Percé), Ducetca (Shuswap), Jack (Thompson), and Ptciza (Kalapuya).[74] On the west coast his tales appear in Chinook, which, by the nineteenth century, was a trade language consisting of mostly French mixed with a few dozen Native tongues and dotted with English.[75]

How did Ti-Jean develop and evolve into the famous fool? As the French became increasingly "tribalized" in the French-Native network, and some Native nations were driven by Haudenosaunee, disease, and alcohol into a world less familiar to them, Ti-Jean influenced Carcajou, Nanabozo, and Coyote tales, resulting in their becoming less regal. Ti-Jean joined with these tricksters, becoming incorporated into a pan-Native folklore, and he was popular precisely because he engendered the qualities of all these local tricksters while erasing their specific sources. Thus Ti-Jean was able to travel widely as a fitting symbol of pan-Native and French unity. This unity became quite literal when, in some tales, Ti-Jean was portrayed as a Native himself.[76] Ti-Jean's Native appearance pops up frequently in Three Rivers, precisely in the St Lawrence town that was founded due to repeated Native requests, where Champlain specifically asked both peoples to intermarry, and which, for the first century of settlement, was the home of most of the fur traders.[77] Yet, in the long perspective, it is not by chance that Ti-Jean appears in the Laurentian heartland of New France as an Amerindian while in the Native centre (Great Lakes, Ottawa region, Illinois country, the west) he was usually portrayed as French. In other words, each region identified him as the Other, meaning that he was a pivotal intercommunal figure across Turtle Island.

It seems that the dialogue between Hellequin and Native America sparked reflections in the metropolis as well. Louis-François de Lisle wrote "Arlequin sauvage" (1721). Arlequin is a Native brought to Europe and who errs out of good-hearted simplicity, yet manages to win his love, Violette, and transmit an unequivocal image of the Noble Savage. This tale of greenhorn Native newcomer in France and sophisticated Frenchmen reversed the Ti-Jean/Gluscap equation, bringing mutual dialogue full circle.[78]

In conclusion, the mythical dialogue between Hellequin and his Algonquian twin (Carcajou in the Atlantic and Nanabozo in the lakelands) gave birth to a uniquely French North American trickster. The thorough fusion of French and Algonquian elements in the Atlantic myths indicates how dialogue dilemmas between French and Algonquian were integrated in an attempt to make mythic sense of socio-historical realities. Unlike twins each brought an entire army of ghosts or beasts to reunite with their communities. Myth became reality, and reality spawned more myth. These developments resulted in an interwoven web of understanding and a mythical métissage.

The Great Lakes area was full of surprises for the early French settlers, and for this reason lakeland Algonquian tales usually had less fusion than did those from other areas. But these tales contained more doubling and incongruous, even incoherent, collaged alternations between worlds. Tales from this area alternate between a French base with Native decorations, a Native base with French decorations, and many in-between. These swatches of influence constitute a modular bricolage, albeit usually with a base that was either French or Native. Social and historical realities suggest that, if the base was French with Native decorations, then it was adapted for a Native audience, and vice versa. Although there is less real integration in inland Algonquian-French mythical dialogue, there seems to be a later mutual dialogue between the synthesized French Canadian Ti-Jean, Nanabozo, and

Coyote. Due to this later dialogue, perhaps Nanabozo became more comic rather than archetypal.

The pivotal liminal mediator between the past and postcontact present must be decoded via Celtic, Nordic, and Algonquian traditions, at the very least. These traditions are deep and have survived the longue durée due to adaptation and the melding of meanings. Ti-Jean's antics have highbooted over the continent to tickle a million funnybones, yet few have searched beyond his buffoonery to discover the older core of his forest ancestors. Hellequin was transformed, as he sailed between worlds, via the beastly metamorphoses of Carcajou and Nanabozo into the Good Hunter, who journeyed within himself by dying and had to be revived with the assistance of the beasts. The Good Hunter remained the focus of both Iroquoian and later Midewiwin healing rites, while Ti-Jean haunted the backwoods of folklore by reincarnating the comic ghost of Champlain and many successive shiploads of newcomers. If the Good Hunter became the formerly wounded healer, Ti-Jean prevented illness through merriment. If Nanabozo's journey was the focus of Native medicine, Ti-Jean's giant peals of laughter still boom over the treetops across North America wherever French and Native met.

PHANTOM CANOES

Contacting ancestors was easier than interpreting their ancestral wisdom in absolute terms (Endzeit). The origin of evil was a particularly sticky question. The seventeenth-century focus upon a Satan independent of divine control was a driving force behind the witch hysteria in Europe, but it was also emblematic of the fragmentation of the conceptual and moral foundation of pre-Reformation Europe.

While British colonies in North America and Protestant areas of Europe were intent derving a maximum profit from nature and human beings, French missionaries were frequently upset because their previously held conceptions of nature and human beings were inadequate in light of what they learned from Native communities in North America. Spiritual and social uncertainty led to an inevitable turning inward, which accompanied a simultaneous turning outward, thus leading to greater tolerance for liminality and the absence of absolute answers. What Jacques Le Goff, Nathalie Zemon Davis, and Homi Bhabha call the hybrid "Third Space"[79] was, at this early time in the inter-Atlantic dialogue, precisely this path between polarities. Wendat neophyte purgatory, as recorded between 1659 and 1671, consisted of passing through a series of wigwams, where one was treated well or badly depending upon one's behaviour on earth. This purgatory was apart from Hell's inhabitants, where the "Ondechonronnons" live in fire and cinders (Notre-Dame-de-Foy).[80] French intermediary purgatorial space, which the Counter-Reformation filled with those departed or absent, was waiting to be redeemed through indulgences (payment) and suffrage prayers. It became crossed with the Native non-judgmental sanctuary, which teemed with ancestors and those not yet officially buried or departed, enlarging the "conceptual powwow ground" between both French and Native souls. The Atisken andahatey reminded the Wendat of the route that the unlike twin brothers took to return to the skyworld towards the end of the third cosmological age reminding humans that they must choose between good and evil.[81] The creation of a Third Space within society and myth was essential in establishing both "common" and "middle" grounds on the St Lawrence and in the Great Lakes, respectively; however, in New France this took place within a context that utilized old frameworks for fresh ideas.

The dialogue of French and Native folk belief and ritual regarding the collective memory of each, ancestors and the deceased, the nature of evil, the identification of a multifarious self, and the nature of penance was especially salient. On the one hand, we have voyageur rituals that marked significant symbols at the checkpoints along the canoe route from the St Lawrence to the Great Lakes fur country. On the other hand, we have the mirror-reversal of this voyage in the classic French Canadian folktale of the Chasse-Galérie, which tells of the coureurs' magical nocturnal canoe flight back to the Laurentian Valley to visit girlfriends as well as the hazardous flight back to fur country. Classically, inversions were used by rebellion leaders and magic-makers, and in New France they had implications for the reconceptualization of French and Native, and good and evil. Don Handelman has rightly suggested that we note not only the world-jump itself but also the measured degrees of "purification" from the otherworld. These voyages mark the crossing from the French to the Native centres of New France itself, the transition from French to Native culture, the journey through time from French immigrant to veteran Canadian and back, which relives the collective memory of the transatlantic voyage as well as the voyage to the Great Lakes. They alluede to the journey of a people from metropolitan France to backwoods Canada, from the celebrations considered to be a witches' sabbath in France to Ononharoia ("the reversing of the brain") in Canada, from the deceased "country of souls" to rebirth, from old age to youth, from paganism to baptism, and from urbanity back to Nature. The power of rebirth was sought in the journey deep into Native territory, which functioned as a "meaning-making" legitimizing collective historical rite of initiation and legend, much like the crossing of the Hebrews from Egypt through Mount Sinai to the Promised Land, celebrated annually in the rite of Passover. The French North American rite also mirrored the great Puritan migration from satanic corrupt Britain to the millennial City on a Hill, as Avihu Zakai has brilliantly reconstructed for New England.[82] The to-and-fro canoe symbol of the essence of New France lent meaning and legitimacy to collective hardships and focused upon communal survival, which depended upon a later reinforcement of communal boundaries and deepened the trusting interdependency between its members. Until the early eighteenth century, expansion and reaching out left vague boundaries; but during the Seven Years War and until the demise of the fur trade, the cradle of the canoe had nourished the nativity of New France. The canoe and its crew became the "symbol of the pioneer community." Having previously sailed together across the stormy ocean, the crew rowed with Native guides in a fragile birchbark canoe that skittered through every rapid, had to be "shot" over the "waterfalls" of obstacles, and would hopefully arrive in the Amerindian heartland. The canoe thus became a literal metaphor for Nativization. Even the contemporary Winter Carnival in Montreal is crowned by ice canoeing across the ice-floe covered St Lawrence onto the snowbound shore.

Whereas initially Wendat traders arrived at Three Rivers, and later Montreal, to trade furs for French goods, after 1649 French youth went en masse to the Great Lakes trappers and were later aided by the Odawa and diaspora Wendat. The transatlantic voyage provided a baseline of "shared understandings" between immigrants, who, although from different localities, began their committed journey together. The early coureur de bois (or, by the eighteenth century, the voyageur), who penetrated the continent via the canoe for furs, metaphorically took the cultural jump of the traversée one step further. The eighteenth-century voyageurs built their repertoire upon seventeenth-century coureurs de bois' knowledge and skills. Their rituals were often based upon survivals of métissages culturels forged by the coureurs and First Nations, of recognizably ancient French or Catholic traditions based upon a Wendat pattern of culture.

Incoming immigrants, in order to pass all the tests for full acceptance and to distinguish themselves from the many temporary winterers and merchants, had to undergo the first mariner's "baptism" of the voyage during the traversée.[83] The second "baptism" drenched them when the voyage was complete and the ship arrived at the mountains of Notre Dame.[84] After being educated with a veteran French Canadian family as an engagé, the male youth was required to pass through the rite of initiation in the heart of fur country in the Great Lakes. The canoe route was an obstacle course of "baptisms" and swearing-in, which the youth had to undergo before being finally admitted into the great male initiation rite of Great Lakes Native living. The rituals constructed by the voyageurs were composed of coureurs de bois themes and rites, which, in the seventeenth century, were generalized among the young male population. These rites became increasingly specialized as fur trade personnel congregated at Three Rivers. The rites were further developed as they were passed to the Montreal area, where fur trading and trapping ran in certain families, and were handed down from one generation to the next.

Several voyageur rituals could serve to illustrate. Joseph-Charles Taché and Grace Lee Nute chronicle the evening preceding the seasonal departure from Lachine. The voyageurs, after smoking, propped up a youth in shirtsleeves with a cock's feather in his knitcap (tuque) beside a veteran in his hooded sweater (capot), multicoloured Métis braided sash, and tobacco pouch (sac à feu). These two were set upon two sacks to sing the Ronde des Voyageurs, while drumming upon two overturned kettles as the company round-danced around them thrice while singing the refrain.

Second, when they reached St-Anne-de-Bellevue, they went to the chapel of "Ste-Anne qui protège les voyageurs" and left money in a special box so the priests would pray for them. Third, the paddlers drank a cup of brandy to avoid the farcical "baptism" of the novices, which was an initiation ceremony at the Point au Baptême, where lots were chosen and the most disagreeable fellow was subjected to a ridiculous group bully session (with his "godfather" upbraiding him to be patient and his "godmother" crushing him with bear hugs). The fourth rite consisted of the initiation into the confrérie des voyageurs: the novice's ceremony consisted of each one, while kneeling, being blessed with a dripping wet cedar branch. From then on they had to follow the voyageur's code of honour.[85] This consisted of never letting a novice pass Point au Baptême without performing the ceremony and never kissing the wife of another voyageur without obtaining his approval.[86]

While entering the Mattawa River from the Ottawa River, they removed their knitcaps and prayed. This was repeated at the site, marked by a cross, where any voyageur had perished en route. When the Great Lakes waves become turbulent, the novices threw tobacco into them and said, "Blow, blow, Old Woman!" ("Souffle, souffle, la vieille!") to conjure a good wind.[87] The novices were warned of the dangers of the Windigo and of the fantastic animals and fish associated with each upcountry site.[88]

The Native allies also had journey rituals that they performed to ensure their health. A dreamlike trance enabled medicine healers to consult with their ancestors, the recently departed, and those absent due to distance. Of all the allies in the seventeenth century, the Wendat were most involved with their ancestors. European epidemics had reduced the Wendat population by at least 50 percent to 90 percent, particularly affecting children and the elderly, and then there was the fall of Wendake. Life now seemed very precious. The shamanic journey was effected through the symbolic agency of special societies of masked beasts, whose aid in providing hunting charms, medicines for the medicine bag, and central roles in the medicine circle all helped the Good Hunter to be resuscitated from the dead and to facilitate human beings' powers of healing.

The origin of this ceremony involved a meeting between the wolf and the owl, who together resuscitated the Good Hunter (a great friend of the wolves) by providing a banquet that brought the dead back to life.[89] This ceremony permitted one to visit beloved deceased and to reunite the living and the dead. The Wendat believed that there were two souls. One of these (esken) walked ahead of the funeral cortège, and wandered back to eat the leftover food of the Aiheonde ("the Great Kettle," or Feast of the Dead). This ceremony took place every seven to ten years, when the bones of the deceased, which were wrapped in furs and placed in a huge pelt-lined pit, were reburied. Then the first soul changed into a turtledove and flew, together with the dead community, straight to the Atisken andahatey, crying "haiiiiii."[90] The second soul, which was within the bones themselves (astiken), stayed in the tomb until sometimes reborn. The avenging spirit of a murder victim's family had to be appeased with a flood of gifts to wash away there tears so that his soul could fly off and thus be "covered."[91] The Native separation of souls occurred by default, unlike in the European pagan conception, where Rhadamanthus's Hall of Judgment sought to punish evil-doers, while the good souls enjoyed Elysium.[92]

The organizing principle of the Wendat afterlife was to unite as many members of families and community allies as possible.[93] Communal and domestic harmony and togetherness were the focus of Wendat life, and this was enhanced by their commercial indispensability to the Algonquian markets. After the fall of Wendake, a Christian Wendat spoke as follows to Bishop Laval, reconstructing the negligible role of the living community in comparison with the illustrious community of the dead: "O Hariouaouagui ... we are nothing more than the debris of a flourishing nation ... What you see is but the carcass of a great people, that the Haudenosaunee has gnawed away at all the flesh ... sucking all the way until ... the marrow ... help your poor children live that are now laid low. For an infinity of peoples depend upon our lives."[94] And, when Prouville de Tracy arrived with the Carignan-Salières regiment to finally attack the Haudenosaunee, they cried for joy: "Great Onontio, you see at your feet ... the remnants of an entire world ... . It is only the carcasses who are speaking ... the Haudenosaunee have only left the bones ... Have courage, desolated people, your bones will be connected to nerves and tendons ... greater than all the governors of the earth, who has had compassion for our miseries."[95] The Wendat found exceptional meaning in reconstituting one large community from links that had been fiercely torn asunder, like Israel's proverbial dry bones that Jeremiah said would be reborn.

Atlantic Algonquians, who lived off the hunt, thought the most obvious way of saving life was to provide enough game; but if this did not work, then they employed shamanism. The Innu told of demiurge Messou, who disguised himself as a mute and presented a thimble pot that was always magically full of food. He told the Innu to keep the secret that he brought all the animals back through the agency of their keepers or elder brothers.[96] Innu tcisaki (medicine healers) tried to contact the Tchipai meskenau ("way of the souls") in the shaking tent ceremony. The Innu traditionalists and converts were buried in common graves.[97] But converted Innu dead were buried with mixed rites: the face was painted red and black, the body shrouded in birchbark covered with linen then blessed by the priest and buried.[98] They then advanced on to the Tchipai Meskenau, where there were blueberry bushes and dancing.[99] By contrast, Mi'kmaq medicine journey traditions were attributed to the myth of the father who lost his only son and voyaged to the realm of the souls to get him (as Norse Odin did for his son Baldur). He was accosted by Papkootparout, the Keeper of Souls, who instructed the Mi'kmaq in everything and who gave him his son's soul as a nut in a sack. In the midst of the festivities welcoming him home, someone accidentally opened the sack, thinking it food. The youth's soul flew back to the realm of the souls, and the father soon died of grief.[100]

Great Lakes Algonquians, as conjectured by Harold Hickerson, evidently held some large funeral ceremonies in the wake of Wendat influence. The inland Algonquians, between 1641 and 1683, also celebrated Feasts of the Dead, and their deceased journeyed to the Tcipaimikan (Anishinabe: Milky Way).[101] These beliefs appear to have been of Wendat origin and their purpose is to unite an otherwise truncated community of partial bands and nations, who lost many loved ones to the Haudenosaunee and the epidemics.[102] According to Hennepin: "they spare nothing to honor their dead ['like the Jews']."[103] The hissing aurora borealis was considered to be the "dance of the dead" for great warriors and medicine healers.[104]

Nanabozo, the culture hero of the Great Lakes and especially of the Anishinabe, had, by the eighteenth century, accepted the founding of the medicine society (the Midewiwin) as the price for his dead brother. Na'patao, his brother the wolf, was responsible for the spirits of the dead. The rattles used at the ceremony were gifts of the rattlesnake, while the loon was a link between the sky and the sea and was represented by drumsticks. The rattles and drums were highly valued because animals could see spirits invisible to humans, even spirits of unborn children. The powers of animals were combined to revive the Good Hunter and to endow him with curative powers.[105] Frequently the formerly ill became Midewiwin healers. The Great Lakes Algonquians' shaman-healers used reversals as a staple of healing – reversing meanings and even magically "shooting" the ill with medicine shells to symbolically "kill" and then resuscitate them.[106] The later Anishinabe Grand Lodge of the Midewiwin's cures was based upon this formula, where the Midewiwin were called Eternal Men. This was the reverse of "casting a spell" upon someone, where the witchcraft victim ostensibly has the foreign object "removed." The Midé's sacred migration recounts the Anishinabe's journey from the Atlantic coast to the interior woods and from there westward. The Ghost Midewiwin (Dzibai) aided the soul on its journey to the land of ghosts. The Dzibai finally helped the family to overcome its overwhelming bereavement.[107] Even the Anishinabe and Lakota had sacred clown healers, called indigokan and Heyoka, who used reversals to obtain healing.[108]

Haudenosaunee medicine societies also revolved around the sacred belief of the Good Hunter, who was revived from the dead by the combined powers of the beasts, who helped humans, especially the powerful Great Horned Serpent Jodigwado and the Otter. Some of the Haudenosaunee societies literally originated with the Wendat, such as the Society of Mystic Animals.[109] The Haudenosaunee also believed, like the Wendat, that, although the main soul (onnonkouat) travels to the "way of the souls," the ghost (uquskenne) stays in the community.[110] Haudenosaunee repeatedly used inversions in order to cast a "white magic" spell to counteract illness. All the dances were counter-clockwise, and the songs reversed meanings. Ancestral spirits must be propitiated with presents, tobacco, food, song, and dance because they are associated with winter, when animals hibernate (although the spirits planted crops on abandoned fields of the living, especially "ghost corn" [dicentra canadensis]). Especially notable was the Ohgiwe ceremony over which the "matrons of the dead preside, while the men who assist are called "hadinehwa" (pelt, or skin).[111] During the ceremony, ghost bread (gahagwagi dawth) was consumed. Death was represented as the Faceless One, which was especially notable because all the medicine society members wore a great variety of masks, particularly beast masks. Haudenosaunee myth also has journeys to the skyworld, and the Ohgiwe society calls for the dissipation of restless spirits that have returned in a dream. By the nineteenth century Handsome Lake, the prophet, tried to suppress both funeral anniversaries and the medicine societies, but even he did not succeed.[112]

The voyageur journey was constructed from both Native and French elements. Native traditions endeavoured to propitiate ancestors via the spirit-power of the beasts to ensure health. French North American customs, while aware of stretching the power of the keeper of the beasts beyond his strength due to the wholesale plunder of pelts, countered ill effects by utilizing the combined power of Christian and Native rites. The Canadians, despite pressure from the missionaries, could not afford to ignore or laugh off Native beliefs. Not only were their own beliefs much closer to Native beliefs than is generally acknowledged, but the life of the settlement also literally depended upon them. This way, St Anne and deceased interpreters, donnés, coureurs, and missionaries, especially those martyred like Father Nicolas Viel, Auhaîtsique, and Cadieux, could provide intercessory suffrages for them in their earthly purgatory.[113]

Even a cursory analysis shows the first rite closely resembles a non-specific Native festival as it follows several set stages of Native protocol: (1.)eating the evening meal, (2) smoking. (3) ritualized speeches on the part of the young military chief and the elder sagamo/sachem, and (4) the choir of dancers imitating the Native "ho, ho, hos," which the company interposes between speeches. The Métis sash is multicoloured while the French king's service wore white, which showed both Canadian insubordination and French-Native taste for finery in clothes.[114] It also seems to function like a swatch of Joseph's "coat of many colours" – which also functioned like the Nordic shaman's coat, which consisted of the combined "powers" of different animal pelts – and protected the canoeman and crew along the journey. The kettle-banging was reminiscent of a charivari and of Native drumming, with both objectives being joined to communicate with the spirits and to chase away vengeful revenants.[115] The kettle, or cauldron, was the time-honoured symbol for the Holy Grail, the adventurous goal of youth, and the healing vessel of the aged and infirm. Concretely, fur trading was what filled the kettle. But this was also true for the Wendat Aiheonde, the Feast of the Dead (i.e., the "Great Kettle"). The kettle nourished life and it was the prime diplomatic symbol for alliance or hostility between Wendat and Haudenosaunee, one of its meanings being inclusion, another being cannibalism.

St Anne was the patron saint of mariners and early New France, and her shrines and churches dotted this country at all the major danger points along its waterways. She was, together with Mary, the favourites among the north Atlantic Algonquians and Wendat. Subsequently, she become the Mi'kmaq patron saint.

At the Point-au-Baptême the main ceremony began. Naturally, at this advanced point, the ceremony was a parody of both Christian and knightly rites, with Native touches. The most unpopular novice was selected for the godfather scolding and godmother smothering. French-style overbearing parenting is parodied, as is the Haudenosaunee ceremony of requickening, wherein a captive is adopted. This ceremony precedes the ascent to the Great Lakes, where French patriarchal and priestly authority were absent. In addition, the sarcasm of the ceremony resembled Haudenosaunee sarcasm towards tortured captives. Those that were not subjected to this guidance had the privilege of drinking alcohol and were admitted to the company of initiated men. Afterwards, receiving water sprinkled from the cedar branch functions as a parody of the sword swearing-in associated with knighthood (again the chevaliers). This dubbing ennobles the profession and introduces, together with the godparents, ties of fictional brotherhood between voyageurs. The cedar branch was probably northern white cedar (thuya occidentalis), which was used extensively in medicine, including in Anishinabe ceremonies, as a purifier for people and objects. The Potawatami used it to exorcise witchcraft.[116] Cedar was and still is the sacred tree, referred to by the Anishinabe as grandmother. It is used to protect against illness, as the axis mundi (central pole) of the Midewiwin lodge, and for totem poles. It was used by the French to install the king's arms and the Cross.[117] It was probably also used as an anti-scurvy medicine (anneda) by Jacques Cartier, who was given it by the St Lawrence Haudenosaunee. Thus it found its way to the French king's Fontainebleau gardens in 1536 or 1542, where it was named the tree of life (arbor vitae).[118] And it seems significant that a branch of the tree of life ("ghost" of the Garden of Eden) inverted the meaning of a metal sword of death and war, the symbol of French noble honneur. From that ceremonial moment, the voyageur's code of honour was to be respected by the newcomers, and this further tied them into the voyageur family framework. This, of course, included symbolically forswearing incestuous acts (i.e., kissing other voyageur's wives without their consent) – quite a contrast to the old French wives-as-possessions idea. This swearing-in ceremony cemented the "knighthood" quality of Canadian "hommes de coeur," whose aristocratic cum-Native values served them well, both in war and in trade.

Along the dangerous routes, fairy beliefs and Odawan and Anishinabe Windigo beliefs, peppered with European monster lore, guided them safely though the dangers of the Great Lakes fur country.[119] They offered tobacco gifts to various sacred and dangerous stone sculptures (Tsakapesh, or the Bear) and waterfalls on the way in order to accomplish this.[120]

In conclusion, the voyageur utilized both north Atlantic French rites and lore and Roman Catholic additions to Native rites of protection along the trade route in order ensure a safe journey. The rocks, rushes, waterfalls, tragic deaths, and Haudenosaunee all menaced coureur de bois well-being. This ritual tradition was continued and elaborated by the later French Canadian voyageurs and Métis of the North West and Hudson's Bay Companies.

The myth of the Chasse-Galérie reversed the geographical direction of the coureur de bois voyage. The classic legend tells of a canoe crew of hunters, coureurs de bois, or voyageurs who sell their souls to the Devil (in the Saguenay version, to an Innu medicine healer) in order to effect a nocturnal flight to the Laurentian Valley to dance with their girlfriends.[121] The only condition was no cursing and no knocking down of crosses on the church tops along the way. They shout "Acabri, Acabra!" was reminiscent of sorcerers casting a spell before setting off. The voyage back was perilous for, rheumy with liquor, they steered off course towards Iroquoia, and one of them swore just as they approached camp, propelling the entire crew pell-mell into the fir trees.[122]

The initiatory or shamanic voyage, in general, was a staple of northwestern French and Native American lore. In the French Canadian popular tradition, the apparition of the Chasse-Galérie canoe was a portent of strange events to come.[123] A phantom vessel with a crew of drowned men sailing the skies to expiate their sins, like the *Flying Dutchman* or Breton vision, is a famous north Atlantic European variant of this apparition.[124] This image reflected the grim reality of canoes becoming the graves of their crew. These martyrs, along with St Anne, numerous Native figures, and far-off deceased, were often petitioned by later coureurs and voyageurs to protect the route.

The Native medicine healer journeyed to the Atisken andahatey in order to consult with the spirits. Yet the magic nocturnal flight was also the sign of the Celtic and Nordic shaman.[125] The Celtic shamanic ship voyage echoes that of Bran's voyage to the otherworld (Annwn, Annwfn, or Annwyn) to retrieve the cauldron of life.[126] Nordic goddess of love Freya's father, Njord, was the god of ships and the sea. Freya's cult involved shamanic soul voyages (seidr) by seers (völva) dressed in the furs of many animals, who invoked spirits and revealed the future.[127] Ships of hollowed out oak tree trunks were often used as the coffins of the privileged Nordic dead, as a symbol of the ship of the sun. In Nordic symbolism the ship departed for the otherworld, as in Beowulf.[128]

Only in purgatory and on the way to Atisken andahatey did the worlds of everyday and the otherworld meet. Jean Delumeau wrote that purgatorial penance was based upon John the Baptist's vow to initiate first through water, then through fire and the Holy Spirit in order to prune the forest of those trees bearing bad fruit.[129] Initiation first through water, then through fire (ignis divinis), and a purgatorial spirit are also elements of both of our voyages, but they were experienced in that order. In their requickening ceremony of war captives, the Haudenosaunee "magically" inverted this initiatory order: first fire (torture), then water (before renaming). The Judeo-Christian heritage affirmed the ritual relationship between water and spirit renewal. In Judaism, the mikva (ritual bath) is at least monthly, while in Catholicism, baptism occurs after birth.[130] Jung treated the liminal baptismal font as representative of a symbolic death and rebirth.[131] It appears that baptism by water was Christian, while baptism by fire was Haudenosaunee. While the coureurs' voyage was through water, the Galérie voyage was through the air. Yet the coureurs' voyage was accomplished via "magic air" (measured in sacred Native tobacco in pipefuls of smoke [pipées]) while going through water.[132] The Galérie voyage was accomplished via French "magic liquid" (brandy) while going through the air. Carlo Ginzburg noted that, in ancient Western Europe, shamans used alcohol to enter the realm of the dead via liquor-induced dreams.[133]

Socially and symbolically, both substances facilitated interethnic communication and métissage between French and Native. Both substances also contained the element of "baptism by fire" as tobacco was smoked by burning while brandy was known as "firewater." Great Lakes Wabeno medicine healers were "firewalkers," equipped with horns, who manipulated fire, assumed beast form at night, interpreted dreams, and healed patients.[134] Haudenosaunee False Face medicine healers also touched hot coals and ashes and blew or rubbed these substances on patients. All these fire associations melded into the primary identification of the satanic and the Haudenosaunee torture fires. Surviving baptisms by water and fire enabled salvation through either the Judeo-Christian Holy Spirit, or shekinah (symbolized by the dove), the Native spirit of nature, or both. In Cadieux's "Complainte," the dying Cadieux sent a bird (ostensibly his soul) to tell his wife that he had been caught by the Haudenosaunee and was doomed to die.[135] But there were also favourable associations. Boiling "tabagie" kettles over dancing council fires was part of the sacred feasts that united various peoples. This was especially so when the peacepipe (calumet) was brought in as it was the most sacred metaphorical Great Lakes Algonquian symbol of unity, melding fragmented First Nations bands with the French. Together, these peoples constituted the Aboriginal melting pot, which later became the key symbol of American social and civic life. French North Americans contributed much to this melting post by offering a unique forum for sharing, exchange, and mixing.

This voyage was courageous due to the numerous obstacles along the way. Initiation trials were headed westward, yet penance trials headed eastward. Ankarloo's comment that the Franciscan and Jesuit nominalists perceived Satan as subservient to God yet tempting to the soul seems to make sense in this context.[136] In Mi'kmaq tradition, the route to the realm of the dead in the west was arduous, but the route back was easy, with two serpents at either side of the road.[137] While the voyageur route entailed canoeing through treacherous water routes, the Chasse-Galérie required canoeing through the air while avoiding swearing or hitting all the crosses along the St Lawrence. Cursing was considered to be a promise to Satan.[138] This obstacle course of crosses echoes the haunted cemetery motif ([âtre périlleux) of the old French miribilia Amadas et Idoine, Perlevaus, and the exempla.[139] Detoxification en route was an essential incremental function of the rite – to gradually strip away what was no longer needed while acquiring that which will prove essential in a new location. The state of what van Gennep called liminality provided opportunities yet was fraught with dangers – flying between two worlds, between life and death – thus exorcisms were necessary.[140] While the voyageur ritual from the St Lawrence to the Great Lakes concentrated upon "detoxifying" the voyageurs from French culture upon entering Amerindian country, the Chasse-Galérie legend attempted to accomplish the reverse. The monde à l'envers of the legend refers to the previous coureur journey by inversely travelling from west to east (from the direction of the Native "country of souls" in the direction of the Judeo-Christian holy city of Jerusalem) while obtaining both Native and Christian suprahuman protection.

The voyage betwixt Heaven and Hell was "purgatorial," but the danger of falling into Hell was great. Cursing almost landed them in Iroquoia, which, as they considered it to be akin to the fires of Hell, was hardly their desired destination. We must note, however, that in the Saguenay region, which was populated mostly by the Innu or Naskapi, the diabolical pact was accomplished with an Innu medicine healer (missionaries sometimes called them sorcerers) who sent the Galérie off by way of magic (which seems therapeutic rather than diabolical). The ambiguity of whether couple dancing was diabolical (according to the post-Trentine Church) or therapeutic (according to the Native medicine healers) was moot. Yet again we are faced with the missionary suspicion that Native healers obtained powers through the Devil because they did not call upon the Judeo-Christian God. Christian legends of pacts with the Devil began with one supposedly concerning a Jewish "magician" who supposedly enticed St Théophilus into signing an agreement for acquiring magic powers. This is how the Faustus legend began.[141] Before the chime of midnight, which was the witching hour because it was the inverse of high noon, the coureurs had to return as the spell would not last longer than that. The last reference to Hell has to do with them almost landing in Iroquoia. This "Hell" could have resulted in them being burned alive and perhaps devoured, even though the French were reputed to be "too salty" for a "tasty" meal.

As the voyageurs travel to and from the St Lawrence, they offer thanks to St Anne, who was associated with baptism just as Satan was associated with firewater. Whereas initially the voyageurs obtained the grace of St Anne, the patron of seafarers, the Chasse-Galérie concludes a pact with the Devil before setting off. Thus, Anne, or her daughter Mary, is again set against Satan, mirroring the same Genetrix versus Satan dynamic as in the Wendat Tree of Dreams. St Anne and Mary were invoked both by coureur Cadieux and his Native wife, as mentioned earlier. Further, baptism signified a return to the womb of the Great Mother and a merging with the spirit of the Holy Ghost.[142] Both of these poles had a role to play as the voyage was purgatorial.

The pivotal figure in the middle, of course, was that erecting stone and water obstructions along the way: Tsakapesh, or the Bear. In the Odanak tale "le courrier du roi," a Frenchman was prevented from contracting a love tie with a Native maid, owing to her pet bear. And in "Tsakapesh l'invincible," of La Romaine, a young Native goes to the mountains to kill the bear that ate his parents.[143] By the eighteenth century the Haudenosaunee and their war deity, Agreskou, were regarded as less "satanic" as their methods became more internalized and the Great Peace of Montreal was finally reached in 1701. On the other hand, Tsakapesh increasingly appeared as an obstacle to the evangelization of the Great Lakes and was called a devil by the missionaries. It is possible that the role of Agreskou and Tsakapesh became somewhat reversed for later evangelization.[144] While Tsakapesh was increasingly being labelled as Satan, Jesus and the French king were both being likened to Agreskou in order to win converts in the Illinois country.

An interesting corollary of the Galérie crew-Tsakapesh relationship is a parallel Gaspésian tale that identifies the Big and Little Dipper as female bears pursued by a canoe of hunters who were guardians of the North Star (urs majores, called Mouhinne; and urs minores, called Mouhinchiche).[145] In other words, the Galérie boys, as guardians of the French sun king, Louis XIV, were being "hunted" by the formidable Tsakapesh. But Mi'kmaq men in the realm of souls as guardians of the North Star were the hunters of the very stars themselves in bear form. In Anishinabe culture, menstruating women were associated with bears and were called "mukowe," meaning to kill a bear with one's bare hands and also to make love. Perhaps they were so called because the scent of childbirth and menstrual blood attracted bears, and because of the eating taboos for women regarding bear meat. The head of the bear was reserved only for the eldest man, and the younger hunters avoided eating the heart for fear that their "Great Man" would forsake them. Several bands regarded the bear as more intelligent and as having greater medicine powers than human beings; indeed, many regarded the bear as merely a less fortunate man, and by 1860 Anishinabe were referring to him as an "Anijinabe" (Native).[146] Native reverence for the masculine qualities of the bear's head (or the enemy scalp in war) corresponds to analogous French perceptions about hats as symbols of male honour.[147] This counterpoint noted not only Native associations of manliness proven through successful human (men in war, women in love) and bear-hunting but also their feeling that the French initially lacked what they considered to be masculinity.

The Chasse-Galérie's almost swerving into Iroquoia was certainly an expression of a close brush with what they conceived of as Hell. Their descent upon fir treetops clearly has associations with the Native, Nordic, and Celtic idea of trees as the intermediate link between the Heavens and Earth.[148] Algonquian dead were laid on tree platforms instead of being buried. Trees of course evoke the Celtic sacred tree (bile) as the axis mundi, and each tribe had its own sacred tree.[149] The Nordic world-tree (yggdrasil), the early missionary symbol of the cross, and the Haudenosaunee tree of peace all had a heaven-to-earth connection, where human and spirit worlds coalesce.[150] John the Baptist warned the people to recognize false prophets, wolves in lamb pelts, by the fruits that they bear. They would be pruned to allow the trees with good fruit to bear their bounty. Why, however, were fir trees chosen among so many other species? North American balsam fir trees (abies balsamea) have abundant aromatic medicinal uses, especially in manufacturing balms for rheumatism and decoctions for upper respiratory infections. And its resin is used as an antiseptic for burns and wounds.[151] It is also used as pitch tar or turpentine. Fir branches were used to line the ground of tipis. These trees are the inverse of the hard oak trees honoured by the Druids, Greeks, and Romans, their wood being light and highly workable.[152] Fir trees were used for the May queens in the British isles (Breton) and for Scandinavian fires on the Eve of St John the Baptist (Norman). Christmas trees were familiar later in French Canada, at the inverse solar nadir of winter, when the axis mundi was most needed to invoke divine aid. The tree also served a similar function to that of the Wendat tree of dreams: the voyage was a shamanic dream-flight that took place by the side of a tree. This enabled the soul to leave and return to earth without getting lost. And finally, luckily for the purgatorial crew, fir trees can bear no bad fruit.

The great irony of the Iroquoia being the symbol of Hell in the Chasse-Galérie is that the Iroquoian flying canoe characterized the heavenly message of the Great White Tree of Peace. Despite many versions of the Deganawida Epic, the flying canoe was also the sign of Hiawatha and the peaceful foundation myth of Deganawida, the founder of the Haudenosaunee League. Briefly, Hiawatha travelled in the air in his white canoe from nation to nation preaching peace with his only child, his daughter Minihaha. One day, the great mystery bird of the heavens took his daughter as a sacrifice to the manitous, just when the Onondagas most needed counsel due to the warring tribes of the north. Hiawatha covered himself in a wildcat skin and grieved for three days. The fourth day, he announced that he would unite the tribes as brothers, that the downfall of one meant the downfall of all. He united them under one fire, one pipe, and one tomahawk, akin to, yet inverting, the French king's absolutist declaration of "one king, one faith, one law" ("un roi, une foi, une loi.") He gathered the white feathers of the heavenly bird and showed them that each tribe represented one feather and that they must join in order to survive. They begged him to stay to help them; but as he left he urged them to take their quarrels to the wisest women, who were the clan mothers and Genetaska, peacemakers. They would turn any strife into friendship if the sachems would only be wise enough to bring disputes to them. Then he flew off into the mists in his white canoe.[153] Thus, instead of going to the supposed Hell in Iroquoia, or the purgatorial Atisken andahatey with the French North Americans, he seemingly flew straight to Heaven where Minihaha awaited him. And he did so on the wings of the bird-soul, like the Holy Ghost. The blind reference to Hiawatha implied in the Chasse-Galérie provided a flying alter-canoe that provided a saintly ideal rather than the implicitly devilish Galérie – to obliterate warfare not only in the League but also among all nations who would bury the hatchet underneath the Great Pine of Peace.

The purpose of the journey to this otherworld was to revive life and to consult with ghosts: ancestors, the departed, and those alive but inaccessible. The Chasse-Galérie journey appears to function as a metaphor for a Native shamanic visit to the "country of souls," generally to heal illness. In the French vein, the spirit journey popular in northwestern French lore was closer to the travels of revenants, who were increasingly demonized.

Rejuvenation was accomplished through some "medicine" derived from the voyage that resuscitated the departed. The medicine kettle that preserved and revived life was composed of ancient elixirs and meanings. The cauldron was not only the object of mediation that assured the dead renewed life in the otherworld but was also the "incarnation of the polity."[154] In functionally non-literate communities, such as those in early and medieval, lightly Christianized, north Atlantic Europe, guidance was not obtained through book learning but, rather, through belonging to a community led by a seer. And it was expressed in ceremonial communal ingestion of a sacred sacrifice. Sacred heads, even after severance, were thought capable of foretelling the future, and full cauldrons persuaded hungry crowds to listen. The prophetic head of John the Baptist, presented on the platter, was a foreshadowing of Jesus' later providing the Eucharist.[155] Jesus' multiplying fish and bread, and wine/blood of the Last Supper, promised divine guidance and community.[156] Supposedly, the Christian source of the Holy Grail is the Passover dish of Jesus' Last Supper, brought by Joseph of Arimathea, 'knight' of Pontius Pilatus, from Jerusalem. It allegedly held magical qualities as a cauldron of plenty that contained the blood of Christ, which promoted healing and could resurrect the dead.[157] Some traditions associate the Grail to the blood-filled chalice at the Cross.[158] Other traditions say the Grail contained a manna-like essence.[159] Still others assert that it is a blood-filled chalice that perhaps links up with earlier Celtic rites. The grave of a high-ranking female Celtic prophet contained a human-size crater, apparently to receive human heads and the blood of war captives, was unearthed and resembled a citation of Strabo referring to the Teutonic Cimbri.[160] Severed heads in broth represented reifications of the wisdom of the departed. The Celtic bowl of plenty (cauldron of Annwn, Annwynn, or Annwfn), which King Arthur sought to bring from the otherworld, follows this tradition, as does the homme de coeur who distributes his plenty after his voyage-purgatorial ordeal.[161] The medicinal unguents of Morgana were boiled to heal the wounded Arthur in the island of Avalon in the "western sea."[162] Celtic and Norse heroic or wise heads swim in the sacred broth of the inexhaustible cauldron, those of Celtic Sual taimh and Bran, the divine Norse mead containing the head of Kvasir, or the prophetic head of giant Mimir, for whom Odin gave his eye.[163] The symbol of the bubbling, toppling "grande marmite" during the Counter-Reformation signified the topsy-turvy instability of French spirituality and community. The French Canadian beast of seven heads (bête-à-sept-têtes) was usually killed by Ti-Jean, which may also signify that a good-natured outlook is more important than seven heads, in social medicine.[164]

Yet Native traditions are also evident. Iroquoian "Big Heads" and Algonquian "rolling heads" dispensed the haunting wisdom of the departed.[165] Enemy scalps, like Celtic decapitated heads and, sometimes, the cannibal feasts of the Iroquoians, were to appease Agreskoué the Iroquoian deity of war, the Haudenosaunee source of strength. Iroquoian captive scalps were adopted by the mourning mothers to "cover" the spirits of their dead children.[166] The medicine potion of plants, stones, and beasts of Wendat, Algonquian, and Haudenosaunee medicine societies were taught by the animals and resurrected the wounded Good Hunter. The seven heads of the dragon of the analogous Anishinabe tale told of the hero-ism of a pair of twins who outwitted the monster. One killed the other out of misplaced jealousy over his wife and finally restored him to life. They parted anyway, one taking the way of God, the other taking the way of the Devil.[167] And finally the Wendat Great Kettle was, of course, the Feast of the Dead. No medicine was more healing than the preventive care of family and com-munal bonds, which ward off myriad diseases. The Chasse-Galérie medici-nal elixir desired at the end of the flight was a combination of liquor and love, which parodies the wine and body of the Eucharist and are the usual medicines desired by humans.

Finally, the circularity of the journey to the Great Lakes and back, which encompasses both Christian crosses and Native nature, signifies the staking out of the spiritual boundaries of the French Canadian pilgrimage into rogations of sacred space. Sacred Judeo-Christian time was linear, but sacred Celtic and Christian space mapped out the journey of human life, the ceremonial circle of seasonal celebrations, fairy rings (ancestral mounds), and Jesus's crown of thorns (penance).[168] The magic circle, from the round-ness of the womb to the roundness of the earth, and the birth to death cycle, was believed to be magically protective for the entire community of the liv-ing, both near and far. The dead were not "entirely dead" when swathed in the protective mantle of caring family, community, and progeny. For, as Odawa chief Nagach8o declared: "My father has always had pity upon me during my life, and although I am dead, I am not entirely dead. I have left a second of myself at Michilimackinac before departing, he holds my place. This is my brother Cabina."[169] Purgatorial Atisken andahatey buffered lives, fragmented between France, the St Lawrence, and the fur trade country, that had to assemble a powwow of all their absent loved ones before the end.

Ambiguity still lurked behind every action whose interpretations were polarized between French and Native. The new context redefined French and Native beliefs and rituals, and the dialogue wove around them to incor-porate, fuse, differentiate, or reject them over time. Convergences and con-trasts aided redefinition. The voyageur route's journey paralleled the Native journey to Astiken andahatey, while the Chasse-Galérie's souls returned, paralleling the return of the Mesnie Hellequin. The protective bond between the living and the dead was common to the Mesnie Hellequin and the Chasse-Galérie, both telling of ambiguously purgatorial souls returning to the living. In Poitou the association between the Chasse-Galérie and

Hellequin's Mesnie was explicit. The Nocturnal Hunt, or the Coach of King Hugo (Carosse du roi Hugon), rode from Rome to Nantes.[170] In Brittany, King Arthur allegedly tried to hunt instead of going to Sunday Mass and was condemned to conduct nocturnal hunts with his dogs after his death.[171] This ancestral Native flight was thus associated with the north Atlantic ancestral cult that was later stigmatized as a witches' sabbath.

In lower Normandy, Cotentin, and the Bocage Virois, a legend was current that told of a sorcerer's apprentice who explicitly ties together the meaning of Celtic, Nordic, and Native beliefs and rites. The apprentice met a naked man on his way to a "witches' sabbath," where men allegedly rubbed the grease of unbaptized children onto their skins, thus transforming them into foxes, skunks, and horses to enable them to fly to the heath ("lande") and revel in dancing, singing, drinking, and playing tricks as well as in making a pact with the Devil, crying "Pic par sus feuilles" ("Jump on the leaves"). This sabbath was believed to usually take place on mont Bonnet, butte Brimbal, the rocks of Clércy, St-Aubert-sur-Orne, mont Margantin, and La Pierre Herpin. The sabbath allegedly took place on St John the Baptist's Eve, when supposedly three suns would dance in the sky.[172]

Interpretation of this legend links early pagan beliefs with their early modern demonization. Thus Carlo Ginzburg's theory that early modern charges of witchcraft involved discrediting early pagan agricultural fertility rites appears to be validated, at least in Normandy.[173] The allusion to La Pierre Herpine seems to suggest that there is some connection to La mère Harpine, who was another alias of Breton and Norman variants of Carlequin, Chéserpine, and Proserpine.[174] Before Aeneus went to the Land of the Dead to search for his deceased father, he sacrificed beasts and fruit to Proserpine and Hecate.[175] Persephone, or Kore, returned to Demeter in spring, yet the farther north one went, the later the renewal of fertility and plants. And St John the Baptist's Eve's fire was associated with Demeter's torch, which she held while searching for her child. Nordic and Celtic lore, the fires of the ancient Celtic Samhain, the rebelliousness of St John the Baptist's Eve, and the "satanic pact" where pre-Christian survivals had been demonized appear to have become melded syncretically. According to Mother Marie de L'Incarnation, a divine sign actually "appeared" when three suns supposedly danced in the sky after the comet on 20 December 1664 during the winter solstice, the significance being that this is exactly the reverse of the calendrical summer solstice of St John the Baptist's eve.[176] Yet Mother Marie said that this sign was divine rather than diabolical. It is also possible that the Nordic Dame Holle, or Holda, who was regarded as the queen of the elves or witches (like Hecate), was also the moon goddess of the ghosts and the dead, entwined with snakes, had three heads, and was also surrounded by a horde of female demons.[177] The circle of associated male and female identities indicates that, whatever the figure was called in that region, she was a seer, chief, mother, or goddess of the dead associated with Orderic Vital's account of Hellequin.

With regard to the Celtic nuances of this Norman sorcerer's apprentice tradition, the fact that all these sabbaths took place on sacred rocky places seems to indicate that the power of the Celtic menhirs was also significant, especially that called mont Margantin, which seems to signal Morgana la Fée or the Morrigan, who was embodied in a corpse-eating crow or the Nordic raven (Valkyrie bird).[178] Thus, both Nordic and Celtic traditions told of sha-manic voyages wherein pagan "magic liquid" and the aid of beasts was required for nocturnal flight. This supposedly took place during the solar solstice of St John the Baptist's Eve – which was the time of the Celtic Beltane fire, the Nordic fires of midsummer – due to the return of the wandering dead. This time entailed festive partying with food, drink, dancing, and rib-aldry, all of which were elements of the Chasse-Galérie legend.

Charivaris seemed to be the medieval link between ancient pagan rites and their contemporary counterparts. The fourteenth-century Roman de Fauvel (1310, 1314) cites a marriage in which a rowdy charivari ("chalivali") broke out. The youths were masked like "sauvages," clashing pots and pans, breaking things, reversing their clothes, dressing transsexually, throwing salt and diarrhea about, and running around with bare backsides, which, according to the author, was something of which only Hellequin and the wildmen of the Mesnie were capable.[179] Fifteenth-century charivari players frequently impersonated bands of roaming dead, reinforcing the connec-tion between ancient belief and contemporary rite.[180] The social point of the charivari was either to reinforce or redefine traditional communal values in a culturally familiar way. Male youth frowned upon widows remarrying quickly due to the "possession rights" of their deceased spouse. Elderly women and men were mocked for marrying the young village eligibles of whom the youth were possessive. But popular belief held that it was to frighten away the vengeful deceased. Mardi Gras monde à l'envers activities in our lifetime includes masking oneself as an animal, phantom, revenant, or sorcerer.[181]

To the French, the Wendat healing ceremony of Ononharoia of the time appeared to be rebellious and suspiciously diabolical. The reversal of nor-mal Wendat life in the Ononharoia ceremony ("reversing of the brain") was supposed to effect healing by bringing the wounded back to life. Unhappi-ness was commanded by a giant who had been socially offended by a Wendat and who later told his people to conduct the Ononharoia in order to coun-teract it.[182] Illness caused by a dream and unspoken desires of the soul (ondinnonc) was the only type of pathology curable through this cere-mony.[183] It was held in midwinter, and a new fire was lit. Belief-wise, the world was in the hold of Ta8iscaron, the fall twin, and his grandmother Aataentsic. Ioskeha rescued the sun and brought spring to counteract the "upside down world" (monde à l'envers) before the New Creation.[184] Dream-guessing, in which others guess the dream of the ailing one and then communally heal him or her, was the heart of the ceremony. It began by singing, then eating. This was followed by singing and dancing, with impersonations of the enemies crying, "Hen, hen, hen, hé, hé, hé, waiiiiiiii."[185] Some shamans (arendiouane) could allegedly turn a rod into a serpent (like Moses) or bring a dead beast back to life.[186] Arendiouane magically killed each other, then brought each other back to life.[187]

Edith Fowkes's later version of the Chasse-Galérie was applied to lumberjacks and took place in Ross in the Gatineau (north of Ottawa). Joe, the hunchback cook, told of his own voyage aboard the Chasse-Galérie, which began when he was drunk, sleeping on the fur-pelt sleigh rug, waiting for the midnight taffy pull on New Year's Eve 1858, when the "souls return to visit." He was wakened by Baptiste Durand, who had not been to confession for seven years (the penance time for outlaws and "werewolves") to fly to the midnight square dance at Lavaltrie to see his girl, Liza Guimbette, with a crew of eight. However, he would have to sell his soul to the Devil and swear not to profane God's name on the journey or hit any crosses. In other words, he was instructed not to drink, to be careful what he said, and to watch where he went.[188] Skirting Two Mountains, they sang a song when they saw the towers of Notre-Dame and flew to Batissette Augé's party in Petite-Misère (trans.:i.e., "little misery") near Contrecoeur (trans.: i.e., "resisting the heart"). Naturally, Liza was dancing with Boisjoli (trans.:i.e.: either "drinks well" or "beautiful forest"), his rival, and Baptiste drank too much. They almost left too late for their midnight curfew, and left "like Indians" – in other words, as they claim, without saying goodbye. Baptist flew them wrong down the Richelieu River (towards Iroquoia). Frightened of "roasting in Hell," the canoe almost landed in a snowbank near Beloeil (trans.: "beautiful eye") Mountain, and Baptist swore. The boys gagged and tied Baptist hand and foot into a human sausage. As they steered, he freed himself and swore, shook like a lost soul, and swung the oar around his head as they all toppled onto a pine tree (the Haudenosaunee peace tree) and fell into a bottomless pit (mirroring Aataentsic's descent from the skyworld to earth via the treehole – but metaphorically, they fell into Iroquoia and thus into an endless abyss). They were found by lumberjacks badly bruised but not in Hell. Afterwards, Joe thought Liza married Boisjoli because of his own less-than-stunning performance that night.[189]

The later Detroit version of this legend based itself upon tradition but became linked to local occurrence. Seeing the Chasse Galérie (Spectral Aerial Hunt) betokened a swift death to one or one's family. It was foreshadowed by the nocturnal lone horseman, with his rifle and his dog pack, who returned every seven years. The phantom canoe of twelve men with the barking dog became connected to Sebastien Lacelle of Askin Pointe, who never returned to his fiancée from the hunt on their wedding day. He only returned as a ghost in his phantom canoe the day she died on Nanabozo's boulders, despite having prayed to St Anne.[190]

As we can clearly see, both tales reconnect with past meaning, as historical facets of the mythical diamond. In the Fowkes version the fur trade has given way to the lumber trade, but the socio-economic problematique of men in the woods has not passed. Yet lumber camps, unlike fur trade posts, were more bereft of women. Joe accomplishes his magic voyage by way of a liquor-induced sleep on the shamanic pelt, which carries him, together with his sinful friend, Baptist (innuendoes of baptism, John the Baptist, repentance, seven years penance, wilderness, baptism by water and fire), to his destination via a pact with the Devil. By way of the mission reserve of Lac-des-Deux-Montagnes and the towers of Notre-Dame, the Freudian allusion to his expectancy of seeing her breasts causes them all to burst into song, even if, ironically, both places are bastions of the Virgin Mary. Also unfortunately, the poor fellow lands only in a "little misery" "against the heart" and finds her, of course, dancing with his opposite twin – the habitant whose "woods" are "beautiful" – or who drinks too much: Boisjoli. Joe reacted by creeping away "like an Indian" and, aloft with his cronies, almost landed near Iroquoia on "beautiful eye" mountain – a metaphor for his sin being that his eye was too hungry for beauty. Sinner Baptist lost control and as converted into a cursing human "sausage" (Freudian?), yet this saved them by causing them to fall into a tree rather than into Hell. His woman friend married the "beautiful woods-drinker" anyway. Lesson? "No drinking, think what you say, and watch where you are going."

The mid-western version of these legends reverses the tradition of its European predecessors: the hunter goes afield and returns in spirit. Here we have come full circle to pagan Europe in the woods of early America. The hunter's apparition returns every seven years, like the hounds of Hades, due to his hyper-hunting hubris, even though his love prayed and waited upon the rocks of Nanabozo-Hellequin. Thus she also perished due to him, and they lost love and a future family.

RUNNING IN PURGATORY

Gathering together dispersed community was a continuing concern in French North America. The charivari, like St John's Eve, assumed a renewed vigour. Naturally, officials and clergy joined hands to curb the noisome ritual, and after a particularly rowdy week-long charivari of a widow who married three weeks after the death of her husband in 1683, Bishop Laval threatened to excommunicate the entire Quebec population. During these charivaris, Cornelius Jaenen writes that the youth pontificated on marriage-related discourses, had a masked spirit of the deceased spouse, asked for masses for the repose of their souls, and did the usual charivari clanging. By the 1750s Bishop Pontbriand also condemned charivaris, which were generally held until the late nineteenth century.[191]

The dead were ever present whenever the meeting or joining of communities occurred. The Wendat Feast of the Dead set a precedent in New France for honouring the dead as the Hospitallers and Ursulines both exchanged and mixed the bones of saintly women in order to signify the joining of their communities.[192] Unlike the repeated use of imported reliquiae and Brébeuf's bones to exorcise or inspire, this act was done, in Wendat fashion, to define a new community.

At the French-Haudenosaunee truce of 1645 the second gift of the seventeen collars of wampum offered during a truce represented the dead ancestor warriors of battles past. "I have heard the voice of my ancestors massacred by the Algonquins ... who cried to me ... A living man is worth more than several dead." ("J'ay oüi la voix de mes Ancestres massacrés par les Algonquins..m' ont crié ... Un homme vivant vaut mieux que plusieurs morts.") The seventeenth gift represented the French killed by the Haudenosaunee. The French reciprocated by giving their fourth gift to the Haudenosaunee to forget the dead: "effacer la pensée des morts."[193] Neither Haudenosaunee nor French could advance to a brotherly future with their dead "uncovered." Yet, whereas the Haudenosaunee heeded the advice of their deceased, the French endeavoured to console the living. Even so, they could not join forces without seeking legitimation from their own ancestors.

The pall that death cast during the Renaissance and early modern era catalyzed the human need for healing and communal bonding.[194] This was especially true concerning the axis that connected the Old World with the New World as the tragedy of the plague in the former gave way to the tragedy of smallpox in the latter. These community decimators were the result of intercontinental encounters that opened up the world from the Middle Ages yet reinforced the urgency of the weaving of an intercommunal dialogue to support overtaxed social and spiritual fabrics. According to Géza Roheim, "The menacing event is the loss of the mother ... is the basis for our fears concerning the definitive adieu ... the Cult of the ancestors and Civilization walk together." ("L'évenement menaçant c'est la perte de [la mère] ... forme la base de nos craintes concernant l'adieu définitif ... . Le culte des ancêtres et la civilisation vont de pair.")[195] This pressing dialogue involved both vertical as well as horizontal dialogue (i.e., a working and reformulation of collective memory as well as cross-cultural exchange and reformulation). Especially in mostly oral cultures, where ancestral tradition looms large, comparisons and blendings of traditions and mythical models served to sharpen self-awareness while joining or dividing diverse communities.

For the French, the inter-Atlantic encounter seemed to be a mythic, reflexive voyage into their own past. The great weight of the encoded Celtic

and Nordic past appeared to be an important element of the cultural survival code of the immigrant population. The enormous preoccupation with
the spirits of the ancestors and martyrs via the wilderness and its animals was
not only a cultural convergence but also a veritable lifeline between their
ancestors, who lived akin to these "wild people," and themselves. Therefore,
the living link between ancestors and descendants also spelled out the
ambiguous meaning of the discovery. Perhaps the French had progressed in
specified subjects, but there was an enormous amount to be reassessed
before determining whether the direction taken by European civilization
would constitute progress or regression. Seeing so many points of comparison only sharpened the ease of positive, as well as negative, comparison and
the re-evaluation of self. In this guise, the philosophic "state of Nature,"
which served as a model for legislation and future utopian visualization, was
a metaphysical journey to the realm of the ancestors. This multilayered dialogue between all these Buberian "ghosts" greatly enriched both understanding of the self, the "Other," and their ultimate interpenetration.

Examining the voyageur journey and its Chasse-Galérie "shadow ghost" in
the French and Native contexts, we notice that, in both cases, a sorcerer-
medicine healer whose powers are akin to those of Satan was required to
allow for a world-jump. The world-jump could be either in time or in space.
The time-jump allowed both French and Native to engage in dialogue with
dead ancestors and thus secure their protection, while the space-jump
allowed a dialogue between French and Native cultures. The sorcerer-medi-
cine healer was required either to protect the living from the revenge of the
deceased or to enable the deceased to protect the living. The sorcerer-medi-
cine healer was also required to journey to the Native Atisken andahatey to
effect healing through the intercession of beasts. While St Anne was obliged
to protect the fur trade canoe route for its voyageurs, only the sorcerer-med-
icine healer was able to reverse the route to allow the Galérie boys to jump
overnight from the Native world to the French world and back in a dream.

The public event of the voyageur canoeing to the Great Lakes, and its
dream-reversed mirror in the Chasse-Galérie myth, depended upon inversion to invoke the ancestral power of protection. In the beginning, the classic Native ritual space-jump involved the Natives going east to the French at
Montreal or Three Rivers, which was an inversion of Native mythical space,
where the west is sacred. Time-wise, this occurred in spring, after the winter
hunting season. In other words, the French ritual space-jump was already
inverted as the French went to the Natives, which was a further inversion of
French sacred space, whose holy centre was Jerusalem (as it was in the Native
sacred direction of the west). It was also inverted time-wise, for this journey
was effected in autumn, while one or several winters were spent in the west.
Therefore, first St Anne (baptism by water), then taking tobacco, then praying for martyrs (baptism by fire) was required to propitiate Tsakapesh (the

Bear) in the form of the waterfall and rocky manitous along the canoe route to fur country. Especially in the seventeenth century, Agreskoué was seen by the French as satanic, and his fire was fought with fire. Winter in the Great Lakes was, according to the Iroquoian conception, the prime time for the propitiation of ancestral spirits with tobacco, food, song, and dance.

The Native mythical time and space-jump inverted the French folkloric direction (i.e., the dead went to the living). For the Natives, the living go to the dead or go back up the world-tree to the skyworld. A Native shaman, arendiouane, or oki was required to journey from the living to the Atisken andahatey to heal illness. Nevertheless, in the French mythical time-jump, the dead came to the living. The hunting Mesnie Hellequin threatened or redeemed the living and was only chased or appeased by a similar reversal of a horned stag party hooting up a racket in a prescriptive ritual – the charivari or the monde à l'envers of the Ononharoia. The rules of the Mesnie and its variants were repeated in the French Canadian mythical space-jump. The flying canoe crew engages in dialogue with the past Mesnie Hellequin and once, on the St Lawrence, was ready for an ancient charivari-Ononharoia-"witches sabbath" party all rolled into one. The crew, like revenants, "return from the dead" (or the past, or Native country) to invade the habitants' party. This was surely an unwelcome visit for habitant boys, who later on were famously jealous of the wilder voyageurs and their ability to attract female attention.[196] The revenants try not only to redeem themselves and the living, but they are also a potentially haunting presence in the Third Space purgatorial Atisken andatahey. They were dreaded by the living, paradoxically seeking both guidance from the past and an innovative rebirth. Thus, the cross-dialogue between the destination of the Galérie, along with the ruckus of the Mesnie, French charivari, "witches' sabbath," and Ononharoia, brought about a dialogue both with the past and between cultures.

At the juncture of the early modern era the Reformation and Counter-Reformation stomped out the last cinders of Celtic and Nordic-inspired bonfires, yet ignited thousands of witch pyres. The dread associated with the pagan past was compounded by the dread of those millions of pagans waiting to be missionized in order to justify the true Christian way. The Christian Heaven and Hell were challenged by the non-judgmental Native "country of souls," which sought to join rather than separate; to gather in rather than to condemn. In New France the fear of the Christian Hell was attenuated by what they imagined to be a living Native "Hell" in Iroquoia, and this heightened the liminal attraction of an ambivalent nocturnal dream flight.

The constant motion of French Canadian youth sought the liminality of purgatorial Atisken andahatey so as to mediate one set of cultural rules with the other. Both French Canadian and Algonquian tales often continue as running episodes. Death, as a final absolute, is coaxed away by being relegated to being mere distance. This involves an Einsteinian formulation, whereby time is converted into space through expending energy. The French Canadian device resembles the Algonquian: "and if he hasn't died, he's running still." ("s'il n'est pas mort, il court encore.")[197] This device was curiously evocative of other French Canadian expressions: "coureur de bois," "courir la dérouine," and "courir l'allumette," all of which referred to either trading, hunting, or woodland romances. These classic French Canadian expressions of this constant motion, which, although powered by "magically suspect" means, escaped geographical, communal, and time limits, eventually landed in the arms of outstretched Nature (fir trees), whose non-judgmental laws suited the perennially youthful runner. The French North Americans "ran" from past to present, and from absence to presence. Those absent seemed less far off, those deceased appeared less dead, those dispersed joined together in the marathon – hunting sustenance, love, community, and the self. It was just a matter of tying those worlds "jumped" together. The French of North America literally "ran," sailed, or mythically flew to escape the Scylla of "official" France and the Charybdis of the Haudenosaunee. They ultimately cobbled together time, place, and cultural rules from one voyage to another. The eternal youthfulness thus obtained in the process was truly a divine gift of a holy ghost ... or a Great Spirit.

CHAPTER EIGHT

Outside in, inside out

Immigration strains the capacities of those who undergo it. Few immigrate without some strong necessity or ideal urging them to disrupt their at least nominally supportive home life. Immigrants become stuck in the liminal, but isolated, passageway between two worlds until they can reorient themselves, reach out to an additional social network, and re-establish themselves. The patchy and ambiguous nature of French settlement in Native North America catalyzed the anomie reverberating within the individual, who mourned the absence of his/her lost world and was surrounded by surprises in the new. The multilayered dialogue set up through twinning with Native nations was not only necessary for the survival of both but also unlocked unknown domains within the self. The trying passage of immigration rallies inner resources that are enriched by the new connections established. "Life-changing dialogue" alleviates the uncertainty and distress caused by what I would call the "inner narrative rupture of emigration," even if the emigration was desired, because of the unprecedented unknowns and range of possible responses one must face in the new location. "Life-changing dialogue" is that "interchange and interinfluence that greatly restructures one's attitudes, feelings, cognitive evaluations, or that fundamentally alters one's emotional, philosophical, motivational, and political set." [1] The narrative threads that continue are rewoven into a fresh environmental context, and the ruptured threads are those that must either be nurtured into adapting or be reevaluated. As anthropologist Milton Singer puts it, even a monologue is always a "dialogue à deux" with an imagined other. [2] The rematching of one current shifting frame of reference with another, still frozen in memory, can be painful when the gap is great or during drastic upheavals. Proust's madeleine epiphany, where a special quality of an inanimate object awakened a flood of vivid memories, stimulated reflection upon his life narrative and the significance of the world of his contemporaries at the Parisian fin de siècle, from an acutely analytical, yet still empathetic perspective. Those myriad ruptured or suspended dormant ties create a sense of mourning, guilt, and distress, while the fresh links, which microdialogue with these disrupted ties, challenge the ability of the self to survive and thrive. The regrowth that binds the wound results from those comparisons and contrasts that were mediated and resolved well after a period of relatively chaotic anomie. Immigration lends urgency before, during, and after the passage, to interpret the inchoate meaning and direction of one's life and the worlds within which one has moved through time and across space.

In a thumbnail review of my multilevel analysis, I begin from the macro and briefly highlight shaping realities and recurrent themes throughout in order to hone several brief microanalyses of those individuals who represent the major themes found at every level of analysis.

The immigrants' north Atlantic French heritage revelled in anti-French riots and rallied its ties to the rest of the north Atlantic world, especially to the older Celtic and Nordic culture that it had in common with Great Britain. Most immigrants were young and male, and thus ripe for rebellion precisely at the historical moment when young males could radically improve their status through mobility, urbanization, literacy, and/or immigration. Thus, their background heritage and economic distress encouraged them to bound forward even though they regretted leaving kin and friends. The majority of female immigrants had less to regret in France since they were often institutionalized orphans. Immigrants were almost invariably ablebodied and mobile. On the Native side, the great mourning created by the epidemics allowed an opening for intercultural dialogue.

Schematically, each of the historical crises that contributed to an evolution in collective identity-formation encouraged Nativization. The Hébert-Couillart family members, who were fully committed to adjusting themselves to North America, after the Kirke invasion of Quebec became colonists without a colony. Being cut off from all French contact, hosting a mixed group of children, and braving the Kirkes, they became bereft immigrants who were required to rely upon and learn from Native friends. During the twin disasters of 1648, immigrants and native-born began to see themselves not as French agents to Native nations but, increasingly, as partners. French administrators and officials were often disregarded if they stood in the way of the budding French North American elite. The formidable bishop and Jesuits were heeded out of apprehension, but whenever their interdicts impeded further adaptation, they were furtively ignored. For the first time, the high-status Wendats were beggared and literally sought French hospitality, thus reversing the power equation between them. Although the French themselves lacked both military and economic autonomy, they learned how to share more liberally, which helped the settlement, the Christian Wendat, and the Algonquians. Last, the battle of the Long Sault crystallized the French image, in both Native and French perceptions, changing it from what the Natives termed the effeminate, theoretical "françois" style (according to which the French only knew how to "argue all at once," duel with their own kinsmen, precipitate and then regret, and substitute bluff for action) into the practical, dignified, manly "canadois" that was their own spitting First Nations image – even if victory was thanks to the veteran Chief Annaotaha at their side.

Due to a life-changing twinship dialogue, social roles and attitudes underwent great transformations. Roles were especially modified across the geographical expanse of the French-Native network, which extended from Acadia to deep into the west, and south to the Gulf of Mexico. In Trois-Rivières and Montreal, men were required by their very occupations to acquire a Native-style sensitivity to shame and humiliation. Self-control (Selbstvange) is an essential ingredient of a maturing civilization, as Norbert Elias writes. Immigrant youth developed this by enduring hardships without a whisper, and embracing the requirements of Native dread of loss of face. This became the supreme goal of the youth rite of passage in canoes travelling along the fur trade route from the St Lawrence to the Great Lakes. Those living in Quebec were more sheltered from the rigours of the fur trade and Haudenosaunee incursions, and Eccles points to the opposition between the Quebec "sheep" and the Montreal "wolves." In the Native centres, and along the peripheries between French or Native centres, the capacity to learn several Native cultures, and the ability to switch between cultures as the need arose, was the skill most valuable to the community. In these volatile intersections, the cloistered Quebec lamb was quickly sheared of its fluffy fleece, yet for those who succeeded, Native North America was well within the grasp of their vast twinship network.

Across this expanse there emerged a levelling metamorphosis that organized society horizontally rather than vertically and in a male-female complementarity rather than hierarchically. The transfer of the new socio-cultural canon was enabled through an extensive didactic process of socializing the young through Native adoptions or veteran French Canadian Nativization, and it was reinforced by necessity.

While selected young Native women, like Katéri Tekakwitha, tried out the feminine self-immolation model of French religious women, many more immigrant French orphan girls preferred the Native sharing ethic, which corresponded closely with noble Frenchwomen's pious "caritas." After all, it was this caritas that had preserved their lives when they were young orphan girls, and now sharing was simply one of the necessities of a new-found settlement – especially for young mothers whose large families and quasi-clanmother standing compensated greatly for what was felt to be their sketchy beginnings.[3] The internship in Native life enabled those who had Nativized to stay in French North America when the survival of the settlement seemed precarious.

Renaming, masking, and rebaptizing between French and Native in Canada were encouraged in the liminal peripheries, which forced a bricolage of one's identity.[4] The naming of newborns or converts in an attempt to re-embody the qualities of Christian saints, or the similar "raising of the dead" through Iroquois adoption and "Requickening" ceremonies, built upon their previous co-opting of Nu-Pieds insurgent "noms de guerre" to demonstrate one's opposition to Crown policies.[5] Native protocol required that one never pronounce one's name publicly. The true self depended upon the power of one's guardian Manitou, or powaganak; the power of the community to both shape and fulfil those inner desires of which one was unaware; and one's capacity for maintaining an imperturbable social face, or mask, that kept social ties on an even keel.

French face slaps were interpreted as menacing to the social mask one was wearing, meaning one's "honneur'; hence the cultural baseline of the French Canadian preoccupation with the obsolete knightly ideal of the homme de coeur, expressed in Corneille's Le Cid. Native conceptions of identity and manhood interacted with this baseline via their own ideals. Natives used face-painting and masks for war and healing ceremonies to conceal their vulnerability and to assume other roles, procedures that the French only permitted during Carnival or the Feast of Fools. Losing face through breaking under torture was one step along the humiliation highway that culminated in having one's head cut off and the scalp sliced off as a trophy to "cover" another's death in a final war of accounting between rivals. Humiliation, or the ultimate loss of face, entailed descending from selfhood to headlessness, to becoming a lifeless corpse devoured by dogs and wild beasts. For the Algonquians, all captured animals, even large fish, received better treatment as their bones were accorded special respect via sacred rites. Yet, according to Radisson, the application of torture in order to force a face-losing humiliation was common Iroquoian military practice, its purpose being to satisfy protocol should their blood not be "covered" by elaborate gift-giving protocol. Blood vengeance that could spiral out of control was not unknown in early modern Europe, as Shakespeare pointed out in Romeo and Juliet, where he talks of the warring Italian city-states, and as Machiavelli pointed out in The Prince. Names, faces, hair, hats, heads, scalps, facepaint, and masks were the emblems of one's social face in a community whose survival often depended upon dissimulation and the muting of emotional expression in close quarters such as the hunting wigwam or longhouse. These emblems served to blur French/Native inside/outside social categories and were rechristenings of new Native-influenced French North

American social types: the burgher-gentleman (bourgeois- gentilhomme), the soldier of God (soldat de Dieu), the militia captain (capitaine de milice), the habitant, and the coureur de bois.

These social configurations were reinforced further through the dialogue between beliefs, and the emergence of intermixed and new figures of faith, such as the rivalry between St Anne and the Wendat and Algonquian Great Serpent, between the Algonquian Gluscap and St John the Baptist, along with the blending of both, as in Ti-Jean and the Chasse-Galérie. These larger-than-life enactments embodied many adaptive problematiques, paradigms, and solutions for survival based upon the amalgamated community's historic development.

Yet, as always, personality and varying degrees of cultural assimilation, alienation, or anomie modified the response of immigrants to their own personal situation. The character of members of the family together with the dynamics of family interaction constitutes a major mediating circle of influence, which, when shorn from the immigrant, carries on a phantom dialogue with him within his mind. Finally, zeroing in from macro to micro, we have the individual. Due to the vast shaping structures and influences setting, moulding, and interacting with the features of one's life, the individual might appear merely as a vessel or pale reflection of these overwhelming interweaving forces over which he may have little power. Yet that is what is so beautiful about it.

Each human being is special, possesses her/his own unique gift and dynamic style of engaging with the multilayered environment. Watching the extinguishment of one human being reminds us that he carried an entire world within himself. The uprooting and recreation of one's entire network of social relations is a complex process. Sociologist Ian Burkitt has even denied that an inside "I" exists and has postulated that there is no core to personality; rather, it is progressively shaped by social and cultural evolution. This melds the theories of Norbert Elias, Karl Marx, and Margaret Mead.[6] Culturally distinct environments that are vitally interdependent and tangled in a ceaseless dialogue create cognitive dissonances, internal contradictions, the transformation of meanings, and differing cultural foci that must be personally worked through. Identity seems to be primarily relational, developmental, and narrative, while the organizing principle constitutes the self. A multidisciplinary approach can go far towards demonstrating the structuring and proportionality of the layers acting in conjunction with one another, of showing how those proportions are modified in each case, and of delineating the core of cross-referenced meanings between layers. To resolve the special life dilemma that one must deal with in this unprecedented colonial contact situation required a creative bricolage of identity, each encoded according to his or her particular life history and providing a unique solution.

FINDING REFUGE

Most females who crossed the Atlantic had numerous difficulties prior to arriving in North America, and this made their social integration and personal fulfillment that much more invested with therapeutic value. Backgrounds of orphanhood, sexual assault, family dramas, and poverty were common for most of the women who left France for Canadian shores. This brief overview cannot possibly do justice to the hard backgrounds of so many later mothers of dynasties. Suffice it to say that their hardships redeemed them from following French ways too slavishly, opened the gates to the wonders of the more liberal Native regimes, and facilitated a cognitive incentive to learn new ways that might boost them and their many children to a better life.

The majority were guided and assisted greatly by the prominent pioneer women who founded families in the first settlement and who became legendary by linking with the female missionaries in devotion. Marie Rollet Hébert and her husband were the first settlers on the St Lawrence, and they stayed in Quebec during the Kirke occupation. She cared for the sick with her husband, Louis Hébert (who was an apothecary), taught French to Native children, and in 1627 prepared a huge baptism feast for Chomina's son, Naneogauchit.[7] According to Azarie Couillard–Desprès, she knew the Huron language so well that she was able to prevent an ambush by two Mohawk reconnaissance men disguised as Wendat, Itahoua and Ginotaha, who came to Quebec. She then negotiated with them to swear not to attack Quebec for ten moons, which they did. However, Chief Itahoua later kidnapped her and tried to save her for torture by hiding her in a tree while her godchild, Pierre Pastedechouan, attacked him and his people with 400 men for recent Wendat deaths and saved her. She then promised Chief Senoka that she would instruct twenty children.[8] Anne Gasnier Bourdon was the celebrated wife of Jean Bourdon, the well respected land engineer of the settlement. She was renowned for her great piety and sharing behavior. Barbe de Boullongne (Governor D'Ailleboust's wife) set a remarkable example of period piety when, as a married women, she decided to become a devotee and to live with her husband platonically. He agreed, and the two did their best to be models of generosity, especially to the needy among the Native nations. The Algonquians called Barbe de Boullonge "Chaouerindamaguetch" (she who pities our poverty). Guillemette Hébert Couillart was the wife of Guillaume Couillart and the daughter of Marie Rollet Hébert. She successfully managed during the difficult Kirke years with several children, the youngest of whom was the famous Louis Couillart de L' Espinay. Marie Leneuf was the first woman to be married in Trois-Rivières, and she pioneered female norms there. Despite using the founders as models of piety in the later 19th-century hagiographies, contemporaries noted the positive atmosphere and energy of the women of the new settlement.

SWEPT AWAY

Religiously inspired women dedicated their entire lives to the betterment of First Nations. Mothers were busy and were devoted to their typically large broods. But their devotion was matched by the maternal devotion of nuns, nurses, and religious women for their Native charges. Missionary women often became entirely self-effacing and even flagellant (in contrast to most of their pious brothers who returned to France) as this was consonant with the prescribed feminine route to self-amelioration and improved social standing. Formally, they were under authoritarian tabs, had little individual autonomy, and managed a budget that was but a tiny fraction of that given the Jesuits. Early pioneer female life-narratives in the settlement were often fraught with a high level of suffering, visions, and self-sacrifice (whether religious or not). Even though Frenchwomen's life narratives were socio-culturally channelled to fit into certain acceptable patterns, once in North America they attempted to mould their narratives and to interpret their sufferings in terms that would be culturally comprehensible while also challenging the strictures of their narrow role in France. Although the missionary men had certain recognizable patterns in Church history, and had several older men to guide them, the women often set out on uncharted territory. This was due to a lack of extensive Latin learning and a dearth of female missionary accounts. There was also great confusion due to the high authority and standing of women in Native communities, especially among the Haudenosaunee in general and the Seneca in particular. Instead of following their pious brothers' prescriptions, these women strung their narratives, like interrelated pearls, in reference to one another. They sought new roles in the New World through cobbling together saint's lives, their own family backgrounds, their striking visions, and what they could include from Native life that did not completely contradict Christian precepts dear to the stern bishop. Their New World spirituality inspired several notable Native girls and women to walk in their footsteps, never knowing that religious womens' lives were much more cloistered and insignificant in old France than on the shore of the St Lawrence.

Many were later famous figures in Quebec, such as Madeleine de la Peltrie, who was a dangerously ill young widow who swore to do great works of charity if only she might live. She spent her great wealth on two main projects, funding the Ursulines of Quebec and helping found Ville-Marie (Montreal). In fact, Marie de L'Incarnation worried that La Peltrie was so occupied with them that she thought her a bit of an airhead. Nevertheless, La Peltrie was described by all the writers as extremely affectionate and as excited about aiding the Native girls who surrounded her as she did her tasks.

Mother Marie de L'Incarnation, the founder of the Quebec Ursulines, was also an unusual and remarkable character. Widowed, she left her adolescent son at boarding school to found another school in Canada. This was very traumatic for him at the time, but soon their correspondence was very prolific and soul-searching. By 1648 her convent instructed eighty girls, both Native and French.[9] She spoke several Native tongues, including Huron, a number of Algonquian languages, Montagnais, and even such Great Lakes tongues as Maskouten. This made her a valuable resource to Native and governor.[10] Yet her many visions indicate great inner struggles over the contradictory demands of motherhood and mission, sexual love and the chastity required of religious women, her analytical capabilities and the impossibility of any official governing role.

Marguerite Bourgeoys, was one of the founders of Montreal, the congregation of Notre-Dame, and a number of girls' schools across the continent. Of a wealthy bourgeois family, after being orphaned at twenty she joined a congregation of which Governor de Maisonneuve's sister Louise was director. She left for Montreal in 1653 as a secular religious "sister" and founded the chapel of Notre-Dame, taught basic literacy and home skills to Native and French girls, toiled as a social worker, and became the chief matchmaker of the orphan filles du roy. She persuaded the king to give her letters patent for her school in 1671, and she established branches in Lachine, Pointe-aux-Trembles, Batiscan, Champlain, and at Montagne mission. Her work was guided by visions of Mother Mary.

Due to these active women, settlement girls became better educated than the boys, and refused to be cloistered. The women modelled their work upon Mary, who never refused help to the needy.[11] One young woman had suffered great stigma in France but turned this around in North America.

Jeanne Supli's parents pleaded with the Quebec Hospitallers to keep her safe after she had been sexually assaulted and abducted by a would-be suitor before she arrived in Canada.[12] We do not know exactly how Jeanne herself thought about any of this. This report was made by later nuns, who may not have known whether she had truly desired to wed a man her parents kept from her by shunting her off to Canada. Hypothetically, however, as a seventeenth-century Frenchwoman, she most likely would not want any history of sexual violation casting a shadow upon her later life overseas. In this age, especially in France, the stigma fell upon her, not him, even if in Normandy and Poitou there were exceptions to this rule. This makes the sexual assault thesis believable. Stigma and rumours can poison the sexual assault victim's social life with undeserved shame that is often skilfully manipulated by those adept at gossip and hungry for tidbits. Today the humiliation is theoretically less, yet even so having to publicly defend oneself often proves to be more destructive than the pain caused by keeping one's silence. This is due to the fragile remedies for female distress within the Western social narrative. In the New World Jeanne Suplis took a new name, Mother Ste-Marie, was treasured by the sisters at the Quebec hospital (Hotel-Dieu), made a valuable contribution to the settlement, and was sorely missed when she died.

Another typical account of religious women's roles is illustrated by Mother Marie de St-Ignace, who was one of the founders of the Quebec Hotel-Dieu. When Marie de St-Ignace was mortally ill (asthma and perhaps a deadly abdominal disorder) she had her sickbed wheeled in to their rooms to comfort the dying. She fed them the fresh meat that was intended for her own illness, and she died at thirty-six due to her sleepless nights of nursing and mortifications. According to Father LeJeune: "she was so satisfied to die in Canada serving these poor barbarians [sic] and was missed by both French and wildmen." The hospital chronicle adds: "the wildmen loved to see her."[13]

Jeanne Mance was another example of a young woman who had a domineering father who inspired her to found the first Native and French missionary hospital and the "folle enterprise" of Montreal (Hotel-Dieu). She persuaded the mighty and wealthy devotees of the Parisian court to found this hospital in a settlement not yet built instead of contributing to their pet causes (such as the Jesuits). This initially displeased everyone, except for the women, yet they obtained backing from the more open-minded Sulpicians and, in the end, finally convinced the first bishop of New France, Mgr de Laval, that it was worth it. Persistence was Jeanne Mance's key, and she insisted that her Hospitallers not be bound to nun's vows, which really required courage considering the era and her lack of communal status as an poor, uneducated single woman without a habit or potential husband. This Jeanne d'Arc-like courage was precisely what thrilled the wealthy devotees, who often strained within their social strictures, needing something more uplifting than paramour intrigue and the petty dramas of the précieuses. The eye of the unorthodox and remarkable governor of Montreal, de Maisonneuve, was caught, and Jeanne and Marguerite Bourgeoys became his two right-hand women. Jeanne returned the governor's favour by donating a large sum for the defence of Montreal when it was riddled by a Mohawk ambush. Two points provide entryway into her character and inner life. As a secular religious hospitaller, she subjected herself to many ascetic rigours and punishments, including limiting her entire daily caloric intake to what she could fit into a tiny cup. We might rightly question, if she was afforded the opportunity to expand her previously inconsequential role as an unmarried woman in France to lead an essential communal task, why did she still so constrict her own life? She appeared to have been indomitable in her fight for control over her great goal and in serving those who needed it badly. In current literature there is a frequent linkage between self-critical women aiming at perfection and eating disorders. French religious women of this age frequently prided themselves upon their ability to sustain the denial that society foisted upon them as their only path to social recognition was through virtue and suffering. These girls had many chores, were not invested in, received little food, and had no land, all of which led their parents to see them as burdens for whom they had to raise a dowry. So, in a bid for social standing that rewarded "virtue," the girls attempted to co-opt and control a parsimonious society. It appears that, while she pioneered irreplaceable roles for women in the New World, Jeanne felt herself inadequate to this unprecedented task and, thus, internalized social censure and punished herself. The second point that offers a glimpse into Jeanne's inner life involved her slipping on the ice and breaking her elbow, which did not heal properly for two years. When this accident occurred she left for France, where her arm was "miraculously" cured in healing waters.[14] Ironically, the excellent fresh waters of Canada could not heal her while the less hygienic waters of France could. Metaphorically, her arms were the tools with which she established so much in Montreal and with which she dug herself out of her former useless social position. Her inability to heal her broken arm, while investing so much of her life healing others, indicates her own uncertainty regarding her capacity not only to fulfill the challenging role as founder but also to control herself and "be perfect" as a pious model. Perhaps in refusing to heal itself her body was rebelling against the meagre sustenance to which she limited herself. Perhaps in France she relaxed her rigidity, not being surrounded by people whom she had to constantly inspire. These religious founders and missionaries established hospitals, schools, and Montreal itself, that were not only remembered and honoured but were imitated by members of later generations, such as Marguerite D'Youville, founder of the devoted Grey Sisters.

SHOOTING WATERFALLS

Most young males were fortunate enough not to find adaptation difficult in North America. All that was required was that they be culturally supple enough to adjust themselves to the demands of their surroundings without seriously damaging their inner identity dilemma, from which they usually benefited significantly. Samuel de Champlain himself, when he was still young, succeeded greatly in adapting to Native life and establishing himself as the major liaison between the French Crown and Native nations. Famous founders, traders, and explorers (such as Jean Bourdon, Jean Nicollet, Louis Hébert, Guillaume and Louis Couillart,[15] Nicolas Perrot, Jean Godefroy de Lintot, Thomas Godefroy de Normanville,[16] Jacques Hertel, Jean Juchereau, Jacques Le Ber, Charles Lemoyne, Olivier LeTardif, and Charles Aubert de la Chesnaye) succeeded very well in adjusting to and learning from Native life. One early settler who did particularly well was commoner Pierre Boucher, who immigrated to Canada as a child. He worked as an interpreter and married a Wendat girl. He was later widowed, became famous for his military valour, and remarried, this time to a French-woman. He received letters of nobility, sizable lands, wrote a now-famous book for the king, and received the governorship of Trois-Rivières. Today, in the new redesignated borough of Longeuil in the Greater Montreal area, Boucherville is a jewel of a suburb, with single-family homes, a private yacht-filled waterside, and long tree-lined bicycle paths winding along the glittering Montreal shore. The Bouchers constitute one of the larger mixed-blood dynasties in North America, with innumerable descendents on both sides of the border.

In the Native centres, contracting a Native-style marriage to a daughter of a respected family, and being loyal to them, their ties, and their nation, was the ordinary way of life for Frenchmen in the extended French-Native peripheries and in the Native centres. The later voyageurs and their descendents, usually Métis, became the bread and butter of the fur-trading North West Company of western Canada. For example, Abenaki chief baron Jean-Vincent d'Abbadie de St-Castin founded a famous Acadian Métis clan after marrying and becoming an Abenaki chief, whose clan was only one of the many mixed-blood families who frustrated the British in their struggle over Acadia.

LOST IN THE WOODS

For those few immigrants possessing a precarious mental state before arriv-ing in North America, their condition worsened with the ambiguous social situation and accompanying dangers. Jean Cavalier de La Salle's well-known mental state, controversial documentation and biographies, and disputed discoveries are too famous and lengthy to be detailed here.[17]

Less due to pathology than to cultural and role confusion, the behaviour of Etienne Bruslé, Nicolas Marsolet, and other interpreters who spent their youth scattered among various tribes indicate identity confusion and some central organizing identity reversals, as has been considered earlier. There were even French who lost contact with the settlement and are only known by their first name (e.g., Grenolle) or by their Native names (e.g., Onraon, Auhaitsique, and Houaonton).

BRANDED BY FIRE

Adoptions were not exclusively innocuous twinning exchanges between will-ing allies. During hostilities between the French-Wendat-Algonquian alli-ance and the Haudenosaunee, the latter formally adopted many of their young captives and attempted to integrate them fully into Haudenosaunee clan society. An in-depth reexamination of war adoptions, and the multiple aspects of the meaning of these adoptions to the adoptees, is essential.[18] James Axtell has suggested that English-speaking "white Indians" frequently refused to return to the colony once they had tasted Native freedom and community.[19] This is important, but their developmental trajectory reveals much more complexity than initially meets the eye. French male youth of Trois-Rivières were the people most frequently captured in ambush, tortured, and then adopted – and who returned to tell the tale. Several of them successfully utilized the cognitive cultural and coping skills that they had acquired through this experience as a jumping off point to become senior diplomats or key trader kingpins. Yet this was not the fate of most who were subjected and/or exposed to captivity. Although life narrations are always unique, those that involve enduring unusually traumatic challenges are usually even more intense, as every twist of fortune requires a sudden marshalling of unprecedented inner resources and extraordinary coping skills.

As the Haudenosaunee fought with nations it regarded as enemies each individual captive's fate depended upon who the clanmothers selected as capable of integration. Thus, while there were many ambushes, killings, and consequent diasporas of Wendat, Neutral, Tionnontati, and Algonquian nations, cultural conversion and incorporation was the goal – never "genocide" or annihilation.[20] Their main concern was to ensure Haudenosaunee incontestability and strength by mounting a "mourning war," carrying off valuable people to incorporate into their society to relive the deceased's social function with his or her name. Adoptees later became valuable assets and perhaps influenced other nations to ally themselves with the Haudenosaunee under the Great White Pine of peace. Incorporation, not coexistence, was the goal. A "mourning war" is quite the opposite of "blood revenge" or "family honour killings" as practiced in the current Arab Middle East. "Blood revenge" leads to killing due to the "mindless fury of grief," in a tit for tat, as was the custom in early modern Europe. And this, of course, can easily spiral out of control. "Redeeming family honour" reinforces the Moslem Sharia code, which gives males the legal right of life and death over female members of their own family. In Haudenosaunee "mourning wars" adoption was almost always preferred over ritual death, alliance over war. Women were not to be dominated; rather, they were those who regulated longhouse disputes, war passions, prisoner-of-war adoptions, and who made all serious decisions concerning life and death.

Seventeenth-century Haudenosaunee adoption commences with torture. This reverses the essential developmental attachment process and, thus, ruins it. It commences with despoiling every possibility of a trusting unequal power relationship by relegating the captive to torture. Then it capitalizes upon the grandiose gesture of snatching the person, literally, out of the jaws of death, thus reinforcing the disempowered hostage relationship that clearly obliterates every vestige of one's prior world and former social identity. This is then called "family," when precisely the reverse has been unfolding. It forcibly attaches the youngster to another community – one that has killed off many of his/her own group – in order to ultimately subordinate and incorporate them. Thus, the process appears to combine a muted variation of two very powerful strategies for disempowering, humiliating, and isolating the youngster. It is only after this "trial-by-literal-fire" process that cordiality crowds around the victim and that the mourning family washes, soothes, initiates, and loves the new brother/sister. Haudenosaunee culture is particularly good at reinforcing family and communal bonds.

Children and youth rely upon their parents for survival. The violation of that life-giving pact constitutes the most essential violation of the role of caregiving.[21] Severe child/youth torture or mutilation, conducted by or in front of the most trusted caretakers of the child/youth and condoned by the entire community, is massively damaging. His predicament causes disbelief in himself, his social sphere, and humanity. Judith Herman's complex disorder of extreme stress (DESNOS) fits this category well, but Ronnie Janoff-Bulman's shattered assumptions only apply to people old enough to have formed assumptions to shatter.[22] The rehabilitation required is complicated by possible prior trauma sensitization[23] and extreme degrees of self-revulsion and humiliation due to the inability to resist harm, which is internalized abuse.[24] This is exacerbated by the community's indifference, avoidance, denial of suffering, bystander guilt, which is much worse when there is communal participation in the torture, such as occurred in early Iroquoia.[25]

The experience of captivity was quite different for each captive. According to the accounts, it appears that the first factor of importance was the age of the captive.[26] The experience of captivity was incised more deeply into the central life-organizing principles at a tender age. If captured when bordering on adolescence, there could be greater resilience. Each brought to the experience his or her own reservoir of health quotient, family support or lack of it, education, life experiences, and self-interpretation.[27] The next factor depended upon whether it was a large-scale ambush that took him together with his family and other community members, whether only his family or part of it was taken, whether only himself and friends, or only himself. The length, degree, kind, and frequency of torture of family or close friends that was witnessed varied greatly for each captive and was immeasurably worse if many community members were involved (as this would mean that many would endure lengthy tortures and atrocious deaths). The frequency, length, kind, and degree of torture that was actually experienced was the next factor that counted.[28] The factor of verbal humiliations and/or death threats counted also. Then there was degree and kind of physical impairments suffered. Which family was taken, and how they treated their charge, was also important.[29] How quickly they integrated into Haudenosaunee society mattered and involved a combination of cultural, emotional, linguistic cognition, physical stamina and capacity for adaptation. Finally, how the escape from captivity was effected, or not, became a highly individualized narrative.[30] Witnessing cruelty upon those very close to one generates conscious thought-restructuring due to the inside-outside nature of experiencing/witnessing this. When it involves many persons of one's closest personal network, the effect is personally disastrous. When it involves family and many figures of one's community network, together or serially, then the effect approaches that of a massacre. When it involves every member of a certain sector, be it defined by religion, tribe, group, or nation, then the effects are catastrophic to the human species, with the most toxic combination of damaging factors possible for the ostensibly obliterated group.[31]

Today, the Harvard Trauma Questionnaire, the Hopkins Checklist, and the Allodi scales try to measure levels of trauma exposure, anxiety symptoms, affective disturbances, somatic complaints, and social difficulties.[32] The mental effects of torture (including sexual assault) are especially severe as it constitutes the most noxious thing that one human being can inflict upon another. The emotional effect is demonstrably more marked upon children than upon adults, upon females than upon males, and upon singles more than upon married couples. And it is always more severe if sexual cruelty is applied.[33]

The variable effect of life-threatening trauma also depends upon prior life events. Many traumatic events can increase vulnerability and anxiety, which results in less resilience to later trauma; but for some people, more trauma desensitizes them, and they are prone to depression. Five core adaptive meanings of the torture seem to be seriously challenging to one's mental health: the sense of safety, attachment, justice, identity-role, and existential-meaning.[34] One may experience panic when one's sense of general safety is impaired, while another may experience depression when one's sense of justice, attachments, self-worth, and meaning is damaged.[35] Perhaps we might also consider that the first reaction may be anxiety, while the second may be depression, these being preliminary stages along the way to a "shattering threshold." This might help to explain why the condition dubbed post-traumatic stress disorder (PTSD) lowers cortisol levels, while depression raises them; but only psychiatric inquiry could explore this question in depth. We might consider that classic allergy treatments work much the same way, in trying to incrementally rebuild a lost tolerance level; however, if one overdoses, then the body overreacts.

We have difficulty understanding why torture was used during this era in both continents, especially during this conflict in which each side claimed to want peace with the other. Mohawk ambushes upon the French settlements were only answered by French retaliation in 1666. Young French male captives had no intention of attacking Iroquoia and were in a vulnerable position. This was in a Native North America that had almost exclusively welcomed them. Champlain's participation in a joint Wendat-Algonquian invasion of Iroquoia in 1609, however, aligned the French with one side during what then was a fierce Iroquoian-Algonquian struggle. First Nations of today are descendents of so many mixed Native and European ancestors that they cannot be separated. Many Haudenosaunee of today were born of former captives.

Torture has been defined as actions whose purpose is to break the will and ultimately destroy the victims' humanity.[36] Whereas in ancient to modern history the torturer was motivated by a will to intimidate, undermine, punish, humiliate, get "information," or a "recantation," today it is a pathological part of contemporary Western media, which included violent pornography and even children's games that can easily be participated in "virtually."[37] Theories regarding the motives of torturers emphasize the processes of regarding the victim as Other, of underrating their predicament, and of excluding them from one's moral universe, thus ostensibly resolving any cognitive dissonance between self-image and actions.[38]

Torture directly harms the mental and physical health of the victim. When life-threatening trauma is acute, the brain generates a quicker than ordinary response to the threat. This emergency response runs through the limbic and endocrine systems located in the brain, through the HPA (hypothalamic/pituitary/adrenal) axis. Initially, the stimuli is sent to the locus ceruleus (pons) in the brain stem,[39] which sends it, via the release of norepinephrine, through the thalamus, and then it is sent directly to the amygdala and locus ceruleus. The amygdala, the high emotion processor, sifts through the stimuli, and then information is sent to the hippocampus, the centre of episodic or declarative memory that contextualizes events, where a cognitive repository for the information is created. Then the information is sent to the right orbitofrontal cortex, where it is processed, and a behavioral and motor response is organized. Yet, when overwhelming arousal is endured for prolonged periods of time, such as that ordinarily endured by adopted captives, the HPA axis that was activated is further acted upon by the hypothalamus, which releases CRH (corticotrophin-releasing hormone) and AVP (arginine vasopressin). These secretions stimulate the release of cortisol from the adrenal medulla and inhibit the release of more ACTH (adrenal corticotrophic hormone from the pituitary gland), which regulates the noradrenergic arousal response and rearranges the long-term stress adaptation response.

Traumatic events that continue over time threaten the limbic system in the brain, which can go haywire if overcapacitated (allostatic load), although we are unsure why.[40] The size of the hippocampus can become reduced, which is a great loss because it contextualizes events and reassures us when a threat is distant and/or has passed.[41] Rachel Yehuda discovered that patients who may have PTSD have reduced cortisol (glucocortisoid) secretion levels from the adrenal glands, and research has since shown that more physiological systems are perhaps involved: opioid, glutaminergic, GABAergic, serotonergic, and neuroendocrinergic pathways.[42] Reactions range on a continuum from normal to dysfunctional, from extraordinary stress, acute trauma, post-traumatic disorders, to PTSD and Herman's DESNOS. It appears that PTSD is the current wastebasket for disparate and/or overlapping disorders that we are not yet able to distinguish.[43] The PTSD has been theorized as a prolonged arousal reaction that has permanently gone haywire, accompanied by extreme avoidance behaviour that restricts activity, dissociation that involves the splitting off of parts of one's identity, reduced sensitivity to pain, an altered sense of time, emotional numbing, hyperarousal of the autonomic nervous system (ANS), sudden intrusional flashbacks, guilt over the suffering and dead, panic, phobias, irritability, unmanageable anger, and nightmares. All this can terminate in suicide, yet, as Young has pointed out, the epistemological trajectory of PTSD inquiry may find a far more complex picture than currently imagined.[44] The capacity to perceive danger enables survival, yet in supposed PTSD sufferers this ability has become incapacitated. Currently it is thought that the strongest predictors of PTSD in captives and POWs are torture and emaciation.[45] Haudenosaunee captors tried to avoid inducing this reaction and even coaxed their captives to eat, revived them, and hid them in trees to bring them safe and sound to the village where the grieving clanmothers decided their fate.

The tortured of today exhibit what many researchers have identified as a "torture syndrome," which includes anxiety, depression, sweating, insomnia, headache, fainting, dizziness, tremors, diarrhea, impulsivity, sexual dysfunction, personality disturbances, difficulty concentrating, confusion, disorientation, memory loss, and many illnesses.[46] Torture victims' symptoms have even acquired some of the characteristics of Terence DesPres' "survivor syndrome," except that Holocaust survivors suffered more numbness and deadening than panic, probably due to the immensity and duration of collective events, the enormous time lapse between events, and the lack of any show of global empathy.[47] These events occurred in a Europe that deliberately misrepresented a little known minority to the gentile public and enabled the wholesale plunder and starvation of almost every Jewish community in its environs. This included the shattering of families, their use as human guinea pigs in pseudo-scientific experiments, the worst deaths, tortures, and humiliations imaginable, and the desecration of corpses, which were treated as inanimate objects to be recycled into ordinary soap, mattresses, and lampshades. This infinitely multiplied the effect of any harm inflicted upon any individual.[48]

If some hope of good treatment or escape is anticipated, high anxiety may be maintained although it is wearing upon the system. Pain-numbing endorphins, the product of fear and arousal, enable the threatened captive to suffer less and so to complete his prescribed tasks and to focus his full attention on survival.[49] Psychologist Peter Levine thinks that endorphins are part of the animal kingdom's freeze response, which induces a numbing immobility when fight or flight is impossible and death is intuited as inescapable.[50] At a later time, if a similar threat arises, the same animal's system shuts down in an immobility response that sometimes induces the attacker to abandon its seemingly lifeless prey. The immobility response is especially strong in children and women, who often cannot escape, while males tend to shift into a fight or flight mode.[51] Paradoxically, the immobility response can precipitate an unusually intimate bond between abuser and victim, the latter trying to pacify the aggressor by becoming whatever the former desires. This, of course, contributes to brainwashing and victim/abuser bonding.

Was Haudenosaunee war adoption a form of brainwashing? Frequently, the most dangerous psychopathological effect of all is an admiration of the abuser – of the one who holds the power of life and death. The victim is very vulnerable to being brainwashed or indoctrinated according to the torturer's pet fancies. Battered women often acquire a "learned helplessness" from being trapped by their intimidators and laws that fail to adequately protect them and their children.[52] In a similar sense, war adoption firmly attaches the adoptee emotionally to the family that has saved his life. This hardly indicates his freely chosen personal preference.[53] Mirroring and cooperation occurs in captivity as a means of survival, whereas constructive identification builds up slowly. The aggressor has chosen to be a foe, not a friend. Although a torture victim of the Inquisition suddenly becomes a reborn Christian, he can hardly be free of the frequently self-damaging sequels of persecution and torture.[54] Haudenosaunee adoption of the enemy must be perceived within this initial framework. The many kindnesses attested to by some who survived and returned indicates an overthankfulness and desire to serve that reflects a state of helplessness and dependency. This attitude only sweetens an inherently bitter pill, which is endured because there is no choice. An abusive relationship is the only one offered.

A notable reorganization of identity, or even personality, could be possible due to what Karen Horney has termed "psychological suicide," which entails the repressing of identity after traumatic experiences have solicited serious internal conflict between one's self-conception and the humiliating experiences one was forced to undergo.[55] Captivity-generated trauma could eventually lead to dissociative identity disorder (DID) due to the splitting of relatively independent structures of experience.[56] The anterior cingulate (responsible for social behaviour and sense of self), which ordinarily exerts a braking action upon amygdala activation, can generate cingulate inhibition and allow the amygdala to be flooded with unchecked fear and arousal to a point that threatens to overwhelm the brain's capacity.[57] Dissociation protects the self from experiencing the full consciousness of pain and trauma by narrowing the focus of conscious attention to a smaller field and often enabling detachment in an out of body experience.[58] Yet this dissociation appears paradoxically self-protective as it fragments the self and hides dangerous memories. Thalamus interruption of consciousness narrows focus upon the danger while numbing other sensory input, as happens during sleep. Outside the narrowed field of intensely focused consciousness, there is a fog that veils extraneous consciousness and numbs the integrated functions of perception, memory, and cognition. Horney's idea of a fugue (flight), which generates a sudden loss of personal identity due to severe disorientation, perhaps affects the action of neuropeptides and neurotransmitters during and after a discrete traumatic event, which results in temporary amnesia.[59] Memory itself is a more complex process than the "false memory" debate of the 1980s and 1990s would have us believe.[60] Perhaps our socio-cultural reading of syndromes reflects our preconceptions. But the autonomic nervous system's memory, especially the startle response, is not forgetful.[61]

We may have illusions about the degree of unity of the self, due to over-simplifying a complex constellation of associated processes. The self evolves over time and outgrows its older self to be continually renewed. Our historical figures seem to validate Goulding and Schwartz's mosaic mind model and Oppenheimer's associative identity disorder,[62] both of which point to a complex, rather than to a monolithic, identity. In other words, the mind's recognition and organization of sets of context-related self-representations may perhaps become neurologically dysfunctional due to endogenous factors or trauma-damage. A coherent self is constructed from interrelated, but imperfectly integrated, components. Perhaps the more components that are added, the more complex the configuration, and the more difficult it is to integrate the entire system under one discernibly coherent unifying principle. Thus, the adding of age, social complexity, cultural multiplicities, and repeated trauma are factors that can make the self-system more intricate, requiring more reflection to manage unusual complexity under the aegis of one central unifying self-principle. Immunological researchers piece together why it is that the body itself does not always quite know what is itself and what is dangerous, as autoimmune disorders such as allergies, rheumatism, lupus, and others attack its own tissues as if they were "enemy" invaders. They have hotly debated the source of the self/non-self distinction: whether it be a cognitive process of somatic evolution, a standard self-marker template, cell differentiation, or whatever.[63] And it is as yet unknown to what extent the reciprocal relations of mind, neurology, and immunology affect one another, although it is certain that the connection is greater than we can trace as of now. Additionally, it had been repeatedly noted that the Western idea of an individual may be matched by an Eastern idea of a we-self.[64] Richard White suggests that the French I-self was in opposition to a Native we-self, but there is more fluidity here than stark opposition. In seventeenth-century Native culture there seemed to be a deeper sense of self together with a more intense sense of community than existed in seventeenth-century French culture, despite a congruity between them when twinned. In other words, the boundaries of the self, while usually interpenetrated by an "interpersonal neurobiology," as Daniel Siegel has suggested become evident at significant "broken narrative" points, when confusion and disarray are evident.[65] Rearrangements become possible either through brainwashing or through the provision of cognitively sound directions to enhance coherency.

In the case of a theorized inborn DID inherently deficient integrative and associative processes in the self-system or the use of several ego-centres instead appear to be a possibility. But it also appears that trauma can radically upset the delicate associational axes by relegating traumatic memory to a location closer to the perception-emotion–arousal emergency processing centre – the limbic system – instead of the ordinary declarative (episodic) memory sites, where most non-emotionally charged information is normally stored. When emotionally charged traumatic information is repeatedly stored in this area, the normal working of the limbic system becomes less efficient. This induces a less orderly scattering of unintegrated consciousness, perception, cognition, and memory, thus resulting in a certain vertical compartmentalization of disorganized emergency material, which is rarely accessible for ordinary memory processing and recall. In a paraconscious state, as during the trauma itself, this memory can be accessed in frightening disjointed flashbacks. These flashbacks often contain pinpoint detail only in the focus area, with accompanying associated sensations (especially scent and area-focused bodily pain), while the rest appears blurred or foggy. Sometimes these paraconscious slivers of memory can be reawakened via touch or scent. But once activated the dissociative response is then stored for future kindling when similar dangers are perceived.[66] Although some postmodernists celebrate fragmented multiple identities, this chaotic state is not an easy one to live with: 90 percent of those diagnosed with ostensible multiple personality or DID were plagued by childhood sexual abuse.[67]

Holocaust survivors and researchers speak of an individual "endurance threshold." They experienced many less comprehensive "breaking points" along the way, but finally arrived at the moment when it appeared that everything was shattered irreparably. A key factor in this shattering seems to be the refusal to live in a world that perpetrated, tolerated, and later ridiculed the Holocaust. This "shattering point" transformed them into "musulmanneren" – Death Camp slang expressing their European view of Islamic indifference to death, which, in context, meant that they were no longer able to resist death. They curled up in the fetal position and died.[68] In this case, Peter Levine's immobility response, for a person under severe inescapable life-threat, may become a massive numbing shock and simply shut down completely.[69] Massive or prolonged life-menacing stress is linked to many hormonal, immunological, neurological, cardiological, and degenerative diseases that have abnormal amounts of cortisol as their source.[70] Nonetheless, we can no longer investigate those who passed their "shattering point" in the camps; we are only looking at those who survived.

Some Haudenosaunee adoptees did not recover well and could not turn their traumatic experience to much benefit. Ostensibly, this was the majority, given that there were many captives and only a few who became subsequently prominent. One might guess that if one could check Father Isaac Jogues' hippocampus, one might find him as one of those so trapped.[71] He was nicknamed Ondessonk, which is Wendat for "bird of prey." He described his time as a war captive as being good for his soul, despite the fact that he made it sound miserable. After he escaped, he returned as a missionary to the very tribe that had mutilated his hands. He was finally axed in the head. It was noticed that Ondessonk had a tendency to put himself in the way of danger. He advocated the values of martyrdom, self-sacrifice, and suffering but also lived them. Even after surviving torture, he actively refused all self-help despite his skill at outrunning Native warriors; he refused to hunt and spent the day praying alone to himself. This made the Wendat suspect that he had antisocial tendencies, and they ended up suspecting him of witchcraft after many sickened following his leaving behind him a number of priestly articles in a black box.[72]

Brother Louis Hennepin and Jean-Robert Cavelier de la Salle set out on an ambitious voyage of discovery together. Hennepin had been an Onondaga war captive and was later adopted by the Sioux. His published adventures appeared in forty-six languages, yet due to his mercurial temperament, he was forbidden to enter the United Provinces, France, and French North America.

There were a few war adoptees who later turned their Mohawk family connections towards diplomacy and/or profit. Guillaume Cousture was a captive who was tortured, adopted by the great-hearted widow of the chief he had killed, and renamed Ihandich. Pierre-Esprit Radisson, while being tortured, still managed to notice the torments of his friend Cousture, who had his joints broken, his hands pierced, a finger cut off, and his nails ripped out – in silence. He became a prudent and conciliatory chief, and accompanied Chief Kiotseaeton, the great Mohawk diplomat-warrior, to a council at Trois-Rivières with Montmagny in 1645. He was not even recognized because it was assumed that he was dead. He was so insistent upon a permanent peace treaty between the French and all Native nations that he returned to Iroquoia so that negotiations with the Wendat could commence. The parlays were broken and Cousture still insisted upon going to Wendake in 1647 to renew the alliance. He returned to the French in 1647, and Father Buteux recorded that, by 1652, both friend and foe regarded him as a highly prized diplomat. Whenever Mohawk negotiated with the French, Cousture had company: "One, who called himself the relation of Mr. Caiture [*sic*] who was a captive in the country of these barbarians [*sic*]" ("un seul, qui se disaoit parent du sieur Caiture, jadis captif au pays de ces barbares" [*sic*]).[73] For himself, in the 1684 census he only admitted to being a simple carpenter. Raymond Douville remarks that his disputes with others in the Conseil Souverain and the seigneury indicate that sometimes his dignity exceeded the Canadian norm, which indicates his feelings of humiliation as a captive, culture shock, and retention of a Native social face after his captivity. His Haudenosaunee family renamed him Achirra, Jean Nicollet's name, as a compliment. François Marguerie was an interpreter-liaison to the Algonquians. He was known by them as the double man (l'homme double.) At this early time he was reputed to have adapted to Native ways better than the rest of the French.[74] This assisted him immensely as a war captive. He saved Trois-Rivières from ambush and freed himself and his companion from captivity. Born later, Charles Lemoyne de Longeuil et de Chateauguay's youthful service in Wendake and later experience as a war captive helped him both in fur trading and in war. He received a title of nobility, became the wealthiest man in Montreal at the time of his death, and left twelve sons who became the most fearsome defenders of New France.

We have a prime subject in Pierre-Esprit Radisson because we can read his own narrative while examining his life. He narrated his life story (which included his two captivities) and proceeded to establish his own fur trade company in London when repeatedly disappointed by the French authorities.[75] His flitting between French, British, Dutch, and French Canadian authorities seems to have been precipitated by his reaction to his youthful Iroquois capture, adoption, escape, and traumatic recapture and torture. Only his Iroquois mother (herself a Wendat captive forty years earlier) saved him from a terrifying death. Radisson's self-narrative appears to support some kind of "breaking threshold" without approaching a final "shattering threshold," such as Holocaust survivors have often experienced. All attempts at conversion conducted in a mildly forcible manner were highly effective, yet when he was recaptured and subjected to frightening amounts of torture, he eventually broke down. This became counterproductive because he was then all the more avid either to devotedly serve (if unavoidable) or to escape (if prudently possible). Although we cannot verify his cortisol levels along the way, his second recapture constituted a real turning point. And there was a profusion of shocking reversals that could easily have thrown him off-centre. He was recaptured by the Haudenosaunee when he was very close to Trois-Rivières; he was jailed by the French authorities after the death of Dollard, when he was hailed as their greatest hero for bringing in canoes full of furs when the settlement was on the brink of economic ruin; and so on.

As Martin Fournier has correctly noted, Radisson's post-recapture behaviour was exemplified by two key long-term patterns: he became very attached to an older male mentor yet studiously avoided committing himself to any one community.[76] In my view, he needed the human closeness of didactic twinning, signifying his need for receiving long-term therapeutic self-revalidation as well as a caring life model. This need appeared to be particularly acute after his disorienting adoption, and he was subsequently in a position to choose his own mentor. Second, thereafter he avoided having his identity defined in terms of any one community as he discovered the benefits of belonging to all to be greater than the benefits of belonging to only one. Radisson could trust loving Mohawk parents with his life, yet he became very apprehensive about volatile youth in the Mohawk community. In the Ericksonian sense, he wildly succeeded in the ego synthesis part but never quite managed the communal commitment part of the stages of maturation. His recapture is an important key as to why.

Bodily illness can be a somatic translation of social, cultural, and psychological trouble in what is called "conversion."[77] Traumatic memory, especially, can become somatized, so that, as historian Pierre Nora puts it, memory becomes a site within the body.[78] Catastrophes over which the individual has little control can trap him in a victim role within his own life narrative as it unwinds about him, or especially, her.[79] For as Laurence Kirmayer emphasizes, the world fails to bear witness to many tragedies that are difficult to bear alone. And Yael Danieli writes that, even if one risks all to bear witness, this still does not mean that the world will listen, learn, change, or become a better place.[80]

In captivity it seems that Radisson developed some sort of disconnect between his face and his stomach, which made eating difficult when he was in situations of severe danger and transition.[81] We shall examine possible sources layered from macro to micro: from geo-historical, socio-cultural, to psychological – as shaping the character of this somatic problem. Radisson's stomach perhaps became a metaphor for his past and inherited identity, while his mouth became a metaphor for his present forced social identity. The trajectory between mouth (Native territory) and stomach (French settlement territory) is the metaphorical hunting and fur trade route, or the flight from the potential enemy to the familiar French environment – the fluid lifeline essential to survival. Young Radisson ignored his friends' fears of ambush and insisted upon hunting. The "portages" and disconnects in this trajectory are also indicative of the emphasis Haudenosaunee culture put on keeping face in all circumstances, especially under torture, if one wished to be considered any sort of man. This cultural orientation certainly could not only have exacerbated Radisson's initial swallowing difficulty but also have reinforced it after torture. There may be a very significant social layer to this analysis as well. Radisson's possible face-stomach disconnect may have been a metaphorical somatic protective procedure that obfuscated the route from the potentially traumatizing Haudenosaunee enemy to the most intimate self. Choking sensations are well known syndromes of Herman's DESNOS survivors, as the constriction of the "globus hystericus" was also a medieval legal test of fear as well as a sign of choking down outrage.[82] Recently, this syndrome has been relabelled as more physiological than mental, and more widespread than had been previously thought, as it has been discovered that high levels of eosinophils can constrict the esophagus, which limits solid food intake. Yet what triggers this? Most significantly, Radisson writes of his repulsion at what he considered to be rotting meat in the Haudenosaunee pot, no matter how hungry he was. It is very unlikely that these men would eat rotten meat during hunting season, when Radisson himself had just supplied them with three geese, ten ducks, a crane, and some teals. It is much more likely that he saw, or thought he saw, them prepare one of his friends for the pot, which better explains why they boiled his meat separately from their sagamité (corn soup with meat). After all, according to Marcel Trudel's useful catalogue of immigrants, his former brother-in-law, Jean Véron dit Grandmesnil, had two domestics, one of whom was Noël Godin, who was injured by the Mohawk when Radisson arrived in Trois-Rivières in May 1651. Godin died shortly after being treated in the Quebec Hospital, while his favourite sister Marguerite's husband was slaughtered by Haudenosaunee on 19 August 1652.[83] This could even be the time Pierre was caught, something he would be extremely ashamed to admit if this were the case.[84] He was caught just after seeing their bloody carcasses and already felt guilty for having scoffed at their previous fears and unknowingly lead them to their deaths. This possibility is not written in his account, but as he was a resident of the old fur trade centre at Trois-Rivières, he surely had been told all about Haudenosaunee ritualistic cannibalism. Due to fright at the reaction of French and British, he would not dare to write this possibility in his first "voyage." During his first capture he tried very hard to please his captors and may have eaten, or seen devoured, his youthful companions. Psychologically, his stomach perhaps envelops his "inner self" (the belly) as if it were a uterine protection from outside danger that was so close that he could not fend it off in any other way. Internalized "geosociotraumatosomatic" reaction?

We can also guess that the protective buffer of his family was not very strong at this time due to his having wandered off beyond what his more experienced friends thought safe, maybe to draw attention to himself by expressing "acting out" behaviour. And perhaps also he was lacking parental notice in the large family because, when he actually returns home after twice being a captive, he does not write a single word about the reaction of his own family; and, indeed, he returns within weeks to Iroquoia.[85] This omission speaks volumes, but of what? It may indicate a deeper reason for his reckless venturing out too far in the first place. Returning home can either soothe or leave one crestfallen, depending upon the reception that one receives.[86] For his evolving self we know that he feels guilty, and this is the reason he waits so long to be saved by the Dutch, because, as he writes, he had "not yet souffred [sic] enough to have merited my deliverance."[87] This guilt may indicate that he actually witnessed the dismemberment of his sister's husband and only then came face to face with her grief and rage, or the bereavement and anger of his dead friends' parents. His somatic focalization upon the face-stomach trajectory precludes him from having relief from his woes of being haunted by guilt over his dead brother-in-law and friends. But what could he do, trapped as an adolescent war captive? In sum, the possible geographical, historical, social, cultural, and psychological layers of his somatization surely were locked into place when he underwent lengthy bodily torture, which underscored physical areas of vulnerability that unlocked the awareness of a whole world of fear and pain. This had to be disconnected from his inner self if he were to survive. And, in the end, he credits his Haudenosaunee family for taking good care of him by offering him meat: "Their care att this was to give me meate. I have not eaten a bitt all that day, and for the great joy that I had conceaved, caused me to have a good stomach, so that I did eat lustily." For a neglected and hungry adolescent boy, especially just released from death, paradise lay in a warm cauldron, surrounded by caring "family" and friends.

His social face, and the trials of maintaining it when his stomach was so much weaker, was a challenge for Radisson. Before being captured he had a premonition after having a nosebleed, as if the French expression "avoir le piff" were the metaphor, blood the concrete result, and his face the social identity. Then he views the severed bloody heads of his friends (or brother-in-law?) who barely left him a moment earlier.[88] Each time his fear surfaced, Radisson found it difficult to swallow or eat, and this was reinforced by being captured and roped about the neck, being secured at night about the neck, seeing cut throats, axed heads, bloody heads, the scalps of those close to him, and cannibalism.[89] In his first, not so traumatic, capture he could not swallow, so his captors boiled his bits of meat separately from the common pot in order to keep him healthy. In his second, traumatic, capture he was forced to cut off the heads of his former Haudenosaunee friends, and his fellow escapee got severely wounded in the neck and had his head sliced off and thrown into the boat next to him – all of which horrified him as he contemplated his own impending torture and possible death.[90] Keeping face was relatively easy for Radisson because he appeared to have an observant eye and rapid cognition, which allowed him to adapt quickly enough to often save his own head and that of others. But he is well attuned to his own queasy skittishness over meals, a sign of sensitivity to oneself that Kirmayer and Robbins note as a marker of somatization. Although they chide him to "keep face" by reminding him of what they expect of him – "Chagon (be happy)" – his stomach seems to be an intimate, private area and an important part of his true acceptance and digestion of what he agrees with and can integrate with his inner self. He keeps a stiff upper lip on his social face: "tried to keep a bould countenance ... always accounted among warriors .... very presumptuous and haughty."[91] But each time he is face to face with another daunting challenge, he cannot swallow, then proceeds cautiously, learns from his mistakes. When the danger has passed, he gets a "good stomach" and then eats "like a beare." But his most crucial sign of fear is his inability to eat – when fear "tooke my stomach." However, in the aftermath of repeatedly traumatizing events, which were dramatically worse the second time around, there seemed to be a switch in his stomach-to-mouth connection.

A few years later, after he returned to Iroquoia as a Jesuit donné, when peace had been established between the Haudenosaunee and the French, there was trouble. Radisson and a few others discerned that the mission and its workers had to escape. Again, Radisson knew the Haudenosaunee happiness in their kettle, so he organized an eat-all feast, after organizing another adoptee to claim as his dream that had to be fulfilled. After this feast, when bellies were full of food and wine and people were sleepy, the raft that had been cobbled together for the French escape fled during the night, to the great bewilderment of the Onondaga.[92] This is the second time Radisson deliberately uses the stupor induced by wine and food to lull his captors as he makes his getaway.

Radisson was often accused of being a traitor by mutual enemies, but his allegiance was necessarily divided. Organizing Native peoples and their French handlers to further the fur trade often fell to British entrepreneurs. He was capable of getting these disparate people to work together in fur commerce. The hierarchical mosaic thus set up was largely due to the neglect of the settlement by the French Crown rather than by British abuse. Radisson knew how to interlink and facilitate work at all levels, from the hungriest Native trappers to the fustiest English aristocrats, having a bit of all of them within himself. It must be remembered that it was the metropolitan French who repeatedly undercut and cheated him, while the British assisted him even if they did not always trust him, due to Desgroseilliers greater ties to New France. Even with this beginning hierarchy spread out over two continents once the French were upcountry, to manage the complex web of intertribal relations with skill and finesse, Native protocol was the primer palette from which they coloured.

Chouart Desgroseilliers, his older mentor, tired sooner than did Radisson of the continual rigours of the fur trade and, especially, of having to manoeuvre between French and British backing and markets. Radisson had to sometimes employ Native usage that, due to his later comfortable British gentleman's life, became ill-fitting even if rerun very smoothly, as he could not, from afar, easily maintain the intense relationships that alliance twinning required.

For real understanding to take place, only a sincere attitude and live exchanges that last longer than a year have any real value when it comes to beginning to understand other cultures and their constraining conditions. This is because it allows one to begin to perceive the conditions through which others see the world. Already by 1682 Radisson managed to win Native nations to his side by continuing the attentions that he indicates he no longer felt: "I spoke to him according to the genius of these peoples ... it is necessary to make oneself well-considered, to brag that one has courage, that one is powerful, and in a position to succour them and protect them against their enemies, one also has to prove, that one will be completely on their side, to be compassionate for them, and above all to give them gifts beforehand, because between themselves this is the great link of friendship ... I told him in his language that I know the world, your friends will be my friends, and that I have come here to bring arms ... . you will not die of hunger nor your wife nor your children ... be courageous I want to be your son, and I have brought you a father."[93] This intimacy was essential in alliances, and while, on the one hand, Radisson voluntarily adopted the chief as his father in order to care for him, he also brought a father for the nation, a missionary, to guide them into the Catholic fold and tighten loyalty and family ties. While he had been adopted by force when young by a nation in conflict with his countrymen, he now brought them a father out of compassion. If the French had to discard their fatherly orientation for a fraternal one, then Radisson masterfully managed to both reassure and commit this nation to his, never challenging their autonomy or authority but becoming more than just another alliance brother by adding a generational continuity at both ends. This is far more than the usual "cousin/uncle" appellation reserved for unallied nations.

The most telling head metaphor came much later in life. An older and increasingly stigmatized Radisson was again forced to defend his social identity in yet another effort to regain his standing among the French North Americans and choose between friend and foe. When a group of tattered Mohawk arrived to trade with the feuding French and English at Hudson Bay, Pierre grabbed the hair of the most prominent older man and asked him his name, which he naturally knew. It was his Mohawk father, who came to plead for better trade conditions. In this Joseph-like situation, after being ill-treated in his youth by the Mohawk and living to benefit from retaining family relations with them, he was now in the position to accord fat or lean years to his persecutors. Does he choose brother or foe? This time, Radisson chose foe, yet when faced with his own Mohawk father's loyalty, he reversed himself yet again. In this dialogic choice he demonstrated several things. By grabbing the hair, he symbolically made his father lose face by holding him like a captive, in a para-scalping and humiliating way. He accentuated the significance of this culturally knowing act by publicly asking his name, as if he did not know it (he writes that he did).[94] He did this in front of his own kinsmen in order to demonstrate that the great chief was now beholden to him, Radisson. But most of all he had internalized the symbolic revenge motif ubiquitous among the Mohawk of the time, reversing his initially captive status and repay them with their own lessons well learned.[95] This action was his most spontaneous, but not his last, response.

The most galling reversal of son-father power equations came when Radisson threatened to "eat sagamité" from the "grandmother's skull" of a dissenter, while he took back his already distributed gifts and said: "go to your brothers the English and tell them my name, that I intend to capture them."[96] This completes the circle that began when he entered Iroquoia incapable of swallowing a bite and now ended in the defiant insult of forcing the eldest clanmother to lose face. In Iroquoian parlance, she is a metaphor for her entire clan because she has given birth to many generations. And corn soup is from corn, the most important of the three life-giving sisters: corn, beans, and squash. Algonquians, in contrast to the Haudenosaunee, were especially careful with any animal head, especially that of the bear, who most resembled a man. The one thing the Haudenosaunee really held in horror was an enemy defacing their grandmother and causing humiliation to them all through insulting the kettle and the generativity of women. The most telling part of this last episode is Radisson's remark after he recounts this incident in English. He explains to the unversed reader that "I had to react thus, in this encounter, or our trade would have been lost, because once one has ceded to Natives, they never let you redeem yourself" ("il fallout que je parlasse ainsi, dans cette rencontre, ou nôtre traite estoit perdue, car quand on a une fois cede aux sauvages jamais ils ne reviennent").[97] This explanation explores the gap between Native and French cultural meanings for a British audience. While the French impetuosity ("fouge") may precipitate them to do things that they may later regret and want to reverse, Native custom forbids hasty actions and, especially, undoing actions. This intercultural translation not only provides the British with a way to understand a perplexing intercultural communication that would otherwise bewilder them but also diverts attention from Radisson's having indirectly menaced British interests.

The spectral bonds that captives feel long after they are free are severed when he rebels against all the torture and terror that he had once felt in their collective presence via this galling metaphor. This metaphor combines sustenance and social face by reversing the grandmother function of providing the face and nourishing everyone to using her skull as a soup bowl and humiliating everyone. In Haudenosaunee diplomacy the cauldron means both "welcome eat with us" and "whoever will not join us may find himself inside the cauldron for the next feast." Radisson's possible somatization metaphor fits well within Haudenosaunee cultural symbolic meaning. This metaphor, in all its horror, expresses his closing the circle and signing off by threatening to "break the kettle" or cut off Mohawk and British relations not due to his lack of understanding but, rather, due to his wanting to adjust them to better fit his current terms. This seems also to be his personal revolt against what he called the Haudenosaunee warriors' method of ambush – falling upon "unsuspecting" victims like "starved dogs or wolves" – which horrified him, especially since the dead (and perhaps cannibalized) from those ambushes haunted him at his table. Now at least he negotiated from a stronger position with a common fount of shared understandings.[98] Feelings of shame are supposedly harder to endure than feelings of grief.[99]

If some French aristocrats became adventurers, then Radisson went the opposite way, from adventurer to aristocrat. But after this negotiation, via much bravado, he, of course, serves his Mohawk father an honorary meal, with special presents, aboard his ship the *Bachelor's Delight*, with a full canon salute.[100] After minding his social face, negotiated via carrots and sticks, he minded his generosity in true homme de coeur fashion, employing the kettle in both Mohawk and ancient Celtic/Nordic diplomatic senses at once.

In this, he expressed a palpable Nativization in taking the lone road. Here, he respected the long-time support of his own Haudenosaunee father. His father himself was willing to counter the will of the entire village in order to save Radisson's life when most screamed for his death. He provided his adopted son with white shirts every day to help him adjust and feel at home in Iroquoia. And when the time came, he allowed Radisson to return to the French, after learning of it from his desperate wife and daughters, because he understood that Radisson desired this second escape, and he acquiesced after the fact. He never became angry whenever he knew Radisson was close by with the Jesuit mission in Ste-Marie de Gannentaha or when he saw him for trade because he understood and respected his former son's decision. For his part, he lost his adoptee at home but gained a powerful son, sometimes with the French and sometimes with the British – a son prominent and independent enough for him to be proud of. Radisson was an Iroquoized, Britified French-man who would always remember his adoption. And he knew what he owed his Haudenosaunee father and former mother, knew the abyss of their mourning a son the second time up close, and loved them despite everything. Yet for a British account, Radisson could not describe these transcultural signallings and crossed meanings in diplomacy and trade. So he writes the incident and its explanation in shorthand, which he probably assumed might make more sense to the practical British.

Disorganized aspects of one's identity, of which one is not fully aware, when perceived through the eyes of a stranger can deepen one's self-consciousness and enhance self-integration. A French soldier at Fort Orange facilitated Radisson's ability to organize an escape from his second capture in Iroquoia by immersing him in a flood of self-awareness: "did verily believe I was French, for all yt I was all dabbled over wth painting and greased. I answered him in ye same language, that no; then he speaks in swearing, desiring me [to tell him] how I fell into the hands of those people. And hearing him speake French, amazed, I answered him, for wch he rejoiced very much. As he embraces me, he cryes out wth such a stirre that I thought him senselesse. He made a shame for all that I was wild but to blush red ... All came about me, ffrench as well as duch ... those of my nation, Iroquoise, who followed me in a great squadroon through the streets, as if I had bin a monster in nature."[101] Was he really red? The French and Flemish drew him into his former frame of reference, and a torrent of humiliation filled him, compounded by being trotted about and stared at as though he were a monster. Radisson began to cry. They sought him out to offer relief from what they saw as his having been kidnapped and humiliated; they brought him to a priest; women plied him with European delicacies and beer. This humiliation differed from the Haudenosaunee humiliation: both were rites of passage from one socio-cultural hearth to another, but where the Iroquoian rite was very bitter, and then very intensely affectionate, this one was very sweet, filled with compassion for his former suffering, admiration for his courage, and the will to advance his standing among their ranks because of it. These are heady draughts for a captive teenager who formerly thought of them as "harmless beerbellies."

Radisson's second capture had regenerated enormous repeat fears that catalyzed his search for models to which to attach himself and serve. He begins doing this by admiring his Haudenosaunee father, whose thigh is cut by the eighteen marks representing the heads he has taken, among them close friends and maybe the brother-in-law of Radisson.[102] Yet, after actually initiating ambush missions in order to prove his fidelity, and carrying home captive slaves, heads, booty, and even "wives" that he certainly could not have obtained in the French settlement in the same fashion, he is rapidly disillusioned with his greatly celebrated victory. The contrast between the methods he must perfect to achieve the ultimate success of a warrior in a Haudenosaunee community, and the celebrity that he achieved by being sought after by one and all in New Netherland, indicated to him that perhaps there was a third option. French and Iroquoian community norms and foibles were very different from one another, and the adolescent Radisson was curious enough to have already appreciated what was best in both, yet could not constantly jump the flames of the fury of each when he desired to forge a kind of allegiance to both.

This third way became possible when he was taken by his helpers to the Dutch governor, who was extremely tolerant of both French and Haudeno-saunee, even when taunted, robbed, or attacked. The worldly, wise, and kind governor perceived Radisson's initial duality between enemy nations not as a source of humiliation but as a diplomatic resource of high worth. The sudden status elevation of Radisson from tortured adopted captive, and maybe "half-cannibal," to a socially celebrated hero who received the open table, ear, and admiration of no less than the governor of all New Netherland, certainly assisted Radisson in mapping out an escape from his captivity. The social support that he found among the tolerant Dutch clearly helped him to reorient himself and, at that particularly vulnerable juncture, the governor himself sat and gave him advice. This advice was received pre-cisely at this most vulnerable yet quiescent adolescent post-traumatic point in time, when Radisson's entire unmanageably contradictory adolescent self was poised at a crossroads for reinterpretation, reorientation, and recon-struction. This is the essence of the value of crucial parental and mentor bonding at critical developmental crossroads or life-crises, especially for adolescents. The governor wisely spoke to him in good enough French to cause Radisson to think him almost a countryman and kindly gave him fresh clothes as well as free trips to Manhattan Island, Amsterdam, and La Rochelle. The governor's advice and attention surely motivated Radisson's own self-interpretative capacities, which were further validated by his crucial bonding and self-exploratory experiences upon returning home. We can deduce that he was probably encouraged to use his new-found abilities, due to a complete silence about how he was viewed, and was received, in France (where he was born) and in Trois-Rivières. This vaulted him back to Iroquoia in short order after his return. The governor may have helped him interpret and ride the waves of the dramatic turns of fortune that he encountered in his life. It seems that the governor introduced the idea that it was due to Providence that Radisson discovered Native nations: "my des-tiny to discover many wild nations, I would not to strive against destinie ... as a thing ordained by God for his greatest glorie."[103] This is clearly the "ad gloriam maioram Dei" and the "praedestinatio" that Dutch Calvinists espoused so dearly at this time.

Recent treatments of victims of torture always emphasize that, in order to get therapy going, an atmosphere of trust and safety must be established. This is precisely what Radisson, for example, perennially lacked, therefore the great value of the governor's talk and his admired mentor and brother-in-law, Desgroseilliers. The catharsis and regression, dealing with guilt feelings, and the reintegration into society via a new self that can engage in a dialogue with the new environment, is the route taken by many centres that treat tortured refugees of today.[104] The most salient feature is to find a "life in the world" interpretation that holds some meaning, as founder of the Viennese school of psychiatry, Viktor Frankl, discovered in Auschwitz.[105] This is the essential link to life beyond trauma. For Radisson, besides benefiting from a therapeutic confession with former captive Jesuit father Joseph Noucet and a merchant in the Dutch colony to whom he declared himself forever grateful,[106] he wrote a travel narrative. As it progressed became more like a cathartic autobiography that, at times, he patched up to suit his present situation and audience. He originally had little scraps of paper in French, and then, with the help of his friend, he "Englished" them. The point of view often shifts dramatically, as the experiences are relived and reworked. Thus, in the first voyage, his Haudenosaunee family and friends are referred to as "those people," as "hungry dogs and wolves," as "my friends," as "my mother and father." Then there are detailed admiring descriptions of them, jumping back and forth from French to English, English to French, as events map themselves out. It is possible that Radisson may have spent more time with the British had Desgroseilliers not returned to the Canadians. The Pennabakerian act of committing it to paper in narrative form commences the distanciation of "oneself as other" that, as the current flow of events rush on, is abandoned periodically for sardonic snickers and outbursts of emotion. For, as Paul Ricoeur writes, we are characters in a story that we keep revising as our lives unfold, searching to find the threads of continuity in all the upheaval.[107] What choice did Radisson have in a world where all the intimate ties he had were with those who, amongst themselves, were enemies? In his case, he was more whole than the divided, warring world around him.

OUTSIDE IN AND INSIDE OUT

The perception of a nebulous and developing inside and outside of society, resulting from an inclusive, yet evolving, socio-cultural porosity and interdependence, was being engaged by an internal multivalence within the individual. A set of not necessarily concentric identities evolved in tandem, competing for prominence, and priorities could shift in the often developing, traumatized, or transculturally oriented personality as environmental necessity frequently warranted. Ostensibly those who possessed a whole gamut of factors had the greatest potential for dramatic Nativization. However, dramatic shifts that were Native-inspired and adaptive were those often most socially celebrated in their own settlement and were accorded great social prominence and recognition.

I have composed a list of elements that tends to catalyze a cultural shift according to macro- to micro-disciplinary layers of analysis. On the level of heritage analysis, those who possessed the weakest link to the officially recognized Parisian French and absolutist heritage were more likely to be influenced. On the geographical level, those who were most geographically

distant from Quebec tended to be farthest away from official French directives. Temporally, those who lived through the greatest amount of formative
crises of settlement tended to realize that adaptation was imperative and
urgent. Socially, the younger one was the more impressionable one was.
During adolescence, the stronger the hormones and conditions of adolescence, the weaker the formative earlier influences and the greater temporary variations could be. Those who had the most tenuous family ties to the
settlement, such as several coureurs de bois, were weak links to anything
French. Culturally and spiritually, those who were less connected to the
orthodoxies and rites of the Catholic faith had less to lose by leaving for
lengthy periods of time. Mind-body analyses would favour seeing that young
males were those most physically exposed to the rigours of the outdoors, the
least socially vulnerable, the most bathed in androgens. This sector, therefore, was permitted the most extreme expression of individual transformations. Lack of laterality in the brain could account for greater legitimized
variability between males as a whole than between females as a whole. Thus,
the most extreme metamorphoses were in individual males who, from an
early age, were most exposed to the rigours of Native life and had the most
to gain from learning from it and putting it to good use. On the other hand,
there is much to be said for the collective shift of women's possibilities as a
whole in the settlement, as they interlinked socially, learned from and transformed one another, and transmitted these lessons to their children.

As for forcible culture change, it appears that Radisson's, Jogues's, and
other captivity narratives point to some difficulties in resisting the cultural
pressure to mould oneself to one's captor's desires.[108] The existence of
death threats and humiliation caused terror and loathing, with ostensibly
insensible victims remembering long afterwards the exact words and gestures that were intended to cut off any empathy for them. As the torture fires
died down, it was immensely significant which family adopted the survivor
and how they treated him or her. And finally, for those who escaped, the
method of escape is important. Did it go against the wishes of their
Haudenosaunee family? or was it part of a prisoner exchange that was never
intended to be lifelong? Did they love their new families?

Those adoptees who possessed a certain facility for effecting one or more
transcultural shifts, and the ability to discern the appropriate application of
each, turned this ability to beneficial use. If they were really talented, they
could, like Radisson, consciously control the application of each transcultural mode and develop the ability to switch appropriately between more
than two cultural domains (e.g., fur trading or diplomacy). This was the
crowning achievement of the often rejected Pierre-Esprit Radisson. Though
beset with seemingly inescapable situations, and mistreated at so many
turns, he managed to think his way through the skillful application of cultural and Zwischenmenschliche twinship rules, to put together a much

larger cooperative enterprise that linked many pairs of unlike twins. This ability enabled him to fight to remain as the founder of the Hudson's Bay Company, which became the main socio-economic base of North America north of the Great Lakes. Radisson exemplifies the height of the refined French ability to Nativize, and he participated in both the north Atlantic French connection as well as the British world.

Radisson is precisely the embodiment of the northern American "métissage culturel" heritage of an "identité bricolé" in all its splendour, which the "mosaic" side of Canada could see as its necessary complement, as the "melting pot" side of the United States could claim. If Champlain was the founder of a multiethnic North America, together with his unlike twin Chief Cherououny, then the torch was carried beyond Champlain by Radisson (and his Haudenosaunee father who rescued him), who, in himself, united French, Native, and British. Radisson's torch was then continued by Louis Riel (and Gabriel Dumont), the Métis who, through a compromise between Métis and European settlements, attempted to unite half-French with half-British First Nations to establish the western provinces. The multiperspectivity allowed by a relatively harmonious interweaving of heritages enabled these individuals to deepen their own reflective capacities in a way that encouraged the growth of norms so favoured by Native social thought. This encouraged the growth of reason, individualism, and independence of thought while protecting the common weal. This expansion of perspectives via Native cultures was enriched by their wisdom not to ignore the seeming irrationality that bubbled up from time to time, especially in the Native dreamworld, whose power could retrieve deeply buried soul-wishes, expose dangerous imbalances, or allow the ghosts of their bereavement to speak. Many succeeded in creatively resynthesizing their lives and selves with the evanescent spectral models within the intricate bricolage that melded multiculturalism with métissage.

Epilogue

Beating Swords into Canoe Paddles

Native peoples ask for no more and no less than do any of us – to be respected, to be listened to, to be honoured, and to be loved.

B. Hudnall and Henry Stamm

During the seventeenth century, blood brotherhood established an inter-continental interdependence through the welcoming adoption of the tiny French band within Native North America. In a land whose resilient bounty promised that no wound need fester, an integrated, more comprehensive analysis of the past can yield some insights into dealing with the future. French Nativization was the fruit of the dialogue of a budding seventeenth-century global dialogue and interdependence, which entailed many layers of belonging. These ranged from that of the broadest scope, through intimate couplehood and twinship, down into the depths of the soul. Habermasian "webs of understanding" can be more easily woven when harsh environmental conditions conducive to bonding, a harmonious inter-lacing of heritages, common geo-economic commercial enterprise match-ing socio-cultural patterns, and individuals with high cognition and initiative work together to ensure common survival. These conditions and abilities led people to define themselves as partners, while issues of race, eth-nicity, religion, economic sophistication, and sometimes even gender topics did not conclusively divide them. People preferred working together for the common weal, while allowing for differing degrees of pluralism and métissage. If this was possible 500 years ago in an age of limited literacy, colonial expansion, and religious extremism, then it is possible today – if we carefully think it through with, as Pierre Lévy says, a higher collective intelli-gence.

This inquiry also looks at the foundational values at the centre of North American uniqueness. Some useful Native lessons that were not wholly embraced at the time, such as the full personhood of children and women, have injured the capacities of democratic societies to cope with the gap between principle and deed. "De-centring the Renaissance" is currently recognized as a historiographical necessity – one that will enable a more well-rounded perspective on the future vis-à-vis the past. We owe some of the finest of European civilization and advancement to North American Turtle Islanders. Albeit neglected and upstaged in international forums, Turtle Island protocols and values are at the core of our North American heritage and, if re-examined, could advance greater social democratization, expand humane sharing, and replant the Pine of Peace in aid of global understanding. Far from the fuzzy reductionism that would seek to brand colonial contact under one banner and cancel "difference" by dumping supposed non-Europeans in one sack, in North America there exists every condition to facilitate the reintegration of Native Americans and Canadian First Nations, and reestablish them at the centre of governmental, socio-economic, and socio-cultural life. Helen Hunt wrote of a century of dishonour, but now two centuries and six generations have past, and the children of the forest, in their own home, now live too often in impoverished squalor struggling to remember what it was that they lost. North American uniqueness is not due to what the otherwise brilliant Samuel Huntington (*Who are We?* 2004) has recently called the British Protestant base, which, like a tomato soup, integrates many disparate immigrants but still remains a British tomato soup. Broadly speaking, the broader Judeo-Christian heritage, and Anglophone component are highly important ingredients. However, First Nations are not just another ingredient in the American Melting Pot: it is their steaming cauldron of corn soup that literally welcomed us on the continent. Hector St John de Crèvecoeur was obviously referring to this when he said "all races are melted into a new race of men" (one can reread "Notes of an American Farmer" to see this) even if Israel Zangwill may not have known its source when he coined the term "Melting Pot" in 1908. Natives are not merely another pebble in the Canadian mosaic: they are both its glue and its keystone. North America was not peopled by elite immigrants, it was the "poor and hungry masses," as poet Emma Lazarus wrote upon the base of the Statue of Liberty, who sought food and often religious refuge from a poorer and more intolerant Europe – and originally learned about liberty while eating corn soup at Native council fires. This intermixed heritage has made North America the young leader of Western civilization, and Quebec unique in the francophone arena. What of the children of the seventh generation?

SURVIVAL VIA ADOPTIVE TWINNING

The case of New France is thus a beacon of light in the otherwise conflictual seventeenth-century colonial worlds, where some of the unprecedented exploitation of later nineteenth- and twentieth-century colonial practices had only been initiated. Despite its tenuous existence, it did survive, unlike New Sweden, New Netherlands, and New Finland, which all tried flexibility but failed to thrive. New Spain had vast numbers of immigrants and large Native cities; the British had moderately large immigrant and Native populations; but New France had a minuscule immigrant population in a Native ocean, which negated the conquest option. Whereas the Spanish conquistadores stole women and silver, and the persecuted sectarian British colonists fought to retain their hold on fertile lands, French pioneers only haggled for beaver skins over an ostensibly amicable drink, and this cemented exchange rather than exclusivity. The Spanish controlled vast areas; the British kept their settlements east of the Appalachian frontier; but the French linked Native-French networks across the continent because Native centres became French fur sources. The British had a few "praying Indians"; New Spain had many rigorous missions; but New France evangelized even those enemies who supposedly intended to devour them. New England consisted of families bound together in a tightly knit autonomous settlement; New Spain installed a rigid hierarchy, putting the mestizo population under increasingly white superiors; while New France encouraged an ethnically penetrable, socio-economically mobile society. New Spain was hierarchically organized according to race; New England was divided along racial frontiers, and Virginia was split along lines of slave or owner status; but New France was mostly split along more egalitarian gender lines, which followed the Native alliance pattern. New Spain had its Inquisition persecuting "heretics"; New England persecuted its "witches"; but New France persecuted its war captives: the Haudenosaunee, the Fox, the Natchez, and the British – based upon the Iroquoian model. Thus, modifying Parkman's dictum, we must conclude that the Spanish despoiled the Natives, the British co-existed uneasily with them, but the French fraternized with them in order to survive. According to the Haudenosaunee, twins are lucky because reciprocity generates renewal.[1]

Epidemic death and phantom absence joined two communities overwhelmed by bereavement in an attempt to achieve common survival. This necessary interdependency neutralized the early modern propensity for a cycle of blood vengeance which, as Michael Ignatieff says, is the principal obstacle to reconciliation. Environmental exigencies were crucial in mapping out the seasonal framework of how the dialogue was negotiated, aided by navigable rivers instead of impassable mountains. The winter freeze further enhanced local interethnic interdependency. Sparse French immigration, and epidemic attacks on Native communities, also increased the dependency of each upon the other. Largely youthful French male immigration, compounded with a Native female surplus, facilitated interdependency and intimate social dialogue between communities. Thus, environment and demography complemented one another to weave a pattern of French-Native interdependency.

The common web of shared meanings constructed from the dialogue between French, Algonquian, and Iroquoian peoples delineated the significance of individual symbolic acts within the broader symbolic social environment. This occurred through the weaving of dialogue over time, as events concretely reinforced the adaptive advantage of social interdependency, which deepened the web of intersubjective understandings encoded in myth. Settlement crises of 1629, 1648, and 1661 all starkly demonstrated the essentiality of good interethnic relations, a successful dialogue, the initial replacement of royal "fathering" by adoptive "twinning" in the fledgling colony, and the adaptive survival value of French Nativization.

Interdependency was nevertheless nuanced over the vast expanse of North America, while each area functioned in flexible tandem with the others. Multicultural diversity became the de facto normative social model for the Laurentian valley (Common Ground) while métissage became the norm for the fur country (Middle Ground), along with the encapsulated syncretism of missions that grew in number and importance by the next century. Aron's integrative Borderlands thesis is based upon the primacy of the political over the economic, geographical, cultural, social, or religious and the idea that these areas were marginal to the functioning of the colonial heartland. New France, nonetheless, must be considered as an exceptional case. Climatic-geographical, socio-economic, and religio-cultural patterns in North America proved ultimately to be more critical than the political strategy of the relatively unreliable French fatherland.

Native alliances created symbolic and actual fraternal bonds between Native and French. Unlike brotherhood required Zwichenmenschliche bonding, which conjured spectres of the past. On the French side, Celtic and Nordic traditions; endemic infectious disease; as well as the merely "sleeping" ghosts of families, relatives, and friends far away in France, compounded the impact of these phantoms. On the Native side a net demographic loss of 50 percent to 90 percent due to epidemic damage catalyzed an acute upsurge in ancestral ghostly consultation that has not completely subsided. Ghosts possessed great immediate import, permitting a re-examination of the past, a re-evaluation of the present, and a hopeful or terrifying vision of the future. Ghosts thus served as "midé-wives" to an expanded repertoire of shared conceptual meanings and helped chart directions in the unknown territory of evolving social interethnic dialogue.

Native bonding policies corresponded with missionary conversionary methods in that they were applied in the cradle, continued throughout youth, and only ended at the tomb. Interethnic adoptions not only produced multicultural attachés but also freed French North American education from severe French "educational" discipline. In adolescence, joint hunting, fishing, and social enterprises were ventured; and, after 1649, French Canadian youth replaced Wendat traders and were introduced into the nexus of the Great Lakes intertribal trade network. Youth is a prime time for identity-searching, rebellion, and social innovation, particularly when matched with friends or lovers of another world. Métissage was encouraged through French male youth enjoying the freedom of movement to and within Native centres (with the king's blessing or obstruction), the attraction of economic gain, and "exotic" Native daughters, which was catalyzed by the lack of Frenchwomen upcountry. Zwischenmenschliche twinning was encouraged by the existential and commercial apprenticeship of the French into the ordinary Native web of life. Adoptions, exchanges, and common projects provided ample opportunities for dialogue into adulthood. Thus, despite Jesuit projects, the early life of the settlement trained French North Americans from birth that Native life would give them the cultural tools they needed to enable their survival and advancement as well as that of the settlement.

Not only people involved in the fur trade, but the Laurentian Valley settlement proper underwent a metamorphosis. Among the men, the old French hierarchy induced so many rivalries that their potential authority was neutralized, while Native egalitarianism seemed a model of opportunity to youth anxious for social mobility. The emerging French Canadian elite complemented or superseded several functions of the French administrative and military elite, especially the articulation of cultural models and the construction of collective solidarity, the latter of which was characteristically weak in the hierarchical and patriarchal seventeenth-century French social fabric. French shock at having been perceived as a "feminine tribe" by their allies perhaps spurred identification with the female "Other," who in France did not possess full rights of personhood. In North America, additionally, they were forced to rely upon women to "hold the fort," work the fields, and participate as full partners in a complementary, horizontal alliance. The total effect of these changes was a socio-economic and political levelling through innovative institutions, which elevated the disadvantaged and reduced those with previously held privileges. Ecostasis and balance codified in mutual respect, and the integrity and equilibrium of all living things, were important Native principles in this transformation.[2] Furthermore, the enhanced reason, decision making, and personal responsibility required of the new Canadian elite heightened the growth of individualism in the settlement, which was encouraged as well by youthful rebellion to authority, a more nuanced understanding of the self due to dialogue, and insightful Native psychological understandings. Immigrant women in Canada were freed from their lowly disinherited French role to become reciprocal socio-economic partners in the Canadian enterprise. This had a favourable effect upon the expanded capacities of the settlement and brought forth a grudging recognition of the female "Other" as a kind of "self." Thus, French settlement society in North America shifted from a vertically hierarchical society, in which most of the population was suppressed, to a horizontal, more democratically organized society – one that afforded an exclusive sphere of expertise for gendered and localized sectors yet retained flexibility between them.

Alongside this profound sociological transformation was the bricolage of French and Native conceptual models, rites, and beliefs. The common web of shared sacred stories constructed from the interethnic dialogue delineated the significance of acts and ideas within the broader social environment. Social models were bricolé from both northwestern French and Native ideals. The cultural model embraced in North America was a métissage culturel of the Native sharing ethic and dread of loss of face with French liberalité and honneur. These last two social values were traits of the heroic self-sacrifice that was part of the French provincial aristocratic ideal of the "homme de coeur." The combining of the two ideals of liberalité and honneur embodied the ancient French ideal of an "homme de coeur," the first of which embodied the Mi'kmaq value of meki'k mkamlamun (great heart); the Algonquian Mistabeo, or Mishtapeu (Great Man); and the Wendat ideal of a Aienda8ati (civilized person). External constraints of French commoners (Fremdzwange) became internal constraints as they advanced up the social scale and as their civilization evolved was obtained by French North Americans who learned it through observing Native self-control (Selbstzwange). The immigrants identified with their noble d'épée local aristocracy as homme de coeur who opposed the Parisian court noble de robe, who were detested as taxmen and lackeys contaminated by their egotism ("amour-propre.") The new French North American model, albeit steeped in an ideal that was already obsolete in France, was infused with a fresh significance owing to its adaptation in the North American physical and social environment. The French North American model challenged and resisted the official egotistical model of the upwardly- mobile bourgeois "honest man" ("honnête homme"), which was embraced by the bourgeois-cum-magistrates of the centralizing French royal court. It also challenged those Parisian administrators, Bordeaux traders, and Alpine military officers who came to the settlement by the next century and who usually abandoned Canada at the Cession/Conquest. Nonetheless, while French North Americans snubbed the French bourgeoisie who flocked to Paris (and later led the French Revolution), they themselves were usually provincial bourgeois-born. They also clamoured for "chiefdom' (noble entitlement) through pelts or war and scalped enemies rather than "guillotining their own delegitimatized elite," as Hannah Arendt and François Furet have pointed out was the case in France.

The extensive Native sharing ethic converged with French aristocratic generosity (liberalité) and Roman Catholic caritas, an attractive combination for socially aspiring immigrant women. Native dread of losing face also had many points of convergence with French military courage (honneur), yet the aspects that did not converge challenged current French conceptions of masculinity. The shift from masterhood to stewardship required the underlying understanding that children, women, and the elderly have familial and communal contributions that are as irreplaceable as is adult male strength. Blood sororial and mother-child solidarity, nourished by clanmother-held land, was the peacefully stable socio-economic foundation upon which Iroquoians built a solid intergenerational familial longhouse. Even patrilocal Algonquians used overall motherly management to good effect. This insight was too contrary to French customs to rehaul the entire patriarchal and hierarchical edifice, Sun King and all. At least at the time.

Sacred belief also paired up in the form of unlike twinship, thus rendering them more easily decipherable to French and Native. Beliefs often "re-presented" social reality, providing a medium for problem-solving and symbolization. Algonquian and Iroquoian peoples held a different type of dialogue with their French partners. Usually, the dialogue between the French and the Algonquian peoples was direct and intimate, while that between the French and Iroquoian peoples was less direct, being generally filtered through mission workers or warfare. Only outright captive adoption by enemy Haudenosaunee combined the "far" view with the "close." French and Algonquian belief dialogue tended to collaging as well as fusion. In the St Lawrence Valley multicultural diversity was tolerated, yet French and Atlantic Algonquian twinning often resulted in belief fusion. In the Great Lakes area social métissage was also ironically complemented by belief collaging instead of a smooth fusing. The reason for this seemingly paradoxical equation could be that, in the early contact areas, where dialogue was continuous and of great antiquity, while there was less wholesale romantic mixing, the belief convergence became more complete. Even more likely, romantic mixing had already taken place in the pioneering days, while afterwards a tolerant multicultural modus vivendi stabilized when cultural identification was not based upon ethnicity but upon religious practice. In contrast, upcountry, where dialogue began later and was discontinuous, the belief fusion was patchier and less coherent, even if the birth of Métis was the norm. Thus, the degree of mythical blending was positively linked to the antiquity and continuity of dialogue, at least for the unequivocally allied Algonquians. The first Atlantic case was characteristic of "first stage dialogue," while the second Great Lakes case was characteristic of "second stage dialogue."

For the Iroquoian peoples, however, polarization-or-inversion, rather than fusion-or-collage, was the basic tenor of French-Wendat or French-Haudenosaunee belief twinning. The French-Wendat belief twinning often resulted in didactic belief polarization, with, in French eyes, the Wendat usually representing the utopian end of the pole and the Haudenosaunee the evil end. The irony of this is that both were Iroquoian peoples, and, since the mid–1650s, many Wendat who were adopted captives in Iroquoia later lived with them as one people. Thus, while the focus of French- Algonquian belief dialogue was upon joining, collaging, and, ultimately, fusing, the focus of French-Wendat and French-Iroquoian belief dialogue was upon moral dualization, with the good pole on the Wendat side and the evil pole on the Haudenosaunee side. This dualism seemed to lay in the geo-sociological reality that both Wendat and Iroquoian dialogues initially took place at a distance, filtered by missionary perceptions. In the Haudenosaunee case, the dialogue generally remained at a distance, while the Wendat almost settled right in Quebec. Thus, the morally infused faith messages embraced a utopian ideal for the Wendat while, through the Mohawk model, justifying the torture and death of Haudenosaunee war captives. The ideal and its inverse was perceived sometimes up close and sometimes from afar, as Jaenen's friend and foe, or Steven Aschheim's brother and stranger.[3] Each pole was relative to the other. The social model of the Noble Savage, Amantacha, stood in contrast to the model of the barbarian traitor Estienne Bruslé. This social dichotomy was echoed in the mythical struggle between the good St Anne (or Mary, or the Jesuit, or Nanabozo) and the evil Great Serpent. Only as the seventeenth century progressed did polarization lessen, when the children of the Great Onontio (French king) joined with the children of the clanmothers beneath the Great Tree of Peace (Haudenosaunee League) in the Great Peace of Montreal in 1701.

Northwestern French and Northeastern Native belief also underwent a metamorphosis in New France. The Tree of Dreams was a didactic construction on the part of Jesuit cultural articulators, and it involved two opposing spiritual and cultural models that had a simultaneous social life. It taught the lesson of post-Trentine free will (librio arbitrio) to choose between good and evil. The twinning of St John the Baptist with Gluscap dealt with the conundrum of the human being within her/himself, which was also transformed by the external interethnic dialogue. The symbolic boundaries of the collectivity were closely associated with symbols of personal identity so that the mixing that occurred in society was echoed in ambiguous personal boundaries. The inward repentant conscience, which moderated the pride of the homme de coeur, had the power to transform the penitent from a wolf into a lamb. The twinning of Hellequin with Carcajou in the Atlantic, and with Nanabozo in the Great Lakes region, filled the need for a formulation regarding communal boundaries, which focused upon the comic trickster who mediated between the living and the dead, thus uniting them. In French Canada the Ti-Jean cycle appeared to be synthesized from these earlier French and Native figures, and united French and Natives in laughter all over the continent.

The coureurs de bois and voyageur journey corresponded with the Chasse-Galérie myth. The myth deals with the liminal flight between two worlds, and it addresses the relationship between humanity and nature, humans within themselves, and the boundaries of communal trust. In the process, Uhrzeit (past time) and Endzeit (end of time) become mythically conflated. This close parallelism with an otherworldly reality reinforced the conceptual polarity between heaven and hell as well as emphasizing a purgatorial métissage culturel to mediate between these poles. The full canoe, a faint echo of the trans-Atlantic voyage, was a prime symbol that held the community together while metaphorically "jumping the rapids" of historical jeopardy, avoiding the crosses of blasphemy, and literally falling into a watery baptism. This canoe voyage was a collective legitimizing rite and myth, much as the Sinai migration to the Promised Land was for the children of Israel, or the flight from satanic Britain to the City on the Hill in Massachusetts.[4]

Metaphors that run through all the beliefs are key symbols of exchange, the ancestral past, communal unity, and rebirth between French and Native peoples. The kettle was the Grail of life and communal unity, as in the Wendat Feast of the Dead. Its Janus face was that of Haudenosaunee diplomatic symbolism: death and cannibalism as the spectral consequence of the boiling over of an untended "Melting Pot." Finally, the pelt as metaphor in New France linked up to a plethora of historically and socially relevant symbols. The keeper of the game as Cernunnos, Arthur, or Hellequin corresponded with Carcajou in his mask disguises and Nanabozo in his rabbit skin. John the Baptist's sheepskin corresponded with Gluscap and his magic belt, the Wendat with his shed "Haudenosaunee-ed" "serpent skin," and the Haudenosaunee with his Medicine Society false face mask. The French Canadian had many incarnations in which the pelt functioned as ghost-double: the revelling charivari celebrant with his mask when young, the contraband fur dealer's hood when in debt, the penitent's cowl after being caught, and finally the repentant elderly Canadien in his hairshirt-capot.

Finally, inner microcosms within the individual reflect and affect the interpenetrating mediating frameworks of environment, the past, the community, and unlike twinning. Intertemporal dialogue with spectres of memory within the individual greatly affected the response to unknown others, who thereafter became tightly laced into necessary interdependencies. Native culture, and the desire for social ascension, accentuated the fashioning of a supple social face that could pass from culture to culture and milieu to milieu, yet be integrated with their less self-conscious pasts and inner selves. Adopted captive Radisson, for instance, feared devouring his friend but also feared being devoured – not only physically but also metaphorically – which was emblematic of the settlement as a whole within adoptive Native America. Differences were sometimes hard to reconcile within a burgeoning complexity of identities. As individualism and independent lifestyles grew as a result of multiple frameworks, multiple belongings and interlinkages resulted both in multiple cultural identities as well as a self-bricolage to retain coherence. The more radical the departure from the familiar, the more effort expended to derive meaning and coherency between brother and foe, between familiar and enemy, resulting in a greater range of possible individual developmental transformations.

European democratic intellectual currents were fuelled by the model of the North American Native as Noble Savage combined with British Enlightenment philosophy and parliamentarianism, all refiltred and interpreted by French philosophes. Enlightenment currents held meaning within the socio-economic atmosphere of the time, served to advance the French Revolution and, through the Napoleonic Empire, spread democratic ideas throughout early nineteenth-century Europe. Seeds of Native influence were nourished along the way by visiting Native chiefs and evangelists, Jesuit missionary and travel accounts, Seven Year War French returnees, some Acadians repatriated in Poitou, baron de Lahontan, French luminaries like the marquis de Lafayette (who participated in the American Revolution), and Americans who visited France (like Benjamin Franklin, Thomas Jefferson, Jeremy Bentham, and Thomas Paine – some of whom received French citizenship). The marquis de Lafayette pointedly handed the key to the Bastille to Thomas Paine so that he could take it to George Washington, which further supported the Sons of Liberty, who supported Chief Tammany, who had been embraced as the patron saint of America. And Canada, due to the alternative accommodating Native-European cooperation at its base, has not yet had its full beneficial influence upon the entire continent. This is due to the confusing struggle to comprehend and interpret its multiplex alternative model and its implications.

IROQUOIS WITHIN OURSELVES

In the grand narrative of American history and culture, ironically, the northwest French collective memory of their ancestral "ghosts," embraced by the early immigrants, was neither very French nor completely Catholic but, rather, was born of ancient Breton and Norman cultures, which preceded the cleavage of France and Britain into separate culture-hearths. In this sense, the early European roots of founding French and British immigrants to Canada converged, and this profound cultural source is only the precedent for over two centuries of common life and Nativization in the New World.

Yet even Siamese twins joined at the waist may defeat themselves by always facing in opposite directions. This is true for Quebec and British North America, as it is for the United States and Canada. Nineteenth-century racism has long been debunked as the basis for discrimination, but petty hierarchies legitimated by it have lingered on. A "speak white" attitude towards Natives and French does a disservice to British North America by taking on the pretensions of the crumbled British Empire in an attempt to chisel other minorities down to insignificant pebbles in the Canadian mosaic. This disdain has only contributed to French North America's collective memory immersing itself in anything that feels "more French than the French" ("plus français que sois"). Selective social snubbing based upon some imagined "ethnicity" also affects other non-Protestant minorities in Canada and the United States. Consider, for example, Huntington's (2004) insistence upon Protestant primacy rather than on understanding that Judeo-Christian civilization is one inalienable whole. Quebecois shame about mixed racial and cultural heritage came to a head at the height of the 1930s, when Gobineauist racism was rife in a Europe anxious to legitimate its extra privileges vis-à-vis the external Other (coloured non-Europeans,)and the internal Other (Jews, Roma, and other Euro-minorities). *Le Devoir*, a prominent Quebec newspaper, warned of the imminent peril of Haudenosaunee hiding within the 100 percent lambswool of the unsuspecting Québecois: "The eternal Iroquois symbolizes those elements around us and more importantly, within us, which diminish and weaken our worth ... All too often the Iroquois resides within ourselves." This was written by none other than Quebec's most eminent nationalist historian, Lionel Groulx.[5] The "eternal Iroquois," after having been repressed for so long in French North American collective memory, still remains quiescent. Ironically, Dollard was celebrated for having internalized Haudenosaunee heroism, while barely a generation ago the Quebecois' "Iroquoian alter-ego" was seen as the spirit of self-defeat. As Mechal Sobel has remarked: "the enemy other is created of rejected inner characteristics ... [and it] remains an important part of the self as well, an inner alien."[6] A stormy forum was provoked in 1979 when Jacques Rousseau claimed that 40 percent of Quebecois possessed Native ancestry. It is due to this misplaced shame that the idealized "Frenchified" Golden Age of New France as the ideal of the "Distinct Society" became the favorite illusion. This cherished historical illusive phantom has often guided Quebecois policies towards its preferred immigrants and refugees, Canada, the United States, other Francophone countries, and international foreign policy. It has also prevented Franco-Americans from popularizing their culture, language, and cuisine all over the continent as Latin Americans have done in the United States, with the exception of Louisiana Cajun country. After the Quebec/New York Festival of September 13th was cancelled after September 11th 2001, sociologist Joseph-Yvon Thériault (*Critique de l'américanité*, 2002) challenged historian Gérard Bouchard's insistence that a larger American vision was the best route for French America, and wrote that the discourse of "Americanity" fell with the Two Towers. A journalist of newspaper *Le Devoir*, Antoine Robitaille, even wrote on September 11th that

Quebec now is more European than American, yet qualified that it is the vision of the EU, not the France of memory, that is being imitated. Yet perhaps with the founding of the Parliament of the Americas a greater vision for the Americas may benefit all parties, especially if Native, children, and women representatives and concerns are heard – Native style.

Internal enemies can sometimes become brotherly partners if an effort is made to comprehend one another in an empathetic, constructive way. French Canadians, over the decades, have had many reasons to prefer to make peace with anglophone North America rather than to wrangle with France. France's pointed effort, since the eighteenth century, to re-Frenchify North American francophones was totally abandoned during the Cession. For a century and a half France could not be bothered with "thirty arpents of snow" in North America, while the Middle East, with its oil, harems, and exotic fruits, beckoned it like a Scheharazadian mirage under a shifting veil of sand. France, holding aloft its Enlightenment and Revolution, chose to carry the beacon of its "mission civilisatrice" to the Arab world, transferring its famous "colonial genius" from the welcoming and democratic North American Aboriginals to the utterly different Arab world. Today, alternately fighting off immigrants, redrawing frontiers, and banning "family honour" killings, genital mutilation, and veils, France itself has unsuccessfully resisted inundation with colonial ex-pats and is currently in a state bordering on internal combustion. The incendiary Left is enmeshed in a war of postcolonial paradigms as both anti-Western totalitarians and anarchists have furiously guillotined the older Dreyfusard-Jaurèsian liberals as scapegoats, prior to lunging at one another's throats. It is France against itself again, and the French dream of "seeding all the winds" ("Je sème a tous vents" [Larousse's motto]) appears to have given way to becoming "seeded by every wind" ("semé par chaque vent") – or what Pierre Taguieff has dubbed "le nouveauisme." Quebec may finally lay to rest its fading French colonial dream and realize its great worth by contributing to the cooperative synthesis of a wider North American and pan-American vision of the future. This might be facilitated the day British North America lays to rest its own fading British colonial dream. North America can hold the future with its own two hands – if it uses the head and heart of a Turtle Islander to keep those hands together.

FACING OUR PHANTOMS IN LIGHT OF OUR FUTURE

This integrated pluridisciplinary inquiry has identified the metaphorical patterning that shapes the macro overview and penetrates deep into the most intricate microcosm within the human being, we cannot help wondering how its dialogue with the phantom past reflects upon our present achievements as a New World Order, a civilization, and an evolutionary era. This emerging self-reflexive consciousness, in the past, has been able to lift the human above the ordinary beast and better his lot. Yet once we lift our heads, to see above the teeming life about us in relation to the ghost of five centuries past, when our ancestors were poised at the cusp of entering into a New World, we struggle to clear our head of borrowed conceptions in order to actually see our achievements, failures, and possibilities in terms of the future. Thus poised, chimerical past, boisterous present, and glimmers of the future in tandem, we must alter some aspects of our civilization's direction before it is too late. We now need a higher level of self-reflective, collective, negotiative intelligence to guide us, as Pierre Lévy of Université d'Ottawa has suggested – with maybe an Iroquoian peacekeeping Genetaska to shepard it.

What kind of species are we if we are capable of inflicting so much suffering upon one another? Instead of the millennium closing gracefully upon the horrendous culmination of a century of global war and ethnically-defined annihilation campaigns – with the fervent hope for an end to this – we stand ready for the next conflagration before we finished grieving the horrors of the recent past. Can we unravel all the strands that are choking off and reversing the progress of civilization?

The scope of the problem appears to be much larger than we can comfortably reconstruct with our limited disciplinary methods. We must see the problem in the round, use multidisciplinary reconstructions to address this problem, and, like Lilliputians capturing a Gulliver of our own making, aim at an overview. As human population density and will for an improved standard of living increases exponentially, requiring many more resources, we must realize that natural resources are finite and that a multitudinous biodiversity of flora and fauna is our life support. Our approach to biodiversity, which supports the balance of ecosystems, is oriented exclusively towards remedying the ills of our own population explosion. We have overrun, continually devoured, and depleted much of the animal kingdom. We have appropriated or devastated much of the plant kingdom in order to build our heavily polluting cities. We are in the process of polluting the globe's vast natural resources through the enormous waste deposits of our galloping technologies. Theoretically, we should recognize that the lack of coordinated effort to protect a healthy social and natural environment will have devastating consequences for our children. World leaders and the international media are too preoccupied with turning conflict to their own political ends to summon a halt to the incitement to hatred and violence. Conflicts based upon resource rivalry, yet couched in political, religious, racial, ethnic or civilizational "legitimating" terms, may already be the consequences of global overpopulation and ecological inaction, of which we may only be half aware. Standing back to see the bigger picture is something we are not socially or educationally conditioned to do. Yet this is part of our responsibility as human beings and as de facto custodians of the world's ecosystems, planning, as our Iroquoian heritage rightly instructs us, for seven generations hence.

The larger picture leads us to conclude that extreme violence in the twentieth century may be partially due to a pathological eco-historical development of which we are either blissfully unaware, indifferent to, or too preoccupied to rectify. Overpopulation (especially as a result of legitimated polygamy and underemphasized female education); pressure on increasingly limited resources; the resistance to pay females and "outsiders" equitably; natural and social environments that encourage poverty and disease in ransacked former colonies; the deprived minorities of mega-metropoli; increasing insensibility to rectifiable but ignored human suffering; and the limits of our own individual intelligences seem to be greater sources of violence than might be guessed from the "reasons" for which wars and endogenous violence have been "justified."

The twenty-first century was preceded by a century ensnared with knotty European wars that drew the entire world into their insanity. We cannot fail to perceive that, despite a degree of inter-European reconciliation, Europe's post-First and -Second World War colonial settling of accounts has unleashed a flood of postcolonial violence and massacres. Native children playing in the nominally violent seventeenth century would have found such a future unthinkable. Will this new century be dominated by another global region that will also draw everyone into its own insanity? The bullying and harming of tiny global minorities who are "world heritage treasures" is the most significant collective indicator of the growing self-destructive, lemming-like direction of humankind.

A microcosm of a common ground for reconciling differences involves North American Native-inspired reasoning sense, reciprocal respect, balance, egalitarianism, and well-chosen interdependencies. These qualities can redirect the world constructively if they can succeed in providing sufficient counterweight to the turmoil currently menacing world peace.

GLOBAL GRAND NARRATIVES: FRONTIERLESS FRONTIERS?

Whereas the precious points of contact between Europeans and the rest of the world were formerly colonial or imperial, in our day ethnocultural interpenetration frequently involves the jump from mixed urban centre to the patchier periphery, in both North America and Europe. The damaged and paralyzed "grand narrative," whose existence is nevertheless made inevitable by the great communications breakthrough, must map an innovative course. Only recently the theoretical struggle between the Frankfurtschüle social thinkers and French postmodernists lay somewhere between locking hingeless doors (for the former) or indiscriminately top billing every novelty (for the latter).[7] The struggle is concrete, not theoretical. Blurring the rest of the world into one amalgamated, collectively exploited "indigenous community" leaves the West astonishingly ignorant of the extreme diversity outside its own enclave. Western media coverage often projects a patronizing "bad colonial West/good indigenous Others" image, where anti-white violent leaders are applauded, thus exacerbating the spread of violence. As Ian Buruma and Avishai Margalit (2004) have pointed out, Occidentalism is a form of condescending reverse Orientalism, as if Westerners are the only ones with the capacity for assuming true responsibility. People of colour in the West are regularly classified as disadvantaged minorities and/or refugees, even if some come from richly resourced and enormous regions. In fact, most of the world is coloured: it is the whites who are in the minority. But the most paradoxical use of the term "Western" occurs when pan-American First Nations, are placed outside the term's conceptual world when, in fact, they are the most Western of us all.

World democratization and the equitable sharing of the world's resources demands, first and foremost, that there be a reasonable balance between world regions — a balance that will enable cooperation. In North America and Europe Jacob Talmon's distinction is still relevant today: a choice must be made between liberal or totalitarian democracy. In the first instance, a Native-grounded respect for human needs and uniqueness is the measure, yet the social contract entails a respect for civility and the common weal. In the second instance, uniformity is more important than common ground rules. Is difference an integral part of the whole that unites around common ground rules? Or can difference profit from an open society and subvert the democratic ground rules of the social contract through hate propagandizing and violence that undermine the basis of shared values, social trust, and harmony? When considering appropriate immigration, the "degree of difference to founding values" may provide the harmonizing element even among quite diverse populations. And, as hate incitement and harm are anathema to the North American entity as a whole, enforcing accountability is an important key. Cultures are not universally irrational entities; rather, they are historically situated entities developed by humans to make sense of the past and present, to enable survival, and to indicate a direction for the future. Thus harmonized difference would tend to blend and complement, as our twins demonstrate, instead of clashing.[8]

Reinvestment in divested world regions is essential if we are to enable complementary regional culture-hearths to flourish; however, this should not include wealthy but retrograde, corrupt regions. Regions of mis-used rich and power disparities could enlist advice from their own emigrants, some of whom currently reside in the West. Perhaps incentives could encourage them to return to improve their own region.[9]

The twentieth century has rightfully been characterized by Eric Hobsawm as a century of extremes, and Samuel Huntington points out the potential clash of civilizations.[10] But the larger picture of the quieter interlinkages, opening up the world due to communications, relations, science, medicine, technology, and postcolonialism, has been neglected as an a priori condition of those extremes, for it is only when frontiers have been torn down that conflicts can erupt. The handicap of twentieth-century history is that it has been written too soon to pinpoint crucial phenomena. The seventeenth century, and its correspondences with our current world, can be a more fruitful endeavor if the effects of rampant overpopulation, diminishing and polluted resources, vastly increased mobility, and communications are factored into the twenty-first century account. History departments often overemphasize the noisy flow of events at the expense of analysis of long-term outcomes. In other words, how harmonious interdependence was carried out in the past and might be maximized in the future might become a more prominent focus of study, than memorizing battlefields out of due respect. It is the lack of trust that must be explained, the lack of reciprocity that must be justified, the missing complementarity that requires an explanation for those steeped in the anti-logic of our most violent of centuries. The best chance we have for constructive amelioration lies in taking a long reflective look at the direction and meaning of human civilization and evolution, refusing to collaborate in partisan or media "spinning," and fulfilling the responsibility to encourage youth to seek beyond appearances, to think for themselves, and to never lose their ethical, empathetic spark of humanity.

FRONTIERLESS FRONTIERS

We have come full circle. An infuriated postcolonialism is currently giving way to an inundated West and the re-erection of frontiers. Our age of unprecedented overpopulation, diminishing and polluted resources, and destabilization caused by massive intercontinental recriminative decolonization, requires that we re-examine our own grounding assumptions. Neither bridges nor barriers are inherently marvellous or reprehensible: it is the appropriate and balanced application of both that constitutes the difference between harmony and trouble. Indiscriminate devotion to decontextualized self-centredness, ideologies, or religious extremism, which ignores the complexity of how we all fit together in a complementary context over the globe, often costs a terrible price.

French-Native fluidity cannot be readily transposed to all and sundry multiethnic global situations without risking another "dialogue of the deaf" (dialogue des sourds.) Northeastern First Nations culture has precious little in common with any other indigenous culture in the world. Trying to force a positive dialogue upon inhospitable prior conditions, inharmonious geo-socioeconomic and cultural patterns, and a cycle of distrust can prove to be dangerous. What we must do is pay attention to points of entry into some mutual understanding and seek alternative solutions to festering conflicts.

For now we have a competing and incoherent globe – a far cry from an "international community." No world community is possible without a well-based trust that cannot be counterfeited. Will there be a negotiated reciprocity between autonomous regions? Ignoring inner destructive forces, such as terror within the family, the undereducation and commodification of women and children, the failure to share resources, and totalitarianism or anarchy, usually worsen both internal and external aggressivity.[11] This puts us in a worse position than in the hopeful seventeenth century. To harm human capacities by living a mockery of civilization, when we demonstrably already know better, is to cripple humankind in the thick of innumerable natural and moral challenges. For, if we are blind to our inner enemy and cannot turn the image of our downfall into a cautious reminder, then we are no more immune to reversing progress than is anyone else entering our transformed Brave New World.

An ounce of prevention is better than more millennia of regret. Constructive peace-making, with preventive solutions for the young, tiny "global minorities," and the defenceless, is preferable to post-catastrophe finger-pointing. Frontierless frontiers have mutual benefit only among those who benefit each other mutually. Survival requires that we know when, and with whom, to bury the hatchet in order to face the greater peril of a necessary interdependence within a larger world we do not entirely trust.

NORTHERN LIGHTS HELPING THE SEVENTH GENERATION

Ignoring the central role of the First Nations within North America (history, culture, land base, political and economic power), and our common future together is tantamount to becoming blinded and lost in a blizzard. The Mohawk crises since 1991 surprised the world with a formerly repressed intensity, yet no hand has yet been fully extended to enable "re-centring" Aboriginal heritage back to the heart of North America to replant the Great Pine of an inclusive democratic peace, although gestures from current Canadian Prime Minister Paul Martin are a first step. The recent Royal Commission on Aboriginal Peoples drew attention to central issues that had long been marginalized.

We can treat the prejudices of our forefathers with respect, while seeking beyond them. Driving at high speed while facing backwards only is a risky endeavour. In the beginning, the shed pelt metaphorically represented the divine will to differentiate the human from the beast, as Abraham saved his son Isaac from human sacrifice by providing an animal substitute. In the Endzeit, every hero struggles with his beast-nemesis, which is how the shaman obtained his multi-pelted coat (similarly to Jacob, who fought with the angel upon Jacob's Ladder and later bequeathed his "coat of many colours" to Joseph). The shed pelt signals the era of a merciful God and the dawn of humanity in an internalized conscience, leaving bestiality behind. In order to enter heaven, one must metaphorically shed one's social mask of pride, rank, race, and gender (like the pelt) and become as a newborn soul, all of whom are equal before God. Jean Baudrillard has remarked that the status of the double in "primitive culture" as the shadow (read twin) or the dead (read ghost) became interiorized as the conscience in modernity, while losing the exchange and continuity, as the modern self-reflexive consciousness emerged.[12] Self-reflexiveness has a longer past of consciousness than we would like to admit, especially among peoples we may think of as "primitive" (read: not us.)

More pointedly, we are hardly free of recent ghosts of the dead in modern times. The death of the Duke of Wellington, David Livingstone, and Queen Victoria, were haunting stepping stones along the road to the fall of the British Empire, not to mention the death of Princess Diana as a mass mourning rite in our time. In France, a generation was guillotined during the French Revolution, as François Furet has argued, while the later death of Victor Hugo plunged France into mourning. Israel is drenched in memory of the Holocaust, while the death of Itzhak Rabin has left generations crying, as did Gandhi for India, and Sadat for Egypt. In the United States, the deaths of Martin Luther King, the two Kennedy brothers, and soldiers who served in Vietnam marked more than a generation. Historians agree that we have not yet processed the enormity of meaning latent within the losses during the world wars of the last generation (Pierre Nora, *Lieux de Mémoire* 1984; George Mosse, *Fallen soldiers: reshaping the memory of the world wars* 1990; Jacques LeGoff, *History and Memory* 1992; Tom Segev, *The Seventh Million* 1993; Reinhart Koselleck and Michael Jeismann, *Der Politische Totenkult: Kriegerdenkmaeler in der moderne* 1993; Thomas Kselman, *Death and the Afterlife in Modern France* 1993; Jay Winter, *War and Remembrance in the Twentieth Century* 1998; Dan Bar-On, *The Indescribable and the Undiscussable: reconstructing human discourse after trauma* 1999; Klaus Neumann, *Shifting memories: the Nazi past in the new Germany* 2000; Paul Ricoeur, *La mémoire, l'histoire, et l'oubli* 2000; Omer Bartov, *Mirrors of destruction: war, genocide, and modern identity* 2000; Peter Honam, *Symbolic Loss: the Ambiguity of Mourning and memory at century's end* 2000.)

We have no right to ruin the future of our children simply out of ethnic fidelity to the past. We must use our humanity and intelligence for the good of humankind. In doing this, we must recognize that First Nations are a prime "global heritage treasure" to be cherished and preserved together with their gifts to humanity. Denying the Native past of North America impoverishes the ancestral thanksgiving for their adoptive succor, imperils far-sighted negotiations in North American statesmanship, prevents us finding enlightening cooperative solutions to the interfacing of Native and European worlds, and denies the essentiality of human biodiversity. First Nations heritage offers many remedies to alleviate the mindless passion of bereavement and to "restore one's sense" in order to survive together in brotherhood/sisterhood under the Great White Pine of Peace. If we have not truly shed the pelt, then our founding clanmother and her twins can be discerned beyond the sobering smoke signals, ghostly northern lights shimmering in the night. After all, we are all children of the same mother. Perhaps human empathy is what we lack most in our great North American grand narrative, which our brilliant eagle feathers could lift skyward.

Notes

ABBREVIATIONS AND ACRONYMS USED
IN THE REFERENCE KEY

Seventeenth-century missionary orthography of Native languages

8 signifies the sound "wa" in English or "oua" in French

Sources and repertories of sources

AAQ   Archives de l'Archévêché de Québec
AFUL   Archives de Folklore de l'Université Laval
AJM   Archives juridiques de Montréal (cited in Grabowski texts)
AQ   *Archives de Québec*, I.
AMR   Archives municipales de Rouen
ANC   Archives Nationales du Canada (now : Bibliothèque et Archives Canada)
ANF   Archives nationales de France
ANQM   Archives nationales du Québec à Montréal
ANQQ   Archives nationales du Québec à Québec
ANQTR   Archives nationales du Québec à Trois-Rivières
AQ   Archives de Québec, I (now ANQ)
ASQ   Archives du Séminaire du Québec
APJM   Massicotte, Edouard-Zotique, *Répertoire des Arrêts, Edits, Mandements, Ordonnances et Réglements conservés dans les archives du Palais de Justice de Montréal 1640–1760*, Ducharme, Montréal, 1919.

ASSSM   Archives du Séminaire de St-Sulpice à Montréal, fonds Faillon
(cited by Jaenen, *Church*, passim.)

Biggar   Biggar, H.P., *The Early Trading Companies of New France*, Argonaut
Press Ltd., NY [1901] 1965.

BNC   Bibliothèque nationale du Canada

BNF   Bibliothèque nationale de France

BSSP   Bibliothèque de St-Sulpice de Paris (cited in Jaenen, *Church*,
passim.)

CIHM   Canadian Institute for Historical Microreproductions
(microfiches)

DRHNF   *Collection de manuscrits contenant lettres, mémoires, et autres documents
historiques relatifs à la Nouvelle-France*, recueilli aux Archives de la
Province de Québec ou copiés à l'étranger, 4 t., Armand Côté et
Cie, Québec, 1879–88.

EO   *Edits, Ordonnances Royaux, Déclarations, et Arrêts du Conseil d'Etat du
Roy*, 3 t., 1854–56.

FHS   French Historical Society

J & D   *Jugements et Délibérations du Conseil souverian de la Nouvelle France
(1863–1716)*, I & II, Armand Côté, Québec, 1885–1891.
(CD-ROM: Chronica 1: 1663–1716)

JJ   Laverdière, Charles Honoré, et Henri Raymond Casgrain, *Journal
des Jésuites d'après le manuscrit original conservé aux archives du
Séminaire de Québec par les abbés Charles Honoré Laverdière et Henri
Raymond Casgrain (1646–1668)*, Valois, Montréal [1871] 1892.
(Kindly lent me by Anya Mali.)

JR(Thwaites)   ibid. (in English)

MNF   Campeau, Lucien, *Monumentae Nova Francia*, 4 t., PUL, Québec,
1980–87.

NT   *Bible, New Testament* (Roman Catholic)

NYCD   O'Callaghan, E., and Brodhead, *Documents Relative to the Colonial
History of the State of New York Procured in Holland, England, and
France*, Weed Parsons, Albany, New York, 1853–87.

OC   Roy, Pierre-Georges, *Ordonnances, Commissions,etc, etc, des
Gouverneurs et Intendants de la Nouvelle-France 1639–1706*, I,
L'Eclaireur Ltée, Beauceville, Québec, 1924.

O'Callaghan   O'Callaghan, E., *Documentary History of the State of New York*, Weed,
Parsons, Albany, New York, 1850–51.

OMM   *Ordonnances de Mr. de Maisonneuve, premier gouverneur de Montréal,
Mémoires et documents publiés par la Société Historique de Montréal*, 3e
livraison, Duvernay frères, Montréal, 1860.

OT   Bible, Old Testament (Jerusalem Bible)

RAPQ   *Rapport de l'Archiviste de la Province de Québec* (and *Archives de Québec*),
1920–60, 1960-present.

REP Charbonneau, Hubert, *Le Répertoire des actes de baptême, mariage, sépulture et des recensements du Québec ancien,* 70 v., PRDH, Université de Montréal, Montréal, 1979.

RJ (Jour) *Relations des Jésuites* (1611–72), 6 t., Ed. du Jour, Presses Payette et Simm, Montréal, 1972.

RJ (inédites) *Relations inédites de la Nouvelle-France 1672–1678,* 2 t., Ed. Elysée, Montréal, 1974.

RJ (Thwaites) Thwaites, Reuben, ed., *The Jesuit Relations and Allied Documents,* 73 vols., Burrow Bros., Cleveland, 1896–1901. (in French)

RJ, year *Relations Jésuites,* CIHM, #fiche (in French)

References

AMDG *Liste des Missionaires Jésuites Nouvelle-France et Louisiane 1611–1800.* Montréal, Collège Ste-Marie, 1929.

DBC Brown, George, Marcel Trudel and André Vachon, eds., *Dictionnaire Biographique du Canada,* I and II, PUL and UTP, Québec and Toronto [1966] 1986.

HNF Trudel, Marcel, *Histoire de la Nouvelle-France,* 5 vols., Fides, Montréal, 1963–97.

RCAP *Royal Commission on Aboriginal Peoples* (*CRPA* in French)

Journals

AA *American Anthropologist*

AHR *The American Historical Review*

ICRJ *American Indian Culture and Research Journal canadienne-française*

BRH *Bulletin des Recherches Historiques*

CHA *Canadian Historical Association*

CHAR *Canadian Historical Association Annual Report*

CHR *Canadian Historical Review*

JAF *Journal of American Folklore*

MSGCF *Mémoires de la Société généalogique*

P & P *Past and Present*

RAQ *Recherches amérindiennes de Québec*

RHAF *Revue d'Histoire de l'Amérique française*

WMQ *William and Mary Quarterly*

INTRODUCTION

1 Michael Heyd, discussion, June 1996.

2 Margry, *Découvertes,* 1:99–100; Intendent Talon au roi, 2/11/1671.

3 Hartz, "Founding," from Saveth, *Immigrants;* Foster, *Conquest,* 12:232–3. George Foster elaborated this idea by concluding that colonial culture was generally "stripped down," or simplified. See Greene, "Transplanting," 224–37; Turner, *Frontier,* introduction; Innes, *Fur;* Eccles, *Frontier;* Bailey, *Conflict.*

4 DRHNF 1:175; Instruction à Courcelles, 1665, cited in Jaenen, *Upper,* 58–9.

5 Durkheim, *Elementary;* Simmel, *Philosophy;* Weber, *Essays;* Foucault, *Archéologie;* Elias, *Outsiders.*

6 Eccles, *Frontier,* 9. On "inclusive" and "exclusive" frontiers see Mikesell, "Frontier," 62–74.

7 ANC, C11A, 103: Réflexions générales (1758); NYCD, 10, 115–7: Abstract of a Plan to excite a Rebellion in Canada (1763); Blaisdell, *Speeches,* 16–21; Peckham, *Pontiac,* passim; Hollmann, *King,* passim; Marquis, Ottawas, passim; Schmalz, *Ojibwa,* ch. 4; Tanner, *Atlas,* 48–54; White, *Middle,* 274; Hurtado and Iverson, *Problems,* 142–5 from Jacobs, *Frontier,* 8–11; Tanner, *Atlas,* 105–23, 151–5; Flanagan, *Reconsidered,* conclusion; Charlebois, *Riel,* passim.; Howard, *Strange,* introduction; McLean, *1885,* passim.; Woodcock, *Dumont,* passim.

8 La Survivance: Ferland, *Histoire;* Faillon, *Histoire;* Sahlins, "Environment," 135–6.

9 Aron, *Sociological,* 2:206.

10 Iouscaha and Ta8iscaron were often compared by the missionaries to Cain and Abel (Lafitau, *Comparée,* 44–7, 58–63; Perrot, *Mémoires,* 3; Hultkranz, *Shamanic,* 65–7). This paradigm continued to be significant: Newberry Library, Ayer Coll., Ayer ms451; Jimmy Johnson on Gar:nyo:diyoh (Handsome Lake) speech, Grand Council of the Confederation of the Haudenosaunee, October 1885. First vision still included the cosmic twins "Sapling" and "Flint."

11 Buber, *Knowledge,* ch. 3; Halbwachs, *Memory,* 169–72; Cooley, *Self;* Mead, *Social;* Handel, *Ethnomethodology;* Stryker, *Interactionism;* Bauman and May, *Thinking;* Habermas, *Moral Conciousness;* Gecas, Social; Lévinas, *Entre nous,* chaps. 11, 17; *Alterity,* chaps. 1, 5–6, 10, 12; *Humanism.*

12 Habermas, *Communicative,* vol. 2.

13 Importance of death prior to and during the Plague: Boas, *Death;* Sutto, *Mort,* esp. 17–30. Early modern importance: Huizinga, *Autumn;* Vovelle, *Mort;* La Roy Ladurie, *Montaillou;* Harding, *Dead,* chaps. 1–45 (contrasts Parisian death rituals with those of London 1500–1670 as indicative of the contrast in their social relations and institutions); Gildea, *Past;* Lucian, *Dialogues,* 107–56; La Motte Le Vayer, *Oeuvres,* 1630–1; Fénélon, *Oeuvres,* 279–510; Salignac, *Dialogue.* Popular beliefs: LeBraz, *Morts,* introduction; Le Goff, *Purgatoire,* 1–27, 140, 439–474; Gennep, *Passage,* 147: the deceased and mourners in sacred state until soul completes journey to Otherworld.

14 Currently, immigrants have been treated based upon the "bereavement model," which works with the uprooting process (Mirsky, "haGira," 208;

Tousignant, "Migration," 167–77). The "mourning liberation process" tries to advance healing and loss to allow for identification, adjustment, and acculturation (Pollock, "Migration," 145–58; Mirsky, "haGira," 2–2–4, 209; Aronowitz, "Adjustment," 237–57.

15 Dewdney, *Scrolls,* ch. 7: the Ghost Lodge; Mooney, *Ghost-dance.*

16 Usually, the revenant in French Canada has traditionally been a recent family or neighborly death, who returned as a ghost, shadow, or headless man around Halloween time [la Toussaint] (Jacob, *Beauce,* passim). On the Other: Memmi, *Portrait,* passim; Gruzinski, L'*imaginaire,* passim; Todorov, *Nous,* passim.

17 Moriarty, *Taste,* 52: "honnesté was the name of an ideal ... with which the traditional aristocracy could redefine its identity ... [and] a means for the new recruit to [enter] the dominant class." See also Norbert Elias, *Civilizing Process;* Bourdieu, *La Distinction.*

18 Weber, *Essays;* Elias, *Civilising.*

19 Background on myth: Lévi-Strauss, *Lynx,* 316; Gregg, Self-Representation, 47; Watlawick, Weakland, and Fisch, *Change,* 18, cited by Sobel, "Inner," in Hoffman, Sobel, and Teute, *Glass,* 171; Lévi-Strauss, *Paroles,* 262–7; Morgan, *Haudenosaunee,* passim; Lévi-Strauss, *Nu,* 580; *Cru,* 20; Jung and Kerenyi, *Myth,* introduction; Jaenen, *Upper,* 23; Lafitau, *Comparée,* ch. 1; Fraser, *Golden,* passim; Fraser, "Fall," in Dundes, *Sacred,* 72–97; Lévi-Strauss, *Structures,* 87–88; *Nu,* 289–290; *Paroles,* 262–7; Ginsberg, *Ecstacies,* 260; Murdock, *Essays,* 85; Vico, *Science,* 141–2; Lilla, *Vico,* 24; Cervantes, *Devil,* 154–6; Malinowski, "Myth," in Dundes, *Sacred,* 199; Murdock, *Culture,* 49; Richards, "Malinowski," in Firth, *Malinowski,* 18–21; Geertz, "Impact," in Cohen, *Man,* 28. Debate over myth: Grim, *Shaman,* 62; Cassirer, *Myth,* 247; Lévi-Strauss, *Tropiques,* 344; *Anthropologie,* 49; Patai, *Modern,* introduction; Foucault, *L'archaelogie;* Cassirer, *Myth,* 237–69; Mosse, *Fallen,* introduction; Ozouf, *Festivals,* introduction; Flood, *Myth,* 46–52, 161–6; Sivan, *Remembrance,* introduction.
Postmodernist debate over the multifold interpretation of reality has been sometimes misused to deny historical events: Vidal-Naquet, "Revisionism," in Furet, *Questions,* chao. 15; High Court of Justice, London, case 1996–1113: *David John Cawdell Irving vs. Penguin Books and Deborah Lipstadt,* 12.4.2000. The historiographical debate over mythicization is particularly interesting regarding the Israeli Historian's debate (Historikerstreit), which examines the origins of the unJewish "New Jew" who can defend himself as either an inversion of the helpless Jewish victim, the delegitimitization of fear as a collective way of coping with endemic dangers, or both (Almog, *HaTsabar,* 124–136; Shapira, *Yehudim,* passim; for Israeli political fragmentation and martyrs: Feige, *Mythos,* introduction). This internal self-critique has metamorphized into a media narrative of a "neo-Nazi colonialist" aggressor that conquers Arab victims who have become "indigenous," although it is the displaced Hebrews who are "aboriginal" while the Arab presence came with

Salah-ed-Din the conqueror from the Arabian peninsula. Within a fifty-year timespan, Jewish minorities have been blamed for being communists, capitalists, Holocaust "sheep," neo-Nazi thugs, and world conspirators. Delegitimizing mythologization of a "global minority" can assume astounding proportions. Eisenstadt's Maybury-Lewis and Almagor, *Opposites*, 345–55.

20 Realm of the dead: Atisken andahatey, or "starry way" (Huron); Tchipai meskenau, or "way of souls" (Innu) (Sagard, *Histoire*, 497–9.); on Purgatory: Delumeau, *Pardon*, 62.

21 Todorov, *Autres*, 104.

22 This paradigm has been mentioned independently by Mechal Sobel in "The Revolution in Selves: Black and White Inner Aliens," in Hoffman, Sobel, and Teute, *Through a Glass Darkly; Teach me Dreams;* and Blum, "From Moccasins to Nus-Pieds"; and "From Savage 'Nobles' to Noble 'Savages.'" We developed mutually reinforcing perspectives, yet were only introduced to one another when I began my dissertation.

23 Elias, *Individuals*, 125. This was due on the European side to Christian reform and post-Trentine currents that emphasised repentence and purgatory, as well as the growing manipulation of the French social face in court via literary and gallant "conversation" and private portraiture. This conciousness met with a Native sensitivity that never shamed the inner self behind the social mask.

24 This began with the French debate over the Noble Savage, which utilized the Wendat as the preferred model due to the baron de Lahontan (*Dialogues curieux entre l'auteur et un sauvage de bon sens qui a voyagé...*, 1703) and Father Quesnel, who inspired François-Marie Arouet Voltaire ("L'ingénu," 1762). Utopian thought that utilized the mediated model of First Nations as their point of reference: *JR* (Thwaites), 27, 152; 31, 223–5; 32, 282–3; *RJ*, 1648, 171–3: Father LeJeune, for example, wrote of Michel the Maskouten: "there is no one so innocent, no one so candid, no one so modest" (il n'y a rien de si innocent, rien de si candide, rien de plus modeste.) This praise reappears frequently in French accounts. A brief list of the far-flung influence of Native American accounts upon French thinkers: Rabelais' *Gargantua* (1542); Michel de Montaigne's *Essais* (1580); the wide reading of the *Relations Jésuites*, less at the time of their writing than in the later 1700s (see Healy, "Jesuits," 143–67); Voltaire's "L'Ingénu," which was supposedly based upon the manuscripts of Father Quesnel; the *Journal de Trévoux* (1701–1734), which was edited by the Jesuit Father Tournemine, François-Xavier Charlevoix's *Journal d'un voyage fait par ordre du roi dans l'Amérique septentrionalle* (1744) and his *Histoire et description générale de la Nouvelle France* (1744); Joseph-François Lafitau's *Moeurs, coutumes, et religions des sauvages americains* and *Moeurs des sauvages amériquains, comparées aux moeurs des premiers temps* (1724); and Louis Armand de Lom d'Arc, Baron de LaHontan's Dario in *Dialogues curieux entre l'auteur et un sauvage de bon sens qui a voyagé...* (1703), among others. The seventeenth-century legal concept of the law of Nature evolved through

investigating a reconstruction of the hypothetical state of Nature in the first human communities. Hobbes conjured beast-like creatures; Spinoza evoked an anarchy of passions; Montesquieu imagined vulnerable, timid creatures; while Rousseau invented the super "wildman" in a state of liberty, based upon the Noble Savage image fostered mainly by Jesuit writings from North America; while van Pufendorf thought early humans to be highly vulnerable without collective protection. The image of the Noble Savage penetrates Rousseau's *Discours sur les sciences et les arts* (1750), *La Nouvelle Héloise* (1761), and *Discours sur l'origine de l'inégalité parmi les hommes* (1755), which served as the basis for *Du contrat social* (1762), the book that was used to legitimate measures taken during the French Revolution. For the use of an exotic "other" to critique European society, see Hazard, *La crise de la conscience européene*. Montesquieu was exceptionally uninterested in the Amerindians in his *L'esprit des lois* (1748), only citing the uncharacteristically hierarchical Natchez as an example, and was more favourably oriented towards the tyrannical Mideast. Denis Diderot's utopian image of a Noble Savage centred around the Tahitian rather than the Amerindian. Malouin François-René Chateaubriand's *Le Génie du Christianisme* (1802), *René* (1802), *Les Natchez* (1800), and *Atala* (1801) captured the romantic side of Native life. Georges-Louis Leclerc de Buffon (*Histoire naturelle, générale et particulière* [1749–1788, 529–46] presented the Amerindians as uncreative and helpless creatures before the forces of Nature. See also abbé G.-T. Raynal, *Histoire philosophique et politique des établissements et du commerce dans les deux Indes* (1780). Then there was utopian thought: Marc Lescarbot, *Histoire de la Nouvelle-France* (1604); and Robert Challes, Augustin-Thierry, *Un colonial au temps de Colbert: Robert Challes, Ecrivain du Roi* (1931), cited by Bennet and Jaenen, *Emerging*, 33. These thinkers, as well as considerations of the state of Nature and the law of Nature, were seized upon by European utopian thinkers of the seventeenth and eighteenth centuries, and Amerindians served as models either for human beings in the state of nature or as grist for utopian thought: Hughes de Groot, *De jure belli ac pacis* (1625); Charles Andrew's, ed., *Famous Utopias, being the complete text of Rousseau 's Contract, More's Utopia, Bacon's New Atlantis, Campanella's City of the Sun*, (n.d.); John Stephenson Spink, *French Free-thought from Gassendi to Voltaire* (1969); René Pintard, *Le libertinage érudit dans la première moitié du xvii e siècle* (1943); Charles Rihs, *Les philosophes utopistes: le mythe de la cité communautaire en France au xviii e siècle* (1970); Jean Ehrard, *L'idée de Nature en France dans la première moitié du xviii e siècle* (1963); Yehoshua Arieli, *Individualism and Nationalism in American Ideology* (1964). The later influence of discussion and accounts of Natives upon European thought was widespread. See Gabrielle Bersier, *Wunschbild und Wirklichkeit: Deutsche Utopien im 18. Jahrhundert* (1981); André Lichtenberger, *Le socialisme au XVIIIe siècle* (1895). Lewis Henry Morgan's *League of the Ho-de-no-Sau-nee or Haudenosaunee* (1851) had an effect upon

Friedrich Engels's *Der Ursprung der Familie, des Privateigentums und des Staats* (1844), which generated utopian, feminist, and communist thought. The correspondence between Lewis Morgan and J.J. Bachofen helped develop the idea of the ancient matriarchy, and the influence of Morgan upon Sigmund Freud's *Totem und Tabu: einige uebereinstimmungen im seelenleben der wilden und der Neurotiker* helped him construct his theory of psychoanalysis through dream analysis (*Die Traumdeutung.*)

25 Davis, "Women," passim; Warkentin, *Decentring*, passim. Late nineteenth-century British-based Spencerian Social Darwinism (Spencer, *Sociology*, 1:621–97); French Gobineauiste racial pseudo-science and the anti-Jewish explosion after the Dreyfus Affair (Gobineau, *Races*, ch. 1; Sicroff, *Pureté*, introduction; Zola, "J'accuse," in Talmon, *Tsarfat:* "J'accuse," "Le Monument Henri"; Drumont, *France*, passim; *Le Temps*, 19–21–1898, *La Libre Parole*, 22–1–1898, both cited in Epstein, *L'antisémitisme*, ch. 1; Barrès, *Déracinés*, passim; Céline, *Bagatelles;* Maurras, *Politiques;* and German and Austrian thinkers and politicians (Mosse, *Fascism;* Sternhell, *Birth;* Yovel, *Riddle*, part 2; Aschheim, *Nietzsche*, introduction; Zimmermann, *Marr*); Schopenhauer's alienation and Angst expressed in Spengler, *Decline;* Nordau, *Degeneration;* Bartov, "Victims," 1177–1194; Margalit, "Gypsies," passim). In North America as well, pre-Boasian evolutionary anthropology served to exonerate colonial racism and exploitation (Smith, *Sauvage*, 8–29, 36–43; Walker, *Indian*, 36–7; Trigger, *Newcomers*, ch. 1). Simultaneously, Natives were herded in a long "trail of tears" onto often infertile reservations (Andrist, *Death*). Exceptions to acquiesence to the Holocaust were made notably by Scandinavian and Bulgarian governments, and other courageous individuals in every country (Hilberg, *Destruction*, 3:991–1044, 1185–1194; Yahil, *Holocaust*, esp. 306–19; Bauman, *Modernity*, appendix; Wistrich, *Survival*, 1–12; Zuroff, *Occupation*, esp. 265–316). For Historian's Debate: Nash et al. *Trial.*

CHAPTER ONE

1 *JR* (Thwaites), 28, 289 in Petrone, *First*, 10.

2 Buber, *Zwichenmenschliche;* Gecas, *Self;* Stryker, *Interactionism;* Lévinas, *Altéréité.*

3 LeClercq, *Gaspésie*, 408.

4 Brébeuf, *Relation*, 143–4.

5 Sagard, *Huron*, 395–403; Brébeuf, *Relation*, 28–30.

6 "de tout le Canada, qui a le plus d'esprit mais ... la dissimulation à un excès ... [il se font] craindre & respecter des autres sauvages, son industrie, son génie fécond, en expédiens & en ressources, son éloquence & sa bravoure ... [ils ont] plus de défauts & plus de vertus" (Charlevoix, *Histoire*, 1:183; White, *Middle*, 433–4).

7 "nos Hurons ont quelque chose de louable par-dessus nous ... possedent des vertus morales ... un maintien humblement graue & modeste ... il s'offensent

rarement & se pardonnent facilement ... à cause de l'amour" (Sagard, *Histoire*, 368–9, 378).

8 Charlevoix, *Histoire* 1:199–222; LeClercq, *Gaspésie*, ch. 10.

9 Brébeuf, *Relation*, 18–20.

10 "le bon sens, l'éloquence naturelle, la Noblesse des sentiments." (Charlevoix, *Histoire* 6, 232).

11 "Dieu se plairoit auec eux, mieux qu'auec nos misérables qui le chassons de nos maisons, par nos tumultes, nos querelles, & nos débats qui ne trouuent iamais fin ... C'est pourquoy i'ay bien peur qu'à la fin il ne nous arriue le chastiment des Juifs" (Sagard, *Histoire*, 277–8).

12 Huddleston, *Indian;* Popkin, *Millenarians,* introduction; Freilich, "Tribes." Ariel Segal Freilich's dissertation, about a Jewish tribe he found in the Amazon, was published by the Jewish Publication Society of Philadelphia.

13 Sagard, *Hurons,* 220; Brébeuf, *Relation,* 29; Boucher, *Histoire,* 98, 115; Lafitau, *Comparée,* 68; Kinietz, *Lakes,* 335, Quebec, 1709: Mémoire concerning the different nations of North America; Perrot, *Mémoires,* 69; La Potherie, *Histoire* 2:70; *JR* (Thwaites), 20, 249.

14 ANC, MG 1, J–1: Sieur de Combes, Copie d'une lettre envoyée de la Nouvelle France, ov Canada, Lyon, Léon Savine (1609), ff. 3–4, 12–15, cited by Jaenen, *Upper,* 273; Zakai, *Puritan; Theocracy,* Ben Israel, Menasseh, *La esperanza de Israel* (1652).

15 Sagard, *Hurons,* 350–1.

16 "oyes babillardes, lorsque trop précipitez & boüillans en leurs actions" (Sagard, *Histoire,* 398–9).

17 *JR* (Thwaites), 20, 249; Bailey, *Conflict,* 84–5.

18 Campeau, MNF 2:439–40, 442, doc. 127, *RJ* 1633.

19 Sagard, *Hurons,* 353.

20 Campeau, MNF 2:411, 414, doc. 127; *JJ,* 1645, 10.

21 Champlain, *Oeuvres* 3:1191–221.

22 Davis, *Archives,* 53, 58.

23 Lossky, *Louis,* 10–15.

24 Deleuze, *Foucault,* 28, writes that the letters were sometimes used by the disadvantaged against the privileged, thus reinforcing royal sovereignty against rival claims.

25 Champlain, *Oeuvres* 1:766–7, 1208–10, 1211–2.

26 LeBlant, "Boullé," 55–69; LeBlant et Baudry, *Nouveaux* 2:330–2, doc. 150, Will of Marguerite Alix, wife of Nicolas Boullé, disinheriting their daughter Hélène Boullé, wife of Samuel Champlain, appended in the revocation of this will (23/5/1636, Paris, 14/2/1614); doc. 149: Déclaration by Nicolas Boulé, and Marguerite Alix disinheriting their daughter Hélène Boullé (13) and revocation and reinstatement, now sole heiress (23/5/1636, Paris, 10/1/1614).

27 Bishop, *Champlain,* 169–178; Trudel, HNF 2:198–201; Trigger, "Champlain," 92–3; Trigger, *Newcomers,* 179.

28 ASQ, Polygraphie, 13, 69: Notes sur Champlain prisonnier des Kirkes (1629); Champlain, *Oeuvres* 3:1228, 1249.

29 Champlain, *Oeuvres* 1:125–6; 2:622–9; 1:296–302.

30 Champlain, *Oeuvres* 2:358–65.

31 De Vignau's story of an English ship in the "Northern Sea" corresponds with our knowledge of Henry Hudson having been sent there by Henri IV himself (Champlain, *Oeuvres* 1:440–73; 2:198–201).

32 Trigger, "Champlain," 86, 89–90, 93.

33 Deleuze, *Foucault*, 35.

34 Champlain, *Oeuvres* 3: ch. 5; Sagard, *Histoire* 2:443, 515; 3:813–822. The surrender of Quebec in Archives du Ministre des Affaires étrangères, Paris, France: Correspondance politique, Angleterre, 43, fol. 192–192v.

35 Champlain, *Oeuvres*, 1146–8.

36 Davis, *Archives*, 36–7.

37 Monter, "Male," 565.

38 "la necessité estoit grande par tout entre nous aussi bien qu'entre les Sauvages ... filer doux & tendre ... [envers] la paix" (Sagard, *Histoire* 1:42–6, 54–7, 226; Champlain, *Oeuvres* 2:601–614; 3:1145–1150; Brébeuf, *Relations*, 39; Lafitau, *Moeurs* 1: 185–7; LeClercq, *Établissement* 1: 117, 121–7; Hennepin, *New* 2:566–571; Charlevoix, *Voyages*, 32–4). La Fourière was also called La Ferrière or La Forière. LeClercq and Hennepin mistake his story for that of a Haudenosaunee chief.

39 LeClercq, *Établissement* 1:, 117.

40 LeClercq, *Établissement* 1:121–7; Hennepin, *New*, 2:566–71; Charlevoix, *Voyages*, 32–4.

41 Sagard, *Histoire* 1:57; Champlain, *Oeuvres* 2:614.

42 Sagard, *Histoire* 1:226.

43 Sagard, *Histoire* 1:42–6; Champlain, *Oeuvres* 2:601–14; 3:1145–50. La Fourière was also called La Ferrière or La Forière.

44 LeClercq, *Gaspésie*, 407–10.

45 White, "Self," in Hoffman, Sobel, and Teute, *Glass*, 414–15.

46 Ricoeur, *Soi-même*, 150–66.

47 Delumeau, *Pardon*, 154.

48 Elias, *Individuals*, 125.

49 Champlain, *Oeuvres* 3:1025–6, 1029–31, 1179.

50 Delumeau, *Pardon*, chaps. 4–6.

51 *JR* (Thwaites), 33, 233–5, cited in Dickinson, "Justice," 24–5.

52 Davis, *Fiction*, 53 in White, "Self," in Hoffman, Sobel, Teute, Glass, *Inner*, 414–7.

53 Grabowski, *Common*, conclusion; Dickinson, "Justice," 31–3.

54 On developmental cognitive schemae: Hartman and Burgess, *Cognition*, 61–86; Pynoos, Steinberg, and Aronson, *Memory*, 293–315; Bruhn, *Earliest*, I.

55 Lévi-Strauss, *Sauvage*, 26–47.

56 Champlain, *Oeuvres* 1:368–370, 397–8; Sagard, *Hurons*, 249, 15n; 333.

57 15 (1615), Du Vernay arrived (1621) [Champlain (Biggar), *Works*, 5, 101];
Grenolle arrived before 1623 [Butterfield, *Brûlé*, 99–108, Trudel, *HNF* 2:229;
Trigger, *Aataentsic*, 372]; 17 among whom were Bruslé, Du Vernay, Guillaume
Chaudron, La Criette, Grenolle, La Montagne, La Vallée, Auhaitsique
(1623–5)[Champlain, (Biggar), *Works*, 5, 129; Sagard (Wrong), *History*, 744,
LeClercq, *Établissement*, 248]; and these same plus La Marche in all probability
until 1627–8 [Sagard (Wrong), *History*, 800; *JR* (Thwaites), 4, 197]; 20 (1628)
[Champlain (Biggar), *Works*, 6, 41]; cited in Trigger, *Aataentsic*, 373.
Generally, they resided among the Attignawantan in Ossossané, Carhagouha,
Quieunonascaran [Sagard, *Hurons*, 193; LeClercq, *Établissement*, 249; also
cited in Trigger, *Aataentsic*, 373.]

58 Erikson *Youth*, 16; Piaget, *Sociological;* Eisenstadt, *Generation*, 171–4.

59 Campeau, *HNF* 2:808–9; Oeullet in Sagard, *Hurons*, 18, 248, 15n.

60 Sagard, *Hurons*, 350–1.

61 Sagard, *Hurons*, 255, 350–3; *Histoire*, 496.

62 Sagard. *Hurons*, 255.

63 Champlain, *Oeuvres* 2:523, 625–9; 3:1065; *JR* (Thwaites), 3, 215; Sagard,
Histoire, 277–8, 406–7.

64 Champlain, *Oeuvres* 3:1065: Bruslé was sent to France 1625–1628, and
reducing his wages from 1000 (100 pistolles) to 400 livres.

65 Erikson, *Youth*, 13.

66 His explorations were sometimes with other truchements, like Grenolle, such
as that around 1621–23 to Sault Ste-Marie (Butterfield, *Brûlé*, 99–108;
Trudel, *HNF* 2:229; Trigger, *Aataentsic*, 372). From Champlain to Kirke:
Champlain, *Oeuvres* 3:1249–51: "vendant maintenant ceux qui vous ont mis le
pain à la main ... on se sert des perfides pour vn temps, vous perdez vostre
honneur, on vous montrera au doigt de toutes parts ... Voilà ceux qui ont
trahy leur Roy & vendu leur patrie, & vaudrait mieux pour vous de mourir
que viure de la façon au monde ... si l'on nous tenoit en France qu'on nous
pendroit." From tribe to tribe: (Trigger, *Aataentsic*, 292); "M de Champlain &
M. le General du Plessis Bochart, nous obligerent grandement l'année passee,
exhortant les Hurons en plein conseil à embrasser la Religion Chrestienne, &
leur disant que c'estoit là l'vnique moyen non seulement destre vn iour
veritablement heureux dans le Ciel, mais aussi de lier à l'avenir vne
très-estroite amitié auec les François, lesquels en ce faisant viendront
volontiers en leurs Pays, se marieroient à leurs filles, leurs apprendroient
diuers arts et mestiers, & les assisteroient contre leurs ennemis, & que s'ils
vouloient amener quelqu-vns de leurs enfans l'an prochain, qu'on les
instruiroit à Kébec." (Brébeuf, *Relation*, 52–3).

67 Sagard, *Histoire*, 166.

68 Champlain, *Oeuvres*, 1065, 1249–50: Bruslé: "fort vicieux, & adonné aux
femmes; mais que ne fait faire l'espérance du gain, qui passe par dessus toutes

considérations." And together with Nicolas Marsolet: "demeurez sans religion, mangeant chair Vendredy & Samedy, vous licentiant en ces desbauches & libertinages désordonnées, souuenez-vous que Dieu vous punira si vous ne vous amendez."

69 Erikson, *Youth,* 3.

70 *JR* (Thwaites), 21, 211; Trigger, *Aataentsic,* 473–5, 479–82, 484–5, 489, 491, 494, 496–7, 509, 518–20, 536, 595, 609, 694.

71 To this feast 2,000 people brought 1,200 gifts to give to the dead, the organizers, and the bereaved families. See also *JR* (Thwaites), 5, 255: the split in Toanché over Bruslé caused both factions to go to separate locations: Wenrio and Ihonatiria. Also *JR* (Thwaites), 5, 255: the split in Toanché over Bruslé caused both factions to go to separate locations: Wenrio and Ihonatiria. *JR* (Thwaites), 10, 311.

72 Champlain, *Oeuvres* 1:107–9; Sagard, *Hurons,* 289–98; Brébeuf, *Relation,* 105–8, 170–1. On linking dead and living community: Mosse, History 121: Lectures, winter 1974; Shamgar-Handelman, *Widows;* Handelman and Shamgar-Handelman, "Presence"; Winter, *Memory,* introduction; Zerubavel, *Roots,* introduction.

73 "I saw where the poor Estienne Bruslé was overcome in a barbaric fashion, which made me think that one day they might treat us in the same way." (Ie vis pareillement où le pauure Estienne Bruslé auoit est, barbarement assommé; ce qui me fit penser que quelque iour on nous pourroit bien traitter de la sorte." [Brébeuf, *Relation,* 12, 161])

74 "Voragine, Dorée, Bibliothèque municipale, Ms. 3, f. 25 v; BNF, ms. Latin 1178, f. 107 v: "Le fantôme d'un damné," in Schmitt, *Revenants,* 44, 100, 173–4.

75 *JJ,* 1646, 69; Brébeuf, *Relation,* ch. 2, 105–12; *JR* (Thwaites), 10, 279–311.

76 Barbeau, "Contes" (1e), 111–12. Dupont, *Légendes,* 38–9; O'Neil, "Légendes," 35; Dupont, *Légendes,* 11; Woodley, *Legends,* 54–62; Dupont, *Légendes,* 14–15; Dupont, *Villages,* 45; Fowkes, *Folklore,* 138; Rouleau, *Légendes,* 25–34; O'Neil, "Légendes," 32. AFUL, Phantoms, A–60: le revenant de Pascal Dion. Dupont, *Légendes,* 51.

77 Barbeau, "Contes (1e)," 131–2.

78 Dupont, *Côte-Nord,* 9. Hamlin, *Detroit,* 97–102: concerns the Keeper of the Gates of the Lakes near the Sleeping Bear sand dunes east of Lake Michigan in 1762. Hamlin, *Detroit,* 40–8, 220–7. For more tales see Jacob, *Revenants,* 91–128.

79 LeFebvre, *L'incroyance,* 410–7; Schmitt, *Revenants,* 167; Morin, "L'homme," 132–56; LeRoy Ladurie, *Montaillou,* 576–611.

80 Bibliothèque Municipale de Lille, ms. no. 795, fos. 588v–589r (BM de Lille, Catalogue des manuscrits, Paris, 1897, 307–310.); Bibliothèque Mazarine, ms. 1337, fos. 90v–91r; all cited in Delumeau, *Peur,* 73–8.

81 Davidson, *Lost,* 88; Delumeau, *Peur,* 81.

82 Van Gennep, *Manuel*, I, 2, 791, 800–1; Brekilien, *Bretagne*, 214–15; Gorel, *Bretagne*, 332–3.

83 Ginsberg, *Ecstacies*, 301; Spence, *Celtic*, 81–2, 160; Gorel, *Bretagne*, 245–354.

84 Spence, *Celtic*, 80; Delumeau, *Peur*, 83.

85 Ginsberg, *Ecstacies*, 264–6.

86 Johnston, *Restless*, 129, 133, 143.

87 Alix, *Contes*, 33–6, 40–3; Féré, *Normandie*, 73–84, 130–6, 137–8; Gorel, *Bretagne*, 271–397.

88 Ariès, *Hour*, 176; 55, 60.

89 Brébeuf, *Relation*, 58, 180; *JR* (Thwaites), 14, 53. Attignawantans burned their lodges due to the malediction of assassination, sure that the later epidemic was due to Bruslé's sister's sorcery (Sulte, *Mémoires*, 126).

90 Brébeuf, *Relation*, 78.

91 Brébeuf, *Relation*, 15, 17; *JR* (Thwaites), 8, 103.

92 *JR* (Thwaites), 10, 79.

93 Trigger, *Aataentsic*, 475.

94 Sagard, *Histoire*, 836–7.

95 Brébeuf, *Relation*, 39; *JR* (Thwaites), 7, 213–15; 8, 69, 139, 149, 151.

96 "The enemy!" This was often reported as the rallying cry of the Algonquians and Wendat against the Haudenosaunee.

97 ANC, MG 6, A 2, 3c, 3; Champlain, *Oeuvres* 3:1252.

98 Brébeuf, *Relation*, 57–8, 60–1.

99 The French gave them iron arrowheads, stood ready with four French arquebusemen, and advised their hosts to build square forts with four guards at each point,which they did at Ossossan (Brébeuf, *Relation*, 63–5.).

100 Mother Juchereau wrote: "They cruelly butchered the Hurons ... and we could not oppose them ... it was sowing season, and there were no men in Quebec ... it was awful to be obliged to abandon them to the fury of these barbarians these poor Christians ... despite the measures that we took ... having built a fort, even put a canon [up for their defence,] they did not receive any help from the French ... We learned this sad news with a general despair." (ils firent une crüelle boucherie des Hurons ... sans qu'on pût s'opposer ... la saison des semences, & qu'il n'y avoit point d'hommes dans le Québec ... affligeante que d'être obligez d'abandonner a la fureur de ces barbares ces pauvres chrétiens ... malgré les mésures qu'on avoit prises ... leur faisant bâtir un fort, ou l'on avoit même mis du canon ... ils ne reçurent aucun secours des François ... On apprit cette triste nouvelle avec une désolation générale" [*RJ*, 1662–3, 36–8, 58, 62–4; *RJ*, 1665, ch. 10, 298; Marie, *Correspondance*, 711–41:8–9/1663, let. CCXV; Juchereau, *Annales*, 127; *BRH* 36, 1930, 18: Du Bois d'Avaugour au ministre, 4/8/1663].)

101 *JR* (Thwaites), 43, 103–25. One could postulate that, if this had occurred at Three Rivers or Montreal, then intervention would certainly have occurred due to the readiness of habitants to fend off the Haudenosaunee as well as to

recent battle deaths: twenty-three in 1652 in Three Rivers and ten from 1648 to 1653 in Montreal far from the Governor General.

102 *RF,* 1648–9, 95.

103 Perrot, *Mémoires,* 158, 192–3. *JR* (Thwaites), 43, 35, 107–23; 45, 115; 53, 121; 70, 207; Juchereau, *Annales,* 91–2. *RJ,* 1648–9, 95. Trigger, *Aataentsic,* 810.

104 *RJ,* 1662–3, 36–8, 58, 62–4; *RJ,* 1665, ch. 10, 298; Marie, *Correspondance,* 711–41:8–9/1663, let. ccxv; Juchereau, *Annales,* 127; *BRH,* 36, 1930, 18: Du Bois d'Avaugour au ministre, 4/8/1663.

105 Carruth, *Trauma,* 3–12. Please refer to Chapter 6 for greater detail on memory and trauma.

106 Erikson, *Youth,* 185–9; Danieli, *Survivors,* passim; Antze and Lambek, *Trauma,* introduction. See Levi, *Saved,* 11–21; Bettelheim, *Heart,* for survivor guilt; for more see the last chapter.

107 *RJ,* 45, 245–61.

108 Dollier, *Montreal,* 252–66; Dickinson, "Palissade," 168, mentions Annaotaha's status versus Dollard's inexperience.

109 Marie (Richaudau), *Lettres* 2:158.

CHAPTER 2

1 Another factor was that the Parisian, Bordelais, and Alpine immigrants who arrived after 1663 were relatively aristocratic or bourgeois, the former being royal officials, the last two being military officers. Choquette's guess about the occupations of the Parisians, Bordelais, and Alpines seems quite correct (Swiss were regularly recruited for European armies, being vigourous mountaineers, and the Bordelais were recruited as mariners). Choquette, *Peasants,* 108.

2 Hartz, *Founding,* introduction; Fischer, *Albion;* Vaughan, *Frontier,* chs. 2–3.

3 Choquette, *Peasant,* 31: a line from Rouen to Toulouse distinguished Atlantic northern France, which had strong ties to North America. Exact numbers for 1608–63 are problematic because Trudel's 1973 book (*Population*) does not concord with the PRDH, and even when it does accord, as in his 1995 book of (*Recensement*), he found 1,212 more names than René Jetté and the PRDH. The figures utilized in this study will be a combination of Leslie Choquette for generalities, with Marcel Trudel for the early period and biographies, particularly if he has the largest figures. Incidentally, Jan Grabowski, in his article on the "petit commerce" (in bibliography), using judicial archival sources, has found people that are present neither in the PRDH nor in Trudel's *Recensement* of 1995. Necessarily we should regard immigration figures as indicative rather than absolute, despite the remarkable work of Quebecois demographers.

4 Please refer to map of immigrant origin in appendix.

5 Bercé, *Revolts,* 291–3.

6 The idea of a general crisis during the seventeenth century was forwarded by Paul Hazard (Hazard, *Crise,* introduction). What constitutes the crisis, the

period referred to, and whether it could be considered universal have all been hotly debated. The economic crisis theory has been debated by Hobsbawm, Mousnier, Trevor-Roper, Porschnev, Coveney, Méthivier, Mandrou, Meuvret, Parker, and others, as against Ivo Schöffler (who cites the contradictory example of the Netherlands), Lubinskaya, and Elliott. The debate on this question goes beyond the scope of our study. For the Little Ice Age, see Le Roy Ladurie, *Climat*, 1; its effect on families: Burguière et al., *Family* 2:16–17.

7 Lossky, *Monarchy*, 5; Le Roy Ladurie, *Royal*, 279: Manifeste des croquants de Perigord.

8 Bercé, *Croquants*, ch. 4. The ration of immigrant versus trader/engagés/administrator populations must be distinguished, as the former stayed in Canada while the latter did not. If they were from the northwest, the bocage areas of Lower Normandy and Poitou encouraged emigration to Canada due to close economic ties. The Perchois were all rural. And those from inland Maine and Anjou left from smaller towns and bocages. Many seventeenth-century "urban" dwellers were rural-born, as many from the countryside flocked to the city to work or "emigrate" (Choquette, *Frenchmen*, 42–4).

9 Coveney, *Crisis;* Bercé, *Croquants;* Benedict, *Rouen;* Bonney, *France;* Mousnier, *Fureurs;* Lubinskaya, *Absolutism.*. Focusing in on problem areas of the Northwest: Foisil, *Nus-Pieds;* Parker, *La Rochelle*, and for a classic analysis see Beik, *Absolutism.*

10 Trudel, *Catalogue;* which concurs with Fournier, "Canada," 108–9; Choquette, *Peasants*, 28–30. The PRDH has agreed that there were 8,527 founding immigrants for the French regime between 1608 and 1760, where the Atlantic northwest (including centre west) contributed 54.4 percent of total immigration (Normandy 1,111 [14.5 percent], Poitou 750 [9.8 percent], Aunis 679 [8.9 percent], Brittany 461 [6 percent], Saintonge 406 [5.3 percent], Anjou 222 [2.9 percent], Perche 217 [2.8 percent], Picardy 162 [2.1 percent], Maine 144 [1.9 percent], Orléanais 137 [1.8 percent], Touraine 115 [1.5 percent], Flanders 57 [.7 percent] (Choquette, *Peasants*, 29–30.) Marcel Fournier found that from 1608–1699, 63.5 percent of immigrants hailed from northwestern France (Normandy, Brittany, Aunis, Bretagne, Saintonge, Anjou, Perche, Picardie, Maine, Angoumois, Orléanais, Artois, and Beauce: 2,916 of 4,589 in absolute numbers [Fournier, "Canada," 111]). Therefore, from 63.5 percent (Fournier) to 54.4 percent (PRDH) total from the northwest from 1608–1760, which means that early immigration was overwhelmingly northwestern. Out of 3,106, only 2033 have been identified. Trudel, *XIII* 3:2, 25.

11 Absolute numbers and statistics, in Trudel, *XIII* 3:2, 24–7.

12 Bercé, *Revolts*, 332.

13 Benedict, *Rouen*, 240; Porschnev, *Soulèvements*, 310.

14 Le Roy Ladurie, *Royal*, 291.

15 Collins, *State,* 43–4.

16 Dewald, *Nobility,* 32, 37.

17 Ibid., 21, 71, 75, 198–200.

18 Pagès, *Monarchie,* 191.

19 *RJ* (Thwaites) 46, 146–8:12/10/1661; Trudel, *XIII* 4:7; LeBlant et Beaudry, *Nouveaux,* 305–21, 4–7–416, 432–41: docs: 143–5; 174–6, 185 about the Montmorencys.
   Dewald, *Nobility,* 93.

20 Out of a sample of 15, 810, and 12,050 people whose origins are known: Brittany 2,035 (16.9 percent), Normandy 1,871 (15.5 percent), Aunis 1,209 (10 percent), Poitou 983 (5.2 percent), Saintonge 311 (2.6 percent), Anjou 300 (2.5 percent), Perche 287 (2.4 percent), Picardy 274 (2.3 percent), Orléanais 184 (1.5 percent), Maine 163 (1.4 percent), Touraine 139 (1.2 percent), Flanders 61 (.5 percent), which gives us 62 percent from northwestern France. (Choquette, *Peasants,* 32, total mine).

21 Goubert, *Paysans.*

22 Bloch, *Caractères,* 223–38.

23 Choquette, *Frenchmen,* ch. 2.

24 Furet and Ozouf, *Reading,* 169, 286–7.

25 Alix, *Contes,* 78–80.

26 The Parisian parlement was not a legislative body, but a consultative one.

27 Collins, *State,* 12; Reese, *Brittany.*

28 Collins, *Brittany,* 25, 276.

29 Collins, *State,* 28; *Brittany,* 275.

30 Furet and Ozouf, *Reading,* 293.

31 Richelieu, *Lettres,* 38–41: lettre 26, 20/2/628, Mémoire de ce qui s'est passé au siège de la Rochelle depuis le départ du roy; Ranum, *Fronde.*

32 Richelieu, *Lettres* 7:94, fol. 158–179, 147: lettre 45. The razing of all these fortifications was consistent with Richelieu's political aim of uniting areas of France that could be had, either through administration or force of arms: "One must flatten all those places which are not frontiers, should not maintain river passages, or that can be used by mutinous ... large cities, but one must fortify in every way those that are frontiers." ("Il faut raser toutes les places qui ne sont point frontières, ne tiennent point les passages des rivières, ou ne servent point de bride aux grandes villes mutines ... ; il faut parfaitement fortifier celles qui sont frontières" – après 16/11/1628); Richelieu, *Mémoires* 7:94, fol. 158–79, lettre 55: Advis donné au roy après la prise de La Rochelle pour le bien de ses affaires (13/1/1629); Richelieu, *Lettres* 36: fol. 48-copie, lettre 26: "Mémoire de ce qui s'est passé au siège de la Rochelle depuis le depart du roy" (20/6/1628); and fol. 279-copie, 143, lettre 42: "Relation de la réduction de la Rochelle, pour l'envoyer aux pays estrangers."

33 Bosher, *Business,* 128–9.

34 "dans les papiers de montaigu il paraissoit liaison d'Angleterre, de Lorraine, Soissons, Rohan, et de la Rochelle contre l'État, dessein de guerre et de soulevation ... consentement de la Reine régnante ... Dès le commencement de l'année, les Rochelois dépêchèrent vers le roi de la Grande-Bretagne, le suppliant de les prendre sous la protection et de les assister jusques à ce qu'ils puissent être délivrés de l'oppression qu'ils disoient souffrier ... Les Anglois firent un trait, avec eux ... de les secourir par mer et par terre à ses dépens ... Les Rochelois à leurs frères des provinces de la Loire, pour les inciter à prendre tous des armes" (Richelieu, *Mémoires*, t. VII, 12–17).

35 Tapié, *France*, 190.

36 They guarded these jealously and were as wary of young Henri IV and Catherine after their escape from Ligue-dominated Paris, as of the Prince de Condé whom they forced to write twenty-two articles confirming their privileges before his entry in Jan. 23 1577. (Vaux de Foletier, *Aunis*, 95–6; Collins, *State*, 29.)

37 Foletier, *Aunis*, 127; Bosher, *Business*, 121; Bercé, *Absolutism*, 98–102. Mandrou, "Canada," 667–675, 671. Richelieu, *Lettres* 46:143: "Les fortifications en sont des plus belles et plus grandes que de plac [sic] du royaulme ... le chastiment de ceste ville rebelle depuis tant d'années ... abattre toutes ces superbes fortiffications ... comme aussy de luy oster tous ses privilèges, qui estoient plus grands que d'aulcune autre ille du royaulme." (lettre 42: Relation de la réduction de la Rochelle, pour l'envoyer aux païs estrangers, 1628, fol. 279-copie).

38 Mandrou, "Canada," 667–675, 671.

39 Bercé, *Absolutism*, 102; Bercé, *Croquants* 2:794–5: ANF, Arch. des Affaires étrangères, Mémoires et documents, France, 1476, fol. 56: Lettre de Robert de Lamont, enseigne des gardes du crops, ... son ami M. de Nesle lors des troubles survenus en Saintonge et Angoumois (8/9/1642): "Tout la Noblesse depuis cinquante ans accoustumée à un tel libertinage qu'il est mal aysé de la ramener à la recognoissance de son devoir [au roi] ... non seulement la Noblesse ne se laisse pas mouvoir, mais, comme si les croquans faisoent ses affaires, il en vient soulz leurs chapeaux, disans que leurs paysans sont ruinez ... sert comme mot de gueté et de ralliement ... toutes les autres provinces du royaume sont en admiration [de Sa Majesté] ... en ce petit coing il y resteroit là ce démon, un esprit Impur, de celuy qui cinquante ans durant y avoit chocqué l'authorité Royalle pour y establir la sienne ... fomente ces désordres."

40 Porschnev, *Soulèvements*, 337, 319.

41 Mandrou, "Canada," 667–675; Moogk, "Exiles", 463–505 (which was kindly sent to me by Cornelius Jaenen). See also Debien, "Engagés", 374–392; Delafosse, "La Rochelle", 469–511.

42 In 1626, Richelieu became governor of Brouage and bought the lucrative "droit de sel" tax, and established the principal naval arsenal there. In 1627,

he bought the seigneurie of Arvert for 159,000 livres. In 1629 Louis XIII made him lieutenant general at Brouage, Oléron, and Ré. On 5/12/1630, he became governor of Ré, Aunis, and La Rochelle and established his control over the whole area. In 1633 he bought the duché-pairie of Fronsac for 600,000 livres, in 1638 he purchased the estates of Saujon for 150,000 livres, 120,000 for the barony of Cozes, Barbézieux for 330,000 in around 1640, and the estates of Mortagne-sur-Gironde and Cosne in 1640. (Bosher, *Business*, 128–9.)

43 Dewald mentions Rouen as only being one and one-half to two days from Paris, travelling by horsepower (Dewald, *Rouen*, 43). Due to the large number of magistrates, which, according to Benedict, was due to the "notorious love of chicanery[,] fueled one of the chief growth industries of the century." He cites 1,346 lawsuits by 1586. Legal officials also became one of the main Rouennais exports (Benedict, *Rouen*, 12, 18).

44 Dewald, *Nobility*, 248–9, 298.

45 Discours, passim.; Deux, passim; Pourtraict, passim.; Troubles, passim., 41; all cited in Benedict, *Rouen*, 102.

46 Benedict, *Rouen*, 217–22.

47 Tapié, *France*, 403; Collins, *State*, 23.

48 Collins, *State*, 62–3.

49 Richelieu, *Lettres* 7:360.

50 Richelieu, *Lettres* 8:360; Hill, *Revolution*. Hugo de Groot, Dutch legal thinker, wrote to Oxenstiern in Sweden that England secretly seemed to support the Nus-Pieds (Grotii, *Epistolae*, 606, cited in Porschnev, *Soulèvements*, 484); also see Porschnev, *Soulèvement*, 476–84.

51 Collins, *State*, 62–4; Tapié, *France*, 395–406.

52 Floquet, *Diaire*, 406; Porschnev, *Soulèvements*, 339.

53 Bercé, *Absolutism*, 147–8.

54 Bercé, *Absolutism*, 71.

55 This is about 51.2 percent of the identified 2,356 non-clerical men. Of the twenty-four feminine engagées, there was only one profession declared: that of a servant (Trudel, *HNF*, 3:2, 52–5). A notable exception to this was the abundance of linen merchants at Rouen, the majority of whom were women (twenty of thirty-six), and whose average tax assessment in 1565 in livres was 31.1 percent, which was higher than the mean average merchant assessment of 18.9 percent. The only professions officially open to female labour were linen-makers (lingères), embroiderers (brodeuses), ribbon-makers (rubannières), and thread-makers (fillacières). (Absolute figures and information from Benedict, *Rouen*, 22–4; calculations mine.)

56 Benedict cites, as early as 1565, only ten masters to sixty journeymen in Rouen (Benedict, *Rouen*, 15; A.C.R., B2, 17/5/1565); Moogk, "Craftsmen," in Cross, *Economy*, 88–119. Choquette also confirms the preponderance of craftsmen (Choquette, *Peasants*, 128.)

57 Trudel, *XIII* 3:2, 52–5; Choquette, *Peasants*, 125, confirms that large proportion of mariners were from Normandy and Brittany.

58 Porschnev, *Soulèvements* (the revolts at Caen, 1630) 350–1, and (the revolts at Rouen, especially 1628, 1634, 1635) 360–4. Choquette, however, indicates that the metalworkers from Maine and Perche were the most numerous (Choquette, *Peasants*, 127).

59 The artisans were well represented in Normandy: in a 1550 royal entry procession, seventy-two professions were in the parade compared to Lille's procession the same year at less than a third of this (Benedict, *Rouen*, 1–9). English cloth imports of 1630–32 all but ruined the Rouen and Darnétal cloth industries due to their quality at bargain prices (Porschnev, *Soulèvements*, 361–2).

60 Choquette, *Peasants*, 124.

61 Ibid., 125–6.

62 LeBlant et Beaudry, *Nouveaux* 2:86–93, 99, 158–9: docs. 50, 54, 59, 80, 88, and Trudel, *Catalogue*, 364, 491, 446, 225, 384, 463, 106. A Dubois-Morel from Perche is listed for 1650. Pierre Moreau dit Morel, 24, couldn't sign, mason, arrived 1641, engagé of 1641, worked for Ursulines 1647–66; Etienne, 21, signature, arrived 1657, Chateau-Richer in 1660, sailor in 1661, captain in 1662; and Thomas, priest, worked in Quebec area 1661–71, and the St Lawrence until 1683, died 1687.

63 Mousnier, *Institutions*, 91–2.

64 All immigrants in Trudel, *Catalogue*, 154, 260, 452, 78: Lafontaine: soldier, personal name unknown, arrived 1645, killed in a duel; sailor, name unknown, arrived 1652, lived in Three Rivers; and many who adopted the epithet "dit Lafontaine" as their nom de guerre, certainly in reference to the renowned Nu-Pieds Lafontaine. Jean de Lalande, arrived 1638, witness in 1639, donné for the Jesuits, in Three Rivers 1642–46, 1646 goes to Iroquoia, killed in October 1646, proclaimed saint by the Church 29 June 1930.

65 Richelieu, *Lettres* 8:360; Porschnev, *Soulèvements*, 479–81.

66 Porschnev, *Soulèvements*, 363.

67 Porschnev, *Soulèvements*, 313, 344–5.

68 Trudel, *Catalogue*, 317, 307, 438, 445, 446: Peronne Dumesnil, Intendant of the Hundred-Associates from Anjou; Marie, Richard, squire; Descartes Dumesnil, baron; who arrived from 1654, 1661.

69 Porschnev, *Soulèvements*, 476.

70 Bergeron, *Légende*, 158.

71 Trudel, *XIII* 3:2, 8–10.

72 Eccles, *Frontier*, 3; Innes, *Fur*, introduction.

73 Champlain, *Oeuvres* 1:263; Trigger, *Aataentsic*, 270, 280.

74 During the sixteenth century, Breton, Norman, and eventually Rochelois fishers had set up their equipment seasonally upon the Grand Bank of Newfoundland to preserve cod to sell on European markets (Denys,

Description, passim.). The Basques had specialized in whaling and had established trade relations with the Mi'kmaq, Maliseet, and Innu in the region, who offered pelts in return for European trade items. The French provided them with labour-saving devices such as metal cauldrons (which replaced heated stones), knives, metal arrowheads, needles and awls instead of bone and wood implements; and glass beads instead of laboriously worked porcupine quills for wampum, blankets, and textiles. And although they were loathe to part with them, sometimes arquebuses were also included. The French were more circumspect about giving firearms to tribes outside the Laurentian Valley due to their thin presence there and eventually only gave them to converts. De Monts and Poutrincourt chose Acadia, largely due to the friendly welcome of the tribes near those areas, their access to furs, and their interest in European goods. Royal directives concerning colonial initiatives were not as yet developed, which left the tentative policies of the merchants to sound out arrangements with the First Nations.

75 Champlain, *Oeuvres* 1, ch. 3I, 296–302; Lescarbot, *Histoire* 5, ch. 2. This sometimes led to trader rivalry, as epitomized by the attempt upon Champlain's life.

76 Grabowski, "Trifluviens."

77 Dickinson, "Haudenosauneee," 31–54, 15; Trudel, *XIII* 3:2, 54 (15.1 percent of total known deaths).

78 Grabowski, "Trifluviens," 18–24.

79 Ossenberg, *Pluralism*, introduction.

80 Lunn, "Contraband;" Grabowski, "Contreband."

81 John Long, an English-speaking fur trader of 1791 even writes of Trois-Rivières fame: "this town ... had formerly a very considerable trade in peltry, and was the second mart in Canada; but in process of time the inhabitants of Montreal contrived to draw almost all the trade to themselves ... and though the residents in Three Rivers live by their commerce with the savages [*sic*], and the manufacturing of birch canoes, yet the town has lost that rank and consequence which it formerly maintained" (Long, *Voyages*, 4).

82 Trudel, *Population*, 67.

83 "The Common Ground: Settled Natives and French in Montreal, 1667–1760" (PhD diss., Université d'Ottawa, 1993).

84 Bartlett, *Europe*, 204–11.

85 Dechêne, *Habitants*, 218–22.

86 ANQ, Coll. de pièces judic., 23: requete du 30/9/1647; Trudel, *XIII* 3:1, 190.

87 The election of Jacques Leneuf de la Poterie as syndic of Three Rivers was recorded in a procès-verbal 10/8/1647 (ASQ, Faribault, 1, 71) signed also by these two interpreters. (syndic election cited by Trudel, *XIII* 3:1, 190, 93n.)

88 *JD*, 353–4, 368–9, 388–9 in Grabowski, Trifluviens," 105–6.

89 Notre-Dame, 26–2, 106, cited and translated in Jaenen, *Church*, 27.

90 Jetten, *Enclaves*, ch. 3; Grabowski, "Contreband."

91 ASQ, Polygraphie 13, 16: Jean de Lauzon ... seigneurie des Onnontagués
   (12/4/1656); 13, 18: Déclaration de Lauzon nommant les Jésuites tuteurs et
   protecteurs des sauvages (16/11/1651); 13,22: Dequen prend possession ...
   sauvages (6/2/1657) [Sillery]; 13,27: Lauzon défend aux sauvages de régir
   leurs biens (12/5/1656); 13, 52: Lauzon concède aux Jésuites la Seigneurie
   des Onnontagués (12/4/1656).

92 Grabowski, "Trifluviens," 25.

93 Kirmayer, "Suicide," 3–58; Kirmayer, "Health," 607–16; Kingsley and Mark,
   Sacred.

94 Their synthesis is based upon the Bolton thesis but constructed from James
   Axtell's *The Invasion Within* (1985), Richard White's *The Middle Ground*
   (1990), Gregory Nobles' *American Frontiers* (1997), and Colin Calloway's *New
   Worlds for All* (1997) in tandem with other Western historians (e.g., Albert
   Hurtado, William Cronon, and Jay Gitlin among others).

95 Adelman and Aron, "Borderlands," 814–17. Jaenen was the first to reexamine
   Bolton in light of his own findings in *Friend and Foe* twenty-five years ago.

96 Dickason, *Louisbourg.*

97 Jaenen, *Friend,* 135: New York and Massachusetts proposed to erect rules of
   war between themselves and New France.

98 ANF, Arch. du Ministère des Affaires étrangères, Paris: Correspondance
   politique, Angleterre, v. 43, fol. 192–192v.

99 Champlain, *Oeuvres* 2:601–14; 3:1145–50, 1178–9, 1194–1205; Sagard,
   Histoire 2:443, 515; 3:813–22.

100 Trigger, *Aataentsic,* 267.

101 Sagard, *Histoire* 4:910–11; Champlain, *Oeuvres* 3:1253–65; Trudel, I, *DBC,*
    204–5.

102 Trigger, "Champlain," 109–10.

103 Sagard, *Histoire,* 829–30.

104 The Kirke brothers, Thomas and David, were only naturalized in Britain in
    1639 (Trudel, *XIII* 3:2, 32n.; *DBC* 1:416–20.). ASQ, Polygraphie, 3, 76:
    Capitulation de Quebec (19/7/1629).

105 Champlain, *Oeuvres* 3:1146.

106 Sagard, *Histoire* 4:833–4.

107 Champlain, *Oeuvres* 3:1194–202, 1204–5.

108 Champlain, *Oeuvres* 3:1195–8; Sagard, *Histoire* 4:842–3: "particularly our
    Napagabiscou [Negabamat] who was full of fervor ... [to Father Joseph] give
    me Brother Gervais, so I can bring him with me to the country of the
    Algonquians ... if you want to give me another of your brothers ... I could feed
    well until ... three. If you suffer from hunger, and if I have something to eat,
    they will also have it" (particulierement nostre Napagabiscou, [Negabamat]
    qui plein de ferueur ... [to père Joseph] que tu me donne Frere Geruais, afin
    que ie l'emmene auec moy au païs des Algoumequins ... si tu veux me donner
    encor un autre de tes freres ... i'en nourriray bien iusques ... trois. Si ie souffre

de la faim ils en souffriront, & si i'ay de quoi manger ils en auront.") They were received with joy and applause ("auec une ioye & applaudissement"), which Sagard attributes to their predilection for religion but which is more likely due to the well known Innu "pity for those suffering," while being angry over the assassination and their personal liking for Brother Gervais. Trigger, *Newcomers*, 86, 199–200.

109 Sagard, *Histoire* 4:854. The Wendat also brought with them eleven to twenty Frenchmen, who only added to the general hunger (Sagard, *Histoire* 4:853: eleven men and 894: fifteen to twenty men; Marcel Trudel writes approximately twenty (Trudel, *XIII* 3:2, 36). Champlain, *Oeuvres* 3:1205–18; Sagard, *Histoire* 4:833–4, 842–3, 853–6, 86. The Innu sold 1,200 eels to Quebec for the 1628 autumn for French-owned beaverpelts (Trudel, *XIII* 3:34).

110 Sagard writes that food portions were small but edifying: "cut again ... each a tiny portion for this little one, which was done for the edification of all, and done with the same gaiety, as if we had already prepared for others" ("retrancher à chacun une partie de la petite portion pour ce petit, ce qui fut fait à l'édification de tous, & auec la mesme gayet, qu'on s'estoit des-ia retranché pour d'autres" (Sagard, *Histoire* 4:856). These three boys were in addition to the several Native children mentioned, as well as La Charité and Lesperence, who had previously been presented to Champlain.

111 The French offered them, when the French ships arrived, a barrel of sea biscuits and two beaver robes for each person they would allow to live with them. According to Marcel Trudel, the total cost value of these were 100 livres and seven beaver pelts (Trudel, *XIII* 2:2, 37).

112 Champlain, *Oeuvres* 3:1150. A root frequently eaten then was Solomon's Seal (le sceau de Salomon, or polygonatum pubescens), boiled up with a throw of barley flour and/or beans and/or acorns, with a bit of fish. However, it was difficult to bring in fresh fish, although they were abundant, due to lack of nets and cords (Sagard, *Histoire* 4:886: he speaks of Sigillum Salomonis [i.e., Solomon's Seal], which was claimed by him as a remedy for hemorroids as well: "cut in slices and worn around the neck on bare skin like a rosary, of which a lady of Paris assured me cured her" ("coupée en rou & portées au col sur la chair nud en chappelets, dont une dame de Paris m'a asseuré en avoir esté guarie").

113 Trigger, *Newcomers*, 199–200.

114 Sagard, *Huron*, 260. Ethnocentric: Trigger, "Champlain," passim.

115 LeBlant et Beaudry, *Nouveaux*, 361–2: doc. 16; Trudel, *Catalogue*, 17–21; DBC 1: passim. ANC, MG 5, A, fols. 194–194v:20/7/1629, Mémoire des armes et autres commoditez qui sont restés après la prise de Quebec. Sagard, *Histoire* 2:443, 515; 3:813–22. Marie Rollet Hébert, Guillaume Couillart: ANC, MG 18, H9, Concession de terre par Champlain ... Guillaume Couillard, 20/6/1627 [Sault-au-Matelot]; Jean Godefroy de Lintot, Thomas Godefroy de

Normanville: ANC, MG 7, 27824 D30413; Jacques Hertel de la Fresnière: ANC MG 7, 31412 D4100; Olivier LeTardif, François Marguerie dit Lahaye, and Jean Nicollet de Belleborne.

116 ASQ, Faribault, 20: Guillaume Couillart; ASQ, Faribault, 20: Olivier Le Tardif; ASQ, Faribault, 20: passim; ASQ, Faribault, 7, Registre A, 560f: Jean Nicollet de Belleborne.

117 ASQ, Séminaire, SME 5: les propriétés et les seigneuries Sault-au-Matelot (1626–76); SME 6: La défense des droits du Séminaire-Famille Couillard-Desprès (1725–59).

118 Sagard, *Histoire* 4:854, 887. Trudel mentions a declaration of 1631 that states that the company storeroom bought from them seven barrels of "pois plain d'orge" (*RHAF* 3:4, 1950, 594); Champlain, *Oeuvres* 3:1144.

119 "Champlain les recommenda ... Guillaume Coliart, gendre de la Dame Hébert, afin qu'il en prit soin, & les gouuernast comme ses filles propres, ce qu'il promist faire, & l'effectua, car il estoit tres-honneste homme & craignant Dieu." (Sagard, *Histoire* 4:910–11); Champlain, *Oeuvres*, 1228, 1253–65; Trudel, *DBC*, 204–5.

120 Collins, *State*, 68.

121 Benichou, *Morales*, passim.

122 Bercé, *Absolutism*, 173, 179.

123 7/ 1652, Articles de l'union de l'Ormée en la ville de Bordeaux; Collins, *State*, 65–78.; Méthivier, *Fronde*, 168–9.

124 Méthivier, *Fronde*, 192.

125 Chéruel, *Histoire*, conclusion; Kossman, *Fronde:* concentrates upon the parlement de Paris; Lorris, *Fronde,* interprets the Fronde as being the last gasp of the power of the great nobility; Moote, *Judges,* passim upon the magistrates; Jacquart, "Princes," 257–90 upon the aristocracy; Lefebvre, "Aspects," 59–106.

126 Bercé, *Absolutism*, 167. Archives de Rouen, Mazarinade, M 14998, 1644: David du Petit-Val, "L'Histoire du temps"; Mazarinade, M 10092: David du Petit-Val et Jean Viret, 886, Déclaration du Msgr le prince de Conti et de messieurs les généraux du 20 mars 1649; Chantilly, XXV A 35, #8, 871: Jean Rousse, Décision de la question du temps; Chantilly, XXV A 35, #8, 414: Jean Rousse, Articles de la paix ... Rueil le 11e mars 1649; Mazarinade, M 19964, 639: Carême des Parisiens; M 10141, 1640: Jacques Besongne, La Fureur des Normands contre le Mazarinistes; Chantilly, XXV A 35, # 21, 113: L'Apologie des Normands; Duranville, "Rouen," 314–35; cited in Carrier, *Mazarinades*, 462–4.

127 Bercé, *Absolutism*, 178.

128 Ibid., 36–7.

129 Richter, *Ordeal*, 3–4; 32–5. This interpretation is strengthened by Father Jogues' letter of 30 June 1643, stating: "The design of the Haudenosaunee as far as I can see, is to take, if they can, all the Hurons; and, having put to death

the most considerable ones, and a good part of the others, to make them both but one people and only one land." (*JR*, Thwaites, 24, 297; Jennings, *Ambiguous*, 93.)

130 Champlain, *Oeuvres*, 253–4; Trigger, *Aataentsic*, 268 (for Wendat).

131 Bruce Trigger had originally adopted a modified George Hunt thesis, that the Haudenosaunee aggression was due to the depletion of beaver in Iroquoia and their greater quantity of firearms, a thesis that is ceding to fresh theories. José Brandao's thesis that the Haudenosaunee endeavoured to preserve their territory from French incursions, capture adoptees to replenish depleting population, and only resorted to force after repeatedly failed diplomatic ventures incorporates much current scholarship while adding the first factor, which is new. John Dickinson has long maintained that Haudenosaunee policy tried to capture and incorporate the Wendat, particularly after some of the latter lived among the former. Daniel Richter and Roland Viau have agreed that the Haudenosaunee policy of war of capture was a major factor in strikes. The Jesuits wrote that, as the Haudenosaunee were "engagez dans de grandes guerres ... [they needed] .... des Hurons pour grossir leurs troupes.." Richter noted that the captive church of the incorporated Wendat in Iroquoia was a major factor in Haudenosaunee diplomacy, and he mentions the truce of 1653, and the Jesuit mission of Ste-Marie Gannentaha, as motivated by the desire to attract Wendat refugees of Lorette and to have adopted Christians in Iroquoia remain in their new homes. Marie-Laure Pilette wrote that peace within the League was only maintained by uniting for war, which builds upon Léo-Paul Desrosiers' idea that only the Oneida and Mohawk were bellicose, while the Seneca, Onondaga, and Cayuga were pacific. Francis Jennings, Alain Beaulieu, and Claude Gélinas counter that militarism was the last option after extensive diplomacy. All of these factors taken together contributed to exacerbate aggression, with an incremental increase of the importance of obtaining captives as the hostilities progressed. Certainly the Mohawk were the most aggressive because they were geographically the most vulnerable, and after 1666 the French struck back with force (Trigger, *Newcomers*, 259–63). Bruce Trigger has argued that C.H. McIlwain's and George Hunt's theories that the Haudenosaunee tried to replace the Wendat as middlemen and funnel all trade to the Dutch is not well grounded (McIlwain, *New York*, introduction; Hunt, *Wars*, introduction). Denys Delâge originally adopted this thesis in *Le Pays Renversé* (1985), ch. 4.; Viau, *Néant*, 40–4. The Jesuits wrote that Haudenosaunee needed the Wendat to assist them in their military conquests: *RJ* (Thwaites), 41, 216–218; *RJ* (Thwaites), 42, 52–8; *RJ* (Thwaites), 44, 150. Richter, *Ordeal*, 108. Pilette, *S'allier*, 24–6, 30–4, ch. 3, 73, 76; Desrosiers, *Iroquoisie*, 93. Matthew Dennis's thesis that warring was effectuated in order to ensure an incorporative peace evokes the diplomatic kettle symbol of both peace (feasting together) and war (devouring the enemy), but it is too selective in its rendition to convey the intricacies of the question (Dennis,

Landscape, 77–90.) Jennings, *Ambiguous,* 8–9; Beaulieu, *Iroquois,* introduction; Gélinas, "Ville-Marie," 119–27. Brandao, *Fyre.*

132 Trigger, *Aataentsic,* conclusion; most avid critique in Campeau, *Mission,* conclusion.

133 Soon after the foundation of Ville-Marie (Montreal) in 1642, the governor of Montreal, Paul de Chomédey de Maisonneuve, was forced to borrow funds from the Montreal hospital to obtain soldiers to defend the settlement. And by 1643 Three Rivers had to enclose its residents within walls for their own safety (Morin, *Véritable,* xxii, 59; Marie, *Correspondence,* 248–49, 14/9/1645: lettre XCI); *JJ,* 1649, 128–12: "the troubles of France etc. And the little hope of ships ... the 20th at night sad news arrived of the destruction of the Hurons and the murder of the three Fathers" ("les troubles de France, & c. & le peu d'esperance de vaisseaux..Le 20. la nuict arriuerent les tristes nouuelles de la destruction des Hurons, & du meurtre des 3. Peres"). Also three ships arrived but one was lost with crew and passengers, and 4,000 livres for the Jesuits. On the effect of Richelieu's death on the Jesuits of Canada, see Lanctôt, *History* 1:190.

134 ASSM, 20/6/1653: 100 workers were recruited by Pierre Boucher, but thirty-five died en route.

135 *RJ,* 1647–8; 1648–1649, chs. 1–4. *RJ,* 1647–8, 18 on the attack of Seneca upon the Aondironnons (Neutrals). For a macroanalysis, see Delâge, *Renversé,* ch. 6; Richter, *Ordeal,* ch. 3; Jennings, *Ambiguous,* ch. 9.

136 *RJ,* 1648–9, 6; Dechêne, *Habitants,* 497, writes that, according to the 1650–1770 censuses, there were about 500 inhabitants in New France in 1648. Raymond Douville estimates that there were barely 600 inhabitants in 1645 (Douville et Casanova, *Canada,* 73).

137 Dickinson, "Palissade," 168–72, who cites Bruce Trigger having postulated this (Trigger, *Aataentsic* 2:805.); Delâge, "Réponse," 114–15.

138 Bercé, *Absolutism,* 111–16.

139 The first outbreak in England claimed 40 to 55 percent of the population in eighteen months (Horrox, *Black,* 3). This unfortunate perspective could easily be due to the distortion introduced by the peephole into Wendat history afforded by the Jesuit Relations, whose aim was to report mission or martyrdom successes. Documents are always written with their own agenda, and it would be a grave mistake to believe that the missions lay at the centre of the Wendat universe.

140 Charlevoix, *Histoire* 5:184; Trigger, *Aataentsic,* 148–50.

141 *RJ,* 1647–8, from 44: The Onondaga delegate, Scandaouati, brought with him fifteen captives and promised to bring about a hundred more.

142 Gélinas, "Ville-Marie," 124.

143 Ragueneau writes of their different strategic approach and of Scandarouati's suicide due to Mohawk disrespect of his diplomatic initiative. (*RJ,* 1647–8, 47–9.)

144 Spiritual factionalization following a catastrophic epidemic is familiar to
Renaissance historians. Written testimonials of individuals living under the
threat of the plague reveal an unleashing of aggressive fanaticism (e.g.,
Savanarola and the Flagellants). Simultaneously, libertine behavior is also
stimulated in some people, such as those described in Giovanni Boccaccio's
Decameron.. Another possibility is the renunciation of one's fate unto
praedestinatio, as Luther and Calvin claimed. This centrifugal effect is no
surprise as it was a decade following the depradations of epidemics
(Fanaticism: Horrox, *Black*, 150–3, 155–7, 119–125, 131–3; Bertrand,
Relation, 212–33; Ziegler, *Death*, 87–9; libertinism: Deaux, *Death*, 145–75;
fatalism: Curson and McCracken, *Sydney*, 169–72.; scapegoating: Horrox,
Black, 207–26; Zeigler, *Death*, 98–111; Curson and McCracken, *Sydney*, 172–6.
Critiques of this are: Philippe Ariès, who argues that the plague not an
important catalyst of change [Ariès, *Hour*, 124–7.) On epidemics, see
Charlevoix, *Histoire* 5:203]).

145 *RJ*, 1648, 37: "on fit courre vn bruit que deux cens Hurons venoient d'estre
deffaits, & que le chamaillis qu'on entendoit, prouenoit de ce combat. A ces
nouuelles le sang se glaça dans les veines, chacun baissa la teste sans mot dire
... Pendant que la tristesse déuoroit le coeur des François, & des Sauuages,
voila paroistre vn canot de Huron."

146 Charlevoix, *Histoire* 5:201.

147 Katz, *Essay*, 133–7; Arendt, "Concentration," 49–164; Fein, *Genocide*,
introduction; Mazian, *Why*, introduction.

148 Note the crossed purposes of the Hungarian Jewish leadership that was
brought to trial in Israel after the war. Dr Israel Kastner was accused of
collaboration and cronyism by other Hungarian Jews, who somehow escaped,
for attempting to save at least some lives in exchange for war materials with
Eichmann. This affair was still a bone of contention fifty-five years later
(Weitz, *Kastner;* Braham, "Councils, "in Furet, *Unanswered*, 252–74).

149 Some joined the religious faction. Some managed to revolt. For example, the
revolt of the Warsaw ghetto was commandeered by a handful of men, women,
and children who held off the Nazi stormtroopers for five days. The Bialystok
ghetto did not fare so well (Arad, Gutman, and Margaliot, *Documents*,
296–322, docs. 137–52; Gutman, *Encyclopaedia:* Warsaw Ghetto Uprising;
Yahil, *Holocaust*, ch. 17). Some fled, joined the partisans, or even revolted
within the extermination camps themselves, like the revolt of the
Zondercommando in Treblinka and the escape from Sobibor (Hilberg,
Destruction, ch. 7; Poliakov, *Breviaire*, ch. 6; Furet, *Unanswered*, 235–51.) Some
looked gentile enough to function in Christian society or were hidden
(especially children), like the adopted Wendat in Iroquoia. In Berlin alone
18,000 Jews were hidden by Berliners opposed to the Reich (George Mosse,
Modern History lectures, winter/spring 1975, University of Madison-
Wisconsin; Oliner et al., *Embracing*, ch. 9; Yahil, *Danish*.) Even though the

great majority of European Jews died anyway (in Poland, 90 percent, Lithuania 95 percent), the bitterness of the loss of life was further aggravated by the ache of the factionalization among those trying to save the community and their families. Currently in Israel, under prolonged existential threat, the middle road is seen as useless, while the entrenchment of the far right and the far left is evident.

150 Bettelheim, *Heart*, ch. 3.

151 *RJ*, 1647–8, ch. 8.

152 The Jesuits write that the Wendat left for hunting and war, Trigger suggests that they left to trade. This attack had been anticipated for almost a year (when the Wendat traders did not descend on New France in the summer of 1647, and St-Ignace was mostly empty from the beginning of winter, due to apprehension of the potential danger (*RJ*, 1647–8, 34; Trigger, *Aataentsic*, 754). *RJ*, 1648–9, 34–5; *RJ*, 1647–8, 14.

153 For fighting and defence: *RJ*, 1648–9, 39–41. For statistics: Trudel, *XIII* 3:2, 36–8.

154 *RJ*, 1648–9, 43–4. Unfortunately, this incident is described as follows: "An old woman who escaped from Taenhatentaron carried news of the Haudenosaunee retreat to Scanonaenrat. Several hundred warriors from that town pursued the Haudenosaunee for two days, but, because they had few guns, they were careful not to confront the enemy. Finally, lacking provisions, they returned home." The text actually reads: "Vne vieille femme eschappée du milieu de cet incendie, en porta des nouuelles au bourg de Sainct Michel, ou il y auoit enuiron sept cens hommes en armes, qui courrent sus ... l'ennemy: mais n'ayans pü l'atteindre après deux iournées de chemin; partie le manquement de viures, partie la crainte de combattre sans auantage vn ennemy encouragé de ses victoires, & qui auoient pour la pluspart des armes ... feu, nos Hurons en ayans fort peu; toutes ces choses les obligerent de retourner sur leurs pas, sans auoir rien fait." In other words, why would 700 Wendat warriors pursue Haudenosaunee who were transporting their own people as war captives for two whole days, only to eventually "avoid" confrontation because they did not possess "guns" to begin with? @@@

155 The distribution of French arquebuses and muskets to the Wendat would have challenged the Haudenosaunee much less than one might imagine, except psychologically. But, concretely, these unsophisticated weapons do not constitute the shadow of a gun, nor would they have been much superior to metal-tipped arrows. The French themselves were not so advanced in military warfare. The battle of Rocroi in 1643, which the prince de Condé led against the feared Spanish pikemen (tercios), was the watershed that heralded the ascendancy of the musket over the pike (Collins, *State*, 54–65.) The Haudenosaunee possessed slightly more advanced military technology: over 500 Dutch "armes à feu," (presumably muskets) as opposed to the 120 French muskets sold to Wendat converts. Although Brian Given wrote that the

difference was marginal (*RJ*, 1648–9, 34; Trigger, *Newcomers*, 262–3: Trigger estimate of number of weapons.) But the eminent clumsiness of these arms precluded dazzling results. The arquebus was a firelock dinosaur of the sixteenth century and could only be shot by lighting a fuse (not with matches) that detonated the firing pin. And then it only fired shot, not a modern bullet. The other weapons used were probably wheellock or flintlock muskets, which required stopping to insert gunpowder with every shot; and in the flintlock muskets, the powder had to be inserted into the barrel as well as into the firing pin. An experienced musket marksman would be able to shoot two shots a minute. (Details on arquebus and musket operation kindly offered by Martin Van Creveld, discussion, winter 1995. Brian Given agrees with van Creveld's estimation [Given, *Gun*], yet his idea that the wars depended upon them is overstated.) Of course, those less experienced, would quickly be larded with arrows while fiddling with the gunpowder.

156 Jaenen, *Relationship*, 161.

157 *RJ*, 1648–9, 34.

158 Feldmarshall Alfred von Schlieffen thought that it was essential to gather a great force, penetrate in several prongs, and move quickly to surprise the enemy (Wallach, *Torot*, 107).

159 British general John Frederick Charles Fuller's strategic theory that whoever dominates the roads will ultimately win also emphasizes the importance of speed when attacking. The Haudenosaunee attack was especially deadly because villages were isolated during winter, the rivers being iced over so that canoe travel was impossible, and escape was difficult over icy cliffs (Wallach, *Torot*, 188, 195).

160 Four hundred people at St-Ignace, 80 Ataronchronon warriors (among them Annaotaha), and 300 Attignawantan warriors from Ossossan and Ste-Magdeleine. Five hundred people of St-Louis escaped from the Haudenosaunee (*RJ*, 1648–9, 34–42).

161 *RJ*, 1648–9, 37–8.

162 *JR* (Thwaites) 33, 101, 77, 257; 34, 199; Trigger, *Aataentsic*, 737. Father Ragueneau states, though, that the bulk of Jesuit food was provided by the Wendat. *JR* (Thwaites) 34, 207.

163 *JR* (Thwaites) 30, 223; 33, 69, 257; Trigger, *Aataentsic*, 739.

164 "Que nous eussions pitié de leur misere; Que sans nous ils se voyoient la proye de l'ennemy; Qu'avec nous ils s'estimoient trop forts pour se defendre auec courage: Que nous eussions compassion de leurs veuues, & des pauures enfans Chrestiens, Que tous ceux qui restoient d'Infideles estoient tous resolus d'embrasser nostre Foy, & que nous ferions de cette Issle, vne Isle de Chrestiens" (*RJ*, 1648–9, 95). Saying this, the Jesuits were presented with ten large wampum collars, which they said were the voices of their women and children. They were presented to Ragueneau to help Echon (Brébeuf) be reborn in him. They were clearly hoping that Ragueneau would henceforth

act with Echon's courage, and were shaming him for having heard their children's cries without responding.

165 *RJ*, 1648, ch. 9 for a description of life at Sillery (pre-Fall). Some joined the Wendat who chose to live about the French habitations at Ville-Marie, Trois-Rivières, and Quebec. "Some Wendat, of those who stayed in our habitations due to fear of their enemies, who like elfs, infest the woods and rivers" ("Quelques Hurons, de ceux qui restent en nos habitations pour la crainte de leurs ennemis, qui comme des lutins infestent les bois & les riuieres." [*RJ*, 1648, 34.])

166 Halbwachs, *Memory*, passim; Levi, *Drowned*, ch. 2; Maurice Barrès, *Les déracinés* (1898) provides an account of the stigma that the uprooted can receive; Shapira, "Debate," 9–40; Zerubavel, *Roots*, introduction.

167 *RJ*, 1647 and 1648, ch. I-IV, 5–23 (part 2: Relation du pays des Hurons).

168 *RJ*, 1647–8, 10–11: "this country has never been so afflicted as we see it today ... Last summer passed almost entirely in waiting and alarms of an enemy army of Haudenosaunee our neighbors, which caused the Hurons not to descend to Quebec, having stayed to defend their menaced country, and afraid that another army of Haudenosaunee Mohawks might wait for them in the passage ... Thus we did not receive any rescue effort and not even a letter from Quebec or even from France." ("iamais ce pays n'a est, plus auant dans l'affliction, que nous l'y voyons maintenant ... L'Esté dernier se passa quasi entier dans les attentes & les alarmes d'vne armée ennemie des Haudenosaunee nos voisins, qui fut la cause que les Hurons ne descendirent point à Quebec, estans demeurez pour defendre leur pays menacé; & craignans aussi d'autre part vne autre armée des Haudenosaunee Annieronnons [Mohawks], qui les attendoient au passage ... Ainsi nous ne receusmes l'an passé aucun secours, & non pas mesme aucune lettre de Quebec, ny de France" [See *RJ*, 1648–9, especially ch. 1–5. Chapter 6 deals with the Wendat diaspora and ways to help them].) They dispersed in the neighbouring forests, lakes, rivers, and islands to neighbouring nations in about two weeks. The Ste-Marie Jesuits decided to go to Ekaentoton (Ste-Marie Island) with their converts, where there was already an Algonquian mission (*RJ*, 1648–9, 92).

169 *RJ*, 1652–3, 150–1.

170 ANC, MGI, C11A, VII, fol. 260–261v:6/2/1685, Mémoire de la Companie du Nord.

171 La Potherie, *Histoire* 2:87–9.

172 Trudel, *XIII* 3:2, 71–5; Moogk, "Exiles," 463–505; Campeau, *Peuplement*, 152: Father Campeau writes that almost 70 percent of the unmarried males in Canada returned to France.

173 During the 1640s, the French wished to respond to Haudenosaunee peace initiatives but refused to cut a separate peace deal that would exclude their allies. In 1641 interpreters François Marguerie and Thomas Godefroy were

captured while hunting, and, being interpreters, they were used as bait to
attack Three Rivers, yet Marguerie warned Governor Champflour and
returned into captivity in order to save the town. Father Ragueneau and Jean
Nicollet were then sent to negotiate and the interpreters were released, which
probably preceded the Mohawk delegation to negotiate a separate peace with
Governor Montmagny, who again refused to abandon Algonquian and
Wendat allies. The Haudenosaunee were committed to a peace, and
proclaimed about Godefroy and Marguerie "[ils] ... sont Haudenosaunee, ils
ne sont plus François ... nous ayons appris a changer les François en
Haudenosaunee ... [ils] sont encor Haudenosaunee, mais tout maintenent ils
seront François; disons plus tost qu'ils seront François et Haudenosaunee tout
ensemble, car nous ne seront plus qu'un peuple." *RJ* (Thwaites), 42, 48–52;
43, 180; 44, 62; Charlevoix, *Histoire* 5:225; VI: the agreement involved
François Marguerie, Champflours, Jean Nicollet, and Father Paul Ragueneau,
262–24: the agreement involved Chief Pieskaret, Chief Negabamat, and
Guillaume Cousture.) Quote: *RJ* (Jour), 1641, 42, cited by Beaulieu, *Peuple,*
introduction.

174 *RJ,* 1644–5; *RJ,* 1645–6; Marie, *Correspondance,* 250–61, 279–81:14–
27/9/1645, let. XCII; 29/8–10/9/1645, let. XCVII. Unprecedented hostilities
in Three Rivers and Montreal finally decided the fate of the 1645 agreement.

175 Dickinson, "Mortalité," 48–54; Brandao, *Fyre,* 287, Appendix F: table F.2:
"French Population Losses to the Haudenosaunee to 1701." Peter Cook
mentioned to me that Brandao probably attributed the numerical difference
to Dickinson's use of parish registers, which seems true.

176 Dickinson, "Mortalité," annexe: 58; Trudel, *XIII* 3:2, 85; Eccles, *Frontier,* 56
writes of 68. In total, 221 dead or presumed dead, 1633–66 (Dickinson,
"Haudenosaunee," appendix; or 159, 1632–62; Trudel, *XIII* 2:2, 84–5)
Haudenosaunee casualties 47.3 percent of 336 deaths (cause known),
excluding infant mortality, out of 604 total deaths, and 143 captivities.
Hennepin, *New* 2:102: fright of torture. ANC, MG 18, H35: Constitution d'une
Communauté, par les habitants de Cap-Rouge pour se protéger des
Haudenosaunee, 19/4/1654. Absolute numbers Brandao, statistics mine
(Brandao, *Fyre,* 287, Appendix F: table F.2: "French Population Losses to the
Haudenosaunee to 1701").

177 Brandao, *Fyre,* 287, Appendix F, table F.2: "French Population Losses to the
Haudenosaunee."

178 Blum, *Nobles,* 64; Blum, *Nu-Pieds,* 64–5. Even after September 11, 2001, fear
far outpaces actual numbers: more than 40 percent of the US population
experienced substantial symptoms of stress after the attacks upon the World
Trade Center towers and the Pentagon. Acute posttraumatic stress disorder
and depression were twice that rate in lower Manhattan five to eight weeks
after the attacks. Television viewing of these attacks were deemed to be
especially harmful to children (Lee, Mohan, and Janca, "Terrorism," 633–7).

179 Morin, *Véritable,* 52–3, 67.
180 Marie, *Correspondance,* 608–18, 25/9/1659–9–10/1659, lets.
CLXXX-CLXXXIII; Juchereau et Duplessis, *Annales,* 91–2; *JJ,* 1660, 282.
181 Dollier, *Montréal,* 80–6.
182 Written in their Acte de décès 3/6/1660, Malchelosse, *Dollard,* 70–1;
Garneau, *Histoire* 1:39; Faillon, *Histoire* 2: 397–40.
183 *RJ,* 1660, ch. 3; Casgrain, *L'Incarnation,* 56; Ferland, *Histoire* 1:455; *BRH,* 1898,
4, 146–7.
184 This account was related to Father Chaumonot and written by Marie de
l'Incarnation to her son, Vachon (Marie, *Correspondence,* 619–30:25/6/1660,
CLXXXIV, *DBC,* 275). Dickinson, "Mortalité," 48–53; Rousseau, "Dollard,"
370–7; Gélinas, "Ville-Marie," 125.
185 Ferland, *Cours* 1:455–62; Faillon, *Histoire* 2:395–420; Groulx, "Dollard."
186 Adair, "Dollard," 121–38.
187 Trigger, *Newcomers,* 281–3.
188 Dollier, *Montreal,* 50.
189 Vachon, *DBC,* 278–9.
190 Massicotte, *Dollard,* 66–9: Donation faits par Jean Valets, 18/4/1660;
Testament faite par Jean Tavernier, 17/4/1660.
191 Marie, *Correspondance* 2:158.
192 Dollier, *Montréal,* 82–3; Vachon, *DBC,* 274; Trudel, *Catalogue,* 388. Marie de
L'Incarnation recorded that Eustache Tsaouonhohoui reported that Dollard
fired the first shot due to distrust in Wendat diplomacy ([Marie Richaudeau],
Lettres 2:158.)
193 Dickinson, "Annaotaha," 178.
194 Jennings, *Ambiguous,* 89–90. Gélinas, "Ville-Marie," 125.
195 Vachon, *DBC,* 266–275; Chevalier, "Warrior," conclusion; Jaenen, *Upper,* 128.
Recently, the Holiday of Dollard has been replaced with the Holiday of the
Patriotes, clearly indicating a shift in historic focus from hostility towards the
Haudenosaunee to hostility towards the British.

CHAPTER THREE

1 Marie, *Correspondance,* 760, 29/10/1665, let. CCXX; Jaenen, *Friend,*
introduction; *Upper,* 7; White, *Middle,* introduction; Grabowski, *Common,*
introduction; Blum, *Nu-Pieds,* introduction.
2 Eccles, *Frontier,* 78–9; Nash, *Red,* 108; White, *Middle,* xv.
3 Trudel, *HNF* 3:1, 400–1. Of the approximately 40,000 French that arrived in
North America only 9,000 stayed (Fournier, "Canada," 109). The enclosure
movement and the jousting of feudal tenants off lands between 1620 and
1642 caused 80,000 British to emigrate, which was then 2 percent of the
population (Bridenbaugh, *Vexed,* 355). Bailyn documents about 21,000
emigrants to New England between 1630 and 1642, and approximately

120,000 emigrants to Ireland during the same period, which demonstrates the enormous exodus of people from England and Scotland during this time. There were apparently 378,000 emigrants from England to the Western hemisphere during the seventeenth century, with 155,000 to the mainland colonies (Bailyn, *Peopling,* 25–6, 61; Trudel, *HNF* 4:7). Of the approximately 40,000 French that arrived in North America, only about 9,000 stayed between 1600 and 1760 (Fournier, "Canada," 109).

4 Archives de Nancy, 3:, 215 et seq. Ordinance 1607 forbid pigs in home cited by Gibson, *Women,* 5

5 Ariès, *Hour,* 176; Burguière, *Family,* 16.

6 Brébeuf, *Relation,* 182.

7 Champlain and Sagard estimated 20,000 for pre-epidemic Wendake. Conrad Heidenreich and Bruce Trigger quote this figure, but later Trigger quotes 18,000 in *The Huron: Farmers of the North* (1969). William Eccles estimates a loss of 15,000 Wendat during the 1630s (Eccles, *Frontier,* 52). Francis Jennings quotes 30,000 and estimated the loss of 9,000 to 10,000 people in ten years (1630–40) or 20,000 people in ten years. John Dickinson and James Axtell give 25,000 to 30,000. Trigger, "Destruction," passim; Trigger, *Farmers,* passim; Jennings, *Ambiguous,* 88; Dickinson, "Huron," 173–80; Axtell, *Invasion,* 341.

8 Nevertheless, Native life had its risks: the use of tobacco, a diet high in animal fats for the Algonquians could have produced high LDL cholesterol levels, and the carcinogenic effects of aspergillus flavus mould, which secretes aflatoxin from all the corn eaten (especially by Iroquoian peoples), could have led to elevated cancer levels. Syphilis and gonorrhoea are under discussion as having originated in the Americas, and tuberculosis at least was a South American disease according to a recent archeological find in Chiribaya, Peru (*Time* magazine, #13, 28/3/1994, 59; Thornton, *Survival,* 60–90; Dobyns, *Thinned,* passim.) Among Iroquoians, eating corn soup twice a day may have instigated some insulin resistance since long periods without food induce a low blood sugar, followed by much corn, which has a high glycemic index, would starve, then flood the body with sugars. Over long periods, has this contributed to the high level of diabetes in Aboriginals that we see today? Among Algonquians, this would be reversed, but due to much subsequent mixing for those in the northeast, did rollercoaster blood sugar levels affect susceptibility to diabetes? Or have many unhealthy environmental conditions, along with poverty and social marginality, exacerbated this too? Despite this later health profile, at the time vigourous exercise and a no-salt regimen probably abetted many cardiological ills. On alcohol: ANC, C11A, 10, 123–124: Denonville au ministre (10/8/1688). Vachon, "L'eau," 266–75.

9 Eleonor Leacock and Carol Devens have documented the Jesuit effort to fit Native life into the patriarchal church mould, which certainly disrupted familial and community constellations that were egalitarian rather than hierarchical.

10 Hennepin, *New*, 475–7. Even after captives were taken in war, the Haudeno-saunee adopted many of them, especially women and children (*JR* [Thwaites], 43, 265: even by 1657 there were more foreigners than Haudenosaunee among them, according to the Jesuits; 51, 123: two-thirds of the Oneida adopted Wendat and Algonquians; 43, 265. By the 1660s, only a third of the Haudenosaunee were born Haudenosaunee. Quoted in Viau, *Enfants*, 63; Gélinas, "Attaques," 125. Adoption was so common that French Canadian folklore also had stories about it, such as Bergeron, *Barbes-Bleues*, 167–86: a young woman at the Rocher-Percé was saved by an adopted Native man.

11 Jaenen, *Church*, 25.

12 Hallowell, "Culture," in Kroeber, *Anthropology*, 599.

13 Choquette, "Compagnonage," 1995 (Cornelius Jaenen kindly allowed me to peruse this article).

14 Axtell, *Invasion*, 53–60.

15 Boyce, *Symphonic;* Keating and Hertzman, *Developmental.*

16 Bowlby, *Attachment;* Mahrer, *Attachment.*

17 Crowne and Marlowe, *Approval,* part 2, especially on conformity, group pressure, and suggestibility; Burkitt, Selves, discusses the internalization of social controls; Elias, *Civilizing,* writes of this internalization of social controls as it has affected mentalités; and Biddle, *Role.*

18 *RJ* (Thwaites), 9, 104; *RJ* (Thwaites), 14, 60–162

19 Deslandres, "Femmes," 280.

20 Marie, *Correspondance,* 718:20/10/1663, let. CCIX.

21 Aries, *Centuries,* 365–6; Bridenthal, *Visible,* 206; Noël, "Femmes," 126.

22 Weisner, *Women,* 52.

23 Burgière, *Family,* 14.

24 Weisner, *Women,* 73.

25 Gibson, *Women,* 70–1.

26 LaRochefoucauld, *Maximes,* 403; Bayle, *Dictionnaire,* art. Andromaque; LaFontaine, *Fables,* 9, nos. 2, 5; 11, n. 2; LaBruyère, *Caractères:* De L'homme, cited by Gibson, *Women,* 12–13.

27 Burguière, *Family,* 15, 21; Flandrin, *Amours,* 40–7; Levitt and Schmitt, *Jeunes,* 367.

28 Furet et Ozouf, *Literacy,* 278–89, 302; Axtell, *Invasion,* introduction.

29 *JR* (Thwaites), 14, 37; Boucher, *Histoire,* 96; Jaenen, *Friend,* 95; Lemieux, *Innocents,* 170–7.

30 LeClercq, *Gaspésie,* 33, 45.

31 Marie, *Correspondance,* 809, 852; LeClercq, *Gaspésie,* 180–4; *JR* (Thwaites), 5, 137; 9, 103; Whitehead, *Micmac,* 62–3; *RJ,* (Thwaites), 44, 264.

32 Szasz, *American,* 311–42.

33 Sagard, *Histoire,* 320, 333.

34 Campeau, *MNF* 2:459, doc. 127: *RJ,* 1633; also cited by Lemieux, *Innocents,* 136.

35 Lahontan, *Mémoires,* 106–7.

36 Charlevoix, *Voyage,* 31.

37 Washburn, *Indian,* 13–14.

38 The kibbutz was also geared for communal support of children. (Sagi et al., *Kibbutz-Reared.*)

39 Perrot, *Voyages,* 32.

40 Jaenen, *Relationship,* 38–41. The Haudenosaunee were particularly adamant that the French regard them as brothers rather than as trustees, a principle that the French subsequently upheld against British claims. See O'Callaghan, *DHNY* 1–2: Magistrates speeches, 28/8/1689, 26/2/1690 in Jennings, *Ambiguous,* 193–4.

41 There seems to be a difference of opinion on this point. Richter, *Ordeal,* 111: "In Indian diplomacy, when enemies made a truce they often exchanged visitors who would lie in each other's villages as face to face reminders of friendship and as an insurance against renewed hostilities." Bruce Trigger, in *Newcomers,* was uncertain as to whether this practice was pre-contact or not, whereas in his earlier *Children of Aataentsic* he referred to the exchange as a Native custom between trading partners.

42 Champlain, *Oeuvres,* 220–22; Lescarbot, Histoire 4: ch. 5; Sagard, *Histoire,* 330–2; Campeau, *MNF* 2:427, doc. 127: *RJ,* 1633; *JR* (Thwaites), 7, 264, 284, 296; *JR* (Thwaites), 7, 284–6; *JR* (Thwaites), 9, 104, 200; *JR* (Thwaites), 7, 9, 30, 34–5, 37; *JR* (Thwaites), 65; *JR* (Thwaites), 11, 90–1, 92–100; *JJ* (Thwaites), 14, 60–2, 256–258; *JR* (Thwaites), 16, 140; *JR* (Thwaites), 10; *JR* (Thwaites), 43, 250; *JR* (Thwaites), 43, 250; *JR* (Thwaites), 47, 220–240. Marie Rollet founded the first mixed school, with her adopted Native and settlement children, and sold her fief for Native evangelization See Couillard- Desprès, *Hébert,* ch. 13, 129; *Colon,* 122–4; Gourdeau, *Délices,* 1994, 53–5; Stanley, "Francisation," 333–48. Of the nations specified, the most numerous were twelve Haudenosaunee, four Wendat, one Haudenosaunee, and over a hundred who were unspecified. One can conjecture that those unspecified were probably Haudenosaunee and other Algonquians. Haudenosaunee and Wendat were usually identified: the Haudenosaunee were enemies until 1701, while the Wendat had a unique status – and a different language. Therefore, most of the familial adoptions during the early days were Haudenosaunee as they were the best Native customers of the Hospital (Hôtel-Dieu), and their community was generally in greater economic distress than the others.

43 Manuscrits 1:235–6: 22/4/1675, Louis XIV ... gouverneur Frontenac. (trans. Jaenen, from Bennett and Jaenen, *Emerging,* 9).

44 Jaenen, "Education," 57–71; *Church,* 25–8; Stanley, "Francisation," 333–48; Gourdeau, *Délices,* 85–99, which points out many ways in which the Ursulines adjusted in order to please their Amerindian pupils. The sending to France of Amerindian children was discouraged by Hundred-Associates Intendant Jean de Lauson in 1634, who often supported Jesuit policy.

45 The Jesuits were not averse to applying physical punishment to their pupils (Magnussen, *Education,* 15). Deslandres, *Intégration;* Gourdeau, *Délices,* 85–89.
46 Lahontan, *Mémoires,* 170.
47 Jetten, *Enclaves,* introduction.
48 Lemieux, *Innocents.*
49 *RJ,* 1648, 10.
50 Moogk, "Sauvages," 36.
51 Magnussen, *Education,* 188–9.
52 Silvy, *Relation,* 4; cited in Moogk, "Sauvages," 17.
53 Lemieux, *Innocence,* 162.
54 Rapson, *American;* Moogk, "Sauvages," 43. Of 40,000 French that arrived in North America, only about 9,000 stayed from 1600 to 1760 (Fournier, "Canada,"
55 All calculations based upon absolute numbers of Trudel, *HNF* 3:2, 36–7. Trudel has the best biographies to accompany his work, and the statistics here are intended to aid in reconstructing the representative, not to revolutionize New France statistics. Male youth were 81.9 percent of all nubiles: young women 521, young men 2,356 (absolute numbers; 60.5 of men were between fifteen and twenty-nine years (1041 out of a total 1720 whose age is known); and 75.8 percent male (2,356 of 3,106 total known immigrants.)
56 Trudel, *HNF* 3:37, 42–4. Trudel mentions that perhaps there were some filles du roy who arrived also in 1654, but Yves Landry does not mention them (Landry, *Filles*).
57 What Jonathan Pearl calls an "abnormal" society. Pearl, "Witchcraft," 204. Ariès, *Centuries,* passim, which has been challenged by other thinkers, notably Laslett, *World,* introduction; Elias, *Civilizing.* Schindler, "Désordres," in Levi and Schmitt, *Jeunes,* 285, 294; Erickson, *Challenge,* passim; Musgrove, *Youth,* 125–149.
58 Eisenstadt, *Generation,* 171–4; Aftenback and Laufer, *Pilgrims,* introduction on Mannheim.
59 Elias, *Civilizing,* introduction.
60 Davis, *France,* ch. 4, 182–4; Estèbe and Davis, "Riot," 127–35; Desan, "Crowds," in Hunt, *Cultural,* 62–3; Muchembled, *Culture,* 202–7.
61 Furet and Ozouf, *Reading,* 304.
62 Trudel, *HNF* 2:2, 8–10. Bercé, *Revolts,* 309.
63 Hallowell, "Rêves," in Caillois et Grunebaum, *Rêve,* 257–76.
64 Washburn, *Indian;* Hallowell, "Psychological," in Johnson, *Man;* Wallace, "Dreams."
65 Bailyn, *Voyagers,* 324.
66 Virginia and Maryland had high rates of indentured servants, especially in the 1650s, until their work was replaced by slaves. New England colonization was mostly a family affair. See Bailyn, *Peopling,* 15, 100–1, 155–6; Smith, "Indentured," 467–72.

67 Moogk, "Sauvages," 26–7.

68 Trudel, *HNF* 2:486.

69 Reported by Trudel, *HNF* 2 281–2.

70 Campeau, *MNF* 2. See biography of Brûlé, 442.

71 Cranston, *Brûlé;* Lanctôt, *Histoire,* 110–13; Trigger, *Aataentsic,* 473–5. Bruce
   Trigger writes that "Coureurs de bois [and] ... agents did not criticize or
   openly challenge the [Natives'] way of doing things ... On the contrary,
   traders such as Bruslé were happy to adopt many outward trappings of Huron
   behavior" (844). What could be considered "inward" or "outward trappings"
   of behaviour, and how can we judge which "trapping" would be "insincere"?

72 Champlain, *Oeuvres,* 440–71, 855; Bishop, *Champlain,* 169–78; Trudel, *HNF*
   2:199–201; Trigger, *Newcomers,* 179.

73 Wallace, *Culture,* 156.

74 During youth there exists a moratorium on adult family and communal
   responsibilites experienced in a peer group setting, which, in the French
   North American Case, was fulfilled through canoing and staying in fur
   country. See Brake, *Youth,* 165–7.

75 Erikson, *Youth,* 11–13.

76 See the litany of ills recited by intendants and governor generals: ANC, MGI,
   C11A, III, 100: lettre de Talon, 1670; ANC, MGI, C11A, IV, 149: lettre de
   31/8/1673; ANC, MGI, C11A, IV, 95: lettre 5/12/1674; ANC, MGI, C11A, IV,
   182: lettre 12/5/1678; ANC, MGI, C11A, IV, 203: lettre 17/9/1678; ANC, MGI,
   C11A, V, 92: lettre 24/4/1679; ANC, MGI, C11A, V, 52–3: Duchesneau au
   ministre, 10/11/1679; ANC, MGI, C11A, V, 331:2/5/1681; ANC, MGI, C11A,
   VI, 173:10/1682; ANC, MGI, C11A, VII, 42–3: Denonville au ministre,
   13/11/1685; ANC, F3 6, 244: Arrêt du Conseil, règlement 29/1/1686; ANC,
   MGI, C11A, VIII, 22: lettre de Denonville, 10/1686; ANC, MGI, C11A, 155:
   lettre de Denonville, 1/1690; ANC, MGI, C11A, XI, 468: Mémoire instructif sur
   le Canada joint ... la lettre de M. de Champigny, intendant, 10/5/1691. See
   Jacquin, *Sauvages,* 276; Cross, *Society,* 33; Paquet and Wallot, "Identities," in
   Canny and Pagden, *Identity,* 95–114; Perrault, *Métissage.*

77 *BRH,* 1926, 32, 187–91:7/12/1653: Ordonnance de Pierre Boucher qui fait
   défense aux soldats, habitants, etc, traiter avec les sauvages (APQ); 26/7/1653: Au
   sujet de ceux qui font la traite sans y avoir droit; 31/7/1654: Au sujet de la traite
   ... *EO* 1:73–4: Ordonnance du Roi au sujet des Vagabonds et Coureurs de bois,
   5/6/1673; Ordonnance du Roy qui défend d'aller à la traite des Pelleteries dans
   les habitations des Sauvages, 15/4/1676, *EO* 86; Ordonnance du Roi qui défend
   d'aller à la chasse hors étendue des terres défrichées et une lieue à la ronde,
   12/5/1678; *EO* 105–96 modified later "si ce n'est qu'avec la permission du
   gouverneur et qu'entre le 15 janvier et le 15 avril de chaque année," 25/4/1679,
   EO, 230–1; Édit du Roi qui défend d'aller à la traite des pelleteries dans la
   profondeur des bois et les habitations des sauvages du mois de mai, 1681, *EO,*
   248–9; Harris, "Land," in Cross and Kealey, *Society,* 33. ANQQ, CPJN (TL5), no. 97,

2e liasse, 1 pièce, 8/9/1671–10/9/1672: Interrogatoire fait à la Prévot, de Québec de trois personnes accusées d'avoir fait la traite dans congé (Pierre Leclerc dit du Tartre, Antoine Bazinet dit la Tour Blansche, Eustache Prévost); ANQQ, Gouverneurs (R1), Frontenac, 2e, ANQQ, Insinuations du Conseil supérieur (TP1, S36) dans *OC* 1:111–13, 27/9/1672: Ordonnance de Frontenac; ANQQ, fonds Gouverneurs (R1), Frontenac; OC 1: 168, 4/8/1674: Ordonnance de Frontenac.; ANQM, Jur. de Montréal, (ZA26/4), OC, pièce no. 204, 15/4/1676: Ordonnance d'Ailleboust; ANQQ, Fond Gouverneur, Régime français (R1), Frontenac, 16/4/1676, Ordonnance du roi (portant défense aux habitants de la Nouvelle France d'aller à la traite des pelleteries dans les habitations des Sauvages et dans la profondeur des bois chez les nations les plus éloignées et au gouverneur et autres officiers de délivrer permis à cet égard); *APJM*, 16–20; ANQQ, J&D (TP1, S28), Chronica 1, 11/5/1676, 11/5/1676: Règlements de police du Conseil supérieur; EO 2; PGR 1; *EO* 2 (Règlements 29–30, 38, 40 all interdict illicit trade). ANQQ, *J&D* (*TP*1, S28), Chronica 1, 2/5/1681, Québec: Arrêt du Conseil souverain condamnant Jean-Baptiste Godefroy all in Delâge, *Histoire*, 82–8, nos. 47–72.

78 Regulations violated: *J&D*, 2/11/1678, 2:260–1.

79 Diamond, *Experiment*, 10; Perrault, *Métissage*, 214.

80 ANC, MGI, C11A, VI, 470: lettre de De Meulles, 12/11/1682 speaks of 130 canoes. Also see Perrault, *Métissage*, 203; Jacquin, *Sauvages*, 74. ANC, MG1, C11A, V, 60: Mémo sur les coureurs de bois, 13/11/1681, Duchesneau au ministre; La Potherie, *Histoire* 2:142 (800 to 1,200 livres); Jacquin, *Sauvages*, 174 (700–1,800 livres); Perrault, *Métissage*, 203 (1,000 francs).

81 ANC, MGI C11A, VI, 479: lettre de nov. 1684; ANC, MGI, C11A, XIX, 24: lettre de Callières, 31/10/1701; Charlevoix, *Histoire* 3:499; Margry, *Découvertes* 5:140, 359; ANC, MGI, C11A, XCI: l4/10/1748, lettre; ANC, MGI, C11A, IV, 70–1: lettre de octobre 1674; ANC, MGI, C11A, IV, 71: 10/1674, lettre de Frontenac; ANC, C11A, V, 8: Frontenac, 10/1679; ANC, MGI, C11A, XV, 297: 10/11/1681, lettre de Duchesneau; Jacquin, *Sauvages, 276*.

82 La Potherie, *Histoire* 2:143.

83 Jacquin, *Sauvages*, 169–172.

84 Dechêne, *Habitants*, 220–2.

85 ANC, MGI, C11A, XIII, 432:4/11/1695, Champigny au ministre.

86 ANC, MGI, C11A, 210:4/11/1683, De Meulles au ministre.

87 "Les Sauvages domiciliés portent aussy la plus grande partie de leur castor ... Orange ... qu'ils apportent ensuite ... Montreal ou ils les traittent avec les Sauvages des nations d'en haut qui y decendent ordinairement tous les ans et même avec les marchands. Ils y vont aussy attendre les Sauvages des nations d' en haut aux passages afin de leur traitter leurs Pelletries, ce commerce est prejudiciable au Royaume, mais il n'est pas possible de l'empescher par la force, il seroit même dangereux" (Mémoire de Vaudreuil et Bégon au ministre, 12/11/1712, 36–7; cited Perreault, *Métissage*, 219–20).

88 27/9/1672, Ordonnance; ANQQ, fonds Gouverneurs (R1), Frontenac, 20?11?1674: Ordonnance de Frontenac; ANQQ, CPJN, no. 221.3, pièces, 24–29/10/1692: Interrogatoires de Gilles Boissel et de Marguerite Boissel, sa soeur in Delâge, *Histoire*, 83, no. 49.

89 ANQQ, *J&D* (TP1, S28), Chronica 1, 5/10/1676: Règlement du Conseil souverain concernant l 'interdiction de traiter avec les Sauvages étrangers ailleurs que Québec, Montréal, et Three Rivers; ANQQ, *J&D* (TP 1, S28), Chronica 1, 21/1/1686: Notification des règlements de police 29 et 30 du 11/5/1676 et de l'arrêt du 26/6/1669 aux Hurons de Lorette et Abénaquis de Sillery.; *EO* 2:111–12, in Delâge, *Histoire*, 85–9, nos. 58, 82, 41.

90 Trudel, *HNF* 2:134.

91 ANC, C11A, V, fol. 298, 13/11/1681, Duchesneau au ministre; Diamond, *Experiment*, 21.

92 "ces Volontaires sont gens Vagabons qui ne se marient pas, qui ne travaillent jamais au défrichement des terres ... et qui commettent une infinité de désordres par leur vie licencieuse et libertine. Ces hommes vivans tousjours ... la manière des Sauvages s'en vont cinq ou six cens lieües au dessus de Quebec pour troquer des paux que ces barbares apporteroient eux-mesmes dans nos habitations."

93 Malchelosse, "Coureurs," 129–30 quotes Duchesneau au ministre in 1680 writing of 800 men. Lejeune, Dictionnaire 1, 443, citation: coureurs de bois. ANC, MGI, C11A, III: Mémoire de Patoulet, 1672, 274. Also 379–80; ANC, MGI, C11A, V, 42:10/11/1679, lettre de Duchesneau; ANC, MGI, C11A, V, 320: 1680 lettre de Duchesneau; ANC, C11A, VI, 470: 10/1684, lettre de de Meulles; ANC, MGI, C11A, VII, 58:20/8/1685, lettre de Denonville; ANC, MGI, C11A, XIII, 432:4/11/1695, lettre de Champigny. Stanley Diamond estimates that the coureurs de bois and hunters depleted Nouvelle-France annually of 33 percent–20 percent of the able-bodied males. Diamond, Experiment, 30; DRHNF 2:323; 25/5/1699, Instructions du roy au gouverneur Louis Hector de Callières; ANC, C11A, V, fol. 209:2/6/1680, Louis XIV ... . Intendant Duchesneau cited in Frégault, *Civilisation*, 91–5. Dechênes, *Habitants*, 218–22.

94 Massicotte, "Engagements, 191–466. Filteau, *Naissance* 2:192–3; Eccles, *Frontenac*, 16.

95 Eccles, "Montcalm, Louis-Joseph de Marquis de Montcalm," in *DBC* 3:458–69, "Rigaud de Vaudreuil de Cavagnial, Pierre de, Marquis de Vaudreuil," *DBC* 4:662–74; Nicolai, "Soldier," 53–75.

96 Perrot, *Histoire*, 131; Giraud, *Métis*, 807–9, 1063–9, especially see Philippe Jacquin's thesis regarding the coureurs de bois in *Sauvages*, especially 134.

97 "Ces déreglemens ... se trouvent bien plus grands dans les familles de ceux qui sont Gentilhommes, ou qui se sont mis sur le pied de le vouloir estre par faineantise ou par vanite n'ayans aucune resource pour subsister q'les bois, car n'estans pas acoutumez a tenir la charrue, la pioche et la hache, toute leur resource n'estant que le fuzil, il faut qu'ils passent leurs vies dans les bois ...

L'on a creu bien longtemps que l'aproche des sauvages de nos habitations estoit un bien tres considerable pour acoutumer ces peuples a vivre comme nous et a s'instruire de notre relligion, je m'aperçoy ... que tout le contraire en est arrivé car au lieu de les acoutumer a nos Loÿs, je vous assure qu'ils nous communiquent fort tout ce qu'ils ont de plus mechant, et ne prennent eux mesmes qu'ce qu'il y a de mauvais et de vitieux en Nous ... a l'egard des autres sauvages qui sont vagabonds et errans autour des Seigneuries particuliers sans estre rassemblez en bourgades comme les autres, vous ne scauriez croire Monseigneur le tort que cela fait ... la dissipline de la colonie, car non seulement les enfants des Seigneurs s'acoutument ... vivre en libertinage comme eux, mais mesme abusent des filles et femmes sauvagesses, qu'ils entretienent avec eux, et menent a leurs chasses dans les bois, ou souvent ils souffrent la faim jusques ... manger leurs chiens" (ANC, MGI, C11A, VII, 13/11/1685: Denonville au ministre).

98 ANC, MGI, C11A, VII, 45–56:13/11/1685, Denonville au ministre. Ttrans. Jaenen, *Emerging*, 12.

99 "plusieurs des gentilhommes et officiers ... et des seigneurs des terres, comme ils s'accoutumera a ce qu'on appelle en France la vie des gentilhommes de campagne qu'ils ont pratiqu, eux-mesmes ou qu'ils ont veue pratiquer font leur plus grande occupation de la chasse et de la pesche et parce que pour leurs vivres et pour leurs habillemens et celuy de leurs femmes et de leurs enfans ... se passer de si peu de chose que les simple habitans & qu'ils ne s'appliquera pas entieremens au mesnage & a faire valloir leurs terres, ils se meslens du commerce, s'endebtens de tous costés, excitans leurs jeunes habitans de courir les bois, & envoyens leurs enfans afin de traiter des pelleteries dans les habitations [des] sauuages & dans la profondeur des bois" (ANC, MGI, C11A, V, fol. 50v–51:10/11/1679, Intendant Duchesneau au ministre).

CHAPTER FOUR

1 Dewald, *Nobility*, 18, 23, 27, 21; Isambert, *Recueil*, 226–38: Edit portant règlement général sur les tailles, sur les usurpations du titre de noblesse ... mars 1600; Ladurie, *Royal*, 297.

2 Dewald, *Nobility*, 32, 73, 199–200. The Brenner Debate suggests that individual refusal to cooperate with the royal authorities was more significant than the revolts themselves. Yet, in northern France, nobles had tax exemptions.

3 Giffard, *Droit*, 214–16.

4 Knachel, *England*, 57–60, 82, 90.

5 Davis, *Archives*, 60.

6 Cohen, "Americanizing," 177–91; Grinde, *Iroquois;* Johansen, *Forgotten;* "Democracy," 277–97; Tooker, "Iroquois," 291–7; Grinde and Johansen,

Exemplar; Delâge, "L'influence," 163–70: Denys Delâge negates the idea of a direct influence on the American Constitution and rightly notes pertinent differences between the two, such as majority rule over consensus, democracy of male citizens rather than democracy founded upon matriarchal descent, concentration of military power rather than its dispersion between clans, and the three-branch system of executive, legislative, and judiciary powers rather than one consultative council where power of decision still lay in the hands of each tribe and village. For more, see: Rony Blum, ed., *First Nations and European Sources of Western Democracy,* 2 v. (Montreal: McGill Institute for the Study of Canada, McGill University, 2001). (Coursepack.)

7 Healy, "Noble," 143–67. European democratic currents such as British parliamentarianism, powerful burghers in the United Provinces, Swiss cantons, and the German free cities had a wider base constituency than those found in the France of Louis XIV.

8 Lescarbot, *Histoire,* 725–7; Perrot, *Moeurs,* 78; La Potherie, *Histoire* 2:78; Clastre, *Society;* Deleuze, *Foucault,* 35; Paine, Thomas, *Common Sense.*

9 "ils ne se conduisent que par la raison, à laquelle ils cedent facilement, & non à la passion, car la violence n'a point de credit chez eux" (Sagard, *Histoire,* 366). Reason was the French philosophes' great basis for Enlightenment thought, while common sense was at the base of Thomas Paine's influential revolutionary stance.

10 Fenton, *Law,* 50–4. Champlain remarks that good judgement was not uncommon (Champlain, *Oeuvres* 1:310).

11 "il n'y en a point qui ne soit capable d'entretien, & ne raisonne fort bien, & en bons termes" (Brébeuf, *Relation,* 137).

12 "l'esprit bon, l'imagination vive, la conception aisée, la mémoire admirable" (Lafitau, *Moeurs,* 67).

13 "ils se croient tous égaux à la vie comme à la mort, sans distinction des chefs" (LeClercq, *Gaspésie,* 43).

14 "Ils n'ont point de Chefs particuliers qui commandent absolument ... l'honneur aux plus anciens & vaillans, qu'ils nomment Capitaines" (Champlain, *Oeuvres* 2:960).

15 "Le sauvage ne sçait ce que c'est d'obéir. Le père n'oserait user d'authorité envers son fils, ny le chef de commandement sur son soldat. Si les chefs ont quelque pouvoir sur eux, ce n'est que par les libéralitez et les festins qu'ils leur font" (Perrot, *Moeurs,* 78).

16 "point voulu souffrir de subordination ... cela est general chez tous les sauvages; un chaqu'un est maître de ses actions sans que personne ose y contredire" (La Potherie, *Histoire* 2:78).

17 Nathalie Zemon Davis wrote that perhaps Haudenosaunee women searched for a more public voice through Christianity. Davis, "Women," in Hendricks and Parker, *Race,* 243–58, 350–61.

18 Deleuze, *Foucault,* 38–44.

19 Le Tac, *Histoire*, 1–30; Morin, *Véritable*, introduction, especially 1–7. SQ, Polygraphie, 3, 1, 30/8/1660: Arrêt Sulpiciens contre Msgr de Laval; Lanctôt, *Maisonneuve*, 30–1.

20 L'Incarnation, *Correspondance*, 630: let. CLXXXV, 17/9/1660; 643: let. CLXXXVIII, 13/10/1660; 652: let. CXCIII, 13/9/1661.

21 ASQ, Séminaire, 15, 2b: Laval au frère de Voyer d'Argenson (20/10/1659); ASQ, Séminaire, 15, 2e: d'Argenson à Louis XIV (21/10/1659); ASQ, 15, 3A: automne 1660: Voyer d'Argenson à son frère; ANC, MGI, C11A, II, 354:7/7/1660: Voyer d'Argenson à son frère; RJ, (Thwaites) 45, 144, 164; JJ, 1659, 263–64.

22 Campeau, "Laval," 103–23.

23 ANF, Colonies, F3 3, 311; Marie, *Correspondance*, 753; let. CCXVII, 30/8/1665.

24 ASQ, Séminaire, 15, 2a, 5/9/1658: d'Argenson à Lalemant; 15, 2b, 20/10/1659, Laval au frère; 15, 2c, 2/10/1659, Lalemant au vicomte d'Argenson; 15, 2d, 14/5/1659: Louis XIV au Voyer d'Argenson; 15, 2e, 21/10/1659: d'Argenson à Louis XIV; 15, 3, 1659: d'Argenson à MM.; 15, 3a, 12/1660: d'Argenson à son frère; 15, 3b, 4/11/1660: d'Argenson; 15, 3c, 14/3/1660: Louis XIV à d'Argenson; ASQ, Lettres, Carton N, 2, 14/5/1657: Insinuation et lettre de cachet Louis XIV à d'Argenson; Carton N, 3, 13/3/1660: Louis XIV à d'Argenson. ASQ, Lettres, Carton O, 59, 12/1681: Ordre de Frontenac pour instruire différend entre Laval et Récollets; Carton O, 60, 4/6/1683: Réponse des Récollets de Québec à Laval; ASQ, Polygraphie, 22, 35, (16/10/1679): Convention entre Frontenac et Conseil Supérieur pour le bien et la paix entre le gouverneur et l'intendant.

25 Charlevoix, *Histoire* 6:236.

26 Ibid., 235.

27 Trudel, HNF 3:2, 74–5. According to province of origin, in descending order, the following are approximative percentage of immigrants who left New France: Normandy 13.4 percent, Perche 16.9 percent left the least, followed by the middling numbers: Saintonge 18.4 percent, Poitou 19 percent, Maine 19.8 percent, Paris 21.4 percent, Aunis 22.8 percent; followed by the greatest returnees: Anjou 25 percent, Champagne 25 percent, Ile-de-France 25 percent, Limousin 25 percent, Berry 50 percent, Lyonnais 50 percent, La Marche and Franche-Comté at 50 percent.

28 RJ, 1648, 167.

29 Porter, *Mosaic*.

30 Elias and Scotson, *Outsiders*.

31 Laberge, *Rouen*.

32 LeTenneur, *Normands*, 207.

33 Inconclusive: Trudel, *Catalogue*, 17 (unlisted origin); Trudel, 1666, 114 (deceased); Fournier, *Bretons*, 55 (not listed); LeTenneur, *Normands*, 61–3, 70–1, 171–2; Vaillancourt, *Conquête*, 74 (not listed).

34 Monter, "Male," 565.

35 RJ, 1635, 4–6.

36　LeTenneur, *Normans,* 66–7.

37　ANF, Arch. du ministère des Affaires Étrangères, Paris, France: Mémoires et documents, Amérique, V, fol. 203, 204–204v. ANC, MGI, C11A, I: Articles accordés entre les Directeurs et Associés en la Compagnie de la Nouvelle France et les députés des habitants du dits pays (6/3/1645), 407–22; *JJ,* 1645, 3. ANC, MGI, C11A, I (6/3/1645), 423–6, 434–7.

38　Hamelin, *Economie,* 43–8.

39　"Communauté des Habitants" in Doucet, *Institutions.*

40　Auguste Gosselin, *BRH,* 4, 1898, 376; *BRH,* 5, 1899, 106–7; OC, I, 6–9: Ordonnance du 6/9/1645; Fillion, "Habitant," 375–401; Trudel, *HNF* 3:, 1, 175; Bertheté, *Seigneurs,* 162–3. Benjamin Sulte, *BRH,* 5, 1899, 106–7: "La lutte dans le Canada a toujours été entre les habitants et les hivernants."

41　Bilodeau, "Liberté," 53.

42　*JJ,* 15/11/1645, 13: "le bruit estant qv'on s'en alloit icy publier la defense qui auoit esté publiée aux Trois Rivieres, que pas vn n'eut ... traiter auec les sauuages, le Vimont demanda ... Mons. de Chastelets commis général si nous serions de pire condition soubs eux que soubs Messieurs de la Compagnie? La conclusion fut que non, & que cela iroit pour nous ... l'ordinaire, mais que nous le fissions doucement." Meaning that if the Jesuits traded discretely, everything would be "fine."

43　Campeau, *Finances.*

44　ANC, MGI, C11A, I, fol. 296:1/7/1656, Règlement du Conseil de Québec.

45　Traité de Montréal, 20/1/1645 cited in Trudel, *HNF* 3:1, 177.

46　ANC, MG18, H 65: Arrest du 27 mars 1647 portant Règlemens pour les habitants de la Nouvelle France (27/3/1647).

47　ANC, MGI, C11A, II, 1:196–200: 15/3/1656, Extrait des Registres du Conseil d'Etat cited by Trudel, *HNF* 3:2, 244n.

48　The habitants requested some kind of council in Quebec and wanted to elect a syndic. *JJ,* 90:29/6/1647: "les habitans furent trouuer M. le Gouuerneur pour luy demander permission d'eslire vn procureur syndic; ils furent renvoyés à l'assemblée generalle; cependant il y eut requeste presentée." ANC, MGI, C11A, I, 438–45: Arrêt portant règlement concernant les habitants du pays du Canada (27/3/1647). ASQ, Séminaire, 6, 23b, 14/2/1645: Election de Michel Le Neuf comme syndic de Three Rivers [signed by Pierre Boucher, Guillaume Habel, Estienne Vien, Gilles Trottier, Hemery Galtos, Urbain Baudry, Jehan Sauuaget, Sebastien Dodier, Jehan Houdan, Elye Simard, Antoine des Boffiers, Jehan Veron, Estienne delafois, Estienne Signeurs, tous les habitants des Three Rivers]. Durocher, "Decree," 11.

49　OC, I, 6–9, 53: Ordonnance du 6/9/1645; Ordonnance du 16/9/1645, which orders all habitants, within fifteen days, under pain of confiscation, to bring all their beaver pelts to the Three Rivers magasin; Ordonnance du 21/9/1646 orders all settlements to render their pelts under pain of confiscation; Ordonnance du 12/8/1646 forbids habitants from climbing aboard French ships without permission; Ordonnance du 25/6/1647 repeats the getting aboard ships interdiction.

50 The Jesuits thought the directors guilty of faulty bookkeeping for 1645–46 and of using community funds for their personal use. Even Montreal governor Maisonneuve refused to sign the gratifications that they requested. This, of course, was what colonial administrators and clerics did regularly, but perhaps this was resented in directors who did not have hefty titles of nobility to shield them from criticism, especially accusations made by the nobility themselves. The Jesuits, for example, although aware of the financial strain upon the Communauté, after complaining that they did not receive subsidized heating under the new system, were touchy about the wood that they did receive, complaining that it was three cords instead of four and that it was of poor quality (*JJ*, 1646) . They complained also about the twenty-two soldiers that they fed for a year in Wendake, which they claimed cost them what seems to be the exaggerated sum of 4,400 livres (200 livres per man), whereas they received 1,980 for it (90 livres per man, a reasonable sum). Perhaps this was to obtain more Jesuit funds. Many habitants certainly lived on less. In the 1590s, ten livres monthly was what a master mason received in wealthy Rouen, according to Philippe Benedict, *Rouen*, 12. Marcel Trudel writes that an engagé received an average salary of 109 livres ten sols for a master craftsman, while the commoners received on average 74 livres 18 sols 10 deniers from 1642 to 1661 (Trudel, *HNF* 3:2, 61–2). Out in the field, the mostly delicate Jesuit fathers endured many privations. Yet, once they were at their retreat, they were less willing to cut their elite standards for the good of the community. Therefore, Communauté directors were hardly immune to accusations both from their "social superiors" and from commoners, who felt left out of all this deregulation. While in France, the orders were chiefly worried about upsetting the hierarchy of things due to the dangerous throngs of "petit people"; in New France they tried to obtain privileges incrementally as individuals instead of as a class. The antipathy between Marsolet and the early pioneers goes back to almost twenty years earlier, when he joined Bruslé and Gros-Iean in siding with the Kirke brothers, an incident not easily forgotten by Louis Couillart de L'Espinay's older sisters, who at the same time were starving and fighting off Marsolet's and Bruslé's unwelcome advances towards their newly acquired Innu sisters, Lesperance and La Charité. With Champlain's anger upon his head, as well as the anger of Lesperance and La Charité, and the Hébert-Couillart family's shock at his behavior after his older friend Bruslé 's death and the Kirke's departure, Marsolet had to invest a much effort to re-establish a respectable reputation.

51 Cahall, *Council*.

52 ASQ, Polygraphie, 13, 34, 15/2/1664: Déclaration des habitants des Three Rivers qui avaient été accusés de ne pas vouloir bâtir un presbytère aux pères Jésuites.

53 Moogk, "Craftsmen," in Cross and Kealey, *Society*, 88–119. Also mentioned by Delâge, "L' influence," 161.

54 *JJ*, 25/6/1647, 90; *RJ*, 1665; Séguin, "Cheval," 227–51, 234–5, 240: the First Nations marvelled at the first "French moose," brought over in 1647, but were the most effective riders on the plains.

55 ANC, MG1, C11A, XVII, 87:26/5/1699, Champigny au ministre; OCGI, I, 2239–240:10/11/1706: OCGI, II, 273: 13/6/1709; IOIQ, I, 104: 28/6/1710; OCGI, 4, 4–5: 29/10/1710; RAPQ, 1947–1948, 176: 12/9/1712. With so many horses in the settlement (684 by 1698 to 1,872 in 1706) by the early eighteenth century, there were ideas about how to limit their number, sell them to the Antilles, and tax ownership; however, the habitants objected and the plans were dropped (Séguin, "Cheval," 222–44, 246–7.) Cross and Kealey, *Society*, 131–2.

56 Trudel, "Censitaire," 3–41.

57 Historians Francois-Xavier Garneau, Lionel Groulx, Guy Gregault, Jean-Pierre Wallot, and historical geographer Richard Harris all concur. Garneau, *Histoire*, I; Groulx, *Histoire* 1:109; Frégault, *Civilisation*, 184 ; Harris, *Seigneurial*, xiii–2; Wallot, *Québec*, 1973, 231.

58 Ouellet, "Societé." He points out that, whereas from 1670–99, 35 percent of landholders were commoners, by 1700–30, 29 percent were landholders, and by 1730–60 only 25 percent were commoners.

59 Mancall, *Deadly*, Introduction; DuCreux, *Histoire* 1:108 cited in Jaenen, *Church*, 24, 131

60 *RJ*, 1648, 167.

61 Grabowski, "Trifluviens," 105–6.

62 Stanley, "Brandy," 489–506; Vachon, "L'eau."

63 *JR* (Thwaites), 20, 241.

64 Perrault, "Métissage," 210.

65 Delâge, *Histoire*, 69: ANQQ, *J&D* (TP1, mS28), Chronica 1, 29/2/1668, 7/3/1657: Interdiction de traiter des boissons énivrantes aux sauvages.

66 Eccles, *Frontier*, 63.

67 Ibid., 65.

68 LeClercq, *Gaspésie*, 411.

69 Grabowski, *Common*, 88–192.

70 ASQ, Séminaire, 15, 6, 24/2/1662, Laval ordonne l'excommunication ... boisson; *JJ*, 282–303; *DBC*, I, 682; Delâge, *Histoire*, 75: no. 4 Têtu et Gagnon, *Mandements*, 30–2, 42–4, 18/4/1661: Excommunication de Pierre par François de Laval pour avoir traité des boissons enivrantes aux sauvages, 24/2/1662; Excommunication contre les traiteurs d'eau de vie aux sauvages, 30/4/1662; Déclaration de l'évêque de Québec sur les boissons données à emporter aux sauvages et contre ceux qui causeront leur ivresse.

71 Delâge, *Histoire*, 75: ANQQ, JDCS (TP1, S28), Chronica 1, 10/10/1678: Ordonnances royale sur les crimes liés à la boisson; Bailey, *Conflict*, 67.

72 Delâge, *Histoire*, 76: no. 8: ANF, coll., F3, III, fol. 392–392v; ANQQ, *J&D* (TP 1, S28), Chronica 1, 28/9/1663; EO, II. ANQQ, *J&D* (TP1, S28), Chronica 1, 23/11/1663: Condamnation de Gilles Esnard pour vente d'eau de vie aux sauvages; *J&D*, 8: Défense à toutes personnes ... boisson enivrante aux sauvages ... amende 300 livres ... au fouet et au bannissement pour la récidive (28/9/1663); *J&D*, 64: Condamnation de Gilles Esnard ... qu'il avait ignoré les défenses qui avaient été faites (23/11/1663).

73 ASQ, Polygraphie, 4, 21: Extraits ... ; ASQ, Polygraphie, 4, 22: Arrêt ... ; *J&D*, 129: Ordre ... témoins contre des Français qui ont vendu des boisins enyvrantes aux sauvages (13/3/1664); *J&D*, 170: Défense ... vendre des boissons enivrantes même de donner le moindre coup aux sauvages sur peine de confiscation de leurs biens et de bannissement et même du fouet (17/4/1664); *J&D*, 181: Nomination de Jean Levasseur pour arrêter tous les sauvages qui seront trouvés ivres, permission à toutes personnes de faire les fonctions, et ordre de prêter main forte sous peine de 10 livres d'amende (24/4/1664); *J&D*, 186: Permission à toutes personnes d'arrêter les sauvages ivres, et ordre à ceux de ce requis de prêter main forte sous peine de dix livres d'amende (24/4/1664); *J&D*, 188: Ordre de retenir en prison deux sauvages sur leur refus de déclarer qui leur a donné de la boisson (11/5/1664); 189: Élargissement des dits deux sauvages après avoir déclaré qui leur avait donné de la boisson (12/5/1664); *J&D*, 274: Ordre au juge des Three Rivers d'informer et procéder contre ceux qui vendent des boissons enivrantes aux sauvages (3/9/1664); *J&D*, 274: Ordre au juge des Three Rivers d'informer et procéder contre ceux qui vendent des boissons enivrantes aux sauvages (3/9/1664); *J&D*, 337: Ordre au sujet d'une sauvagesse emprisonnée pour ivresse (24/4/1665); *J&D*, 337: Interrogatoire de Levasseur, concierge des prisons au sujet de l'évasion, d'une sauvagesse (24/4/1665); *J&D*, 340: Défense itérative de donner des boissons aux sauvages, même en exerçant l'hospitalité (29/4/1665); *J&D*, 342: Ordre du Conseil au sujet de certaine personnes trouvées ivres et bataillant dans les rues, le procès contre elles devant être plus amplement instruit (4/4/1665); *J&D*, 368: Ordonnance contre ceux qui donnent des boissons enivrantes aux sauvages (6/12/1666).

74 *J&D*, 370: Commission au Sieur Pierre Duquet notaire, et à Levasseur ... contre ceux qui traitent de boissons aux sauvages, en la seigneurie de Lauson (10/1/1667); *J&D*, 373: Commission au Sieur de Villeray pour procéder à l'instruction du procès de Serreau St Aubin accusé d'avoir traité des boissons aux sauvages (24/1/1667); *J&D*, 388: Nomination du Sieur Gorribon pour recevoir les plaintes contre ceux qui donnent des boissons aux sauvages (26/4/1667); Delâge, *Histoire*, 69, Annexe (B): ANF, Colonies, F3, 3, fol. 334–334v; ANQQ, *J&D* (TPP1, S28), Chronica 1, 5/1/1667: Défense de traiter des boissons aux sauvages.

75 ANQQ, *J&D* (TP1, S28), Chronica 1, 23/11/1663 (Gilles Esnard); 8/2/1664 (Jean et François Pelletier); 11/5/1664 (Ta8iskaron et Anaka8abemat);

24/4/1665 (Geneviesve sauvagesse). ANQTR, Juridiction de Three Rivers (ZA
33/4), pièce détachée no. 139, 10/5/1665: Condemnation de Jean Peré..
ANQTR, Greffe des notaires, Jacques de la Touche, Cap-de-la-Madeleine,
20/6/1666: Enquête (Joseph On Dessonke[a] du dit Lamouche, Jeanne
A8oubiay [Wendat]). JRAAD, 46, 164, 186 in Delâge, *Histoire*, Annexe (B);
Vachon, *DBC* 1:681–2, cited by Grabowski, "Trifluviens," 30; *J&D*, 406: Sentence
contre divers habitants st sauvages accusés d'avoir contrevenu à l'ordonnance relative à la traite des boissons aux sauvages (20/6/1667); *J&D*, 410: Confiscation
d'eau de vie offerte en vente aux sauvages (20/6/1667); *J&D*, 422: Amende de
20 livres contre René Lévesque pour avoir donné de l'eau de vie à un sauvage
(18/7/1667); *J&D*, 423: Amende de 50 livres contre Rochereau pour vente de
boisson aux sauvages, et Crevier, son interprète (18/7/1667); *J&D*, 474:
Ordonnance contre ceux qui traitent des boissons aux sauvages (29/2/1668);
J&D, 477: Ordonnance qui défend, après la bâtisse d'une brasserie, l'importation
de vin et eau de vie sans en avoir obtenu congé du Roy, laquelle importation ne
devra pas excéder douze cents barriques en tout, dont deux tiers de vin et un tiers
d'eau de vie (5/3/1668); *J&D*, 544: Sentence contre ceux une sauvagesse
huronne pour s'être enivrée et avoir calomnié (16/2/1669); *J&D*, 558: Défense
aux habitants d'aller dans les bois à la rencontre des Sauvages pour leur porter
des boissons, sous peine de 50 livres d'amende pour la première fois, et de
châtiment pour récidive et peine de deux heures de carcan et de deux castors
gras contre les sauvages qui s'enivrent (26/6/1669).

76 *J&D* 1:353–4, 368–9, 388–9; ANQTR, Sentences et Jugements, 1667–77;
1752–59; ANQTR, Juridiction royale de Three Rivers, I, fol. 157–180; ANQTR,
Juridiction seigneuriale, 1638–1753, pièces détachées; ANQTR, Juridiction
seigneuriale du Cap-de-la-Madeleine, 1659–85, fols. 119–83 cited by
Grabowski, "Trifluviens," 1–36.

77 Delâge, *Histoire*, Annexe (B): ANQQ, *J&D* (TP 1, S28), Chronica 1,
10/11/1668 et 26/6/1669: Permission de vendre de toutes boissons aux
sauvages. APJM, 15; OC, I, 174–5: Permission de vendre de toutes les boissons
aux sauvages qui voudront leur en acheter; ANQQ, *J&D*, Chronica 1,
10/11/1668; ANQTR, Juridiction de Three Rivers, pièce détachée no. 162.

78 ASQ, Polygraphie, 4, 25: Permission ... ; ASQ, Polygraphie, 4, 26: Défense ... ;
ASQ, Polygraphie, 4, 20: Discours ... ; ASQ, Polygraphie, 4, 27: Réponse ... ;
ASQ, Polygraphie, 4, 35: Règlements généraux de la Police (11/5/1676), art.
16–20: "Deffences à leurs femmes et Enfans d'esennyures soubs peine de
punion corporelle;" LeClercq, *Gaspésie*, 412–14.

79 ASQ, Polygraphie, 4, 28: Ordonnance du roi ... Frontenac et Duchesneau de
faire assemblée des 20 principaux habitants pour opiner; ASQ, Polygraphie, 4,
28a: Réponse aux raisons qui prouvent qu'il faut laisser la liberté de traiter
des boissons aux sauvages (1678).

80 ANQQ, *J&D* (TP 1, S28), Chronica 1, 7/11/1678: Ordre du conseil au sujet des
informations faites contre les traiteurs d'alcool; Eccles, *Frontier*, 67–8.

81 Delâge, *Histoire*, 69–71: ANC, Colonies, C11A, III, fol. 19–20v, 10/11/1668: Arrêt du Conseil supérieur de Québec qui permet à toute personne de vendre des boissons aux Sauvages, défense à eux de s'enivrer sous les peines y portées. OC 1:277–8; ICFS 3: 280, 11/5/1680: Défense à tout cabaretier de donner des boissons aux sauvages et défense de leur vendre des boissons enivrantes. APJM, 29: Ordonnance de Lefebvre de la Barre faisant observer l'ordonnance du roi du 14/5/1679.

82 Delâge, *Histoire*, 72–89: ANQQ, *J&D* (TP1, S28), Chronica 1, 21/1/1686: Défense d'enivrer les sauvages signifié aux Hurons de Lorette uniquement; EO 2:111–12; Notification du règlement de police 29 & 30 de 11/5/1676 et l'arrêt du 26/6/1669 aux Hurons de Lorette et Abénaquis de Sillery suivant l'arrêt du Conseil du 9/1/1686. ANF, Col., F3, III, fol. 387–288; ANQQ, J&D (TP1, S28), Chronica 1, 26/6/1669; 29/2/1668: Interdiction d'apporter des boissons dans les bois ... APJM, 7–8, 12/7/1670: Ordonnance sur le commerce de l'eau -de-vie dans les bois. ANQQ, *J&D* (TP1, S28), Chronica 1, 7/10/1675: Contrat ... Lorette. OC 1:238–40, 22/9/1678: Défense à tout habitant de Prairie de la Madeleine de tenir cabaret ou de vendre des boissons ... ANF, Colonies, A, I, 2335–236, fol. 64; EO 1:235–36; ANQQ, *J&D* (TP1, S28), Chronica 1, 16/10/1679: Interdiction de porter ou de faire porter de l'eau de vie aux sauvages. OC 1:318–22; APJM, 27–8; *ICFS* 3:282: Défense de porter ou de faire porter/envoyer eau de vie dans les bourgades des sauvages éloignées des habitations françaises. OC, 35, 24/4/1683: Défense de traiter aucune eau de vie avec les sauvages dans les pays du sud et du nord; ANQQ, Fonds Gouverneur (R1), OC 2:37; Grabowski, "Trifluviens," 17; Grabowski, "Contrebande," 48–9.

83 Têtu et Gagnon, *Mandements* 1:511–12:1666 Edit contre le blasphème.

84 ASQ, Séminaire, 15, 5, 1/1/1662: Consultation de la Sorbonne sur l'excommunication ... boisson.

85 Bilodeau, "Economique," 53: "Les Canadiens possédaient un gouvernement équivalent presque à l'indépendance, un 'self-gouvernment' dans le cadre de l'empire français."

86 Lagrave, *Liberté*, 31–3.

87 ANC, MGI, C11A, II, fol. 106–117v, 129–166. ASQ, Polygraphie, 2, 32, 1664: Difficulté entre Mésy et Laval touchant la création d'un nouveau conseil; Marie, *Correspondance*, 710: let. CCVII, 9–10/1663; *J&D*, I, 3: Arrêt à Mezy au gouverneur (18/9/1663); 127: Différends entre le Gouverneur et L'Évêque (5/3/1664); 346: Ordre à papiers à Mezy (13/4/1665).

88 ANC, MGI, C11A, II, fol. 106–117v, 129–166: Mémoire de Jean Peronne Dumesnil (20/9/1663); *J&D*, 4: Pouvoir donné au Sieur de Villeray de faire rechercher dans la maison habitée par Péronne Dumesnil des papiers appartenant au Conseil, concernant le service de Sa Majesté, et ordre au dit Dumesnil de vider la dite maison (20/9/1663); 6: Ordre du Sieur Gaudais ... Dumesnil contre ... Villeray, de la Ferté, D'auteuil et de Tilly (22/9/1663);

27: Arrêt – Inventaire ... papiers du dit Dumesnil (10/10/1663); 35: Arrêt condamnant à du Mesnil à payer au Sieur de la Chesnaye ... (20/10/1663); 131: Ordre de représenter ... les papiers du Sieur du Mesnil (13/3/1664); 135–36: Ordre de faire l'ouverture du coffre ... papiers du Sieur du Mesnil (18/3/1664); 136: Liste de certains papiers trouvés ... (18/3/1664); 136: Liste de certain papiers ... (18/3/1664).

89 *J&D*, 115: Condamnation de Jean et François Pelletier ... pour avoir accusé ... D'auteuil (8/2/1664); 116: Déclaration des dits Pelletier ... contre le sieur D'Auteuil (2/8/1664).

90 ANC, MGI, C11A, VII, 45–56: Denonville au ministre (13/11/1685)..

91 Ironically, many older sword families whose titles were excellent were stripped, while the newer literate and wealthy bourgeois obtained the bonus titles. This was due, in the sixteenth century, to the sudden influx of South and Central American silver stolen by Spanish conquistadors. The glut of Spanish silver deregulated prices, stimulated the growth of commerce, urbanization, a prospering merchant class, schooling for bourgeois boys, and it also devalued land. All of this challenged sword country aristocratic privileges. Many aristocrats living in their manors lacked the means to frequent the court and obtain royal favour and influence. And fearing the vengeance that exploded during the Fronde, the young king and his bourgeois-cum-robe nobles were very anxious to strip them of their titles. Isambert, *Recueil*, 226–38, mars 1600: Edit portant règlement général sur les tailles, sur les usurpations du titre de noblesse ... ; ANC, MGI, C11A, XI, fol. 265v: 10/5/1681.

92 "les principaux deffauts des personnes etablies en Canada est principalement des nobles et de ceux qui'enorgueulissent sans lestre ... il est bien en consequence de ne pas [donner] des lettres de noblesse a aucun, a moins qu'on veuille aug-menter le nombre des gueus ... Mr. L'Intendant sauroit fait recherche contre ces pretendus nobles pour representer leurs titres" (Eccles, *Frontier*, 101).

93 Moogk, "Craftsmen," in Cross and Kealey, *Society*, 88–119; Dewald, *Nobility*, 18, 21.

94 This was, ironically, after Henri IV forbade ennoblement by military service in France. Jaenen, *Friend*, 197; Hamelin, *Economie*, 65–71; Ouellet, "Société."

95 Weisner, *Women*, 201.

96 Merrick, "Fathers," 281–303; (Knachel, *England*, 57–60, 82, 90).

97 *RJ* (Thwaites), 10, 44.

98 Boucher, *Histoire*, 94.

99 Wallot and Paquet, "Quebec," in Canny and Pagden, *Atlantic*, 95–114.

100 Nish, *Gentilhommes*; Diamond, "Feudalism," 33–4. "It cannot be too strongly emphasized that the habitant ... during the French regime was anything but a docile and unenterprising peasantry ... habitants remained a vigourous, independent temperament who probably differed little from the coureurs de bois" (Harris, in Cross and Kealey, *Society*, 38).

101 Cameron Nish, Jean-Pierre Wallot, and Sigmund Diamond. Unlike Molière's figure, the French Canadian bourgeois-gentilhomme sought work rather than leisure. Eccles, *Frontier*, 75; Diamond, "Experiment," 27; Frégault, *Civilisation*, 176–7.

102 LeClercq, *Gaspésie*, 19–38.

CHAPTER FIVE

1 Haase Dubosc et Viennot, *Femmes*, 9.

2 Bodin, *Commonwealth*, 14–17, 19–20, 746, 782; Richelieu, *Lettres*, 6, 539; Weisner, *Women*, 243.

3 Delumeau, *Peur*, ch. 10–12; Weisner, *Women*, 147, 199, 244; Hanley, *Lit;* Stone, *Aristocracy;* Burguière, *Family*, 28.

4 Fagniez, *Femme*, 99–116.

5 Muchembled, *Culture*, 202–7 and ch. 5; Gibson, *Women*, passim.

6 Gibson, *Women*, 39.

7 ASQ, Polygraphie, 4, 69a: extrait ... ; ASQ, Polygraphie, 5, 20: Édit du roi Henri II sur le fait des femmes grosses et enfants morts-nés (2/1556); Weisner, *Women*, 102.

8 Davis, Archives, 85–7; Weisner, *Women*, 52.

9 Tallemant, *Historiettes* 5:58; 7, 158, 224; 8, 230; St-Simon, *Mémoires* 4:293, 344, all cited in Gibson, *Women*, 61, 64–5, 84–86; also Davis, *Archives*, 11–13, 141–2.

10 Rabelais, *Tiers*, ch. 28, cited in Davis, *Archives*, 190, n. 18.

11 Davis, *Archives*, ch. 3, appendix B.

12 du Faël, *Rustiques*, 37.

13 Bossy, "Lent," in Burke, *Popular*, ch. 8.

14 Weisner, *Women*, 103, 125, 129, 195–6, 199, 201, 207.

15 Bacon, *Mothers;* Rapley, *Dévotes*, passim.

16 Rapley, *Dévotes*, 8.

17 Beauchamp, "Women," 31–3, 137–9; Lafitau, *Moeurs* 1:66–71; Morgan, *Ancient*, 72.

18 Johnson, *Valley*, 30–1, 28–9: NYSL, MSS nos. 13350–1.

19 Lafitau, *Moeurs* 1:568, 579; Charlevoix, *Voyage* 2:24–8; Trigger, "Matrilineality," 55–65; Trigger, *Newcomers*, 208; Carré "Haudenosaunee," 215; St John, *Haudenosaunee*, 34. Norman Clermont writes that refuting the idea of matriarchy occurs due to a distorted reading of the sources (Clermont, "Iroquoiennes," 288). Naming, "de-horning" of chiefs, and power to save captives (Lafitau, *Moeurs* 1:308; 2:71; Morgan, *Ancient*, 72, 85).

20 JR (Thwaites), 68, 93.

21 Hennepin, *New*, 490; Champlain, *Oeuvres* 2:951–2; Lahontan, *Mémoires*, 140.

22 Johnson, *Valley*, 30–1: NYSL, MSS nos.13350–1.

23 Brébeuf, *Relation*, 21–30; LeClercq, *Gaspésie*, 416; JR (Thwaites), 5, 133; 6, 233.

24 *JR* (Thwaites), 5, 174.

25 Lafitau, *Moeurs* 2:564.

26 Champlain, *Oeuvres* 2:952–4; Boucher, *Histoire*, 104–5; Perrot, *Mémoire*, 64–5; Lahontan, *Mémoires*, 139; Hennepin, *New*, 478–83.

27 Perrot, *Histoire*, 22; Lafitau, *Moeurs* 1:589.

28 Champlain, *Oeuvres* 2:953; Lahontan, *Mémoires*, 141. Lack of jealousy did not indicate lack of attachment, for when wives died often husbands either died of melancholy or threw themselves into warfare (LeClercq, *Gaspésie*, 185–6, 416).

29 Lafitau, *Moeurs* 1:555.

30 La Potherie, *Histoire* 2:32; Lafitau, *Moeurs* 1:585–7.

31 *JR* (Thwaites), 39, 283; 15, 181–3; Clermont, "Iroquoiennes," 287; Dickinson, "Justice," 36.

32 Fenton, *Longhouse*, 112.

33 Sagard, *Histoire*, 357.

34 Noël, "Femmes," in Francis and Smith, *History*, 123–46; I. Foulch-Delbosc, "Women," in Prentice and Trofimenkoff, *Majority;* Séguin, "Canadienne." John Bosher has written the contrary view in Bosher, *Business*, ch. 9.

35 Charlevoix, *Histoire* 5 180. For a dissident view see Dawson, "Protestant," 34.

36 Davis, *Society*, ch. 5.

37 Choquette, *Peasants*, 51.

38 Jetté, *Dictionnaire*, passim; Trudel, *Catalogue*, passim; Trudel, *1663*, passim; Landry, *Orphelines*, passim.

39 Jaenen, *Church*, 154–5. See rash of rape prosecutions in *J&D*, 129: Ordre aux pères Jéuites et à un certain nombre d'habitants et chefs de tribus sauvages de s'assembler pour prendre leur avis sur une accusation de viol contre un sauvage (13/3/1664); Arrêt soumettant les sauvages à la peine portée par les lois et ordonnances de France pour crime de meurtre et de viol (17/4/1664); 399: Sentence contre Claude Maugrain, condamné au fouet pour tentative de viol (6/6/1667); 463: Sentence de mort contre Jean Ratté, convaincu de viol (29/11/1667); 517: Sentence contre Pierre Pinelle, convaincu de viol, portant qu'il sera rasé, foutté aux verges et envoyé en France pour servir sur les galères pendent 9 ans (1/10/1668); 572: Distribution des deniers provenant de la vente des biens d'Antoine Gaboury antérieurement condamné aux galères pour tentative de viol (12/8/1669); 575: Sentence de mort contre Jacques Nourry, coupable de viol (19/9/1669); 578: Bannissement pour six mois de Nicolas Palmy, convaincu de viol sur la personne de Marie Anez (14/10/1669); 649: Appel mis à néant en amendant la sentence de mort contre Jean Bourgois atteint et convaincu de viol sur la personne de Jeanne Jaquereau, âgée de six à sept ans, condamnation du dit Bourgeois à être battu de verges aux carrefours, marqué à la joue droite de la fleur de lys, et banni à perpetuité (10/3/1670); 656: Question ordinaire et extraordinaire pour crime de viol à Jean Gongnard (18/8/1670).

40 Séguin, "Canadienne," 503; Lanctôt, *Filles*, 210–13; Noël, "Femme," 124–8, 134.

41 This is the frequent experience of today's widows, single women, and divorcées due to childcare and family responsibilities, obstacles to professional advancement, much lower salaries, and the ostracism of coupled-up society. See Shamgar-Handelman, *Widows*.

42 Trudel, *HNF* 2:2, 564s, 622, 625; *J&D*, 68: Défense à toute personne d'empêcher les filles venues de France aux dépens du Roy de se marier quand bon leur semblera (24/11/1663).

43 *DBC*, 114; Juchereau, *Annales*, 33; Dollier, *Montréal* 2:46–7; Morin, *Véritable*, 54–65; *DBC*, 115; Marie, *Correspondance*, 643–5: let. CLXXXIX, 13/10/1660; 652–657: let. CXCIII, 13/9/1661.

44 Quote: *RJ*, 1648, 173–4. On Laval: Marie, *Correspondance*, 285–6: let. XCVII, 28/8/1646–10/9/1646.

45 Trudel, *HNF* 2:2, 71–5.

46 *J&D*, 639: Arrêt pour l'enregistrement ... rente à dix enfants et plus à 20 livres à leurs noces (20/10/1670). Yves Landry documents that the average spacing between children shortened in Canada: while in France from 1670 to 1769 the interval was between eleven and nine months, the immigrants filles du roi had shortened that interval to nine to seven months, while the Canadian women were busy with the dizzying interval of five to six months (Landry, *Orphelines*, 224).

47 Dawson, "Protestant," 74.

48 *RJ*, 1637, 11–12.

49 Morin, *Véritable*, 18; Juchereau, *Annales*, 75–6.

50 Eccles, *Frontier;* Trudel, *HNF* 2:2. Trudel, *HNF* 2:108–9.

51 Weisner, *Women*, 86.

52 Dechêne, *Habitants*, 204–9, 393; Foulch-Delbousc, "Women," 25; Lunn, "Illegal," 61–75; Moogk, *House*, 60–4; Noël, "Femmes," 139–42: Agathe de St Père (founded textile industry); Marie-Anne Barbel veuve Fornel worked the Tadoussac fur trade, among other enterprises; Louise de Ramezay developed the sawmill; and women pioneered auxiliary industries essential to construction: Plamondon, "Barbel," 165–85: guaranteed the division of her and her deceased husband's assets equally between her five children of either gender, and generated assets from her own mother's bequeathment to her and her siblings.

53 Bosher, "Family," 7; Noël, "Femmes," 142. Child support is included in these figures.

54 Lafitau, *Moeurs*, 86; Clermont, "Femme," 286–90; Tooker, *Huron*, 128; Morgan, *League*, 78–104.

55 *J&D*, 540: Sentence sur conviction d'adultère contre Marie Chauvet ... rasée et fouettée ... complices Vivien et LeRoy ... tenir prison pendant 8 jours, les fers aux pieds et aux mains, et au pain et à l'eau (14/1/1669).

56 *J&D,* 660: Sentence de mort contre Françoise Duverger convaincu d'avoir caché sa grossesse et d'avoir tué son enfant l'instant après être couchée (7/9/1670); *J&D,* 669: Arrêt pour l'exécution de la sentence contre Françoise Duverger condamnée à être pendue (17/11/1671). Seven women were accused of infanticide during the French Regime, and sentences were more severe than after the Cession, three being killed for it: the case just mentioned, Madeleine Gibaut of Montreal (1697) and Marie-Anne Sigouin of Quebec (1732) (Cliche, "Infanticide," 45).

57 ANC, Affaires Étrangères Amérique, V: Frontenac au ministre, nov 13, 167, fols. 324–5.

58 Boyer, *Crimes,* 326–9, 340, 350, 361–2; cited in Noël, "Femmes," 135.

59 *JR* (Thwaites), 5, 177–80; 18, 106–8.

60 *JR* (Thwaites), 22, 81–6; 115–27, cited in Etienne and Leacock, *Colonization,* 34.

61 ASQ, Série MS, 216: Pierre Cholenec, Sur la vie de quelques femmes sauvages (1676–80); Béchard, "Gandeacteua, Catherine, " in *DBC,* 330; Jaenen, *Friend,* 78; Marie, *Correspondance,* 117, 181–2, 531, 975, cited in Deslandres, "Femmes," 281–3.

62 Jaenen, "Miscegenation"; Peterson, *In Between;* Peterson and Brown, *Métis;* Gorham, "Mixed"; Harrington, "Half Breed; Perrault, *Métissage.* For the West: Giraud, *Métis;* Dickason, "New," 1–21; Sprague and Frye, *Genealogy;* Brown, *Strangers;* Van Kirk, *Tender.*

63 Jaenen, *Church,* 28; Lachance, "Déséquilibre," 214; Harris, *Atlas,* plate 47: Native resettlement 1635–1800.

64 Peterson, *In Between,* passim; Perrault, *Métissage.*

65 Nash, *Red,* 104: The French "exhibited no embarrassment at this mixing of blood and were hard put to understand English qualms about interracial relations." Romance, however, did not always need official prodding. In Acadia, the French taught the Mi'kmaq womens how to deep kiss, which could have aroused curiosity, while the Native men were anxious to see the Frenchwomen who supposedly had beards (Lescarbot, *Histoire* 3:141; also in Bailey, *Conflict,* 18). One cannot underestimate the cultural shock of scantily covered Native young people upon the French, both men and women, who were brought up on Counter-Reformation and Protestant severity (Champlain, *Oeuvres,* 134; Tooker, *Ethnography,* 20–1). Consider how trundelled up common Frenchwomen were, with collars that choked, sleeves that dripped into their work, skirts that swept the floor, and white caps upon the girls' heads, compared to some Native women's bare breasts and scanty skirts. These women were also often decorated with various matachias, feathers, porcupine quillwork, furs, and careful coiffures.

66 *EO* 1:10: Acte d'établissement des Cents-Associés, art. 17; ANC, C11A, 2, I, 44655; Trudel also cites the arrêt of 5/3/1658 (Trudel, *HNF* 3:1, 11; Jaenen, *Church,* 25.)

67 *JR* (Thwaites), 5, 205, 211; Bailey, *Conflict,* 41.

68 *JR* (Thwaites), 14, 15–17; Trigger, *Aetaentsic,* 539. They were probably referring to Bruslé, and perhaps Grenolle, Guillaume Chaudron, Auhaitsique, and others.

69 Daveluy, *Notre-Dame,* unpaginated.

70 ANC, MGI, C11A, II, fol. 199–199v, 206v:5/4/1666, Colbert à intendant Talon; Bailey, *Conflict,* 107; Nash, *Red,* 104; Kidwell, "Mediators," 97–107.

71 ANC, AC, F1A, Fonds des Colonies, I-X; O'Callaghan and Brodhead, *NYCD,* 9, 207, La Barre au ministre, 4/11/1683; cited by Dickason, *First,* 171.

72 Gary Nash points out that later some English regretted this policy: William Byrd and Robert Beverley lamented English "false delicacy" on the early Chesapeake, which kept them from making "prudent alliances" (Nash, *Red,* 105).

73 Dickason, *First,* 160.

74 For St-Castin, Jaenen writes of the twelve children of the Baron and cites d'Entremont, "St-Castin," 9–28, cited in Jaenen, *Friend,* 165; Casgrain, "L'Acadie," 101–2; Maillard, "Account," 89–90, cited in Dickason, *First,* 170; Beaumont, "L'Acadie," 101–2; Bailey, *Conflict,* 18, 112; Maurault, *Abénaquis,* 75.

75 Mancall, *Deadly,* conclusion. Peter Mancall rejects this idea.

76 LeClercq, *Gaspésie,* 412; Vachon, "L'eau," 22–32.

77 *RJ* (Thwaites), 16, 62; Margry, *Découvertes* 5:107; Lahontan, *Mémoires,* 132; Kinietz, *Lakes,* 367, Raudot, letter 40, Québec, 1709; La Potherie, *Histoire* 2: 1–28.

78 Lahontan, *Mémoires,* 133–4.

79 Champlain, *Oeuvres* 2:953.

80 ASQ, Polygraphie, 4, 35: Règlements généraux de la Police (11/5/1676), art. 16–20.

81 *J&D,* 129: Ordre aux Pères Jésuites et à certain nombre d'habitants et chefs de tribus sauvages de s'assembler pour prendre leur avis sur une accusation de viol contre un sauvage (13/3/1663); *J&D,* 174: Arrêt soumettant les sauvages à la pleine portée par les lois et ordonnances de France pour crime de meurtre et de viol (21/4/1664); *J&D,* 399: Sentence contre Claude Maugrain au fouet pour tentative de viol (6/6/1667); *J&D,* 463: Sentence de mort contre Jean Ratté convaincu de viol (29/11/1667); *J&D,* 517: Sentence contre Pinelle convaincu de viol, portant qu'il sera rasé, fouetté de verges, et envoyé en France pour servir aux galères pendant 9 ans (1/10/1668); *J&D,* 572: Distribution des deniers provenant de la vente des biens de Antoine Gaboury antérieurement condamné aux galères pour tentative de viol (13/8/1669); *J&D,* 575: Sentence de mort contre Jacques Nourry, coupable de viol (19/8/1669); *J&D,* 578: Bannissement pour 6 mois de Nicolas Palmy, convaincu de viol sur la personne de Marie Anez (14/10/1669); *J&D,* 649: Appel mis à néant en amendant la sentence de mort contre Jean Bourgeois

atten et convaincu de viol sur la personne de Jeanne Jaquereau, âgée de 6 à 7
ans; condamnation du dit Bourgeois à être battu de verges aux carrefours,
marqué à la joue droite de la fleur de lys, et banni à perpetuité (10/3/1670);
J&D, 656: Question ordinaire et extraordinaire pour crime de viol à Jean
Gongnard (18/8/1670). Delâge, *Histoire*, 76–77: ANQQ, *J&D* (TP1, S28),
Chronica 1, 13/3/1664, Quebec: Déliberations du Conseil souverain sur la
nécessité de continuer le procès commencé contre Robert Hache, Algonquin,
et d'assujettir les sauvages aux lois françaises. ANQQ, *J&D* (TP1, S28), Chronica
1, 21/4/1664: Assemblée de différents chefs amérindiens au sujet de la
condamnation de Robert Hache pour le viol de Marthe Hubert; *EO*, II, fol. 14,
21/7/1664.

82 ANQM, AJPD, pièces détachées, 14/10/1676; ANC, C11A, 9. 27 (6/11/1687);
    ANQM, AJPD, 17/6/1686; ANQM, AAJPD, 12/7/1689; ASSSM, FF 30, 4/8/1689
    all cited in Grabowski, "Contrebande," 49, 51.

83 Dollier, *Montreal*, 31–3.

84 Theresa Schenk on the Cadotte family in Brown et al, *Revisited*.

85 ANC, F3, 24: (1732) Mémoire concernant les Illinois; ANC, F3, 20, f. 85:
    (16/5/1735) Bienville et Salmon au ministre; ANC, C13A, 23: (1738)
    Mémoire sur les mariages des sauvagesses avec les françois; cited by White,
    Middle, 214, n50. Têtu and Gagnon, *Mandements*, 502–3, cited in Jaenen,
    Emerging, 65.

86 Lex Pacis Castrensis (1158) Frederick Barbarossa had the noses of the
    prostitutes cut off to keep the soldiers away from them. The Lombard Laws
    and the Laws of the Alamans (Cnut) allowed the mutilation of female noses
    (European mutilation: Rose, *Venice*, 50, 69; Amerindian mutilation; Native:
    Kinietz, *Lakes*, 94, 184–5, 207, 389).

87 In Louisiana, even local commanders, such as Vaudreuil and LeMoyne de
    Bienville, were sometimes opposed to metissage. The Natchez were even more
    rigidly hierarchical than the French. By 1706, uncharacteristically, the French
    waged a fierce war against them and killed thousands. Governor of Louisiana,
    Bienville, burned three Natchez villages and demanded that Tattooed
    Serpent, the Natchez ruler, send him the head of a lesser chief. By 1729,
    when major hostilities broke out, the French and Choctows killed 1,000
    Natchez, burned many others, and sold around 400 into slavery in Santo
    Domingo. In addition, the Native female surplus seemed to suit Frenchmen.
    Cornelius Jaenen recounts that, when twelve filles du roi were sent to Bayou
    La Fourche, the men ignored all but two of the girls and returned to the
    Native women whom they found to be prettier. "M. de Clairambault should
    pay attention rather to the figure than to virtue ... they still preferred the
    native women with whom they marry." Jaenen even cites that abbé Jean-
    François Buisson de St-Cosme, who decried French and Native debauchery,
    nevertheless became the lover of the female Natchez ruler. In sum, Louisiana
    brought out the most extreme passions of the French, for better or worse.

See Perrot, *Moeurs*, 178, n1; Raudot letter 40, Quebec, 1709 in Kinietz, *Lakes*, 36; cited by Jaenen, "Miscegenation," 11; from Gabriel Marest to Louis Germain, 9/11/1712 in Kipé Missions, 199, 204, cited by Jaenen, "Miscegenation"; De Gannes (DeLiette) Memoir, IHC, 23, 327, 335–7, cited by White, *Middle*, 62; Kellogg, *Narratives*, 243.

88 Juchereau, *Annales*, 31–2. Charbonneau, "Note," 265–6.

89 ANC, MGI, C11A, V, 52–53:10/11/1679, Duchesneau au ministre; ANC, MGI, VII, 42–6:13/11/1685, Denonville au ministre; ibid., XI, M,moire instructif sur le Canada, joint à la lettre de M. de Champigny, intendant, 10/5/1691, 468. Most historians ignore or sweep this aspect under the rug, but it was mentioned by Wrong, *Fall* 1:394–6; Diamond, "Experiment," 11; Harris, "Land," in Cross and Kealey, *Society*, 33.

90 ANC, MGI, C11A, III, fol. 257:2/11/1672, Frontenac au ministre.

91 Charbonneau et al., *Naissance*, ch. 5; Landry, *Orphélines*, 196–8. Both Hubert Charbonneau and Yves Landry note that Canadian women had greater fertility than women of northwestern France due, perhaps, to improved nutrition but that the filles du roi's fertility was slightly more than that of Frenchwomen but slightly less than that of Canadian women.

92 Delâge, "L'Influence," 142; Moogk, "Sauvages," in Parre, *Childhood*, 17.

93 Têtu et Gagnon, *Mandements*, 4/3/1665, 51–53, 56–66: Mandement pour l'établissement de la Confrérie de la sainte famille, Règlements de la Confrérie de la Sainte Famille; Marie, *Correspondance*, 735:19/8/1664, let. CCXIII: 1663 for Montreal, in 1664 for Quebec by Boullogne and Bishop Laval.

94 Cited by Jaenen, *Popular*, 8–9; ANC, MGI, C11A, VII, 84:6/5/1686, Denonville au ministre.

95 Têtu et Gagnon, *Mandements* 1:269 cited by Jaenen, "Popular," 9.

96 Mémoires de Pierre de Sales Laterrière et de ses traverses, Quebec, 1873, 61, cited in Jaenen, "Popular," 8.

97 Dechêne, *Habitants*, 27–8: "un certain nombre [of Natives] habitent dans la ville et dans les côtes. Il y a ceux qui refusent de se déplacer avec les missions et restent derrière, ceux qui rejettent la tutelle des prêtres mais recherchent le commerce des habitants, enfin ceux qui sont chassés des missions pour mauvaise conduite," while she adds that the Natives along the coasts, like those at Châteauguay (baillage, procès verbal, October 1679), were protected by the habitants there and in Montreal. This is attested to by several witnesses and inquiries in the archives du baillage of Montreal. The Montreal governor wrote that there were many Natives roaming around the seigneuries (ANC, C11A, 7, f. 90), and the Sulpicians said the same (Mémoire sur les missions, 1684, ASSP, dossier 109, pièce 1, article 23).

98 Jaenen, "Pelleteries," 107–14; Gagnon, *Sauvages;* Dickason, *Savage.*

99 Con to métissage: Intendant the Marquis de Denonville, Governor Rigaud de Vaudreuil, Lousiana commander Jean-Baptiste Le Moyne de Bienville (all cited by Jaenen, "Miscegenation," 7, 11).

100 White, *Middle,* 70. For Cadillac's later reversal on intermarriage: ANC, C11A, 4, f. 255: Marriage des françois avec des sauvagesses. Some Frenchmen wanted two wives, trying to imitate Wendat chiefs, who sometimes married pairs of sisters. The difference is that the French tried to keep two women without knowledge one of the other, which was hardly the same thing. Two French envoys, Paul Le Moyne de Maricourt and Louis-Thomas Chabert de Joncaire, had both French and Native wives. The latter were Haudenosaunee, who themselves did not permit polygamy (although the Seneca sometimes practised polyandry). Dickason remarks that this pattern was repeated in their families as well: ANC, MGI, C11A 18:82, 147–8; Giraud, *Métis* 1:232–4. O'Callaghan and Brodhead, Documents, IX, 580; *DBC*, vols. II, III, IV under Chabert de Joncaire.

101 As stated "Le Conseil déclare les sauvages exclus des successions Français. Celle des femmes 'sauvages' mourants [sic] sans enfants seront déclarée au domaine de la compagnie. Les Sauvagesses veuves ne pourront disposer des biens fonds ... de leur mari qui seront mis à la garde de tuteurs pour leur payer une pension annuelle du tiers du revenu, le restant, aux enfants et héritiers lorsqu'il y en aura. Défense aux français de contracter mariage avec des 'Sauvagesses' jusqu'à ce qu'il ait plu au roi de faire connaître sa volonté." ANF, Coll., II, fol. 178–179v:18/10/1728, Arrêt de Conseil de la Chambre du Canada.

102 Mitchell, *Boucher,* 65: Contrat de mariage de Pierre Boucher, copie de M.B. de la Bruère.

103 *JR* (Thwaites), 64, 201–3; White, *Middle,* 69; Cadillac's plan for Détroit involved extensive mixed marriages: 18/10/1700, Cadillac au ministre.

104 ANC, MGI, C11C, 16, pièce 28:6/7/1746, Maurepas, unsigned letter. Eventually restrictions were placed on Native women with regard to inheriting their husbands' property. These rules are unmistakably to reduce their preponderant role in the family, whose high status the newer French, in particular, found offensive. Then a 1735 edict required the consent of the governor or commanding officer for a mixed marriage, but for different reasons than in the British case. This measure was to prevent the abuse of wife-stealing and trading that sometimes occurred and ruined relations (Jaenen, *Friend,* 164–5.)

105 *RJ* (Thwaites), 45, 148.

106 RAPQ, 1942–3, 420:14/11/1709, Vaudreuil et Bégon au ministre cited in Grabowski, "Trifluviens," 32.

107 Perrault, *Métissage,* 212, 233.

108 By the eighteenth century there were increasing numbers of children born out of wedlock, who were called the "enfants du roi." We must conjecture that they were probably the result of mixed liaisons between Canadian women and Native men. These children of the pale between legitimacy and public shame had a standing of their own. Even marginally European-looking children were

automatically passed off as the offspring of the legal father. Only if a child was obviously Métis, would a woman be cornered. And these children assuredly were the fruit of Christian, usually French, women because unofficial mixed-blood children born to Native women were automatically part of the tribe. By 1718 the Council of the Marine mentions a problem of "little savage slaves" that the Canadians kept for sexual favours and that the king should be responsible for educating. Thus there appears to be a growing gap between the rapidly rising standing of "legitimate" children, those born "illicitly," and those obtained probably due to war. Charlevoix, *Histoire* 3, 311, cited in Delâge, "L'influence," 164; "Ecologiques," 342.

109 "We have declared and now declare that, taking the very saintly and very glorious Virgin as a special protector of our realm, we consecrate particularly to our state, our crown, and our subjects, to plead of Her to try to inspire such a saintly conduct, and defend with so much care this realm against the effort of all Her enemies ... we will construct anew the great altar of the Parisian cathedral, with an image of the Virgin ... we will be represented at the feet and Son of the Mother, as we offer our crown and sceptre." ("nous avons déclaré et déclarons que, prenant la très saincte et très glorieuse Vierge pour protectrice spéciale de nostre royaume, nous luy consacrons particulièrement à nostre personne, nostre Estat, nostre couronne et nos sujets, la suppliant de vouloir nous inspirer une sy saincte conduitte, et deffendre avec tant de soin ce royaume contre l'effort de tous ses ennemies ... nous ferons construire de nouveau le grand autel de l'église cathédrale de Paris, avec une image de la Vierge ... nous serons représenté aux pieds et du filz et de la mère, comme leur offrant nostre couronne et nostre sceptre.") Déclaration pour la protection de la Vierge, fin décembre, 1637: Richelieu, *Lettres* 5:910–11; *RJ*, 1648–9, 60; Dewald, *Rouen*, 56.

110 Gibson, *Women*, 171.

111 Fain, *Rouen* 2:60

112 Benedict, *Rouen*, 63.

113 Ibid.; Dewald, *Rouen*, 56.

114 Chaumonot, *Autobiographie*, 32–3. *RJ*, 1648–9, 60 for Brébeuf; Barbeau, *Contes* (7e), 129: "Le miracle de Ste-Anne." Charlevoix, *Histoire* 7:313.

115 Gold, *Lady*, 71–4; Warner, *Alone*, 153; Bynum, *Jesus*, 18–19; Weisner, *Women*, 184.

116 Blouin, *Hurons*, 292. Archives Paroissiales de Notre Dame de Quebec, Répertoire, Série III, carton 1, nos 20–1:28/5/1649, Lettre patente from Father Charles Thibault for the erection of the confrérie du Saint Rosaire at Quebec, signed by Father Jérôme Lalemant de Quebec, 23/10/1650 cited by Bibeau, "Marial," 415–28; Sicotière, *Percheronne*, 11–12.

117 LeClercq, *Gaspésie*, 12.

118 Archives paroissiales de Notre Dame de Québec, Répertoire, Série III, Carton 1, nos 20–21 :28/5/1649, Lettre patente from Father Charles Thébault for

the erection of the confrérie du Saint Rosaire at Quebec, signed by Father
Jérôme Lalemant de Quebec, 23/10/1650 cited by Bibeau, "Marial," 415–28,
Sicotière, *Percheronne*, 11–12.

119 ASQ, Séminaire, 66: *Recueil de Chants hurons* par Paul Tsaouenhohi Picard.

120 Desdouits, *Caux*, 410; Cliche, "Mort," 85: the confréries of the Congregation
de la Vierge (for men), Ste-Anne, Ste-famille (for women), and the Tiers
Ordres (for both) received donations from the wills of the deceased. The first
received the overwhelming majority (76 at 7,484 livres, the second received
47 at 1,581 livres, the third received 42 at 1,509 livres, and the last received
12 at 607 livres).

121 Benedict, *Rouen*, 105, 150.

122 ASQ, Polygraphie, 14, 18: Authentique de la relique de Ste-Anne par Laval
(12/3/1670).

123 Méthivier, *Fronde*, 100.

124 Marie, *Correspondance*, 754–6: let. CCXVII, 30/9/1665; Rand, *Mi'kmaq*, 282;
Clark, *Legends*, 153–4.

125 Weisner, *Women*, 184–5, 192–3.

126 Delâge and Dubois, "L'Eau," 7.

127 *BRH*, 1846, II, 73: ANC, MG18, H4, 1657: requête pour confrérie de Ste-Anne.

128 Beaudoin, *L'été*, 167–173; Jaenen, *Church*, 144. Brébeuf, *Relations*, 24–5;
Blouin, *Hurons*, 269–71.

129 Rand, *Mi'kmaq*, 449–52.

130 Whitehead, *Mi'kmaq*, 191–3; Prins, *Mi'kmaq*, 172–3.

131 ASQ, Polygraphie, 13, 2: Relation des miracles opérés à la Ste-Anne de
Beaupré par l'abbé Thomas Joseph Morel (24/6/1680); ASQ, MS, 257:
Thomas Morel, Miracles opérés à la Bonne Ste-Anne; ASQ, Polygraphie, 4, 44:
Récir des miracles opérés à la Ste-Anne de Beaupré (1662–1768); Dupont,
Héritage, 325; Trudel, *HNF* 3:, 2, 475; Rand, *Mi'kmaq*, 31; Bailey, *Conflict*, 141.

132 Supposedly Jean Cadieux of Montreal or Boucherville (12/3/1671-May
1709: AFUL, coll. Luc Lacoursière, no. 1043; Barbeau, "Complainte"; 163–83;
Taché, Forestiers; Larue, "Chansons," 371; Bailey, *Conflict*, 185; Béland,
Chansons, 133–6; Barbeau, "Cadieux," 163–183; Fowkes, *Folktales*, 109–115,
Woodley, *Legends*, 19–25; Taché, *Forestiers*, 134–42. Kohl, *Kitchi-Gami*, 261–5;
Nute, *Voyageurs*, 148–50.

133 Beaudoin, *L'été*, 167–173; Trudel, *HNF* 2:2, 475.

134 Lachance, "Mentalité," 229–38; Upton, *Mi'kmaqs*, 146: No racial slurs appear
on the record in New France. None compared to the "dirty squaw" slur
current in eighteenth- to nineteenth-century British Nova Scotia, as
mentioned by Leslie Upton.

135 Dollier, *Montréal*, 11.

136 Charlevoix, *Histoire* 5:207.

137 Marie, *Correspondance*, 478: let. CXLII, 1/9/1652; Dollier, *Montréal*, 56;
Charlevoix, *Histoire* 5:207.

138 Dollier, *Montréal*, 89, 46–7; *JJ*, 174; *JR* (Thwaites), 37, 50–2; Godbout, "LeMoyne," 539.

139 Charlevoix, *Histoire* 5:207. However, the popular French image of female "unruliness" was undoubtedly a result of a much harsher life than could be conceived of by celibate male clergy and idle male nobles around whom governmental and social institutions revolved. Prominent Frenchwomen of the time had been forced to assume military rules during the Wars of Religion and the revolts. They were familiar with duelling, handling weapons, and sometimes joined or formed armies. The Princess of Condé frequently interceded for family members, while Catherine de Lorraine and the duchesse of Nevers led troops. The duchesse de Chevreuse, duchesse de Longueville, and the princesse Palatine were allegedly "capable of turning ten states upside down" during the Fronde. Tax collectors during the Norman Nu-Pieds rebellion were tortured by both sexes. And the fictional Talestris, Hermione, Menalippe, and Melandre were all "amazones." (Mercure Gallant, v. 1679, 55–8; nov. 1681, 56 et seq., avril 1687, 95, sept. 1692, 328–31, mai 1695, 211–12, cited by Gibson, *Women*, 148, 155–6; Floquet, *Diaire*, 420; Foisil, *Nu-Pieds*, 174. In addition, owing to idealism, those Frenchwomen who actually had the courage to risk coming to New France were probably not inclined to show their delicate, personal side in public.

140 J.C.B., *Voyage*, 43; cited by Eccles, *Frontier*, 97; and later by Delâge, "L'influence," 157–8.

141 Marie, *Correspondance*, 735: let. CCXIII, 19/8/1664, Stanley, "Francisation," 332–7; Deslandres, "Femmes," 280.

142 Maybury-Lewis and Almagor, *Dualistic*, 345–55.

143 Eisenstadt, "Dual," in Maybury-Lewis and Almagor, *Dualistic*, 345–55.

144 Bailey, *Conflict*, 170.

145 Barbeau, *Huron*, 219–21, 307–9, 317–25; Quebecois sea serpent tales: Meurger, *Monsters*. Dupont, *Villages*, 30–1; Barbeau, *Huron*, 317–26: collected 1816 in Vieille Lorette from Ohiarek8en Grandlouis by Aubert de Gasp,; LeMoine, *Legends*, 188–92.

146 Lévi-Strauss, *Lynx*, ch. 1.

147 Mesopotamian Enuma Elish describes the mother of gods, the sea monster Tiamat (*Enuma Elish* 4, 101); Egyptian Isis was surrounded by snakes (Apuleius, *Metamorphoses* 11:3.); Juno had serpent associations in Lanuvium (Properius, *Elegies* 4:88, w. 3–14). Greek Python slain by Apollo at Delphi (Ovide, *Métamorphoses* 1:416–51). Cassandra had been left there as a child so she acquired the power of prophecy (Homer, *Iliad*); Perseus slew the snake-haired Medusa; Heracles killed the Hydra; Artemis, Demeter, and Hecate were associated with snakes (Apollonius Rhodius, *Argonautica* 3:1211–15.) Athena guarded Erichthonius, the sacred snake who guards the Acropolis; Roman Hygieia was the goddess of health; Roman Minerva sent snakes to attack Lacaoon (Virgil, *Aeneid* 2:225–7). Roman Cupid forbade Psyche to look on him in his serpent form

(Apuleius, *Metamorphoses* 4:29), cited in Chaunu, *Morts,* 23. Cadmus and Harmony were transformed into serpents (Ovide, *Métamorphoses* 4:563–603).

148 Homer, *Iliad* 23:5–109; Lucretius, *Nature* 1:. 130–5; 4: 58–62.

149 *OT,* I Samuel 28:6–28; I Kings, 28; Chronicles 10:13–14; Ecclesiastes 46:23.

150 The snake, for the Hebrews, was the symbol of evil. This was due to Hebrew opposition to the fertility religions of Asia minor, where serpents were the soothsayers of the future and were interpreted by high priestesses (*OT,* Genesis 3; Isaiah 27:1; Psalms 74:13. N.B.: in Hebrew "tanin" means crocodile).

151 Littleton and Malcor, *Camelot,* ch. 7.

152 Davidson, *Scandinavian,* 58–60.

153 Moricet, *Normandie,* 165–9; Bosquet, *Norman,* 208.

154 Spence, *Magic,* 21–2, 95; McCana, *Celtic,* 45–7, 53–4.

155 Squier, *Serpent,* 243–7.

156 Williams, *Dominion,* 5, 23–9, ch. 2.

157 Danu was the Celtic sea goddess who lent her name to many rivers, including the Danube. "Tradition," from Melusine, *Niort,* 207–25. Baraton et al., "Poitou-Charentes," 176–8.

158 Erdoes and Ortiz, *Myths,* 181–4.

159 Squier, *Serpent,* 227–31.

160 Gill and Sullivan, *Mythology,* 192.

161 Squier, *Serpent,* 137–44.

162 Watson-Hamlin, *Detroit,* 40–8.

163 Dupont, *Villages,* 63; Côte-Nord, #13: serpent de mer Havre St-Pierre.

164 Henry, *Travels,* 176.

165 Barbeau, *Huron,* 276.

166 Barbeau, *Huron,* 308-9, from Connelley, *Wyandotte,* 87–88 and "Wyandottes," 117–18.

167 Barbeau, *Huron,* 219–21. The informants of 1911 claimed that the serpent was still either in Lac St-Charles, Richardson, or Lawrence and that he was one to two feet thick and thirty feet long.

168 Ranum, *Fronde,* 35.

169 Lachance, "L'injure"; Moogk, "Buggers," 524–47.

170 Sobel, "Inner," in Hoffman, Sobel, and Teute, *Glass,* 188.

171 Brébeuf, *Relation,* 118–19.

172 Steckley, "Warrior," 478–509.

CHAPTER 6

1 Dollier, *Montréal,* 5.

2 Prins, *Mikmaq,* 20–2, 219.

3 Bercé, *Absolutism,* 206; *Revolts,* 285–7. Like other insurgents over France, they dubbed themselves "Knights of the Straw," a tongue-in-cheek conjugation of nobility with it's opposite: peasant symbols.

4 Mollat, *Poor*, ch. 12: From charity to policing of the poor; Gutton, *Pauvres*, introduction; Braudel, "Misère," 129–42; Collins, *State*, 34; Rapley, *Devotes*, 7, 195: Zeller, *Institutions*, 384.

5 Porschnev, *Soulèvements*, 363.

6 Davis, *Gift*, 25.

7 Neuschel, *Noble*, 198; Davis, *Gift*, 34–42, 85–99.

8 Jaenen, *Church*, 156.

9 Rapley, *Devotes*, 77; Collins, *State*, 34; Weisner, *Women*, 88–9, 94, Gibson, *Women*, 225.

10 Du Fail, *Rustiques*, 20 translated and cited by Davis, *Gifts*, 43.

11 Jaenen, "Presents," 231–51.

12 Champlain, *Oeuvres* 1:70–1; Lescarbot, *Histoire* 2:534.

13 Brébeuf, *Huron*, 13, 29, 137.

14 Sagard, *Histoire*, 41–2.

15 LeClercq, *Gaspésie*, 110–12, 374, 406–8.

16 Boucher, *Histoire*, 98, 115.

17 Sagard, *Histoire*, 370.

18 LeClercq, *Gaspésie*, 110–12, 374, 406–8.

19 Brébeuf, *Relation*, 137.

20 Perrot, *Moeurs*, 69.

21 Quoted in Ryerson, *Founding*, 16; Lahontan, *Mémoires*, 126.

22 Lafitau, Comparée, 68; *Mémoires* 2:100.

23 Boucher, *Histoire*, 42–4.

24 Kinietz, *Lakes*, 355: Quebec, 1709, Memoir concerning the different Indian Nations of North America.

25 La Potherie, *Histoire* 2:70.

26 LeClercq, *Gaspésie*, 403–4.

27 Trigger, *Newcomers*, 192.

28 Champlain, *Oeuvres*, 588.

29 Sagard, *Hurons*, 48.

30 *JR* (Thwaites) 10, 19–20.

31 Price, "Sharing," 6.

32 *JR* (Thwaites) 20, 249; Bailey, *Conflict*, 84–5.

33 Perrot, *Moeurs*, 71.

34 Brébeuf, *Relation*, 138–41.

35 Boucher, *Histoire*, 98, 115; Lafitau, *Moeurs* 1:68; Kinietz, *Lakes*, 355, Quebec, 1709, Mémoire concerning the different Indian nations of North America; la Potherie, *Histoire* 2:70; Perrot, *Mémoires*, 69.

36 Hennepin, *New* 1:37, cited in Jaenen, *Friend*, 88.

37 LeClercq, *Gaspésie*, 110–13.

38 The first fief in Canada, Sault-au-Matelot, was accorded to Louis Hébert in 1626, of which half later devolved upon his daughter, Guillemette Hébert, and her husband, Guillaume Couillart, who was also ennobled in December

1654 "en faveur des services rendus au pais du Canada." (ASQ, Faribault, 6, 2:15/9/1634, Partage fait entre Guillaume Couillard; ASQ, Faribault, 20; Guillaume Hubou et sa femme pour servir ... Guillaume Hébert.) Couillart or Couillard's coat of arms is a golden dove with open wings [symbol of Holy Ghost], carrying an olive branch [symbol of peace], with the saying "Dieu aide au premier colon" (God helped the first colonist). Ville, *Rollet*, 70.

39 Campeau, *MNF* 2:411, 414: doc. 127: *RJ*, 1633; *JJ*, 1645, 10.

40 *JJ*, 1645, 10, 15; Charlevoix, *Histoire* 7:302.

41 Canny and Pagden, *Colonial*, 100.

42 LeClercq, *Gaspésie*, 95–6.

43 *JJ*, 1645, 19.

44 Bellmare, *BRH*, 279–81; Roy, *BRH*, 577–9.

45 Trudel, *HNF* 3:1, 240–2, 244; *Seigneurial*, 71.

46 Dollier, *Montréal*, 9–10: "A generosity without example ... giving nourishment that he himself was missing down to the food upon his own table ... not trying to derive anything from it, but due to a pure and cordiale generosity" ("une générosité sans exemple ... donner des vivres il en a manque lui-même, leur distribuant jusqu'aux mets de sa table ... ne faisait pas pour retirer aucun bien, mais par une pure et cordiale générosité").

47 Hospitallers: "we have never seen a better example of the power of charity" ("jamais on n'a vit mieux jusqu'où va le pouvoir de la charité") (Charlevoix, *Histoire* 5:208).

48 ASQ, Polygraphie, 3, 44: Mme. de la Peltrie. "[she] reduced her needs to lack the basics to clothe the children ... all her life ... it was but a tissue of the most heroic charitable acts ... . to the great advantage of the colony" ("se réduire à manquer du nécessaire, pour vêtir les Enfants ... toute sa vie ... qu'un tissu d'actions de la plus héroïque charité ... au grand avantage de toute cette colonie") (Charlevoix, *Histoire* 5:208).

49 *JR* (Thwaites), 61, 194–208; 63, 154–82.

50 Boucher, *Histoire*, 1–2.

51 Cliche, "Testaments," 70–82:1663–1700 requests to do good works were 81.5 percent while requests for mass was 50 percent, but during the later 18th century, 57.5 percent requested good works, yet the popularity of masses to requite their sins rose to 80.7 percent. Vovelle, *Provence*, 420–1.

52 Campeau, *MNF* 2:439–40, 442: doc. 127: *RJ* 1633.

53 Jaenen, "Présents," 232–3.

54 NFDH I, 52:30/6/170, roi au Vaudreuil. On the suppression of accepting gifts: ANC, MGI, B, 30 (2), 359–360:6/7/1709, ministre au Vaudreuil; ANC, MGI, B, 30 (2), 319:6/7/1709, ministre au Raudot. On the French king trying to convert a reciprocal relationship to one of sharing largesse (or in French terms, charity): ANC, MGI, B, 23–1, 137:1702, roi au Callières: "His Majesty is pleased to have them observe with regard to these presents ... that they look upon them as relief for their needs coming from his Majesty's goodness and

charity and not as a means of continuing their disorders, nor as the price of our friendship" (trans. Jaenen): all cited in Jaenen, "Presents," 245-6, 249.

55 Williams, "Bounty," introduction; Jaenen, "Presents," 232, cites Jacobs, *Wilderness*, 13–17.

56 Turgeon, Fitzgerald, et Auger, "Échanges," 152–167.

57 Mauss, *Sociologie*, introduction; Lojkine, "Don"; Godelier, *Rationalite*, introduction; Davis, *Gift*, 24.

58 *RJ*, 1648–9.

59 Trigger, *Natives*, 184–194.

60 *JJ*, 1645, 20, 29.

61 Desdouits, *Caux*, 63; Beaudoin, *L'été*, 157; Trudelle, "Pain," 157–8.

62 Massicotte, "Guignolée," 365–7; Desdouits, *Caux*, 72–81.

63 Quêteux had categories: that from afar (interesting stories), from the neighbouring parish (Carapet, Gras d'Ours, Beau-Carosse, who usually got the pretty girl), the charlatan, the spellbinder, and the poor quêteux of the parish (Joe-la-Galette, Ferme-pas-Juste, L'Anguille) (Proteau, *Légendes*, 32–40). Bergeron, *Légendes*, 138–9: the quêteux was thought to be a good healer but, if vexed, could throw spells, and slept in the sofa bed. Recently, architectural students in Montreal recycled the "banc-lit" of the quêteux into the "vagabanc" (Lanctôt, *Contes*, 228–31).

64 Rouleau, *Légendes*, 25–34.

65 Champlain, *Oeuvres*, 527–528; Campeau, *HNF* 2:142, doc. 50; Perrot, *Mémoires*, 77; Boucher, *Histoire*, 120–32; Radisson, *Voyages*, 50–7.

66 Eccles, "Military," 1.

67 Neuschel, *Honour*, 198, 204; Schalk, *Pedigree*, ch. 7, explains the shift from military valour to pedigree in the early seventeenth century.

68 Levi et Schmitt, *Jeunes*, 312–13.

69 Dewald, *European*, 198.

70 Ariès, *Death*, 145.

71 Dubois, "Coeur," 21.

72 Jaenen, *Friend*, 147.

73 Caroll, *Catholic*, cited by Delâge, "Religion," 75 (with no page number).

74 Benichou, *Grand*.

75 Floquet, *Diaire*, 415–417.

76 Bartlett, *Europe*, 89.

77 Bluche, *Louis XIV*, 235; Collins, *State*, 83–5; Castiglione, *Courtier*, 67–8, in Dewald, *Nobility*, 35.

78 Delumeau, *Peur*, 3–5; Montaigne, *Essais* 1:106; 2: ch. 28.

79 Tapié, *Richelieu*, 166–9, 183, 186.

80 Benichou, *Grande*; Floquet, *Diaire*, 415–17; Morin, *Véritable*, 76, 83–4. General conscription further encouraged the "military ethos" of the settlement. See Eccles, *Frontier*, 1.

81 Charlevoix, *Histoire* 5:212. Paul, *Mi'kmaq*, 20–2.

82 Lafitau, *Comparée*, 68.

83 LeClercq, *Gaspésie*, 18–19.

84 Ibid., 418–19.

85 Campeau, MNF 2:142, doc. 50.

86 LeClercq, *Gaspésie*, 404, 406. This is also discussed by Prins, *Mi'kmaq*, 219, who uses the term for Great Heart.

87 Charlevoix, *Voyage*, 32.

88 Sagard, *Histoire*, 373.

89 Lafitau, *Comparée*, 68.

90 LeClercq, *Gaspésie*, 404, 406.

91 Roy, *d'Argenson*, 15.

92 JR (Thwaites), 42, 51; 1, 277; cited by White, "Inner," in Hoffman, Sobel, and Teute, *Glass*, 416; Iroquois phrase in Fenton, *Law*, 160.

93 Boucher, *Histoire*, 97.

94 Perrot, *Moeurs*, 77.

95 LeClercq, *Gaspésie*, 407.

96 Ibid.; La Bruyère, *Caractères*, 24–8, 64–71; LaFayette, *Clèves;* Delumeau, *L'aveu*, introduction.

97 LeClercq, *Gaspésie*, 428–9.

98 Kinietz, *Lakes*, 362–3: Raudot, Québec 1709, letter 37; Sagard, *Histoire*, 372.

99 Giguère, *Champlain*, 77.

100 La Potherie, *Histoire* 2:76.

101 Young, *Hybridity*, introduction.

102 Kinietz, *Lakes*, 378: letter 51: Raudot, Québec 1710; Perrot, *Mémoire*, 103; Hennepin, *New* 2:510.

103 Marie, *Correspondance*, 256–7:14–27/9/1645, let. XCII.
The Third Estate was approximately 90 percent during the early seventeenth century, whereas by the Revolution it had decreased to 85 percent.

104 ASQ, MS, 66: Recueil de chants hurons par Paul Tsaouenhohi Picard.

105 RJ, 1672–1673, 72, 76.

106 RJ, 1670 and 1671, 95–102.

107 Lescarbot, *Histoire* 5, ch. 5; Sagard, *Histoire*, 331–2.

108 Davis, *Fiction*, 37–9.

109 Albert-Petit, *Normandie*, 252; Sealy and Kirkness, *Tipis*, ch. 55–70.

110 Salon, *Colonisation*, 89: "They excel at exploiting French fury. It is for them a game to heat up thins and then trap us in a trap, or for a diversion, to hide their veritable intentions, and to bring us to disarm, while suddenly they apply their most vigorous effort against us. It is by a manoeuvre of this kind that in 1653 when they were two fingers from penetrating, without flinching, into Three Rivers." ("Ils excellent à exploiter la furia française. C'est pour eux un jeu que de l'échauffer et de nous attirer dans un piège, ou, pour une diversion, de nous donner le charge sur leurs intentions véritables et de nous amener à dégarnir de combattants le point ou soudain se portera leur plus

vigoureux effort. C'est par une manoeuvre de cette sorte qu'en 1653 ils ont
été à deux doigts de pénétrer, sans coup férir, aux Three Rivers.") Salon's
tends to write not about the "French Canadians" in history but about "us."

111 *RJ*, 1648, 16–17.

112 Marie, *Correspondance*, 768:16/10/1666, let. CCXXIII.

113 Ibid., 770–1:2/11/1666, let. CCXXIV.

114 Jaenen, *Friend*, 132–4; White, *Middle*, 80.

115 "Le Cid" of Pierre Corneille, a Rouennais, was written in 1636 and dedicated
     in 1637 to Marie-Madeleine de Beauvoir Du Roure de Combalet d'Aiguillon,
     who was the financial founder of the Québec Hôtel-Dieu Hospital, among
     other charitable works (*JJ*, 1652, 16/4/1652; Héraclius: *JJ*, 1651, 4/12/1651).
     "Héraclius, empereur d'Orient" (1642) was dedicated to Chancellier Séguier,
     who was not only the protector of the Académie but also the one who crushed
     the Nu-Pieds revolt. Héraclius deals with the familiar Jesuit theme about
     controlling tyranny and concerns two boys whose wetnurse exchanged their
     identities, also an interesting theme for French Canadians. Molière's
     "Tartuffe," about a falsely pious man who tries to dupe others sexually and
     financially, so incensed Bishop St Vallier, that he thundered about it from
     the pulpit and paid Governor Frontenac not to play it. See Corneille,
     Molière.

116 Posner, *Nobility*, ch. 4.

117 *JJ*, 1646; Fauteux, *Duel*, 10.

118 Charlevoix, *Histoire* 5:201.

119 Juchereau, *Annales*, 91–2; *RJ* (Thwaites) 43, 107–13.

120 Bettelheim, *Heart*, ch. "Extreme;" expressed in Primo Levi, *I Sommersi e i
     salvati, (The Drowned and the Saved)* 1986; Wallace, *Extreme*.

121 Narrative; *DBC* 1:399–402.

122 Trigger, *Newcomers*, 279; Three Rivers: *JR* (Thwaites) 43, 103–25.

123 *RJ* (Thwaites) 43, 107–13. The bulk of the population was scandalized. See
     Trigger, *Aataentsic*, 810.

124 Dollier, *Montréal*, 40.

125 Juchereau, *Annales*, 91–2.

126 *RJ* (Thwaites) 19, 90–120; Marie, *Correspondance*, 104–7:4/9/1640, let. XLV.

127 Moogkt, "Exiles," 503.

128 Details in Boucher, *Histoire*, 151; Trudel, *HNF* 2:1, 203.

129 Eccles, "Military," 1–22.

130 Marie, *Correspondance*, 143–4:16/9/164, let. LIX.

131 Morin, *Véritable*, 63.

132 Charlevoix, *History* 7, 285; Eccles, *Frontier*, 97.

133 *JR* (Thwaites) 8, 10; Ragueneau, "Mémoires touchant la mort et les vertus des
     pères Isaac Jogues, etc.," Archives du Collège de Ste-Marie à Montréal, re
     RAPQ, 1924–5, 3–70, passim. *RJ*, 1648–9; Marie, *Correspondance*,
     364–367:9/1649, let. CXXI; Charlevoix, *Histoire* 7:290.

134 ANC, MG 18, H10 (1): Lettres de noblesse accordées à Pierre Boucher;
Boucher, *Histoire*, 48–9. After the Battle of Three Rivers in 1653 Governor
Lauzon promoted Pierre Boucher, to commander and, within a few months,
to city governor; Commission as governor of Three Rivers: ANQ, Insinuations
du Conseil Souverain, I, fol. 5, Québec, 28/10/1663.

135 Morin, *Véritable*, 69; Dollier, *Montréal*, 29–31. Juchereau, *Annales*, 40–1:
According to Mother Juchereau, Montréal governor Maisonneuve and twenty
Montrealers ran to save four soldiers trapped in the watchout from 800
Iroquois. Perhaps the numbers are exaggerated, but he became a hero just
the same. See Dollier, *Montréal*, 18.

136 *BRH*, 1927, 33, 157–9: lettre Canadien captif des Iroquois.

137 ASQ, Lettres, M, 21, 38; 317000; "d'Iberville," *BRH*, 21, 1915, 224; Frégault,
Iberville; Crouse, d'Iberville.

138 ANC, MG 18, H16: Marie Magdelaine De Verchère, 19 October 1699. *DBC*,
246. Marie-Madeleine Jarret de Verchères' sudden courage could have been
mobilized by the traumatic memory of the Iroquois attack upon her own
mother in 1690. Her mother's life was saved by Thomas Crisafy, chevalier de
Malte. She also later saved the life of her own husband. See Patterson, *Battles*,
32.

139 Marie, *Correspondance*, 767:16/10/1666, let. CCXXIII.

140 The French used ruses in battle that impressed even the Iroquois: apparently
Radisson induced an Iroquois adopted son to tell of his dream, which
precipitated an eat-all feast, which occupied them while the threatened
mission stealthily prepared a raft. When the Iroquois awoke the next
morning, they thought the black robes had flown away like birds because all
the canoes were intact. See *JR* (Thwaites) 44, 177, 179; Marie, (Richaudeau)
Lettres 2:128–37. And for a picturesque rendering of this incident see
Parkman, *France*, 1128–33. Colonel Braddock and his British contingent was
unfamiliar with Native strategy and was roundly routed at Monongehela by
the French; some officers disguised as Natives; Abenaki, Wendat, Potawatami,
Ojibwa, Shawnee, and Kahnewake Iroquois; and Ottawa under Pontiac.
George Washington wrote of the Canadians who mixed with their allies, and
on 18 July 1759, one was caught naked, painted red and blue with feathers on
his head, scalping the British (Washington, *Washington*, 55.)
The first Ursulines danced in the Native fashion with their students; the
Canadians danced in their allied villages; during the Great Peace in 1701 at
Montreal, three Canadians danced Native style; Frontenac was depicted doing
a Native war dance; when he visited the Sisters of the Congregation Pehr
Kalm was treated to Amerindian dances by Canadian girl pupils whose
families lived in Amerindian communities. And in the Mauricie area, the
makusham is still danced. All of the foregoing is cited in Delâge,
"L'influence," 136–8.

141 Nikolai, *Courage*, 73.

142 Louise Dechêne writes of the gentlemen-soldiers who arrived in New France : "Values that they have brought as their only baggage were so close to those of Native society that instead of speaking of influence, one should speak of an encounter." ("Les valeurs qu'ils apportent pour tout bagage sont si près de celles qui ont cours dans la société indienne qu'au lieu de parler d'influence, il faudrait parler de rencontre.") Unfortunately, Dechêne does not pursue this fruitful idea any farther (Dechêne, *Habitants*, 50).

143 Tocqueville, *Democracy*, 256–7.

144 Légaré, *Beau*, 7–115; Barbeau, *Contes* 7e, 137–141; Lanctôt, *Contes* 5e, 383–7: Pierre sans peur.

145 Elias, *Individuals*, 100–2.

146 Michaelson, "Mi'kmaq," 33; Bailey, *Conflict*, 186.

147 Leland, *Legends*, 15, 89, 125–7; Leland, "Edda," 127, 228; Bailey, *Conflict*, 159–61, 167, 184–7.

148 Clements, *Folklore*, 129–154.

149 Ibid., 134.

150 Ibid., 136–7.

151 Rand, *Mi'kmaq*, 233–7.

152 Ibid., 288, 292.

153 Leland, *Edda*, 15; Dixon, *Algonkins*, 1–10.

154 Bailey, *Conflict*, 187.

155 Clements, *Folklore*, 133–4.

156 Speck, *Breton*, 59; Rand, *Mi'kmaq*, 45.

157 Speck, *Breton*, 60.

158 Speck, *Mi'kmaq*, 59; Leland, *Legends*, 15, 89, 125–7; Leland, "Edda," 127, 228; Bailey, *Conflict*, 159–61, 167, 184–7. Parsons, *Mi'kmaq*, 55; Bailey, *Conflict*, 185–8.

159 Speck, *Breton*, 60; Bailey, *Conflict*, 185–8.

160 Clements, *Folklore*, 138.

161 Ibid., 144–5.

162 Clarke, *Legends*, 43–6; Thompson, *Tales*, 5–8.

163 NT, Matt. 5:1–16 (Sermon on the Mount).

164 Ortiz and Erdoes, *Myths*, 365–7.

165 Rand, *Mi'kmaq*, 233–7, 254; Clark, *Legends*, 34–6.

166 Dirks, Eley, and Ortner, *Theory*, 19.

167 Josephus, *Wars*, 375.

168 Ibid., 371.

169 Desdouits, *Caux*, 304; Provencher, *Saison*, 198.

170 Bercé, *Absolutism*, 203.

171 Desdouits, *Caux*, 287–97; in Cyrano de Bergerac's *Histoire comique des Estats et Empires de la Lune: Voyages imaginaires à la recherche de la vérité humaine* (1628) the hero finds himself in Québec, and the contraption with which he intended to fly to the moon was thrown into the bonfire by Canadian soldiers. So instead of flying, he celebrated the St-Jean-Baptiste in Quebec.

172 *NT,* Matt. 3; Mark 1:1–13; Luke 1:57–80, 3; John 1–2.

173 The Druids used to drive cattle between two great bonfires as a protection against disease (Renel, Gaule; Anwyl, *Celtic;* Squier, *Serpent,* 125).

174 Squier, *Serpent,* 125.

175 Brekilien, *Bretagne,* 214–15.

176 The St John fires are still lit in Scandinavia today, despite the Reformation, due to the strength of their Celtic and Nordic sources (Davidson, *Lost,* 88.)

177 Greilsammer, *Heresy,* 25.

178 Delumeau, *Catholicism,* ch. 3.

179 *NT,* Mark 6:22; Josephus, *Wars,* Ant. 2:202; Josephus, *Wars,* Excursis 1:371–5; Nitzan, "Repentance," in Flint and Vanderkorn, *Assessment,* 145–70; Evans, "Jesus," in Flint and Vanderkorn, *Assessment,* 573–98; Yadin, *Milhamot,* 222–6.

180 Porschnev, *Soulèvements,* 320–1, Tapié, *France,* 396–7.

181 Berce, *Revolts,* 309.

182 Gaspé, *Anciens,* 86.

183 Jaenen, *Church,* 145–6.

184 Hamelin, *Détroit,* 161.

185 Desdouits, *Caux,* 304–5; Provencher, *Saisons,* 198.

186 Dollier, *Histoire,* 89; Morin, *Histoire,* 86.

187 Desdouits, *Caux,* 289.

188 Jaenen, *Church,* 146.

189 AFUL, coll. Gui Giguère, "le dernier char du défilé,: St-Jean-Baptiste et son mouton (Ste-Anne de Beaupré).

190 Johnston, *Restless,* 133.

191 Sébillot, *Folklore* 4:63.

192 Gibson, *Women,* 77.

193 Schmitt, *Revenants,* 233.

194 Molière, "Tartuffe," 3:2

195 Sagard, *Histoire,* 40; *RJ* (Thwaites), 3, 7–8, 22: neophyte penitents insisted on lacerations, which sometimes caused early deaths, as with Catherine Tekakwitha.

196 Jaenen, *Church,* 142–4.

197 Cliche, "Testaments," 62, 90.

198 Desdouits, *Caux,* 299–300.

199 He wore a woven camelhair coat (*NT,* Matt. 3:4; Mark 1:6), yet in early modern France he was traditionally dressed in a sheep- or lambskin.

200 Benedict, *Rouen,* 1, for reproduced emblem.

201 Ovide, *Métamorphoses* 7:1–158; Johnston, *Restless,* 167.

202 Monter, "Male," 582–4.

203 Dollier, *Montréal,* 60.

204 Jetten, *Enclaves,* 103–6.

205 *OT,* Exodus, 12–13:1–16.

206 *RJ,* 1646, 64–5.

207 Barbeau, "Contes 1st," 102–5.

CHAPTER 7

1 Eusebius Pamphili, *Episcopi Chronicon*, s.a. 1509; Biggar, *Precursers*, 66; all cited in Dickason, *Savage*, 72–84.

2 Caesar, *Gallico*, 18; Ross, *Britain*, 152; Rhys, *Celtic*, 202–3; Rhys, *Heathendom*, 250–1; Lloyd-Jones, *Geir*, 37; Duvel, *Gaule*, 306–7; Martin, *Religion*, passim; Renel, *Gaule*, 187, 246, 261; Green, *Celts*; Anwyl, *Religion;* Davidson, *Pagan*, 209; Davidson, *Lost*, 46; McCana, *Celtic*, 44–53. YHWH is the Hebrew abbreviation for the God of the Old Testament. The name of God should ideally never be uttered, due to its holiness.

3 Dickason, *Savage*, 289, 63n.

4 *Babylonian Talmud*, Tractate Gittin, 68a-b, cited by Gaster, "Apocrypha." Loomis, *Literature*, 32; Loomis, *Celtic*, 125; Tolstoy, Quest, 28–9, 141.

5 Tolstoy, *Quest*, 146–7; O Riain, "Wild," 179–206.

6 Pliny, *Natural*, 14, 95; Caesar, *Bello Gallico*, 4. MacCana, *Celtic*, 43.

7 Ms. cotton Titus A. xix; cited by Le Rouzic, *Carnac*, 173.

8 Grisward, *Epopée*, 183–228; Widengren, "Harlekintracht," 41–111, cited in Schmitt, *Revenants*, 122–40.

9 Spence, *Magic*, 92–3.

10 Schmitt, *Ghosts*, 111–19.

11 Tilbury, *Traditions*, 289.

12 Baraton, et al, *Vendée*, 176.

13 Bibiliothèque municipale d'Alençon, ms 2653, fol. 5r–14r; Chibnall, *Orderic* 1:17, which included Bishop Hugues de Lisieux, abbé Mainier de St-Evroult, and abbé Gerbert de St-Wandrille Moricet, *Normandes*, 177–94: The Wild Hunt [E 501] occurred at the church of St-Aubin de Bonneval; Schmitt, "Jeunes," 106–22; Schmitt, *Ghosts*, ch. 5; LeGoff and Schmitt, *Charivari*, 134–6.

14 Desdouits, *Caux*, 397–400.

15 Ovid, *Metamorphoses*, cited by Schmitt, *Revenants*, 201–32; Ariès, *Death*, 23.

16 Davidson, *Lost*, 77, 99.

17 Bernheimer, *Wild*, 1–33; Dickason, *Savage*, 72–80; van Gennep, *Folklore* 4:622; 1:924; *Populaires*, 20, 1905, 177–86; Moricet, *Normandie*, 177–94.

18 Le Héricher, *Littérature*, 51; Moricet, *Normandie*, 193.

19 Dickason, *Savage*, 74; Schmitt, *Ghosts*, 113–15.

20 Schmitt, *Ghosts*, 115–20; Delumeau, *Peur*, 87.

21 Lecouteux, *Fantômes*, 24–5; Davidson, *Lost*, 138–43.

22 Guillaume d'Auvergne, *De universo*, III, ca XII, in *Opera Omnia*, Paris, 1674, I, 593–1074 in Schmitt, *Revenants*, 143–5.

23 Schmitt, *Ghosts*, 109–16.

24 Revelard et Kostadinova, *Masques*, passim.

25 Exorcist manual: *Livre d'Egidius*, doyen de Tournai cited in Delumeau, *Peur*, 73.
26 Regismäl and Sigidrifum 1:, 20; Davidson, *Lost*, 137–8; Ginsberg, *Ecstacies*, 301; also Norman: Moricet, *Normandes*, 157: "La fosse Arthur." He is buried between Mortain and Domfront in Barenton, while Arthur and Guinevere haunt it as crows. Moricet, *Normandie*, 157–8; Lecoeur, *Esquisses*, 372–4. Soul as a bird: Thompson, *Folktale*, 258: E732.
27 Baldrs Draumar, Volsinga Saga, Harbardsljojd, Ynglinga Saga, Grimnism cited in Davison, *Lost*, 77, 109.
28 Clements, *Folklore*, 146.
29 Bibliothèque D'Alençon, Ms. no. 2653, fol. 164.
30 Massignon, *Ouest*, 160–3.
31 Cureau, *Traité*, ch. 2,2,2<???>; ch. 3,1,1<???>; ch. 3; ch. 4; ch. 5: the ability of humans to metamorphose into animals and vice versa was a common belief among the people, yet it was vehemently denied by the elite, who insisted that animals had no souls and were incapable of thought. LaFontaine (*Les Fables*, *L'âme des bêtes*) was the sole defensor of animals among them. Roheim, *Culture*, ch. 2: le culte des morts et la civilization. Virgil, *Ecologues*, VIII, 70; St. Augustine, *Civitate*, 18, 18; Institutoris et Kraemer, *Malleus*, II, q. 1, 298–301 cited in Roberts, "Circe," in Barry et al., *Witchcraft*, 183–206.
32 Clements, *Folklore*, 135.
33 Rand, *Mi'kmaqs*, 89; Clements, *Folklore*, 135–41.
34 Clements, *Folklore*, 140–1.
35 Leland, *Edda*, 228; Bailey, *Conflict*, 167.
36 Clements, *Folklore*, 142.
37 La Potherie, *Histoire* 2:6; *JR* (Thwaites), 6, 159–60. Radin, *Ojibwa*, # 1327; Barnouw, *Wisconsin*, ch. 2–3; Speck, *Timiskaming*. Thompson, *Tales*, 8–13; Clarke, *Legends*, 5–6; Erdoes and Ortiz, *Myths*, 347–52.
37 Hennepin, *New* 2:538–9.
39 Sagard, *Histoire*, 514, *JR* (Thwaites), 6, 159–61.
40 Grim, *Shaman*, 86–91; Warren, *Ojibway*, 110; Hallowell, "Ontology," 228; Helbig, *Nanabozhoo*.
41 Ritzenthaler, *Lakes*, 128–32.
42 Barnouw, *Wisconsin*, 30–4, 85.
43 Sagard, *Histoire*, 510; LaPotherie, *Histoire* 2:6.
44 *JR* (Thwaites), 12, 15; 15, 99; 23, 155; 24, 209; 31, 191; 33, 25; 39, 15; 53, 283; 54, 127–9; 57, 297.
45 Delumeau, *Catholicism*, ch. 3.
46 Grim, *Shaman*, 88; Dewdney, *Scrolls*, 115.
47 Radin, *Trickster*, 202; Roheim, *Hero*, 190–4.
48 Joué-du-Plain, Bibliothèque d'Alençon, ms. n. 2653, fol. 73 r–74 r; Lecoeur, *Esquisses* 1:265–6; Moricet, *Normandie*, 109.
49 Martin, *Keepers*, 94–112 (this book was kindly given to me by Cornelius Jaenen). Altherr, "Flesh," 275; Armitage, *Homeland;* Martin, *Keepers*, 131–44:

tularemia (pasteurella or Francisella tularensis), ectoparasites, enzootic, epizootic, zoonoses.

50 Martin, *Keepers,* ch. 1–2; Speck, *Naskapi;* Hendrickson, *Hunters;* Tanner, *Cree.*

51 Sagard, *Histoire,* 510.

52 LeClercq, *Gaspésie,* 307. The Mi'kmaq especially respected the bones of female beavers, porcupines, and birds. See *JR* (Thwaites), 6, 211–13.

53 *JR* (Thwaites), 1, 177; Martin, *Keepers,* ch. 3.

54 *Edda,* 178; Clements, *Folklore,* 150; Davidson, *Lost,* 119.

55 Moricet, *Normandie,* 65–80; Lecoeur, *Esquisses* 2:403–4; Du Bois, *Recherches,* 299.

56 Ariès, *Hour,* 170; Davidson, *Lost,* 81; Ginsberg, *Ecstacies,* 244–6. The Celtic myth of the Children of Lir held that seals and swans were king's children under a spell who needed their pelts to remain free. See Spence, *Magic,* 92–5.

57 MacNeill and Gamer, *Penitentials,* 276–7.

58 Diamond, "Disease," in Dickason, *Imprint,* 155–67.

59 Proteau, *Légendes,* 57.

60 Desdouits, *Caux,* 397–402.

61 *RJ* (inédite), 2, 79.

62 Cliche, "Mort," 63–8.

63 Lévi-Strauss, *Lynx,* 245–6; Racine, *Oeuvres,* 123–40. Jean Racine used this character's name in Les Plaideurs, and the simpleton can later be found in the early eighteenth-century metropolitan evolution of Jean le Teigneux and Robert le Diable. In the Vendée, there was also a "Jan le Sot." See Gautier et Quellec, *Vendée,* 72–9.

64 Fowkes, *Folktales,* 30–3.

65 Barbeau, *Contes* 1e, 134–5: Four men hunted and saved a bird for the one who had the best dream. The first dreamt that he married a beautiful princess, while the second saw Mother Mary. The third went to Heaven to see God, but the fourth dreamt that he had eaten the bird, which they soon afterward discovered had not merely been a dream (also in Fowke, *Folktales,* 12). Analogous tales: "Prince de l'épée verte," where the prince was a hunter (Barbeau, *Contes* 1e, 61–70); and "Ti-Jean ti-bois," in Barbeau, Contes 1e, 80–7. Perhaps its Norman predecessor is "Language des bêtes," in Tenaille, *Normandie,* 9–17.

66 The inverse of the Rose Latulippe legend, where the most desirable belle of the parish is almost whisked away by a mysterious dancing stranger, who is the Devil in disguise. this mars her life. See Dupont, Tadoussac, # 10:"Diable beau danseur" (Sept Îles); Dupont, *Villages,* 44–5: "le survenant du Mardi Gras" (Îles d'Orléans); Woodley, *Legends,* 26–33; Fowkes, *Folktales,* "Le diable à la danse."

67 *OT,* Daniel, 6.

68 Assiniwi, *Contes,* 25.

69 Rand, *Mi'kmaqs,* 14.

70 Mechling, Maliseet, 219–58; Bailey, *Conflict*, 180–3.

71 Assiniwi and Myre, *Contes*, 87–98.

72 Bailey, *Conflict*, 180.

73 Ibid.

74 Lévi-Strauss, *Lynx*, 242; Barnouw, *Wisconsin*, 213–14.

75 Lévi-Strauss, *Nu*, 247–8.

76 Légaré, *Beau*, 3–18.

77 Ibid.; 171–80; 191–206; 207–16; Légaré, *Têtes*, 17–40; 55–60; 151–62.

78 Dickason, *Savage*, 80–1.

79 Le Goff, *Purgatory*, 1–14; Nathalie Zemon Davis, discussion summer 1998; Bhabha, *Culture*, passim.

80 Sagard, *Histoire*, 497–9. *RJ* (inédites) 6:12; 5:5, cited in Jetten, *Enclaves*, 111.

81 St-John, *Haudenosaunee*, 43.

82 Legitimating historical legends, called "foundation legends" by Tudor, *Myth*, chs. 3–4. Zakai, *Exile;* but especially *Theocracy.*

83 Sagard, *Hurons*, 42–3.

84 *RJ*, 1648, 101.

85 Nute, *Voyageurs*, ch. 4.

86 Taché, *Forestiers*, 145.

87 Pomerleau, *Coureurs*, 90.

88 Teicher, *Windigo;* Landes, *Midewiwin*, 7, 12–14, 13, 39, 58; Barnouw, *Wisconsin*, ch. 5; Fogelson, "Psychological," in Spiro, Anthropology, 74–99; Parker, "Wiitiko," 603–23; Brown, "Windigos," 20–3; Hay, "Windigo," 1–19; Rohrl, "Windigo," 97–101. Upcountry: the old pays d'en haut, the Upper Country, Old Northwest (i.e., Great Lakes).

89 Sagard, *Huron*, 113–14; *JR* (Thwaites), 10, 177, 183, 325.

90 Champlain, *Oeuvres* 2:962: raven (1616); Brébeuf, *Relation*, 105–8, 171: turtledove (1636).

91 The elderly and the children did not have the strength to do this, and they remained and occupied abandoned fields and homes. Suicides and war dead were not permitted entry into the village of souls as their souls frightened the others. On the way to the Astiken andahatey, the esken pass a rock (Ecaregniondi) that holds the lodge of Oscotarach (Pierce-head), who removed the brains from the skulls. See Brébeuf, *Relation*, 138–41. Then the esken has to pass a river (like the Roman Cocytus) over a tree bridge guarded by a dog (like the Roman Cerberus). Here some of the souls fell into the river. See Le Braz, *Morts* 2:104–23; Le Braz, *Morts* 2:86–7. Then the soul flies away. In île de Bréhat, geese or black cat; in Cornwall, black crow (like King Arthur); in Ireland, dove or black cat or dog.

92 Sagard (Wrong), *Hurons*, 211–14; Brébeuf, *Relation*, 105–8, 171; *JR* (Thwaites), 10, 279–311.; Kinietz, *Lakes*, 99–120. The Christian concept of a separate Heaven and Hell came from the European pagan separation of souls. Its Hebrew root, She'ul, did not separate families.

93 Champlain, *Oeuvres* 2:962: "United in friendship and concordance, like parents and friends, without being able to separate from these bones which were mixed this way." ("Unis en amitié & concorde, comme parents & amis, sans s'en povuoir se séparer ces os estans ainsi meslez.")

94 "nous ne sommes plus que les debris d'une nation florissante ... Ce que tu vois n'est que la carcasse d' un grand peuple, dont L'Haudenosaunee a rongé toute la chair ... sucer jusques ... la moelle ... fais vivre tes pauvres enfants qui sont aux abois. De notre vie depend celle d'une infinité de peuples." See *RJ* (Thwaites), 45, 40–2; Vachon, *Eloquence*, 75.

95 "Grand Onontio, tu vois ... tes pieds ... les restes d'un monde entier ... Ce ne sont que les carcasses qui te parlent ... l'Haudenosaunee n'a laissé que les os ... Courage peuple désolé, tes os vont être liés de nerfs et de tendons ... plus grand des Onontios de la terre, qui a eu compassion de nos misères." See *JR* (Thwaites), 49, 226–34.

96 Sagard, *Histoire*, 508–14.

97 *JR* (Thwaites), 8, 23; 33, 24.

98 Ibid., 8, 259.

99 *JR* (Thwaites), 16, 191. Other Algonquians: Ketaguswowt or Spirit's Path (Abenaki).

100 LeClercq, *Gaspésie*, ch. 8.

101 Chamberlain, "Algonkian," 275.

102 *JR* (Thwaites), 23, 209–23; 55, 137–9; 62, 201; Radisson (Skull), *Voyages*, 199–201, 217–19; Perrot, *Histoire* 1:86–8; Margry, *Découvertes* 5:104–6; Hickerson, "Feast," 81–107, 92–8.

103 Hennepin, *New* 1: ch. 28.

104 Squier, *Serpent*, 70. Northern Lights: Wababanal (Abenaki) or Wasetibikan (Anishinabe). For a modern Cree rendition of a song based upon this belief, see Bass and Green, *Heartbeat*, song 33. Northern Lights: "Listen to the Heavens / the spirits are singing / Listen to the heavens / the spirits are dancing / Listen to the songs / the spirits are singing" (Crying Woman Singers of Thunderchild Reserve in Saskatoon, Saskatchewan).

105 Skinner, *Menomini*, 299–307.

106 Kinietz, *Lakes*, 160; Skinner, *Menomini*, 291–4.

107 Grim, *Shaman*, 71–6.

108 Hirschfelder and Molin, *Religions*, passim.

109 Parker, "Seneca," 161–85.

110 Hewitt, "Soul," 112–15.

111 Fenton and Kurath, *Dead*, 145–7.

112 Newberry Library, Ayer Ms 451, a translation of the speech by Jimmy Johnson (Sosheowa) at the Grand Council of the Haudenosaunee 1851 (on the code of his grandfather Handsome Lake [Skaniadario or Ganyadaiyo]); also Fenton, *Longhouse*, 114–16, 3rd vision 5/2/1800 and 3rd dictum.

113 Sagard, *Histoire* 3:789; *RJ* (Jour) 4:170. Auhaîtsique was a French interpreter whose only known name today is in Huron, the people amongst whom he

sojourned. He and Father Viel drowned, perhaps due to Wendat intent, at the descent from the Rivière des prairies at what is even today called "Sault au récollet."

114 Bercé, *Absolutism,* 149. The drum in Native culture chased away sorrow and illness by inducing life-giving dance.

115 *RJ* (Jour), 3, 14–15; Eliade, *Shamanism,* 147.

116 Moerman, *Medicine,* 483.

117 Grim, *Shaman,* 76–8. Hennepin, *New* 1:245–6; *RJ,* 1670–1, 95–102; Landes, *Midewiwin,* 49; 63; Woodley, *Legends,* 12–18.

118 Rousseau, "L'Annéda," 201.

119 For windigo beliefs, see Blum, "Windigos."

120 *JR* (Thwaites), 10, 158–67; 33, 226; 50.

121 Bergeron, *Royaume,* 144; in St-Jérôme (Lac St-Jean) the priest sings midnight mass before the Chasse-Galérie arrives. Dupont, *Villages,* 17 legend 17 "le curé en Chasse-Galérie"; Dupont, *Côte-Nord,* 19, the Chasse-Galérie Hunter Valère goes hunting on snowshoes. Good Friday sees the Chasse-Galérie with Satan visibly forking at them.

122 Beaugrand, *Chasse-Galérie,* 19–32; Bergeron, *Royaume,* 139–42.

123 *BRH,* 4, 282; Pearl, "Witchcraft," 195.

124 Le Braz, *Mort* 2:1639; Delumeau, *Peur,* 85–6.

125 Eliade, *Mythes,* 126–38.

126 Davidson, *Celtic,* 18–19, 33; Column, *Myths,* 152–61; Spence, *Magic,* 74, 129–31, 174; Green, *Celtic,* 141–2.

127 Davidson, *Scandinavian,* 74–92; Davidson, *Lost,* 137.

128 Davidson, *Scandinavian,* 23, 92–3; Osseberg ship, ship graves at Tuna in Västmanland; Davidson, *Lost,* 158.

129 Le Goff, *Purgatory,* introduction.

130 *OT,* Ezechiel, 36:25–6; Yoel, 3:1–2; Isaiah, 33:15–18; 55: 1–10.

131 Jung, *Symbols,* vol. 5.

132 Noted by Delâge and Dubois, "L'eau," 14.

133 Ginsberg, *Ecstacy,* 176, ft. 26.

134 Hirschfelder and Molin, *Religions,* passim; Grim, *Shaman,* 65–70.

135 Sobel, "Inner," in Hoffman, Sobel, and Teute, *Glass,* 182. In early Christianity, the dove had always been the symbol of the Holy Ghost, which was derived, according to Mechal Sobel's certainly correct deduction, from the Kabbalistic vision of the Shekinah, or the soul's basic femaleness. Beland, *Chansons,* 133–6.

136 Ankarloo and Henningson, *Witchcraft,* 45–51.

137 Rand, *Mi'kmaq,* 233–7.

138 Schmitt, *Ghosts,* 113.

139 Marx, *Graal,* 281–4; Schmitt, *Ghosts,* 80–1.

140 Van Gennep, *Initiation,* introduction; Mahdi, Foster, and Little, *Betwixt,* 461.

141 Levack, *Witchcraft,* 35–6.

142 Neumann, *Mother*, 326.

143 Dupont, *Villages*, 3; Côte-Nord, 18.

144 Delâge and Dubois, "L'eau," 14.

145 LeClercq, *Gaspésie*, 359; Barnouw, *Wisconsin*, 298.

146 Kohl, *Kitchi-Gami*, 408; Landes, *Midewiwin*, 27–8; Hallowell, *Bear*, 135–7; Skinner, *Saulteaux*, 68–76; Tanner, *Cree*, 170–80; Martin, *Keepers*, 117–18; Grim, *Shaman*, 96–7; Barnouw, *Chippewa*, 139.

147 Nathalie Davis on Frenchmen and hats: Davis, *Fiction*, 31, 38, 171n13, 174n38.

148 Don Handelman, discussion, 9/2/1998.

149 McCana, *Celtic*, 50; Sheldrake, *Worlds*, 48; Davidson, *Lost*, 31, 68–78, 98.

150 Hultkranz, "Pillar."

151 Van Dam, *Saints*, 116–41.

152 Carpentier, *Arbres*, 24–5; Moerman, *Medicinal*, 1–2; Vogel, *Medicine*, 277–9. McCana quotes *Strabo* 12:5, diunemeton (oak sanctuary) in *Celtic*, 16; Fraser, *Golden*, 159–61, "druid" means "oak man."

153 Erdoes and Ortiz, *Myths*, 193–9.

154 Turgeon, "Kettle," 11, 16.

155 Aus, "Beheading," ch. 1. Symbols could aid interpretation: the head of the beloved Father St-Père was shorn on the Eve of St John the Baptist and allegedly haunted the Haudenosaunee unceasingly, thus preserving New France (Dollier, *Montréal*, 68–9).

156 *NT*, Matt. 15:36–9; Mark, 8:1–10.

157 Loomis, *Arthurian*, 210. Lévi-Strauss mentions the correspondence of the Grail in both the Old World and the New World but points to different aspects than those mentioned here (Lévi-Strauss, *Lectures*, ch. 6).

158 BNF, fr. 99, fol. 563: Li Roumans du bon chevalier Tristan cited in Malcor, *Chalice*, 42 and Littleton and Malcor, *Camelot*, ch. 8.

159 Troyes, *Oeuvres*, 760–8, lignes 3004–363.

160 Strabo, *Geographia* 7:2.3, cited by Davidson, *Lost*, 14–17; Green, *Celtic*, 147: 5th century BCE crater of 1.63 metres with gorgon heads and warriors on handles, surmounted by a strainer decorated with the statuette of a woman at Vix, Burgundy, that is one of the richest burial sites of the period in Central Europe.

161 Taliesin, *Preiddeu Annwn*, cited in Markale, *Brocéliande*, 278; Spence, *Magic*, ch. 8; also Green, *Celtic*, 142.

162 Strabo, *Geographia* 7:2.3, priestess at Cimbri gathered the blood and heads of slain war captives; cited in Davidson, *Lost*, 14–17, 96; McCana, *Celtic*, 31.

163 Davidson. *Lost*, 72–3, 78; Davidson, *Scandinavian*, 96.

164 Légaré, *Mauricie*, 19–40; Woodley, *Legends*, 96–100.

165 Thompson, *Tales*, 163; Erdoes and Ortiz, *Myths*, 230–6.

166 Viau, *Enfants*, 116–17; Gélinas, "Attaques," 122.

167 Légaré, *Tête*; Thompson, *Tales*, 201–4.

168 Sheldrake, *Worlds,* 50–4.
169 Charlevoix, *Journal,* 136, cited in White, *Middle,* 178.
170 Van Gennep, *Folklore* 1:632–40; Bernheimer, *Wild,* 65; Dickason, *Savage,* 74–5; Baraton, *Hommes,* 176.
171 Bergeron, *Légende,* 140.
172 Moricet, *Normandie,* 89–91, 93; Lecoeur, *Esquisses,* 36–7.
173 Ginsberg, *Benandanti,* introduction.
174 Jung and Kerenyi, *Mythology,* 94; Neumann, *Mother,* 310.
175 Virgil, *Aeneid,* IV.
176 Marie, *Correspondance,* 740–3:28/7/1665, let. CCXV.
177 Neumann, *Mother,* 80, 140, 169–70, 228–31, 231, 273, 311, 326, 332; Stone, *Mirrors,* 354–6.
178 Neumann, *Mother,* 164–5.
179 BNF, ms., fr. 146: Gervais du Bus, Roman de Fauvel (1310 et 1314), cited in Schmitt, *Revenant,* 191–3.
180 Ginsberg, *Ecstacies,* 303.
181 Desdouits, *Caux,* 160.
182 Sagard, *Hurons,* 113–14; *JR* (Thwaites), 10, 177, 183, 325; 17, 167–71, 181; 23, 53, 103; 30, 101; 42, 155–65; 55, 61.
183 Sagard, *Hurons,* 112–13, 118; *JR* (Thwaites), 8, 121; 10, 13, 61, 169–79, 185, 225; 13, 55, 155, 191; 15, 73, 99, 105, 159–61, 177–9, 187; 17, 15, 97, 137, 155, 161–3, 191–5; 21, 161–3; 23, 45, 171, 153–5; 26, 245–9; 33, 189–93, 199, 201, 203–5.
184 *JR* (Thwaites), 15, 99; 21, 161; 23, 153–9; 51, 235; 53, 265, 295–197; St-John, *Haudenosaunee,* 66.
185 Brébeuf, *Relation,* 120–5; *JR* (Thwaites), 10, 183.
186 *JR* (Thwaites), 33, 221.
187 Brébeuf, *Hurons,* 131–6; *JR* (Thwaites), 10, 199–209. Another life-giving ceremony was the Andacwander, requested sometimes by the ill, which consisted of the woman and youth making love in front of him or her to revive the spirits (*JR* [Thwaites], 167, 147).
188 In the logger version recorded by Bergeron (*Légendes,* 139–42) they cried: "Ramons, ramez, ramons, ramez les anges vont nous porter."
189 Fowkes, *Folktales,* 118–24.
190 Hamlin, *Detroit,* 126–33.
191 AAQ, registre A, # 173, 131; Têtu et Gagnon, *Mandements,* I, 114 cited in Jaenen, *Church,* 140.
192 Marie, *Correspondance,* 737:19/8/1664, let. CCXIV.
193 Ibid., 248–263:14–27/9/1645, let. XCII.
194 Lucretius, *Nature* 3: w. 952–78; Bossuet, "Sermon sur la mort," 267: "Tout nous appelle à la mort"; Pascal, *Pensées;* Delumeau, *Renaissance,* 386; Ariès, *Death,* 124–6.
195 Roheim, *Culture,* 147.

196 Beland, *Chansons*, 147–9: Coll. E.-Z Massicotte, MN, #842; MN, #1087.
Example: "In Chicoutimi, there is a brunette / ... who says that the habitants
are savages or Natives ... / the young girls say amongst themselves, the
Voyageurs arrive, each one for herself / see the habitants, each to her own /
See the habitants, they are greatly ashamed, / ... So they be, their girlfriends
... / See a habitant at work / Full of cow excrement up to the face / See the
Voyageur at work ... Full of vivacity and courage." ("C"est dans Chicoutimi il
y'a-t-il une brune / ... dit que les habitants sont des sauvages ... / les jeunes
filles se disent entre eux autres/ – les voyageurs qui arrivent, chacun les
nôtres. / Voyez les habitants, ils ont grand honte, / ... leurs-z-êtent, leurs
blondes ... / Voyez un habitant ... son ouvrage / Plein de marde de vache
jusqu'au visage. / Voyez un voyageur ... son ouvrage. / Plein de vivacité, plein
de courage.")

197 Erdoes and Ortiz, *Myths*, 352; Bailey, *Conflict*, 174–5.

CHAPTER 8

1 Term and quote in Attinasi and Friedrich, "Dialogic," 51, in Tedlock and
Mannheim, *Emergence*.

2 Singer, *Glassy*, 80, cited in Attinasi and Friedrich, "Dialogic," 34, in Tedlock
and Mannheim, *Emergence*.

3 Landry, *Orphélines*.

4 James Axtell, Jan Grabowski, Richard White, and Nancy Shoemaker, *Negotiators of Change*, 60–1, have noted the importance of renaming. Some immigrant noms de guerre were identical with those of the Nu-Pieds – Lafontaine,
Larose, Lafleur, Laverdure, Sans Regret – indicating that the rebel models
symbolized the urge for self-renewal. The nicknames Bassompierre and
Gassion, after commanders who suppressed the rebellion, were clearly not
intended as compliments. Names compared from Floquet, *Diaire*, passim;
Bercé, *Revolts*, 285–7; Foisil, *Nu-Pieds*, index; Trudel, *Catalogue*, passim.

5 *JR* (Thwaites), 5, 22–3; 10, 201–3, 206–9; 13, 231; 26, 17, 157, 176–7; 20, 30;
42, 154–5, 160–1, 163, cited in Fenton, *Faces*, 496–500.

6 Burkitt, *Selves*.

7 Ethel Bennet, *DBC*, 591–2; Couillard-Desprès, *Premiers*, 19, 37, 46 : Marie
sought out Wendat girls and women to teach them French and catechism,
53–6: she converted Pierre Pastedechouan, and was often the godmother of
several new converts. At the baptism feast, she cooked fifty-six Canada geese,
twenty teals, two barrels of peas, one barrel of sea biscuits, twenty pounds of
prunes, and five small pails of corn, which she mixed as it bubbled in a bucket
attached to a beanpole. The meat was brought in with a rake; 70: She visited
the sick and brought them nourishment, even when her husband was upset
that many habitants were digging up his garden. She carried two barrels of
peas to the Recollects during the Kirke siege.

8 Couillard-Desprès, *Premiers,* 84–127.

9 *RJ,* 1648, 160.

10 *RJ,* 1648, 172–3; Gourdieu, *Délices.*

11 ACND, MS, M1, V1, V2, Écrits autographes de soeur Marguerite Bourgeois; ACND, MS: Charles Glandelet, *Le vray esprit de Marguerite Bourgeoys et de L'Institut des soeurs seculières de la Congregation de Notre-Dame établie à Ville-Marie en L'Isle de Montréal en Canada* (1701); Faillon, *Bourgeoys;* Bernier, *Bourgeois.*

12 Jûchereau, *Annales,* 32–3.

13 *RJ,* 1641, 161–3; Trudel, *HNF* 1:178; Trigger, *Aataentsic,* 269; *DBC,* 351.

14 For more about traditional and modern French beliefs about healing waters, see Weisz, "Spas"; Szabo, *Lourdes.*

15 ASQ, Faribault, 20; Champlain, *Oeuvres,* passim; *RJ* (Thwaites), passim; *JJ,* passim; Couillard-Desprès, *Premiers; Hébert; Seigneurs;* "Dictionnaire," 91–4; "Annoblissement," 221–4; "En marge"; *J&D* 3:641; Audet, "Seigneurie"; *DBC* 2000, on-line. Guillaume's coat of arms was a dove with outspread wings and an olive branch in its beak, against a blue background, under which was written: "Dieu aide au premier colon" ("God helps the first settler"). Louis was not only well known as an intrepid fisherman who once caught 1,000 cod in a day in 1656, but he also caught 220 seals in 1649 and discovered a mine, which won him 1,000 livres, in 1664. His seal enterprise produced an export of oil to the Antilles. His motto was "Prix des travaux n'a rien de vil." His was the kernel of the present Couillard dynasty on the Rivière du Sud, at what he called "La Couillardière."

16 Bouwer, "Clinic," 316–8: Tortured and imprisoned young South African males displayed panic disorder and high anxiety levels (18.7 on the Montgomery-Ashberg Depression rating score).

17 ANC, MG 7, Bibliothèques de France, Coll. Margry (Margry slants his material unduly to cast a more favourable light upon La Salle); Muhlstein, *La Salle.*

18 Blum, *Moccasins,* 140–1; Blum, *Noble,* 220–7.

19 Axtell, "White."

20 Krystal, *Integration;* Yehuda, Steiner, Kahana, et al., "Alexithymia," 93–100; Mollica et al., "Cambodian," 158–66: impact of genocide upon Cambodian refugees.

21 Scaer, *Burden,* 5.

22 Gurris, "Torture," 37, in Graessner, Gurris, and Pross, *Torture,* 29–56.

23 Shalev, "Psychophysiology," 143–62: today heart rate at trauma linked to PTSD. True and Lyons, "Twins," 61–78, in Yehuda, "Risk," 93–12: Today there is a possible predisposition in high-risk groups, due to low cortisol, such as Holocaust survivors' children.

24 Herman, "Complex," 97. Shame and guilt: Wenk-Ansohn, "Psychosomatic," in Graessner, Gurris and Pross, *Survivors,* 57–69, 66; Herman, 90–2.

25 Danieli, "Holocaust," 298–9, in Figley, *Trauma,* ch. 12: "conspiracy of silence." Livanou, Basoglu, Marks, De Silva, Noshirvani, Lovell, and Thrasher,

"Beliefs, 157–65: torture victims today are noted for their mistrust, feelings of helplessness, loss of meaning, and feelings of there being great injustice in the world.

26 Captive children were in a worse situation than refugee children and frequently witnessed the violent death of their mothers as well as the torture, death, and scalping of their fathers/brothers. Trauma symptoms can be less potent on much younger children if they have support during the trauma (Dougherty, "Gulag," 1–19). But value system reconstruction thereafter is harder, and Dougherty himself emphasizes that exposure to human remains exacerbates PTSD. Refugee adolescents, in contrast, often exhibit less risky behaviour than do their native-born controls if they are settled in a healthy and safe refuge. According to Rousseau, the refugee process can either lead to specific risks or special competences (Rousseau and Drapeau, *Influence*, 110–11); Howard and Hodes, "Psychopathology," 368–77.

27 For today: Hermansson, Timpka, and Thyberg, "Refugees," 374–80: war wounded refugees from nine countries assessed in Sweden eight years later yielded worse results for those with combined factors of higher education, unemployment, and poor health.

28 Today, burns in particular can be associated with permanent body–image impairment (Ilechukwu, "Burn Unit").

29 Vroegh, "Adoptees," 568–75. Cross-racial adoptions today differ little from racially matched adoptions. Vonk, " Transracial," 246–55; Hoksbergen and te Laak, "RAD," 291–308. Reactive Attachment Disorder (RAD), a sometime result of a badly matched adoption, may lead to psychic homelessness. McCarthy, " Adoption," abstract. Today, how parents redefine themselves vis-à-vis adopted children also influences the course of adoption.

30 Wenzel, "Forensic," 611–5. There seems to be no universal model for captivities.

31 The terms "genocide" and "ethnic cleansing" both draw from long discredited pseudoscientific grounds for exclusion and death, yet retention of the terms
does not relegate the flawed concepts to oblivion, where they belong.

32 Holtz, "Tibetan," 24–34; Silove, Steel, McGorry, Miles, and Drobny, "Tamil," 49–55.

33 Currently, groups of veterans, POWs, rape victims, and refugees were examined for the symptoms that characterized each group. There were more symptoms for rape victims and POWs, with the former exhibiting more avoidance symptoms, while the others presented more hyperarousal symptoms (Henigsberg, Folnegovic-Smalc, and Moro, "Characteristics," 543–50; Stein and Kennedy, "Violence," 133–8); Rossman, Bingham, and Emde, "Symptomatology," 1089–1097; Palacios, "PTSD," 19–26; Creamer, Burgess, and McFarlane, "Australian," 1237–47: women are at higher risk than men, and much more for single women.

34 Silove, *Integrated.*

35 Janoff-Bulman, *Shattered.*

36 Stower and Nightingale, *Breaking,* 5.

37 Wenzel, "Sequels," 611–5. Over half of children exposed to war meet PTSD criteria, as it overwhelms their coping skills (Allwood, Bell-Dolan, Husain, "Children's," 450–7).

38 Staub, "Torturers," 49–76.

39 Bremner, Krystal, Southwick, Charney, "Noradrenergic," 28–38: Noradrenergic neurons form the locus ceruleus project into the cerebral cortex and limbic system, especially the hippocampus, amygdala, thalamus, and hypothalamus, where they quickly and globally modulate brain function responding to the environment. Increased norepinephrine is associated with fear conditioning and sensitization.

40 Bremner, *Damage,* 290; McEwen, "Neurobiology," 469–72; Hull, "Neuroimaging," 102–10.

41 Scaer, *Burden,* 65.

42 Yehuda et al., "Cortisol," 366–9; Yehuda et al., "Holocaust," 982–6; Hageman, Anderson, and Jorgensen, "PTSD," 411–22.

43 Grossman, Buchsbaum, and Yehuda, " Neuroimaging," 317–9: recommends multidisciplinary verifications of PTSD; also Wong, "Psychoneuroimmunology," 369–70.

44 Young, "Neurosis," 661–83; Schutzwohl and Maercker, "Anger," 483–9.

45 Eitinger, *Camp,* 219–30, in Levin, *Society;* Kolb, "Neuropsychological," 989–95; Tennant et al., "Forty," 833–9; Miller, "Prisoners of War," 110.

46 Stover and Nightingale, *Breaking,* 71–2; Somnier et al., "Psycho-social," 62; Basoglu and Marks, "Torture," 1423–4; Miller, "POW," 111–14, in Basoglu, *Torture.*

47 "The Survivor Syndrome or K-Z Syndrome or the Concentration Camp Syndrome": Herman, "Complex," 91–2, in Krystal, *Trauma;* Eitinger, "Syndrome"; Krystal and Niederland, "Syndrome"; DesPres, *Survivor;* Eaton, W., John Sigal, and Morton Weinfeld, "Impairment," 773–7; Dasberg, Distress," 243–56.

48 Basoglu and O'Brien somehow bypass the pioneering work of Holocaust psychiatrists, social workers, and therapists who write about treatment for torture and genocide victims. A chapter in Basoglu attempts to discredit their findings, supposedly due to lack of good conditions and more organized methods. Yet this was the courageous pioneering work before systematization was agreed upon. It was conducted in deplorable conditions, and it laid the pioneering groundwork for present torture victim, hostage, and PTSD treatments, so credit might be given where credit is due.

49 Endorphins: Scaer, *Burden,* 14.

50 Freezing: Levine, *Tiger;* cited also in Rothschild, *Remembers,* 13; Scaer, *Trauma,* 15–22.

51 If boys are traumatized early enough, they also can freeze.

52 Walker, *Battered*.

53 Berman, "Identifying," 141–51.

54 Muchnik, "Hazards," 571–609, examines reasons for conversions.

55 Herman, "Complex," 95: losing the sense that one has a self or being reduced to a non-human life form.

56 Mahrer, *Experiencing*, 28–30, in Rowan, *Subpersonalities*, 96–7. Famous cases of what was thought to be multiple personality: Thigpen and Cleckley, *Faces;* Shreiber, *Sybil;* Keyes, *Milligan*. Tauber, "Survivors," 228–37; Ingel, "Extreme," *Genocide*, 167–84; Devereux, *Ethnopsychoanalysis*, ch. 8. Wada, "Psychopathology," 335–54 : intense and chronic trauma into personality organization reorganized around it.

57 Also Ramasubbu, "Conversion," 118–22: parietal lobe infarct can induce a dissociative experience as well.

58 Rieber, "Duality," 3–17; Aldridge-Morris, *Deception;* Kenney, "Disease," 449–54; Merckelbach, "Alters," 481–97.

59 "Fugue behaviour": Horney, *Personality*. Bremner et al., "Mechanisms," 71–82.

60 Bremner and Marmar, *TMD*, ch. 12; Bremner, et al., "False," 71–82: Neuropeptides and neurotransmitters affected by stress can modulate memory in hippocampus, amygdala, and so on, which can alter these neuromodulators long-term, thus affecting memory.

61 Graessner, Gurris, and Pross, *Survivors*, 142–52, 153–68; 184–97.

62 Oppenheimer, "Self," 97–128: deficient integrative and associative processes in the self system or use of several ego centres instead of one. Also, cognitive complexity of the neurological system may be a factor in AID. Brown, "MP," 437–47: Brown's idea is that the failure to integrate alternative autobiographical memory schemata that cross-classify a human life can be called associative identity disorder. The schemata provide a variety of frameworks with associated clusters of general event memory. These intersecting autobiographical memories, which gracefully switch social or cultural roles, behavioural repertoire, and emotional dispositions, are hard to access with this disorder.

63 Moulin and Cambrosio, *Singular*, 44, 66, 75–83.

64 Csordas, *Sacred;* Crapanzano, *Rethinking;* Suarez, Orozon, and Spindler, *Anthropology;* also Daniel Siegel's "interpersonal neurobiology."

65 Kirmayer, "Broken," in Mattingly and Garro, *Narratives*.

66 Krystal, Bremner, D'Souza, Anand, Southwick, and Charney, "Neurobiology," ch. 22, in Shalev, Yehuda, and McFarlane, *Handbook;* Rivère, *Childhood;* Gast et al., "Dissociative," 249–57; Griffin, Resick, and Mechanic, "Dissociation," 1081–8; Shalev, Bonne, and Eth, "Treatment," 165–82; Lenzenwanger and Hooley, *Experimental*, ch. 16 about experimental approaches to the recovered memory controversy; Kenny, "Disease," 449–54; Rodin, De Groot, and Spivak, "Dissociation," ch. 5, in Bremner and Marmar, *Memory*.

67 Bremner and Marmar, *TMD*, ch. 12; Glass, *Shattered*, 157–61; Girard, *Scapegoat:* "mirror of doubles."

68 Frankl, *Meaning;* Levi, *Drowned.* This corresponds with what is now called the "living dead." (Jacobsen and Vesti, *Survivors,* 14; Hunter, "POW," 162: even some US POWs in the Korean and Vietnam Wars gave up like this.)

69 Nijhuis, E., J. Venderlinden, and Spinhoven, *Traumatic,* 23–260.

70 Besedovsky, del Rey, and Sorkin, "Immune," 342–6; Rothwell and Hopkins, "Cytokines," 130–6; Sundar, Cierpial, Kilts, Ritchie, and Weiss, "Brain," 3701–6; Claman, "Lymphoid," 388–97; Ader, Felton, and Cohen, *Psychoneuroimmunology,* 2 v.

71 Van der Kolk, "Reenactment," 389–410.

72 *JJ*, 1646, 8/1/1646, 26; 15/4/1646, 42; *JR*, 1647, 84–129.

73 Cousture: *RJ,* 1648, 36. More on Cousture: *J&D* 1:417, 438; 2:674; Roy, *Couture;* Godbout, *Trifluvienne;* Desrosiers, *Iroquoisie;* Delanglez, *Jolliet.*

74 Douville, *DBC* 1:500.

75 We have utilized the famous account that he wrote in English published by Gideon Skull, his notes about the fur trade in NAC, as well as an earlier French account called the Rawlinson manuscript of Windsor, entitled *Relations des Voyages de sieur Pierre Esprit Radisson escvyer, au nord de l'Amerique es années 1682, 1683, et 1684* (Londres 1685, 133), very generously copied for me by Martin Fournier of UQAR. He wrote two recent books about Radisson, and this manuscript was given to him as a gift by the Radisson's descendents, who still live in Quebec.

76 Fournier, *Radisson,* conclusion.

77 Kirmayer and Robbins, *Somatization,* conclusion; Kleinman's "Sociosomatics."

78 Ishikura and Tashiro, "Conversion," 381–90: patients seeking love and who couldn't find it tended to dissociation, while those who sought a frustrated self-actualization (and also had dysfunctional mothers) tended towards conversion disorders. Both situations, once resolved, tended to dissipate.

79 Antze and Lambek, *Tense,* xii–xix; Kirmayer, "Landscapes."

80 Danieli, *Multigenerational,* 308.

81 Mantero and Crippa, "Eating," 1–16: Between eating disorders (ED) and PTSD, there is some co-morbidity. Perry, Silvera, Rosenvinge, and Holte, "Eating," 405–16.

82 Herman, "Complex," 90.

83 Radisson, *Voyages,* 3: May 24 1651.

84 *JJ*, 1651; *RJ*, 36, 126; Trudel, *Catalogue,* 103, 158, 166, 226, 253, 568.

85 Radisson, *Voyages,* 86: "I mean not to tell you the great joy I preceavd in me to see those persons that I never thought to see more … In my absence peace was made between the French & ye Iroquoits, wch was ye reason I stayed not long in a place."

86 Hunter, "POW," 167.

87 Radisson, *Voyages,* 81.

88 ANC MG 7, I, A–5, fol. 649–50, Bibliothèque Nationale, Coll. Clairambault, no. 1116, Mémoire de Radisson sur la traite; Radisson, *Voyages*, 29.

89 Radisson, *Voyages*, especially 35–71.

90 Ibid., 46–9.

91 Ibid., 51.

92 Ibid., 125–31.

93 "Je luy parlay selon le genie de ces peoples...il est necessaries pour se faire consider, de se vanter qu'on a du courage, qu'on est puissant, et en estat de les secourir, et proteger contre leurs ennemis, il faut aussi leur temoigner, qu'on entre tout afait dans leurs interets, avoir de la complaisance pour eux, sur tout leur faire d'abord des presents, car c'est entre eux le grand lien de l' amitié ... je luy disais en sa langue, Ie connois toute la terre, tes amis seront mes amis, et je suis venu icy t'aporter des armes ... tu ne mourras pas de faim ni ta femme ni tes enfans .... prend courage je veux estre ton fils, et je t'ay amené un pere" (Rawlinson, 21–2).

94 Rawlinson, 80–1.

95 Freud's idea of "Nachträglichkeit" might apply to his response. Early trauma can be comprehended only later, when its impact is fully understood. On this term, see de Levitas, "Onset," 97–8.

96 "va t'en ver tes freres les anglois dis leur mon nom, et que je veux les aller prendre" (Rawlinson, 80–1).

97 Rawlinson, 81.

98 Radisson, *Voyages*, 53–71: "cutt pieces of flesh from all parts of the body and broyle them, get you to eat it, thrusting it into yor mouth."

99 Rothkegel, "Dreamwork," 95–111.

100 Rawlinson, 88.

101 Radisson, *Voyages*, 80.

102 Ibid., 61–3.

103 Ibid., 80.

104 Allodi and Cowgill, "Torture," 98–102; Stover and Nightingale, *Breaking*, 73–6.

105 Frankl, *Auschwitz*. Robert Jay Lifton and Aaron Antonovsky agree.

106 Radisson, *Voyages*, 85.

107 Ricoeur, *Oneself*, 140–1; Pennebaker, James.

108 Stover and Nightingale, *Breaking*, 66–9: Allodi Trauma scale. Mollica et al., "Harvard," 111–16: HTQ.

EPILOGUE

1 Fenton, *Law*, 50–64.

2 The principles of balance and complementarity are essential to Native civic philosophy, according to Donald Grinde (personal communication, 1/4/2003).

3 Aschheim, *Brothers*, analyzes the ambiguous relationship between the Germans and the German Jews, who were highly assimilated, constituted a

certain bourgeois elite, and often intermarried prior to the Second World War, yet acted as intermediaries between the Germans and the Eastern European Ashkenazi Jews (Ostjuden), whose relationship was hostile.

4 akai, *Theocracy, Exile, Reenchantment.*

5 Delisle, *Traître,* 43–4, 139: Omer Héroux, "Les Iroquois, c'est là qu'ils sont maintenant!" *Le Devoir,* 24/5/1938, 1 (editorial); and *Le Devoir,* 26/5/1938, "Dollard."

6 Sobel, "Inner," in Hoffman, Sobel, and Teute, *Glass,* 171; *Dreams,* conclusion.

7 Poster, " Debate," in Goux and Wood, *Terror,* 104–18.

8 Talmon, *Totalitarian.* His argument links up with Hannah Arendt's argument concerning the nature of totalitarianism. Arendt, *Totalitarianism.*

9 Gibbon, *Fall;* Lewis, *Islam;* Trigger, *Civilizations:* some civilizations contain many decivilizing elements, and their rapid fall or improvement are not inevitable.

10 Hobsbawm, *Extremes.* Hobsbawm incidentally condenses the history of the Holocaust to a mere paragraph, which literally mirrors Jean-Maire LePen's comment about it being no more than this. Huntington, *Clash.*

11 Mennel, "Decivilizing," in Salumets, *Elias,* 32–49. Mennel names different processes than the ones I outline, but his chapter spurred thought on this subject.

12 Baudrillard, *L'Échange,* 216–17.

Bibliography

ARCHIVAL SOURCES

Canada

ONTARIO

Archives Nationales du Canada, Ottawa (ANC) (formerly, Archives publiques du Canada)

MG I: Archives des Colonies

C11A. Correspondance génerale, Canada, v. 1–9, 120, 125

MG6: Archives départementales, municipales, maritimes et de bibliothèques (France)

B1 bob. c–7202 (Amerindian medicines and herbs sent to pharmacy in Dieppe)

MG7: Bibliothèques de France à Paris

I – A3: Collection Margry, (F–177, v. 9269–9389)

Ms. 24225 "Histoire naturelle, ou la fidelle recherche du tout ce qu'il y a de rare dans les Indes occidentales," par Louis Nicolas

MG8: C6: PIAF

MG18: C2: Communauté des Habitants (1646)

H4: Confraternité de Ste-Anne (1657, 1660)

H10: (1) Lettres de noblesse accordées à Pierre Boucher

H16: Madeleine de Verchères (1699)

H27: De la Mission des Hurons de Notre-Dame de Lorette en 1676

H44: Coll. de la famille Aubert de Gaspé 1677–1977, bob. H–2346–2349 #1792

N1: Québec, Capitulation (1629)

Pierre Radisson, *Voyage to North America 1682–1682*, British Museum add. Mss., v. 11626 (purchased by Rodd 8/7/189)

Metropolitan Toronto Library Board, Toronto:

Lettres Canadiennes 1700–1725, Baldwin Canadiana Rm., Metropolitan Toronto Library Board, Toronto. (kindly lent me by Cornelius Jaenen)

QUÉBEC

Archives de l'Archeveché de Québec (AAQ)

Archives de folklore de l'Université Laval (AFUL)

A11: anges gardiens; A16: fées; A20: loups-garous; A50: esprits et génies; A60: fantômes; A70: chasses fantastiques; B12: saints populaires; B20: personnages historiques; B22: faits historiques; B37: morts; B39: captivité; B40: guérisseurs; B41: dons; B42; B50: rêves: B501: croyances sur les rêves; C13: lieux hantés et tabous; C5: vaisseaux fantômes; C7: métamorphoses; M16: carnaval; M19: St-Joseph; M31: la St-Jean; M34: la Ste-Anne; M42: La Toussaint (1 nov); M43: le jour des morts (2 nov); N1: rites de passage; N115: Baptême; N118: Adoption; N1352: Charivari; N15: mort; W32: Chasseur/Trappeur/Coureur. Archives Jean Du Berger.

Archives du Collège de Ste-Marie à Montréal

Paul Ragueneau, "Mémoires touchant la mort et les vertus des pères Isaac Jogues, etc.," rep. RAPQ, 1924–5.

Archives Nationales de Québec (ANQ)

(ANQQ for Québec, ANQM for Montréal, ANQTR for Trois Rivières):

Collection de seigneurie de Sillery (1637–1695), mf. M–69, 1 bobine.

Fonds Juridiction de Montréal (ZA26) 1677–1762.

Juridiction de Montréal: Documents et ordonnances (1675–1705), mf. M–31, 4 bobines.

Juridiction royale de Trois-Rivières: Ordonnances (1646–1759), mf. M–38, 5 bobines.

Archives paroissiales de Notre Dame de Québec

Répertoire, Série III, carton 1, nos 20–21: 28/5/1649, Lettre patente du père Charles Thébault pour une confrérie du Saint Rosaire à Québec, 23/10/1650.

Archives du Séminaire de Québec (ASQ): (special thanks to Mme. Mireille St-Pierre)

• Faribault

7, Registre A, 560f: Jean Nicollet de Belleborne

20: Guillaume Couillard

passim: Jean Godefroy de Lintot, Olivier LeTardif

P29: Rapport Druillettes ambassadur à Nouvelle-Angleterre (1651)

Viger-Verreau, P32: Correspondence Rémy de Courcelles, gouv. de Trois Rivières(1665)

• Polygraphie

2, 32: Difficulté entre Mésy et Laval touchant la création d'un nouveau conseil (1664)

2: Extraits de la vie de soeur Marie des Vallées [écrit par La Peltrie?] (1671)

3, 11: Arrêt Sulpiciens contre Msgr de Laval (30/8/1660)

3, 44: Testament olographe de Mme. de la Peltrie (18/7/1669)

3, 74: Mariage entre Guillemette Hébert et Guillaume Couillard et note généalogique (21/8/1621)

3, 76: Capitulation de Québec (19/7/1629)

4, 20: Discours des sauvages hurons (1675)

4, 35: Règlements de la police (11/5/1676)

4, 54: Edit de 'l'Etablissement du Conseil Souverain à Québec (4/1663)

4, 69a: Extrait de l'Edit du roi Henri II qui établit peine de mort contre les femmes qui étant devenues enceintes par voies illicites cachent leur grossesse (2/1556)

4, 20: Discours des sauvages hurons qui demandent aux seigneurs de M. des terres dans leurs île et demandent qu'on ne leur traite point de boissons et réponses (1675)

4, 21: Extraits de Lois de Boston ... l'eau de vie et sauvages (1666)

4, 22: Arrêt Conseil Supérieur déffendant à toutes personnes de vendre des boissons énivrantes, même de donner un coup aux sauvages, sous peine de confiscation de leurs biens, de banissement et même du fouet (17/4/1664)

4, 25: Permission à tous les français habitants de la Nouvelle-France, de traiter des boissons aux sauvages (10/11/1668)

4, 26: Défense aux habitants d' aller porter des boissons aux sauvages sous peine de 50 livres d'amende pour la première fois et de châtiment pour recidive et peine de 2 h de carcan et de castors gras contre les sauvages qui s'énivrent (26/6/1669)

4, 27: Réponse de six professeurs de la Sorbonne sur les deux cas ... alcohol et sauvages (8/3/1675)

4, 28: Ordonnance du roi à Frontenac et Duchesneau de faire assemblée des 20 principaux habitants pour opiner sur la traite de l'eau de vie aux sauvages (12/5/1678)

4, 28a: Réponse aux raisons qui prouvent qu'il faut laisser la liberté de traiter des boissons aux sauvages (1678)

4, 35: Règlements généraux du Conseil Supérieur de Québec pour la police (11/5/1676)

4, 36: Règlement du Roi qui exclut des officiers militaires d'avoir rang dans les églises (2/3/1668)

4, 36a: Déclarations du roi concernant les conventions matrimoniales en Canada (6/5/1733)

4, 43: grammaire hébraïque, s.d.

4, 44: Recit des miracles opérés à Ste-Anne de Beaupré (1662–1768)

10, 25: Notes sur l'affaire LeGardeur de Repentigny et Philibert, s.d.

13, 2: Relation des miracles opérés à Ste-Anne de Beaupré par l'abbé Thomas Joseph Morel (24/6/1680)

13, 3: Mémoire à Louis XIII par Champlain (circa. 1630)

13, 4: Sermon en l'église d'Angers ... baptême de Pierre Antoine Pastedech8an (29/4/1621)

13, 16: Jean de Lauzon ... seigneurie des Onnontagués (12/4/1656)

13, 18: Déclaration de Lauzon nommant les Jésuites tuteurs et protecteurs des sauvages (16/11/1651)

13, 22: Dequen prend prise de possession...sauvages (6/2/1657) [Sillery]

13, 27: Lauzon défend... sauvages de laisser.... (12/5/1656)

13, 34: Déclaration des habitants des Trois Rivières qui avaient été accusés de ne pas vouloir bâtir un presbytere aux pères Jésuites (15/2/1664)

13, 52: Lauzon concède aux Jésuites la Seigneurie des Onnontagués (12/4/1656)

13, 53: Plan et description des terres aux Trois Rivières, s.d.

13, 69: Notes sur Champlain prisonnier des Kirkes (1629)

14, 18: Authentique de la relique de Ste-Anne par Laval (12/3/1670)

15, 20: Edit du roi Henri II sur le fait des femmes grosses et enfants morts-nés (2/1556)

22, 4: Mémoire sur la première chapelle de Notre-Dame de Lorette (2/3/1673)

22, 35: Convention entre Frontenac et Conseil Supérieur pour le bien et la paix entre le gouverneur et l'Intendant (16/10/1679)

22, 42: Charles Couillard des Islets achète un banc à la basilique de Québec (12/5/1669)

#13, 16: Concession pour les Onontages (1656)

#13, 27: Lauson déffend aux sauvages de régir leurs biens

• Lettres

Carton N: Aubert de la Chesnaye

Carton N:1: 31/3/1659, Anne d'Autriche à d'Argenson [honour Laval]

Carton N: 2: 14/5/1657, Insinuation et lettre de cachet Louis XIV à d'Argenson ["]

Carton N: 3: 13/3/1660, Louis XIV à d'Argenson ["]

Carton O: 59: 12/1681, Ordre de Frontenac pour instruire différand entre Laval et Récollets

Carton O: 60: 4/6/1683, Réponse des Récollets de Québec à Laval

Carton P: 51: 31/5/1686, Instructions du roi à de Champigny

Carton R: 186: Lettre incomplète du père Julien Garnier, missionaire chez les iroquois (circa. 1686)

Carton S: 93: 12/5/1677, Jean Dudouyt, prêtre à Laval sur l'eau de vie

Carton Z: 18: 15/8/1669, lettre de Marie de St-Ignace à Madeleine de St-Xavier

• Séminaire

I–38

I, 15, 7/12/1677, Bénédiction du Petit Séminaire de Québec et autres extraits du journal au sujet des élèves jusqu'à 8/3/1678

I, 17, 8/4/1680, SME de Paris retrocède Sault-au-Matelot à Laval (vendu 5/10/1666) – donation au Séminaire

6, a, Jean-Paul Godefroy

6, passim: Olivier LeTardif

6, 2, 15/9/1634, Partage fait entre Guillaume Couillard, G. Huboust et sa femme pour servir à Guillemette Hébert

6, 15,22/7/1646, Guillaume Couillard déclare que le Lac St-Charles ne lui appartient pas mais réclame le droit de pêche

6, 17, 14/2/1645, Séparation des terres entre les Jésuites et Guillaume Couillard à la rivière St-Charles

6, 23b, 14/2/1645, Election de Michel Le Neuf comme syndic de Trois Rivières (signed by Pierre Boucher, Guillaume Habel, Estienne Vien, Gilles Trottier, Hemery Galtos, Urbain Baudry, Jehan Sauuaget, Sebastien Dodier, Jehan Houdan, Elye Simard, Antoine des Boffiers, Jehan Veron, Estienne delafous, Estienne Signeurs, tous les habitants des Trois Rivières)

6, 28, 24/10/1639, Inventaire des biens de Guillaume Hébert

6, 30 & 30a, 25/6/1665, Ratification pour Mme. Guillaume Couillard de 100 arpents de terre par Talon

6, 31, 10/7/1644, Vente faite entre Hubou et Couillard

6, 35, 9/12/1643, Marché entre Giffart, Couillard, et Hubou

6, 38, 21/8/1645, Inventaire des meubles Hubou et Rollet

6, 39, 8/12/1641, Quittance réciproque entre Giffart, Couillard, et Hubou

6,41, 3/5/1642, Permission à Marsolet de Launay et autres, aller à Tadoussac et ordre de surveiller les navires étrangers

15, 2, 5/9/1658, d'Argenson au baron Chevrier de Fancan

15,2a, 5/9/1658, d'Argenson à Lalemant

15, 2b, 20/10/1659, Laval à d'Argenson à Paris

15, 2c, 2/10/1659, Lalemant au vicomte d'Argenson

15, 2d, 14/5/1659, Louis XIV au Voyer d'Argenson

15, 2e, 21/10/1659, d'Argenson à Louis XIV

15, 3, 1659, d'Argenson à MM.

15, 3a, 12/1660, lettre d'Argenson

15, 3b, 4/11/1660, lettre d'Argenson

15, 3c, 14/3/1660, Louis XIV au d'Argenson

15, 5, 15,5,1/1/1662, Consultation de la Sorbonne sur l'excommunication ... boisson

15, 6, 24/2/1662, Laval ordonne l'excommunication .... boisson

15, 48, 19/9/1687, Prières publiques ... guerres contre les iroquois

26–27, tutelles des enfants orphélins (1680–1759)

35: 25A: Olivier LeTardif

35: 27–27L: Olivier LeTardif

36, 1, 11: Olivier LeTardif

37, 3, 4: Olivier LeTardif

SME 2.1: lettres qui se rapportent aux Amérindiens 1660–1879

SME 5: les propriétés et les seigneuries Sault-au-Matelot (1626–1676)

SMA 6: La défense des droits du Séminaire-Famille Couillard-Desprès (1725–1759)

SME 8: le Petit Séminaire

SME 12.2.4: Soeurs de la Congrégation de Notre-Dame

SME 13: Le journal du siège de Québec

SME 15: Coll. cartographique – nouvelles découvertes des voyageurs

- Série MS

Pierre Marquette, Facsimilé livre de prières en illinois

C4: Aubert de la Chesnaye

C17: Aubert de la Chesnaye

2: A. J. M. Jacrau, Annales du Petit Séminaire de Québec (1700)

20: Aubert de la Chesnaye

61: M. L'abbé Girault de Villeneuve, "Hurons de la Jeune Lorette" (1762); "Des Missions" (1639) Sillery; Sermonnaire en iroquois et notice sur les hurons; Prières chrétiennes en outaouais

64: Cahier catéchisme micmac à la mission de Miramichi (1810)

66: Recueil de chants hurons par Paul Tsaouenhohi Picard

71: Lesueur, Catéchisme abénaquis (1730)

71b: APOnt. Mss. hurons du RP Potiers

165: Registre des baptêmes des Sauvages Lac St-Jean (1669–92), T–19A

170: Documents pour l'histoire du Canada (1629–32)

171: Documents pour l'histoire du Canada (1663–91)

216: Pierre Cholenec, Sur la vie de quelques femmes sauvages (1676–80)

257: Thomas Morel, Miracles...opérés à la Bonne Sainte-Anne

309: livre de prières et cantiques en françois, anglais, iroquois, illinois

310: Chansons

- Seigneuries'

3, 10: Olivier LeTardif

- Carton B.B.

"Vie de Cathérine Tekakwitha par père Pierre Cholenec," CIHM, #04137.

- Fonds Verreau, 036: lettres Renjart négotiant de la Rochelle: #2 10/10/1740; #5 31/10/1740, 2/11/1740, 30/11/1740.

- Landes Collection, McLennan Library, McGill University.

France

Archives municipales de Rouen (AMR)

David du Petit-Val, L'Histoire du temps (1644), Mazarinade, M 14998; David du Petit-Val et Jean Viret, Déclaration du Msgr le prince de Conti et de messieurs les généraux du 20 mars 1649 (886), Mazarinade, M 10092; Jean Rousse, Décision de la question du temps (871), Chantilly, XXV A 35, #8; Jean Rousse, Articles de la paix ... à Rueil le 11e mars 1649 (414); Carême des Parisiens (639), Mazarine, M 19964; Jacques Besongne, La Fureur des Normands contre le Mazarinistes (1460), M 10141; L'Apologie des Normands (113), Chantilly, XXV A 35, #21.

Archives nationales de France (ANF)
   Fonds des Colonies, Sous-Série F3, Coll. Moreau de St-Méry
• Bibliothèque nationale de France (BNF) (also found in ANC)
   Fond français, Ancien Gratoire.162.Fr. 24225: Histoire Naturelle des Indes
   Occidentales par L. N. (Louis Nicolas?)
   Coll. Clairambault
   Fonds français
   Mélanges Colbert
   Nouvelle acquisitions

United Kingdom

WINDSOR:
privately owned copy of Pierre-Esprit Radisson's Rawlinson manuscript, *Relations des
   Voyages dv sieur Pierre Esprit Radisson escvyer au nord de l'Amerique es années 1682,
   1683, 1684* (London, 1685) by Dr Jean Radisson, which was kindly reproduced
   for me by Dr Martin Fournier of Université de Québec à Rimouski. Many thanks
   to both of them for this privilege.

United States, Illinois

NEWBERRY LIBRARY
   Ayer Collection
   Ayer Ms 451 box: A translation of the speech by Jimmy Johnson [Sosheowa] at the
   Grand Council of the Iroquois 1851 [on code of his grandfather Handsome Lake
   (Skaniadario or Ganyadaiyo)]

SOURCES: PRINTED AND REFERENCED

Anonyme (circa 1700). "Nation Iroquoise: Abrégé des Vies et Moeurs et autres
   Particularitez de la Nation Irokoise laquelle est divisée en Cinq villages, Scavoir
   Agnez Onney8t Nontagué Goyog8an et Sonnont8an." *RAQ* 26 (1996): 31–47.
Aquinas, Thomas. *Summa Theologica.* Blackfriars, London, 1964–68.
Apollonius Rhodius. *Jason and the Golden Fleece: The Argonautika.* Oxford University
   Press, New York [1993] 1998.
St. Augustine. *City of God.* Trans. John Healey, Dent, London, 1945.
Bacqueville de la Potherie, Claude Charles. *Historie de l'amérique septentrionale
   ...1534–1701.* 4 vols., Rouen, 1722. CIHM #28221, 28222, 32233, 32234.
Bayle, Pierre. *Dictionnaire historique et critique.* University of Chicago, ARTFL Project,
   1998.
Bible, related sacred books: (Scrolls translated into English in Martínez, *Scrolls,* pp.
   95–125).
   Midrash

Babylonian Talmud, Moed Katan, Tractate Gittin

Talmud, Baba Batra

Zohar, Exodus

Dead Sea Scrolls: 1QWar Scroll (1QM [+1Q33]); 4QWar Scrolla (4Q491 [4QMa}); 4QWar Scrollb (4Q492 [4QMb]; 4QWar Scrollc (4Q493 [4QMc]); 4QWar Scrolld (4Q494 [4QMd]); 4QWar Scrolle (4Q495 [4QMe]); 4QWar Scrollf (4Q496 [4papQMf]).)

Bibaud, Maximilien. *Biographies des Sagamos illustres.* L'Amérique Septentrionale, Lovell and Gibson, Montréal, 1848.

Blaisdell, Bob. *Great Speeches by Native Americans.* Dover Thrift Ed., Mineola, New York, 2000.

Blendec, Charles. *Cinq histoires admirables ... Soissons,* Guillaume Chaudière. Paris, 1582.

Bodin, Jean. *Les Six Livres de la République.* Jacques Du Puys, Paris, 1577, 1599.

– *The Six Books of the Commonwealth: A Facsimile Reprint of the English Translation of 1606.* Harvard University Press, Cambridge, 1962.

Boucher, Pierre. *Histoire Véritable et Naturelle Des Moeurs and Productions du Pays de la Nouvelle-France Vulgairement dite Le Canada.* Florentin Lambert, Société Historique de Boucherville [1664] 1964.

Bourgeoys, Marguerite (ed. A.J. Roque). "Documents inédits." *RHAF* 20 (1965): 75–107.

– *Marguerite Bourgeoys: Textes choisis et présentés.* Fides, Montréal, Collection Classiques Canadiens, 1958.

Brébeuf, Jean de. *Les Relations de ce qui s'est passé au pays des Hurons (1635–1648).* Librairie Droz, Genève, 1957.

Brunet, Michel; Frégault, Guy; et Trudel, Marcel, éds. *Histoire du Canada par les textes.* Editions Fides, Ottawa, 1952.

BRH: *Bulletin des Recherches Historiques* 3 (1922–3): 191–265; (1926): 296–300; (1931–32): 243–365;

Brut y Tywysogion (Chronicles of the Princes) (ed. and trans. J. Williams Ithel). Rolls Series, London, 1860.

Buffon, George-Louis LeClerc de (ed. Jean Piveteau). *Oeuvres philosophiques de Buffon.* Corpus général des philosophes français, Presses universitaires de France, Paris, 1954.

Bumstead, J.M., ed. *Documentary Problems in Canadian History.* Vol 1: *Pre-Confederation,* Irwin-Dorsey, Georgetown, 1969.

Calloway, Colin, ed. *The World Turned Upside Down: Indian Voices of Early America.* Bedford Books, St Martin's Press, Boston and New York, 1994.

Campeau, Lucien, éd. *MNF: Monumenta Nova Franciae.* Vol. 1: *La première mission des Jésuites en Nouvelle France 1611–1613;* Vol. 2: *Etablissement à Québec (1616–1634).* Presses de l'Université Laval, Québec, 1980.

– *Gannentaha: Première mission iroquoise 1653–1665.* Bellarmin, Montréal, 1983.

– *La mission des Jésuites chez les Hurons 1634–1650.* Institutum Historicum, Bellarmin, Rome et Montréal, 1987.

– *Catastrophe démographique sur les Grands Lacs: Les premiers habitants de Québec.* Bellarmin, Montréal, 1986.

– "Le Testament de Champlain." *Cahiers des Dix* 42 (1979): 49–60.

Castiglione, Baldassarre, conte de. *The Courtier; or the complete gentleman and gentlewoman. Being a treatise of the politest manner of educating persons of distinction of both sexes and the qualifications requuisite in people of all ranks from the prince to the private gentleman ...*, Curtis, London, 1729.

Champlain:

Biggar, H.P. *The Works of Samuel Champlain.* 6 vols., The Champlain Society, Toronto, 1922–1936.

LeBlant, Robert, and Baudry, René. *Nouveaux documents sur Champlain et son époque. I: 1560–1622,* APC, #15, Ottawa, 1967.

Champlain. *Oeuvres:* Giguère, George-Emile, éd. *Oeuvres de Champlain.* 3 v., Ed. du Jour, Montréal, 1973.

Charlevoix, Pierre-François-Xavier de. *Histoire et déscription générale de la Nouvelle France.* 3 vols., Nyons et fils, Paris, 1744, CIHM #33219.

– *Journal d'un voyage fait par ordre du roi dans l'Amérique septentrionale.* 2 vols., PUM, Montréal [1744] 1994.

– *Journal of a voyage to North America.* 2 vols., March of America Facsimile, # 36, University Microfilms, Ann Arbor [1744] 1966.

Chaumonot, Pierre-Joseph Marie. *Autobiographie du père Chaumonot de la Companie de Jésus et son complément par Félix Martin.* Oudin, Paris, 1885, CIHM #08575.

– "Mémoire concernant la nation iroquoise, 1666." *RAQ* 26 (1996): 5–9.

Chibnall, Marjorie, ed. *The Established History of Orderic Vitalis.* 5 vols. Clarendon Press, Oxford, [1696] 1975, bks. 9 and 10.

Cholenec, Pierre. "The Life of Katharine Tegakouita (1696)." In *The Positio ... on the Introduction of the Cause for Beatification and Canonization and on the Virtues of the Servant of God Katherine Tekakwitha, the Lily of the Mohawks,* 239–5. Fordham University Press, New York, 1940.

Chrétien de Troyes. *Oeuvres complètes.* Gallimard, Paris, 1994.

Cicero, Marcus Tullius. *De Divinatione.* Packard Humanities Institute, Los Altos, CA, 1991.

Collection de manuscrits contenant lettres, mémoires et autres documents historiques relatifs à la Nouvelle-France. 4 vols., Province de Québec, Côté et Cie., Québec, 1883.

Combes, Sieur de. *Coppie d'une lettre Envoyée de la Nouvelle France ou Canada, par le Sieur de cobes, Gentilhomme poictvin a un sien amy.* Jean Savine, Lyons, 1609.

Commager, Henry Steele, ed. *Documents of American History.* 2 vols., F.S. Crofts and Co., New York, 1943.

"La Communauté des Habitants:" documents inédits." *RHAF* 5 (1951): 118–25.

Companie des Cents-Associés. *Edits, ordonnances, déclarations, et arrêts relatifs à la tenure seigneuriale demandés par une adresse de l'Assemblée Législatif.* Ottawa, 1851, CIHM #61642.

Condorcet, Marie-Jean Antoine Nicolas de Caritat, marquis de. Outlines of a Historical View of the Progress of the Human Mind: "The Future of Man." offprint.

- *De l'influence de la révolution d'Amérique sur l'Europe.* S.I., s.d., 1786, ch. 1.

Corneille, Pierre. *Oeuvres complètes.* Ed. du Seuil, Paris, 1963.

Couillard-Després, Azarie. "Acte de Concession de l'arrière-fief de Lespinay (4/8/1671)." *BRH* 31 (1925): 93.

Coyre, James, ed. *Exploration of the Great Lakes, 1669–1670, by de Casson and de Galinée.* Ontario Historical Society, Toronto, 1903.

Crèvecoeur, Michel Guillaume St-Jean de. *Letters from an American Farmer and Sketches of eighteenth century America.* Signet, New York, 1963.

Cureau de la Chambre, Marin. *Traité de la Connaissance des animaux où tout ce qui a esté dit Pour, & contre le raisonnement des bestes est examiné (1645).* Arthème Fayard, Paris, 1989.

Cyrano de Bergerac. "Histoire comique des Estats et Empires de la Lune" (1628). In *Voyages imaginaires à la recherche de la vérité humaine.* Lettres Modernes, Paris, 1977.

Daveluy, Marie-Claire. *Les Véritables motifs des Messieurs et Dames de la Société de Notre-Dame de Montréal pour la Conversion des Sauvages.* NLC, Paris, 1643.

Delafosse, Marcel. "Documents inédits: Séjour de Champlain à Brouage en 1630." *RHAF* 9 (1956): 571–8.

Delâge, Denys, ed.. *Histoire des Amérindiens.* Faculté des lettres et Sciences Sociales. Université Laval, Québec, Automne 1997. (Contains *Registre de la Prévoté de Québec, Ordonnances sur la traite des boissons, Inventaire chronologique des documents;* extraits de Chronica 1.)

- "Les premiers contacts selon un choix de récits amérindiens publiés aux XIXe et XXe siècles." *RAQ* 22 (1992): 101–15.

Denys, Nicolas. *Description geographique et historique des costes de l'Amérique septentrionale.* 2 vols., Paris, 1672, CIHM #34784.

- *Histoire Naturelle Des Peuples, des Animaux, des Arbres & Plantes de l'Amérique Septentrionale, & de ses divers Climats Avec une Description exacte de la Pesche des Moluës, tant sur le Grand Banc qu'a la Coste, & de tout ce que s'y pratique de plus particulier, & c.* Claude Barbin, Paris (1672) Ottawa, CIHM #34785.

De Grenaille, François, sieur de Chatounières. *L'Honnête Mariage.* Vol. 3. Toussainct Quinet, Paris, [1640] 1969.

Deux chroniques de Rouen. Armand Heron, Rouen, 1900.

Dewdney, Selwyn. *The Sacred Scrolls of the Southern Ojibway.* University of Toronto Press, Toronto, 1975.

Discours abbregé et mémoires d'aulcunes choses advenues tant en Normandye que en France depuis de commencement de l án 1559, et principalement en la ville de Rouen. Armand Heron, Rouen, (s.d.) 1900.

"Dollard et ses compagnons." *BRH* 6 (1900): 123–4.

Dollier de Casson, François. *Histoire de Montréal, 1640–1672.* Ottawa, Mémoires de la Société Historique de Montréal [1672] 1869, CIHM #27036.

Dreuillette, Gabriel (1610–1681?). *Narré du voyage faict pour la mission des Abnaquois, 1648–1649.* Weed Parsons, Albany, 1855, CIHM # 38214.

Drimmer, Frederick, ed. *Captured by the Indians: 15 Firsthand Accounts, 1750–1870.* Dover Pubs., New York, 1961.

Drolet, Gilles. *Notre-Dame de Lorette et le père Chaumonot: choix de textes*. Ed. Sigier, Ste-Foy, Québec, 1985.

DTV – *Atlas zur Weltgeschichte: Karten und chronologischer Abriss*, I & II, 7, Deutscher Taschenbuch Verlag, München, BRD, 1964.

Du Creux, François du. *Historiae Canadensis, sue Novae Franciae Libri decem, ad annum usque 1664*. Paris, 1664, CIHM #47682.

Dupâquier, Jacques et Jean-Pierre Bardet, éds., *Paroisses et communes de France: Dictionnaire d'histoire administrative et démographique*. CNRS, Paris, 1974–1991.

Edda Saemundar (The Poetic Edda). Trans. Lee Hollander, University of Texas Press, Austin, TX, 1962.

Fail, Noël du. *Propos Rustiques suivis de Baliverneries*. Garnier, Paris, 1928.

Faribault-Beauregard, Marthe. *La population des forts français d'Amérique (XVIIIe siècle)*. 2 t., Ed. Bergeron, Montréal, 1982.

Floquet, A. *Diaire ou journal du voyage du Chancellier Séguier en Normandie après la Sédition des Nu-Pieds (1639–1640)*. Edouard Frère, Rouen, 1842.

Fournier, Marcel. *Les Européens au Canada des origines à 1765*. Ed. du fleuve, Montréal, 1989.

Franquet, Louis. *Voyages et mémoires sur le Canada en 1752 et 1753*. Ed. Elysée, Montréal, 1974.

Gagnon, Soeur Claire et François Rousseau, éds. *Deux Inventaires des Archives de l'Hôtel-Dieu de Québec*. Archives, 70.1, 1973.

Gendron, François. *Quelques particularites du pays des Hurons en la Nouvelle-France*. Bechet et Billiance, Troyes et Paris, 1640, CIHM #26088.

Geoffrey of Monmouth. *The History of the Kings of Britain*. Folio Society, London [1966] 1984.

– *Life of Merlin: Vita Merlini*. University of Wales, Cardiff [1973] 1985.

Gottschalk, Louis. *Lafayette between the American and the French Revolution (1783–1789)*. University of Chicago Press, Chicago, 1950.

Gouhier, Pierre, et al. *Atlas historique de Normandie (1636–1789)*, Centre de recherches d'histoire quantitative, Caen, 1967.

Grimshaw, Polly. *Images of the Other: A Guide to Microform Manuscripts on Indian-White Relations*. University of Illinois Press, Urbana, IL, 1991.

Grotius, Hugo, *Grotii Epistolae quotquot reperiri potuerunt; inquibus praetas hactenus editas, plurimae theologici, juridici, philogici, historici, & politici argumenti occurunt*, Wolfgang, Waasberge, Boom à Someren and Goethals, Blaev, Amstelodami, 1687.

William of Auvergne (Guillaume d'Auvergne). *The Universe of Creatures*. Medieval philosophical texts in translation, #35, Marquette University Press, Milwaukee [1674] 1998.

Hamlin, Marie Caroline Watson. *Legends of Le Détroit*. Thorndike Nourse, Detroit, 1884, rep. Gale Research Co., Book Tower, Detroit, 1977, pp. 264–317: Early French Families.

Harris, Richard Cole, ed., *Historical Atlas of Canada*. University of Toronto Press, Toronto, 1980.

Hébert, Léo-Paul. *Le Registre de Sillery (1638–1690).* Coll. Tekouerimat, Presses de l'Université de Québec à Chicoutimi, Québec, 1994.

Hennepin, Louis. *A New Discovery of a Vast Country in America.* 2 vols., McClurg and Co., Chicago, 1903.

Henripin, Jacques. *La population canadienne au début du XVIIe siècles.* Presses Universitaires de France, Paris, 1954.

Hirschfelder, Arlene and Paulette Molin. *Encyclopedia of Native American Religion: an Introduction.* Facts on File, New York, 2000.

Homer. *The Odyssey.* Penguin Classics, Baltimore, 1946.

Hoxie, Frederick. *Encyclopaedia of the Native American Indian.* Houghton Mifflin, New York, 1996.

– *Treaties: A Sourcebook.* D'Arcy McNickle Center for the American Indian History, Chicago, 1998.

Hurtado, Albert, and Peter Iverson, eds. *Major Problems in American Indian History: Documents and Essays.* Heath and Co., Toronto, 1994.

"Index des actes notariés du Régime français à Trois Rivières." ANQ, mf. M–99, 1 bobine.

"Inventaire des Archives du Séminaire des Trois Rivières. " RAPQ, 1961–64, 69.

"Inventaire sommaire des Archives conservées au Palais de Justice des Trois Rivières." RAPQ, 1920–21, 328–49.

Jourdan, Decrucy et François Isambert. *Recueil général des anciennes lois françaises depuis l'an 1420 jusqu`a la Révolution de 1789.* 27 vols. Belin la Prieur, Paris, 1822–30.

Jaenen, Cornelius J. *The French Régime in the Upper Country of Canada during the Seventeenth Century: Documents.* Champlain Society, Toronto, 1996.

Jamet, Denys. "Coppie de la lettre Escripte Par de R.P. Denys Jamet, Commissionare des PP. Recollectz de Canada, A monsieur de Rance, grand vicaire de Pontoyse." 16/8/1620, CIHM, s.d.

Jaenen, Cornelius J., ed. *The French Régime in the Upper Country of Canada during the Seventeenth Century.* Champlain Society, Toronto, 1996.

J.C.B. *Voyage au Canada fait depuis l'an 1751 à 1761.* Paris, Aubier-Montaigne, 1978.

Jogues, Father Isaac. *Narrative of a Captivity among the Mohawk Indians and a Description of New Netherlands in 1642–1648.* New York Historical Society, New York, 1856.

Jesuit Sources (utilized whichever editions available on research visits):

Lallement, Charles, "Copie de Trois lettres escrittes es années 1625 et 1626." A. Albanie, Paris, 1870. CIHM.

RJ: *Relations des Jésuites,* CIHM #50858, 36491, 29165, 36492, 52013, 52015, 29126, 63120, 35136, 44703, 36103, 48657, 36188, 53094, 53098, 62717, 90076, 63303, 36241, 63754, 36195, 63308, 36037, 42270, 36102, 56259, 63302.

Johnson, Charles. *The Valley of the Six Nations: A Collection of Documents on the Indian Lands of the Grand River.* Champlain Society, Toronto, 1964.

Josephus. *The Jewish Wars.* Trans. G.A. Williamson, Steimatzky's, Pelican Press, 1959.

Journal de ma vie: Mémoire du maréchal de Bassompierre. Vol. 3. Société d'histoire de France, Le Marquis de Chantérac, Paris, 1870–77, pp. 305–415.

Juchereau de St-Ignace, Jeanne-Françoise, et Marie Andrée Duplessis de Ste-Hélène. *Les Annales de l'Hôtel-Dieu de Québec 1636–1716*. Hôtel-Dieu de Québec, Québec [1751] 1939.

Jurgens, Olga "Documents inédits: Le Testament de Samuel Champlain, 17/11/1635." *RHAF* 17 (1963): 269–86.

Kagan, Hilde Heun, ed., *The American Heritage Pictorial Atlas of US History*. Heritage Pub. Co., Inc., New York, 1966.

Kalm, Pehr. *Voyage de Pehr Kalm au Canada en 1749*. Trad. Jacques Rousseau, Béthune et Morisset, Montréal, 1977.

Kappler, Charles, ed. *Indian Treaties, 1778–1883*. Amereon House, Mattituck, New York, 1972.

Kinietz, Vernon. *The Indians of the Western Great Lakes, 1615–1760*. Ann Arbor Paperbacks, University of Michigan Press, Ann Arbor [1949] 1965.

Labé, Louise. *Oeuvres*. Slatkine Reprints, Genève, 1968.

LaBruyère, Jean de. *Les caractères, accompagnés des caractères de Théophraste et du Discours à l'Académie*. Didier, Paris, 1926.

La Coudrette. *Le Roman de Mélusine ou Histoire de Lusignan*. Klinksieck, Paris, 1982.

Lafayette, Marie-Madeleine de. *La Princesse de Clèves*. Hachette, Paris, 1961.

Lafitau, Joseph-François. *Moeurs des sauvages américains comparées aux moeurs des premiers temps*. Vol. 1. Maspéro, Paris, 1866, CIHM #38670.

– *Moeurs, coutumes, et religions des sauvages amériquains*. 1839, CIHM, #38670–38672.

LaFontaine, Jean de. *Fables de la Fontaine*. Hachette, Paris, 1930.

Lafrenière, Denis. *Repertoire des personnages indiens au 17e siècle et description de leurs rôles*. GREL, UQAM, cahier #3, juin 1991.

Lahontan, Louis-Armand, baron de. *Dialogues curieux entre l'auteur et un sauvage de bon sens qui a voyagé…* Oxford University Press, London [1703] 1931.

– *Mémoires de l'Amérique septentrionale, ou la suite des voyages de Mr. le baron de La Hontan*. Vol. 2. Amsterdam, ed. Elysée, Montréal [1705] 1974.

– *Oeuvres complètes*. (Éd. Réal Ouellet), Presses de l'Université Laval, Sillery, 1984.

Lallemant, Charles. *Copie de Trois lettres escrittes es années, 1625–1626*. Albanie, Paris, 1870, CIHM #29485.

La Motte le Vayer. *Dialogues faits à l'imitation des anciens*. Fayard, Paris, 1988.

Landry, Yves. *Orphélines en France, pionnières au Canada: les filles du roi au XVIIe siècle*. Leméac, Montréal, 1992.

La Rochefoucauld, François, duc de. *Réflexions, sentences et maximes morales: mises en nouveau ordre, avec des notes politiques & historiques*. Chez Ganeau, Bauche D'Houry fils, Paris, 1754.

Larose, André. *Les registres paroissiaux au Québec avant 1800*. Presses de l'Université Laval, Québec [1979] 1981.

Larouche, Léonidas et François de Crépieul. *Le Seconde régistre de Tadoussac 1668–1700: transcription*, Coll. Tekouerimat. Presses de l'Université de Québec, Montréal, 1972.

LaSicotière, Léon de. *L'Emigration Percheronne au Canada pendant le XVIIe siècle*. Société historique de l'Orme, 27/10/1887, Alençon, 1887. CIHM #09059.

Le Clercq, Chrestien. *Nouvelle-Relation de la Gaspésie qui contient les moeurs & la religion des sauvages Gaspésiens Porte-Croix, adorateurs du Soleil, & autres peuples de l'Amérique Septentrionale. dite le Canada*. Chez Amable Auroy, Paris [1691] 1791 in Ganong, William, ed. *New Relation of Gaspesia*. Champlain Society, Toronto, 1946.

– *Premier établissement de la foi dans la Nouvelle-France contenant la publication de l'Evangile, l'histoire des colonies françaises et des découvertes qui s'y sont faites jusqu'à présent*. 2 vols. Amable Auroy, Paris, 1691, CIHM #36369.

Leabhar Gabhala (Book of the Conquests of Ireland). Ed. and trans. R.A.S. Macalister and J. MacNeill. Dublin, n.p., n.d.

Lefebvre, Fernand. "Documents inédits:" Testament de Noble homme Charles Le Moyne Escuyer, Sieur de Longueuil." *RHAF* 6 (1952): 274–5.

Legendre, Ghislaine, éd. *Histoire simple et véritable: annales de l'Hôtel-Dieu de Montréal. 1659–1725 par Marie Morin*. Presses de l'Université de Montréal, Montréal, 1979.

Le père Chaumonot de la companie de Jésus: Autobiographie et pièces inédites. Henri Oudin, Auguste Carayon, 1869

Leland, Waldo. *Guide to Materials for American History in the Libraries and Archives of Paris*. Carnegie Institution of Washington, Washington, DC, 1932, Kraus reprints, New York, 1965.

Lescarbot, Marc. *Histoire de la Nouvelle France suivie par des Muses de la Nouvelle France depuis sa découverte jusqu'en l'an 1632*. CIHM #09060, Tross, Paris, 1866, CIHM #36380–36382.

Les textes poétiques du Canada français, 1606–1867. Vol. 1. Fides, Montréal, 1987.

Le Tac, Sixte. *Histoire chronologique de la Nouvelle France ou Canada par le Père Sixte Le Tac. Récollet*. Editions Elysée, Montréal, 1975.

Le Tenneur, René. *Les Normands et les origines du Canada français*. Presses de l'imprimerie

Le Vary Pourtraict de la ville de Rouen assiegée et pris par le roy Charles 9. Paris, n.d.

Leymarie, A.-Léo. "Pages d'histoire: Inédit sur le Fondateur de Québec." *Nova Francia* 1 (1925): 80–5.

"Relation des troubles excités par les calvinistes dans la ville de Rouen depuis l'an 1537 jusqu'en l'an 1582." en *La Revue de Rouen et de la Normandie*. Rouen, 1837.

Livy. *Roman History*. Appleton, New York, 1901.

Lom d'Arce, Louis-Armand de, baron de Lahontan. *Dialogue curieux entre l'auteur et un sauvage de bon sens qui a voyagé et Mémoires de l'Amérique Septentrionale*. Éd. Gilbert Chinard. Oxford University Press, Oxford, 1931.

– *Mémoires de l'Amérique septentrionale de Mr. le Baron de LaHontan*. Editions Elysée, Montréal, 1974.

– *Voyages du Baron de LaHontan dans l'Amérique septentrionale*. Editions Elysée, 1974

Mabinogion: the Text of the Mabinogion and other Welsh Tales from the Red Book of Hergest. Ed. J. Rhys and J. Evans, Oxford University Press, Oxford, 1887.

Malchelosse, Gérard et Roy Régis. *Le régiment de Carignan, son organisation et expedition au Canada (1665-1668): Officiers et soldats qui s'établirent en Canada.* Ducharme, Montréal, 1925.

Malory, Sir Thomas. *La Morte d'Arthur.* Ed. Keith Baines. Dent, London, 1947.

Margry, Pierre. *Découvertes et établissements des Français dans l'ouest et dans le sud de l'Amérique septentrionale, 1614-1754.* 6 v., Maisonneuve, Paris, 1879-1888.

Marie de L'Incarnation (éd. Oury, Guy). *Correspondance.* Solesmes, Abbaye de St-Pierre, 1971.

Marquette, Jacques. *Voyages.* University Microfilms Incorporated, Ann Arbor, MI, 1966.

– *Voyages et découvertes de quelues pays et nations de L'Amérique septentrionale par le Père Marquette et Sieur Joliet, Etienne Michelet, Imp. de Maulde et Renou.* [1681] 1845.

Marshall, Joyce. *Word From New France: The Selected Letters of Marie de L'Incarnation.* Oxford University Press, Toronto, 1967.

Martin, Jacques. *La Religion des Gaulois tirées des Plus Pures sources de l'antiquité.* 2 t., Saugrain, Paris, 1722.

Massicotte, Edouard-Zotique. *Dollard et ses compagnons: notes et documents.* Comité des monuments, Montréal, 1920.

– "La milice de 1663." *BRH* 32 (1926): 405-18

– "Les colons de Montréal de 1642 à 1667." *BRH* 33 (1927): 170-92, 224-39, 312-20, 379-384, 433-48, 467-82, 538-48, 613-25, 650-2; 37, 1931, pp. 757-9 (corrections).

– "A Propos de congés." *BRH*, 1926, 296-300.

– "Les congés de traite déposés aux Archives Provinciales de Québec." *RAPQ*, 1922-23, 192-265.

– "Les congés de traite déposés aux Archives Provinciales de Québec enrégistrés à Montréal." *RAPQ*, 1921-22, 189-225.

– "Congés et permis déposés ou enregistrés à Montréal sous le Régime français." *RAPQ*, 1921-22, 189-225.

– "Repertoire des engagements pour l'Ouest aux Archives Juridiques à Montréal 1670-1778." *RAPQ*, 1929-30, 191-466; 1931-32; 1932-33.

McLeod, Peter. "The Anishinabeg Point of View: The History of the Great Lakes Region to 1800 in 19th-Century Mississauga, Odawa, and Ojibwa Historiography." *CHR* 73 (1992): 194-210.

MacNeill, John and, Helena Gamer, eds. *Medieval Handbooks of Penance.* Columbia University Press, Ann Arbor, MI [1938] 1958.

"Madame de Champlain." *BRH* 4 (1898): 304-5.

Mead, Margaret, and Bunzel, Ruth. *The Golden Age of Anthropology.* George Braziller, New York, 1920.

Méchoulan, Henry. *Manasseh ben Israel's Mikveh Israel (The Hope of Israel).* Trans. Moses Wall, 1652, Littman Library, Oxford University Press, New York, 1987.

"Mémoires de feu M. Boucher, seigneur de Boucherville, et ancien gouverneur des Trois-Rivières (extraits)." *BRH* 32 (1932): 398-404.

Mémoires et documents relatifs à l'histoire du Canada, Ordonnances de Paul de Chomedey, sieur de Maisonneuve, premier gouverneur de Montréal. ANQM, Montréal, 1860.

Mercure Gallant:

fév. 1679, pp. 55–8; nov. 1681, pp. 56 et seq., avril 1687, p. 95, sept. 1692, pp. 328–31, mai 1695, pp. 211–12.

"La Minute notariée du Contrat de mariage de Champlain." *Nova Francia* 5 (1930): 142–55.

Molière, Jean-Baptiste Poquelin, dit. *Oeuvres complètes*. Éd. R. Joanny. Garnier Frères, Paris, 1962.

Montaigne, Michel de. *Essais*. Vol. 2. Thibaudet, Paris, 1965.

Montesquieu, Charles de Secondat, baron de. Éd. Gilbert Chinard. *Pensées choisis de Montesquieu: tirées du 'Commonplace Book' de Thomas Jefferson*. Les Belles Lettres, Paris, 1925.

Morice, Adrien Gabriel. *Dictionnaire Historique des Canadiens et des Métis de l'ouest*. 2e ed. aug., Garneau, Québec, 1912.

Motier, Gilbert du. *Marquis de la Fayette in the Age of the American Revolution: Selected Letters and Papers 1776–1790*. Cornell University Press, Ithaca, New York, 1977.

Munro, W.B., ed. *Documents relating to the Seigneurial Tenure in Canada, 1598–1854*. ANC: Public Archives of Canada, 1908.

Nabokov, Peter, ed. *Native American Testimony: A Chronicle of Indian White Relations from Prophecy to the Present, 1492–1991*. Viking, New York [1978] 1991.

"Nation Iroquoise: Abrégé des vies et Moeurs et autres Particularitez de la Nation Irokoise laquelle èst divisée en Cinq villages. Scavoir Agnez Onney8t Nontagué Goyog8an et Sonnont8an, anonyme, c. 170." *RAQ* 26 (1996). (Bibliothèque Mazarine, MG7, IV, 1964, 1–17.)

Nennius. *Historia Britonum*. W. Gunn, London, 1819.

Nicolas, Louis. "Grammaire Algonquine ou des Sauvages de l'Amérique Septentrionale." *BNF*, fond américain, #1.

Nies, Judith. *Native American History: A Chronology of a World's Vast Achievements and their Links to World Events*. Ballantine Books, New York, 1996.

Nish, Cameron, ed. *Le Régime français I: Histoire du Canada: textes et documents*. Prentice-Hall of Canada, Ltd., Scarborough, ONT, 1966.

"Ordonnances de M. de Lauzon au sujet de Pierre Boucher (18 novembre 1653)." *BRH* 32 (1926): 735.

"Ordonnances inédites de Pierre Boucher, gouverneur des Trois Rivières." *BRH* 32 (1926): 187–92.

Ouellet, Réal, ed. *Sur Lahontan: comptes rendus et critiques 1702–1711*. L'Hêtrière, Québec, 1983.

Ovide. *Les métamorphoses*. Garnier Flammarion, Paris, 1992.

Patin, Guy. *Lettres du temps de la Fronde*. Bossard, Paris, 1921.

Paullin, Charles, *Atlas of the Historical Geography of the United States*. Carnegie Institute of Washington, D.C., #401, Greenwood Press, Westport CN, 1932.

Pausanias. *Description of Greece.* 5 vols. William Jones, Harvard University Press, Cambridge, 1959.

Petit Larousse. 19e éd., Librairie Larousse, Paris [1959] 1964.

Perrot, Nicholas. *Mémoire sur les moeurs, coustumes et relligion des sauvages de l'Amérique Septentrionale par Nicolas Perrot.* A. Franck, Paris, 1864, CIHM #49784.

Petrone, Penny, ed. *First People, First Voices.* University of Toronto Press, Toronto, 1991.

Peyser, Joseph. *Letters from New France: The Upper Country, 1686–1783.* University of Illinois Press, Urbana, 1992.

Plinius, Secundus. *Pliny's Natural History.* Ed. Lloyd Haberly. Ungar, London, 1957.

Polybius. *Historiae.* Heinemann, London [1922] 1967.

Provencher, Gérard. *Répertoire des mariages de l'Ancienne Lorette (1695–1966).* Société canadienne de généalogie, Québec, 1968, #25.

Prucha, Francis, ed. *Documents in United States Indian Policy.* University of Nebraska Press, Lincoln, NB [1975] 1990.

Public Archives of Canada. *General Inventory: Manuscripts.* Information Canada, Ottawa, 1974.

Quaker Spirituality: Selected Writings. Paulist Press, New York, 1984.

Rabelais, François. *Gargantua: Édition critique sur le texte de édition dite définitive, pub. en 1542 à Lyon par Frère Juste.* Henri Champion, Diff. Slatkine, Genève, Switzerland, 1995.

– *Oeuvres complètes.* Garnier, Paris, 1962.

Racine, Jean. *Oeuvres complètes.* Ed. du Seuil, Paris, 1962.

Radisson, Pierre Esprit. *Voyages of Pierre-Esprit Radisson: Being an account of his travels and experiences among the North American Indians from 1652 to 1684.* Trans. Gideon Skull. Prince Society, London, 1885, CIHM #09232.

"Correspondance échangé entre la cour de France et le Gouverneur de Frontenac, pendant sa première Administration 1672–1682." *RAPQ,* 1926–27, 1–144.

Documents inédits: La communauté des Habitants de la Nouvelle-France. *RHAF* 5 (1951):118-25.

Raguenau, Paul. *La Vie de la Mère Catherine de St-Augustin, Religieuse Hospitalière de la Miséricorde de Québec en la Nouvelle-France.* CIHM, Ottawa [1671] 1992.

"Raisons qui m'engage à habiter ma seigneurie que j'ay nomée Boucherville." *RAPQ,* 1921–22, 58.

Ramenovsky, A. *The Archaeology of Population Collapse: Native American Response to the introduction of Infectious Disease.* University of Washington, Seattle, WA, 1982.

RAPQ: Rapports des Archives du Province de Québec (specific citations)

"Correspondance d'Intendant Jean Talon.," *RAPQ,* 1930–31, 1–182

"Correspondance échangée entre la Cour de France et le gouverneur de Frontenac." *RAPQ,* 1926–27, 1–144.

"L'ambassade de M. Legardeur de Courtemanche chex les Outaouis en 1691." *RAPQ,* 1921–22, 233–6.

Labrèque, Lucile, "Inventaire de Pièces détachées de Cours de Justice de la Nouvelle-France (1638–1760)." *RAPQ,* 1971, 5–25.

"Mémoire sur ce qui concerne le commerce des castors et ses dépendances (1715). *RAPQ*, 1922–23, 69–79.

"Première concession de terre faite sur la Rive Sud du St-Laurent (15/5/1647)." *RAPQ*, 1923–24, 71–3.

"Requête du Procureur général Jean Bourdon avec jugement de l'Intendant Talon." *RAPQ* 1927–28, 48–9. "Répertoire de la Collection Couillard-Després." *RAPQ*, 1972, 33–81.

Relation des troubles excités par les calvinistes dans la ville de Rouen depuis l'an 1537 jusqu'en l'an 1582. (Publication de *La Revue de Rouen et de la Normandie*, Rouen, 1837.)

Richaudeau, abbé, éd. *Marie de l'incarnation: Lettres.* Librarie Internationale-Catholique, 1876, vol. 2, 154–62.

Richelieu, Armand Jean DuPlessis, duc de. *Testament politique: Edition critique.* Robert Laffont, Paris, 1947.

– *Lettres.* Ministère des Affaires étrangères, Paris, s.d.

– *Mémoires de Cardinal de Richelieu.* t. VIII, Institut de France-Académie Française, 1628, Honoré Champion, Paris, 1927.

Rochemonteix, Camille de. *Les Jésuites et la Nouvelle-France aux XVIIIe siècle.* Paris, 1895–1896, 3 vols. LeTouzey et ainé, Paris, 1895–1896, CIHM #12671–12673.

Rowlandson, Mary. *The Captivity of Mrs. Mary Rowlandson of Lancaster, who was taken by the French and Indians.* Hori Brown, Brookfield, Ottawa, 1811, CIHM #37783.

Roy, Pierre-Georges. *Inventaire des greffes des notaires du régime français.* 27 t., APQ, Québec, 1943–76.

– *Inventaire d'une Collection de pièces judiciaires, notariales, etc., etc., conservéees aux Archives de Québec.* I, L'éclairieur, Beauceville, Québec, 1917.

– *Inventaire des concessions en fief et seigneurie.* 6 vols., Province de Québec, 1927–29.

– *La Réception de Monseigneur le Comte d'Argenson par toutes les nations du païs du Canada à son entrée du gouverneur de la Nouvelle-France.* Léger-Brosseau, Québec, 1890.

– "Lettres de noblesse, généalogies, érections de comtés et baronnies insinuées par le Conseil souverain de la Nouvelle-France." *APQ*, 2 vols., vol. 1. Beauceville, L éclaireur, 1920.

Sagard, Gabriel. *Histoire du Canada et voyages que les frères mineurs recollects ont faicts pour la conversion des infidèles depuis l'an 1615, avec un dictionnaire de la langue huronne.* 2 v., nouvelle ed., Libraire Tross, 1886, CIHM #47347–47351. (Denys Delâge generously gave me his extra copy.)

– *Le grand voyage dv pays des Hurons: situé en l'Amérique vers la mer douce és dernières confins de la nouuelle France, dite Canada; avec un dictionnaire de la langue Huronne, pour la commodité de ceux qui ont à voyager dans le pays, & ont l'intelligence d'icelle langue suivi du Dictionnaire de la langue huronne,* éd. Critique. Presses de l'Université de Montréal, Montréal [1632] 1998. (This was kindly sent me overseas by Ramsay Cook.)

Saint-Simon, Louis de Rouvroy, duc de. *Mémoires: Scènes et portraits.* Fayard, Paris, 1950.

de Salignac, François, de la Motte Fénélon. *Dialogues des morts suivis de quelques dialogues de Boileau, Fontenelle, d'A'lembert* ... Hachette, Paris, 1878.

Saulnier, Carole. *Etat général des fonds et des collections des Archives de folklore.* 2e ed., rev. et aug., Presses de l'Université Laval, Québec, 1990.

Seno, William, ed. *Up Country: Voices from the Midwestern Wilderness.* Round River Publications, Madison, WI, 1985.

Sicotière, Léon de la. *L'émigration percheronne au Canada pendant le XVIIe siècle.* E. Renault-de-Broise, Alençon, 1887.

Silvy, Antoine. *Relation par lettres de L'Amérique septentrionale 1709–1710.* ed. Camille de Rochemonteix, Mika Pub., Belleville, ON [1904] 1980.

Snow, Dean, Charles Gehring, and William Starna, eds. *In Mohawk Country: Early Narratives about a Native People.* Syracuse University Press, Syracuse, 1996.

Squier, E.G. "Historical and Mythological Traditions of the Algonquins: With a Translation of the 'Walum-Olam,' or Bark Record of the Linni-Lenape." In William Clements, ed., *Native American Folklore in 19th Century Periodicals.* Swallow Press, Ohio University Press, Athens, OH, 1986.

Sturluson, Snorri. *Two versions of the Snorra Edda from the 17th Century.* Ed. Anthony Faulkes, 2 vols. Stofnun Arna Magnussonar, Reykjavik, 1957.

Surtees, Bob. *Canadian Indian Policy.* D'Arcy McNickle Center for American Indian History, Chicago, 1982.

Tacitus. *Germania.* Ed. Rives, Clarendon University Press, Oxford, 1999.

Tallemant, Réaux des. *Historiettes.* 8 vols, Gallimard, Paris, 1967.

"Le Testament de Samuel de Champlain, premier gouverneur de la Nouvelle-France." *RAPQ,* 1920–21, h.t. au début.

Têtu, Mgr. H., and abbé Gagnon, C.O., éds. *Mandements, lettres pastorales et circulaires des évêques de Québec.* Vols. 1 and 2. Coté, Québec, 1887–88.

Tanguay, Mgr C. *Dictionnaire genealogique des familles canadiennes-françaises depuis la fondation de la colonie.* 7 t., Senecal, Montréal, 1871–90.

Tanner, Helen Hornbeck, *Atlas of Great Lakes Indian History.* University of Oklahoma Press, Norman, OK, 1987.

– *The Ojibwas.* D'Arcy McNickle Center for American Indian History, Chicago, 1976.

Têtu, H. et Gagnon, C.O. *Mandements, lettres pastorales, et circulaires des évêques de Québec 1659–1887.* 6 vols., vol. 1. Côté, Québec, 1887–1890.

Thompson, Davis. *Narrative 1784–1812.* Ed. Richard Glover. Champlain Society, Toronto, 1962.

Tougard, A., ed. *Les Trois siècles palinodiques, ou histoire générale des Palinods de Rouen.* Dieppe, etc. ... S.I., Rouen, 1898.

Troyes, Chrestien de. *Oeuvres complètes.* Gallimard, Paris, 1997.

Trudel, Marcel. *Atlas de la Nouvelle-France,* Presses de l'Université Laval, Québec, 1968.

– *Catalogue des immigrants, 1632–1662.* Cahiers du Québec, coll. Histoire, Editions Hurtubise, Montréal, 1983.

– *Dictionnaire des esclaves et leurs propretiaires au Canada français.* Cahiers du Québec, Histoire, Editions Hurtubise, nouv. ed., Montréal, 1990.

– *La population du Canada en 1663.* Fides, Montréal, 1973.

– *La population du Canada en 1666: recensement reconstitué.* Septentrion, Silléry, 1995.

Trudel, Pierre. "On découvre toujours L'Amérique: l'arrivée des Européans selon des récits cris recueillis à Whapmagoostui." *RAQ* 22 (1992): 63–70.

Vachon, André. *Dreams of Empire: Canada before 1700.* ANC: Archives Publiques du Canada, Ottawa, 1982.

– *Eloquence indienne.* Fides, Montréal, 1968.

Vachon de Belmont, François. *Histoire du Canada 1608–1700, d'après un manuscrit à la Bibliothèque du Roi à Paris.* Société littéraire de Québec, Québec, 1840, S.I., s.n.

Vaillancourt, Emile. *Le conquête du Canada par les Normands.* Ducharme, Montréal, 1930.

Van den Bogaert, Harmen Meyndertsz. *A Journey into Mohawk and Oneida Country 1634–1636.* trad. Charles William Starna, Syracuse University Press, 1988.

Vanderwerth, W.C. *Indian Oratory: Famous Speeches by Noted Indian Chieftains.* University of Oklahoma Press, Norman, OK, 1971.

Villiers, Baron Marc de. *Les Raretés des Indes (Codex Canadiensis).* Les Ed. de Boutons d'or, Montréal, 1974.

Virgil. *The Aeneid.* Wordsworth Classics, Norhaven, 1995.

– *Ecologues and Georgics.* Trans. T. F. Royds, Everyman's Library, London [1907] 1965.

Visière, Isabelle et Louis, eds. *Peaux-Rouges et Robes Noires.* coll. Outre-mers, Ed. de la différence, Paris, 1993. (This was kindly given to me by Gérard Lipovetzky.)

Vogel, Virgil. *A Documentary History of the American Indian.* Harper and Row, New York, 1969.

Voragine, Jacobus de. *The Golden Legend of Jacopus de Voragine: Trans. and adapted from the Latin.* Arno Press, New York, 1969.

Waldman, Carl, *Atlas of the North American Indian,* Facts on File, New York and Oxford, 1985.

Watson, Marie Caroline. *Legends of Le Détroit: Early French Families.* Gale Research Co., Book Tower, Detroit [1884] 1977.

Washburn, Wilcomb, ed. *The Indian and the White Man: Documents.* New York University Press, New York, 1964.

Washington, George. *George Washington: A Biography in his Own Words.* 2 vols., Ed. Newsweek publications, Dist. Harper and Row, New York, 1972.

Wright, John, ed., *Atlas of the Historical Geography of the United States.* Carnegie Institute of Washington, Pub. #401, Greenwood Press, Westport, CN, 1932.

Zoltany, Yves. *The French Tradition in America: Documentary History of the United States.* Harper and Row, New York, 1969.

SECONDARY SOURCES

Abraham, Claude. *Norman Satirists in the Age of Louis XIII: Papers on French Seventeenth Century Literature.* Paris-Seattle-Tübingen, 1983.

Ackerman, Robert. *The Myth and Ritual School: Theorists of Myth Theories,* vol. 2. Garland Publishers, New York, 1991.

Adair, E.R. "Dollard des Ormeaux and the Fight at the Long-Sault: A Reinterpretation." *CHR* 13 (1932): 121–38.

Adelman, Jeremy, and Stephen Aron. "Forum Essay: From Borderlands to Borders: Empires, Nation-States, and the Peoples in Between in North American History." *AHR* 104 (1999): 813–41.

Aftenback, Philip, and Robert Laufer. *The New Pilgrims: Youth Protest in Transition.* David Melley, New York, 1972.

Agulhon, Maurice. *Marianne into Battle.* Cambridge University Press, Cambridge, 1981.

Alberro, Solange. "L'Acculturation des Espagnols dans le Mexique colonial: déchéance ou dynamisme culturel." *L'homme* 32 (1992): 149–64.

Albert-Petit, Armand. *Histoire de Normandie.* Ancienne Librarie Furne, Boivin et cie, 12e ed., 1927.

Aldridge-Morris, Ray. *Multiple Personality: An Exercise in Deception.* Lawrence Erlbaum Associates, Hove and London, 1989.

Alix, Pierre. *Autres Contes populaires et légendes de Bretagne.* Ar Vorenn, Nantes, 1984.

Allaire, Gratien. "Officiers et marchands: les sociétés de commerce des fourrures 1715–1760." *RHAF* 40 (1987): 409–245.

Altherr, Thomas. "'Flesh Is the Paradise of a Man of Flesh:' Cultural Conflict over Indian Hunting Beliefs and Rituals in New France as Recorded in The Jesuit Relations." *CHR* 64 (1983): 267–77.

Amsell, Jean-Loup. *Logiques métisses.* Payot, Paris, 1990.

AMDG. *Liste des Missionaires Jésuites: Nouvelle-France et Louisiana, 1611–1800.* College Ste-Marie, Montreal, 1929.

Anderson, Fred, and Andrew Cayton. "The Problem of Fragmentation and the Prospects for Synthesis in Early American Social History." *WMQ* 50 (1993): 299–310, 311–28.

Aron, Raymond. *Peace and War.* Weidenfeld and Nicolson, London, 1966.

Les Amériques françaises. Université d'Ottawa, 48e Congrès de l'RHAF, 20–21/10/1995.

Anderson, Benedict. *Imagined Communities: Reflections on the Origin and Spread of Nationalism.* Verso, London, 1991.

Anderson, Karen. *Chain Her by One Foot: The Subjugation of Women in Seventeenth-Century New France.* Routledge, London, 991.

Andrist, Ralph. *The Long Death: The Last Days of the Plains Indians.* Macmillan, New York, [1964] 1966.

Ankarloo, Bengt, and Gustav Henningsen, ed. *Early Modern Witchcraft: Centres and Peripheries.* Oxford University Press, Oxford, 1982.

Antti, Aarne, and Stith Thompson. *The Types of the Folktale.* Suomaleinen Tiedeakatemia, Academia Scientiarum Fennica, Helsinki, 1961.

Antze, Paul, and Michael Lambek. *Tense Past: Cultural Essays in Trauma and Memory.* Routledge, New York, 1996.

Anwyl, Edward. *Celtic Religion.* Open Court, Chicago, 1906.

Arad, Itzhak, Israel Gutman, and Avraham Margaliot. *Documents on the Holocaust.* Yad VaShem, Jerusalem, 1981.

Arendt, Hannah. *The Origins of Totalitarianism.* George Allen and Unwin, London, 1967.

– "Social Science Techniques and the Study of Concentration Camps." *Jewish Social Studies* 12 (1950): 49–164.

Arieli, Yehoshua. *Individualism and Nationalism in American Ideology.* Harvard University Press, Cambridge, 1964.

Ariès, Philippe. *Centuries of Childhood.* Knopf, New York, 1962.

– *L'Homme devant la mort.* Seuil, Paris, 1977.

– *The Hour of Our Death.* Penguin, Harmondsworth, [1981] 1983.

Arieti, Silvano, and Johannes Meth. "Rare, Unclassifiable, Collective, and Exotic Psychiatric Syndromes." In Silvano Arieti, ed., *The American Handbook of Psychiatry.* Basic Books, New York, [1974] 1981, 546–64.

Armitage, Peter. *Homeland or Wasteland?* Ottawa, Naskapi Montagnais Innu Association, 1989.

Armstrong, Joe. *Champlain.* Macmillan, Toronto, 1987.

Aron, Raymond. *Main Currents in Sociological Thought.* Trans. Richard Hoard and Helen Weaver. Pelican, Harmondsworth, Middlesex, 1967.

Aronowitz, M. "Adjustment of Immigrant Children as a Function of Parental Attitudes to Change." *International Migration Review* 26 (1992): 89–110.

Aschheim, Steven. *Brothers and Strangers Reconsidered.* Archivio Guidoizzi, Rome, 1998.

– *Culture and Catastrophe: German and Jewish Confrontations with National Socialism and other Crises.* Macmillan, London, 1996.

– *The Nietzsche Legacy in Germany 1890–1990.* University of California Press, Berkeley, 1992.

Auerhahn, N., and Dore Laub. "Intergenerational Memory of the Holocaust." In Danieli Yael, *International Handbook of Multigenerational Legacies of Trauma.* Plenum, abstract. Plenum, New York, forthcoming.

Ashley-Montagu, Sir, ed. *The Concept of the Primitive.* Free Press, New York, 1968.

Assiniwi, Bernard, and Isabelle Myre. *Contes adultes des territoires Algonkins.* Ottawa: Ed. Leméac, coll. Ni-T'Chawama, 1985.

Aubert de Gaspé, Philippe. *Les Anciens Canadiens.* Beauchemin, Montreal, 1938.

Aubry, Claude et Saul Field. *Le violon magique et autres légendes du Canada français.* Ed. des Deux Rives, Montreal, 1968.

Auger, Léon. *Pionniers vendéens au Canada aux XVIIe–XVIIIe.* Sables d 'Olonne, 1990.

Aus, Roger. *Water into Wine: The Beheading of John the Baptist.* Brown Judaic Studies, 150, Scholar's Press, Atlanta, GA, 1988.

Ayalon, Ofra. "Posttraumatic Stress Recovery of Terrorist Survivors." In John Wilson and Beverley Raphael, eds. *International Handbook of Traumatic Stress Syndromes*, 855–66. Plenum Series on Stress and Coping, New York, 1993.

Axtell, James. *The European and the Indian: Essays in the Ethnohistory of Colonial America.* Oxford University Press, Oxford, 1981.

– *The Invasion Within: The Contest of Cultures in Colonial North America.* Oxford University Press, Oxford, 1985.

– *Native and Newcomer: The Cultural Origins of Native America.* Oxford University Press, New York, 2000.

– "The White Indians of Colonial America." *WMQ* 32 (1975): 55–88.

– *White Indians of Eastern America.* Ye Galeon Press, Fairfield, WV, 1991.

Babcock, Barbara, ed. *The Reversible World: Symbolic Inversion in Art and Society.* Cornell University Press, Ithaca, NY, 978.

Bachofen, Johann Jakob. *Myth, Religion, and Mother Right: Selected Writing of J.J. Bachofen.* Princeton University Press, Princeton, 1992.

Bacon, Margaret. *Mothers of Feminism: The Story of Quaker Women in America.* Friends General Conference, Philadelphia, 1995.

Badinter, Elisabeth et Robert. *Condorcet.* Fayard, Paris, 1991.

Badone, Ellen. "The Construction of National Identity in Brittany and Québec: review." *American Ethnologist* 19 (1992): 806–17.

Bailey, Alfred Goldsworthy. *The Conflict of European and Eastern Algonkian Cultures.* 2nd. ed. University of Toronto Press, Toronto, 1969.

Bailyn, Bernard. *The Peopling of British America: An Introduction.* Vintage Books, New York, 1988.

Bailyn, Bernard, and Philip Morgan. *Strangers within the Realm: Cultural Margins of the First British Empire.* University of North Carolina Press, Chapel Hill, NC, 1991.

Baker, Alice. *True Stories of New England Captives Carried to Canada during the Old French and Indian Wars.* Cambridge University Press, Cambridge, MA, 1897.

Bakhtin, Mikhail. *L'oeuvre de Rabelais et la Culture Populaire au Moyen Age et sous la Renaissance.* trad. Andrée Robel, Gallimard, Paris, 1976.

– *The Dialogic Imagination.* University of Austin, Austin, 1981.

Baraton, Angélique, Ogam Bonnin, Xavier Cheseseau, Philippe Randa, Jean-Pierre Raffarin. *Hommes et Traditions populaires Poitou-Charentes et Vendée.* Martelle Ed., Amiens, 1993.

Barbeau, Marius. *L'arbre des rêves.* Lumen, Montréal, 1948.

– "Dialectes Hurons-Iroquois." *RHAF* 12 (1958): 178–83.

– "La Complainte de Cadieux, coureur de bois." *JAF* 67 (1954): 163–83.

– "Contes Populaires Canadiens." *JAF* 29 (1916): 23–137 (1e série).

– "Contes Populaires Canadiens." *JAF* 30 (1917): 1–141 (2e série).

– "Contes de la Beauce (Evelyn Bolduc)." *JAF* 32 (1919): 1–76 (3e série).

– "Contes populaires Canadians." *JAF* 39 (1926): 372–447 (5e série)

- "Contes populaires Canadians." *JAF* 53 (1940): 89–190 (7e série: coll. Adélard)
- *Mots sauvage en français chez nous*. Archives de Folklore de l'Université Laval.
- *Mythologie huronne et wyandotte*. Presses de l'Université de Montréal, Montréal, 1994.

Barsh, Russel. "Indigenous Peoples and the Idea of Individual Human Rights." *Native Studies Review* 10 (1995): 35–56.

Baird, Jay. "Goebbels, Horst Wessel, and the Myth of Resurrection and Return." *Journal of Contemporary History* 17 (1982): 633–50.

Barnett, Homer. *Innovation: The Basis of Cultural Change*. McGraw-Hill, New York, 1953.

Barnouw, Victor. "Chippewa Social Atomism." *AA* 63(1961): 1006–13.
- "A Psychological Interpretation of a Chippewa Origin Legend." *JAF* 68 (1955): 73–85; 68 (1953): 211–23; 68: 341–55.
- *Wisconsin Chippewa Myths and Tales: And Their Relation to Chippewa Life*. University of Wisconsin Press, Madison, 1977.

Barocas, H. "Children of Purgatory: Reflections of the Concentration Camp Survivor Syndrome." *International Journal of Social Psychiatry* 21 (1975): 87–92.

Bartlett, Robert. *The Making of Europe: Conquest, Colonization, and Cultural Change 950–1350*. BCA, London, 1993.

Barrès, Maurice. *Les déracinés*. Plon, Paris, 1937.

Barry, Jonathan. "Introduction: Keith Thomas and the problem of Witchcraft." In Barry, Jonathan, Marianne Hester, and Gareth Roberts, eds.. *Witchcraft in Early Modern Europe: Studies in Culture and Belief*. Cambridge, New York [1996] 1998, 1–48.

Barry, Jonathan, Marianne Hester, and Gareth Roberts, eds. *Witchcraft in Early Modern Europe: Studies in Culture and Belief*. Cambridge, New York [1996] 1998.

Bartov, Omer. "Defining Enemies, Making Victims: Germans, Jews, and the Holocaust." *AHR* 103 (1998): 771–816; 103 (1998): 1170–94.

Bar Yosef, Rivka. "Desocialization and Resocialization: The Adjustment Process of Immigration." *International Migration Review* 2 (1982): 27–43.

Barrett, D. "Through a Glass Darkly: Images of the Dead in Dreams." *Omega: Journal of Death and Dying* 24 (1992): 97–108.

Basoglu, Metin, ed. *Torture and Its Consequences: Current Treatment Approaches*. Cambridge University Press, Cambridge, 1992.

"La basse-normandie et ses poètes à l'époque classique." *Cahiers des Annales de Normandie*, #9, Centre Nationale de Recherche sur le Société, Caen, 1977.

Baudrillard, Jean. *L'échange symbolique et la mort*. Gallimard, Bibliothèque de Sciences humaines, Paris, 1998.

Bauman, Zygmunt. *Debating Cultural Hybridity: Multicultural Identities and the Politics of Anti–Racism*. Zed Books, Atlantic Highlands, NJ, 1997.

Bauman, Zygmunt, and Tim May. *Thinking sociologically*. Blackwell Pubs., Oxford, Malden, MA, 2001.

Beauchamp, William. "Heroic Deeds of Glooscap." *JAF* 1 (1888): 85–159.

- "Iroquois Notes." *JAF* 4 (1891): 39–46.
- "Onondaga Customs." *JAF* 1 (1888): 177–94.
- "Onondaga Notes." *JAF* 8 (1895): 209–21.
- "Onondaga Tales." *JAF* 6 (1893): 173–84.
- "Onondaga Tales." *JAF* 2 (1889): 261–70.

Beaudoin, Thérèse. *L'été dans la culture Québecoise*. Institut québécois de recherche sur la culture, Québec, 1987.

Beaudry, René. "Mme. de Champlain." *Cahiers des Dix* 33 (1968): 13–53.

Beaugrand, Honoré. *La Chasse-Galérie: légendes canadiennes*. coll. du Nénuphar, Fides, Paris, [1900] 1973.

Beaulieu, Alain. *Convertir les fils de Caën: Jésuites et amérindiens nomades en Nouvelle-France 1632–1642*. Nuit Blanche, Québec, 1990.

- "Ne faire qu'un seul peuple?: Iroquois et français à l'âge héroïque de la Nouvelle-France (1600–1660)." PhD, Université Laval, 1992.
- "Les pièges de la judiciarisation de l'histoire autochtone." *RHAF* 53 (2000): 541–51.

Beaulieu, Victor-Lévy. *Les contes québecois du grand-père forgeron à son petit fils Bouscotte*. Ed. Trois-Pistoles, Trois-Pistoles, 1998.

Beard, Mary. "The Roman and the Foreign: The Cult of the 'Great Mother' in Imperial Rome." In Nicolas Thomas and Caroline Humphrey, eds., *Shamanism, History, and the State*, ch. 3. University of Michigan Press, Ann Arbor, MI, 1996.

Beauregard, Yves, Serge Goudreau, Andrée Héroux, Michèle Jean, Rénald Lessard, Johanne Noël, Lucie Paquet, Alain Laberg. "Note de Recherche: Famille, Parenté, et Colonisation en Nouvelle-France." *RHAF* 39 (1986): 391–405.

Beauroy, J., et al. *The Wolf and the Lamb: Popular Culture in France from the Old Regime to the Twentieth Century*. Stanford, Stanford University Press, 1976.

Béchard, Henri. "Gandeacteua, Cathérine." *DBC*, I (n.d.): 330.

Bechtel, Guy. *La sorcière et l'Occident: la déstruction de la sorcellerie en Europe des Origines aux grand bûchers*. Plon, Paris, 1997.

Behringer, Wolfgang, ed. *Hexen und Hexenprozesse in Deutschland*. München, 1988.

- *Shaman of Oberstdorf: Conrad Stoeckhlin and the Phantoms of the Night*. University Press of Virginia, Charlotteville, VA, 1998.

Beik, William. *Absolutism and Society in Seventeenth Century France: State Power and Provincial Aristocracy in Languedoc*. Cambridge Series in Early Modern History, Cambridge, 1985.

Béland, Denise. "Le costume des voyageurs." *BRH* 48 (1942): 235–6.

Beland, Madeleine. *Chansons des Voyageurs et des forestiers*. Presses de l'Université Laval, Québec, 1982.

Bellmare, Raphael. "Le bureau des pauvres de Montréal." *BRH* 5 (1899): 279–81.

Benedict, Philip. *Rouen during the Wars of Religion*. Cambridge University Press, Cambridge, 1981.

Benedict, Ruth, *Patterns of Culture*. Houghton Mifflin Co., Boston, [1934] 1959.

Benichou, Paul. *Morales du grand siècle*. Gallimard, Paris, 1948.

Bennett, Paul, and Jaenen, Cornelius J. *Emerging Identities: Selected Problems and Inter-pretations in Canadian History.* Prentice-Hall Canada, Scarborough, ON, 1986.

Ben Yehuda, Nachman. *The Masada Myth: Collective Memory and Mythmaking in Israel.* University of Wisconsin Press, Madison, 1995.

– "Witchcraft and the Occult as Boundary Maintenance Devices." In Jacob Neusner, Ernest Fredrichs, and Paul Flesher. *Religion, Science, and Magic.* Oxford University Press, Oxford, 1989.

– "The Sociology of Moral Panics: Toward a New Synthesis." *Sociological Quarterly* 27 (1986): 495–513.

Bercé, Jean-Marie. *The Birth of Absolutism: A History of France, 1598–1661.* Trans. Richard Rex, Macmillan, London, 1996.

– *Histoire des Croquants: études des soulèvements populaires au XVIIe siècle dans le sud-ouest de la France.* 2 t., mémoires et documents, Droz, Genève, 1974.

– *History of Peasant Revolts.* Cornell University Press, Ithaca, New York, 1990.

Berger, Carl. *Approaches to Canadian History.* University of Toronto Press, Toronto, 1967.

Bergeron, Bertrand. *Au royaume de la légende.* Ed. JCL, Chicoutimi, 1988.

– *Les Barbes-bleues: contes et récits du Lac Saint-Jean.* Musée national de l'homme, Quinze, 1980.

– *Au royaume de la légende.* Ed. JCL, Chicoutimi, 1988.

Berman, E. "Identifying with the Other: A Conflictual, Vital Necessity – Commentary on Paper by Jay Frankel." *Psychoanalytic Dialogues* 12, 1 (2002): 141–51.

Bernard, Jean-Paul. "L'historiographie canadienne récente (1964–1994) et l'histoire des peuples du Canada." *CHR* 76 (1995): 321–53.

Bernheimer, Richard. *Wildmen in the Middle Ages.* Harvard University Press, Cambridge, 1952.

Berthet, Thierry. "L'autonomisation des colonies de peuplement: la cas de Nouvelle-France." PhD, Université de Montréal, 1992.

– *Seigneurs et Colons de Nouvelle-France: émergence d'une société distincte.* Ed. de l'E.N.S., Paris, 1992.

Bertrand, Carmen, et Serge Gruzinski. "Métissages du nouveau monde." Dans Chérif Khaznader et Jean Davignaud, eds. *Le métis culturel.* International de l'Imaginaire, serie I, Maison des cultures du monde, Babel, 1994.

Bettleheim, Bruno. *The Informed Heart.* Penguin, Harmondsworth, UK [1960] 1986.

Bhabha, Homi. *Nations and Narration.* Routledge, London, 1990.

– *The Location of Culture.* Routledge, London, 1994.

Bibaud, Maximilien F.M. *Biographie des Sagamos illustres de l'Amérique septentrionale.* Lovell et Gibson, Montréal, 1848.

Bibeau, Hector. "Le climat marial en Nouvelle-France à l'arrivée de Mgr de Saint-Vallier." *RHAF* 22 (1968): 415–28.

Biddle, Bruce. *Role Theory: Expectations, Identities, and Behaviors.* Academic Press, New York, 1979.

Billacois, François. "La Crise de la noblesse européene, 1550–1650: une mise à point." *Revue d'histoire moderne et contemporaine* 23 (1976): 258–77.

Bilodeau, Rosario. *Champlain*. Editions Hurtubise Ltée, Figures Canadiennes, Montréal, 1961.

– "Liberté économique et politique des Canadiens sous le régime français." *RHAF* 10 (1956): 49–68.

Bilu, Yoram. "The Other as a Nightmare: The Israeli-Arab Encounter as Reflected in Children's Dreams in Israel and the West Bank." *Political Psychology* 10, 3 (1989): 365–87.

Binger, Tilde. *Asherah: Goddesses in Ugarit, Israel, and the Old Testament*. Sheffield Academic Press, Sheffield, 1997.

Birette, Charles. *Dialecte et Légendes du Val de Saire*. A. Richard, Paris, 1927.

Bishop, Charles, "Ojibwa Cannibalism." Paper for Ninth International Congress of Anthropological and Ethnological Sciences, Chicago, IL, Aug-Sept. 1973.

– *The Northern Ojibwa and the Fur Trade*, Holt, Rinehart, and Winston, Toronto, 1974.

Bishop, Morris. *Champlain: A Life of Fortitude*. McClelland and Stewart, Carleton Library Series, #64, 1963.

Black, Jean, and Richard Yarnell. *Algonquin Humour*. AAA, 28/11–2/12/1975, New Orleans, LA Offprint, DIAND files.

Bissonnette, Alain. *L'Influence du Régime français sur le statut et les droits des peuples autochtones du Canada*. RCAP, 1994, DIAND.

Blackwell, Richard. "Disruption and Reconstitution of Family, Network, and Community Systems Following Torture, Organized Violence, and Exile." In Wilson, John and Beverley Raphael, eds. *International Handbook of Traumatic Stress Syndromes*, 733–42. Plenum Series on Stress and Coping, New York, 1993.

Blain, Jean. "Economie et Société en Nouvelle-France: historiographie des années 1960." *RHAF* 30 (1976): 323–61.

– "Notes Critiques: La moralité en Nouvelle-France: Les phases de la thèse et de l'Antithèse." *RHAF* 27 (1973): 408–16.

Blakeslee, Donald. "The Calumet Ceremony and the Origin of Fur Trade Rituals." *Western Canadian Journal of Anthropology* 7 (1977): 81–2.

Blanchard, David. *Kahnawake: aperçu historique*. Kanien'kehaka Raotitiohkwa Press, Kahnawake, 1980.

– "To the Other Side of the Sky: Catholicism at Kahnawake 1667–1700." *Anthropologica* 24 (1982): 77–102.

Blémus, René. *Jean Nicollet en Nouvelle-France: Un Normand à la découverte des grands lacs Canadiens*. Carnets d'histoire, Isoète, Cherbourg, 1988.

Bloch, Marc. *Les caractères originaux de l'histoire rurale française*. Armand Colin, Paris, 1952.

– *French Rural History: An Essay on it Basic Characteristics*. Trans. Janet Sondheimer, University of California Press, Berkeley, 1966.

Bloom, Harold. *The Closing of the American Mind*. Simon and Schuster, New York, 1988.

Blouin, Anne-Marie. *Histoire et iconographie des Hurons de Lorette du XVIIe et XVIIIe siècles*. 2 t., thèse de doctorat, Université de Montréal, 1987.

Bluche, François. *Louis XIV.* Hachette littéraire, Paris, 1986.

Blum, Rony. "From Savage Nobles to Noble Savages": The Nativity of Unlike Twins in New France 1608–1663." PhD, Hebrew University of Jerusalem, October 2000.

– "From Nus-pieds to Moccasins: The Historical Inception of French North American Nativisation." MA thesis, Hebrew University of Jerusalem, 1995. (Listed as Blum Lipovetzky.)

– "HaAtzil haPere vehaPere haAtzil: Tehalih ha'Yeledizatsia' bekerev haMehagrim haTsarfatim beTsarfat haHadasha 1608–1663 [Savage Nobles and Noble Savages: The Process of Nativization of French Immigrants to New France 1608–1663]." *Historia* 1 (1998): 21–54. (Listed as Blum Lipovetzky)

– "Windigos and Werewolves: Possession and Belonging in Native North America." Jerusalem Conference on Canadian Studies, June 25–29, 2000.

Blummer, Herbert. *Four Sociological Traditions: Selected Readings.* Oxford University Press, Oxford, 1994.

Boas, Franz. *The Mind of Primitive Man.* Macmillan, New York, 1938.

– *Race. Language, and Culture.* Macmillan, New York, 1940.

– "Dissemination of Tales among the Natives of North America." *JAF* 4 (1891): 13–20.

– "Mythology and Folktales of the North American Indians." *JAF* 27 (1914): 374–410.

Boas, Marie. *The Scientific Renaissance, 1450–1630.* The Rise of Modern Science, II, Harper and Bros., New York, 1962.

Boase, Thomas. *Death in the Middle Ages: Mortality, Judgement, and Remembrance.* Library of Medieval Civilization, McGraw-Hill, New York, 1972.

Bock, Philip. *Continuities in Psychological Anthropology.* W. Freeman and Co., San Francisco, 1980.

Bois, Guy. *The Crisis of Feudalism: Economy and Society in Eastern Normandy, 1300–1550.* Cambridge University Press, Cambridge, 1984.

Boldt, Menno. "Enlightenment Values, Romanticism, and Attitudes toward Political Status: A Study of Native Leaders in Canada." *Canadian Review of Sociology and Anthropology* 18 (1981): 545–65.

Bonichon, Philippe. *Des cannibales aux castors: les découvertes françaises de l'Amérique.* France-Empire, Paris, 1994.

Bonnefoy, Yves. *Mythologies.* 2 v., University of Chicago Press, Chicago, 1991.

Bonney, Richard. *Political Change in France under Richelieu and Mazarin.* Oxford University Press, Oxford, 1978.

Borch-Jacobsen. *Jacques Lacan: The Absolute Master.* Trans. Douglas Brick, Stanford University Press, Stanford, 1991.

Boscq de Beaumont, Gaston du. comp. and ed. "Les derniers jours de l'Acadie." *Le Canada Français* 1 (1888): 101–2.

Bosquet, Amélie. *La Normandie romanesque et merveilleuse: tradition, légendes, et superstitions populaires de cette province.* Le Brument, Rouen, 1845.

Bosher, John. *Business and Religion in New France (1600–1760): 22 Essays.* Canadian Scholar's Press, Toronto, 1994.

Bossy, John. "The Counterreformation and the People of Catholic Europe." *Past and Present* 47 (1970): 51–70.

Bouchard, Martin. *Gérer le patrimoine familiale en Nouvelle-France: la famille Boucher et la seigneurie de Boucherville aux XVIIe et XVIIIe siècles.* mémoire de maîtrise, Université de Montréal.

Boucher, Philip. *Les Nouvelles-Frances: France in America 1500–1815.* John Carter Brown Library, Providence, RI, 1989.

Boulette, T.R., and S.M. Anderson. "Mind Control and the Battering of Women." *Community Mental Health Journal* 21, 2 (1985): 109–18.

Bourdieu, Pierre, and Wacquant, Loïc J. D. *An Invitation to Reflexive Sociology.* University of Chicago Press, Chicago, 1992.

– *La Distinction: critique sociale du jugement.* Editions de minuit, Paris, 1979.

– *The Logic of Practice.* Stanford University Press, Stanford, 1990.

– *Outline of a Theory of Practice.* Trans. Richard Nice, Cambridge University Press, Cambridge, 1977.

Bourgeois, Emile. *Les sources de l'histoire de France, XVIIe siècle.* A. Picard, Paris, 1913–35.

Bouwsman, William. "Lawyers and Early Modern Culture." *AHR* 78 (1973): 310–11.

Boyd, William, ed. *William Byrd's Histories of Dividing Line between Virginia and North Carolina.* North Carolina Historical Commission, Raleigh, NC, 1929.

Boyer, Stephen, and Paul Nissenbaum. *Salem Possessed: The Social Origins of of Witchcraft.* Cambridge University Press, Cambridge, MA, 1974.

Braham, Randolf. "The Jewish Councils." In François Furet, ed., *Unanswered Questions: Nazi Germany and the Genocide of the Jews.* Schocken, New York, 1989, ch. 13, 252–74.

Brake, Mike. *The Sociology of Youth Culture and Youth Subidentities.* Routledge and Kegan Paul, London, 1980.

Brandao, José. "The Treaties of 1701: A Triumph of Iroquois Diplomacy." *Ethnohistory* 43 (1996): 209–44.

– *"Your Fyre Shall Burn No More:" Iroquois Policy toward New France and Its Native Allies to 1701.* University of Nebraska Press, Omaha, 1997.

Brandes, D., G. Ben Shahar, G., Gilboa, O. Bonne, S. Freedman, and A. Shalev. "PTSD Symptoms and Cognitive Performance in Recent Trauma Survivors." *Psychiatry Research* 110, 3 (2002): 231–8.

Braudel, Fernand. *Ecrits sur l'histoire.* Flammarion, Paris [1969] 1984.

– "Misère et Banditisme." *Annales* 2 (1947): 129–42.

Braun, Bennett. "Multiple Personality Disorder and Posttraumatic Stress Disorder: Similarities and Differences." In John Wilson and Beverley Raphael, eds., *International Handbook of Traumatic Stess Syndromes,* 35–48. Plenum Series on Stress and Coping, New York, 1993.

Brebner, J.B. "Subsidized Intermarriage with the Indians." *CHR* 6 (1925): 33–6.

Breen, Theodore. *Horses and Gentlemen: The Cultural Significance of Gambling among the Gentry of Virginia.* S.I., N/A, 1977.

– *Puritans and Adventurers: Change and Persistence in Early America*. Oxford University Press, New York, 1980.

Brékilien, Yann. *Histoire de la Bretagne*. Ed. France-Empire, Paris, 1993.

– *Les Mythes traditionels de Bretagne*. Ed. du Rocher, Monaco, 1998.

Bremner, Douglas. *Does Stess Damage the Brain? Understanding Trauma-Related Disorders from a Mind-Body Perspective*. Norton, New York, 2002.

Bremner, Douglas, John Krystal, Dennis Charney, Steven Southwick. "False Memory Syndrome." *American Journal of Psychiatry* 153, 75 (1996): 71–82.

– "Neural Mechanisms in Dissociative Amnesia for Childhood Abuse." *American Journal of Psychiatry* 153, 75 (1996): 71–82.

Bremner, Douglas and Charles Marmar, eds. *Trauma, Memory, and Dissociation*. Progress in Psychiatry, #54, American Psychiatric Press, Washington, DC, 1998, chs. 9, 11.

Bridenthal, Renate. *Becoming Visible: Women in European History*. Houghton-Mifflin, New York [1987] 1998.

Briggs, Robin. *Early Modern France: Witches and Neighbors: The Social and Cultural Context of European Witchcraft*. Penguin, New York, 1998.

– *Communities of Belief: Culture and Socil Tension in Early Modern France*. Oxford University Press, Clarendon Press, Oxford, 1989.

Brinton, Daniel. "The Myths of Manibozo and Ioskeha." In William Clements, ed. *Native American Folklore in 19th Century Periodicals*, 61–73. Ohio University Press, Athens, OH, 1986.

Brink, J.R., A.P. Coudert, and M.C. Horowitz, eds. *The Politics of Gender in Early Modern Europe*. 16th century Essays and Studies 12, Kirksville, KY, 1989.

Brom, Danny, and Rolf Kleber. *Coping with Trauma: Theory, Prevention, and Treatment*. Swets and Zeitlinger, Amsterdam, 1992.

Brown, Charles. *Sea Serpents: Wisconsin Occurrences of these Wierd Water Monsters in the Four Lakes, Rock, Red Cedar, Koshkonong, Geneva, Elkhart, Michigan, and Other Lakes*. Madison, WI, American Folklore Society, 1941.

Brown, Jennifer. "Children of the Early Fur Trades." In Joy Parr, ed. *Childhood and Education in Canadian History*, 44–68. McCLelland and Stewart, Toronto, 1982.

– "The Care and Feeding of Windigos: A Critique." *AA* 73 (1971): 20–3.

– *Strangers in Blood: Fur Trade Companies in Indian Country*. University of British Columbia Press, Vancouver, 1980.

Brown, Jennifer, and Robert Brightman. *Orders of the Dreamed: George Nelson on Cree and Northern Ojibwa – Religion and Myth* [1823], Manitoba Studies in Native History, Winnipeg, MN [1988] 1998.

Brown, Jennifer, William Eccles, and Donald Heldman, eds. *The Fur Trade Revisited: Selected Papers of the Sixth North American Fur Trade Conference*. Mackinac Island, MI, 1991, Michigan State University Press, East Lansing, MI, 1994.

Brown Jennifer, and Elisabeth Vibert, eds. *Reading beyond Words: Contexts for Native History*. Broadview Press, Peterborough, 1996.

Brown, Kathleen. "Brave New Worlds: Women's and Gender History." *WMQ* 50 (1993): 311–28.

Brown, M. "Multiple Personality and Personal Identity." *Philosophical Psychology* 14, 4 (2001): 435–47.

Brown, Wallace. "Wa-ba-ba-nal, or Northern Lights." *JAF* 3 (1890): 213–14.

Bruneau, Marie-Florine. *Women Mystics Confront the Modern World: Maire de l'Incarnation and Madame Guyon.* SUNY, Albany, New York, 1998.

Buber, Martin. *Das Dialogische Prinzip.* 5., Durchgesehene Aufl., Lambert Schneider, Heidelberg, 1984.

– *The Knowledge of Man.* Allen and Unwin, London, 1965.

– *I and Thou.* 2nd. ed., trans. Ronald Gregor Smith, Clark, Edinburgh, 1958.

– *The Letters of Buber: A Life of Dialogue.* Schocken, New York, 1991.

– *On Intersubjectivity and Cultural Creativity.* University of Chicago Press, Chicago, 1992.

Bumstead, J.M., ed. *Canadian History before Confederation.* 2nd ed., Irwin-Dorsey, Georgetown, 1979.

– "Carried to Canada: Perceptions of the French in British Colonial Captivity Narratives, 1690–1760." *American Review of Canada Studies* 13 (1983): 79–96.

Burger, Carl. *Beaverskins and Mountain Men.* Dutton and Co., New York, 1968.

Burgess, J. "Windigo." *The Beaver* 277 (1947): 4–5.

Burgess, Olive. "Death Possessions and Communal Memory in the Middle Ages." In Bruce Gordon and Peter Marshall, *The Place of Death: Death and Remembrance in Late Medieval and Early Modern Europe.* Cambridge, Cambridge University Press, 2000.

Burguière, André, Christiane Klapish-Zuber, Martine, Segalen, Martine, and Françoise Zonabend, eds.*A History of the Family.* Cambridge, Polity Press, Cambridge, 1996.

Burke, Peter. *Popular Culture in Early Modern Europe.* Temple Smith, London, 1978.

– *The Fabrication of Louis XIV.* Yale University Press, New Haven, 1992.

– *New Perspectives on Historical Writing.* Penn State University Press, University Park, 1991.

Burkitt, Ian. *Social Selves: Theories of the social Formation of Personality.* Sage, London, 1991.

Burt, Alfred. "The Frontier in the History of New France." *CHAR,* Ottawa, 1940, 93–99.

Butterfield, Consul Wilshire. *History of Etienne Brûlé's discoveries and explorations 1610–1626.* Helman Taylor, Cleveland, 1898, CIHM #00368.

Bynum, Caroline Walker. *Jesus as Mother: Studies in the Spirituality in the Middle Ages.* University of California Press, Berkeley, CA, 1982.

Cabrette. "Pierre LeMoyne d'Iberville et Mlle. Picoté, de Bellestre." *BRH* 21 (1915): 224.

Caciok, Nancy. "Wraiths, Revenants, and Ritual in Medieval Culture." *Past and Present* 152 (1996): 40–5.

Cahall, Raymond Dubois. *The Sovereign Council of New France.* Columbia University Press, New York, 1929.

Caillaud, René. *Normandie, Poitou, et Canada français.* Fides, Montréal, 1945.

Callois, Roger et Gustave von Grunebaum, éds. *Le rêve et les sociétés humaines.* Gallimard, Paris, 1967.

Calloway, Colin. *Dawnland Encounters: Indians and Europeans in New England.* University Press of New England, Hanover and London, 1991.

– *New Directions in American Indian history.* University of Oklahoma Press, Norman, OK, 1988.

– *New Worlds for All: Indians, Europeans, and the Remaking of Early America.* John Hopkins University Press, Baltimore, 1997.

– *North Country Captives: Selected Narratives of Indian Captivity from Vermont and New Hampshire.* University Press of New England, Hanover, NH, 1990.

– *The Western Abenakis of Vermont, 1600–1800: War, Migration, and the Survival of an Indian People.* #197, The Civilization of the American Indian, University of Oklahoma Press, Norman, 1990.

Campeau, Lucien. *Les Cents-Associés et le peuplement de la Nouvelle-France (1633–1663).* Bellarmin, Cahiers d'histoire des Jesuites, #2, Ed. Bellarmin, Montréal, 1974.

– *Les finances publiques de la Nouvelle-France sous les Cent Associés, 1632–1665.* Bellarmin, Montréal, 1975.

– "Le fief des Sauvages et l'organisation de Québec." *Cahiers des Dix* 48 (1993): 9–44.

– "Les Jésuites ont-ils retouché les écrits de Champlain?" *RHAF* 5 (1951): 340–61.

– "Mgr de Laval et les Hosptialières de Montréal (1659–1684)." L'Hôtel-Dieu de Montréal, 1642–1973, Cahiers de Québec, Editions Hurtubise, Montréal, 1973, 103–23.

– "La route commerciale de l'Ouest au dix-septième siècle." *Cahiers des Dix* 48 (1994): 21–49.

Campisi, Jack, and Lawrence Hauptman. *The Oneida Indian Experience: Two Perspectives.* Syracuse University Press, Syracuse, 1988.

"La Canada militaire." *RAPQ,* 1949–51, 312–14; Guillaume Couture, 520; François Hertel, 391–2; Nicolas Juchereau.

Canny, Nicolas, and Anthony Pagden, eds. *Colonial Identity in the Colonial World, 1500–1800.* Princeton University Press, Princeton [1987] 1989.

Careless, J.M.S. "Frontierism, Metropolitansm, and Canadian History." *CHR* 35 (1954): 1–21.

Carmona, Michel. *Les Diables de Loudun, Sorcellerie et sous Richelieu.* Fayard, Paris, 1988.

Caron, abbé Ivanhoe. *La colonisation du Canada sous la domination française.* Québec, 1916.

Caron, Diane. "Les postes de traite de fourrure sur la Côte-Nord et dans l'Outaouais." Dossiers #56, Min. des Affaires Culturelles, Québec, s.d.

Carrier, Hubert. *Les muses guerrières: les mazarinades et la vie littéraire au milieu du XVIIe Siècle.* Klinksieck, Paris, 1996.

– *La presse de la Fronde, 1648–1653: les Mazarinades.* Droz, Genève, 1989–1991.

Carrion, V., C. Weems, R. Ray, B. glaser, D. Hessl, A. Reiss. "Diurnal salivary cortisol in pediatric posttraumatic stress disorder." *Biological Psychiatry* 51, 7 (2002): 575–582.

Carroll, Michael. *Catholic Cults and Devotions*. McGill-Queen's University Press, Montréal, 1989.

– *The Cult of the Virgin Mary: Psychological Origins*. Princeton University Press, Princeton, 1986.

– "Lévi-Strauss, Freud, and the Trickster: A New Perspective upon an old Problem." *American Ethnologist* 8 (1981): 301–13.

Carson, William. "Ojibwa Tales." *JAF* 30 (1917): 491–3.

Carruth, Cathy, ed. *Trauma: Explorations in Memory*. John Hopkins Press, Baltimore, 1995.

Carruthers, Mary. *The Book of Memory: A Study in Medieval Culture*. Cambridge University Press, Cambridge, 1990.

Casgrain, Henri. *Champlain, sa vie et son caractère*. Imprimerie de Demers et frère, Québec, 1898.

– "Coup d'oeil sur l'Acadie." *Le Canada Français*, II, 1888, 101–2.

– *Oeuvres complètes*. III, Légendes Canadiennes et oeuvres, Darveau, Québec, 1873.

Cassirer, Ernst. *The Philosophy of Symbolic Forms, II: Mythical Thought*. Trans. R. Manheim. Yale University Press, New Haven, 1966.

– *Symbol, Myth, and Culture: Essays and Lectures of Ernst Cassirer, 1935–1945*. Ed. Donald Verene. Yale University Press, New Haven, CN, 1979.

Castel, Robert. "'Problematization' as a Mode of Reading History." In Jan Goldstein, ed., *Foucault and the Writing of History*. Basil, Blackwell, Oxford, 1994.

Catherwood, Mary. *The Chase of St-Castin and Other Stories of the French in the New World*. Houghton Mifflin, Boston and New York, 1894.

Cazelles, Brigitte. *The Unholy Grail: A Social reading of Chrétien de Troyes's Conte du Graal*. Stanford University Press, Stanford, CA, 1996.

Ceinture fleche. L'Etincelle. Montréal, 1973, Bulletin 93, National Museum of Canada.

Célestin, Roger. *From Cannibals to Radicals*. University of Minnesota, Minneapolis, 1996.

Céline, Louis Ferdinand. *Bagatelles pour un massacre*. Ed. DeNoël, Paris, s.d.

Cellard, André. "Book Review Histoire de la folie au Québec de 1600 à 1800." *CHR* 73 (1992): 81–2.

Centre méridionale de rencontre sur le XVIIe siècle: Colloque. Marseille et Cassis, Université de Provence, 1988.

Certeau, Michel de. *Heterologies: Discourse on the Other*. Trans. Brian Massumi, Theory and History of Literature, 17, University of Minnesota, Minneapolis, 1986.

– *La possession de Loudun*. Paris, 1970.

Cervantes, Fernando. *The Devil in the New World: the Impact of Diabolism in New Spain*. Yale University Press, New Haven and London, 1994.

Chadwick, Henry. *The Early Church*. Penguin, London [1967] 1993.

Chamberlain, Alexander. "Nanibozhu amongst the Otchiwe, Mississagas, and Other Algonkian Tribes." *JAF* 4 (1891): 193–215.

– *The Contributions of the American Indian to Civilization*. American Antiquarian Society reprint, Philadelphia, 1903.

– "A Mississaga Legend of Na'niboju." *JAF* 5 (1892): 291–2.
– "Nanabozhu amongst the Otchipwe, Mississaugas, and other Algonkian Tribes." *JAF* 4 (1891): 191–213.
– "Some Items of Algonkian Folklore." *JAF* 8 (1900): 274–7.
– "Tales of the Mississaugas." *JAF* 3 (1890): 149–55.

Chapdelaine, Claude. "L'Origine des Iroquoiens dans le Nord-Est." *RAQ* 22 (1992): 3–4.

Charbonneau, Hubert et al. *Naissance d'une population: les français établis au Canada au XVIIe siècle.* Presses de l'Université Laval, Québec, 1987.

– "Note Critique: Refléxions en marge d'Habitants et marchands de Montréal de Louise Dechêne." *RHAF* 30 (1976): 265–6.

– "Note Critique: Réflexions en marge de La Population au Canada en 1663 de Marcel Trudel." *RHAF* 27 (1973): 417–24.

Charlebois, Peter. *The Life of Louis Riel.* NCP, Toronto [1975] 1978.

Chartier, Roger. *The Cultural Origins of the French Revolution.* Duke University Press, Durham, NC, 1991.

– "Text, Symbols, and Frenchness." *Journal of Modern History* 57 (1985): 682–95.

"La Chasse-galérie." *BRH* 6 (1900): 282–4.

Chaunu, Pierre. *La mort à Paris: 16e, 17e, 18e siècles.* Fayard, Paris, 1978.

Cheruel, Adolphe. *Histoire de la France pendant la minorité de Louis XIV.* 4 v., Hachette, Paris, 1878–1880.

Chevalier, Jacques. "Myth and Ideology in Traditional French Canada: Dollard, the Martyred Warrior." *Anthropologica* 21 (1979): 143–76.

Chiasson, Anselme. *Le diable Frigolet et autres contes des Iles de la Madeleine.* Ed. Acadie, Moncton, NB, 1991.

Chibnall, Margery., ed. *The Ecclesiastical History of Orderic Vital.* 6 vols. Clarendon Press, Oxford, 1969–1980.

Chinard, Gilbert. *L'Amérique et le rêve exotique dans la littérature française au XVIIe siècle.* Droz, Paris, 1934.

– *The American Enlightenment.* University of Rochester Press, Rochester, New York, 1993.

– *L'éxotisme américaine dans la littérature du XVIe d'après Rabelais, Ronsard, et Montaigne.* Hachette, Paris, 1911.

– *The French-American Connection: 200 Years of Cultural and Inellectual Interaction.* Institut français de Washington, Chapel Hill, NC, 1994.

– *Lafayette in Virginia: Unpublished Letters from the Orginal Manuscript in the Virginia State Library and Library of Congress.* Johns Hopkins Press, Baltimore, 1928.

– *La vie américaine de Guillaume Marie d'Aubigne Volney et l'"Amérique.* Johns Hopkins Press, Baltimore, 1923.

Chodoff, P. "Late Effects of the Concentration Camp Syndrome." *Archives of Clinical Psychology* 8 (1963): 323–33.

Choquette, Leslie. *Compagnonnage in 18th Century Canada.* Assumption College, June, 1995.

- "'Les amazones du Grand Dieu:' Women and Mission in XVIIe century Canada." *FHS* 17 (1992): 327–55.
- *Frenchmen into Peasants: Modernity and Tradition in the Peopling of French Canada.* Harvard Historical Studies, #123, Harvard University Press, Cambridge, 1997.

Choquette, Robert. *Le sorcier d'Anticosti et autres légendes canadiennes.* Fides, Montréal, 1975.

Church, William. *The Impact of Absolutism in France: National Experience under Richelieu. Mazarin, and Louis XIV,* J. Wiley, New York, 1969.

Cioranescu, Alexandre. *Le masque et le visage: du baroque espagnol au classicisme français.* Droz, Genève, 1983.

Clapin, Sylvia. "Mots d'origine sauvage." *BRH* 6 (1800): 294–305.

Clark, Ella Elisabeth. *Indian Legends of Canada.* McClelland and Stewart, Toronto, 1992.

Clastres, Pierre. *Society against the State: The Leader as Servant and the Humane Uses of Power among the Indians of the Americas.* Trans. Robert Hurley, Mole Ed., Urizen Books, New York, 1977.

Clements, William, ed. *Native American Folklore in 19th century Periodicals.* Ohio University Press, Athens, OH, 1986.

Clermont, Norman. "L'acceptation de l'Autre: la conversion en Huronia." *RAQ* 21 (1991): 53–66.
- "Le Gougou de Champlain et les Croyances Algonquiennes." *RHAF* 35 (1981): 377–81.
- "La place de la femme dans les sociétés iroquoiennes." *RAQ* 13 (1983): 286–90.
- "Les kokotchés à Weymontachie." *RAQ* 8 (1978): 139–46.
- "Le pouvoir spirituel chez les Iroquoiens de la période du contact." *RAQ* 28 (1988): 61–8.

Cliche, Marie-Aimée. "Les attitudes devant la Mort d'après les clauses testamentaires dans le gouvernement sous le Régime français." *RHAF* 32 (1978): 57–250.
- "L'infanticide dans la région de Québec 1660–1969." *RHAF* 44 (1990): 31–59.

Clifford, James. *The Invented Indian: Cultural Fictions and Governmental Policies.* Transaction Publishers, New York, 1990.

Clifton, James. *Hurons of the West: Migrations and Adaptations of the Ontario Iroquoians, 1650–1704.* offprint, n.d., DIAND files.

Coffey, Rebecca. *Unspeakable Truths and Unhappy Endings: Human Cruelty and the New Trauma Therapy.* Sidran Press, Lutherville, Maryland, 1998.

Collaboration, éd. *L'histoire du Saguenay depuis l'origine jusqu'à 1870.* Publication de la Société du Saguenay, Ed. du Centenaire, #3, vol. 1, Chicoutimi, 1938.

Collectif Clio. *L'histoire des femmes au Québec depuis quatre siècles.* Quinze, Montréal, 1982.

Cloutier, J.-E.-A. "Anecdotes de L'Islet." *JAF* 33 (1920): 274–94.

Coates, Ken. "Writing First Nations into Canadian History: A Review of Recent Scholarly Works." *CHR* 81 (2000): 99–114.

Cocchiara, Guiseppe. *Il Mito del Buon Selvaggio: Introduzione alla storia delle teorie etnologiche.* rep., G. d'Anna, Messina, Italia [1934] 1997.

Coffin, Margaret. *Death in Early America: The History and Folklore of Customs and Superstitions of Early medicine, Funerals, Burials, and Mourning.* Nelson, Nashville, 1976.

Cohen, Felix. "Americanizing the White Man." *American Scholar* 21 (1952): 177–91, DIAND files.

Cohen, Yehudi, ed. *Man in Adaptation.* Aldine, Chicago, 1968.

Cohn, Bernard. "History and Anthropology: The State of Play." *Comparative Studies of Society and History* 22 (1980): 198–221.

Cohn Norman. *Europe's Inner Demons: An Inquiry into the Great Witchhunt.* Sussex University Press, London, 1975.

– "Myth of Satan and His Human Servants." In Douglas, *Witchcraft*, ch. 1.

Colby, Charle., *The Founder of New France.* Brook and Co., Glasgow, 1915.

Collins, James. *Classes, Estates, and Order in Early Modern Brittany.* Cambridge Studies in Early Modern History, Cambridge University Press, Cambridge, 1994.

– *The State in Early Modern France.* Cambridge University Press, Cambridge, 1995.

Collins, Randall, ed. *Four Sociological Traditions: Selected Readings.* Oxford University Press, Oxford, 1994.

Colombo, John Robert. *The Mystery of the Shaking Tent.* Hounslow Press, Toronto, ON, 1993.

– *Windigo.* Western Producer Prairie Books, Saskatoon, SAS, 1982.

Conan, Laure. *Louis Hébert, premier colon du Canada.* Imp. de l'evenement, Québec, 1912.

Congrès de Niort, 1896, "La tradition en Poitou et Charentes." *Société d'Ethnographie nationale et d'art populaire*, Brissaud, Poitiers, 1981.

Conkling, Robert. *Social and Cultural change among the Wabnaki in French Colonial Times 1600–1750.* NLC, Ottawa, 1970.

Connelley, W.W. *Ontario Archaeological Report, 1899–1900.* "The Wyandottes," 1899–1900: 117–18.

– *Wyandotte Folklore*, 87–8. N/A.

Connerton, Paul, ed. *Critical Sociology.* Penguin Modern Readings, Markham, ON [1976] 1978.

Contes montagnaises. Conseil internationale de la langue française et Agence de cooperation culturelle et technique. Edicef, Paris, 1983.

Cooper, John Montgomery. "The Cree Witiko Psychosis." *Primitive Man* 4 (1949): 33–48.

– "The Northern Algonquian Supreme Being." *Primitive Man* 6 (1934): 41–111.

– *Snares, Deadfalls, and other Traps of the Northern Algonquians and Northern Athapaskans.* AMS rep., New York [1938] 1978.

Cook, Ramsay, ed. *The Maple Leaf Forever: Essays on Nationalism and Politics in Canada.* University of Toronto Press, Toronto, 1977.

Cooley, Charles. *On Self and Social Organization.* University of Chicago, Chicago, 1998.

Corlett, William Thomas. *The Medicine-Man of the American Indian and his Cultural Background.* Charles Thomas, Springfield, IL, 1935.

Côté, Louise, Tardivel, Louis et Vaugeois, Denis. *L'Indien Généreux: ce que le monde doit au Amériques*. Boréal, Montréal, 1992.

Couillard-Desprès, Azarie. *Histoire des Seigneurs de la Rivière du Sud*. Imp. de la Tribune, Ste-Hyacinthe, 1912.

– *Louis Hébert: premier colon canadien et sa famille*. Imprimerie des sourds-muets, Montréal, 1918.

Courteau, Henri. *La Fronde à Paris*. Firmin Dodot, Paris, 1930.

Courville, Serge. "Espace, Territoire, et Culture en Nouvelle-France: une vision géographique." *RHAF* 37 (1983): 417–29.

Coveney, Richard, ed. *France in Crisis*. Macmillan, London, 1968.

Cox, Isaac. "The Indian as a Diplomatic Factor in the History of the Old Northwest." Ohio Archaeology and Historical Society Pubs., 18, 1909, offprint, DIAND files.

Craigie, William. *The Religion of Ancient Scandinavia*. Archibald Constable, London, 1906.

Cranston, Herbert. *Etienne Brûlé: Immortal Scoundrel*. Ryerson Press, Toronto, 1949.

Creighton, Donald. *Dominion of the North*. Macmillan, Toronto [1957] 1997.

Creamer, M., P. Burgess, A. McFarlane. "Posttraumatic Stress Disorder: Findings from the Australian National Survey of Mental Health and Well-Being." *Psychological Medicine* 31, 7 (2001): 1237–47.

Cross, Michael, and George Kealey. *Economy and Society during the French Regime to 1759: Readings in Canadian Social History*, vol. 1. McClelland and Stewart, Toronto, 1983.

Crouse, Nellis. *LeMoyne d'Iberville, soldier of New France*. Ryerson, Toronto, 1954.

Crouzet, Denis. *Les guerriers de Dieu: La violence au temps des troubles de religion vers 1525-vers 1610*. 2 t., Epoques Champ Vallon, Paris, 1990.

Crowne, Douglas, and David Marlowe. *The Approval Motive*. John Wiley and Sons, New York, 1964.

Csordas, Thomas. *The Sacred Self: A Cultural Phenomenology of Charismatic Healing*. University of California Press, Berkeley, CA (1994) 1997.

Cunningham, Hugh. *Children and Childhood in Western Society since 1500*. Longman, London, 1995.

Danieli, Yael. "Diagnostic and Therapeutic Use of the Multigenerational Family Tree in Working with Survivors and Children of Survivors of the Nazi Holocaust." In John Wilson and Beverley Raphael, eds., *International Handbook of Traumatic Stress Syndromes*, (1987). Plenum Series on Stress and Coping, New York, 1993.

– "International Handbook of Multigenerational Legacies of Trauma." Plenum Press, New York, in *PTSD Research Quarterly* 8, 1 (1997). Avaliable on-line.

– "Treating Survivors and Children of Survivors of the Nazi Holocaust." In John Daniels, "The Indian Population of North America in 1492." *WMQ* 49 (1992): 298–320, at 278–93.

Darnton, Robert. *The Great Cat Massacre and other Episodes in French Cultural History*. Vintage Books, New York, 1985.

Dasberg, Haim. "Psychological Distress of Holocaust Survivors and Offspring in Israel: Forty Years Later – A Review." *Israel Journal of Psychiatry and Related Sciences* 23 4 (1987): 243–56.

Daveluy, Marie-Claire. "Le Drame de la recrue de 1653." *RHAF* 7 (1953): 157–70.

– *La société de Notre-Dame de Montréal, 1639–1663, Les véritables motifs.* N.p.

Davidson, H.R. Ellis. *Myths and Symbols in Pagan Europe: Early Scandinavian and Celtic Religions.* Manchester University Press, Manchester, 1988.

Davis, Nathalie Zemon. *Fiction in the Archives: Pardon Tales and Their Tellers in 16th-Century France.* Polity Press, Cambridge, 1987.

– *The Gift in Seventeenth Century France.* Princeton University Press, Princeton, 1998.

– "Iroquois Women, European Women." In Margo Hendricks and Patricia Parker, *Women, "Race," and Writing in the Early Modern Period.* Routledge, New York, 1994.

– *Society and Culture in Early Modern France.* Stanford University Press, Stanford, CA, [1965] 1975.

– "Polarities, Hybridities: What Strategies for De-Centring?" In Germaine Warkentin and Carolyn Podruchny, ed., *Decentering the Renaissance: Canada and Europe in Multidisciplinary Perspective, 1500–1700,* draft. University of Toronto Press, Toronto, 1998 (Pre-press offprint kindly given to me in 1997.)

– *Women on the Margins: Three Seventeenth Century Lives.* Harvard University Press, Cambridge, MA, 1995.

Dawson, Nelson-M. "The Filles du roy Sent to New France: Protestant, Prostitute, or Both?" *Historical Reflections* 16 (1989): 55–77.

Day, John. *God's Conflict with the Dragon: Echoes of a Canaanite Myth in the Old Testament.* Cambridge University Press, Cambridge, 1985.

Debien, Gabriel. "Engagé pour le Canada au XVIIe siècle, vus de la Rochelle." *RHAF* 3 (1952): 374–92, 4; 1952, 177–233.

De Bolt, Joseph. "Belief Systems and Evolution: a Distinction between Magic and Religion and its implications for Socio-Cultural Change." *Canadian Review of Sociology and Anthropology* 6 (1969): 80–91.

Dechêne, Louise. *Habitants et Marchands de Montréal au XVIIe siècle.* Plon, Paris, 1974.

– *Le partage des subsistances au Canada sous le Régime français.* Boréal, Montréal, 1994.

De Jong, J. P. B. de Josselin. *Original Odzibwe Texts.* Baessler Archiv, Leipzig and Berlin, 1913.

Delafosse, Marcel. "La Rochelle et la Canada au XVIIe siècle." *RHAF* 4 (1951): 469–511.

Delâge, Denys. "Essai sur les Origines de la Canadianité." Séminaire de la CEFAN, 15 juillet 1997. (Several works of Denys Delâge kindly given to me by the author.)

– "L'alliance franco-amérindienne 1660–1701." *RAQ* 19 (1989): 3–30.

– "Les Amérindiens dans l'imaginaire des Québécois." *Liberté* 33 (1991): 15–28.

– "L'histoire des Premières Nations, approches et orientations." *RHAF* 53 (2000): 521–7.

– "L'influence des Amérindiens sur les Canadiens et les Français au temps de la Nouvelle-France." *Lekton* 2 (1992): 103–191.

– *Le pays renversé: amérindiens et européens en Amérique du nord-est 1660–1664.* Boréal Express, Montréal, 1985.

– "Les premières nations d"Amérique sont-elles à l'origine des valeurs écologiques et démocratiques contemporaines?" dans Turgeon, Laurier, Denys Delâge, Réal Oueillet, éds.. *Transferts culturels et métissages Amérique/Europe*. Presses de l'Université Laval, Québec, 1996.

– "La religion dans l'alliance franco-amérindienne." *Anthropologies et Sociétés* 15 (1991): 55–87.

– "La rencontre des deux mondes." *Anthropologies et Sociétés* 15 (1991): 5–12.

– "Réponse de l'auteur." *RAQ* 16 (1986): 112–15.

Delâge, Denys et André Dubois. "L'eau, les Amérindiens et les Franco-Canadiens: Mythes et réalités en Amérique du Nord au XVIIe et XVIIIe siècles." Conférence biennale internationale, Associazione Italiana di Studi Canadasi, Sienne, 1er juillet 1997.

Delâge, Denys and Tanner, Helen Hornbeck. "The Ojibwa-Jesuit Debate at Walpole Island, 1844." *Ethnohistory* 41 (1994): 195–321.

Delâge, Denys, Jean-Pierre Sawaya, Marc Jetten, et Régent Sioui. "'Le français, l'anglais, et l'indien allaient être égaux:' autochtones du Québec dans l'histoire." *Rapport RCAP*, 1995.

Delangley, Jean. *Louis Jolliet: vie et voyages*. Les Etudes de l'Institut d'Histoire de l'Amérique française, Chicago, 1950.

Delarue, Paul, et Marie-Louise Tenèze. Le Conte Populaire Français. 2 vols. Maisonneuve et Larose, Paris, 1963.

Delcambre, Etienne. "La psychologie des inculpés lorrains de sorcellerie." In William Monter, *European Witchcraft*, J. Wiley, New York, 1969.

Deleuze, Gilles, and Félix Guattari. *Anti-Oedipus: Capitalism ad Schizophrenia*, vol. 1. Viking, New York, 1977.

– "On the Line." Trans. John Johnston. *Semiotext(e)* n.v. 1983: n.p.

De Levitas, David. " Late Onset of Symptoms in Holocaust Survivors." In Linda Hunt, Linda Marshall, and Cherry Rawlings, eds. *Past Trauma in Late Life*, 95–107. Jessica Kingsley, London, 1997.

Delisle, Esther. *Le traître et le juif*. Etincelle, Outremont, 1992.

Deloria, Vine. *God is Red: A Native view of Religion*. Fulcrum Publishing, Golden, CL [1993] 1994.

Delpech, Jeanine. *L'âme de la Fronde: Mme. de Longueville*. Fayard, Paris, 1957.

Delumeau, Jean. *Catholicism between Luther and Voltaire*. Burns and Oates, London, 1977.

– *L'aveu et le pardon: les difficultés de la confession XIIIe-XVIIIe siècle*. Fayard [1964] 1992.

– "Ignorance Religieuse et mentalité magique sous l'Ancien Régime." offprint, pp. 1–24.

– *La Peur en L'Occident*. Fayard, Paris, 1978.

Demos, John. *The Unredeemed Captive: A Family Story from Early America*. Alfred Knopf, Random House, 1994.

– *Entertaining Satan: Witchcraft and the Culture of Early New England*. Oxford University Press, Oxford, 1982.

Dening, Greg. "Introduction: in Search of a Metaphor." In Ronald Hoffman, Mechal Sobel, and Frederika Teute, eds. *Through a Glass Darkly: Reflections on Personal Identity in Early America*, intro. Omohundro Institute of Early American History and Culture, Williamsburg, VA. University of North Carolina Press, Chapel Hill, NC, 1997.

Dennis, Matthew. *Cultivating a Landscape of Peace: Iroquois-European Encounters in 17th-Century America*. Cornell University Press, Ithaca, New York, 1993.

Densmore, Francis. *Indian Use of Wild Plants for Food, Medicine, and Crafts*. Dover Pub., New York [1928] 1974.

– "Winnebago Beliefs Concerning the Dead." *AA* 33 (1931): 659–60.

Deroy-Pineau, Françoise. *Madeleine de la Peltrie (Alençon 1603-Québec 1671): Amazone du nouveau Monde*. Bellarmin, Montréal, 1992.

Desan, Susan. "Crowds, Community, and Ritual in the Work of E.P. Thompson and Nathalie Davis." In Lynn Hunt, *The New Cultural History*, 62–3. University of California, Berkeley, LA, 1989.

Desbarats, Cathérine. "Essai sur quelques éléments de l'écriture de l'histoire amérindienne." *RHAF* 53 (2000): 491–520.

Deschesnes, Donald, et Michel Courchesne. *Légendes de chez-nous: récits fantastiques de l'Ontario français*. Centre français-ontarien de folklore, Sudbury, ON, 1996.

Desdouits, Anne-Marie., *La vie traditionelle au pays de Caux et au Canada français: le cycle des Saisons*. Presses Universitaires de France, Ed. du Centre national de la recherche scientifique, Québec et Paris, 1987.

Desgraves, Louis. *Catalogue de la Bibliothèque de Montesquieu*. Droz, Genève, 1954.

Deslandres, Dominique. "Le modèle d'intégration socio-religieuse 1600–1650: missions intérieures et premiers missions canadiennes." PhD, Université de Montréal, 1991.

– "Marie de L'Incarnation et la femme amérindienne." *RAQ* 13 (1983): 277–89.

Despres, Terence. *The Survivor: An Anatomy of Life in the Death Camps*. Oxford University Press, New York, 1976.

Desrosiers, Léo-Paul. *Iroquoisie*. Etudes de l'institut d'Histoire de l'Amérique française, Imp. Populaire, Montréal, 1947.

– "Les Onnontagués." *Cahiers des Dix* 18 (1953): 45–66.

– "Dollard des Ormeaux, dans les textes." *Cahiers des Dix* 10 (1945): 41–86.

– *Les engagés du Grand-Portage*. Fides, Montréal, 1957.

– *Paul de Chomédey, Sieur de Maisonneuve*. Fides, Montréal et Ottawa, 1967.

Dessureault, Christian. "L'égalitarisme paysan dans l'ancienne société rurale de la vallée du du Saint-Laurent: Eléments pour une Réinterpretation." *RHAF* 40 (1987): 373–407.

Detienne, Marcel. *The Creation of Mythology*. Trans. Margaret Cook, University of Chicago Press, Chicago, 1986.

Devens, Carol. *Countering Colonization: Native American Women and Great Lakes Missions, 1630–1900*. University of California, Berkeley, 1992.

Devereux, Georges. *Basic Problems of Ethnopsychiatry*. Trans. Basia Miller Gulati and George Devereux, University of Chicago Press, Chicago, 1980.

– "Rêves pathogènes dans les sociétés non occidentales." dans Callois, Roger et Gustave von Grunebaum, éds. *Le rêve et les sociétés humaines.* Gallimard, Paris, 1967.

Devèze, Michel. *La vie de la forêt française du XVIe siècle.* 2 vols. Presses Universitaires de France, Paris, 1961.

Dewald, Jonathan. *Aristocratic Experience and the Origins of Modern Culture: France 1570–1715.* University of California Press, Berkeley, 1993.

– *The European Nobility, 1400–1800.* Cambridge University Press, Cambridge, 1996.

– *The Formation of a Provincial Nobility: the Magistrates of the Parlement of Rouen (1499–1610).* Princeton University Press, Princeton, 1980.

Diamond, Jared. "The Arrow of Disease." In Olive Patricia Dickason, *Native Imprint: The Contribution of First Peoples to Canada's Character.* 155–67. Athabaska University Press, Athabaska, AL, 1996.

Diamond, Sigmund. "An Experiment in Feudalism: French Canada in the 17th century." *WMQ* 18 (1961): 3–34.

Dickason, Olive Patricia. *Canada's First Nations: A History of Founding Peoples from Earliest Times.* McClelland and Stewart, Toronto, 1993.

– "Book review of Convertir les Fils de Caïn by Alain Beaulieu." *CHR* 73 (1992): 250–1.

– "From 'One Nation' in the Northeast to 'New Nation' in the Northwest: A Look at the Emergence of the Metis." *AICRJ* 6 (1982): 1–21.

– *The Myth of the Savage and the Beginnings of French Colonialism in the Americas.* University of Alberta Press, Edmonton, 1984.

– *Louisbourg and the Indians: A Study of Imperial Race Relations, 1713–1760.* Natural Parks and Sites, 1976.

– *Native Imprint: the Contribution of the First Nations to Canada's Character to 1815.* Raincoast Books, Vancouver, 1995.

Dickins, A.G. *The Counter-Reformation.* Harcourt, Brace, and World, New York, 1969.

Dickinson, Joh., "La justice seigneuriale en Nouvelle-France: le cas de Notre-Dame-des-Anges." *RHAF* 28 (1974): 323–46.

– "Annaotaha et Dollard vus de l'autre côté de la palissade." *RHAF* 35 (1981): 163–78.

– "La guerre Iroquoise et la mortalité en Nouvelle-France 1608–1666." *RHAF* 36 (1982): 31–54.

– "Native Sovereignty and French Justice in Early Canada." *Essays in the History of Canadian Law,* 5, Crime and Criminal Justice, Osgoode Society for Canadian Legal History, Toronto, 1994, 17–40.

"Le differand du gouverneur de Mézy, avec MM. Jean Bourdon et Louis de Villeray." *RAPQ* (1921–22): 96–101.

Dimsdale, John, ed. *Survivors, Victims, and Perpetrators: Essays on the Nazi Holocaust.* Hemisphere Pubs., Washington, 1980.

Dinnerstein, Leonard, Roger Nicols and David Reimer. *Natives and Strangers: Ethnic Groups and the Building of America.* Oxford University Press, New York, 1979.

DiNicola, Vincenzo. "Ethnocultural Aspects of PTSD and Related Disorders among Children and Adolescents." In Spero Manson, Jannette Beals, Theresa O'Nell,

Joan Piasecki, Donald Bechtold, Ellen Keane, and Monica Jones, *Wounded Spirits, Ailing Hearts: PTSD and Related Disorders among American Indians,* chap 10. American Psychological Association, Washington, DC, 1996.

Dionne, Narcisse-Eutrope. "Etudes généalogiques: Olivier LeTardif." *MSGCF* 12 (1961): 4–20.

– *Samuel Champlain, fondateur de Québec et père de la Nouvelle-France.* Armand Côté, Québec, 1891.

Dirks, Nicholas, Geoff Eley, and Ortner, Sherry, eds. *Culture/Power/History: A Reader in Contemporary Social Theory.* Princeton University Press, Princeton, 1994.

Dobyns, H.F. *Their Number become Thinned: Native Population Dynamics in Eastern North America.* University of TN Press and the Newberry Library Center for the Study of the American Indian, Knoxville, TN, 1983.

"Documents inédits." *RHAF* 3 (1950): 587–97.

Dodds, Muriel. *Les récits de voyages: sources de* L'Esprit des lois *de Montesquieu.* Slatkine, Genève [1929] 1980.

Dominiguez, Virginia. *White by Definition: Social Ostracism in Creole Louisiana.* Rutgers University Press, New Brunswick, NJ, 1986.

St John, Donald. "The Dream-Vision Experience of the Iroquois: Its Religious Meaning." PhD, Fordham University, New York [1981] 1982.

"Don mutuel entre Louis d'Ailleboust, gouverneur de la Nouvelle-France, et Barbe de Boulogne, son épouse." *RAPQ* (1920–21): 136.

Donald, Leland. *Aboriginal Slavery on the Northwest Coast of North America.* University of California Press, Berkeley, 1997.

Doniger, Wendy, ed. *Off with Her Head! Denial of Women's Identity in Myth, Religion, and Culture.* University of California, Berkeley, 1995.

– *Myth and Method.* University of Virginia Press, Charlottesville, VA, 1995.

Dorsey, Owen. "Nanibozhu in Siouan Mythology." *JAF* 5 (1892): 293–304.

Dorson, Richard. *Canadiens: Bloodstoppers and Bearwalkers.* Cambridge University Press, Cambridge, 1959.

Doty, William. *Mythography: The Study of Myth and Rituals.* University of Alabama Press, Tuscaloosa, AL, 1986.

Doucet. *Society and Institutions in Early Modern France.* University of Georgia Press, Athens, GA, 1991.

Douglas, Mary, ed. *Purity and Danger: An Analysis of the Concepts of Pollution and Taboo.* rep., Routledge, New York, 2000.

– *Natural Symbols: Explorations in Cosmology.* Pantheon, New York, 1982.

– *Witchcraft Confessions and Accusations.* Tavistock, London, 1970.

Dougherty, M.J. "Stalin's Gulag Prisoners and Prevalence of Post-Traumatic Stress Disorder." *Journal of Loss and Trauma* 6, 1 (2001): 1–19.

Douville, Raymond. *La vie quotidienne en Nouvelle-France: La Canada de Champlain à Montcalm.* Imp. Nationale de SA, Monaco, 1964.

– "Quelques inédites sur Nicolas Perrot et sa famille." *Cahiers des Dix* 28 (1963): 43–62.

Douville, Raymond, and Jacques Casanova. *La vie quotidienne des Indiens du Canada à l'époque de la colonisation française.* Hachette, Paris, 1967.

Doyon-Ferland, Madeleine. *Coustumes et croyances populaires.* "Influence du costume des Indiens sur celui des Blancs," Actos do Congreso Internacional de Etnografica, Coloquio de Ethnografia Comparada, 4, 10/7/1963–18/7/1963., BMDF, Lisboa, 1965.

Dowd, Gregory Evans. "The French King Wakes Up in Detroit: 'Pontiac's War' in Rumor and History." *Ethnohistory* 37 (1990): 254–78.

Drake, Samuel, ed. *Indian Captivities, or life in the wigwam: being true narratives of captives who have been carried away by the Indians from the frontier settlements of the United States from the earliest period to the present time.* Saxton, New York, 1859.

Driver, Harold. *Indians of North America.* University of Chicago Press, Chicago, 1961.

Druke, Mary Becker. "Farmers and Hunters of the Eastern Woodlands: A Regional Overview." In R. Bruce Morrison and C. Roderick Wilson, *Native Peoples, the Canadian Experience,* 317–22. McClelland and Stewart, Toronto [1986] 1995.

Drumont, Edouard. *La France juive.* Marpion et Flammarion, Paris, 1886.

Dubé, Dollard. *Légendes indiennes du St. Maurice.* Les Pages trifluviennes, Trois Rivières, 1933.

Du Berger, Jean. "Le loup garou et autres mauvais esprits." *Démons et merveilles,* Maison Radio-Canada, Montréal, 17 dec. 1984.

Dubois, Elfrieda. "Some Interpretations of the Notion of Coeur in Seventeenth Century France." *17th Century French Studies* 9 (1987): 4–25.

Dubois, Page. *Torture and Truth.* Routledge, New York, 1991.

Duby, Georges, and Michelle Perrot, eds. *A History of Women in the West.* 3 vols. Trans. Arthur Goldhammer, Harvard University Press, Belknap Press, Cambridge and London, 1992.

Dufour, Andrée. "Book Review: Education in New France, Roger Magnussen, McGill-Queen's University Press, Montréal, 1992." *CHR* 74 (1993): 632–4.

Dugas, Georges. *Un voyageur des Pays d'en haut.* Beauchemin, Montréal, 1904.

Duigan, Peter. "Early Jesuit Missionaries: A Suggestion for Further Study." *AA* 60 (1958): 725–32.

Dumont-Johnson, Micheline. *Apôtres ou Agitateurs?* Boréal Express, Montréal, 1970.

Duker, Avraham. "Acculturation and Integration." In Judd Teller, *Acculturation and Integration: A Symposium by American, Israeli and African Experts,* introduction. American Histadrut Cultural Exchange Institute, 1965.

Dumas, Silvio. *L'Exploit du Long-Sault: les témoignages des contemporains.* Société historique de Québec, Québec, 1960.

– "Le Lieu de l'exploit du Long Sault." *RHAF* 14 (1960): 353–67.

Dumézil, Georges. *Mythe et Epopée III: Histoires romaines.* Gallimard, Paris, 1973.

Dumont, Micheline et al. *L'histoire des femmes au Québec depuis quatre siècles.* Quinze, Montréal, 1982.

Dumouchel, Paul. *Violence and Truth: On the work of René Girard.* Stanford University Press, Stanford, 1988.

Duncan, Scott. *Traditional History of the Confederation of the Six Nations, Prepared by a Committee of the Chiefs.* Mémoires de la Société Royales du Canada, sect. 2, 1911, 195–246.

Dundes, Alan. *Sacred Narrative: Readings in the Theory of Myth.* University of California Press, Berkeley, 1984.

——, ed. *The Study of Folklore.* Prentice Hall, Englewood Cliffs, NJ, 1965.

Dupont, Jean-Claude. *Héritage d'Acadie.* Léméac, Montréal, 1977.

– *Légendes de la Côte-Nord de Tadoussac à Blanc-Sablon.* Ed. Dupont, Ste-Foy, Québec, 1996.

– *Légendes du St-Laurent.* Ed. Dupont, Ste-Foy, Québec, 1985.

– *Légendes des Villages.* Ed. Dupont, Ste-Foy, Québec, 1978.

– *Mélanges en l'honneur de Luc Lacoursière: folklore français de l'Amérique.* Leméac, Ottawa, 1978.

– *Le monde fantastique de la Beauce Québecoise.* Centre Canadien d'études sur la culture traditionelle, coll. Mercure, dossier 2, Ottawa, 1972.

– "Le père loup-garou," [Rivière-du-Loup, St-Antonin] *Légendes des villages.* Marquis Ltée, Montmagny, 1988.

Dupont, Jean-Claude. *Héritage d'Acadie.* Leméac, Ottawa, 1977.

Dupouy, Auguste. *Histoire de Bretagne.* Ancienne Librarie Furne, Boivin et Cie., Paris, 1932.

Duran, E., Duran, B., Braveheart-Jordan, M., and Yellowhorse-Davis, S. "Healing the American Indian Soul Wound." In Yael Danieli, *International Handbook of Multigenerational Legacies of Trauma,* Plenum, New York, forthcoming (abstract), p. 4.

Durand, André. *Pierre-Esprit Radisson.* Lidec, Montréal, 1993.

Duranville, Joseph-Léon de. "Quelques pages sur les mazarinades imprimées à Rouen en 1649." *Précis analytique des travaux de l'Académie de Rouen année 1874–1875,* Rouen, 1875, 314–35.

Durkheim, Emile. *Textes: Religion, Morale, Anomie.* Editions de Minuit, Paris, 1975.

– *The Elementary Forms of the Religious Life: A Study in Religious Sociology.* Collier Books, New York, 1961.

Durocher, Gilles. "Canada's First Consitutional Document: The Decree of 1647." *The Archivist* 19 (1992): 11.

Duvel, Paul-Marie. *La vie quotidienne en Gaule pendant la Paix Romaine.* Hachette, Paris, 1952.

Eaton, W., John Sigal, and Morton Weinfeld. "Impairment in Holocaust Survivors after 33 Years." *American Journal of Psychiatry* 139 (1982): 773–7.

Eccles, William. *Canada under Louis XIV, 1663–1701.* McClelland and Stewart, Toronto, 1964.

– *The Canadian Frontier, 1534–1760.* Holt, Rinehart, Winston, New York, 1969.

– *Essays on New France.* Oxford University Press, Toronto, 1987.

– *France in America.* Michigan State University, East Lansing, MI, 1990.

– "Frontenac and the Iroquois 1672–1682." *RHAF* 36 (1955): 1–16.

– "Frontenac's Military Policies 1689–1698: A Reassessment." *RHAF* 37 (1956): 201–24.

- "The Fur Trade and Eighteenth-Century Imperialism." In Olive Patricia Dickason, ed., *Native Imprint: The Contribution of First Peoples to Canada's Character*, 345–69. Athabaska University Press, Athabaska, AL, 1996.
- "The History of New France According to Francis Parkman." *WMQ* 18 (1961): 163–75.
- "The Social and Political Significance of the Military Establishment in New France." *CHR* 52 (1971): 1–22.
- "Sovereignty-Association, 1500–1783." *CHR* 65 (1984): 475–510.

Edmunds, R. David. "Native Americans, New Voices: American Indian History 1895–1995." *AHR* 100 (1998): 717–40.

Eggan, Fred. *The American Indian.* Weidenfeld and Nicolson, London, 1966.

Eisenstadt, Schmuel. *The Absorption of Immigrants.* Glencoe Free Press, Glencoe, IL, 1955.
- *From Generation to Generation: age groups and social structures.* Transaction, New Brunswick, [1998] 2003.
- ed. *Approche comparative de la civilisation européenne: études de la relation entre la culture et la structure sociale.* Presses Universitaires de France, Paris, 1994.
- "Generation Conflict and Intellectual Antinomianism." In Philip Altback and Robert Laufer, *The New Pilgrims: Youth Protest in Transition.* David McKay Co., New York, 1972.
- *Martin Buber. On Intersubjectivity and Cultural Creativity.* Heritage of Sociology Series, University of Chicago Press, Chicago, 1992.
- *Power, Trust, and Meaning: Essays in Sociological Theory and Analysis.* University of Chicago Press, Chicago, 1995.

Einstein, Albert. *Why War? The Correspondence between Albert Einstein and Sigmund Freud.* Trans. Fritz and Anna Moellenhoff, Chicago Institute for Psychoanalysis, 1978.

Eliade, Mircea. *Le Chamanisme et les techniques archaïques de l'extase.* Payot, Paris, 1951.
- *Mythes, rêves, et mystères.* Gallimard, coll. idées, Paris, 1957.
- *Myth and Reality.* Trans. Willard Trask, Harper Torchbooks, New York, 1968.
- *Shamanism: Archaic Techniques of Ecstacy.* Trad. Willard Trask, Bollingen Series, #76, Princeton University Press, Princeton, 1964.

Elias, Norbert. *The Civilizing Process.* 2 vols. Basil, Blackwell, Oxford, 1982.
- *The Society of Individuals.* Trans. Edmund Jephcott, Basil Blackwell, London, 1991.

Elias, Norbert, and John Scotson. *The Established and the Outsiders: A Sociological Inquiry into Community Problems.* Sage, London, 1994.

Eliav-Feldon, Miriam. *Realistic Utopias: The Ideal Imaginary Societies of the Renaissance, 1516–1630.* Clarendon Press, Oxford, 1982.

Ellis, Harold. *Boulainvilliers and the French Monarchy: Aristocratic Politics in Early 18th-Century France.* Ithaca, New York, 1988.

Ellison, Ralph. *The Invisible Man.* Modern Library, New York, 1992.

Elsass, Peter. *Strategies for Survival: The Psychology of Cultural Resistance in Ethnic Minorities.* Trans. Fran Hopenwasser, New York University Press, New York, 1992.

Engels, Friedrich. *Der Ursprung der Familie, des Privateigentums und des Staats.* Deitz, Berlin, 1961.

D'Entremont, Clarence. "The Children of the Baron de St-Castin." *French Canadian Genealogical Review* 3 (1971): 9–28.

Epstein, Simon. *L'antisémitisme français: aujourd'hui et demain.* Belfond, Paris, 1984.

Ehrard, Jean. *L'idée de Nature dans la première moitié du XVIIe siècle.* Albin Michel, Paris, [1963] 1994.

Eitinger, Leo. "The Concentration Camp Syndrome and Its Late Sequelae." In Joel Dimsdale, ed., *Survivors, Victims, and Perpetrators,* 127–62. Hemisphere. Washington, DC, 1980.

Erdoes, Richard and Alfonso Ortiz, eds. *American Indian Myth and Legends.* Pantheon, New York, 1984.

Erikson, Erik. *The Challenge of Youth.* Doubleday, Garden City, New Jersey, 1965.

Estèbe, Janine, and Nathalie Zemon Davis. "Debate on the Rites of Violence: Religious Riot in Sixteenth Century France, Comment and Rejoinder." *Past and Present* 67 (1975): 127–35.

Ettawageshik, Fred. "Witchcraft in Menomini Acculturation." *AA* 54 (1952): 539–93.

Etienne, Mona, and Eleanor Leacock. *Women and Colonization.* Praeger Special Studies, JF Bergin Pub. Book, New York, 1980.

Evans-Prichard, E.E. *Anthropology and History.* Manchester University Press, Manchester, 1961.

– *Witchcraft, Oracles, and Magic among the Azande.* Clarendon Press, Oxford, 1937.

Everly, George, and Jeffrey Lating, eds.. *Psychotraumatology: Key Papers and Core concepts in Post-Traumatic Stress.* Plenum Press, New York, 1995.

Everstine, Diana and Louis. *The Trauma Response: Treatment for Emotional Injury.* Norton, New York, 1993.

Ewert, Charles. *No Man's Brother: The Story of Etienne Brûlé.* Avon, Scarborough, ON, 1984.

Fabian, Johannes. *Time and the Other: How Anthropology Makes Its Object.* Columbia University Press, New York, 1983.

Fagniez, Gustave. *La Femme et la société française dans la première moitié du XVIIe siècle.* Gamber, Paris, 1929.

Faillon, E.M.. *Histoire de la colonie française au Canada, Paris, 1865–1866.*

– *L'exploit de Dollard, Bibliothèque de l'Action française,* Montréal, s.d.

– "Famille Marsolet de St-Aignan," *BRH* 40 (1934): 383–409.

Flannery, Regina. *An Analysis of Coastal Algonquian Culture.* Catholic University of America, #7, Catholic University of America Press, Washington, DC, 1939.

Fanon, Franz. *Black Skin, White Masks.* Grove, Weidenfeld, New York [1951] 1991.

Fauteux, Aegidius. "La Chasse-galérie." *BRH* 32 (1920): 693–4.

Fauvel, Jacques. *La Fronde des Généraux.* Arthaud, Paris, 1961.

Favret-Saada, Jeanne. *Deadly Words: Witchcraft in the Bocage.* Cambridge, 1980.

Fawke, Edith. *Folktales of French Canada.* Ed. Marquis, Montmagny, 1979.

Febvre, Lucien. *A Geographical Introduction to History.* Barnes and Nobles, New York, 1966.

– *The Problem of Unbelief in the 16th Century: The Religion of Rabelais.* Harvard University Press, Cambridge, 1982.

Feige, Michael. *Tnuot Hevratiot, Hegemonia, veMithus Politi: Behina Mashva shel haIdeologia shel Gush Emunim veShalom Achshav.* Universita Ivrit, Yerushalayim, 1995 (in Hebrew).

Fein, Helen. *Genocide: A Sociological Perspective.* Sage Pubs., London, 1993.

Feldman, Burton and Robert Richardson. *The Rise of Modern Mythology, 1680–1860.* University of Indiana Press, Bloomington, IN, 1972.

Fenton, William. *The False Faces of the Iroquois.* University of Oklahoma, Civilization of the American Indian Series, University of Oklahoma Press, Norman, OK, 1987.

– *The Great Law and the Longhouse: A Political History of the Iroquois Confederacy.* University of Oklahoma Press, Norman, OK, 1998.

– "Masked Medicine Societies of the Iroquois." In Elisabeth Tooker, *An Iroquois Source Book, III: Medicine Society Rituals,* 397–465. Garland, New York, 1986.

– "Songs from the Iroquois Longhouse: Program Notes for an Album of American Indian Music form the Eastern Woodlands (1942)." In Elisabeth Tooker, *An Iroquois Source Book, III: Medicine Society Rituals,* 1–40. Garland, New York, 1986.

– "The Training of Historical Ethnologists in America." *AA* 54 (1952): 328–39.

Fenton, William, and Gertrude Kurath. "The Feast of the Dead, or Ghost Dance, at Six Nations Reserve, Canada (1951)." In Elisabeth Tooker, *An Iroquois Source Book, III: Medicine Society Rituals,* 143–65. Garland, New York, 1986.

Féré, Octave. *Légendes et Traditions de la Normandie.* Charles Haulard, Rouen, 1845.

Ferland, J.B.A. *Cour d'histoire du Canada.* I, Armand Côté, Québec, 1861.

Fernandez, James. "Historians Tell Tales of Cartesian Cats and Gallic Cockfights." *Journal of Modern History* 60 (1988): 113–27.

Figley, Charles. *Trauma and Its Wake: The Study and Treatment of Post-Traumatic Stress Disorder.* Brunner/Mazel Psychosocial Stress Series, #4, Brunner/Mazel, New York, 1985.

Fillion, Konrad. "Essai sur le l'évolution du mot habitant (XVIIe-XVIIIe siècles)." *RHAF* 24 (1970): 375–401.

Filteau, Gérard. *La naissance d'une nation: tableau du Canada en 1755.* Ed. de l'ACF, Montréal, 1937.

Finkielkraut, Alain. *La défaite de la pensée.* Gallimard, Paris, 1987.

– *La vaine mémoire.* Gallimard, Paris, 1989.

Finkler, Kaja. *Spiritualist Healers in Mexico: Successes and Failures of Alternative Therapies.* Bergin and Garvey, New York, 1985.

Finley, M.I. "Myth, Memory, and History." In *History and Theory* 4 (1965): 281–302.

Firth, Raymond, ed. *Man and Culture: an Evaluation of the Work of Bronislaw Malinowski.* Routledge and Kegan Paul, London, 1957.

Fisher, Robin. *Contact and Conflict: Indian-European Relations in British Columbia, 1774–1890.* UBC Press, Vancouver, 1977.

Fisher-Tayler, Gail. "In the Presence of Ghosts: Transforming Reality." In Margo Rivera, *Fragment by Fragment: Feminist Perspectives on Memory and Child Sexual Abuse.* Gynergy Books, Charlottetown, PEI, 1999.

Flaherty, Gloria. *Shamanism and the 18th Century.* Princeton, NJ, 1992.

Flanagan, Thomas. *Riel and the Rebellion: 1885 Reconsidered.* University of Toronto Press, Toronto [1983] 2000.

Flandrin, Jean-Louis. *Les amours paysannes: amour et sexualit, dans les campagnes de l'ancienne France (XVIe-XIXe).* Gallimard/Julliard, Paris, 1975.

– *Families in Former Times: Kinship, Household, and Sexuality.* Cambridge University Press, Cambridge, 1979.

Flint, Valerie. *The Rise of Magic in Early Medieval Europe.* Princeton University Press, Princeton and Oxford, 1991.

Flood, Christopher. *Political Myth: A Theoretical Introduction.* Garland, New York, 1996.

Flower, Harriet. *Ancestor Masks and Aristocratic Power in Roman Culture.* Clarendon Press, New York, 1996.

Fogelson, R. "Psychological Theories of Windigo 'psychosis' and a Preliminary Application of a Models Approach." In Melvin Spiro, ed. *Context and Meaning in Cultural Anthropology,* 74-99. Free Press, New York, 1965.

Foisil, Madeleine. *La révolte des Nus-pieds et les révoltes de 1639.* Presses Universitaires de France, Paris, 1970.

Fondation Héritage Côte-du-Sud, Contes et Légendes de la Côte-du-Sud. SA, Ministre des Transports, Septentrion, Québec, 1994.

Forbes, G. "Les Iroquois de Caughnawaga." *BRH* 6 (1900): 116–17.

Forbes, Jack. "The Americanization of Education in the United States." *The Indian Historian* (now *Wassaja*) 37 (1974): 15–21.

Forbes, Thomas. *The Midwife and the Witch.* Yale University Press, New Haven, 1966.

Ford, Richard. *An Ethnobiology Sourcebook: The Uses of Plants and Animals by American Indians.* Garland, New York, 1986.

Forster, Robert, and Greene, Jack, eds. *Preconditions of Revolution in Early Modern Europe.* Baltimore, MD, 1970.

Foster, Don. *Detention and Torture in South Africa: Legal and Historical Studies.* St. Martin's Press, New York, 1987.

Foster, George. *Culture and Conquest: America's Spanish Heritage.* Chicago, 1960.

– "What is Folk Culture?" *AA* 55 (1903): 159–73.

Foster, Michael, Jack Campisi, and Marianne Mithun, eds. *Extending the Rafters: Interdisciplinary Approaches to Iroquoian Studies.* SUNY Press, Albany, New York, 1984.

Foucault, Michel. *L'archaeologie du savoir.* Bibliographie des sciences humaines, Gallimard, Paris, 1994.

Foulch,-Delbosc, Isabelle. "Women of New France." *CHR* 21 (1940): 132–49.

– "Women of Trois-Rivières, 1651–1663." In A. Prentice and S. Trofimenkoff, eds. *The Neglected Majority.* Toronto, McClelland and Stewart, Canadian Social History Series, 1977.

Fournier, Marcel. *Dictionnaire biographique des Bretons en nouvelle-France 1600–1765.* Etudes et recherches archivistiques, #4, ANQ, 1981.

– "L'immigration européenne au Canada des origines à 1765." *MSGCF* 42 (1991): 106–24.

Fournier, Martin. *Pierre-Esprit Radisson : Coureur de bois et homme du monde (1652–1685)*. Nuit Blanche, Québec, 1996.

– *Pierre-Esprit Radisson: aventurier et commerçant*. Septentrion, Sillery, Québec, 2001.

Fowke, Edith. *Folktales of French Canada*. North Canadian Press Ltd., Toronto, 1979.

Francis, Daniel, and Toby Morantz. *Partners in Furs: A History of the Fur Trade in Eastern Canada*. McGill-Queen's University Press, 1983.

Frankl, Viktor. *Man's Search for Meaning*. Washington Square Press, New York [1959] 1984.

Fraser, James Georges. *Aftermath: A Supplement to the Golden Bough*. Macmillan, New York, 1937.

– *Fear of the Dead in Primitive Religion*. Arno Press, New York [1933–36] 1977.

– *The Golden Bough: A Study in Magic and Religion*. Macmillan, New York, 1949.

– *The Worship of Nature*. Macmillan, New York, 1926

Fréchette, Louis. *Le Loup-garou: Contes d'autrefois*. Beauchemin, Montréal, 1946, 113–34.

– "La messe du revenant." *BRH* 4 (1898): 166–72.

Freedy, John, and Steven Hobfoll, eds. *Traumatic Stress: From Theory to Practice*. Plenum Press, New York, 1995.

Freeman, Mark. *Rewriting the Self: History, Memory, Narrative, Critical Psychology*. Routledge, New York, 1993.

Frégault, Guy. *Iberville le conquérant*. Ed. Pascal, Montréal, 1944.

– *Le XVIIIe siècle canadien*. Hurtubise, Montréal, 1968.

– *La Civilisation de la Nouvelle-France*. Hurtubise, Montréal, 1944.

Freud, Sigmund. *The Interpretation of Dreams*. Trans. James Strachey, George Allen and Unwin, London 1967.

Friedl, Ernestine. "Persistance in Chippewa Culture and Personality." *AA* 58 (1956): 814–25.

Friedländer, Saul. "Trauma, Transference, and 'Working Through' in Writing the History of the Shoah." *History and Memory* 4 (1992): 52–3.

Friedrich, C. J., and Z. Brzezinski. *Totalitarian Dictatorship and Autocracy*. Frederick and Praeger, New York, 1961.

Frisch, Jack. "Cognatic Kinship Organization among the Northeast Algonquians." MA thesis, Indiana University, 1964.

Fullerton, Carol, and Robert Ursano, eds. *Posttraumatic Stress Disorder: Acute and Long-Term Responses to Trauma and Disaster*. Progress in Psychiatry Series, #51, American Psychiatric Press, Washington, DC, 1997.

Furet, François. *Interpreting the French Revolution*. Cambridge University Press, Cambridge, 1981.

– ed. *Unanswered Questions: Nazi Germany and the Genocide of the Jews*. Schocken, New York, 1989.

Furet, François and Jacques Ozouf. *Reading and Writing: Literacy in France from Calvin to Jules Ferry*. Cambridge Studies in Oral and Literate Culture 5. Cambridge University Press, Cambridge, 1982.

Furet, François and Mona Ozouf, éds. *The French Revolution and the Creation of Modern Political Culture.* Vol. 3: *The Transformation of Political Culture, 1789–1848.* Pergamon, Oxford, 1987–94.

Gaboury, Lorraine. *La noblesse de Nouvelle-France: familles et alliances.* Editions Hurtubise, coll. Cahiers de Québec, LaSalle, 1992.

Gaboury, Lorraine, Yves Landry, Hubert Charbonneau. "Démographie differentielle en Nouvelle-France: villes et campagnes." *RHAF* 38 (1985): 357–78.

Gagnon, François-Marc. *Ces hommes dits sauvages.* Libre Expression, Montréal, 1984.

– *La conversion par image.* Bellarmin, Montréal, 1975.

Gagnon, Jean-Philippe. *Rites et croyances de la naissance à Charlevoix.* Leméac, Ottawa, 1978.

Gagnon, Serge. *Mourir hier et aujourd'hui: De la mort chrétienne dans la campagne québecoise au XIXe siècle à la mort techniste dans la cité sans Dieu.* Presses de l'Université Laval, Québec, 1987.

– *Québec and its Historians, 1840–1920.* Trans. Yves Brunelle, Harvest House, Montréal, 1982.

Gallant, Melvin. *Ti-Jean: contes acadiens.* Fides, Montréal, 1984.

Galloway, Patricia. *La Salle and his Legacy.* University Press of Mississippi, Jackson, 1982.

Garneau, François-Xavier. *Histoire du Canada.* Vols. 1 and 2. Edition de l'arbre, Montréal, 1944.

Gastel, Ada van. "Van der Donck's Description of the Indians: Additions and Corrections." *WMQ* 47 (1990): 411–21.

Gaster, Moses. "Magic, Modern Romance, Hebrew Apocrypha, and Samaritan Archaelogy." In *Studies and Texts in Folklore,* vol. 2, Ktav, New York, 1971.

Gaster, Theodor. "Myth and Story." *Numen* 1 (1954): 184–212.

Gatschet, Albert. "Water Monsters of American Aborigines." *JAF* 12 (1899): 255–60.

Gautier, Michel. *Contes populaires de Vendée, Le Cercle d'or, Geste paysanne.* UPSCP, Nantes, 1952.

Gecas, Viktor. "The Self as a Social Force." In Tim Owens, Sheldon Stryker, and Norman Goodman, eds. *Extending Self-Esteem Theory and Research: Social and Psychological Trends.* Cambridge University Press, New York, 2000.

– "Self and Identity." In Karen Cook, Gary Alan Fre, and James House, eds. *Perspectives in Social Psychology.* Allyn and Bacon, New York, 1995.

Geddes, Virginia. *Various Children of Eve: (AT 758): Cultural Variants and Antifeminine Images.* Etnologiska Institutionen, Uppsala, 1986.

Geertz, Clifford. *After the Fact: Two Countries, Four Decades, One Anthropologist.* Harvard University Press, Cambridge, 1995.

– *Available Light: Anthropological Reflections on Philosophical Topics.* Princeton University Press, Princeton, 2001.

– "History and Anthropology." *New Literary History* 21 (1989–90): 321–35.

– *Myth, Symbol and Culture: Essays.* Norton, New York, 1971.

– "Impact of the Concept of Culture on the Concept of Man." In Yehudi Cohen, ed., *Man in Adaptation*, 16–28. Aldine, Chicago, 1974.

Gélinas, Claude. "La Nature des attaques Iroquoises contre Ville-Marie 1642–1667." *RAQ* 24 (1994): 119–27.

Geras, Norman. *The Contract of Mutual Indifference: Political Philosophy after the Holocaust.* Verso, New York, 1999.

Gergen, Kenneth. *Historical Social Psychology.* Erlbaum Association, Hillsdale, NJ, 1984.

Gergen, Kenneth. "Narratives of the Self." In S Hinchman, ed., *The Idea of Narrative in the Human Sciences*, 161–84. University of New York Press, Albany, New York, 1997.

Germain, Pierre. "Les Récits de Voyages de Pierre-Esprit Radisson: études d'histoire Bibliographique." *RHAF* 34 (1980): 407–14.

Gerth, Hans, and Wright Mills, eds. *From Max Weber: Essays in Sociology.* Oxford University Press, New York, 1946.

Gervais de Tilbury, *Revue des Traditions populaires* 18 (1903): 289.

Getty, Ian, and Antoine Lussier, *As Long as the Sun Shines and the Water Flows: A Reader in Canadian Native Studies.* UBC Press, Vancouver, 1983.

Gibbon, Edward. *The Rise and Fall of the Roman Empire.* Harper and Row, New York, 1900.

Gibson, Wendy. *Women in 17th-Century France.* Macmillan, Basingstoke, 1989.

Giddens, Anthony. *Central Problems in Social Theory: Action, Structure, and Contradiction in Social Analysis.* Cambridge University Press, Cambridge, 1979.

Giesey, Ralph. *The Royal Funeral Ceremony in Renaissance France.* Droz, Genève, 1960.

Giffard, A.E. *Précis de droit romain.* Vol. 1. Dalloz, Paris, 1938.

Gildea, Robert. *The Past in French History.* Yale University Press, New Haven, 1994.

Gille, Johannes. *Der Manabozho-Flutzyklus der Nord, Nordost-, und Zentralalgonkin.* Trüte, Göttingen, 1939.

Gillot, Hubert. *La Querelle des anciens et des modernes en France.* Slatkine, Genève [1914] 1968.

Gilman, Carolyn. *Where Two Worlds Meet: The Great Lakes Fur Trade.* St Paul, MN, 1982.

Ginsberg, Carlo. *Ecstacies: Deciphering the Witches' Sabbath.* Trans. Raymond Rosenthal, Hutchinson Radius, London [1989] 1990.

– *The Night Battles: Witchcraft and Agrarian Cults in the 16th and 17th Centuries.* Johns Hopkins University Press, Baltimore, 1983.

Girard, Camil, and Normand Perron. *Histoire du Saguenay-St-Jean.* coll. les Régions du Québec, 2, Institut Québecois de Recherche sur la Culture, 1995.

Girard, René. *Le Bouc émissaire.* Librarie générale française, Paris, 1986.

– *Violence and the Sacred.* Johns Hopkins University Press, Baltimore, 1972.

Giraud, Marcel. *The Metis in the Canadian West.* University of Alberta Press, Edmonton, 1986.

Giroux, T.E. "La medecine indienne et le traitement du cancer." *Laval Medical* 38 (1967): 954–62.

Given, Brian. *A Most Pernicious Thing: Gun Trading and Native Warfare in the Early Contact Period.* Carlton University Press, Ottawa, 1994.

Glass, James. *Shattered Selves: Multiple Personality in a Postmodern World.* Cornell University Press, Ithaca, 1993.

Gnoli, Gherardo. *La mort, les morts, dans les sociétés anciennes.* Cambridge University Press, Cambridge, 1982.

Gobineau, Arthur, comte de. *Essai sur l'inégalité des races humaines.* Chez Firmin-Didot, Paris, 1884.

Godbeer, Richard. *The Devil's Dominion: Magic and Religion in Early New England.* Cambridge University Press, Cambridge, 1992.

Godbout, Archange. "Les Origines de la famille LeMoyne." *RHAF* I (1947–48): 539.

– "Origine d'Olivier LeTardif." *MSGCF* 9–11 (1958–60): 151.

Godbout, Jacques and Alain Caillé. *The World of the Gift.* Trans. Donald Winkler, Montreal, McGill-Queen's University Press, 1998.

Goddard, Peter. "The Devil in New France: Jesuit Demonology, 1611–1650." *CHR* 78 (1997): 40–62.

– "Science and Scepticism in the 17th-Century Mission to New France." offprint.

Goddard, Ives. "Agreskou,: A Northern Iroquoian Deity." In Michael Foster, Jack Campisi, and Marianne Mithun, eds. *Extending the Rafters: Interdisciplinary Approaches to Iroquoian Studies,* 229–36. SUNY Press, Albany, New York, 1984.

Godelier, Maurice. The Enigma of the Gift. Trans. Nora Scott. Chicago, University of Chicago, 1999.

Gold, Norman. *Who Wrote the Dead Sea Scrolls? The Search for the Secret of Qumran.* Scribner, New York, 1995.

Gold, Penny. *The Lady and the Virgin: Image, Attitude, and Experience in 12th-Century France.* University of Chicago Press, Chicago, 1985.

Golden, Richard. *The Godly Rebellion: Parisian Curés and the Religious Fronde, 1652–1662.* University of North Carolina Press, Chapel Hill, NC, 1981.

Goldstein, Robert. *French-Iroquois Diplomatic and Military Relations (1609–1701).* Mouton, Den Haag, 1969.

Goode, Erich. *Deviant Behavior.* Prentice Hall, NJ [1978] 1997.

Goody, Jack. *The Domestication of the Savage Mind.* Cambridge University Press, Cambridge, 1977.

Gordon, Evian, ed. *Integrative neuroscience: Bringing Together Psychology and Clinical Models of the Human Brain.* Harwood Academic Pubs., Amsterdam, 2000.

Gorel, Les, éd. *Contes popularies et légendes de Bretagne.* Richesse du Folklore de France, Presses de la Renaissance, Paris, 1974.

Gorham, Harriet. "Families of Mixed Descent in the Western Great Lakes Region." DIAND files paper.

Gorny, Yosef, Yaakov Oved, and Idit Paz, eds. *Communal Life: An International Perspective.* The International Conference on Kibbutz and Communes, May 1985, Yad Tabenkin and Transaction Books, Efal and New Brunswick, NJ, 1987.

Gosselin, Auguste. *Jean Bourdon et son ami l'abbé de Saint-Sauveur.* Dusault & Proulx, Québec, 1904.

Goubert, Pierre. *La vie quotidienne des paysans français au XVIIe siècle.* Hachette, Paris, 1982.

Goudsboum, Johan. "Les Grandes epidémies et la civilité des moeurs." *Actes de la Recherche en Science Sociale* 68 (1987): 3–14.

Gould, C., and L. Cozolino. "Ritual Abuse, Multiplicity, and Mind Control." *Journal of Psychology and Theology* 20, 3 (1992): 194–6.

Goulet, Denis, and André Paradis. *Trois siècles d'histoire médicale au Québec. 1639–1939*, coll. Etudes Québecoise, VLB d., Montréal, 1992.

Gutman, Israel. *Encyclopaedia of the Holocaust.* 4 vols. Macmillan, New York, 1990.

Forman, Jack, and Robert Kertzner, eds. *Psychoimmunology update.* Progress in Psychiatry, #35, American Psychiatric Press, Washington DC, 1991.

Gouger, Lina. *L'acculturation des Algonquians au XVIIe siècle.* Presses de l'Université Laval, Sillery, 1987.

Goulding, Regina, and Richard Schwartz. *The Mosaic Mind: Empowering the Tormented Selves of Child Abuse Survivors.* Norton, New York, 1995.

Gourdeau, Claire. *Les Délices de nos coeurs: Marie de l'Incarnation et ses pensionaires amérindiennes, 1639–1672.* Cahiers du Célat, Septentrion, Québec, 1994.

Goux, Jean-Joseph, and Philip Wood, eds. *Terror and Consensus: Vicissitudes of French Thought.* Stanford University Press, Stanford, 1998.

Grabowski, Jan. "Les amérindiens domiciliés et la 'contrebande' des fourrures en Nouvelle-France." *RAQ* 24 (1994): 45–52.

– "The Common Ground: Settled Natives and French in Montréal, 1667–1760." PhD., Université de Montréal, 1993.

– "French Criminal Justice and Indians in Montreal, 1670–1760." *Ethnohistory* 43 (1996): 405–29.

– "L'historiographie des Amérindiens au Canada: quelques données et commentaires portant sur les directions de la recherche et sur les travaux en cours." *RHAF* 53 (2000): 552–60.

– "Le 'petit commerce' entre les Trifluviens et les Amérindiens en 1665–1667." *RAQ* 28 (1998): 105–21. (Pre-press copy kindly given me in 1997 by author.)

Graf, Fritz. *La Magie dans l'Antiquité gréco-romaine.* Belles-lettres, Paris, 1994.

Grant, John Webster. *Moon of Wintertime: Missionaries and the Indians of Canada in Encounters since 1534.* University of Toronto Press, Toronto, 1984.

Graessner, Sepp, Norbert Gurris, and Christian Pross, eds. *At the Side of Torture Survivors: Treating a Terrible Assault on Human dignity.* Johns Hopkins University, Baltimore, 2001.

Green, Frederick. *The Ancien Régime: A manual of French Institutions and Social Classes.* Edinburgh, Edinburgh University Press [1958] 1960.

Green, Miranda. *The Gods of the Celts.* Alan Sutton, Gloucester, 1986.

– *Celtic Goddesses: Warriors, Virgins, and Mothers.* British Museum Press, London, 1995.

Greene, Jack. *Interpreting Early America: Historiographical Essays.* University Press of Virginia, Raleigh, VA, 1996.

– "Interpretive Frameworks: The Quest for Intellectual Order in Early American History." *WMQ* 48 (1991): 515–30.

– *The Intellectual Construction of America: Exceptionalism and Identity from 1492–1800,* University of North Carolina Press, Chapel Hill, 1993.

- "Transplanting Moments: Inheritance in the Formation of Early American Culture." *WMQ* 48 (1991): 224–37.

Greene, Jack, and J.R. Pole, eds. *Colonial British America.* Johns Hopkins University Press, Baltimore, 1984.

Gregg, Gary. *Self-Representation: Life Narrative Studies in Identity and Ideology.* Greenwood Press, New York, 1991.

Grenier, Hélène. "Les étrangers au Canada sous le Régime français." Thèse de maîtrise, Université de Sherbrooke, 1992.

Griffin, M., P. Resnick, M. Mechanic. "Objective Assessment of Peritraumatic Dissociation: Psychopathological Indicators." *American Journal of Psychiatry* 154 (1997): 1081–8.

Grim, John. *The Shaman: An Interpretation of This Religious Personality Based on Ethnological Data from the Siberian tribes and the Woodland Ojibway of North America.* University Microfilms Incorporated, Ann Arbor, MI, 1980.

Grinde, Donald, Jr. *Iroquois and the Founding of the American Nation.* The Indian Historian Press, Inc., 1977.

Grinde, Donald, and Bruce Johansen. *Exemplar of Liberty: Native America and the Evolution of Democracy.* American Indian Study Center, Los Angeles, CA, 1991.

Grisward, J.H. *Archéologie de l'épopée médieval.* Payot, Paris, 1981.

Grossman, James. *The Frontier in American Culture: Essays by Richard White and Patricia Nelson Limerick.* Exhibition at Newberry Library, Aug. 26, 1994-Jan. 7, 1995, University of California Press, Berkeley, 1996.

Groulx, Chanoine Lionel. *Chez nos ancêtres.* L'action française, Montréal, 1920.

- *Histoire du Canada depuis la découverte.* Fides, Montréal, 1962.
- *Histoire du Canada français.* 2 t., Fides, Fleur de Lys, Montréal, 1960.
- *Dollard est-il un mythe?* Fides, Ottawa, 1960.
- "Le bonnet phrygien." *BRH* I (1895): 92–4.

Groulx, Patrice. *Pièges de la Mémoire: Dollard des Ormeaux, les Amérindiens, et nous.* Ed. Vents d'Ouest, Hull, 1998.

Gruzinski, Serge. *La colonisation de l'imaginaire: sociétés indigènes et occidentalisation dans le Méxique espagnol XVIe-XVIIIe siècle.* Gallimard, Paris, 1988.

- *La pensée métisse.* Fayard, Paris, 1999.
- "S'ensauvager: Quand les français du Brésil et du Canada choisissaient de vivre parmi les indiens XVIe-XVIIe siècles." *Cahiers de Sociologie économique et culturelle* 18 (1992): 19–28.

Guérin, Léon. *Aux sources de notre historie: les conditions economiques et sociales de la colonisation en Nouvelle-France.* Fides, Montréal, 1946.

Gutman, Yisrael. "Social Stratification in the Concentration Camps." *The Nazi Concentration Camps,* Yad VaShem, Jerusalem, 1984, 143–76.

Gutton, Jean-Pierre. *La Société et les Pauvres en Europe.* Presses Universitaires de France, Paris, 1974.

Guz, H., Z. Doganay, A. Ozkan, E. Colak, A. Tomac, G. Sarysoy. "Conversion and Somatization Disorders: The Dissociative Symptoms and Other Characteristics." *European Psychiatry* 17 (2002): 207S.

Haase Dubosc, Danielle, et Eliane Viennot. *Femmes et pouvoirs sous l'ancien régime.* Rivages, Histoire, Paris, 1991.

Habermas, Jürgen. *Between Facts and Norms: Contribution to a Discourse Theory of Law and Democracy.* MIT, Cambridge University Press, Cambridge [1996] 1998.

– *Communication and the Evolution of Society.* Beacon Press, Boston, 1979.

– *Moral Conciousness and Communicative Action.* Polity Press, Cambridge, 1990.

– *The Past as Future: "Vergangenheit als Zukunft."* University of Nebraska, Lincoln, 1994.

Hacking, Ian. *Rewriting the Soul.* Princeton University Press, Princeton, 1995.

Hagar, S. "Micmac Customs and Traditions." *AA* 8 (1895): 31–42.

– "Micmac Magic and Medicine." *JAF* 9 (1896): 170–7.

Hageman, I, H.S. Anderson, and M.B. Jorgensen. " PTSD: A Review of Psychobiology and Pharmacotherapy." *Acta Psychiatrica Scandinavica* 104, 6 (2001): 411–22.

Halbwachs, Maurice. *On Collective Memory.* Trans. Lewis Coser. University of Chicago Press, Chicago, 1992.

Hale, Horatio. "Huron Folklore." *JAF* 1 (1888): 177–83; 2 (1889): 249–54; 4 (1891): 289–306.

– *The Iroquois Book of Rites and Hale on the Iroquois.* Iroqrafts, Ohsweken, ON, 1989.

Hale, Katherine. *Pierre-Esprit Radisson.* Ryerson Press, Toronto, n.d.

Halifax, Joan. *Shamanic Voices: A Survey of Visionary Narratives.* Penguin, Harmondsworth [1979] 1980.

Hall, David. *Witchhunting in 17th-Century New England: A Documentary History, 1638–1692.* Northeastern University Press, Boston, 1991.

Hallpike, C.R. "Some Problems in Cross-Cultural Comparison." In T.O. Beidelman, *The Translation of Cultures: essays to E.E. Evans-Prichard,* 123–40. Tavistock Pubs., London, 1971.

Hallowell, A. Irving. *Contributions to Anthropology: Selected Papers of A. Irving Hallowell.* University of Chicago Press, Chicago, 1976.

– "Culture and Mental Disorder." *Journal of Abnormal and Social Psychology* 29 (1963): 1–9.

– "The Impact of the American Indian on American Culture." *AA* 59 (1957): 201–17.

– "Myth, Culture, and Personality." *AA* 49 (1947): 544–55.

– *The Role of Conjuring in Saulteaux Society.* University of Pennsylvania Press, Philadelphia, 1942.

– "Le rôle des rêves dans la culture Ojibwa." In Roger Caillois et Gustave von Grunebaum, eds. *Le rêve et les sociétés humaines.* Gallimard, Paris, 1967, 257–76.

Hamelin, Jean. *Economie et société en Nouvelle-France.* Presses de l'Université de Laval, Québec, 1970.

Hamilton, J.C. "Two Algonquin Legends." *JAF* 7 (1894): 201–4.

Hamilton, Roberta. *Feudal Society and Colonization: A Critique and Reinterpretation of the Historiography of New France.* Langdale Press, Gananoque, ON, 1988.

Handel, Warren. *Ethnomethodology: How People Make Sense.* Prentice-Hall, Englewood Cliffs, New Jersey, 1982.

Handelman, Don. "Critiques of Anthropology: Literary Turns, Slippery Bends." *Poetics Today* 15 (1994): 341–81.

– *Models and Mirrors: Towards an Anthropology of Public Events.* Cambridge University Press, Cambridge, 1990.

Handler, Richard. *Nationalism and the Politics of Culture in Quebec.* University of Wisconsin Press, Madison, WI, 1988.

Hanley, Sarah. *Le Lit de Justice of the Kings of France: Constitutional Ideology in Legend, Ritual, and Discourse.* Princeton University Press, Princeton, 1983.

Harding, Vanessa. *The Dead and the Living in Paris and London: 1500–1670.* Cambridge University Press, Cambridge, 2002.

Harrington, M.R. "Da-ra-sa-kwa: A Caughnawaga Legend." *JAF* 19 (1906): 127–9.

Harding, Robert. *Anatomy of a Power Elite: The Provincial Governor of Early Modern France.* Yale University Press, New Haven, 1978.

Harel, Zev, Boaz Kahana, and Eva Kahana. "Social Resources and Mental Health of Aging Nazi Holocaust Survivors and Immigrants." In John Wilson and Beverley Raphael, eds. *International Handbook of Traumatic Stress Syndromes,* 241–52. Plenum Series on Stress and Coping, New York, 1993.

Harkness, Laurie. " Transgenerational Transmission of War-Related Trauma." In John Wilson and Beverley Raphael, eds. *International Handbook of Traumatic Stress Syndromes,* 635–44. Plenum Series on Stress and Coping, New York, 1993.

Harrington, Carolyn. "Development of a Half Breed Community in the Upper Great Lakes." DIAND files paper.

Harris, Jay. *How the Brain Talks to Itself: A clinical Primer of Psychotherapeutic Neuroscience.* Haworth Academic, New York, 1998.

Harris, Richard Colebrook. *The Seigneurial System in Early Canada.* University of Wisconsin Press, Madison, WI, 1966.

Hartz, Louis. *The Founding of New Societies.* Harcourt, Brace and World, New York, 1964.

– "Violence and Legality in the Fragment Cultures." *CHR* 50 (1969): 123–40.

Hastrup, Kirsten. "The Dynamics of Anthropological Theory." *Cultural Dynamics* 9 (1997): 351–71.

– ed. *Other Histories.* New York and London, Routledge, 1992.

Hatch, Elvin. "Theories of Social Honor." *AA* 91 (1989): 341–53.

Havard, Gilles. "La Grande Paix de Montréal de 1701: Les voix de la diplomatie franco- Amérindienne." *RAQ,* Montréal, 1992.

Hay, Thomas. "The Windigo Psychosis: Psychodynamic, Cultural, and Social Factors in Aberrant Behavior." *AA* 73 (1971): 1–19.

Hayden, Colin and William Doyle, eds. *Robespierre.* Cambridge University Press, Cambridge, 1999.

Hazard, Paul. *La crise de la conscience européenne.* 2 t., Librairie Arthème Fayard, Paris, 1961.

Healy, George. "The French Jesuits and the idea of the Noble Savage." *WMQ* 15 (1958): 143–67.

Heard, Norman. *White in Red: A Study of the Assimilation of White Persons Captured by the Indians.* Metuchen, NJ, 1973.

Heelas, Paul, and Andrew Lock, eds. *Indigenous Psychologies: The Anthropologies of the Self.* Academic Press, London, 1981.

Heidenreich, Conrad. *Huronia: A History of the Huron Indians, 1600–1650.* McClelland and Stewart, Toronto, 1971.

Helbig, Althea. *Nanabozhoo: Giver of Life.* Green Oak Press, Brighton, MI, 1987.

Hendricks, Margo, and Patricia Parker. *Women, "Race," and Writing in the Early Modern Period.* Routledge, London, 1994.

Hendrickson, George. *Hunters in the Barrens: The Naskapi on the Edge of the White Man's World.* 6th ed., Institute of Social and Economic Research, Memorial University of Newfoundland, St John's, 1981.

Henigsberg, N., V. Folnegovic-Smalc, and L. Moro. "Stressor Characteristics and PTSD Dimensions in War Victims." *Croatian Medical Journal* 42, 5 (2001): 543–50.

Henry, Bruce. *Friends of God: The Early Huron Church in Canada.* Tomiko, North Bay, 1991.

Herman, Judith. "Complex PTSD: A Syndrome in Survivors of Prolonged and Repeated Trauma." In Geroge Everly and Jeffrey Lating, eds., *Psychotraumatology: Key Papers and Core Concepts in Post-Traumatic Stress,* 87–100. Plenum Press, New York, 1995.

Herrick, James. *Iroquois Medical Botany.* Syracuse University Press, Syracuse, New York, 1994.

Hertel de Rouville, Jean-Baptiste-Melchior. "Généalogie de la famille Hertel." *Nova Francia* 5 (1930): n.p.

Herzfeld, Michael. *Anthropology through the Looking Glass: Critical Ethnography on the Margins of Europe.* Cambridge University Press, Cambridge, 1987.

Hester, Marianne. *Lewd Women and Wicked Witches: A Study in the Dynamics of Male Domination.* London, 1992.

– "Patriarchal Reconstruction and Witch Hunting." In Jonathan Barry, Marianne Hester, and Gareth Roberts, eds., *Witchcraft in Early Modern Europe: Studies in Culture and Belief,* 288–308. Cambridge, New York [1996] 1998.

Hewitt, J.N.B. "The Iroquoian Concept of the Soul." *JAF* 8 (1895): 107–16.

Hickerson, Harold. *Ethnohistory of the Chippewa of Lake Superior.* Garland, New York, 1974.

– "The Feast of the Dead among Seventeenth-Century Algonkians of the Upper Great Lakes." *AA* 62 (1960): 81–107.

– "The Socio-Cultural Significance of Two Chippewa Ceremonials." *AA* 65 (1963): 67–86.

Hilberg, Raul. *The Destruction of the European Jews.* 3 vols. Holmes and Meier, New York, 1985.

Hilgard, Ernest. *Divided Consciousness: Multiple Controls in Human Thought and Action.* expanded ed. Wiley Series in Behavior, Wiley and Sons, New York, 1986.

Hill, Christopher. *A Century of Revolution.* Routledge, London, 1991.

– *The World Turned Upside Down.* Viking Press, New York, 1972.

Himmelfarb, Gertrude. "Some Reflections on the New History." *AHR* 94 (1989): 661–70.

Hinrichs, E. *"'Charivari' und Regebrauchtum in Deutscheland. Forschungsstand und Forschungsaufgaben" in Brauchforschung,* M. Scharfe, Darmstadt, 1991.

Hirschfelder, Arlene, and Martha Kreipe de Montano. *The Native American Almanac: A Portrait of Native America Today.* Macmillan, New York [1993] 1998.

L'histoire du Saguenay depuis l'origine jusqu'à 1870. vol. 1, Edition du Centenaire, Société Historique de la Saguenay, #3, Chicoutimi, 1938.

"Historical Anthropology: The Unwaged Debate." *Focaal: Tijdscrift voor Antropologie.* (1996): 26–27.

Hobsbawm, Eric. "Barbarism: A User's Guide." *New Left Review* 206 (1994): 44–54.

Hobsbawm, Eric, and Terence Ranger. *The Invention of Tradition.* Cambridge University Press, Cambridge, 1983.

Hoeykaas, R. *Religion and the Rise of Modern Science.* Eerdman's, Grand Rapids, MI, 1972.

Hoffer, Peter Charles. *The Devil's Disciples: Makers of the Salem Witchcraft Trials.* Johns Hopkins University Press, Hampton Station, Baltimore, MA, 1991.

Hoffman, Ronald, Mechal Sobel, and Frederika Teute, eds. *Through a Glass Darkly: Reflections on Personal Identity in Early America.* Omohundro Institute of Early American History and Culture, University of North Carolina Press, Chapel Hill, NC, 1997.

Hoffman, W. J. *The Midewiwin or "Grand Medicine Society" of the Ojibwa.* Bureau of American Ethnology Annual Report, 7, 1885–1886, WA, DC, Smithsonian, Institution, 1891.

– "Pictography and Shamanistic Rites of the Ojibwa." *AA* 1 (1888): 209–29.

Hoksman, René and Jan ter Laak. "Adult Foreign Adoptees: Reactive Attachment Disorder May Grow into Psychic Homelessness." *Journal of Social Distress and the Homelessness.* 9, 4 (2000): 291–308.

Holt, Mack. *The French Wars of Religion, 1502–1629.* Cambridge University Press, Cambridge, 1995.

Honigman, John. *Personality in Culture.* Harper and Row, New York, 1967.

Horowitz, Mardi. *Stress Response Syndromes.* 4th ed., Jason Aronson, New Jersey, 2001.

Horrox, Rosemary. *The Black Death.* Manchester University Press, Manchester, 1994.

Houmans, Peter. *Symbolic Loss: The Ambiguity of Mourning and Memory at Century's End.* Charlottesville and London, University of Virginia, 2000.

Howard, Joseph. *Strange Empire: A Narrative of the Northwest.* Minnesota Historical Society, St. Paul, MN (1952) 1994.

Hoxie, Frederick. *Indians in American History: An Introduction.* Arlington Heights, IL, 1988.

Hubert, Henri and Mauss, Marcel. *Sacrifice.* Trans. D. Halls, Cohen, and West, London, 1964.

Huddleston, Lee Eldridge. *Origins of the American Indians: European Concepts, 1492–1729.* University of Texas Press, Austin, TX, 1967.

Huizinga, Johann. *The Autumn of the Middle Ages.* University of Chicago Press, Chicago, 1991.

Hultkrantz, Ake. *Shamanic Healing and Ritual Drama: Health and Medicine in Native North American Religious Traditions.* Crossroads, New York, 1992.
– "A New Look at the World Pillar in Arctic and Subarctic Religion." Paper presented at IAHR Regional Conference on Circumpolar and Northern Religions, Helsinki, 1997.
Hull, A.M. "Neuroimaging Findings in Posttraumatic Stress Disorder: Systematic Review." *British Journal of Psychiatry* 181 (2002): 102–10.
Hunt, George. *The Wars of the Iroquois: A Study in Intertribal Trade Relations.* University of Wisconsin Press, Madison, 1940.
Hunt, Lynn. *The New Cultural History.* University of California, Berkeley, 1989.
Hunter, Edna. "The Vietnam Prisoner of War Experience." In John Wilson and Beverley Raphael, eds., *International Handbook of Traumatic Stress Syndromes.* Plenum Series on Stress and Coping, New York, 1993.
Huppert, George. *Les Bourgeois Gentilhommes: An Essay on the Definition of Elites in Renaissance France.* University of Chicago, Chicago, 1977.
Hurley, John. *Children or Brethern: Aboriginal Rights in Colonial Iroquoia.* University of Saskatchewan, Native Law Centre, Saskatoon, 1985.
Hutton, Patrick. "Of Death and Destiny: the Ariès-Vovelle debate about the history of mourning." In Peter Houmans, *Symbolic Loss: The Ambiguity of Mourning and Memory at Century's End.* Charlottesville and London, University of Virginia, 2000.
Huyssen, Andreas. *Twilight Memories: Marking Time in a Culture of Amnesia.* Routledge, London, 1995.
Ilechuckwu, S.T. "Psychiatry of the Medically Ill in the Burn Unit." *Psychiatric Clinics of North America* 25, 1 (2002): 129–34.
Innis, Harold. *The Fur Trade in Canada.* Yale University Press, New Haven, 1930.
Irwin, Lee. "Contesting World Views: Dreams among the Hurons and Jesuits." *Religion* 22 (1992): 259–70.
Ishikura, R., and N. Tashiro. "Frustration and Fulfilment of Needs in Dissociative and Conversion Disorders." *Psychiatry and Clinical Neurosciences* 56. 4 (2002): 381–90.
Jack, Edward. "Maliseet Legends." *JAF* 8 (1895): 193–207.
Jacob, Paul. *Les revenants de la Beauce.* Boréal Express, Montréal, 1977.
Jacobsen, Lone. *Torture Survivors: A New Group of Patients.* Danish Nurses' Organization, Copenhagen, 1990.
Jacquart, Jean. "La Fronde des princes." *Revue d'histoire moderne et contemporaine* 7 (1960): 257–90.
Jacquin, Philippe. *Les Indiens Blancs.* Pyot, Paris, 1987.
– et Daniel Royot. *Le mythe de l'Ouest: L'Ouest américain et les 'valeurs' de la Frontière.* Editions Autrement, série Monde HS, #71, Paris, 1993.
Jacquin, Philippe, Véronique Weisinger, et Sylvie Péharpré. *Sur le Sentier de la découverte: rencontres franco-indiennes du XVIe au XXe siècle.* Musée national de la coopération franco-américaine, Aisne, 27/6–12/10/92.
Jaenen, Cornelius J. 'Amerindian Views of French Culture in the Seventeenth Century." *CHR* 55 (1974): 261–91. (Countless material kindly given to me by the author.)

- "Conceptual Frameworks for French Views of America and Amerindians." *French Colonial Studies* 2 (1978): 1–22.
- "Education for Francisation: The Case of New France in the Seventeenth Century." *Canadian Journal of Native Education* 2, 1 (1983): 1–19.
- "Evangelisation des Amérindiens de la Nouvelle-France au xviie siècle." *La Société Canadienne d'Histoire de l'Eglise Catholique,* Sessions d'Etude, 35, pp. 33–46.
- *De France en Nouvelle-France: société fondatrice et société nouvelle.* Presses de L'Université d'Ottawa, Ottawa, 1994.
- *The French Régime in the Upper Country of Canada during the Seventeenth Century.* Champlain Society, Toronto, 1996.
- *The French Relationship with the Natives Peoples of New France and Acadia.* DIAND, Ottawa, 1984.
- *Friend and Foe: Aspects of French-Amerindian Cultural Contact in the 16th and 17th Centuries.* McClelland and Stewart, Toronto, 1976.
- "The Indian Problem in the Seveteenth Century." In J.M. Bumstead, ed., *Documentary Problems in Canadian History;* Vol. 1: Pre-Confederation, 1–24. Irwin Dorsey, Georgetown, 1969.
- *The Meeting of the French and Amerindians in the Seventeenth Century.* NLC, Ottawa, 1970.
- "Miscegenation in Eighteenth Century New France." *Second Laurier Conference on North American Ethnohistory and Ethnology,* Huron College, London, 11–14/5/1983, DIAND files paper.
- "Pelleteries et Peaux-Rouges: perceptions françaises de la Nouvelle-France et de ses peuples indigènes aux xvie, xviie et xviiie siècles." *RAQ* 13 (1983): 107–14.
- "Repression or Suppression: Popular Culture in New France." Paper read at Huron College.
- The Rôle of the Church in New France. *CHA,* Ottawa [1976] 1985.
- "The Rôle of Presents in French-Amerindian Trade." In Duncan Cameron, ed., *Explorations in Canadian Economic History,* n.a. University of Ottawa Press, Ottawa, 1985.
- "'Les Sauvages Amériquains': Persistence into the Eighteenth Century of Traditional French Concepts and Constructs for Comprehending Amerindians." *Ethnohistory* 29 (1982): 43–56.
- James, Bernard. "Some Critical Observations Concerning Analyses of Chippewa 'Atomism' and Chippewa Personality." *AA* 56 (1954): 283–6.
- Janoff-Bulman, Ronnie. *Shattered Assumptions: Towards a New Psychology of Trauma.* Macmillan, Free Press, New York, 1992.
- "Jean Bourdon et la Baie d'Hudson." *BRH* 2 (1896): 2–9.
- Jenness, Diamond. *The Indians of Canada.* University of Toronto Press, Toronto, 1977.
- Jennings, Francis. *The Ambiguous Iroquois Empire: The Covenant Chain Confederation of Indian Tribes with English Colonies.* W.W. Norton, New York, 1984.
- "Francis Parkman: A Brahmin among Untouchables." *WMQ* 42 (1985): 305–28.
- *The Invasion of America: Indians, Colonialism, and the Cant of Conquest.* University of North Carolina Press, Chapel Hill, 1975.

– ed., *Iroquois Indians: A Documentary History of the Diplomacy of the Six Nations and their League.* Research Publications, Woodbridge, CT, 1985.

– "A Vanishing Indian: Francis Parkman versus His Sources." *Pennsylvania Magazine of History and Biography* 87 (1963): 306–23.

Jennings, Francis, William Fenton, and Mary Druke, eds. *The History and Culture of Iroquois Diplomacy: An Interdisciplinary Guide to the Treaties of the Six Nations and Their League.* Newberry Library Center for the History of the American Indian, Syracuse Press, Syracuse, 1985.

Jesch, Judith. *Women in the Viking Age.* Boydell Press, Woodbridge, 1994.

Jetten, Marc. *Enclaves amérindiennes: Les "réductions" du Canada, 1637–1701.* Cahiers Célat, Septentrion, Québec, 1994.

La reconnaissance et l'acquisition de la propriété autochtone en Amérique du Nord (17e – 19e siècles): Les cas des nations domiciliées du Canada. CRPA, 13/12/1993, DIAND.

Jochens, Jenny. *Old Norse Images of Women.* University of Pennsylvania Press, Philadelphia, 1996.

Johansen, Bruce. "Native American Societies and the Evolution of Democracy in America. 1600–1800," *Ethnohistory* 37 (1990): 288–90.

Jouhaud, Christian. *Mazarinades: La Fronde des mots.* Aubier, Paris, 1985.

Johnson, Norris. "Cannibals and Culture: The Anthropology of Montaigne." *Dialectical Anthropology* 18 (1993): 153–69.

Johnston, A.L.B. *Proceedings of the French Colonial Historical Society* 15 (1992): 178–88.

Johnston, Sarah Iles. *Restless Dead: Encounters between the Living and the Dead in Ancient Greece.* University of California Press, Berkeley, 1999.

Jolicoeur, Cathérine. *Le vaisseau fantôme.* 2 vols. AFUL, Presses de l'Université Laval, Québec, 1970.

Colins, Colin. "Hospitals in Seventeenth-Century France." *17th-Century French Studies* 7 (1988): 139–52.

Jones, W. "The Algonkin Manitou." *JAF* 18 (1905): 183–90.

Jongleur Songs of Old Québec. Rutgers University Press, New Brunswick, NJ, 1962.

Josephy, Alvin. *The Indian Heritage of America.* Jonathan Cape, London, 1968.

Jouan, Henri. *Jean Nicolet, interprète-voyageur du Canada 1618–1642.* CIHM, #07663.

Judkins, Russell. "An Iroquois Death Messenger Vision." *New York Folklore Quarterly* 29–30 (1973–74): 153–22.

Jung, Karl. *Man and His Symbols.* Dell, New York [1964] 1979.

Jung, Carl, and Carl Kerenyi. *Introduction to the Science of Mythology.* Routledge and Kegan Paul, London, 1970.

Jürgens, Olga. "Recherches sur Louis Hébert et a famille." *MSGCF* 7 (1956): 107–12, 135–45; 9–11 (1958–60): 24–31.

Kafka, Franz. *Metamorphosis and Other Stories.* Penguin Books, London, 1961.

Kapferer, Bruce. *Legends of People, Myths of State: Violence, Intolerance, and Political Culture in Sri Lanka and Australia.* Smithsonian Institute Press, Washington, DC, 1988.

Kaplan, David, and Robert Manners. *Culture Theory.* Foundations of Modern Anthropology Series, Prentice-Hall, Englewood Cliffs, New York, 1972.

Kaplan, Steven, ed. *Understanding Popular Culture.* Mouton, New York and Berlin, 1984.

Kapler, C. *Monstres, démons, et merveilles à la fin du Moyen Age.* Payot, Paris, 1980.

Karlsen, Carol. *The Devil in the Shape of a Woman: Witchcraft in Colonial New England.* Norton, New York and London, 1987.

Kates, Gary, ed. *The French Revolution: Recent Debates and New Controversies.* Routledge, New York, 1998.

Katz, Steven. "Quantity and Interpretation: Issues of the Comparative Historical Analysis of the Holocaust." In *Holocaust and Genocide Studies* 4 (1998): 127–48, esp. 133–7.

Kellogg, Louise. *The French Regime in Wisconsin and the Northwest.* Cooper Square, New York, 1968.

Kennedy, J.H. *Jesuit and Savage in New France.* Yale University Press, New Haven, 1950.

Kenny, Michael. "Disease Process or Social Phenomenon?" *Journal of Nervous and Mental Disease* 186, 8 (1988): 449–54.

– "Trauma, Time, Illness, and Culture: An Anthropological approach to Traumatic Memory." In Paul Antze and Michael Lambek, 151–71. *Tense Past: Cultural Essays in Trauma and Memory.* Routledge, New York, 1996.

Kertzer, David, and Peter Laslett. *Aging in the Past: Demography, Society, and Old Age.* University of California Press, Berkeley, 1995.

Kestenberg, Judith, and Eva Fogelman, eds. *Children during the Nazi Reign.* Praeger, Westport, CT, 1994.

Kidwell, Clara Sue. "Indian Women as Cultural Mediators." *Ethnohistory* 39 (1992): 97–107.

Kieckhefer, Richard. *Forbidden Rites: A Necromancer's Manual of the Fifteenth Century.* Pennsylvania State University Press, University Park, PA, 1997.

– *Magic in the Middle Ages.* Cambridge Medieval Textbooks, Cambridge, 1989.

Kierkegaard, Soren. "Concluding Unscientific Postscript." In *Fear and Trembling, and Sickness and Death,* conclusion. Trans. David Swenson, Princeton, University Press, 1941.

Kim, Uichol, and John Berry, eds. *Indigenous Psychologies: Research and Experience in Cultural Context.* Cross-Cultural Research and Methodology Series, 17, Sage, London, 1993.

Kimmel, Michael. *Absolutism and Its Discontents: State and Society in 17th-Century France and England.* Transaction Books, New Brunswick, NJ, 1974.

Kimmerling, Baruch. *Social Interruption and Besieged Societies: The Case of Israel.* Council on International Studies, SUNY, Special Studies, #121, Amherst, New York, 1979.

Kingsley, Cherry, and Melanie Mark. *Sacred Lives.* National Aboriginal Consultation Project, on-line.

Kinietz, W. Vernon. *The Indians of the Western Great Lakes, 1615–1760.* University of Michigan Press, Ann Arbor Paperbacks [1940] 1965.

Kip, William. *The Early Jesuit Missions in North America.* Wiley and Putnam, New York, 1846.

Kirmayer, Lawrence. "Confusion of the Senses: Implications of Ethnocultural Variations in Somatiform and Dissociative Disorders for PTSD." In Anthony Marsella,

Matthew Friedman, Ellen Gerrity, and Raymond Scurfield, eds., *Ethnocultural Aspects of Postraumatic Stress Disorder: Issues, Research, and Clinical Applications*, ch. 6. American Psychological Association, Washington, DC, 1996.

– ed. *Current Concepts of Somatization, Research and Clinical Perspectives*. American Psychiatric Association, Washington, DC, 1991.

– "Landscapes of Memory: Trauma, Narrative, and Dissociation." In Paul Antze and Michael Lambek, *Tense Past: Cultural Essays in Trauma and Memory*, 173–98. Routledge, New York, 1996.

– "The Mental Health of Aboriginal Peoples: Transformations of Identity and Community." *Canadian Journal of Psychiatry* 45 (2000): 607–16.

Kirmayer, L., G. Brass, C. Tait. "Suicide among Canadian Aboriginal peoples." *Transcultural Psychiatric Research Review* 31, 1 (2000): 3–58.

Kittredge, George. *Witchcraft in Old and New England*. Cambridge University Press, Cambridge, MA, 1929.

Klaits, Joseph. *Servants of Satan: The Age of the Witchhunts*. University of Indiana Press, Bloomington, 1985.

Klein, Laura, and Lillian Ackerman, eds. *Women and Power in Native North America*. University of Oklahoma Press, Norman, 1995.

Kloos, Carla. *YHWH's Combat with the Sea Serpent: A Canaanite Tradition in the Religion of Ancient Israel*. Van Oorschot, Amsterdam, 1986.

Kluckhohn, Clyde. "Myths and Rituals: A General Theory." *Harvard Theological Review* 35 (1942): 45–79.

– *Navaho Witchcraft*. Papers of the Peabody Museum of American Archaeology and Ethnology, 22, #3, Harvard University Press, Cambridge, 1944.

Kluckhohn, Richard, ed. *Culture and Behavior: Essays of Clyde Kluckhohn*. Free Press, New York, 1962.

Knachtel, Philip. *England and the Fronde: the Impact of the English Civil War and the Revolution on France*. Folger Shakespeare Library, Cornell University Press, Ithaca, New York, 1968.

Knauft, Bruce. "Theoretical Currents in Late Modern Cultural Anthropology." *Cultural Dynamics* 9 (1997): 277–300.

Kogan, Ilany. *The Cry of Mute Children: A Psychoanalytic Perspective of the Second Generation of the Holocaust*. Free Association Books, London, 1995.

Kohl, J.G. *Kitchi-Gami: Legend and Lore of the Ojibway Indians of the Lake Superior Country*. Ross and Haines, Inc., Minneapolis, MN [1860] 1956.

Kohut, H. *The Restoration of the Self*. International Universities, Press, New York, 1977.

Koppedrayer, K.I. "The Making of the First Iroquois Virgin: Early Jesuit Biography of the Blessed Kateri Tekakwitha." *Ethnohistory* 40 (1993): 277–306.

Kors, Alan, and Edward Peters. *Witchcraft in Europe 1100–1700: A Documentary History*. University of Pennsylvania Press, Phildelphia, 1972.

Kossman, Ernst. *La Fronde*. Universitaire pers Leiden, Leiden, 1954.

Kristeva, Julia. *Strangers to Ourselves*. Columbia University Press, New York, 1991.

Kroeger, J. *Identity Development: Adolescence through Adulthood*. Sage, London, 2000.

Krystal, Henry, and W. Niederland. "Clinical Observations on the Survivor Syndrome." In Henry Krystal, *Massive Psychic Trauma*. International Universities Press, New York, 1969.

– *Integration and Self-Healing: Affect, Trauma, and Alexithymia*. Analytic Press, Hillsdale, New Jersey, 1988.

– *Massive Psychic Trauma*. International Universities Press, New York, 1969.

Krystal, Henry. "The Emerging Neurobiology of Dissociative States: Relevance to PTSD." In Arieh Shalev, Rachel Yehuda, and Alexander McFarlane. *International Handbook of Human Response to Trauma*, 307–17. Kluwer Academic/Plenum, New York, 2000.

Kselman, Thomas. *Death and the Afterlife in Modern France*. Princeton University Press, Princeton, 1993.

Kubany, Edward, and Stephen Abueg. "Development and Validation of the Trauma-Related Inventory (TRGI)." *Psychological Assessment* 8 (1996): 428–44.

Kuper, Adam. "The Historian's Revenge: Book Review of George Stocking's Functionalism Historicized: Essays on British Social Anthropology." *History of Anthropology*, vol. 2, University of Wisconsin, Madison, 1984.

– *The Invention of Primitive Society*. Routledge, London, 1998.

Kügler, Dietmar. *In der Wildnis die Freiheit: Trapper, Mountain Men, Pelzhändler, der amerikanische Pelzhandel*. Verlag für Amerikanistik, Wyk auf Foehr, BRD, 1989.

Kurath, Gertrude. "Notes and Queries: The Iroquois Ohgiwe Death Feast." *JAF* 63 (1905): 62–3.

La Barre, Weston. "Le rêve, le charisme, et le héros culturel." Dans Roger Callois et Gustave von Grunebaum, éds. *Le rêve et les sociétés humaines*. Gallimard, Paris, 1967.

Laberge, Lionel. *Rouen et le commerce du Canada de 1650 à 1670*. Ed. Bois Lotinville, l'Ange-gardien, 1972.

Laberge, Yves. *L'Ouest français et la francophonie nord-américaine*. Actes du Colloque international de la francophonie tenu à Angers, 26–29/5/1995, Angers, 1996.

Lacapra, Dominick. "Chartier, Darnton, and the great symbol massacre." *Journal of Modern History* 60 (1988): 95–112.

– *Rethinking Intellectual History: Texts, Contexts, Language*. Academic Paperback Editions, Cornell University Press, Ithaca, New York, 1983.

Lacey, Laurie. *Micmac Medicines: Remedies and Recollections*. Nimbus Publishing, Halifax, 1993.

Lachance, André. *Le bourreau au Canada français sous le Régime français*. Société historique de Québec, Québec, 1966.

– "Une étude de mentalité: les injures verbales au Canada au XVIIIe siècle (1712–1748)." *RHAF* 41 (1977): 229–38.

Lachance, Paul. "L'effet du déséquilibre des sexes sur le comportement matrimonial: comparaison entre la Nouvelle-France, St-Domingue, et la Nouvelle-Orléans. *RHAF* 39 (1985): 211–31.

Lafaille, Anne-Cathérine. "Une altérité radicale: rencontre avec le cannibale du nouveau monde." *Canadian Folklore Canadien* 18 (1996): 129–55.

Laflèche, Guy. *Les saints martyrs Canadiens*. 5 vols. Ed. du Singulier, Laval, 1990–95.

Lafleur, Norman. *La vie traditionelle du coureur de bois aux XIXe et XXe siècles*. Leméac, Ni-t'chawama (mon ami mon frère), Montréal, 1973.

Laforce, Hélène. *Histoire de la sage-femme dans la région de Québec*. coll. Edmond-de-Nevers, #4, IQRC, 1985.

Lagarde, André et Laurent Michard. *XVIIIe siècle*. Collection Textes et Litérature, Larousse- Bordas, Paris, 1997.

– *XVIIe siècle*. Collection Textes et Litérature, Larousse-Bordas, Paris, 1998.

Lagrave, Jean-Paul. *La liberté d'expression en Nouvelle-France, 1608–1760*. Ed. de Lagrave, Montréal, 1975.

Lahaise, Robert. "Rabelais et la médecine populaire au Québec." *Ethnologie québecoise*, I, Les cahiers de Québec, Hurtubise HMH, Montréal, 1972, 45–69.

La Horbe, Florian. *L'incroyable secret de Champlain*. Ed. du Mont Pagnote, Paris, 1959.

Lambert, Monique. *Le premier ménage trifluvienne: Jean-Godefroy et Marie Leneuf*. Société régionale de Trois Rivières, Trois Rivières, 1959 (?).

Lambert, Serge. "Les pauvres et la société à Québec de 1681–1744." PhD, Université, Laval, Québec, 1990.

Lamontagne, Sophie-Laurence. *L'hiver dans la culture québecoise XVIIe-XIXe siècles*. IQRC, Québec, 1983.

Lanctôt, Gustave. "Une accusation contre Monseigneur de Laval." La société Canadienne d'histoire de l'église catholique, *Rapport*, 1944–45.

– "Contes populaires Canadiens." *JAF* 36 (1923): 205–71 (4e série)

– "Contes populaires Canadiens." *JAF* 44 (1931): 225–95 (6e série)

– "The Elective Council of Québec." *CHR* 15 (1934): 123–32.

– *A History of Canada*. Vol. I. Clarke, Irwin, and Co., Toronto, 1963.

– *Montréal sous Maisonneuve 1672–1665*. Beauchemin, Montréal, 1966.

– "Position de la Nouvelle-France en 1663." *RHAF* 11 (1958): 517–32.

Landes, Ruth. "The Abnormal among the Ojibwa." *Journal of Abnormal and Social Psychology* 33 (1938): 14–33.

– *Ojibwa Religion and the Midewiwin*. University of Madison Wisconsin Press, Madison, 1968.

– *The Ojibwa Woman*. Columbia University Press, New York, 1938.

Langer, Lawrence. *Admitting the Holocaust: Collected Essays*. Oxford University Press, New York, 1995.

– *Holocaust Testimonials: The Ruins of Memory*. Yale University Press, New Haven, 1991.

Langlois, Georges. *Histoire de la population Canadienne-Française*. Albert Levesque, Montréal, 1935.

Lannoy, Richard. *The Speaking Tree: A Study of Indian Culture and Society*. Oxford University Press, Oxford, 1971.

Lapierre, Guy. "Note: les Attitudes devant la Mort: sur deux ouvrages récents." *RHAF* 32 (1978): 251–5.

Laqueur, Walter, ed. *The Terrorism Reader: A Historical Anthology*. Signet Classics, New York, 1978.

Larin, Robert. *La contribution du Haut-Poitou au peuplement de la Nouvelle-France.* Ed. d'Acadie, Moncton, NB, 1994.

Larner, Christina. *Enemies of God: The Witchhunt in Scotland.* Oxford University Press, Blackwell, London [1980] 1983.

– *Witchcraft and Religion: The Politics of Popular Belief.* Basil Blackwell, Oxford, 1984.

Larocque, Robert. "Le rôle de la contagion dans la conquête des Amériques." *RAQ* 18 (1988): 5–15.

LaRose, André. *Les registres paroissiaux au Québec avant 1800.* Presses de l'Université Laval, Québec, 1979.

Larue, Hubert. "Les chansons populaires et historiques du Canada." *Le Foyer canadien,* vol. 1, Québec, 1869.

Lavie, Peretz, and Hanna Kaminer. "Sleep, Dreaming, and Coping Style in Holocaust Survivors." In Deidre Barrett, ed., *Trauma and Dreams,* 114–24. Harvard University Press, Cambridge MA, 1996.

Leach, J. "Personality Profiles of Potential Prisoners of War and Evaders." *Military Psychology* 14, 1 (2002): 73–81.

Leacock, Eleonor. *The Montagnais "Hunting Territory" and the Fur Trade.* American Anthropological Association, 56, #5, part 2, memoir #78, 1950.

– *Myths of Male Dominance: Collected Articles on Women Cross-Culturally.* Monthly Review Press, New York, 1981.

Leavitt, Robert, and David Francis. *Wapapi Akonutomakonol, The Wampum Records: Wabnaki Traditional Laws.* Micmac-Maliseet Institute, University of New Brunswick, Frederickton, NB, 1990.

Le Ber, Joseph. "Les Origines de la famille Le Moine." *RHAF* 1 (1948): 101–7.

LeBlant, Robert. "Documents inédits: Notes sur Madame de Bullion Bienfaitrice de l'Hôtel-Dieu de Montréal 1587–1664." *RHAF* 12 (1958): 112–25.

– "La Famille Boullé, 1586–1639." *RHAF* 18 (1963–64): 55–69.

Le Blant, Robert, et Marcel Delafosse. "Les Rochelais dans la Vallée du St-Laurent 1599–1618." *RHAF* 10 (1956): 333–63.

LeBraz, Anatole. *La Légende de la mort chez les Bretons armoricans.* 2 vols., Honoré Champion, Paris, 1990.

LeBrun, François et Normand Séguin, éds. *Sociétés villageoises et rapports villes-campagnes au Québec et dans la France de l'ouest XVIIe-XXe siècle.* Actes du colloque franco-québécois de Québec, Centre de Recherche en études québécoises, Université du Québec à Trois Rivières, et Presses Universitaires de Rennes, Trois Rivières et Rennes, 1987.

LeClerc, Jean. "Denonville et les Galériens Iroquois." *RHAF* 14 (1960): 408–558.

Lecouteux, Claude. *Fées, sorcières, et loups-grous au Moyen âge.* Imago, Paris, 1992.

Lecouteux, Claude et Philippe Marcq. *Les esprits et les morts.* Champion, Paris, 1990.

Lee, Alyssa, Isaac Mohan, and Alexander Janca. "Postraumatic Stress Disorder and Terrorism." *Current Opinion in Psychiatry* 15, 6 (2002): 633–7.

Lee, Ronald, J. Colby Martin. *Psychology after Kohut: A Textbook of Self Psychology.* The Analytic Press, Hillsdale, NJ, 1991.

Lefebvre, Madeleine. *Tsakapesh, récit montagnais-naskapi.* Série cultures amérin-diennes, Ministère des Affaires Culturelles, Québec, 1974.

Lefebvre, P. "Aspects de la fidelité en France au XVIIe siècle." *Revue historique* 20 (1973): 59–106.

Lefort, Claude. "La Révolution comme religion nouvelle." In François Furet and Mona Ozouf, éds. *The French Revolution and the Creation of Modern Political Culture.* Vol. 3. Pergamon, Oxford, 1987–94, 391–9.

LeFranc, Abel. *La vie quotidienne au temps de la Renaissance.* Hachette, Paris, 1938.

Legaré, Clément. *Beau Sauvage et autres contes de la Mauricie.* coll. Mémoires d'homme, Presses de l'Université de Québec, Silléry, 1990.

– *Pierre la Fève et autres contes de la Mauricie.* coll. Mémoires d'hommes, Quinze, Montréal, 1982.

– *La bête à sept têtes et autres contes de la Mauricie.* Quinze, Montréal, 1980.

Le Goff, Jacques. *The Birth of Purgatory.* Trans. Arthur Goldhammer, University of Chicago, Chicago [1981] 1984.

– *La naissance du Purgatoire.* Gallimard, Paris [1981] 1991.

– *L'Imaginaire médievale: essais.* Gallimard, Paris, 1985.

Le Héricher. *Littérature populaire de Normandie.* Mémoires de la Société d'archaeo-logie, 1littérature, sciences et arts de arrondissements d'Avranches et de Mortain, 7, 1885.

Leiblich, Amia. *Seasons of Captivity: The Inner World of POWs.* New York University Press, New York, 1994.

Leland, Charles Geoffrey. *The Algonquin Legends of New England or Myths and Folklore of the Micmac, Passamaquoddy, and Penobscot Tribes.* Houghton Mifflin, Boston, 1884.

– "The Edda among the Algonquin Indians." In William Clements, ed., *Native Ameri-can Folklore in 19th-Century Periodicals.* Swallow Press, Ohio University Press, Athens, OH, 1986.

– "Liberty, Equality, and Fraternity: Was the Indian Really Egalitarian?" pp. 145–68, offprint, DIAND.

Lemay, Diane. "La perception de la femme amérindienne par les missionaires de la Nouvelle- France." Thèse de maîtrise, Université d'Ottawa, 1992.

Lemay, Michel. "Le voyageur dans le pays d'en haut à travers quelques romans et quelques Récits." *Ethnologie québecoise,* 1, Les cahiers de Québec, Éditions Hurtubise, Montréal, 1972, 127–30.

Lemieux, Denise. *Les petits innocents: L'enfance en Nouvelle-France.* Institut Québécois de la Recharche sur la Culture, Québec, 1985.

Le Moine, Sir James. *The Legends of the St. Lawrence.* Holliwell, La Cie d'imprimerie de Québec, Seaside series, 1898.

Le rossignol y chante, Répertoire de la chanson folklorique française au Canada. Vol. 1. Musée nationale de l'homme, Bulletin #175, #52 Série anthropologique [1979] 1982.

Le Roux de Lincy, Antoine Jean Victor, ed. *Registres de la ville de Paris pendant la Fronde: suivis d'une relation de ce qui s'est passé dans la ville et l'abbaye de St-Denis à la même époque.* Renouard, Paris, 1846.

Le Roy Ladurie, Emmanuel. *L'argent, l'amour, et la mort en pays d'Occitane.* Ed. du Seuil, Paris, 1980.

– *Histoire du climat depuis l'an mil.* Flammarion, Paris, 1983.

– *The Royal French State, 1460–1610.* Basil Blackwell, Oxford, 1994.

LeTenneur, René. *Les Normans et les origines du Canada français.* Presses de l'Imp. OCEP, Coutances, 1973.

Létourneau, Henri. *Henri Létourneau raconte ....* Ed. Bois-Brûlé, Winnipeg, 1980.

Lessard, Rénald. "Les faux sauniers et la peuplement de la Nouvelle-France." *L'Ancêtre* 14 (1987): 83–95; 14 (1987): 138–46; 14 (1988): 175–9.

Levack, Brian. *The Witchhunt in Early Modern Europe.* Longman, London and New York [1987] 1995.

Levi, Primo. *The Drowned and the Saved.* Trans. Raymond Rosenthal, Abacus, Simon and Schuster [1986] 1988.

– *Survival in Auschwitz.* Summit, New York, 1986.

Levinas, Emmanuel. *Altereity and Trancendence.* Trans. Michael Smith, Columbia University Press, New York, 1999.

– *Entre nous: On Thinking-of-the-Other.* Trans. Michael Smith and Barbara Harshav, Columbia University Press, 1998.

– *Humanism of the Other.* Trans. Nidra Poller, University of Illinois Press, Urbana and Chicago, 2003.

Levine, Peter. *Waking the Tiger: Healing Trauma – The Innate Capacity to Transform Overwhelming Experiences.* North Atlantic Books, Berkeley, CA, 1997.

Lévy-Bruhl, Lucien. *L'âme primitive.* Alcan, Paris, 1927.

Lévi-Strauss, Claude. *Anthropology and Myth: Lectures 1951–1982.* Trans. Roy Willis, Basil Blackwell, London, 1984.

– *Histoire de lynx.* Plon, Paris, 1991.

– *L'homme nu.* Plon, Paris [1971] 1997.

– *Myth and Meaning.* Schoken, New York, 1979.

– *Paroles données.* Plon, Paris, 1984.

– *La pensée sauvage.* Plon, Paris, 1962.

– *Race et Histoire.* Gonthier, Paris, 1968.

– *Le regard éloignée.* Plon, Paris, 1983.

– *Les structures élémentaires de la parenté.* Presses Universitaires de France, Paris, 1949.

Lifton, Robert. *Thought Reform and the Psychology of Totalism: Brainwashing in China.* Pelican, Harmondsworth, 1961.

Lilla, Mark. *Giovanni Bernard Vico: The Making of an Antimodern.* Cambridge, MA, 1993.

Limerick, Patricia Nelson. "Turnerians All: The Dream of a Helpful History in an Intelligible World." *AHR* 100 (1995): 697–716.

Lincoln, Bruce. *Myth, Cosmos, and Society.* Harvard University Press, Cambridge, 1986.

Lips, Julius. *Naskapi Law: Lake St. John and Lake Mistassini Bands – Law and Order in a Hunting Society.* American Philosophical Society, 1947 (DIAND).

– *The Savage Hits Back.* Yale University Press, New Haven, CN, 1937.

Littlefield, Lorraine. "Women Traders in the Maritime Fur Trade." In Bruce Cox, *Native Peoples, Native Lands: Canadian Indians, Inuit, and Métis,* 173–85. Carleton University Press, Ottawa, [1987] 1992.

Littleton, C. Scott and Linda Malcor. *From Scythia to Camelot: A Radical Reassessment of the Legends of King Arthur, the Knights of the Round Table, and the Holy Grail.* Garland, New York, 1994.

Livanou, M., M. Basoglu, I.M. Marks, P. De Silva, H. Noshirvani, K. Lovell, S. Thrasher. "Beliefs, Sense of Control, and Treatment Outcome in Postraumatic Stress Disorder." *Psychological Medicine* 32, 1 (2002): 157–65.

Lloyd, Christopher. *Explanation in Social History.* Basil Blackwell, Oxford, 1986.

Loomis, Arthur. *Celtic Myth and Arthurian Romance.* Columbia University Press, New York, 1927.

– *Arthurian Literature in the Middle Ages.* Clarendon Press, Oxford, 1959.

Lorris, Pierre-Georges. *La Fronde.* Albin Michel, Paris, 1961.

Lossky, Andrew. *Louis XIV and the French Monarchy.* Rutgers University Press, New Brunswick, NJ, 1994.

Lowenthal, David. *The Heritage Crusade and the Spoils of History.* Cambridge University Press, Cambridge, 1998.

– *The Past Is a Foreign Country.* Cambridge University Press, Cambridge, 1985.

Lubinskaya, Maya. *French Absolutism: The Crucial Phase, 1620–1629.* Cambridge University Press, Cambridge, 1968.

Lucas, Colin, ed. *Rewriting the French Revolution.* Oxford University Press, Oxford, 1991.

Lunn, Jean. "The Illegal Fur Trade Out of New France, 1713–1760." *CHAR,* 1939, ch. 2.

Lynch, Kathryn. *The High Medieval Dream Vision.* Stanford University Press, Stanford, 1988.

Maccoby, Hyman. *The Sacred Executioner: Human Sacrifice and the Legacy of Guilt.* Thames and Hudson, London, 1982.

MacCana, Proinsias. *Celtic Mythology.* Hamlyn, London, 1970.

MacCulloch, John. *The Celtic and Scandinavian Religions.* Hutchinson's University Press, London, 1948.

MacFarlane, Alan. *Witchcraft in Tudor and Stuart England: A Regional and Comparative Study.* Harper and Row, New York, 1970.

Macksoud, Mona, Atle Dyregrov, and Magne Raundalen. "Traumatic War Experiences and Their Effects upon Children." In John Wilson and Beverley Raphael, eds., *International Handbook of Traumatic Stress Syndromes,* 625–34. Plenum Series on Stress and Coping, New York, 1993.

MacLeod, Peter. "Microbes and Muskets: Smallpox and the Participation of the Amerindian Allies in New France in the Seven Years War." *Ethnohistory* 39 (1992): 42–64.

Magnussen, Roger. *Education in New France.* McGill-Queen's University Press, Montréal, 1992.

Mahdi, Louise Carus, Steven Foster, and Meredith Little, eds. *Betwixt and Between: Patterns of Masculine and Feminine Initiation.* Open Court, LaSalle, IL, 1987.

Maher, Alvin. *Experiencing: A Humanistic Theory of Psychology and Psychiatry.* University of Ottawa Press, Ottawa, 1989.

Mahler, Margaret. *The Selected Papers of Margaret Mahler.* Aronson, New York, 1979.

Maier, Charles. *The Unmasterable Past: History, Holocaust, and German National Identity.* Harvard University Press, Cambridge, 1988.

Mailhot, José. "La glorification du mâle dans le vocabulaire cri et montagnais." *RAQ* 13 (1983): 291–7.

Maland, David. *Europe in the Seventeenth Century.* Macmillan, London [1961] 1967.

Malchelosse, Gérard. "Nicolas Perrot au Fort St-Antoine." *Cahiers des Dix* 17 (1952): 111–36.

– "Peuples sauvages de la Nouvelle-France (1600–1670)." *Cahiers des Dix* 28 (1963): 63–92.

Mali, Anya. "The Dynamics of Conversion: The Mystical and Missionary Experience of Marie de L'Incarnation." PhD, Hebrew University of Jerusalem, 1990.

Mali, Joseph. "Narrative, Myth, and History." *Science in Context* 7 (1994): 121–42.

Malinowski, Bronislaw. *The Dynamics of Culture Change.* Yale University Press, New Haven, CT, 1945.

– "Myth in Primitive Psychology." In *Magic, Science, and Religion and other Essays.* Anchor Books, Doubleday and Co., New York, 1954.

Mancall, Peter. *Deadly Medicine: Indians and Alcohol in Early America.* Cornell University Press, Ithaca, New York, 1995.

Mandrou, Robert. "Les français hors de France au XVIe et XVIIe siècles." *Annales* 14 (1959): 662-75.

– *Magistrats et sorciers en France au XVIIe siècle: une analyse de psychologie historique.* Plon, Paris, 1968.

– *Possession et sorcellerie au XVIIe siècle: textes inédits.* Fayard, Paris, 1979.

Manson, Spero, Janette Beals, Theresa O'Nell, Joan Piasecki, Donald Bechtold, Ellen Keane, and Monica Jones. "Wounded Spirits, Ailing Hearts: PTSD and Related Disorders among American Indians." In Anthony Marsella, Matthew Friedman, Ellen Gerrity, and Raymond Scurfield, éds. *Ethnocultural Aspects of Postraumatic Stress Disorder: Issues, Research, and Clinical Applications,* chap. 10. American Psychological Association, Washington DC, 1996.

Mantero, M., and Crippa, L. Eating Disorders and Chronic Post-Traumatic Stress Disorder: Issues of Psychopathology and Co-Morbidity." *European Eating Disorders Review* 10, 1 (2002): 1–16.

Marin, C., and Carron, R. "Historical Development of the Concept of Somatisation." *Evolution Psychiatrique* 67, 3 (2002): 506–15.

Marcuse, Herbert. *Eros and Civilisation: A Philosophical Inquiry into Freud.* Beacon, Boston [1955] 1965.

Margalit, Gilad. "HaIsuk haGizani beTsoanim beGermania misof haMea haTsha Esre vead 1945 veMkorotea." *Historia,* The Historical Society of Israel, Jerusalem, 1998, 95–120.

Marion, Séraphin. *Pierre Boucher: un pionnier canadien.* Proulx, Québec, 1927.

Markale, Jean. *Brocéliande et l'enigme du Graal.* Pygmalion, Gérard Watelet, 1988.

Markussen, Eric, and David Kopf. *The Holocaust and Strategic Bombing: Genocide and Total War in the 20th Century.* Westview Press, Boulder, CO, 1995.

Marquis, Thomas. *The War Chief of the Ottawas: Chronicle of the Pontiac War.* Series Chronicles of Canada, 15, University of Toronto Press, Toronto [1915] 1964.

Marr, Wilhelm. *Der Seig des Judenthums über das Germanthum.* 12 Aufl., Constable, Bern, 1879.

Martijn, Charles. "Les Malécites et la traite des fourrures." *RAQ* 24 (1994): 25–43.

– ed. *Les Micmacs et la mer.* Collection Signes des Amériques, Montréal, 1986.

Martin, Calvin. *Keepers of the Game: Indian-Animal Relationships and the Fur Trade.* University of CA, Berkeley, 1978.

Martinez, José. *Dead Sea Scrolls: Study Edition.* Brill, Leiden, 1997–98.

Marx, Jean. *La légende Arthurienne et le Graal.* Presses Universitaires de France, Paris, 1952.

Massicotte, Edouard.-Zotique. "Chirurgiens, Apothécaires, etc., sous le Régime Français." *BRH* 31 (1925): 166–70.

– *Dollard des Ormeaux et ses compagnons: notes et documents.* Comité du Monument Dollard des Ormeaux, Montréal, 1920.

– "La guignolée." *BRH* 28 (1922): 365–7.

– "Les chirurgiens, médecins, etc., etc., de Montréal, sous le régime français." *RAPQ* 3 (1922–23): 131–55.

– "La petite histoire." dans *La Presse,* Montréal, 6/2/1924.

– "Les seigneuries de Jean Bourdon." *BRH* 42 (1936): 336–40.

Massignon, Geneviève, éd. *Contes de l'Ouest, Brière-Vendée-Angoumois.* Ed. Erasme, Paris, 1954.

– ed. *Folktales of France.* University of Chicago Press, Chicago, 1968.

Masta, Henry. *Abenaki Indian Legends.* Voix des Bois-Francs, Victoriaville, Quebec, 1932.

Matthews Grieco, Sara. *Ange ou Diablesse: la representation dela femme au XVIe siècle.* Flammarion, Paris, 1991.

Mattingly, Cheryl, and Linda Garro. *Narrative and the Cultural Construction of Illness and Healing.* University of California, Berkeley, 2000.

– *Narrative Representation of Illness and Healing,* Pergamon, Exeter, UK, 1994.

Maurras, Charles. *Mes idées politiques.* Fayard, Paris [1937] 1973.

Maurault, Joseph. *Histoire des Abenaquis depuis 1605 jusqu'à nos jours.* Johnson rep., Mouton, Den Haag, 1969.

Mauss, Marcel. *Sociologie et anthropologie.* Quadridge, Presses Universitaires de France, Paris, 1993.

Mavromatis, Andreas. *Hypnogogia.* Routledge, London and New York [1987] 1991.

Maybury-Lewis, David and Uri Almagor, eds. *The Attraction of Opposites: Thought and Society in a Dualistic Mode.* University of Michigan Press, Ann Arbor, MI, 1989.

Mayer, Arno. *Why Did the Heavens Not Darken? The Final Solution in History.* Pantheon Books, New York, 1990.

Mazian, Florence. *Why Genocide? The Armenian and Jewish Experiences in Perspective.* Iowa State University Press, Ames, Iowa, 1990.

McCarthy, Dolores. "Identity Issues of Parents Who Adopt Children Internationally." Dissertation Abstracts International, University Microfilms, Ann Arbor, MI, Oct 1999.

McDougall, John. "The Frontier in the History of New France." *CHAR* n.v. (1929): 121–6.

McEwen, B. "The Neurobiology and Neuroendocrinology of Stress: Implications for Posttraumatic Stress Disorder from a Basic Science Perspective." *Psychiatric Clinics of North America* 25, 2 (2002): 469–70.

McGee, H.F. *The Native Peoples of Atlantic Canada: A History of Ethnic Interaction.* Carleton Library Series, McClelland and Stewart, Toronto, 1974. pp. 199–214.

– "Windigo Psychosis." *AA* 74 (1972): 244–6.

McGee, Whitehead. *The Micmac.* Nimbus Pubs., Chelsea Green, White River Junction, VT, 1991.

McIlwain, C.H., ed. *An Abridgement of the Indian Affairs .... Transacted in the colony of New York from the year 1678 to the year 1751,* by Peter Wraxell. Harvard Historical Studies #21, Cambridge, 1915.

McLaughlan, Virginia. *Immigration Reconsidered: Historical Sociology and Politics.* Oxford University Press, Oxford, 1990.

McLean, Donald. *1885: Métis rebellion or government conspiracy?* Pemmican Pubs., Winnipeg, 1985.

McNeill, William. "Mythistory, or Truth, Myth, History, and Historians." *AHR* 91 (1986): 1–10.

McNickle, D'Arcy. *Native American Tribalism: Indian Survivals and Renewals.* Institute of Race Relations, Oxford University Press, Oxford, 1973.

McPherson Le Moine, James. *The Legends of the St. Lawrence.* Holiwell, Québec, 1898.

Mechling, W.H. "Maliseet Tales." *JAF* 26 (1913): 219–58.

Mead, George. *On Social Psychology: Selected Papers.* University of Chicago, Chicago, 1964.

Meinig, D.W. *The Shaping of America: A Geographical Perspective on 500 Years of History.* Vol. 1: *Atlantic America, 1492–1800.* Yale University Press, New Haven, 1986.

Mélusine. Congrès de Niort, "La tradition en Poitou et Charentes." Société d'Ethnographie nationale et d'art populaire, 1896, rep. 1981, Brissaud, Poitiers.

Memmi, Albert. *The Coloniser and the Colonised.* Souvenir, London, 1991.

Menkis, Richard. "Historiography, Myth, and Group Relations: Jewish and Non-Jewish Quebecois on Jews and New France." *Canadian Ethnic Studies* 23 (1991): 24–38.

Mennell, Stephen. "The American Civilizing Process." In Thomas Salumets, ed., *Norbert Elias and Human Interdependencies.* 226–44. McGill-Queen's University Press, Montreal, 2001.

– "The Other Side of the Coin: Decivilizing Processes." In Thomas Salumets ed. *Norbert Elias and Human Interdependencies,* 32–49. McGill-Queen's University Press, Montreal, 2001.

Merckelbach, H. Devilly, G. Rassin, E. "Alters in Dissociative Identity Disorder: Metaphors or Genuine Entities?." *Clinical Psychology Review* 22, 3 (2002): 481–97.

Merlin, Hélène. *Public et littérature en France au XVIIe siècle.* coll. Histoire, les belles lettres, Paris, 1994.

Merrell, James. *The Indian's World: The Catawbas and Their Neighbors from European Contact through the Era of Their Removal.* Chapel Hill, NC, 1989.

– "Some Thoughts on Colonial Historians." *WMQ* 46 (1989): 94–119.

Merrick, Jeffery. "Fathers and Kings: Patriarchalism and Absolutism in 18th-Century French Politics." *Studies on Voltaire and the 18th Century* 308 (1993): 281–303.

Meshulam, M. Marsel. *Principles of Behavioral and Cognitive Neurology.* 2nd ed., Oxford, New York, 2000.

Méthivier, Hubert. *La Fronde.* série Historien, PUF, Paris, 1984.

Meurger, Daniel. *Monstres des lacs de Québec: Mythes et troublantes réalités.* Stanké, Montréal, 1992.

Meyer, Jean. *La noblesse bretonne au XVIIIe siècle.* 2 vols. N.p. Paris, 1966.

Micha, Alexandre. *Etudes sur le Merlin de Robert de Boron.* Droz, Genève, 1980.

Michaud, Jean. *La Renaissance et les temps modernes 1492–1789.* coll. Isaac, Classiques Hachette, Paris, 1970.

Michaelson, Truman. "Micmac Tales." *JAF* 33 (1925): 33–133.

Michelet, Jules. *Des Jésuites.* Pauvert, Paris, 1966.

– *La Sorcière.* Garnier-Flammarion, Paris [1862] 1966.

Midelfort, Eric. *Witchhunting in Southwestern Germany, 1562–1684.* Stanford University Press, Stanford, CA, 1972.

Migliore, Sam. "The Doctor, the Lawyer, and the Melancholy Witch." *Anthropologica* 25 (1983): 163–92.

Mignolo, Walter. *The Darker Side of the Renaissance: Literacy, Territoriality, and Colonization.* University of Michigan Press, Ann Arbor, 1997.

Mikesell, Marvin. "Comparative Studies in Frontier History." *Annals of the Association of American Geographers* 50 (1960): 62–74.

Miller, Christine, Patricia Chuchryk, with Maria Smallface Marule, Brenda Manyfingers, and Cheryl Deering, eds. *Women of the First Nations: Power, Wisdom, and Strength.* University of Manitoba, Winnipeg, 1996.

Miller, Thomas, ed. *Clinical Disorders and Stressful Life Events.* International Universities Press, Stress and Health Series, #7, Madison, CT, 1997.

Millett, Kate. *The Politics of Cruelty: An Essay on the Literature of Political Imprisonment.* Norton, New York, 1994.

Milner, Clyde, II, ed. *A New Significance: Reenvisioning the History of the American West.* Oxford University Press, Oxford, 1996.

Milot, Jocelyn. *Encyclopaedie de la dévotion à sainte Anne,* Presses de l'Université Laval, Québec, 1978.

Minois, Georges. *Histoire des Enfers.* Fayard, Paris, 1991.

– *History of Old Age from Antiquity to the Renaissance.* Trans. Sarah Tenison, University of Chicago Press, Chicago, 1989.

Mirsky Julia. "HeVetim Psychologim beHagira: Skirat Sefrut." *Psychologia* 5 (1996): 199–214.

Mitchell, E. *Messire Pierre Boucher, seigneur de Boucherville 1622–1717.* Librairie Beauchemin, Montréal, 1967.

Mithus veZicharon: Gilgulaya shel haToda'a haIsraelit. Machon Van Leer, Yerushalayim, 1996. (In Hebrew.)

Moerman, Daniel. *Medicinal Plants of Native America.* 2 vols. University of Michigan Museum of Anthropology, Technical Reports, #19, Research Reports in Ethnobotany, #2, Ann Arbor, 1986.

Mollat, Michel. *Histoire de Rouen.* Univers de la France et des pays francophones, série Histoire des villes, Toulouse, 1979.

– *The Poor in the Middle Ages: An Essay in Social History.* Trans, Arthur Goldhammer, Yale University Press, New Haven, 1986.

Mollica, Richard, Xingjia Cui, Keith McInnes, and Michael Massagli. "Science-Based Policy for Psychosocial Interventions in Refugee Camps: A Cambodian Example." *Journal of Nervous and Mental Disease* 190, 3 (2002): 158–66.

– "The Trauma Story: Psychiatric Care of Refugee Survivors of Violence and Torture." In *Posttraumatic Stress Disorder Therapy and Victims of Violence,* 295–314. Brunner/Mazel Pubs., Psychosocial Stress, Series #11, 1988.

Mondoux, Soeur. "Les 'hommes' de Montréal." *RHAF* 2 (1948): 59–80.

Monter, Edward William. *European Witchcraft.* Wiley and Sons, New York, 1969.

– *Ritual, Myth, and Magic in Early Modern Europe.* Harvester Press, Sussex, 1983.

– "The Pedestal and the Stake: Courtly Love and Witchcraft." In Renate Bridenthal and Claudia Koonz, eds. *Becoming Visible: Women in European History.* Boston, 1977.

– *Ritual, Myth, and Magic in Early Modern Europe.* Harvester Press, Sussex, 1983.

– "Toads and Eucharists: The Male Witches of Normandy, 1564–1660." *French Historical Studies* 20 (1997): 563–95.

– *Witchcraft in France and Switzerland: The Borderland during the Reformation.* Ithaca, New York, 1976.

Moogk, Peter. *Building a House in New France.* McClelland and Stewart, Toronto, 1968.

– "In the Darkness of a Basement: Craftsmen Associations in Early French Canada." In Michael Cross and George Kealey, *Economy and Society during the French Regime to 1759,* 88–119. Readings in Canadian Social History, I, McClelland and Stewart, Toronto, 1983. 88–119.

– "Les petits Sauvages: The Children of 18th-Century New France." In Joy Parr, ed., *Childhood and Family in Canadian History,* 17–43. McClelland and Stewart, Toronto, 1982.

– "'Thieving Buggars' and 'Stupid Sluts': Insults and Popular Culture in New France." *WMQ* 36 (1979): 524–47.

– "Reluctant Exiles: Emigrants from France in Canada before 1760." *WMQ* 46 (1989): 463–505.

Mooney, James. *The Ghostdance Religion and the Sioux Outbreak of 1890.* University of Nebraska Press, Lincoln, NB [1896] 1991.

Moore, James. *Indian and Jesuit.* Loyola University Press, Chicago, 1982.

Moote, A.L. *Revolt of the Judges: The Parlement of Paris and the Fronde, 1643–1652.* Princeton University Press, Princeton, 1971.

Morelly. *Code de la Nature ou le véritable esprit des lois de tout temps négligé ou méconnu.* Ed. Sociales, Paris, 1970.

Morgan, Lewis. *Ancient Society: Researches in the Lines of Human Progress from Savagery through Barbarism to Civilisation.* Meridien, New York [1877] 1963.

— *The League of the Iroquois.* Corinth Books, New York, 1962.

Moore, R.A. *The Formation of a Persecuting Society: Power and Deviance in Western Europe 950–1250.* Oxford University Press, Oxford, 1991.

Moriarty, Michael. *Taste and Ideology in Seventeenth-Century France.* Cambridge University Press, Cambridge, 1988.

Moricet, Marthe. *Récits et contes des veillées normandes.* Cahier des Annales de Normandie, #2, Caen, 1963.

Morisset, Gérard. *Coup d'oeil sur les arts en Nouvelle-France.* Autopublie, Québec, 1941.

Morisset, Jean. "Miroir indigène, reflet eurogène: Essai sur l'américanité et la fabrication de l'identité canadienne." RAQ 28 (1998): 285–312.

— "Paroles du Québecois traduites du Tchippeyan." RAQ 22 (1992): 117–20.

Mosse, George. Winter 1973–1974 Lectures, History 120, University of Wisconsin-Madison.

— *Fallen Soldiers: Reshaping the Memory of the World Wars.* Oxford University Press, New York, 1990.

— *The Fascist Revolution: Toward a General Theory of Fascism.* Fertig, New York, 1999.

— *Nazi Culture: Intellectual, Cultural, and Social Life in the Third Reich.* Universal Library, Grosset and Dunlap, New York, 1966.

Mosse, Werner. *The German-Jewish Elite 1820–1935: A Socio-Cultural Profile.* Oxford, Clarendon Press, 1989.

Morton, Desmond. *A Short History of Canada.* McClelland and Stewart, Toronto [1983] 2001.

Mother-Worship: Theme and Variations. University of North Carolina, Chapel Hill, NC, 1982.

Moulin, Anne-Marie, and Alberto Cambrosio. *Singular Selves: Historical Issues and Contemporary Debates in Immunology.* Amsterdam, New York, 1994.

Mousnier, Roland. *Fureurs paysannes: les payans dans les révoltes du XVIIe France, Russie, et Chine.* Calmann-Lévy, Paris, 1969.

— *The Institutions of France under the Absolute Monarchy, 1598–1789: Society and the State.* Trans. Brian Pearce, University of Chicago Press, Chicago, 1979.

— *La Plume, la Faucille, et le Marteau: Institutions et Société en France du Moyen Age à la Revolution.* Presses universitaires de France, Paris, 1970.

— *La vénalité des offices sous Henri IV et Louis XIII.* Ed., Maugard, Rouen, n.d.

Mouzelis, Nicos. *Sociological Theory: What Went Wrong? Diagnosis and Remedies.* Routledge, London, 1995.

Muchembled, Robert. *Culture populaire et Culture des elites dans la France moderne, XV-XVIIIe Siècle.* Flammarion, Paris, 1978.

— ed. *Magie et sorcellerie en Europe du Moyen Age à nos jours.* Armand Colin, Paris, 1994.

— *La sorcière au village XVe siècles.* Gallimard-Julliard, Paris, 1979.

– *Le roi et la sorcière: l'Europe des bûchers XVIe-XVIIIe.* Desclée, Paris, 1993.

Muchnik, Naomi. "From Judaism to Catholicism: The hazards of Faith in the Seventeenth Century." *Revue historique* 623 (2002): 571–609.

Muhlstein, Anka. *Cavalier de la Salle ou l'homme qui offrit l'Amérique à Louis XIV.* Grasset, Paris, 1992.

Muise, D.A., ed.. *Approach to Native History in Canada.* National Museum of Canada, Ottawa, 1977.

Mukerji, Chandra, and Michael Schudson. *Rethinking Popular Culture: Contemporary Perspectives in Cultural Studies.* University of California, Berkeley, 1991.

Munck, Thomas. *Seventeenth-Century Europe: State Conflict and the Social Order in Europe, 1598–1700.* Macmillan, Houndmills, 1990.

Murdock, George. *Culture and Society.* University of Pittsburgh Press, Pittsburgh, 1965.

Murray, Margaret. *The Witch Cult in Western Europe.* Oxford University Press, Oxford, 1921.

Musgrove, F. *Youth and the Social Order.* Indiana State University, Bloomington, 1965.

Nadel, Siegfried. *Witchcraft in Four Societies: An Essay in Comparisons,* Bobbs-Merrill, Indianapolis, IN, 1952.

Narrative of a Captivity among the Mohawk Indians and a Description of New Netherlands in 1642–3 by Father Isaac Jogues. New York Historical Society, New York, 1856.

Nash, Gary. *History on Trial: Culture Wars and the Teaching of the Past.* Purdue University Video Archives, West Lafayette, IN, 1997.

– *Red, White and Black: The Peoples of Early America.* Prentice-Hall, Englewood Cliffs, NJ, 1974.

Neumann, Erich. *The Great Mother: An Analysis of the Archetype.* Trans. Ralph Manheim, Bollingen Series 47, Princeton University Press, Princeton, NJ [1955] 1974.

Neuschel, Kristen. *Word of Honor: Interpreting Noble Culture in 16th-Century France.* Ithaca, New York, 1988.

Nicolai, Martin. "A Different Kind of Courage: The French Military and the Canadian Irregular Soldier during the Seven Years War." *CHR* 70 (1989): 53–75.

Niederland, W. "Clinical Observations on the Survivor Syndrome." *International Journal of Psychoanalysis* 49 (1949): 313–15.

– "The Problem of the Survivor: Some Remarks on the Psychiatric Evaluation of Emotional Disorders in Survivors of the Nazi Persecution." *Journal of the Hillside Hospital* 10, 3–4 (1949): 233–47.

Nirenberg, David. "Mass Conversion and Genealogical Mentalities: Jews and Christians in Fifteenth-Century Spain." *P&P* 174 (2002): 3–41.

Nish, Cameron. *Les bourgeois-gentilshommes de la Nouvelle-France, 1729–1748.* Fides, Montréal, 1968.

Nitzan, Bilhah. "Repentence in the Dead Sea Scrolls." In Peter Flint, and James Vanderkam, *The Dead Sea Scrolls after 50 Years: A Comprehensive Assessment.* Brill, Leiden, 1999.

Nobles, Gregory. *American Frontiers: cultural encounters and continental conquest.* Penguin, London, 1998.

- "Breaking into the Backcountry: New Approaches to the Early American Frontier 1750–1800." *WMQ* 46 (1989): 642–70.

Noël, Jan. "New France: les femmes favoris." In R. Douglas Francis and Donald Smith, *Readings in Canadian History: Pre-Confederation*, 123–46. Holt, Rinehard, and Winston of Canada Ltd., Toronto, 1990.

Noonan, John. *Contraception: A History of Its treatment by Catholic Theologians and Canonists.* Cambridge, MA., Belknap Press of Harvard University Press [1969] 1986.

Nora, Pierre. *Lieux de mémoire.* Paris, Grasset, 1984.

Nordau, Max. *Degeneration.* Fertig, New York, 1968.

Normand, Silvio. *Les droits des Amérindiens sur le territoire sous le Régime français.* CRPA, 1994.

"Les notaires au Canada sous le régime français." *RAPQ* 1921–22, 14: Guillaume Couture.

Noy, Dov, "Madua haMachshafa hi tamid Isha?" [Why is the Witch always a Woman?] *Davar* 30,4 (1995): n.p. (In Hebrew.)

Numbers, Ronald. *Medicine in the New World: New Spain, New France, and New England.* University of Tennessee Press, Knoxville, TN, 1987.

Nute, Grace Lee. *Caesars of the Wilderness: Médart Chouart, sieur des Groseilliers, and Pierre Esprit Radisson, 1618–1710.* Arno Press, New York [1943] 1977.

- *The Voyageur.* Appleton and company, New York and London, 1931.

O'Brien, Stephen. *Traumatic Events and Mental Health.* Cambridge University Press, Cambridge, 1998.

Ochberg, Frank, ed. *Post-Traumatic Stress Therapy and Victims of Violence.* Psychosocial Stress Series #1, Brunner/Mazel Pubs., New York, 1988.

Oesterreich, Traugott, trans. D. Ibberson. *Possession: Demonical and the Other among the Primitive Races in Antiquity, the Middle Ages, and Modern Times.* Routledge, London [1930] 1999.

Ohnuki-Tierney, Emiko, ed. *Culture through Time: Anthropological Approaches.* Stanford University Press, Stanford, 1990.

Oliner, Pearl. *Embracing the Other: Philosophical, Psychological, and Historical Perspectives on Altruism.* New York University Press, New York, 1992.

Olivier-Martin, François. *Histoire du droit français: des origines à la Révolution.* Presses Universitaire de France, Paris, 1970.

O'Meara, Walter. *Daughters of the Country: Women of the Fur Traders and Mountain Men.* HBW, New York, 1968.

O'Neil, Huguette. "Quelques légendes du Québec en remontant le st-Laurent." *Culture vivante*, Ministère des affaires culturelles du Québec, 18, 1970, 32–5.

O'Neill, Sean Patrick. *Conversion on the Frontier: Attitudes of Jesuit Missionaries and American Indians Toward Baptism in Seventeenth-Century New France.* University of California, Santa Barbara, 1991.

Opler, Morris. "Themes as Dynamic Forces in Culture." *American Journal of Sociology* 51 (1945): 198–206.

Oppenheimer, L. "Self or Selves? Dissociative Identity Disorder and Complexity of the Self-System." *Theory and Psychology* 12, 1 (2002): 97–128.

O'Riain, Padraig. "A Study of the Irish Legend of the Wild Man." *Eigse* 19 (1972): 179–206.

Ortiz, Alfonso. "Some Concerns Central to the Writing of "Indian' History." *The Indian Historian,* 10 (1977): 17–22.

– "Some Central Concerns to the Writing of 'Indian' History." *The Indian Historian* 10 (1977): 17–22.

Ortiz, Alfonso, and Richards Erdoes, ed. *American Indian Myths and Legends.* Pantheon Fairy Tale and Folklore Library, New York, 1984.

Ossenberg, Richard, ed. *Canadian Society: Pluralism, Change, and Conflict.* Prentice-Hall, Scarborough, 1971.

"Ou a eu lieu le combat de Dollard?," *BRH* 4 (1898): 146–7.

Ouellet, Fernand. "La formation d'une société dans la vallée du St-Laurent: d'une société sans classes à une société de classes." *CHR* 62 (1981): 1–21.

Ozouf, Mona. *Festivals and the French Revolution.* Harvard University Press, Cambridge, MA, 1988.

Pagels, Elaine. *The Origin of Satan.* Random House, New York, 1995.

Pagès, Georges. *La Monarchie de l'Ancien régime en France.* Armand Colin, Paris, 1946.

Paine, Robert. *Dam a River, Damn a People? Saami (Lapp) Livelihood and the Alto/Kautokeino Hydroelectric Project and the Norwegian Parliament.* Copenhagen, NW, International Work Project for Indigenous Peoples, 1982.

Pannekoek, Frits. *The Fur Trade and Western Canadian Society, 1670–1870.* CHA, Ottawa, 1987.

Paquette, Lyne et Réal Bates. "Les naissances illégitimes sur les rives du St-Laurent avant 1730." *RHAF* 40 (1986): 239–52.

Parent-Brousseau, France. *Les femmes et la justice en Nouvelle-France.* maîtrise, Université Laval, 1990.

Park, Willard. *Shamanism in North America: A Study in a Cultural Relationship.* Northwestern University Press, Evanston, 1938.

Parker, Arthur. *The Constitution of the Five Nations or the Iroquois Book of the Great Law.* Iroqrafts, Ohsweken, ON [1916] 1984.

– "Secret Medicine Societies of the Seneca" [1909], in Elisabeth Tooker, *An Iroquois Source Book, III: Medicine Society Rituals,* 161–85. Garland, New York, 1986.

Parker, David. *La Rochelle and the Monarchy.* Royal Historical Society, London, 1980.

Parker, Geoffrey, and Lesley Smith. *The General Crisis of the Seventeenth Century.* Routledge and Kegan Paul, London, 1978.

Parker, Seymour. "The Wiitiko Psychosis in the Context of Ojibwa Personality and Culture." *AA* 62 (1960): 603–23.

Parkman, Francis. *France and England in North America.* 2 vols. Literary Classics of the USA, Viking Press, New York, 1983.

Parman, Susan. *Dream and Culture: An Anthropological Study in the Western Intellectual Tradition.* Praeger, New York, 1991.

Parson, Erwin. "Ethnicity and Traumatic Stress: The Intersecting Point in Psychotherapy." In Charles Figley, *Trauma and Its Wake: The Study and Treatment of Post-*

Traumatic Stress Disorder, 314–37. Psychosocial Stress Series, #4, Brunner/Mazel, New York, 1985.

– "Posttraumatic Narcissism: Healing Traumatic Alterations in the Self through Curvilinear Group Psychotherapy." In John Wilson,and Beverley Raphael, eds., *International Handbook of Traumatic Stress Syndromes*, 821–40. Plenum Series on Stress and Coping, New York, 1993.

Parsons, Elsie. "Micmac Folklore." *JAFL* 38 (1925): 55–133.

Patai, Raphael. *Myth and Modern Man*. Prentice-Hall, Englewood Cliffs, NJ, 1972.

Patterson, E. Palmer. *The Canadian Indian: A History since 1500*. Collier-Macmillan, Don Mills, ON, 1972.

Patterson, T.W. *Canadian Battles and Massacres*. Stagecoach Publications, Ltd., Langley, BC, 1977.

Paul, Daniel. *We Were Not the Savages: A Micmac Perspective on the Collision of European and Aboriginal Civilization*. Nimbus, Halifax, 1993.

Paul, Jocelyn. "Croyances religieuses et changement social chez les Hurons de Lorette." Thèse de MA, Université de Montréal, 1992.

Pearl, Jonathan. "Witchcraft in New France in the Seventeenth Century: the Social Aspect." *Historical Reflections/Réflexions historiques* 4 (1977): 191–205.

Peckham, Howard. *Pontiac and the Indian Uprising*. University of Chicago Press, Chicago, 1961.

Peers, Laura. *The Ojibwa of Western Canada 1780–1970*. University of Manitoba Press, Winnipeg, 1994.

Péguy, Charles. *Morceaux choisis*. Gallimard, Paris, 1927.

– *Jeanne d'Arc*. Gallimard, Paris, 1948.

Pelletier, Jean-Roland. *Jean Bourdon 1601–1668*. Société historique de Québec, Québec, 1978.

Pels, Peter. "Anthropology and Mission: Towards a Historical Analysis of Professional Identity." In R. Bonsen, H. Marks, and J. Miedena, eds. *Focaal, The Ambiguity of Rapprochement: Reflections of Anthropologists on their Controversial Relationship with Missionaries*. Nijmegen, 1990.

Pernot, Michel. *La Fronde*. Ed. de Fallois, Paris, 1994.

Perrault, Isabelle. *Le métissage en Nouvelle-France*. mémoire de maîtrise, Université de Montréal, 1982.

– "Traite et métissage: un aspect du peuplement de la Nouvelle-France." *RAQ* 12 (1982): 86–94.

Perrault, Jean-Alfred. "Nicolas Perrot a-t-il tenté d'empoisonner Cavalier de la Salle." *RHAF* I (1948): 49–53.

Perroy, Edouard. "Social Mobility among the French Noblesse in the Later Middle Ages." *P & P* 21 (1962): 25–38.

Perry, J., D. Silvera, J. Rosenvinge, A. Holte. "Are Oral, Obsessive, and Hysterical Personality Traits Related to Disturbed Eating Patterns?" *Journal of Personality Assessment* 78, 3 (2002): 405–16.

Peters, Edward. *Torture*. Oxford University Press, Oxford, 1985.

Peterson, Jacqueline. "The People in Between: Indian-White Marriage and the Genesis of a Métis Society and Culture in the Great Lakes Region, 1680–1830." Phd, University of Chicago, Chicago, 1981.

Peterson, Jacqueline and Jennifer Brown, eds. *The New Peoples: Being and Becoming Métis in North America.* Manitoba Studies in Native History 1, University of Manitoba Press, Winnipeg, 1985.

Peterson, Kirtland, Maurice Prout, and Robert Schwartz. *Post-Traumatic Stress Disorder: A Clinician's Guide.* Plenum Series on Stress and Coping, Plenum Press, New York, 1991.

Peterson, Nicolas. "Demand Sharing: Reciprocity and the Pressure for Generosity among Foragers." *AA* 95 (1993): 860–72.

Piaget, Jean. *Behavior and Evolution.* Routledge and Kegan Paul, London, 1978.

— *Entretiens sur les notions de genèse et de structure.* Mouton, Paris, 1965.

— Intellectual Evolution from Adolescence to Adulthood. *Human Development* 15 (1972): 1-12.

— *Play, Dreams and imitation in Childhood.* Norton, New York, 1962.

— *Sociological Studies.* Routledge, London, 1995.

Pilette, Marie-Laure. "S'allier en combattant et combattre pour s'allier ou les deux paramètres du cannibalisme mythique et social des Iroquois des 16e et 17e siècles." PhD, Université Laval, Québec, 1991.

— "Un dilemme iroquois: Combattre pour s'allier et s'allier pour combattre." *RAQ* 21 (1991): 71–8.

Pillorget, René et Suzanne, France Baroque. *France classique 1589–1715.* coll. Bouquins, Robert Lafont, Paris, 1995.

Pintard, René. *Le Libertinage érudit dans la première moitié du XVIIe siècle.* 2 t., Ancienne Librarie Furne, Boivin et Cie., Paris, 1943.

Plamondon, Lilianne. "Une femme d'Affaires en Nouvelle-France: Marie-Anne Barbel, Veuve Fornel." *RHAF* 31 (1977): 165–85.

Plaut, A. "A Case of Tricksterism illustrating Ego Defenses." *Journal of Analytical Psychology* 5 (1959): 35–54.

Poliakov, Léon. *Breviaire de la haine: le IIIe Reich et les juifs.* Calmann-Lévy, Paris, 1951.

— *Histoire de l'antisémitisme.* 5 t., Calmann-Lévy, Paris, 1955.

— *The Aryan Myth: A History of Racist and National Ideas in Europe.* Trans. Edmund Howard. Chatto, London, 1974.

Pollock, G. "On Migration: Voluntary and Coerced." *Annual of Psychoanalysis* 17 (1989): 145–58.

Pollack Linda. *Forgotten Childhood: Parent-Child Relations 1500–1900.* Cambridge University Press, Cambridge, 1983.

Pomerleau, Jeanne. *Les coureurs de bois.* Dupont, Ste-Foy, Québec, 1994.

Pope, Kenneth. *Recovered Memories of Abuse: Assessment, Therapy, Forensics.* American Psychological Association, Washington D.C., 1996.

Popkin, Richard. *The History of Scepticism from Erasmus to Spinoza.* University of California Press, Berkeley, 1979.

– *Sceptics, Millenarians, and Jews.* Brill, Leiden, 1990.

Porschnev, Boris. *Les soulèvements populaires en France de 1623–1648.* SEVPEN, Paris, 1968.

Porter, John. *The Vertical Mosaic: An Analysis of Social Class and Power in Canada.* University of Toronto Press, Toronto, 1965.

Porterfield, Amanda. *Female Piety in Puritan New England: The Reemergence of Religious Humanism.* Oxford University Press, Oxford, 1992.

Posner, David. *The Performance of Nobility in Early Modern European Literature.* Cambridge Studies in Renaissance Literature and Culture, #33, Cambridge University Press, Cambridge, 1999.

Poster, Mark. "Postmodernity and the Politics of Multiculturalism: The Lyotard-Habermas Debate over Social Theory." In Jean-Joseph Goux and Philip Wood, *Terror and Consensus: Vicissitudes of French Thought,* chap. 5. Stanford University Press, Stanford, 1998.

Potvin, Pascal. *Le Chevalier des mers: Pierre LeMoyne d'Iberville.* Ateliers de L'Action Catholique, Québec, 1934.

Pouliot, Adrien. "L'Exploit du Long-Sault." *RHAF* 14 (1960): 1–15; 157–70.

Price, John. "Sharing: The Integration of Intimate Economies." *Anthropologica* 17 (1975): 3–27.

Price, John, *Alabi's World.* Johns Hopkins Press, Baltimore, 1990.

Prins, Harald. *The Mi'kmaq: Resistance, Accommodation, and Cultural Survival.* Case Studies in Cultural Anthropology, Harcourt Brace College Pubs., Holt, Rinehart, and Winston, Orlando, FL, 1996.

Propp, Vladimir. *The Morphology of the Folktale.* 2nd ed., American Folklore Society, #9, Austin TX, 1968.

Proteau, Lorenzo, ed. *Contes et légendes (19e et 20e siècles).* Ed. des Amitiés Franco-Québécoises, Boucherville, 1997.

Proulx, Gilles. *Between France and New France: Life aboard the Tall Sailing ships.* Dundurn Press, Toronto, 1984.

Puckle, Bertram. *Funeral Customs: Their origins and Development.* Frederick Stokes Co., New York, 1926.

Purich, Donald. *The Métis.* James Lorimer, Toronto, 1988.

Purkhardt, Brigitte. *La chasse-galérie: De la légende au mythe.* Théorie et littérature, XYZ, Montréal, 1992.

Pynoos, Robert, and Nader, Kathi, "Issues in the Treatment of Posttraumatic Stress in Children and Adolescents." In John Wilson and Beverley Raphael, eds. *International Handbook of Traumatic Stress Syndromes.* Plenum Series on Stress and Coping, New York, 1993.

Quaife, G.R.. *Godly Zeal and Furious Rage: The Witch in Early Modern Europe.* Croom Helm, Beckenham, 1987.

Quimby, George, *Indian Life in the Upper Great Lakes 11,000 BC – 1800 AD.* University of Chicago Press, Chicago, 1960.

Rabb, Theodore, *The Struggle for Stability in Early Modern Europe.* Oxford University Press, New York, 1975.

Radin, Paul. *The Trickster*. Philosophical Library, New York, 1956.
- "Ojibwa Myths and Tales." *JAF* 41 (1928): 61–146.
- *Quelques Mythes et Contes des Ojibwa du Sud-Est d'Ontario*. Canada Ministere des Mines Commission Géologique, Mémoire 48, #2 Série Anthropologique, Government Printers, Ottawa, 1916.
- *The Story of the American Indian*. John Murray, London, n.d.
Ralston, Helen. "Religion, Public Policy, and the Education of Micmac Indians in Nova Scotia." *Canadian Review of Sociology and Anthropology* 18 (1981): 470–7.
Ramasubbu, R. "Conversion Sensory Symptoms Associated with Parietal Lobe Infarct: Case Report, Diagnostic Issues, and Brain Mechanisms." *Journal of Psychiatry and Neuroscience* 27, 2 (2002): 118–22.
Ramenofsky, A.F. *The Archaelogy of Population Collapse: Native American Response to the Introduction of Infectious Disease*. University of Washington, Seattle, WA, 1982.
Rand, Silas. *Legends of the Micmacs*. Longman's, Green, and Co., 1894, rep. Johnson Reprint Corp., New York and London, 1971.
Randle, Martha. "Psychological Types from Iroquois Folktales." *JAF* 65 (1952): 13–21.
- "The Waugh Collection of Iroquois Folktales." *Proceedings of the American Philosophical Society* 97 (1953): 611–33.
Ranke, Kurt. *Die Zwei Brüder*. Folklore Fellows Communications. XVIII, n. 114, Helsinki, Suomi, 1934.
Rankin, Herbert. *Celts and the Classical World*. Routledge, London [1987] 1989.
Ranum, Orest. *The Fronde: A French Revolution, 1648–1652*. Norton, New York, 1993.
Rapley, Elisabeth. *The Dévotes: Women and Church in 17th-Century France*. McGill-Queen's University Press, Montreal, 1990.
Rapson, Richard. *Denials of Doubt: an interpretation of American History*. University Press of America, Washington, DC, 1978.
Rasmussen, David. *Reading Habermas*. Blackwell, Oxford, 1990.
Ray, Arthur. *"I Have Lived Here since the World Began: An Illustrated History of Canada's Native People*. Key Porter, Toronto, 1996.
- *Indians in the Fur Trade*, UTP, Toronto, 1974.
Reagan, Albert. "Medicine Songs of George Farmer." *AA* 24 (1922): 332–45.
- "Some Chippewa Medicinal Receipts." *AA* 23 (1921): 246–9.
Redfield, Robert. "The Folk Society." *American Journal of Sociology* 52 (1947): 293–308.
- *The Little Community*. University of Chicago Press, Chicago, 1967.
Reece, Jack. *The Bretons against France*. University of North Carolina Press, Chapel Hill, 1977.
Reed, Charles. *The First Great Canadian: The Story of Pierre LeMoyne Sieur d'Iberville*. McClurg and Co., Chicago, 1910.
Rémy, Nicholas. *Démonolatrie*. Trans. Montague Summers, Redker, London, 1930.
Renel, Charles. *Les Religions de la Gaule avant la Christianisme*. Vol. 21. Ernest Leroux, Paris, 1906.

Revelard, Michel et Guergana Kostadinova. *Le Livre des masques*. La Renaissance du livre, Tournai, Belgium, 1998.

Reviere, Susan. *Memory of Childhood Trauma: A Clinician's Guide to the Literature*. Guilford Press, New York, 1996.

Reyna, Stephen. "Theory in Anthropology in the Nineties." *Cultural Dynamics* 9 (1997): 325–50.

Reynes, Geneviève. *Couvents de femmes: La vie des religieuses cloîtrées dans la France des XVIIe et XVIIIe siècles*. Fayard, Paris, 1987.

Rhéalt, Joanne. "Les postes de traite et les routes de canot (1760–1821)." en *Aspects du Nouvel-Ontario au XIXe siècle*, University of Sudbury, coll. Documents historiques, #73, pp. 11–21.

Rhys, John. *Celtic Folklore, Welsh, and Manx*. Oxford University Press, Oxford, 1901.

– *Lectures on the Origin and Growth of Religion as Illustrated by Celtic Heathendom*. London, 1888.

Rich, E.E. *The Fur Trade and the Northwest to 1857*. Canadian Centenary Series, McClelland and Stewart Toronto, 1967.

Richards, Audrey. "The Concept of Culture in Malinowski's Work." In Raymond Firth, ed., *Man and Culture: an Evaluation of the Work of Bronislaw Malinowski*, 15–32. Routledge and Kegan Paul, London, 1957.

Richards, David. *Masks of Difference, Cultural Margins*. Cambridge University Press, Cambridge, 1994.

Richter, Daniel. *The Ordeal of the Longhouse: The Peoples of the Iroquois League in the Era of European Colonization*. University of NC Press, Chapel Hill, NC, 1992.

– "War and Culture: The Iroquois Experience." *WMQ* 40 (1983): 526–659.

– "Whose Indian History?" *WMQ* 50 (1993): 388–93.

Richter, Daniel, and James Merrell, eds., *Beyond the Covenant Chain: The Iroquois and Their Neighbors in Indian North America, 1660–1800*. Syracuse Press, Syracuse, 1987.

Ricoeur, Paul. *Soi-même comme un autre*. Seuil, Paris, 1990.

Ridington, Robin. "Wechuge and Windigo: A Comparison of Cannibal Belief among Boreal Forest Athapascans and Algonkians." *Anthropologica* 18 (1976): 107–30.

Rieber, R. "The Duality of the Brain and the Multiplicity of Minds: Can You Have It Both Ways?" *History of Psychiatry* 13, 49 (2002): 3–17.

Rihs, Charles. *Les philosophes utopistes: Le mythe de la cité communautaire en France au XVIIe Siècle*. Marcel Rivière, Paris, 1970.

Rioux, Marcel, Martin, Yves, eds. *French Canadian Society*. Carleton Library Series #18, McClelland and Stewart, Toronto, 1965.

– "La notion de culture en anthropologie." *RHAF* 4 (1950): 311–21

– "Les sociétés paysannes." *RHAF* 5 (1952): 493–504.

Ritzenthaler, Robert. "The Ceremonial Destruction of Sickness by the Wisconsin Chippewa." *AA* 47 (1945): 320–4.

Ritzenthaler, Robert, and Pat Ritzenthaler. *The Woodland Indian of the Western Great Lakes*. Milwaukee Public Museum, Milwaukee, WI, 1983.

Roach, Joseph. *Cities of the Dead: Circum-Atlantic Performance.* Columbia University Press, New York, 1996.

Rouanet, S.P. "Irrationalism and Myth in Georges Sorel." *Review of Politics* 26 (1964): 45–69.

Robbins, Russel, Hope. *The Encyclopeadia of Witchcraft and Demonology.* Crown Pubs., New York, 1959.

Roberts, Gareth. "The Descendents of Circe: Witches and Renaissance Fictions." In Jonathan Barry, Marianne Hester, and Gareth Roberts, eds., *Witchcraft in Early Modern Europe: Studies in Culture and Belief.* Cambridge, New York [1996] 1998.

Robin, Robert, Barbara Chester, and David Goldman. "Cumulative Trauma and PTSD in American Indian Communities." In Anthony Marsella, Matthew Friedman, Ellen Gerrity, and Raymond Scurfield, eds, *Ethnocultural Aspects of Postraumatic Stress Disorder: Issues, Research, and Clinical Applications,* ch. 9. American Psychological Association, Washington DC, 1996.

Rodrigue, Denise. *Le Cycle de Pâques au Québec et dans l'Ouest de la France.* Les Archives de France, #24, PUL, Laval, 1983.

Rogers, Edward, and Jean Rogers. *The Individual in Mistassini Society from Birth to Death.* National Museum of Canada Bulletin, #190, Contribution to Anthropology, Part 2, DIAND, Ottawa, 1960.

Rogers, Spencer. *The Shaman: His Symbols and His Healing Power.* Charles Thomas Pub., Springfield, IL, 1982.

Roheim, Géza. *Origine et fonction de la culture.* Trad. Roger Dadoun, coll. idées, Gallimard, Paris, 1972.

Rohrl, Vivian. "The Nutritional Factor in Windigo Psychosis." *AA* 72 (1970): 97–101.

– "Comment on 'The Cure and Feeding of Windigos': A Critique." *AA* 74 (1972): 242–4.

Ronda, James, and Jeanne Ronda. "The Missionary as Cultural Revolutionary: Two Seventeenth-Century Examples." Paper presented at Great Lakes Regional History Conference, May 1975.

Roots, Maria. "Women of Colour and Traumatic Stress in 'Domestic Captivity'": Gender and Race as Disempowering Statuses." In Anthony Marsella, Matthew Friedman, Ellen Gerrity, and Raymond Scurfield, eds., *Ethnocultural Aspects of Postraumatic Stress Disorder: Issues, Research, and Clinical Applications,* chap. 10. American Psychological Association, Washington DC, 1996.

– *The Sillery Experience: A Jesuit-Indian Village in New France, 1637–1663.* Mss, 1975.

Roper, Lyndal. *Oedipus and the Devil: Witchcraft, Sexuality and Religion in Early Modern Europe.* Routledge, London, 1994.

– "Witchcraft and Fantasy in Early Modern Germany." In Jonathan Barry, Marianne Hester, and Gareth Roberts, eds., *Witchcraft in Early Modern Europe: Studies in Culture and Belief,* 207–36. Cambridge, New York [1996] 1998.

Rose, Mary. *Violence in Early Renaissance Venice.* Rutgers University Press, New Brunswick, 1980.

Rosenbaum, Alan, ed. *Is the Holocaust Unique? Perspectives on Comparative Genocide.* Westview Press, Boulder, 1996.

Ross, Anne. *Pagan Celtic Britain.* Routledge and Kegan Paul, London, 1967.

Rossman, B., Bingham, Richard, Emda, Robert. "Symptomatology and Adaptive Functioning for Children Exposed to Normative Stressors, Dog Attack and Violence." *Journal of the American Academy of Child and Adolescent Psychiatry* 36 (1997): 1089–97.

Rothschild, Babette. *The Body Remembers: The Psychophysiology of Trauma and Trauma Treatment.* Norton, New York, 2000.

Rouleau, C.-E. *Légendes Canadiennes.* Granger frères, Montréal, 1930.

Rousseau, Cecile. *Influence des factuers psychosociaux sur la santé mentale des adolescents Réfugiés.* 2ᵉ étape : rapport préesentée au Conseil québécois de la recherche sociale, Département de Psychiatrie, Hôpital de Montrèal pour Enfants, 1999.

Rousseau, Français. "L'Hôpital et Société en Nouvelle-France: L'Hôtel-Dieu de Québec à la fin du XVIIIe siècle." *RHAF* 31 (1977): 29–47.

– *L'oeuvre de chère en Nouvelle-France: le régime des malades à l'Hôtel-Dieu de Québec.* Cahiers d'histoire de l'Université Laval, PUL, Québec, 1983.

Rousseau, Jacques. "'L'affaire Dollard' de Fort Orange au Long-Sault." *RHAF* 14 (1960): 374–5.

– "L'annéda et l'arbre de vie." *RHAF* 8 (1954): 201.

– "Le Canada aborigène dans le contexte historique." *RHAF* 18 (1964): 39–63.

– "Le lieu de l'exploit du Long-Sault." *RHAF* 14 (1960): 353–77.

Rowan, John. *Subpersonalities: the People Inside Us.* Routledge, London, 1990.

Roy, Carmen. *Contes populaires Gaspésiens.* coll. La Grande Aventure, Fides, Montréal, 1952.

– *La littérature orale en Gaspésie.* Musée National du Canada, Ottawa, 1962.

Roy, Joseph-Edouard. *Guillaume Coûture: premier colon de la Pointe-Lévy.* CIHM #12722.

Roy, Pierre-Georges. "Le bureau des pauvres de la Sainte-Famille de l'Ile d'Orléans." *BRH* 33 (1927): 577–9.

– "La ceinture fléchée." *BRH* 3 (1897): 172–3.

– *La famille Aubert de Gaspé.* Mercier. Lévis, 1907.

– *La famille Godefroy de Tonnancourt.* Mercier, Lévis, 1904.

– *La famille Juchereau Duchesnay.* Mercier, Lévis, 1903.

– "La famille Marsolet de St-Aignan." pamphlet, Lévis, 1934, 26–9.

– "Les Iroquois sur les galères." *BRH* 4 (1898): 123–5.

– "Légendes Canadiennes." *Cahiers des Dix* 2 (1937): 45–92.

Rubel, Arthur, Carl O'Nell and Rosaldo Collado-Ardon. "Susto: a Folk Illness." *Comparative Studies of Health Systems and Medical Care.* University of California Press, Berkeley, 1984.

Russell, Diane. *The Secret Trauma.* Basic Books, New York, 1986.

Russell, Diane and Karen Trocki. "Evidence of Harm." In *Making Violence Sexy,* 194–213. Athene series, Columbia University Press, New York, 1993.

Russell, James. *The Germanization of Early Medieval Christianity: A Socio-Historical Approach to Religious Transformation.* Oxford University Press, New York, 1994.

Ryerson, Stanley. *The Founding of Canada: Beginnings to 1815*. Progress, Toronto, 1960.

Sack, Benjamin. *History of the Jews in Canada*. Harvest House, Montreal, 1965.

The Sacred Heritage: The Influence of Shamanism on Analytical Psychology. Routledge, New York, 1997.

Safley, Thomas Max, Ed. *The Reformation of Charity: The Secular and the Religious in Early Modern Poor Relief*. Boston, Brill Academic Publishers, 2003.

Sahlins, Marshall. "Culture and Environment." In Sol Tax, *Horizons in Anthropology*. Aldine, Chicago, 1964.

– *How "Natives" Think: About Captain Cook for Example*. University of Chicago Press, Chicago, 1995.

– *Islands of History*. University of Chicago Press, Chicago, 1985.

Sahlins, Peter. *Forest Rites: The Wars of the Demoiselles in 19th-Century France*. Harvard University Press, Harvard, 1994.

Sainte-Marie, Paule. *Madame Bourdon: L'histoire véritable de la France nouvelle*. Guérin, Montréal, 1987.

Saint-Pierre, Georges. *Exhibition de tableaux 23/1/1975–23/2/1975*. Musée de Québec, Ministère des affaires culturelles, Québec, 1975.

Salisbury, Neal. *Manitou and Providence*. Oxford University Press, New York, 1982.

– "The Best Poor Man's Country as Middle Ground? Mainstreaming Indians in Early American Studies." *Reviews in American History* 26 (1998): 498–503.

Salmon, J.H. "History without Anthropology: A New Witchcraft Synthesis." *Journal of Interdisciplinary History* 19 (1989): 481–6.

– *Renaissance and Revolt: Essays in Intellectual and Social History of Early Modern France*. MIT Press, Cambridge, MA, 1987.

– "Venal Office and Popular Sedition in 17th-Century France: Review of a Controversy." *P & P* 37 (1967): 21–43.

Salone, Emile. *La colonisation de la Nouvelle-France: Étude sur les origines de la nation Canadienne-Française*. Guilmoto, Paris, 1906.

Salumets, Thomas, ed. *Norbert Elias and Human Interdependencies*. McGill-Queen's University Press, Montreal, 2001.

Sanders, Ronald. *Lost Tribes and Promised Lands: The Origins of American Racism*. Little and Brown, Boston, 1978.

Santino, Jack. *Halloween and Other Festivals of Death and Life*. University of Tennesee Press, Knoxville, TN, 1994.

Sargeant, Margaret. "Seven Songs from Lorette." *JAF* 6 (1950): 175–80.

"Le sauvage Amantacha en France." *BRH* 13 (1907): 215–23.

Sauzet, Robert. "Sorcellerie et possession en Touraine et Berry aux XVIe-XVIIe siècles." *Annales de Bretagne et les pays de l"Ouest* 101 (1994): 69–83.

Savard, Pierre. *La Religion populaire*. Colloques internationaux du Centre nationale de la recherche scientifique, #576, Centre nationale de la recherche scientifique, 17–19/10/1977.

Savard, Rémy. *Carcajou et le sens du monde: récits Montagnais-Naskapi.* Série cultures amérindiennes, Ministère des Affaires Culturelles, 1972.

– *La voix des autres.* Positions anthropologiques, L'Hexagone, Montréal, 1985.

Sawaya, Jean-Pierre. *La Fédération des Sept Feux de la vallée du St-Laurent (XVIIe au XIXe siècle).* Septentrion, Québec, Sillery, 1998.

Scaer, Robert. *The Body Bears the Burden: Trauma, Dissociation and Disease.* Hawroth Medical Press, New York, 2001.

Scarry, Elaine. *The Body in Pain: The Making and Unmaking of the World.* Oxford University Press, New York, 1987.

Schaaf, Gregory. *Wampum Belts and Peace Trees: George Morgan, Native Americans, and Revolutionary Diplomacy.* Fulcrum Pub., Golden, CL, 1990.

Schalk, Ellery. *From Valor to Pedigree: Ideas of Nobility in France of the 16th and 17th century.* Princeton University Press, Princeton, 1986.

Scheff, Thomas. "Unpacking the Civilizing Process: Interdependence and Shame." In Thomas Salumets, ed., *Norbert Elias and Human Interdependencies,* 99–115. McGill-Queen's University Press, Montreal, 2001.

Schindler, Norbert. "Les gardiens du désordres." In Giovanni Lévi and Jean-Claude Schmitt, ed., *Histoire des Jeunes en Occident: De l'Antiquité à l'époque moderne.* Trad. Jean-Pierre Bardos, I, Seuil, Paris, 1996.

Schmalz, Peter. *The Ojibwa of Southern Ontario.* University of Toronto Press, Toronto, 1991.

Schmitt, Jean-Claude. *Ghosts in the Middle Ages: The Living and the Dead in Medieval Society.* Trans. Teresa Fagan, University of Chicago, Chicago, 1998.

– *Les revenants: Les vivants et les morts dans la société médiévale.* Gallimard, Paris, 1994.

Schoolcraft, Henry. *Indian Legends* (ed. Mentor Williams). Michigan State University Press, East Lansing, MI, 1956.

Schrift, Alan, Ed. The Logic of the Gift: Toward an Ethic of Generosity. New York and London, Routledge, 1997.

Schultz, Richard, Jr, and Stephen Sloan. *Responding to the Terrorist Threat: Security and Crisis Management.* Pergamon Policy Studies on International Politics, Oxford, 1980.

Schwartz, Barry. "The social psychology of the gift." In Aaflae Komter, Ed. *The Gift: an interdisciplinary perspective.* Amsterdam, Amsterdam University Press, 69–80.

Schwartz, Barry, Yael Zerubavel, and Bernice Barnett. "The Recovery of Masada: A study in Collective Memory." *Sociological Quarterly* 27 (1986): 147–64.

Schwartz, Stuart, ed. *Implicit Understandings: Observing, Reporting, and Reflecting upon the Encounters between Europeans and Other Peoples in the Early Modern Period.* Cambridge University Press, New York, 1994.

Schweder, Richard. *Thinking through Cultures: Expeditions in Cultural Psychology.* Harvard University Press, Cambridge, 1991.

Scott, Colin. "La rencontre avec les Blancs d'après les récits historiques et mythiques des Cris de la Baie James." *RAQ* 22 (1992): 59–61.

Scott, Hamish, ed. *The European Nobilities in the 17th and the 18th Centuries.* Vol.1: *Western Europe.* Longman, London, 1995.

Scott, James. *Weapons of the Weak: Everyday Forms of Resistance.* Yale University Press, New Haven, CN, 1990.

Scott, Joan Wallach. "History in Crisis?" *AHR* 94 (1989): 680–92.

Sealey, D. Bruce and Verna Kirkness. *Indians without Tipis: A Resource Book by Indians and Metis.* Book Society of Canada, Agincourt, Ontario, 1974.

– ed. *Stories of the Métis.* Manitoba Métis Federation, Winnipeg, 1973.

Sebeok, Thomas. *Myth: A Symposium.* American Folklore Society, 1955, rep., Indiana University Press, Bloomington, IN, 1965.

Sébillot, Paul. *La folklore de France.* Ed. Imago, Paris, 1982.

Segal Freilach, Ariel. "The 15th- to 18th-Century Theological Debate about the Origins of Native Americans Judaizing and Relinquishing Hebrew-Indian Theories." Offprint (kindly given to me by author).

Segal, Robert. "In Defense of Mythology." *Annals of Scholarship* 1 (1980): 3–49.

– *Joseph Campbell: An Introduction.* New American Library, New York [1987] 1990.

Segev, Tom. *The Seventh Million: The Israelis and the Holocaust.* Hill and Wang, New York, 1993.

Seignolle, Claude. *Contes populaires et légendes de Bretagne.* Richesse du folklore de France, Pub. de la Renaissance, Paris, 1974.

Séguin, Robert-Lionel. *La civilisation traditionelle de habitant aux XVIIe et XVIIIe siècles.* Fides, Montréal, 1967.

– "L'apprentissage de la chirurgie en Nouvelle-France." *RHAF* 20 (1967): 593–9.

– "L'apport européen à la civilisation traditionalle du Québec." *Cahiers des Dix* 39 (1974): 21–41.

– "Le cheval et ses implications historiques dans l'Amérique française." *RHAF* 5 (1951): 227-51.

– *La vie libertine en Nouvelle-France.* 2 t., Leméac, Montréal, 1972.

– "La Canadienne aux XVIIe XVIIIe siècles." *RHAF* 13 (1960): 492–508.

– *La sorcellerie au Québec du XVIIe au XIXe siècle.* Leméac, Québec, 1978.

Sévigny, André. *Les Abénaquis: Habitat et migrations (17e et 18e siècles).* Cahiers d'histoire des jésuites, #3, Bellarmin, Montréal, 1976.

Shahar, Shulamith. *Childhood in the Middle Ages.* Routledge, London, 1990.

– *Growing Old in the Middle Ages: Winter Clothes Us in Shadow and Pain.* Routledge, London, 1997.

– *The Fourth Estate: A History of Women in the Middle Ages.* Trans. Chaya Galai, Methuen, London, 1983.

Shalev, Arieh. "Acute to Chronic: Etiology and Pathophysiology of PTSD – a Biopsychological Approach." In Carol Fullerton and Robert Ursano, eds., 209–40. *Posttraumatic Stress Disorder: Acute and Long-Term Responses to Trauma and Disaster,* Progress in Psychiatry series, #51, American Psychiatric Press, Washington, DC, 1997.

Shalev, Aryeh, Omer Bonne, and Eth Spencer. "Treatment of PTDS: A Review." *Psychosomatic Medicine* 58, 2 (1996): 165–82.

Shamgar-Handelman, Lea. *Israeli War Widows: Beyond the Glory of Heroism.* Bergin and Harvey, South Hadley, MA, 1986.

Shapira, Anita. "Politics and Collective Memory: The Debate Over the 'New Historians' in Israel." *History and Memory* 7 (1995): 9–40.

– *Yehudim Hadashim, Yehudim Yashanim.* Am Oved, Tel-Aviv, 1998.

Sheehan, Bernard. *Savagism and Civility.* Cambridge University Press, Cambridge, 1980.

Sheldrake, Philip. *Living between Worlds: Place and Journey in Celtic Spirituality.* Darton, Longman, and Todd, London, 1995.

Shils, Edward. *Centre and Periphery.* University of Chicago, Chicago, 1975.

Shimony, Anne-Marie. "Iroquois Witchcraft." In Deward Walker, *Systems of North American Witchcraft and Sorcery,* 239–65. University of ID Press, Moskow, ID, 1970.

Shoemaker, Nancy. *Negotiators of Change: Historical Perspectives on Native American Women.* Routledge, New York, 1995.

Shortridge, James. *The Middle West: Its Meaning in American Culture.* University Press of KA, Lawrence, KA, 1989.

Shultz, Richard, Jr, and Stephen Sloan. *Reponding to the Terrorist Threat: Security and Crisis Management.* Pergamon Policy Studies on International Politics, Oxford University Press, Oxford, 1980.

Sicroff, Albert. *Les controverses des statuts de "pureté de sang" en Espagne du 15e au 17e Siècle.* Didier, Paris, 1960.

Siegfried, André. *Tableau politique de la France de l'Ouest sous la III Republique.* Imprimerie nationale éditions, Paris, 1913.

Segal, John, E. Hunter, and Z. Segal. "Universal Consequences of Captivity: Stress Reactions among Divergent Populations of Prisoners of War and Their Families." *International Journal of Social Science* 28 (2000): 593–609.

Silove, Derrick. "The Impact of Torture on Posttraumatic Stress Symptoms in War-Affected Tamil Refugees and Immigrants." *Comprehensive Psychiatry* 43, 1 (2002): 49–55.

– "The Psychosocial Effects of Torture, Mass Human Rights Violations, and Refugee Trauma: Toward an Integrated Conceptual Framework." *Journal of Nervous and Mental Disease* 187, 4 (1999): 200–7.

Silver, Steven, and John Wilson. "Native American Healing and Purification Rituals for War Stress." In John Wilson, John, Zev Harel, and Boaz Kahana, *Human Adaptation to Extreme Stress: From the Holocaust to Vietnam,* 337–55. Plenum Press, New York, 1988.

Silver, Timothy. *A New Face to the Countryside: Indians, Colonists, and Slaves in South Atlantic Forests, 1500–1800.* Cambridge University Press, Cambridge, MA, 1990.

Silverblatt, Irene. *Moon, Sun, and the Devil: Inca and Colonial transformation of Andean Gender Relations.* Princeton University Press, Princeton, 1987.

Simard, Jean-Paul. "Le meeting de m8chau 8raganich." *RAQ* 6 (1976): 13–16.

Simmel, Georg. "Faithfulness and Gratitude." In Aaflae Konter, ed. *The Gift: An Interdisciplinary Perspective.* Amsterdam, Amsterdam University Press, 1996.

Simon, Ronald, and Charles Hughes, eds. *The Culture-Bound Syndromes: Folk Illnesses of the Psychiatric and Anthropological Interest.* Reidel, Dordrecht, 1985,

Sioui, Anne-Marie. "Les Onze Portraits d'Indiens du 'Codex canadiensis." *RAQ* 11 (1981): 281–96.

Sioui, George. *Les Wendats: une civilisation méconnue.* PUL, Québec, 1994.

– *Pour une autohistoire amérindienne: Essai sur les fondements d'une morale.* PUL, Québec, 1989.

Skinner, Alanson. "European Folktales Collected among the Menominee Indians." *JAF* 26 (1913): 64–80.

– "European Tales from the Plains Ojibwa." *JAF* 29 (1916): 330–40.

– "Final Observations on the Central Algonkin Dream Dance." *AA* 27 (1925): 340–3.

– "Songs of the Menomini Medicine Ceremony." *AA* 27 (1925): 290–314.

Slattery, Brian. *Official French Attitudes toward American Indian Territories, 1500–1599.* Native Law Centre, Saskatoon, SAS, 1980.

Smandych, Russel and Gloria Lee. "Women, Colonization and Resistance: Elements of an Amerindian Approach to the Study of Law and Colonialism." *Native Studies Review* 10 (1995): 21–46.

Smith, Abbot. "The Indentured Servant and Land Speculation in Seventeenth Century Maryland." *AHR* 40 (1935): 467–72.

Smith, Daniel. "A Perspective on Demographic Methods and Effects on Social History." *WMQ* 39 (1982): 442–68.

Smith, Dennis. *The Rise of Historical Sociology.* Temple University Press, Philadelphia, 1991.

Smith, Donald Boyd. "Le Sauvage: The Native People in Quebec – Historical Writing on the Heroic Period." Ottawa, National Museums of Canada, 1974, offprint, DIAND files.

Smith, James G.E. "Notes on the Wiitiko." In William Cowan, ed., *Papers of the Seventh Algonquian Conference*, 1975, Carleton University, Ottawa, 1976, 18–28.

Stryker, Sheldon. *Symbolic Interactionism: A Social Structural Version.* Benjamin/Cummings, Menlo Park, CA, 1980.

Snynerman, George. Behind the Tree of Peace: A Sociological Analysis of Iroquois Warfare. PhD, University of PA, Philadelphia, 1948.

Sobel, Mechal. "The Revolution in Selves: Black and White Inner Aliens." In Ronald Hoffman, Mechal Sobel, and Frederika Teute, eds. *Through a Glass Darkly: Reflections on Personal Identity in Early America.* Omohundro Institute of Early American History and Culture, University of NC Press, Chapel Hill, NC, 1997.

– *Teach Me Dreams: The Search for Self in the Revolutionary Era.* Princeton University Press, Princeton, 2000.

– *The World They Made Together: Black and White Values in 18th-Century Virginia.* Princeton University Press, Princeton, 1987.

Soboul, Albert. *La civilisation et la révolution française.* Arthaud, Paris, 1970.

– *Les sans-culottes parisiens en l'an II.* Clavreuil, Paris, 1958.

Society and Institutions in Early Modern France. University of Georgia Press, Athens, 1991.

Soeur Marie-Ursule. *Civilisation traditionelle des Lavalois.* AFUL, PUL, 5–6, 1951, 184–68.

Solomon, Zahava. *Combat Stress Reaction: The Enduring Toll of War.* Plenum Press, New York, 1993.

— "Transgenerational Effects of the Holocaust: The Israeli Research Perspective." In Yael Danieli, International Handbook of Multigenerational legacies of Trauma. Plenum, New York, forthcoming (abstract), 4.

Soman, Alfred. *Sorcellerie, justice et justice criminelle: Le parlement de Paris 16e–18e siècles.* Variorum, Hampshire, GB, 1992.

Speck, Frank Goldsmith. "The Eastern Algonkian Wabanaki Confederacy." In Robert Leavitt and David Francis, *Wapapi Akonutomakonol (the Wampum Records): Wabnaki Traditional Laws,* intro. Micmac-Maliseet Institute, University of New Brunswick, Frederickton, NB, 1990.

— "Montagnais and Naskapi Tales from the Labrador Peninsula." *JAF* 38 (1925): 1–32, 38–9, 61.

— "Malecite Tales." *JAF* 30 (1917): 479–85.

— *Myths and Folklore of Timiskamong Algonquin and Timagami Ojibwa.* Canadian Dept. of Mines Geological Survey, memoire 71, #9, Anthropological series, n.d.

— *Naskapi: Savage Hunters of the Labrador Peninsula.* University of Oklahoma Press, Norman, OK, 1935.

— *A Northern Algonquin Sourcebook: Papers.* Garland, New York, 1985.

Spence, Lewis. *The Magic Arts in Celtic Britain.* Constable, London [1945] 1995.

Spencer, Herbert. *The Evolution of Society.* ed. Robert Carneiro, University of Chicago Press [1967] 1974.

Spengler, Oswald. *The Decline of the West.* Knopf, New York, 1950.

Spindler, Louise. "Menomini Witchcraft." In Deward Walker, *Systems of North American Witchcraft and Sorcery,* 183–220. University of Idaho Press, Moskow, ID, 1970.

Spink, John. *French Free Thought from Gassendi to Voltaire.* Greenwood, New York, 1969.

Spiro, Melford. *Context and Meaning in Cultural Anthropology.* Free Press, New York, 1965.

Spittal, William, ed. *Iroquois Women: An Anthology.* Iroqrafts, Ohsweken, ON [1990] 1996.

Sprague, D.N., and R.P.Frye. *The Genealogy of the First Metis Nation.* Pemmican Pubs., Winnipeg, 1983.

Spreen, Otfried. *Developmental Neuropsychology.* Oxford University Press, New York, 1995.

Springer, Sally. *Left Brain, Right Brain: Perspectives on Cognitive Neuroscience.* Freeman, New York, 1998.

Squier, E.G. "The Serpent Symbol and the Worship of the Reciprocal Principles of Nature in America." *American Archaelogical Researches,* I, Kraus Reprint, Millwood, New York, [1860] 1975.

Stamm, B. Hudnall, and Henry Stamm. "Trauma and Loss in Native North America: An ethnocultural Perspective." In Kathleen Nader, Nancy Dubrow, and B. Hudnall Stamm, eds., *Honouring Differences: Cultural Issues in the Treatment of Trauma and Loss,* 49–75. Brunner/Mazel, Philadelphia, 1999.

Stanley, George F.G. "The First Indian Reserves in Canada." *RHAF* 4 (1950): 178–210.

– "The Policy of Francisation as Applied to the Indians during the Ancien Régime." *RHAF* 3 (1949): 333–48.

– "The Indians and the Brandy Trade during the Ancien Regime." *RHAF* 6 (1953): 489–505.

Stannard, David. *American Holocaust: The Conquest of the New World*. Oxford University Press, Oxford, 1992.

Steblin-Kamenskij, M.I. *Myth*. University of MI Press, Ann Arbor, MI, 1982.

Steckley, John. "The Warrior and the Lineage: Jesuit Use of Iroquoian Images to Communicate Christianity." *Ethnohistory* 39 (1992): 478–509.

Stewart, T., and Marshall Newman. "An Historical resumé of the Concept of Differences in Indian Types." *AA* 53 (1951): 19–36.

Stocking, George. *Functionalism Historicized: Essays on British Social Anthropology, History of Anthropology*. 2 vols. University of Wisconsin Press, Madison, 1984.

Stonechild, Blair, and Bill Waiser. *Loyal till Death: Indians and the Northwest Rebellion.* Fifth House Pubs., Calgary, 1997.

Stover, Eric and Elena Nightingale. *The Breaking of Bodies and Minds: Torture, Psychiatric Abuse and the Health Professions*. Freeman, New York, 1985.

Strauss, Claudia. "Partly Fragmented, Partly Integrated: An Anthropological Examination of 'Postmodern Fragmented Subjects.'" *Cultural Anthropology* 12 (1997): 362–404.

Strenski, Ivan. *Four Theories of Myth in the 20th Century: Cassirer, Eliade, Lévi-Strauss, and Malinowski*. University of Iowa Press, Iowa City, 1987.

Sugarman, Susan. *Piaget's Construction of the Child's Reality*. Cambridge University Press, Cambridge, 1987.

Starna, William, and Ralph Watkins. "Northern Iroquoian Slavery." *Ethnohistory* 38 (1991): 34–55.

Sternhell, Ze'ev. *Etranger: Fascisme, antisémitisme, racisme*. Institut de recherches sociologiques et anthropologiques, Montpellier, University, Paul Valéry, 1998.

– *The Birth of Facist Ideology: From Cultural Rebellion to Political Revolution*. Princeton University Press, Princeton, 1994.

Stipes, Millard Fillmore. *Radisson and Radisson in the Mississippi Valley*. Jamesport, Missouri, self-published, 1906.

Stone, Bailey. *The French Parlements and the Crisis of the Old Regime*. University of NC Press, Chapel Hill, NC, 1986.

Stone, Lawrence. *The Crisis of the Aristocracy, 1558–1641*. Oxford University Press, Oxford, [1965] 1966.

Stone, Lyle, and Donald Chaput. "History of the Upper Great Lakes Area." DIAND files.

Staub, Ervin. "The Psychology and Culture of Torture and Torturers." In Peter Suedfeld, *Psychology and Torture*. The Clinical Series in Clinical and Community Psychology, Hemiphere, New York, 1990.

Sulte, Benjamin. "Habitant et Hivernant." *BRH* 5 (1899): 106–7.

– "Les Canadiens-français et les sauvages." *BRH* 4 (1898): 360–3.

– "Etienne Brûlé." Mémoires de la Société Royale du Canada, Ottawa, 1907, 97–126.

– *Radisson in the Northwest, 1661–1663.* Copp-Clark, Ottawa, 1904.

– *Histoire des Canadiens-français. 1608–1880,* Montréal, Wilson, 1884.

– "La Légende de Cadieux." *BRH* 3 (1897): 173–4.

– "Les Mots sauvages." *BRH* 3 (1897): 139–40.

– La St-Jean-Baptiste (1636–1852). Ed. Edouard, Garand, Montral, 1929.

Surtees, Robert. *The Original People.* Holt, Rinehart and Winston of Canada, Ltd., Toronto, 1971.

Sutto, Claude. *Le Sentiment de la mort au Moyen Age.* Institut d'études medievales, L'aurore, Montréal, 1979.

Szasz, Margaret. *Indian Education in the American Colonies, 1607–1783.* University of New Mexico Press, Albuquerque, NM, 1988.

Taché, Joseph-Charles. *Forestiers et voyageurs.* Fides, Montréal [1884] 1946.

Taguieff, Pierre-André. *La Force du préjugé: Essai sur le racisme et ses doubles.* Gallimard, Paris, 1987.

Talmon, Jacob Leib. *The Myth of the Nation and the Vision of Revolution: The Origins of Ideological Polarization in the 20th Century.* Weidenfeld and Nicolson, London, 1981.

– *The Origins of Totalitarian Democracy.* Penguin, Middlesex, 1952.

Tanner, Adrian. *Bringing Home Animals: Religious Ideology and Mode of Production of the Mistassini Cree Hunters.* St. Martin's Press, Syracuse, 1970.

Tapié, Victor. *La France de Louis XIII et de Richelieu.* Flammarion, Paris, 1967.

Tauber, Yvonne. "The Traumatized Child and Adult: Compound Personality in Child Survivors of the Holocaust." *Israel Journal of Psychiatry and Related Sciences* 33 (1996): 228–37.

Tax, Sol, ed. *Indian Tribes of North America.* Selected Papers of the 29th International Congress of Americanists, University of Chicago Press, Chicago, 1952.

Tedlock, Barbara. *Dreaming: Anthropological and Psychological Interpretations.* Cambridge University Press, Cambridge, 1987.

Tedlock, Dennis and Barbara, eds. *Teachings from the American Earth: Indian Religion and Philosophy.* Liveright, New York, 1975.

Tedlock, Bruce, and Bruce Mannheim, eds. *The Dialogic Emergence of Culture.* University of Illinois Press, Urbana, IL, 1995.

Tehariolina, Marguerite, et Savignac, Pierre. *La Nation Huronne: Son histoire, sa culture, son Esprit.* Ed. du Pelican, Montreal, 1984.

Teicher, M., S. Anderson, A. Polcari, C. Anderson, and C. Navalta. "Developmental Neurobiology of Childhood Stress and Trauma." *Psychiatric Clinics of North America* 25, 2 (2002): 397–404.

Teicher, Morton. *Windigo Psychosis: A Study of the Relationships between Belief and Behavior Among the Indians of Northeastern Canada.* Proceedings of the American Ethnological Society, Seattle, 1960.

Tenaille, Marie. *Contes de Normandie,* coll. Vermeille, Hachette, Paris, 1977.

Tessier, Albert, et Byron Hervé. *Vers le Pays d'en haut.* Beauchemin, Montréal, 1890.

"Testament de Jean Bourdon." *BRH* 2 (1896): 39–43.

Testard de Montigny, Louvigny. *Mémoires et Comptes rendus de la Société royale du Canada.* 3e serie, 47, 1953, sect. 1, pp. 1–32.

Thomas, Keith. *Religion and the Decline of Magic.* Scribner's, New York, 1971.

Thomas, Nicolas. "The Inversion of Tradition." *American Ethnologist* 19 (1982): 213–32.

– *Out of Time: History and Evolution in Anthropological Discourse.* Cambridge University Press, Cambridge, 1989.

Thomas, Nicolas, and Caroline Humphreys, eds. *Shamanism, History, and the State.* Ann Arbor, MI [1994] 1996.

Thompson, Michael, Richard Ellis, and Aaron Wildavsky. *Cultural Theory.* Westview Press, Boulder, CO, 1990.

Thompson, Stith. *European Tales among the North American Indians.* Colorado, College Pubs., General Series nos. 100–101, Language Series, vol. 2, no. 34, Colorado Springs, 1919.

– *Tales of the North American Indians.* Indiana University Press, Bloomington, IN, 1973.

Thornton, Russell. *American Indian Holocaust and Survival: A Population History since 1492.* University of Oklahoma Press, Norman, OK [1987] 1990.

Tiffany, Sharon and Kathleen Adams. *The Wild Woman: An Inquiry into the Anthropology of an Idea.* Schenkman Pub. Co., Cambridge, MA, 1985.

Tiger, Lionel. *Men in Groups.* Vintage Books, New York, 1970.

Tocqueville, Alexis de. *De la démocratie en Amérique.* 2 t., I, folio Histoire, 1986.

– *Democracy in America.* 2 vols. Garden City, NJ, 1970.

Todorov, Tzvetan. "L'Etre et l'Autre: Montaigne." *Yale French Studies* 64 (1983): 113–14.

– *Nous et les autres: la réflexion française sur le diversité humaine.* Seuil, La couleur des idées, Paris, 1989.

Tooker, Elisabeth. "Commentary on the Iroquois and the Constitution: Rejoinder to Johansen." *Ethnohistory* 37 (1990): 291–7.

– *An Ethnography of the Huron Indians, 1615–1649.* Smithsonian Institute, Bureau of American Ethnology, Bulletin 190, US Printing Office, Washington, DC, 1964.

– *The Iroquois Midwinter Ceremony.* Syracuse University Press, Syracuse, 1970.

– "The United States Constitution and the Iroquois League." *Ethnohistory* 35 (1988): 305-36.

– ed., *The Development of Political Organization in Native North America.* Proceedings of the American Ethnological Society, 1983.

– ed. *Native North American Spirituality of the Eastern Woodlands.* Paulist Press, Mahwah, NJ, 1979.

– ed. *An Iroquois Source Book, ii: Calendric Rituals.* Garland, New York, 1985.

Tousignant, Michel. "Migration and Mental Health: Some Prevention Guidelines." *International Migration Quarterly* 3 (1992): 167–77.

Traditional Adoption Practices in Africa, Asia, Europe, and Latin America. Research for Action. #6, International Planned Parenthood Federation, Philip Kreager, 1980.

Treasure, Geoffrey. *Mazarin: the Crisis of Absolutism in France.* Routledge, London, 1995.

Trémaudan, Auguste-Henri de. *Histoire de la nation métisse dans l'Ouest canadien.* Ed. du Blé, St-Boniface, Manitoba, 1979.

Tremblay, Daniel. *Au cœur du quotidien: La vie matérielle à Trois-Rivières au XVIIIe siècle.* mémoire de maîtrise, Université de Sherbrooke, 1978.

Trevor, Aston, ed.. *Crisis in Europe, 1560–1660.* Garden City, NJ, 1967.

Trevor-Roper, H.R. *The Crisis of the 17th Century: Religion, the Reform, and Social Change.* Harper and Row, New York, 1968.

Trigger, Bruce. "Champlain Judged by His Indian Policy: A Different View of Early Canadian History." *Anthropologica* 13 (1971): 85–114.

– *The Children of Aataentsic.* 2 vols. McGill-Queen's University Press, Montreal, 1982.

– "The Historian's Indian: Native Americans in Canadian Historical Writing from Charlevoix to the Present." *CHR* 67 (1986): 315–42.

– *The Huron: Farmers of the North.* Holt, Rinehart, and Winston, Inc., New York, 1969.

– *Natives and Newcomers: Canada's "Heroic Age" Reconsidered.* McGill-Queen's University Press, Montreal, 1985.

Trofimenkoff, Susan Mann. *The Dream of Nation: Social and Intellectual history of Québec.* Gage Publishing, Toronto, 1983.

Troyansky, David. *Old Age in the Old Regime: Image and Experience in 18th-Century France.* Ithaca, New York, 1989.

Trudel, Marcel. *Catalogue des immigrants, 1632–1662.* Cahiers du Québec, coll. Histoire, Hurtubise HMH, Montréal, 1983.

– *Les débuts du régime seigneurial au Canada.* Fides, Montréal, 1974.

– *Les Écolières des Ursulines de Québec, 1639–1686: Amérindiennes et Canadiennes.* Editions Hurtubise, Montréal, 1999.

– *Histoire de la Nouvelle-France.* 4 vols. Fides, Montréal, 1963–1970.

– "Jean Nicollet dans le Lac Supérieur et non dans le Lac Michigan." *RHAF* 34 (1980): 183-96.

– *La population du Canada en 1663.* Fides, Montréal, 1973.

– *La population du Canada en 1666: recensement reconstitué.* Septentrion, Sillery, Québec, 1995.

– "Les obligations du censitaire, à l'époque des Cents-Associés." *RHAF* 27 (1973): 3–41.

– "La rencontre des cultures." *RHAF* 18 (1965): 477–516.

Trudel, Pierre. "Histoire, neutralité, et Autochtones: une longue histoire…" *RHAF* 53 (2000): 528–40.

Trudelle, Charles. "Le pain bénit." *BRH* 18 (1912): 158–72.

Tudor, Henry. *Political Myth.* Pall Mall Press Ltd., London, 1972.

Turgeon, Laurier. "French Fishers, Fur Traders, and Amerindians during the Sixteenth Century: History and Archaology." *WMQ* 55 (1998): 585–610.

– "The Tale of Kettle: Odyssey of an Intercultural Object." *WMQ* 44 (1997): 1–29.

– "Les objets des échanges entre français et Amérindiens au xvie siècle." *RAQ* 22 (1992): 152–67.

Turgeon, Laurier, Denys Delâge, et Réal Ouellet. *Transfers culturels et métissages Amériques/Europe XVIe-XXe siècle.* Presses de l'Université Laval, Québec, 1996.

Turner, David. "Windigo Mythology and the Analysis of Cree Social Structure." *Anthropologica* 19 (1977): 63–73.

Turner, Frederick Jackson. *The Rise and Fall of New France.* Minnesota Historical Society, St. Paul, MN, 1937, 383–98.

– "The Significance of the Frontier in American History." *AHA Annual Report for the Year 1893,* Washington DC, 1894.

Turner, Stuart, and Caroline Gosrt-Unsworth. "Psychological Sequelae of Torture." In John Wilson and Beverley Raphael, eds. *International Handbook of Traumatic Stress Syndromes,* 703–14. Plenum Series on Stress and Coping, New York, 1993.

Tylor, Edward. *Primitive Culture.* 2 vols. Murray, London, 1891.

Ulman, Richard, and Doris Brothers. *The Shattered Self: A Psychoanalytic Study of Trauma.* Analytic Press, Hillsdale, New Jersey, 1988.

Ulrich, Laurel. *Good Wives: Image and Reality in the Lives of Women in Northern England, 1650–1750.* Oxford, New York [1982] 1993.

"Un conseil de guerre tenu par M. de Longueuil en 1700." *BRH* 37 (1931): 45–8.

Upton, Leslie. *Micmacs and Colonists: Indian-White Relations in the Maritimes, 1713–1867.* UBC Press, Vancouver, 1979.

Usner, Daniel, Jr. *Indians, Settlers, and Slaves in a Frontier Exchange Economy: The Lower Mississippi Valley before 1783.* University of North Carolina Press, Chapel Hill, 1992.

Vachon, André. "L'Eau de vie dans la société indienne." *CHAR* n.v. (1960): 22–32.

Vaillaneix, Paul. "Réformation et Révolution." In François Furtet and Mona Ozouf, éds., *The French Revolution and the Creation of Modern Political Culture,* 359–74. Pergamon, Oxford, 1987–94.

Van der Kolk, Bessel. "The Compulsion to Repeat the Trauma: Reenactment, Revictimization, and Masochism." *Psychiatric Clinics of North America* 12, 2 (1989): 389–410.

– ed. *Post-Traumatic Stress Disorder: Psychological and Biological Sequelae.* American Psychiatric Press, Inc., Washington, DC, 1984.

Van Gennep, Arnold. *Coutumes et croyances populaires en France.* Le Chemin vert, Paris, 1980.

– *Manuel du Folklore français.* Picard, Paris, 1946–58.

– *Les Rites de passage.* Picard, Paris [1909] 1994.

– *The Rites of Passage.* Routledge and Kegan Paul, London, 1977.

Vandiveer, Clarence. *The Fur Trade and Early Exploration.* Cooper Square Pubs., New York, 1971.

VanItallie, T. "Stress: A Risk Factor for Serious Illness." *Metabolism: Clinical and Experimental* 51, 6 (2002): 40–5.

Van Kirk, Sylvia. *Many Tender Ties: Women in Fur Trade Society 1670–1870.* University of Manitoba, Winnipeg, 1980.

Varkey, Joy. "Local Political Initiatives in French Imperialism: The Case of Louisbourg, 1713–1758." PhD, University of Ottawa, 1996.

Vaugeois, Denis. *Les Hurons de Lorette.* Septentrion, Sillery, Québec, 1996.

– *La fin des alliances franco-indiennes.* Boréal, Septentrion, Montréal, 1995.

– *Les juifs et la Nouvelle-France.* Boréal Express, Trois Rivières, 1968.

Vaughan, Alden. *New England Frontier: Puritans and Indians, 1620–1675.* 3rd ed., University of OK Press, Norman, OK [1965] 1995.

Vaux de Foletier. *Histoire d'Aunis et de Saintonge.* Boivin, Paris, 1929.

Vecsey, Christopher. *The Paths of Kateri's Kin.* Vol. 2: *American Indian Catholics.* University of Notre Dame Press, Notre Dame, Indiana, 1997.

– ed. *Religion in Native North America.* University of Idaho. Moskow, ID, 1990.

– *Traditional Ojibwa Religion and Its Historical Changes.* American Philosophical Society, Philadelphia, 1983.

Vecsey, Christopher, and William Starna, eds. *Iroquois Land Claims.* Syracuse University Press, Syracuse, 1988.

Vennum, Thomas. "Ojibwa Origin-Migration Songs of the Mitewiwin." *JAF* 91 (1978): 753–91.

Verene, Donald Philip, ed. *Symbol, Myth, and Culture: Essays and Lectures of Ernst Cassirer, 1935–1945.* Yale University Press, New Haven, 1979.

Verrette, Michel. "L'alphabetisation au Québec, 1660–1900." PhD., Université Laval, 1990.

Verschelden, Marie-Claude. "Le mariage mixte: Espace d'altérité et rencontre des identités." *Canadian Folklore Canadien* 18 (1996): 171–82.

Vestal, Stanley. *King of the Fur Traders: The Deeds and Deviltry of Pierre-Esprit Radisson.* Houghton-Mifflin, Riverside Pubs., Boston, 1940.

Vesti, Peter and Marianne Kastrup. "Treatment of Torture Survivors: Psychosocial and Somatic Aspects." In John Freedy and Stevan Hobfoll, eds., *Traumatic Stress: from Theory to Practice,* 339–64. Plenum Press, New York, 1995.

Vetromile, Eugene. *The Abenakis and Their History.* James Kirke, New York, 1866.

Viau, Roland. *Enfants du néant et mangeurs d'âmes: Guerre, culture et société en Iroquoisie Ancienne.* Boréal, Montréal, 1997.

Vico, Giambattista. *The New Science of Giambattista Vico.* Anchor Books, Garden City, New York, 1961.

Vidal-Naquet, Pierre. *Les assassins de la mémoire.* Ed. de la Découverte, Paris, 1986.

Vijker, Fons van de, and Giel Hutschemaekers. *The Investigation of Culture: Current Issues in Cultural Psychology.* Tilburg University Press, Tilburg, Netherlands, 1990.

Ville, L,on, Marie Rollet. *Les premiers colons franco-Canadiens.* s.p., Paris, 1928.

Villeneuve, Larry. *The Historical Background of Indian Reserves and Settlements in the Province of Québec.* Updated by Daniel Francis, DIAND offprint, 1984.

Vincent, Catharine. *Des charités bien ordonnées: les confréries normandes de la fin du XIIIe siècle au début du XVIe siècle.* Ecole normale supérieure, Paris, 1988.

Vincent, Marguerite. "Un siècle de réclamations de la seigneurie de Sillery par les Hurons." *RAQ* 12 (1982): 21–25.

Vincent, Sylvie. "Comment peut-on être rasciste?" *RAQ* 11 (1987): 3–16.

Vincent, Sylvie et Arcand Bernard. *L'Image de l'Amérindien dans les manuels scolaires du Québec*. Coll. Cultures amérindiennes, Cahiers du Québec, Hurtubise, Québec, 1978.

Vizenor, Gerald Robert. *The People Named the Chippewa*. University of Minnesota, Minneapolis, 1984.

Vogel, Virgil. *American Indian Medicine*. University of Oklahoma Press, Norman, OK, 1970.

– *A Documentary History of the American Indian*. Harper and Row, New York, 1972.

Von Franz, Marie-Louise. *On Dreams and Death*. Shambhala, Boston, 1986.

Vonk, Elisabeth. "Cultural Competence for Transracial Adoptive Parents." *Social Work* 46, 3 (2001): 246–55.

Vovelle, Gaby et Michel. *Vision de l Mort et de l'au-dela en Provence d'après les autels des âmes du Purgatoire aux XVe-XXe siècles*. Armand Colin, Paris, 1970.

Vrough, Karen. "Transracial Adoptees: Developmental Status after 17 Years." *American Journal Orthopsychiatry* 67, 4 (1997): 568–75.

Wade, Ira. *The Intellectual Origins of the French Revolution*. Princeton University Press, Princeton, 1971.

Wuthnow, Robert. *Cultural Analysis: The Work of Peter Berger, Mary Douglas, Michel Foucault, and Jürgen Habermas*. Routledge and Kegan Paul, London, 1984.

Walker, James. "The Indian in Canadian Historical Writing." *CHAR* n.v.1971.

Walker, Lenore. *The Battered Woman Syndrome*. Springer, New York, 1984.

Walker, Louise. "Indian Feast of the Dead." *JAF* 62 (1949): 428.

Wallace, Anthony. *Culture and Personality*. Random House, New York, 1961.

– "Dreams and Wishes of the Soul: A Type of Psychoanalytic Theory among the Seventeenth-Century Iroquois." *AA* 60 (1958): 234–48.

– *Human Behavior in Extreme Situations: A Survey of the Literature and Suggestions for Further Research*. Committee on Disaster Studies, #1, National Academy of Science and National Research Council, pub. # 390, Washington DC, 1956.

Wallach, Yehuda. *Kriegstheorien ihre Entwicklung im 19. und 20. Jahrhundert*. Israeli Ministry of Defence, Jerusalem, 1978. (In Hebrew: Torot Tzvaiot.)

Wallis, Ruth, and Wilson Wallis. *The Micmac Indians of Eastern Canada*. University of Minnesota, Minneapolis, 1955.

Wallot, Jean-Pierre. *Un Québec qui bougeait*. Boréal Express, Montréal, 1944.

Wallot, Jean-Pierre, and Gilles Pacquet. "New France/Quebec/Canada: A World of Limited Identities." In Nicolas Canny and Anthony Pagden, *Colonial Identity in the Atlantic World, 1500–1800*, chap. 4. Princeton University Press, Princeton, 1987.

Warkentin, Germaine, ed. *Decentring the Renaissance: New Essays on Early Modern Canada*. University of Toronto Press, Toronto, 1998.

– "Discovering Radisson: A Renaissance Adventurer between Two Worlds." In Jennifer Brown and Elisabeth Vibert, eds., *Reading beyond Words: Contexts for Native History*, 43–70. Broadview Press, Peterborough, ON, 1996.

Warner, Marina. *Alone of All Her Sex: The Myth and Cult of the Virgin Mary*. Vintage Books, New York [1976] 1983.

Warren, William Whipple. *History of the Ojibwa Nation*. Boréalis, Minnesota Historical Society Press, St Paul, MN, 1885.

Washburn, Wilcomb. *The Garland Library of Narratives of North American Captivities*. 96, Smithsonian Institute, New York and London, 1978.

Washburn, Wilcomb and William Fenton. *American Indian and White Relations to 1830: An Essay*. Institute of Early American History and Culture, University of North Carolina Press, Chapel Hill, NC, 1957.

Watelet, Hubert. *De France à la Nouvelle-France: Société fondatrice et société nouvelle*. Presses de L'Université d'Ottawa, Ottawa, 1994.

Watkins, Alan. *Mind-Body Medicine: A Clincian's Guide to Psychoneuroimmunology*. Churchill Livingstone, New York, 1997.

Watkins, Mary. *Invisible Guests: The Development of Imaginal Dialogues*. Analytic Press, Hillsdale, New Jersey, 1986.

Watrous, Blanche. "A Personality Study of Ojibwa Children." Phd, Northwestern University Press, Evanston, IL, 1949.

– *The Indian and the White Man*. New York University Press, New York, 1964.

Wear, A., R. French, and I.M. Lonie, eds. *The Medical Renaissance of the 16th Century*. Cambridge University Press, New York, 1985.

Weatherhead, Jack. *Native Roots: How the Indians Enriched America*. Crown Pubs, New York, 1991.

Weber, Max. *Economy and Society: An Outline of Interpretive Sociology*. Bedminster, New York, 1968.

Weir, Alison. *Sacrificial Logics*. Routledge, London, 1995.

Weir, Perry John. *Roots of Renewal in Myth and Madness: The Meaning of Psychotic Episodes*. Jossey-Bass, San Francisco, CA, 1976.

Weisner, Merry. *Women and Gender in Early Modern Europe*. Cambridge University Press, Cambridge, 1993.

Wenzel, Thomas. "Forensic Evaluation of Sequels to Torture." *Current Opinion in Psychiatry* 15, 6 (2002): 611–15.

White, Bruce. "Encounters with Spirits: Ojibwa and Dakota Theories about the French and Their Merchandise." *Ethnohistory* 41 (1994): 369–406.

White, Richard. *The Middle Ground: Indians, Empires, and Republics in the Great Lakes Region, 1650–1815*. Cambridge Studies in North American Indian History, University of Cambridge Press, Cambridge, 1991.

Whitehead, McGee. *The Micmac*. Chelsea Green Pub., White River Junction, VT, 1992.

Whitehead, Ruth. *The Old Man Told Us: Excerpts from Micmac History, 1500–1950*. Nimbus Pubs, Halifax, 1991.

Widener, Alice, ed. *Gustave LeBon: The Man and His Works*. Liberty Press, Indianapolis, 1979.

Widengren, Georg. "Harlekintracht und Münchszkutte, Clownhut und Derwischmütze." Orientalia Suedana, II, fasc. 2/4, Uppsala, 1953, 41–111.

Williams, Gerhild Scholz. *Defining Dominion: The Discourse of Magic and Witchcraft in Early Modern France and Germany*. University of MI, Studies in Medieval and Early Modern Civilization, Ann Arbor, MI, 1995.

Williams, Lyon. *Encyclopaedia of Native American Shamanism: Sacred Ceremonies of North America*. ABC-Clio, Santa Barbara, CA, 1998.

Williams, Mentor, ed. *Schoolcraft's Indian Legends*. Michigan State University Press, Ann Arbor, 1956.

Williams, Paul. "The King's Bounty: A Short History of the Distribution of Indian Presents 1764–1858." offprint, 1979, DIAND files.

Willis, Debra. *Malevolent Nature: Witchhunting and Maternal Power in Early Modern England*. Cornell University Press, Ithaca, New York, 1995.

Wilson, John, Zev Harel, and Boaz Kahana, eds. *Human Adaptation to Extreme Stress: From the Holocaust to Vietnam*. Plenum Press, New York, 1993.

Winter, Jay. *Sites of Memory, Sites of Mourning: The Great War in European Cultural History*. Cambridge University Press, Cambridge, 1995.

Wistrich, Robert. *Terms of Survival: The Jewish World since 1945*. Routledge, New York, 1995.

Wolfe, John. *Great Deaths: Grieving, Religion, and Nationhood in Victorian and Edwardian Britain*. British Academy, Oxford University Press, 2000.

Wong, C. "Posttraumatic Stress Disorder: Advances in Psychoneuroimmunology." *Psychiatric Clinics of North America* 25, 2 (2002): 269–377.

Woodcock, George. *Gabriel Dumont: The Métis Chief and His Lost World*. Hurtig, Edmonton, AB, 1976.

Woodley, Edward. *Legends of French Canada*. Thomas Nelson and Sons, Toronto, 1931.

Wright, Louis, ed., Robert Beverley. *The History and Present State of Virginia*. University of North Carolina Press, Chapel Hill, NC, 1947.

Wrong, George. *The Rise and Fall of New France*. Macmillan, New York, 1928.

Wyman, David, ed. *The World Reacts to the Holocaust*. Johns Hopkins Press, Baltimore, 1996.

Yadin, Yigal. *The Message of the Scrolls*. Simon and Schuster, New York, 1957.

– *Milhamet Bnei haOr leBnai haHosech: MiMegillot Midbar Yehuda*. Mossad Bialik, Jerusalem, 1957.

Yahil, Leni. *The Holocaust: The Fate of European Jewry*. Oxford University Press, New York, 1990.

– *The Rescue of Danish Jewry: Test of a Democracy*. Jewish Publication Society, Philadelphia, [1969] 1993.

Yard, Francis. *Légendes et histoires du beau pays de Normandie, Editions Bertout, La mémoire normande*, s.d.

Yehuda, Rachel, Ann Steiner, Boaz Kahana, Karen Binder-Brynes, Steven Southwick, Shelly Zemelman, Earl Giller. "Alexithymia in Holocaust Survivors with and without PTSD." in *Journal of Traumatic Stress*, 10, 1, 1997, pp. 93–100.

– ed.. *Risk Factors for Posttraumatic Stress Disorder*. Progress in Psychiatry, American Psychiatric Press, Washington, 1999.

Young, Allan. "An Alternative History of Stress." In Arieh Shalev, Rachel Yehuda, and Alexander McFarlane, eds. *International Handbook of Human Response to Trauma*, 51–66. Kluwer, New York, 2000.

– "Bodily Memory and Traumatic Memory." In Paul Antze and Michael Lambek, ed. *Tense Past: Cultural Essays in Trauma and Memory*, 89–102/ Routledge, New York, 1996.

– "Our Traumatic Neurosis and Its Brain." *Science in Context* 14, 4 (2001): 661–83.

– *The Harmony of Illusions: Inventing Post-Traumatic Stress Disorder*. Princeton University Press, Princeton, 1995.

Young, David. *Cry of the Eagle: Encounters with a Cree Healer*. University of Toronto Press, Toronto, 1990.

Young, J.L. and E. Griffith. "A Critical Evaluation of Coercive Persuasion as Used in the Assessment of Cults." *Behavioral Sciences and the Law* 10, 1 (1992): 89–101.

Young, Robert. *Colonial Desire: Hybridity in Theory, Culture, and Rac.*, Routledge, London, 1995.

Youngblood Henderson, James. *The Mi'kmaw Concordat*. Fernwood, Halifax, 1997.

Yovel, Yirmiahu. *Dark Riddle: Hegel, Nietzsche, and the Jews*. Polity Press, Cambridge, 1998.

Zakai, Avihu, ed. *Europa veHaOlam HeHadash: Gilui America veKibusha alYadei Medinot Europa be Mayot ha–1500–1700*. Mekorot veTeudot, Akademon, Jerusalem, 1993.

– *Exile and Kingdom: History and Apocalypse in the Puritan Migration to America*. Cambridge University Press, Cambridge, 1992.

– *Theocracy in Massachusetts: Reformation and Separation in Early Puritan New England*. Mellen University Press, Lampeter, UK, 1994.

Zeller, Gaston. *Les Institutions de la France au XVIe siècle*. Presses universitaires de France, Paris, 1948.

Zerubavel, Yael. *Recovered Roots: Collective Memory and the Making of Israeli National Tradition*. University of Chicago Press, Chicago, 1995.

Zicklin, Gilbert. *Countercultural Communes: A Sociological Perspective*. Contributions in Sociology, #44, Greenwood Press, Westport, CN, 1983.

Zoltvany, Yves. "Esquisse de la coutume de Paris." *RHAF* 25 (1971): 365–84.

Zuroff, Ephraim. *Occupation: Nazi Hunter – The continuing Search for the Perpetrators of the Holocaust*. KTAV, Hoboken, NJ, 1994.

Index